Costumes & Chemistry

A Comprehensive Guide to Materials and Applications

Sylvia Moss

Costume & Fashion Press

an imprint of

Quite Specific Media Group, Ltd.

New York & Hollywood

Dedication

To Cecily, Aaron, and Bob for your inspiration, patience, and encouragement.

COPYRIGHT © SYLVIA MOSS 2001

FIRST PUBLISHED 2001. PRINTED IN CHINA BY MIDAS PRINTING.

COVER PHOTOS, CLOCKWISE FROM UPPER LEFT: DESIGN BY CHERI TROTTER FOR *MAD FOREST* AT
UNIVERSITY OF CALIFORNIA, LOS ANGELES. CONSTRUCTION BY ROBERT SECRIST, PHOTO BY ROBERT ZENTIS, DESIGN BY JENNIFER LANGEBERG
FOR THE REDWOOD ICE ARENA. PHOTO BY KEN SCIALLO; PREFORMED ACRYLIC USED TO MAKE JEWELRY, PHOTO BY RICHARD S. BAILEY.
DESIGN BY DEBORAH NADOOLMAN FOR *THE WAITING ROOM* AT MARK TAPER FORUM, LOS ANGELES, PHOTO BY CRAIG SCHWARTZ/JAY THOMPSON.

PRODUCTION EDITOR: JUDITH DURANT

ART DIRECTION AND DESIGN: JAMES MORE

COSTUME & FASHION PRESS AN IMPRINT OF QUITE SPECIFIC MEDIA GROUP LTD., 7373 PYRAMID PLACE, HOLLYWOOD, CA 90046
BUSINESS OFFICE (212) 725-5377 VOICE, (212) 725-8506 FAX, EMAIL:INFO@QUITESPECIFICMEDIA.COM

OTHER QUITE SPECIFIC MEDIA GROUP LTD. IMPRINTS:
DRAMA PUBLISHERS
BY DESIGN PRESS
ENTERTAINMENTPRO
JADE RABBIT
HTTP://WWW.QUITESPECIFICMEDIA.COM

ISBN: 0-89676-214-9

Table of Contents

Table of Contents *(continued)*

PART FOUR

Acknowledgments

I wish to thank the many fine and talented costume craftspersons, designers, and technical experts who have shared their ideas and knowledge to make this book possible. Miriam Reed for editorial and writing assistance. Bill Malone, Uncommon Conglomerates; Thurston James, Prop Maker; Robert Secrist, Prop Maker; Phillip Hitchcock, Philip Hitchcock Designs; Phillip Berman, FLIP Enterprises; M. David Torosian, Cinema FX and Paul Bailey, GM Foam, Inc. for information on materials. Monona Rossol, Industrial Hygienist, Arts and Crafts and Theatre Safety (ACTS) for health and safety information.

For sharing creative ideas of costume design and construction I thank the following designers and craftspersons and apologize to anyone that I may have overlooked: Alan Apone, Alan Armstrong, Henry Bagdasarian, Frau Baronowky, Mine Barral Bergez, Moielle Bickel, Francoise Boudet, Peg Brady, John Brandt, Inge Cabsella, Carter Church, Shirley and Anthony Columbo, Judy Corbett, Tracy Cunningham, Sylvie Dehayes, John Dodds, Marilyn Dozier-Chaney, Denise Dreher, Jack Edwards, John Fifer, Robert Fletcher, Achim Freyer, Lizzie Gardiner, Tony Gardiner, Caroline Gordon, Louise Gordon, Rodney Gordon, Frau Heyman, Frau Himmerich, Maribeth Hite, Liz Honeybone, Ann Hould-Ward, Noel Howard, Pamela Howard, David Janzow, Elinor Kleiber, Jean Hunnisett, Doreen Johnson, Jane Klugston, Edward Maeder, Elaine Maser, Donna May, Janet Mayo, Sasha McMullen, Frau Meyer, Patry McCrory, Chuck Olson, Tommy O'Neill, Priscilla Parshall, Sally Ann Parsons, Janice Pullen, Michael Scott, Lois Sembach, Methbild Sengof, Ted Shell, Sylvia Strahammer, Bill Strawbridge, Ellen Rifkin, Bob Ringwood, Francis Rowe, Doug Spesert, Claire Springer, Anita Trammel, Joe Venturini, Denise Wallace, Chip Wickett, Stan Winston, Andy Wilkes, Erica Young, Larry Youngblood, and Gina Zeh. For help in testing and researching materials, I thank my many assistants, who include Rochelle Anthony, Gail Bowman, Dale Cunningham, Elizabeth Luce, Ann McEntee, and Cornelius Skates.

I thank the many chemists, technicians, and salespeople and manufacturers of plastic materials who answered my endless questions and supplied me with samples, brochures, books, and other technical literature: 3M Company, Four D Rubber Company Ltd., Aleene's Division of Artis Inc., American Art Clay, Inc. (AMACO), Beacon Chemical Company, BF Goodrich, Bond Adhesives, Cadillac Plastic and Chemical Company, Canal Rubber and Supply Company, Inc., Cementex Latex Corporation, Cerulean Blue, Ltd., ColorCraft, Ltd., CPC International, Decart Inc., Delta Technical Coatings, Inc., Dow Chemical, E.I. du Pont de Nemours and Company, Federated Linen and Uniform Service, Foamex Products, Inc., The Hygenic Corporation, Hysol Adhesives, Industrial Polychemical Service Corporation (IPS), The Kleerdex Company, Koh-I-Noor Inc., Laird Plastics, Pebeo Industries, Pink House Studios, Rosco Laboratories Inc., Savoir-Faire, Sculptural Arts Coating, Inc., Slomons Laboratories, Inc., Spartech Corporation, Spectra Dynamics Products, Stabond Corporation, Textile Resources, UnNatural Resources, Voltek, and Ward Engineering. For many generous research grants, I thank the senate of the University of California, Los Angeles.

Preface

For many years, I searched libraries and bookstores for a reference that explained how to make such unusual costume pieces as wings for insects, helmets for superheroes, and heads for animals. I never found such a book. Thus, as a designer-craftsperson receiving commissions to design and often to make nonsewn costumes, I had to learn my craft by trial and error. When I was asked to construct sewn costumes, I was able to turn to the hundreds of books available that detail tailoring and dressmaking techniques—techniques that have been passed down through centuries. But when constructing nonsewn pieces, I, like so many others, was on my own, working with no guide but my own ingenuity and working, of necessity, with those materials most readily available.

The available materials were modern materials—often plastics or man-made—many developed for commercial use and not for costume construction. Methods for their use were similarly commercial methods. Methods for other uses were, once again, left to the ingenuity of the new user. I continued to long for a handy reference guide that offered information on manmade materials.

Later, as an educator in costuming, I rediscovered the need for such a reference. As I observed students trying to repair shoes with white glue, paint leather with acrylic scene paint, and repair torn seams with hot-melt glue, I longed to hand them a book that explained How to Use these materials correctly.

Finally, after receiving several generous grants from the University of California, where I was teaching, I was able to begin this much-needed reference. During summers and sabbaticals, I traveled the globe, interviewing craftspersons, designers, and costume makers. I found a world of ideas, an abundance of novel methods, and much of the valuable information that has gone into this book.

At home in Los Angeles, I purchased both tried and untried materials, such as adhesives, coatings, and various plastics, and hired student laboratory assistants to aid me in testing their many uses. For over fifteen years, my lab assistants and I experimented with modern materials and methods practical for costume construction. Some of the materials and methods discussed in this book have seldom, or never, been used in costume making. Most, however, have proven to be tried and dependable through repeated use by skilled technicians.

This reference will extend the costume-making possibilities for imaginative designers and craftspersons by setting out the tested methods and reliable corroborate that work with these new materials and technologies. It is my hope that this reference—so long a part of my life through so many years of travel and testing—will help my colleagues and aspiring designers of the future to avoid, at the very least, those problems that so troubled my own career throughout the long and hazardous path of learning that is trial and error.

Introduction

During the past twenty years, a wealth of man-made materials and extensive new technologies have been developed by diverse, nontheatrical industries. Many of these materials are unknown or have seldom been considered for costume making; yet manmade materials properly handled can be of great value to the theatrical designer, who must often be highly ingenious and who will take the most unusual materials to implement creative design concepts.

Today, the innovative designer faces a two-fold challenge: The sheer variety alone of today's manmade materials can overwhelm all but the most experienced professional, and almost all information on How to Use plastic materials has been gathered through trial and error or by word of mouth, with only minimal working instructions recorded. Nevertheless, working with plastic materials—adhesives, coatings, and certain paints—is a new requirement for the professional costumer.

Most of the materials discussed in this book are plastics. The word plastic refers to qualities of a material or to the name of a certain group of synthetic materials. Natural latex rubber, glass, clay and wax are plastic in that they are formable—they may be shaped. Polyester, vinyl, acrylic, and epoxy are plastics because they are man-made, or synthetic, materials. Both plastic materials and plastics share a characteristic feature—the ability to be molded or formed into a desired shape.

To select the plastic most suitable for developing a design, the designer needs to be familiar with the many uses of each material as well as the wide variety of materials available.

Though a great many materials are listed in this book, they are only a few of the vast number that can be used, and these are limited to those that I have researched, either through actual testing, or learned about through interviews and study. It is impossible to discuss in one volume every material that modern costumers use; the materials I have chosen to discuss are those that are most popular with costumers as well as those that show creative potential for the field of costume.

This book is timely and both general in background and specific in guidance. Part One offers guidelines and safety advice for working with plastics and modern synthetics. Because most of these materials include hazardous chemicals in their makeup, it is especially important that the user be aware of and take the specific safety steps necessary to protect health. Almost as important, certainly to the success of the project, is the discussion on proper surface preparation. Finally, because life casts form the basis of many of the costumes described in Part Three, descriptions of the techniques for making full-body and head life casts are included.

In Part Two are discussions of the many modern materials preferred by costume craftspersons. The materials fall under two headings: *Materials to Apply to Costumes* and *Materials for Forming Costumes*. Under the former heading are adhesives, coatings, colorants, and metallizers, and under the latter are casting materials and sheetings.

These categories are listed alphabetically as are the sections under each category, and within each section, individual products are listed alphabetically. Although most of these products are discussed only once, many more may be employed for a variety of uses and are, therefore, not limited to one categorical discussion. For example, a substance such as acrylic matte medium that changes and coats a surface may also function as an adhesive. An adhesive like hot-melt glue may be cast to create jewelry.

Each of the many sections under the categories of adhesives, coatings, colorants, and metallizers begins with a list of the brands of the subject material that we have tested for laundering and dry cleaning. Sometimes included at the end are names of additional, untested brands and manufacturers, so that the reader may learn of other brands available.

Some of the products described herein are best known by brand names: Kydex, a form of acrylic-polyvinyl chloride sheeting; Super Glue, a brand of cyanoacrylate adhesive; Scotchguard, a spray-on silicone coating. Although familiar brand names are often given, I have emphasized the generic names of products. Brand names change as manufacturers go in and out of business and products' formulas are changed. Familiarity with generic names offers the user the advantage of investigating and comparing like products as well as exploring competitive pricing.

Products similar to those mentioned in this book are known by other brand names in Europe and the United Kingdom. When it was possible to identify those brands, the names have been included. Products known by generic rather than brand names are identified as "usually sold by generic name," though sometimes the brand name will also be mentioned. Should the reader require further details on a specific brand, inquiry can be made of the distributors and manufacturers. Most manufacturers are very cooperative and will supply the information requested.

Concluding the discussions of each individual category of adhesives, coatings, colorants, and metallizers are detailed charts noting the effects of dry cleaning and laundering on fabrics treated with the subject material. For over fifteen years, my lab assistants and I subjected nineteen different surfaces to laundering and dry cleaning tests, checking for strength of bond, for the effect that the subject material may have on the fabric, and for stability. All these are important considerations when selecting materials. I would advise, however, that before using our recommended substances, additional testing be carried out, for fabrics can vary widely within their own category. A woven cotton fabric can be simply or highly processed, closely or tightly woven, with or without pile, and with or without additional processing, all of which can affect the extent to which paints, adhesives, and other substances adhere to the surface of the fabric.

Costumes made from casting materials and sheetings are rarely laundered or dry-cleaned; obviously, no testing was done of those materials.

Because the emphasis in this book is on materials and because both materials and projects can be idiosyncratic, the discussion of both is limited to general and basic.

guidelines. Be aware that conditions such as variable temperatures and humidity can affect a material. For example, extreme cold may crack and freeze, and extreme heat may melt adhesives: Headdresses shipped by air have been known to fall apart because the cold in the cargo compartment of the airplane was so severe; other costumes adhered with rubber cement melted and separated in the desert heat.

When describing techniques for developing specific projects, I refer the reader to other, more specialized texts that deal in greater detail with working methods. Manufacturers and distributors will usually supply brochures and specific technical data, if requested.

Part Three describes the creation of actual costumes and costume pieces, based mostly on my interviews with designers and craftspersons throughout the United States and Europe. Techniques range from the simple, low-budget to the most sophisticated and costly. In following any of these techniques, however, I suggest that the reader also refer to the sections of Part Two that discuss the specific materials involved.

Part Four, the Appendix, includes several sections that should be of particular help to the costumer. The section on solvents offers advice for their use, along with cautions on the hazards involved, for solvents are invariably toxic and punishing to health. The pages on stain removal are useful to anyone working in costumes, for stains occur in the shop as well as on a stage or working set. In addition, a section on measurements offers assistance in translating between the U.S. systems and the European metric system. Also included are an extensive glossary, a list of distributors, and a bibliography. In the bibliography can be found information on all the titles mentioned within the text.

The Appendix also includes two resource lists many of the manufacturers and most of the workshops mentioned in this book. Since this writing, some groups may have gone out of business or changed their addresses or telephones. Please note also that the manufacturers and distributors listed are only those referred to in this book; many others exist who can supply the same and similar materials.

In the credits for both picture captions and acknowledgments, I have presented all the material I could gather, and I hope to be forgiven for any I have omitted. I have in all cases included the title of the theatrical production. Playwrights' names are cited to identify a theatre piece only when more than one version of the work exists. Names of theatres are included when referring to stage productions. Films are identified by year only when more than one versions of a film has been made. Where actors' names have been available, they have been included.

The many photographs and drawings included in *Costumes & Chemistry* illustrate graphically the methods described within these pages and give as well an idea of the final results. Other photographs exist that would have contributed to this book, but obtaining all the necessary copyrights from photographers and legal departments was impossible. Should the reader find particular costumes of interest, pictures of many may be found in videos and, sometimes, magazines.

In writing this reference, I have kept in mind the busy designer or craftsperson who may use it to look up very specific information. With that in mind, some information is repeated in different sections. For example, the Body Padding section contains descriptions of body padding that are also included in descriptions of the complete costumes for which the padding was designed.

Costume design offers endless opportunity for experimentation and creation. It is my hope that the materials and examples included here will excite and stimulate all ranks of designers and craftspersons to become even more creative. So, "Break a leg!" my readers, as you gather your Tonys, Emmys, and Oscars. Remember that your work are special because you bring beauty and joy to the world.

Getting Started

PART ONE

Health and Safety

Costume craftspersons work in a dangerous business. For years, people working in theatres have been exposed to toxic substances contained in the materials they handle and released into the air they breathe. Few in theatre have the chemistry background to understand the extent of the toxicity, and only since the 1970s have the hazards been acknowledged, as government and private organizations devoted to public health and safety have begun enacting and reinforcing safety codes and regulations.

Even when aware of the necessity for taking safety precautions, theatre artists are too often in a hurry, under pressure, oblivious to all but the current deadline. Ultimately more interested in personal expression and forgetful of everything but the creative process at hand, little energy is left for dealing with safety measures.

Costume shops are often small, and setting up a properly ventilated workspace in which to isolate toxic materials can be difficult and expensive. Costume craftspeople must work quickly with many materials in a short time, moving efficiently from needle and thread to spray paint to adhesives. Yet this commonplace routine has dangerous potential. Adhesives and coatings can self-ignite in the presence of flammable materials. Dust from plastics, paints, and dyes can cause lung cancer.

Some of the known illnesses resulting from exposure to toxic chemicals are various forms of cancer, birth defects, nervous system disorders, and chronic respiratory diseases. The following symptoms may be noted: headaches, breathing problems, intestinal disorders, memory loss, fatigue, and depression. Bodily functions may be permanently damaged. A recently discovered disorder, Multiple Chemical Sensitivity (MCS), has been found to be caused by massive exposure to chemicals in the environment, by either one single strong exposure or by repeated low-dose exposures. Ordinary allergies—resulting in dermatitis, hay fever, and asthma—are more common.

Some substances, particularly those found in solvents, can cause infertility in both men and women and can contribute to birth deformities. Many experts agree that almost all solvents at the right dose can cause reproductive and developmental problems, ranging from reduced sex drive and performance to infertility and fetal damage. Ethyl alcohol is also associated with these problems. And the same serious reproductive problems can be caused by solvents other than ethyl alcohol in much lower doses. Particularly damaging are the glycol ethers. Representatives of this group of solvents are likely to be found in water-based paints and inks, pump spray cleaners, aerosol products, photo resists, permanent markers, and paint strippers. Other strong reproductive hazards come from toluene, xylene, and the glycidyl ethers in epoxy resins and paints. Men and women planning families should reduce exposure to all solvents as much as possible and avoid all contact with chemicals toxic to the reproductive system.

In all cases, to protect your health, choose chemicals that are the least toxic. Whenever possible, substitute water-based products for solvent-based products. Yet be aware that water-based products may also present hazards, as mentioned above. Some other hazards have been mentioned in individual discussions within this book. Always read the Material Safety Data Sheet (MSDS) when using any chemical.

Heating plastics, when heat-forming and melting, also has dangers. Hot molten material can cause burns, and fumes may damage the eyes, throat, and nose as well as release toxins into the atmosphere. To avoid danger from fumes emitted by heated plastics, wear a respirator or work in a well-ventilated area and avoid contact with skin. Wear padded gloves to avoid burned hands. Neither respirator cartridges nor respiratory system protectors guard against emissions from heating plastics. Plastics in a hot, liquid state can also be volatile.

Dyes and pigments can be dangerous. Colors containing lead are especially toxic, and their poisonous quality has long been known. Interestingly, the pigments derived from nature are more likely to be hazardous than the synthetic colors. Those pigments that have been studied are only a small percentage of the many in use, and results show that some are toxic, others not, and still others cause cancer in animal studies. Some pigments can impair the ability of the blood to carry oxygen, while others can cause birth defects, allergies, and health problems. Powder pigments can be inhaled, or they can be absorbed through the skin and are thus more hazardous than colors already mixed into a liquid suspension. For more complete information on the hazards of specific colors, see Monona Rossol's charts in *The Artist's Complete Health and Safety Guide.*

The individual sections on materials contain more specific information on possible hazards as well as how to use the materials safely.

Toxic Effects

Illnesses stemming from toxic materials can be acute (short and severe), or chronic (long-term). Acute illnesses usually result from massive exposure to a toxic chemical. Massive exposure to lacquer thinner, turpentine, and other highly volatile solvents can cause dizziness, or result in nausea, unconsciousness, and even death. A brief exposure offers the hope of complete recovery; however, longer exposure can damage the brain, liver, and/or kidneys.

With acute illness, the symptoms are seen shortly after exposure. On the other hand, chronic, long-term effects may not show up immediately, for the body may initially be able to resist the toxicity. Symptoms may be vague, for they are often caused by a buildup of toxicity over a long period of time and may last a lifetime. Because chronic symptoms can be so long separated in time from the cause, they are often difficult to explain. Chronic conditions can include damage to the nervous system, psychological problems, ongoing liver and kidney problems, and dermatitis.

Sensitizers, or chemicals that can cause an allergy, are a part of many of the chemicals used in costume making. For example, epoxy resins and their curing agents have been shown to cause such allergic responses as dermatitis or asthma in over 50 percent of their users. Turpentine, isocyanates (used in foaming polyurethane and other substances), formaldehyde, and fiber-reactive dyes are also the source of allergic reactions in some users. It is important to treat allergic reactions seriously; if ignored, the exposed individual may develop life-long allergies to many related chemicals.

Toxic chemicals are inhaled, ingested, or enter the body through contact with the skin. Inhalation can cause nosebleeds, chemical pneumonia, chronic respiratory damage, as well as cancer and kidney and liver damage (these last three resulting from substances passing through the lung tissue and into the blood stream). Fumes from heating plastics, chemical dusts, spray paints, and solvents used in paints, adhesive, coatings, plastic formulation and dry-cleaning preparations are all dangerous to inhale.

Skin contact with acids, caustics, solvents, and bleaches can break down the skin's barrier of waxes and oils. Some chemicals will literally pass rapidly through the skin and into the bloodstream from where they can reach any organ in the body. These include methyl alcohol, toluene, mercury (from thermometers), glycol ethers, and many of the highly toxic impurities in organic dyes and pigments such as aniline, dioxins, and PCBs. Many of these will also permeate various types of chemical gloves without visually changing the appearance of the gloves. Any cuts or breaks in the skin will allow chemicals immediate entrance into the body and bloodstream.

Eye contact with most chemicals, through both vapor or liquid contact, can be damaging. Direct contact with toxic liquids is especially harmful and, if not immediately remedied, can cause irreversible damage.

Ingestion can be caused by eating, smoking, or drinking while working, as well as by touching the mouth with contaminated hands. Always wash hands before touching food, and be sure to keep solvents in proper containers. Children, and even adults, in the workplace have often mistaken solvent-filled cups for beverages. Ingestion also occurs from breathing the fine dust produced by sanding and sawing.

Individual Protection

Ventilation

Opening a window does not ensure adequate ventilation and the dispersion of toxic fumes. For good reason, government standards for adequate ventilation have been set. Costume shops cannot be set up safely in buildings that have merely a standard recirculating ventilation system. Ensuring that an adequate ventilation system has been installed is the craftsperson's first priority.

There are two types of ventilation systems that can be used for control of toxic air contaminants in costume shops:

1. *Dilution ventilation* (also called *mechanical* or *general ventilation*) uses fans and air inlets to push fresh air into the room as an exhaust fan is drawing contaminated air out of the same space. These systems are recommended only for removal of small amounts of gases or vapors of low toxicity. An example might be a shop that has many workstations, each using small amounts of solvents such as those in permanent markers or the small application of solvent-containing glues. Care must be taken not to build partitions or organize shop furniture in any way that interferes with the flow of the outgoing air.

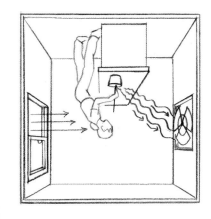

Dilution ventilation uses an electric fan and a draft from an open window to push fresh air into the room, while the exhaust fan draws contaminated air out of the same space.

2. *Local-exhaust ventilation* systems capture air pollutants before they get into shop air and exhausts them directly to the outside air. Examples are canopy hoods over dye vats or spray booths. It is important that the local exhaust system be powerful enough to capture contaminants as they are created. For example, spray booths must have a flow of air designed to capture the paint as fast as it is ejected from the nozzle of the gun.

Beware of salesmen touting ventilation systems that filter and return the air back into the room. There are only a few very limited applications for these systems, none of which are suitable for costume-shop work.

Every costume shop where solvents and paints are sprayed should have a spray booth. If more than occasional aerosol-can spraying is done, the spray booth will come under fire regulations, which require that the booth and the room in which it is located be explosion-proofed.

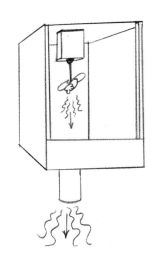

Local-exhaust ventilation from a spray booth captures pollutants before they enter the local indoor air and exhausts them directly to the outside.

Respirators

Respirators, properly fitted to the wearer, reduce the inhalation of toxic particles from dust, mists, and fumes when they reach the appropriate filters. Respirators are equipped with specific cartridges and filters that are designed to trap specific gases, vapors, fumes, dusts, and mists. A well-fitting respirator (hard if not impossible to do with facial hair) will prevent toxins from passing between the wearer's face and the mask. Each worker needs a personal respirator, and if the same respirator is to be shared by two workers, it should be sterilized before being transferred. A variety of cartridges are available to filter specific substances.

Following is a list of available cartridges, from Monona Rossol's *The Artist's Complete Health and Safety Guide.* Chemical cartridges are effective for approximately eight hours of use or for two weeks after air exposure. Cartridges are usually stamped with an expiration date.

Organic-vapor respirators contain cartridges and filters that catch gases, vapors, and fumes as well as dusts and powders.

Dust/mist respirators are designed to filter dust and powder.

Cartridge Name, Abbreviation and Use for Cartridges and Filters

Acid Gas (AG)	Acid gases rising from bleaches, etching and pickling baths, photochemicals, etc.
Ammonia (NH3)	Ammonia from diazo copiers, cleaners, etc.
Organic Vapor (OV)	Vapors from evaporating solvents, solvent-containing products, etc.
Formaldehyde (CH2O or FOR)	Formaldehyde from plywood, formalin, urea formaldehyde glues, etc.
Paint, Lacquer, and Enamel Mist (PLE)*	Sprays and aerosols from solvent-containing paints and other products.
Pesticides (PEST)	Pesticide sprays and dusts.
Asbestos (A)	Air-supplied respirators are needed.
Dusts (D)	Toxic and fibrosis-producing dust (e.g., silica) having a Threshold Limit Value of not less than 0.05 milligrams per cubic meter (mg/m3).
Mists (M)	Water-based mists having a Threshold Limit Value of not less than 0.05 mg/m3.
Fumes (F)	Fumes (e.g. metal fumes) having a Threshold Limit Value of not less than 0.05 mg/m3.
High Efficiency (H)	Dusts, mists, and fumes of highly toxic materials with Threshold Limit Values of 0.05 mg/m3 or less such as lead, and radionuclides.

*PLE cartridges are organic vapor cartridges preceded by a spray mist prefilter to keep mists from soaking into and saturating the chemical cartridge.

CHART REPRODUCED WITH PERMISSION FROM THE ARTIST'S COMPLETE HEALTH AND SAFETY GUIDE, MONONA ROSSOL, ALLWORTH PRESS, NEW YORK, 1994.

Gloves Various types of protective *gloves* are available, but no one type provides protection against all contaminants. The MSDS that accompanies the product or chemical to be handled should list the contents of the product. With this information, it is the responsibility of the user to contact a glove manufacturer who will advise on the type of glove offering the maximum protection.

Though surgical and other thin vinyl gloves may keep hands clean, they are easily permeated by toxic liquids. The wearer may feel only dampness on the hands when the hands are actually being bathed in chemicals that have passed through the thin vinyl.

The most effective gloves may be purchased from chemical supply companies and from companies selling safety equipment. Most companies will readily supply information and advice. The 3M Company is one that sells safety equipment and offers a brochure with comprehensive safety information.

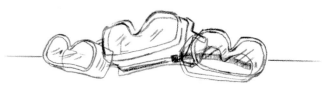

Goggles can protect against toxins present in sprays and accidental splashes

Goggles/Eyewash Stations Especially helpful to dyers are the chemical *goggles* that protect their wearers from splashes of dye, bleach, color remover, etc., as well as from toxins that may be present in sprays. The Occupational Safety and Health Association (OSHA) requires that *eyewash* be kept always available when workers are using chemicals such as bleach, silver nitrate, 56 percent acetic acid, or any chemical that could harm the eyes.

Metal Storage Cabinets Flammable materials require special storage to guard against fire. All flammable materials and solvents, such as cleaning fluid, aerosol paints, and solvent-based paints, should be stored in *metal cabinets* with close-fitting doors. These metal cabinets should be placed as far as possible away from exits, ensuring a clear escape in the event of a fire.

Labeling If products are poured into unlabeled containers and stored, the law (OSHA 1910-1200) requires the creation of new *labels* that give the name of product and its potential hazards.

Waste Disposal Hazardous waste is a by-product of the vapors, liquids, plastics, powders, and other chemicals frequently used. By definition, *hazardous waste* is any substance that cannot be legally disposed of in a normal landfill or a refuse incinerator designed to handle ordinary refuse. According to the Environmental Protection Association (EPA), hazardous waste has the four following characteristics:

- *Ignitable*: It can catch fire and burn.
- *Corrosive*: It is capable of corroding solids and metals.
- *Reactive*: It is capable of detonation and violent reaction.

• *Toxic*: It contains toxic gases and other contaminants.

For years, artists and craftspeople have been disposing of waste products by pouring them into sinks and dumping them into garbage cans. Today, to protect the environment, extensive regulations govern the disposal of toxic wastes, and business and industry must conform to these regulations and ensure that toxic wastes are disposed of properly. To learn the appropriate regulations, contact the agency in your state that has jurisdiction over the EPA regulations. Craftspersons working at home are not regulated by the EPA, though they, too, need to be protective of the environment by disposing carefully of solvents at Household Waste Round-Ups.

Large institutions like universities and film studios have personnel whose sole duty is to manage and dispose properly of hazardous chemicals. It is important to notify these trained persons when chemicals are to be disposed.

Regulatory Agencies

The Environmental Protection Agency (EPA), founded in 1970, is a U.S. governmental agency that has enacted regulations that are the basis for laws that are under the jurisdiction of the health services or the environmental division of individual states.

The Occupational Safety and Health Administration (OSHA) is a federal agency. States have their own agencies. In many cases, as in California and New York, the regulations of the state agency are more strict than those of the national government; California has the strictest safety and environmental laws of any state.

Protective Laws

The Occupational Safety and Health Act (OSHAct) was created to protect those working in dangerous situations or with hazardous materials. It mandates that an "employer shall furnish . . . a place of employment which is free from recognized hazards." In Canada, the OSHAct (Occupational Safety and Health Act) regulates that employers "take every precaution reasonable in the circumstances for the protection of a worker."

OSHA offices, under the U.S. Department of Labor, have employees who will answer questions about safety measures. OSHA also publishes a detailed book entitled *General Industry Standards*.

The general industry standards for theatres apply to working surfaces, entrances and exits, fire protection, tools, electricity, welding equipment, health and environmental control (including ventilation), and toxic and hazardous substances. Many of the regulations apply specifically to businesses involved in the arts as well as to schools. OSHA sets minimum standards for the release of air pollutants such as solvent vapors of the types found in cleaners, paints, dusts, and fumes. Unfortunately, the OSHA standards are often unknown to many shop supervisors and theatre owners. Costume craftspersons unfamiliar with these regulations will need to obtain copies of the laws from the federal and state Department of Labor.

Infractions of any of the OSHA laws can result in large penalties and fines. As of 1997, maximum penalties were $7,000 per violation. There is a minimum penalty of

$5,000 and a maximum of $70,000 for a willful violation, and a penalty of up to $70,000 for a repeat violation. These are hefty sums to be paid by struggling artists and theatre companies. Moreover, employers can be sued for costs of accidents and illnesses incurred by the craftsperson because of *deliberate* infractions of regulations. Some U.S. employers are currently in prison for such violations.

The federal right-to-know laws, instituted in 1988, require employers to develop formal hazard-communication programs, to maintain open inventories and data sheets for all potentially hazardous chemicals, and to set up training programs for those working with hazardous materials. Included in these programs are directions for working with paints, dyes, solvents, metals, and cleaning materials. Craftspeople and others exposed to such materials should be informed about their use and the dangers involved. Though most manufacturers of materials print warnings on their labels, the information given is scarcely adequate for understanding all of the possible hazards.

All employees in the United States are covered by right-to-know, or federal hazard communication laws. Employees in Canada are covered by the Workplace Hazardous Materials Information System (WHMIS). And all employers involved with such materials must, by law, develop programs and train employees to work safely with hazardous materials. An excellent text for such training programs is Monona Rossol's *Stage Fright*. Training programs can be accomplished in one day and should be held for new employees and to introduce new materials. Some states mandate an annual training session for all employees.

Craftspersons and artists who are self-employed and working alone at home are not covered by these laws. Yet, if they work at a site where employees are present, all uses of hazardous materials and of materials brought to the workplace must conform to the hazard communication laws or Workplace Hazardous Materials Information System labeling requirements.

Teachers have a special responsibility: They must train their students to use hazardous materials safely, since, by law, teachers are liable for any harm that comes to students through classroom activity. Again, *Stage Fright* is an excellent reference for such training.

Some manufacturers who claim that certain art materials are nontoxic and therefore exempt from MSDS rulings are not willing to distribute the MSDS sheets; however, by law, it is their obligation. Consumer products are not necessarily any safer than those marketed for industry. Since art materials are often used in ways not originally intended, the law requires that workers be informed of the potential for danger. All costumers are familiar with spraying brush-on paints, melting waxes and crayons, and sprinkling powder onto costumes; all of these techniques can pose hazards to health through ingestion, inhalation, or when the toxic substances come in contact with the skin.

To comply with the Hazard Communication Standard of the United States and the WHMIS of Canada, first call the local department of labor to learn if compliance should be with either the state, province, or federal right-to know laws. Obtain applicable copies of the law as well as additional information.

General requirements by the United States and Canada are similar. Each mandates that employers take necessary steps toward compliance with the law, including inventorying of all workplace chemicals, identifying any hazardous products, and ensuring that there are Material Safety Data Sheets for all hazardous products. Employers must have these sheets on file and available to employees.

*A **Material Safety Data Sheet** (MSDS), front. These sheets must be made available by manufacturers for workers' protection.*

Material Safety Data Sheet

May be used to comply with
OSHA's Hazrd Communication Standard
29 CFR 1910.1200. Standard must be consulted for
specific requirements.

U. S. Department of Labor

National Safety and Health Administration
(Non-Mandatory Form
Form Approved
OMB No. 1218-0072

IDENTITY *(As Used on Label and List)*

Note: Blank spaces are not permitted. If any item is not applicable, or no information is available, the space must be markede to indeicate that.

Section I

Manufacturer's Name	Emergency Telephone Number
Address *(Number, Street, City, State and ZIP Code)*	Telephone Number for Information
	Date Prepared
	Signature of Preparer *(optional)*

Section II — Hazardous Ingredients/Identity Information

Hazardous Components (Specific Chemical Identity: Common Name(s)	OSHA PEL	ACGIH TLV	Other Limits Recommended	% *(optional)*

Section III — Physical/Chemical Characteristics

Boiling Point		Specific Gravity ($H_2O = 1$)	
Vapor Pressure (mm Hg.)		Melting Point	
Vapor Density (AIR = 1)		Evaporation Rate (Butyl Acetate = 1)	
Solubility in Water			
Appearance and Odor			

Section IV — Fire and Explosion Hazard Data

Flash Point (Method Used)		Flammable Limits	LEL	UEL
Extinguishing Media				
Special Fire Figthting Procedures				
Unusual Fire and Explosion Hazards				

(Reproduce Locally)

Section V – Reactivity Data

Stability	Unstable		Conditions to Avoid
	Stable		

Incompatibility *(Material to Avoid)*

Hazardous Decomposition or Byproducts

Hazardous	May Occur		Conditions to Avoid
			Will Not Occur

Section V – Reactivity Data

Route(s) of Entry: Inhalation?   Skin?   Ingestion?

Health Hazards *(Acute and Chronic)*

Carcinogenicity?   NTP?   IARC Monographs?   OSHA Regulated?

Signs and Symptoms of Exposure

Medical Conditions

Emergency and First Aid Procedures

Section V – Reactivity Data

Steps to Be Taken in Case Material is Released or Spilled

Waste Disposal Method

Precautions to Be Taken in Handling and Storing

Other Precautions

Respiratory Protection *(Specify Type)*

Ventilation	Local Exhaust	Special
	Mechanical *(General)*	Other
Protective Gloves		Eye Protection

Other Protective Clothing or Equipment

Work/Hygenic

OSHA has regulated that manufacturers and distributors of hazardous products distribute a MSDS along with the product. The MSDSs detail the hazards of specific materials so that workers can protect themselves. MSDSs include extensive chemical terms and are therefore difficult to interpret; thus, they must be read with care.

The MSDS should accompany the items ordered and should be requested when materials are ordered. It can also be obtained independently. The MSDS gives the following information:

- Product's brand name and chemicals included
- Product's properties and its hazardous health effects
- Type of protective gear necessary
- Safest way to handle the product
- Appropriate first-aid treatment in case of accident.Most efficient response to accidents
- Medical problems that could be aggravated by use of the product

MSDSs accompany the following categories of products:

- Adhesives
- Catalysts and Resins
- Dry media
- Dyes and Pigments
- Flame Retardants
- Inks
- Lacquers and Clear Finishes
- Oil Soluble Paints
- Primers and Sealers
- Solvents
- Water Soluble Paints

Surface Preparation

Before applying any kind of coating—whether an adhesive, a protective coating, or a paint—to any surface, that surface must be clean. Any residue left on the surface should be removed before spreading on a new covering. Additionally, most smooth surfaces require abrasion, or roughening, which permits a mechanical bond and thus increased bonding power. Generally, if a surface is not properly prepared, the new coating will not last well.

The techniques offered below are for bonding adhesives, paints, and coatings on surfaces that receive only light or moderate wear and pressure. To create a bond that can survive stress and strong pressure, more involved and hazardous methods must be used. Such methods, which are employed by industry, are beyond the scope of most costume and prop shops. Should industrial methods be required, refer to *Industrial Adhesives and Sealants* or *Adhesives*, both listed in the bibliography.

Some General Guidelines

New surfaces accept coatings better than do old ones.

Some roughness on a surface increases bonding power.

Extreme roughness may decrease bonding power.

The surface, before cleaning, always bears some contaminants.

Bond the surfaces as soon as possible after cleaning.

Health and Safety

When working with solvents, observe the health and safety precautions described in the Health and Safety section. Use a water-based solution or the solvent with the highest Threshold Limit Value (TLV) whenever possible. TLV is the maximum airborne concentration of a material to which most healthy individuals on the average work schedule can be exposed without experiencing adverse health effects. Standards are determined by the American Conference of Government Industrial Hygienists.

Follow these measures for safety when working with solvents.

- Work in a well-ventilated space or wear the correct type of respirator and avoid contact with skin.
- Wear appropriate gloves for hand protection.
- Keep away from stoves and heating elements.
- When abrading surfaces that release dust into the air, wear a particle mask.

SAFETY MEASURES WHEN WORKING WITH SOLVENTS

Fabrics	Before applying dye or other coatings such as paint to launderable fabric, wash the fabric well to remove sizing or other chemicals. This will allow the new dye or coating material to adhere more strongly to the fibers of the fabric. If the fabric cannot be laundered, as with woolens and most silks, do not try to wash it.
Plastic Sheetings	Plastic sheetings can be cleaned with any of the variety of plastic cleaners available at most plastics supply outlets or from plastics manufacturers, or they can be wiped and abraded by solvents. Abrasion usually follows the solvent cleaning, with yet a second solvent cleaning after the abrasion.
— Acrylic	Wipe with isopropyl or methyl alcohol on a soft, clean cloth. No further preparation is necessary.
— Chloroprene Rubber (Neoprene)	Wipe with acetone on a clean cloth. No further preparation is necessary.
— Expanded (Foamed) Rubber or Plastic	Degrease with solvent or detergent and water; refer to specific polymer. Do not abrade.
— Fiberglass Reinforced Plastic Laminate	Wash with warm detergent, rinse with distilled water, and dry. Then abrade with emery cloth and wipe well.
— Polyester Film (like Mylar)	Wipe with acetone. Scrub with a cleaning powder (like Ajax or Dutch Cleanser), then rinse and dry.
— Polyester Resin	Wash with detergent and warm, preferably distilled, water, and dry. Abrade with an emery cloth. No further preparation is necessary.
— Polyethylene Film	Wipe with acetone on a clean cloth.
— – Polyethylene Sheet	Wipe with acetone on a clean cloth, abrade with sandpaper, and wipe again with acetone.
— – Polypropylene	Wipe with acetone on a clean cloth, abrade with sandpaper, and wipe again with acetone.
— – Polystyrene	Wash with detergent in warm water, preferably distilled, and then dry. Abrade with an emery cloth and wash again in detergent and water. No further preparation is necessary.

— Polyvinyl Chloride (PVC), Rigid	Wipe with acetone or isopropyl alcohol, abrade with sandpaper, and wipe as before. No further preparation is necessary.
— Polyvinyl Chloride, Soft and Elasticized	Wipe with mineral spirits. No further preparation is necessary.
— Polyurethane	Wipe with acetone on a clean cloth, abrade with fine sandpaper or an emery cloth, and wipe again with acetone. No further preparation is necessary.
Metals	Metal surfaces may be covered with grease, dust, dirt, oil, and other contaminants from the air. To clean the metal, use a combination of a solvent and an abrasive. For a bond of light to medium strength, wipe the metal with acetone or isopropyl alcohol on a clean cloth, and then wipe dry. Abrade lightly with dry, fine-grit sandpaper. Wipe again with the solvent and dry, repeating the first stage.
Cork	Abrade the surface with sandpaper until a fresh surface is exposed. Remove loose particles by vacuuming.
Glass	Wipe with acetone or a glass cleaner on a clean cloth.
Leather	Abrade with an emery cloth or sandpaper.
Plaster	Abrade with an emery cloth or sandpaper.
Rubber	Wipe with acetone on a clean cloth. Abrade with sandpaper or a wire brush, and wipe again with acetone.
Wood	Fine sanding leaves dust that fills the pores and interferes with a good mechanical bond. Most adhesives usually bond more strongly to wood that has been roughened with a rasp or coarse sandpaper. Care must be taken, however, not to damage the wood's surface, or the bond may not endure. Most wood joints fail because the wood separates at the glue line, or at the glue's edge, where the wood fibers have been damaged in preparation for the bond. After sanding, wipe away all dust with a damp rag. Especially oily woods should be wiped with mineral spirits, dry woods with water. Allow the surface to dry before applying glue. Make sure that all matching surfaces fit well and that the joints contain enough space for the glue film. If there are gaps, choose a glue with body, like white glues formulated for woodworking or use epoxy putty or cyanoacrylates.

PART TWO

Materials and Methods

Descriptions and Uses

Materials to Apply to Costumes

Adhesives

Adhesives are also known as *glues, cements,* and *bonding agents.* Originally, adhesives were made from natural products like milk, horse hooves, and tree fibers, and bonding applications were limited. Today, a wide variety of adhesives are synthesized from increasingly more complex polymers that bond practically everything, offering unique convenience to the modern costumer.

The most popular adhesives used by modern costume shops are *white glue* (polyvinyl acetate or PVA); *synthetic rubber cements,* such as those used by shoe-repair shops; and *hot-melt resins,* sold as web-like sheets (Stitch Witchery), or as sticks to be applied with a special heat gun. No one adhesive is suitable for all purposes, though for every surface a suitable adhesive is available.

Using adhesives can save time and therefore cut costs. Adhesives are often the most practical medium for adhering small items like jewelry, sequins, and other decoration to various surfaces. Borders and three-dimensional motifs can be created with hot glue or silicone sealant for other decorative effects. Fragile appliqué and delicate fabric may be protected with adhesives and unfinished fabric edges sealed.

Many costumers modify fabric with adhesives, stiffening costume parts, for instance, where a unique modification is desired. The modified fabric can then be further decorated or distressed as desired.

The use of adhesives brings certain disadvantages, however. The service life of the fabric that has been treated with adhesives is not well known, and most costume makers are concerned that the fabric may deteriorate when costumes are stored over a long period. Certainly, in many cases, discoloration and increased brittleness of fabric and dissipation of the original bond occur over time. Adhesives also bring hazards into the costume shop, for their inherent solvents and resins discharge vapors and liquids that can cause harm to both workers and the environment, as noted earlier under Health and Safety.

When working with adhesives, correct procedures must be followed carefully, for different adhesives bond in different ways. A chemical adhesion is based on a chemical interaction, for the adhesive alters the molecular structure of the substrate (the surface of the material that is being bonded), forming a bridge between the two substrates, each of which has been chemically altered. A mechanical bond interlocks adhesive into the interstices of the substrate, but does not alter its chemistry. Porous fabrics, like those of natural fibers, provide an effective surface for a mechanical bond. For example, an adhesive bonding a piece of fabric actually captures the fibers in its mass and holds it fast as the adhesive hardens. The best bond is one which is both chemical and mechanical, as when an adhesive both locks itself into the fibers and alters the molecular structure. Such bonds last well and are apt to survive varying conditions including laundering and cleaning.

To successfully bond surfaces other than textiles, particular care must be taken, and the adhesive must be applied to the surface exactly as directed. For information on surface preparation, see the Surface Preparation section on pages 25-27.

Dense and rigid plastic surfaces are often most successfully bonded by solvent bonding, or welding. (Do not confuse solvent bonding with solvent reactivation bonding, which is described on page 33.) For information on solvent bonding and other methods of adhering plastic sheetings, read Working Methods in the Plastic Sheetings section. Specific bonding information is included with each of the plastics covered.

Chemists classify adhesives on the basis of their chemical composition, but costumers more often classify adhesives according to their use by the costume industry. This reference book follows both types of classification. For example, many so-called jewel glues are actually specifically designed PVAs, or white glues; and because they are identified in stores as designed specifically for bonding jewelry, we have listed them as such. In other cases, rubber-based glues, including those sold for shoe repair, have many other uses, and thus are listed according to their composition. Adhesives come in various containers, which are designed to facilitate specific usage, i.e. in bottles, jars, cans and spray cans, tubes, dropper bottles, squeeze bottles, and one- and two-part syringes. Adhesives also come in many forms: powder, thin liquid, thick paste, thin paste, putty, sticks, webbing, and gel. Applications are by brush, spatula, roller, silk screen, dipping, dropper bottle, syringe, and spray. Bonding may require heat, evaporation, or pressure or all of these, and curing time can vary greatly.

Because adhesives are so various, it is imperative that the manufacturer's directions be followed explicitly. It is also important to understand that, for some adhesives, there are no solvents whatsoever. Once stuck is forever stuck. Other adhesives dry quickly, and working time is extremely limited. Shelf life is also limited for most liquid adhesives; thus, it is advisable not to overstock supplies. Most adhesives can be highly toxic (both from fumes or by skin contact) to the user and to the environment. Different materials require different methods, and the costumer must consider the number of pieces being assembled, and the type of workspace, as well as deadline constrictions. Package directions and technical data sheets usually specify the most practical techniques for using each kind of adhesive. To prevent excessive stiffening or cracking, try always to select adhesives that are more flexible than the surfaces to which they will adhere. Although adhesives can be convenient and efficient, because of the environmental toxic and safety hazards they present they are not necessarily to be preferred over sewing and other mechanical fastening methods, particularly when sewing and mechanical fastening methods will work just as effectively.

We have tested all of the adhesives described in the following sections. All have been applied to these eighteen listed substrates: acetate fabric, acetate sheeting, acrylic fabric, acrylic sheeting, cotton fabric, glass, leather, linen, metal, Mylar sheeting, nylon fabric, nylon spandex, polyester fabric, polyurethane foam (upholstery type), rayon, silk, styrofoam, vinyl upholstery sheeting (topside), and wool. All those that bonded were separated into two groups and subjected to as many as fifteen launderings and fifteen dry cleanings. The results are recorded in the accompanying charts. Results may vary, however, depending on the following factors: the quality of a fabric being bonded—its thickness, its openness of weave or knit, its stretchability, its smoothness or texture, and its surface treatment (like embossing). Other factors that influence bonding are heat and humidity in the environment, the amount of adhesive applied, and the time taken for bonding the materials together.

The charts may serve as guides for bonding like materials or unlike materials. For instance, if a specific adhesive bonds leather together and also bonds metals together, it will most likely bond metal to leather just as satisfactorily.

Working Methods Adhesives which are liquid are usually applied in one of three ways:

1. The adhesive can be applied to one surface only; in this case, allow the adhesive to become tacky and then press the parts together.

2. The adhesive can also be applied to both surfaces being bonded; this is contact bonding. In contact bonding, apply the adhesive to both surfaces and allow it to become tacky before joining.

3. For an even stronger bond, use the solvent reactivation technique. Apply the adhesive to both surfaces, allow it to dry, and then wet the adhesive with itself or its solvent, and bring the two surfaces together.

Many solvent types of adhesives can be thinned with their solvent for spray application. Spray only in a space that has adequate ventilation and follow the appropriate safety precautions. Spraying adhesives is messy, and the workspace will need protective covering. Some adhesives lose their effectiveness when thinned. Read the technical literature or contact the manufacturers if there is any question.

Adhesives can be applied by many means. In most cases, an appropriate-size brush, spatula, or smooth stick is suitable. To achieve a fine line, use a squeeze bottle with a fine tip; for an even finer line, wrap masking tape to the correct size or purchase a packet of four sizes of small metal tips, like those made by Plaid Enterprises, to fit onto the end of squeeze bottles; they are available at many craft stores. The finest lines can be drawn with syringes. Some, like Aleene's brand of syringes, are obtainable at craft stores. A large medical syringe can also be used. Be sure to clean thoroughly all syringes and metal tips so they can be reused.

Keep handy the correct solvent for quick cleanup of spills and miscalculations. Make sure that surfaces to be used are clean and dry.

In almost any kind of bonding method, pressure adds strength. An exception is when the adhesive is full bodied, or thick, and the thickness is a factor in creating the bond. Heat frequently strengthens a bond, even as it hastens the bonding process.

The working life of adhesives varies from less than a minute to a few hours, depending upon the rate of evaporation of the inherent solvent. In any bonding procedure, if the bonding time is not respected, inferior bonds will result.

Curing time is the time required for chemicals to set, or to complete their action. Since curing can take up to several days, it is wise to wait before applying pressure or laundering or dry cleaning or otherwise actually using items bonded by adhesives. Curing time can vary according to conditions of temperature and humidity. Again, refer to technical literature for exact timing.

Health and Safety Precautions for specific adhesives are listed individually below.

When it is possible to use a water-based adhesive, do so. When working with solvent-based adhesives, follow these safety measures:

- Wear a respirator or work in a well-ventilated space and avoid skin contact.
- Protect hands from solvents with the correct kind of gloves. Read MSDSs for content of the product and contact a glove manufacturer who offers advice on the best kind of gloves for protection against particular contents.
- Do not use near a stove or heat element.
- *Do not smoke or use near flames, and keep away from food and drink.*

Acrylic Cements

Brands Tested	Manufacturers
Cadco Acrylic Adhesive SC-125	Cadillac Plastic and Chemical Company
Weld-on 4	Industrial Polychemical Service Corporation, Inc. (IPS)
Weld-on 16	Industrial Polychemical Service Corporation, Inc., (IPS)

Examples of Use
- Bond acrylic and other rigid parts, such as crowns, armor, purses, and jewelry.
- Use only for bonding acrylic and the other rigid plastics, as mentioned below, to themselves or to other surfaces. This adhesive is not recommended for bonding other substrates to themselves.

Description *Acrylic cement* was created specifically to cement acrylic plastic sheets together. This adhesive will also adhere to and bond several other rigid plastics; the two Weld-on adhesives also bond polystyrene, butyrates, and polycarbonates. All three adhesives bond most other materials to acrylic. Acrylic cements are of high strength and cure quickly, varying in viscosity from water-thin to syrup consistency. They adhere by actually dissolving the substrate, so that in their softened states, they will bond, or weld, to themselves and other surfaces. Of the adhesives we tested, Cadco Acrylic Adhesive SC-125 and Weld-on 4 are low-viscosity adhesives. SC-125 is fast-setting and Weld-on 4 is moderately fast-setting, while Weld-on 16 is of high viscosity and quick-setting.

The brands listed above are available in consumer size and convenient for use by the costume shop. Other brands of acrylics come only in bulk size, more suitable for industrial use.

How to Use First sand and clean hard surfaces. With Cadco SC-125 and Weld-on 4, use a brush or other suitable applicator to completely coat one or both surfaces. In a few seconds, press parts together while still wet. Use a clamp or weight to press together until dry. The bond forms quickly, curing in 48 hours. With Weld-on 16, which is more viscous, squeeze a bead from the tube onto one surface, hold or clamp, and allow 24 hours for cure.

Acrylic can also be bonded by capillary cementing. Using masking tape, tape acrylic pieces to a jig (or clamp them together), then drip cement into the joint. Hold together until dry.

To bond plastic sheeting by the capillary-cement method, first place the plastic sheeting in a grooved jig and secure with masking tape to prevent seepage before applying the cement.

Solvent for Cleanup Acetone.

Precautions To prevent acrylic adhesives from deteriorating, store in a refrigerator.

Acrylic adhesives stiffen fabrics.

Health and Safety Use in well ventilated area or with respirator. Avoid contact with skin. Keep away from heat sources.

Some Untested Brands Crafts' size: Hal-Tech 3001, Halcraft USA. Industrial Polychemical Service Corporation, Inc. (IPS), has an extensive line of acrylic cements.
Industrial size: 3M Co., Loctite Corp., IPS, Inc., and Lord Corp. manufacture extensive lines of acrylic cements.

Where to Find Plastics supply shops and craft stores.

Sizes 1½ oz. - 1 gal.

ACRYLIC CEMENTS **LAUNDER** DRY-CLEAN

Surface	Cadco		Weld-on 4		Weld-on 16	
Acetate Fabric	0	0	0	0	E	G
Acetate Sheeting	0	0*	0	0*	P	F*
Acrylic Fabric	0	0	0	0	P	P
Acrylic Sheeting	E	P	P	F	P	P
Cotton	0	0	0	0	E	P
Glass	0	0	0	0	P	P
Leather	0	0	0	0	G	E
Linen	0	0	0	0	P	E
Metal	0	0	0	0	E	P
Mylar	0	0	0	0	P	P
Nylon	0	0	0	0	G	F
Nylon Spandex	0	0	0	0	E	P
Polyester Fabric	0	0	0	0	E	G
Polyurethane Foam	0	0	0	0	E	P
Rayon	0	0	0	0	E	E
Silk	0	0	0	0	E	G
Styrofoam	0	0	0	0	P	P
Vinyl	0	0	0	0	E	E
Wool	0	0	0	0	P	P

0 =Does not bond.
P =Poor bond: Bond fails with first laundering or dry cleaning.
F = Fair bond: Materials stay bonded for up to five launderings or dry cleanings.
G = Good bond: Materials stay bonded for up to fourteen launderings or dry cleanings.
E = Excellent: Bond appears permanent.

Note: Acrylic cements stiffen fabrics.
*Material disintegrates in dry cleaning

Cyanoacrylates (Super Glues)

Brands Tested / Cyanoacrylates (Superglues)	Manufacturers
Devcon Super Glue	Devcon Corporation
Devcon Super Glue Gel	Devcon Corporation
Duro Quick Gel Super Glue	Loctite Corporation
Frame Fast Screen Adhesive	Uncommon Conglomerates, Inc.
Krazy Glue	Krazy Glue, Inc.
Zap-A-Gap	Pacer Technology

Examples of Use

- Create and repair jewelry.
- Adhere small pieces and decorations onto nontextile accessories.
- Texture or glaze a surface.

Cyanoacrylates are most effective for bonding small areas like jewelry, decorative pieces, and nontextile accessories. When the work can be done quickly and when the time to dry and cure is not limited, cyanoacrylates can be the product of choice.

Cyanoacrylate was carefully dropped into place from its container onto the fabric to create an illusion of beads.

Cyanoacrylate gel can also be used for texturing, by dripping small beads of the glue onto a costume surface. The desert tortoise skin described in Part Three was textured with cyanoacrylate. In the film *Fellini's Casanova*, droplets of jewel-like cyanoacrylate enliven many headdresses.

Description   *Cyanoacrylate* (superglue) is especially effective for quickly bonding nonporous materials such as glass, metals, and most sheet and film plastics to themselves and to other materials. Though the cyanoacrylates available in hardware stores do not usually bond porous substances, other brands are especially formulated for such use. These are available only through their manufacturers. Cyanoacrylates are colorless and transparent and set quickly within a work time of only a few seconds, or at the most, within one minute, since they cure by exposure to air. Hundreds of different formulas are available, with viscosities ranging from as thin as water to the thickness of gels. Cyanoacrylates are packaged in tubes and dropper bottles. Surfaces must be cleaned carefully for successful bonding, and application is usually by squeezing or dropping. A spray activator may be used in conjunction with the adhesive for a stronger bond and a wider range of bonding surfaces.

In industry, cyanoacrylates replace screws and nails, but the bond can degrade when subjected to moisture. It is most important not to bring cyanoacrylates in contact with the skin, because the bonding is both immediate and damaging to the skin.

How to Use   Cyanoacrylates bond best on hard nonporous surfaces like glass, metals, ceramics, and hardwood. Surfaces must be dry and completely clean before bonding. Sand lightly and wipe with a cloth moistened with a solvent such as alcohol, to be sure the surfaces to be bonded fit exactly (though with cyanoacrylate gels, the gel usually provides enough thickness to fill small gaps). Drop the adhesive onto one surface only, using two drops per square inch. Spread by rubbing the two surfaces together. Apply some pressure. The bond begins to set in a few seconds, though the maximum bond comes twelve to twenty-four hours later. Do not use with polyurethane, for the cyanoacrylate-polyurethane combination could ignite.

If using with a spray activator, first spray the surfaces before applying the glue. Spray activators also make bonding fabric using cyanoacrylates easier. Hold fabric in place. Apply both the adhesive and the activator, applying either one first.

Gels are thicker, stronger, and preferable for applying small decorative items onto larger surfaces.

Solvent for Cleanup   Cyanoacrylate debonders are designed specifically for cyanoacrylate removal. Other solvents that have a more limited effect include acetone and nail polish remover.

Precautions   Cyanoacrylates stiffen fabrics.

Water catalyzes cyanoacrylate polymerization. When the humidity is high, the polymerization will result in weak or brittle bonds. To see this reaction dramatized, put a small drop of water on a bead of superglue and watch it. The result will be a white powdery substance rather than a clear strong plastic material.

Do not use cyanoacrylate on polyurethane—it could ignite.

Health and Safety   Cyanoacrylates are highly volatile and should be used in an open space, preferably near an exhaust fan. A respirator should protect against organic vapors. Cyanoacrylates stick to most surfaces, including skin, and will mar all surfaces, often permanently. We advise keeping a debonder solvent nearby when working with this product.

Vapors from cyanoacrylates are damaging to the eyes.

Some Untested Brands   Pronto Instant Adhesives, 3M Co.; Super Glue, Bond Adhesives Company; Super Glue, Evo-stick, Evode Ltd. (UK); Loctite 404 and 480, Loctite Corp.; and other brands from Pacer, Ross, Quicktite, and Uncommon Conglomerates.

Where to Find   For small quantities: hardware, paint, and hobby stores.

The Uncommon Conglomerates, Loctite Corp. and 3M Co. products are only available through the manufacturer. Many Pacer products are only available through the manufacturer, though many of Pacer's Zap products are sold in hobby and hardware stores.

Activator: Uncommon Conglomerates

Sizes For crafts use: .06 oz. - 1 oz.
For industrial use: 1 oz. - 1 lb.

CYANOACRYLATES (SUPER GLUES) **LAUNDER** DRY-CLEAN

Surface	Devcon Super Glue		Devcon Super Glue Gel		Duro Quick Gel Super Glue		Frame Fast Screen Adhesive		Krazy Glue		Zap-A-Gap	
Acetate Fabric	F	F	P	P	F*	F*	0	0	P	P	E	P
Acetate Sheeting	P	P	P	0	P	P	0	0	F	F	E	0
Acrylic Fabric	P	P	F	P	F	P	0	0	P	P	E	F
Acrylic Sheeting	P	P	P	P	P*	P*	E	0	P	P	E	F**
Cotton	F*	P*	G*	F*	G	F	P	0	P*	P*	0	0
Glass	E	E	G	G	E	G	P	P	E	E	F	G
Leather	P	P	P	P	F	F	0	0	P	P	F	F
Linen	P	P	F	F	F	F	0	0	P	P	0	0
Metal	P	F	F	G	P	F	P	P	F	F	E	E
Mylar	P	F	P	P	F*	P*	0	0	F	F	P	P
Nylon	F*	F*	G*	G*	G*	F*	0	0	G*	F*	E*	P*
Nylon Spandex	0	P	F	P	F	P	0	0	P	P	0	0
Polyester Fabric	0	F*	F*	F*	G*	P*	0	0	F*	F*	0*	0
Polyurethane Foam	P	P	F	F	F	P	P	F†	P	P	F	F
Rayon	F	P	F	F	G*	P*	0	P	P	P	P	P
Silk	0	P	F	F	F*	F*	0	P	P	P	E	E
Styrofoam	0	0	0	0	0	0	P	P	0	0	P	P**
Vinyl	F	P	E	P	G	F	P	F††	P	P	E	G
Wool	0	P	P	F	P	P	0	P	0	0	0	0

0 = Does not bond.
P = Poor bond: Bond fails with first laundering or dry cleaning.
F = Fair bond: Materials stay bonded for up to five launderings or dry cleanings.
G = Good bond: Materials stay bonded for up to fourteen launderings or dry cleanings.
E = Excellent: Bond appears permanent.

Note: Cyancacrylates stiffen fabrics.
*Adhesive stains.
**Material dissolves.
† Material crumbles.
†† Surface dissolves.

Epoxies

Brands Tested	Manufacturers
Five Minute Epoxy	Devcon Corporation
Five Minute Epoxy Gel	Devcon Corporation
Aradite Gel	Ciba-Geigy Corporation, U. K.
Devcon EK 2 Kit Clear Epoxy	Devcon Corporation
Duro Master Mend	Loctite Corporation
Duto Quick Mix Syringe E-Pox E 5	Loctite Corporation
Scotch-Weld 2216 A/B	3M Company

Examples of Use

- Bond metal to nonporous materials such as rigid plastics, glass, porcelain, and ceramics to make jewelry.
- Apply decorations to solid costume pieces, such as rigid plate armor.
- Use as casting material.

Epoxies are useful to the costumer for making and repairing jewelry as well as for creating additional three-dimensional decorative pieces on armor, headdresses, etc. Epoxies can also be used for casting and creating dimensional, or relief, decoration. See examples on pages 203-208 of the Casting Plastics section.

Description

Epoxies are high-strength adhesives that effectively bond metals, glass, ceramic, nylon, and phenolics. They have good resistance to solvents, water, and the environment, although prolonged immersion in water is not recommended. Epoxies are packaged in cans, tubes, and syringe dispensers, and are available in varying viscosities, ranging from syrup to putty. Large quantities can be purchased in cans from industrial suppliers. Color varies from amber to gray.

The tested epoxies are all two-part systems, with differing means of application. They are available in kits—one part is epoxy and the other is a hardener or setting agent. Mixing and application directions are packaged with the product, and it is of utmost importance to follow instructions exactly; otherwise, there may be no bond or the bond may never dry. Epoxies sold in tubes, rather than syringes, are more reliable, because syringes sometimes disperse unevenly.

To bond large quantities of materials, buy epoxy from an industrial adhesive specialist, whose quality can be more dependable than in the smaller "crafts" containers.

Araldite: Two-part system in twin-tube syringe, one part clear, the other yellow. This epoxy bonds to most surfaces, and survives on most through repeated laundering and dry cleaning.

Devcon 5 Minute Epoxy: Kit includes two one-ounce tubes, clear in color and of thick viscosity. Spread with a stick or spatula. Fairly successful in laundering.

Devcon 5 Minute Epoxy Gel: Two-part system in twin-tube syringe; thick gel; white; apply by syringe or spatula.

Devcon EK 2 Kit Clear Epoxy: Kit includes two self-metering tubes (one of clear epoxy and the other a hardener), two mixing paddles and full instructions and medium liquid of clear amber color. According to our testing, this epoxy proved the most successful and bonded all surfaces, with only styrofoam losing its adhesion after washing and dry cleaning. Like all epoxies, however, it stiffens fabrics.

Duro Master Mend: A twin-tube set, with one-ounce tubes of yellow; thick viscosity. Spread with a stick or spatula.

Duro Quick Mix Syringe E-Pox-E5: Two-part system packaged in twin-tube syringe with attached static mixer; mixes as it is extruded out of the parallel tubes and through the mixer tube; medium syrup; pale yellow. This epoxy was the least satisfactory when subjected to washing and dry cleaning.

Scotch-Weld 2216 A/B: A two-part system of medium viscosity; medium gray. Mix equal amounts from each of two tubes, following enclosed instructions; apply with a special gun, spatula, or trowel. Although many of the materials tested lasted through fifteen washings and dry cleanings, this adhesive stiffened and discolored fabrics more than most, even cracking some.

How to Use Nonporous surfaces require careful cleaning before using, and following package directions with utmost care, for different epoxies have different specifications. Bonding or setting time varies from four minutes to several hours, depending on composition of the epoxy.

Only mix as much as will be used, and mix according to package directions. Polyethylene sheeting makes a good mixing surface, since epoxy does not adhere to it. If bonding surfaces need to be held together while drying, use a clamp or masking tape.

Store epoxy in refrigerator when not being used and warm to room temperature before using.

Solvent for Cleanup Mineral spirits, paint thinner, acetone, or nail polish remover can be used in some cases before the curing process is under way. Devcon 5 Minute Epoxy can be cleaned with soap and water while still wet. After epoxies are dry and set, they cannot be cleaned up.

Precautions Epoxies are not recommended for bonding fabric to fabric; epoxies are stiff and brittle, best used on hard surfaces. A full-length laundering cycle can soften epoxies, causing the bond to weaken.

Health and Safety MSDSs on epoxies are crucial because literally dozens of chemicals can be contained in them. Some epoxies are much more toxic than others.

Epoxies are highly flammable and combustible. Do not use near a flame or while smoking. Use with local ventilation or wear respirator. Goggles, protective gloves, and protective clothing are also needed for large jobs. Glycidyl ethers, used in some epoxy formulations, can cause birth defects as well as reproductive and blood diseases in animals. Among workers exposed to epoxy daily, almost 50 percent have developed allergies.

Some Untested Brands Scotch-Weld Epoxy Adhesives, 3M Co.; Epoxy Adhesive, Ross.

Where to Find Hardware stores, home-improvement stores, and manufacturers. Consult yellow pages for local manufacturers.

Sizes 1 oz. - 4 oz.

EPOXIES   **LAUNDER** DRY-CLEAN

Surface	Araldite		Devcon 5 Ninute Epoxy		Devcon 5 Minute Epoxy Gel		Devcon EK2 Kit Clear Epoxy		Duro Master Mend		Duro Quick Mix Syringe E-Poxes		Scotch Weld 2216 A/B	
Acetate Fabric	E	E	E	E	P	P	E	E	P	P	G*	G*	E*	P*
Acetate Sheeting	E	G	P	P	P	P	E	E	P	P	P	P	G	E
Acrylic Fabric	E	E	E	E	E	E	E	E	P	G	E*	G*	E*	P*
Acrylic Sheeting	F	P	P	P	F	P	E	E	F	P	P	P	E	P
Cotton	E	E	E	G	G	E	E	E	G	P	E	E	E	F
Glass	G	E	E	E	G	G	E	E	E	E	E	E	P	E
Leather	F	G	P	G	P	P	E	E	F	F	P	P	G	F
Linen	E	E	E	E	E	F	E	E	E	E	E	E	E	F
Metal	E	E	E	E	E	E	E	E	E	E	G	P	E	E
Mylar	E	E	P	P	P	P	E	E	P	P	P	P	E	G
Nylon	E	E	P	P	P	P	E	E	P	P	G	F	E	G
Nylon Spandex	E	E	P	O	P	P	E	E	P	P	P	P	P	P
Polyester Fabric	E	E	G	G	G	G	E	E	G	G	F	P	E	E
Polyurethane Foam	E	E	E	F	E	G	E	E	E	G	G	P	E	P
Rayon	E	E	G	G	G	G	E	E	G	F	E	G	E	E
Silk	E	E	P	E	E	E	E	E	P	F	G	P	E	G
Styrofoam	E	P	E	P	E	P	P	P	E	P	G	P	E	E
Vinyl	E	G	P	P	P	P	E	E	P	P	G	F	F	P
Wool	E	E	P	E	E	E	E	E	P	P	E	F*	G*	G*

O = Does not bond.
P = Poor bond: Bond fails with first laundering or dry cleaning.
F = Fair bond: Materials stay bonded for up to five launderings or dry cleanings.
G = Good bond: Materials stay bonded for up to fourteen launderings or dry cleanings.
E = Excellent: Bond appears permanent.

Note: Epoxies stiffen fabrics.
*Adhesive stains.

Fabric Adhesives

Brands Tested	Manufacturers
Bridal Adhesive	Manny's Millinery Supply
Evo-Stik for Fabric	Evode Limited, UK
Fray Check	Dritz Corporation
Magic Mender	EZ International
OK to Wash-It	Aleene's (Product of Duncan Enterprises)
Stitchless Fabric Glue	Delta Technical Coatings, Inc.
Stop Fraying	Aleene's (Division of Artis, Inc.)
Unique Stitch	W. H. Collins, Inc.

Examples of Use

- Substitute for basting.
- Mend patches onto fabric.
- Finish raw edges of fabric.
- Appliqué small decorations onto fabric.

Mending, patching, and appliquéing small cloth items to flexible surfaces can be easily achieved with these adhesives.

Fray Check and Stop Fraying are designed specifically to prevent fabric from fraying. Fray Check and Stop Fraying bond some textiles, but when so used, the bond lasts through laundering and dry cleaning.

Description

Fabric adhesives are usually found in the notion counters of fabric stores and are designed for quick repairs: basting, trim application, and fray prevention. Bridal Adhesive can be obtained through millinery suppliers and is widely used by costume shops to apply trim. OK to Wash-It, Unique Stitch, and Stitchless have a vinyl base in a water solution, similar to white glue, and these are soluble in water when still wet. Bridal Adhesive, Evo-Stik, Fray Check, and Magic Mender are solvent-based and cannot be thinned or cleaned up with water. For personal safety and health, the water-based adhesives should be used whenever possible.

How to Use

Use directly from the squeeze bottle or brush onto one surface being glued. For the white, water-based brands, let set for a few minutes until tacky. Then press together the two pieces being bonded for best results. Wait at least twenty-four hours before washing or dry cleaning.

The solvent-based brands dry more quickly, with a shorter working time. To speed up results with either type, use a hair dryer, iron, or hot-air gun.

Solvent for Cleanup

OK to Wash-It, Stitchless, and Unique Stitch: water.
Fray Check: alcohol.
Bridal Adhesive, Evo-Stik, and Magic Mender: acetone.

Precautions

Do not use when a soft, pliable hand—or draping quality—is a factor, for these adhesives will stiffen and sometimes stain fabrics. Stretch fabrics lose their elasticity. Not all of these adhesives remain bonded to all fabrics through washing and dry cleaning.

Health and Safety   Use personal safety precautions. Bridal Adhesive and Fray Check are extremely flammable as well as harmful to inhale. Use all these adhesives with adequate ventilation, avoid skin contact, and keep away from flames and food. When possible, substitute water-based adhesives for these solvent-based ones.

Some Untested Brands   Water-based: Fabric Glue #430, and Waterproof Victory, Bond Adhesives Company; Plexi 400 Stretch Adhesive, Tom Jones; Magique.

Solvent-based: Bridal Glue, Washington Millinery; Darn Fabric Mender, Woodhill Permatex; Fabri Tac, Beacon Chemical Co.; Fabric Cement, Magic Mender; Liquid Stitch, Dritz; Magna-tac Bridal Glue, Beacon Chemical Co. Inc.; No-Fray Spray, Sprayway.

Where to Find   Fabric stores.

Sizes   ¾ oz. (Fray Check) through 8 oz. (Stitchless)

FABRIC ADHESIVES TO PREVENT FRAYING   **LAUNDER**   DRY-CLEAN

Surface	Fray Check		Stop Fraying	
Acetate Fabric	E	E	E	G*
Acrylic Fabric	E	E	G	E *
Cotton	E	E	E	G*
Linen	E	E	E	P
Nylon	E	E	P	E*
Nylon Spandex	E	E	P	E*
Polyester Fabric	E	E	E	E*
Rayon	E	E	G	G*
Silk	E	E	E	G*
Styrofoam	E	E	E	P*
Vinyl	E	E	G	P*
Wool	E	E	E	E*

0 = Does not bond.
P = Poor bond: Bond fails with first laundering or dry cleaning.
F = Fair bond: Materials stay bonded for up to five launderings or dry cleanings.
G = Good bond: Materials stay bonded for up to fourteen launderings or dry cleanings.
E = Excellent: Bond appears permanent.

Note: Edges coated with Stop Fraying should be hand laundered.
* Samples stuck together in the first dry cleaning.

FABRIC ADHESIVES **LAUNDER** DRY-CLEAN

Surface	Bridal Adhesive		Evo-Stick		Magic Mender		OK to Wash-It		Stitchless		Unique Stitch	
Acetate Fabric	P	P	E	F	P	P	G	P	G	G	E	E
Acetate Sheeting	E	G	P	G	P	P	G	G	P	P	G	E
Acrylic Fabric	E	G	G	P	P	P	G	G	P	P	E	F
Acrylic Sheeting	E	G	E	P	P	P	G	G	F	F	G	P
Cotton	E	G	E	F	P	P	G	G	G	G	E	E
Glass	O	G	F	P	P	P	P	P	O	O	P	E
Leather	E	G	F	F	P	P	G	G	G	G	E	E
Linen	E	G	E	F	P	P	G	G	E	E	E	E
Metal	P	G	F	E	P	P	F	G	E	E	E	G
Mylar	E	G	E	G	P	P	G	G	G	E	E	G
Nylon	P	G	F	P	P	P	G	G	G	F	F	F
Nylon Spandex	P	P	E	F	P	P	E	F	E	G	E	G
Polyester Fabric	P	E	E	F	P	P	E	F	F	G	F	F
Polyurethane Foam	E	F	E	P	E	P	G	G	G	G	F	F
Rayon	P	E	F	F	E	P	E	P	G	E	E	E
Silk	E	P	E	F	P	P	E	P	G	E	E	E
Styrofoam	E	P	P	P	P	P	G	F	E	P	E	P
Vinyl	E	P	E	F	P	P	G	G	P	G	E	E
Wool	E	E	E	F	P	P	G	F	G	E	E	E

O = Does not bond.
P = Poor bond: Bond fails with first laundering or dry cleaning.
F = Fair bond: Materials stay bonded for up to five launderings or dry cleanings.
G = Good bond: Materials stay bonded for up to fourteen launderings or dry cleanings.
E = Excellent: Bond appears permanent.

Glue Sticks

Brands Tested	Manufacturers
Glue-Stic	Avery Dennison Incorporated
Glue Stick Purple/White	3M Company
UHU Stic	Eberhard Faber

Examples of Use

- Replace hand basting for appliqués and hems.
- Make emergency repairs.
- Stop runs in nylon hosiery and tights.

This glue can fill gaps in nonporous materials and can be used as a base for textured matter. Such bases can also hold objects like wires, flowers, or feathers.

Glue sticks are also useful for applying motifs of glitter or flocking. Simply draw or stencil a design with the glue stick onto a fabric and sprinkle glitter or flocking before the glue dries. This technique should not be used on items to be washed.

Description *Glue sticks* are popular vinyl-based adhesives for adhering papers. We have found that they also have a place in the costume shop. They are conveniently packaged in easy-to-use cylindrical lipstick-like cases. Both 3M and Avery Dennison make sticks that are temporary. 3M also makes permanent glue sticks in purple as well as the standard white. An advantage to a colored stick is its visibility to the user.

How to Use Push the glue up and out of the container, like a lipstick, and rub onto a surface. Press the two surfaces together immediately, since it dries in two to three minutes. Optimum adhesion occurs in one minute after contact.

For emergency repairs and quick basting, roll on a thick line of glue. Do not place glue on the machine stitching line, for this can gum up the sewing machine needle.

Some fabrics bonded with glue sticks can be dry-cleaned. Refer to the charts that follow.

Solvent for Cleanup Water.

Precautions Keep cap on tightly, and do not wash. dry cleaning is successful on some surfaces.

Health and Safety Avoid eye contact and prolonged or repeated skin contact. Repeated contact can cause redness, swelling, pain, and itching.

Some glue sticks marketed for children contain detergent so they wash out easily.

Some Untested Brands Elmer's Washable Glue Stick, Elmer's Products, Inc.
Ross Stik, Ross Adhesives

Where to Find Stationery and office supply stores.

Sizes .26 oz. - 1 oz. in containers from 3 ¼" - 4 ½" long.

GLUE STICKS   **LAUNDER** DRY-CLEAN

Surface	Glue-Stic		Glue Stick		UHU Stic	
Acetate Fabric	P	E	P	E	P	F
Acetate Sheeting	P	G	P	G	P	F
Acrylic Fabric	P	G	P	G	P	F
Acrylic Sheeting	O	O	O	O	O	O
Cotton	P	E	P	E	P	F
Glass	O	O	O	O	P	P
Leather	P	E	P	E	P	F
Linen	P	G	P	G	P	F
Metal	O	O	O	O	P	P
Mylar	P	G	P	G	P	F
Nylon	P	G	P	G	P	F
Nylon Spandex	P	G	P	G	P	F
Polyester Fabric	P	E	P	G	P	F
Polyurethane Foam	P	G	P	G	P	F
Rayon	P	P	P	G	P	F
Silk	P	E	P	G	P	F
Styrofoam	P	P	P	P	P	F
Vinyl	P	G	P	G	P	P
Wool	P	E	P	E	P	F

O = Does not bond.
P = Poor bond: Bond fails with first laundering or dry cleaning.
F = Fair bond: Materials stay bonded for up to five launderings or dry cleanings.
G = Good bond: Materials stay bonded for up to fourteen launderings or dry cleanings.
E = Excellent: Bond appears permanent.

Hot-Melt Resins:
Glue Sticks, Fusible Web Film, Pellets, and Powder

Hot-melt resin adhesives are formulated from a variety of polymers, which accounts for their differing properties. The most common plastics used for hot melts are ethyl vinyl acetate (EVA), polyamides (nylons), polyesters, and silicones. Hot melts are solid at room temperature and are melted by heat into a molten state. Upon cooling, they return to a solid form, allowing them to function as adhesives or sealants. The advantages and disadvantages of using hot melts vary with the intended purposes. Hot melts bond materials and create a moderately flexible bond that with some brands and on some substrates may be laundered or dry-cleaned. The various forms of hot melts are described on the following pages.

Hot-Melt Glue Sticks

Brands Tested	Manufacturers
Bostik 6330	Bostik Inc.
Jet-Melt Adhesive 3762	3M Company
Jet-Melt Adhesive 3764	3M Company
Hot-Melt Glue Sticks	Stanley Fastening Systems

Examples of Use
- Use as an adhesive when a thick base must hold jeweled pieces, chains, metallic ornaments, etc.
- Create raised ornamental designs such as fake embroidery, braids, and jewels on fabric, or place raised decoration on nontextile accessories.
- Cast in plaster molds for jewelry. See pages 208-210 of Casting Plastics section for casting hot-melt glue sticks.

Since hot-melt glue sticks are thick-bodied, they work best as adhesives on heavy fabric or on nontextile accessories.

Description *Hot-melt glue sticks* are applied by special heat applicators, or glue guns. The sticks may vary in size, from one half to one inch in diameter and two to twelve inches in length, and must fit the gun. Most costume shops use a very small gun that requires small sticks. Gun prices vary widely, and one with safety features is a solid

Five different found objects of various materials were bonded onto this helmet with hot-melt glue sticks.

CONSTRUCTION: RICHARD TAUTKUS.

investment. Some other features are safety stands, temperature control, and battery operation.

Companies like 3M and Bostik have an extensive line of guns with different features for use with different size sticks. Make sure that the stick size and gun size match up. The high-temperature sticks that bond many materials are manufactured by industrial adhesive manufacturers like 3M, Bostik, and Thermogrip.

Craft and hobby stores sell low-temperature glue guns for low-temperature, small-size sticks. Though a low temperature is safer, it may not be hot enough to adhere a given stick to a specific substrate. These do not bond to as many surfaces, nor do the bonds survive well in washing and dry cleaning.

How to Use Insert the glue stick into the gun and push the lever to operate. Use plenty of glue because a thin amount will not bond. Work fast, as the glue cools and hardens quickly. If your project requires careful handling, first heat up the surfaces with an iron or heat gun to slow down the cooling and hardening process.

Solvent for Cleanup To clean up, peel and scrape the cooled glue from the work surface. To clean from small items, place the items in a freezer and then chip off the frozen glue.

Precautions Do not use hot-melt glue sticks on very flexible surfaces. Hot-melt glue has only moderate flexibility and is not appropriate for gluing such items as rubber shoe soles.

Health and Safety Hot-melt glue can easily and seriously burn the skin. Because of this, do not be tempted to hand manipulate this glue, and take special care not to place fingers near the tip of the gun.

The hot-melt glue odor is from volatilization of plasticizers that manufacturers will tell you are harmless. For this reason, most manufacturers do not identify these chemicals on their MSDSs. Actually, most plasticizers have never been studied for long-term hazards, even though many are chemically related to known toxic and/or cancer-causing substances. Until more is known about these plasticizers, it is wise to use hot glue with ventilation.

Burning or overheating hot-melt glue is known to release highly toxic chemicals.

Some Untested Brands Industrial grade: 3M, Bostik, and Thermogrip all have a long line of these products.

Hobby and craft grade: FloralPro, Adhesive Technologies Inc.; Pow'r Stix, H.B. Fuller Company. Hot-melt glue sticks are also sold by Ad-Tech and Technocraft.

Where to Find Hardware stores, some fabric stores, and manufacturers.

Sizes ½" - 1" diameter, 1" - 12" length.

HOT-MELT GLUE STICKS **LAUNDER** DRY-CLEAN

Surface	Bostik 6330		Jet-melt 3762		Jet-melt 3764		Stanley Hot-Melt Glue Sticks	
Acetate Fabric	F	F	P	P	F	P	G	F
Acetate Sheeting	F	G	O	O	E	G	F	F
Acrylic Fabric	F	F	E	P	E	F	F	F
Acrylic Sheeting	E	F	E	P	E	P	E	F
Cotton	E	F	P	P	E	P	E	F
Glass	F	E	P	P	E	E	F	F
Leather	F	F	P	P	E	P	F	F
Linen	F	F	P	P	E	P	E	F
Metal	F	F	P	P	F	E	F	F
Mylar	F	F	P	P	F	G	F	F
Nylon	F	F	P	P	E	P	G	F
Nylon Spandex	F	F	P	P	E	P	G	F
Polyester Fabric	F	F	P	P	E	P	G	F
Polyurethane Foam	E	F	G	P	E	P	G	F
Rayon	F	F	F	P	F	P	F	F
Silk	F	F	P	P	E	P	F	F
Styrofoam	E	P	E	P	E	P	E	F
Vinyl	E	F	P	P	F	P	G	F
Wool	F	F	P	P	E	G	F	F

O = Does not bond.
P = Poor bond: Bond fails with first laundering or dry cleaning.
F = Fair bond: Materials stay bonded for up to five launderings or dry cleanings.
G = Good bond: Materials stay bonded for up to fourteen launderings or dry cleanings.
E = Excellent: Bond appears permanent.

Fusible Web Films

Brands Tested	Manufacturers
Stitch Witchery	Bostik inc.
Wonder Under	Pellon Corporation
Wonder Web	Pellon Corporation

Examples of Use

- Appliqué for short-term use when not requiring cleaning or washing.
- Baste large appliqués that could be difficult to hand-sew.

Use on woven and felted fabrics of thin to moderate thickness. Most fusible webs are not stretchy, and so are not successful with stretch fabrics. There are, however, some specifically made to use with knits. Thin fabrics fuse more strongly because the iron's heat can easily reach through to the layer of web.

Description   *Fusible web films* are tissue-thin sheets of adhesive resin, packaged in several-yard rolls, which can be cut to the size needed. Several weights are available in most brands. Web films also come as iron-on tapes. Web films and tapes that come with a paper backing are generally easier to use.

How to Use   Cut the webbing to the correct shape, placing it between the two layers of fabric. Set an iron on the wool steam setting, cover the fabric's surface with a wet press cloth and press firmly for ten to fifteen seconds. Repeat until the entire area is covered, overlapping the ironed spots for thorough coverage.

Precautions   Since a hot iron must be used, the heat may be too hot to fuse fabrics like synthetics with a low melting point. Wool, nylon, and acetate as well as plastic sheeting, vinyl, and leather are materials that may not fuse as successfully as others.

Unfortunately, in most cases, web films will not withstand dry cleaning, though they tolerate laundering better.

Some Untested Brands   Full-width rolls: Heat N Bond, Therm O Web; Hot Stitch, Aleene's (Division of Artis, Inc.).

Iron-on Tapes: Heat N Bond, Therm O Web; Hem N Trim, Dritz.

Where to Find   Fabric stores.

Sizes   15" × 15 yd.

FUSIBLE WEB FILM   **LAUNDER**   DRY-CLEAN

Surface	Stitch Witchery		Wonder Under		Wonder Web	
Acetate Fabric	P	P	G	G	P	P
Acetate Sheeting	O	O	O	O	O	O
Acrylic Fabric	F	F	G	G	P	F
Acrylic Sheeting	O	O	O	O	O	O
Cotton	F	F	G	E	P	F
Glass	O	O	O	O	O	O
Leather	P	P	G	G	P	P
Linen	P	P	G	E	P	P
Metal	O	O	O	O	O	O
Mylar	O	O	O	O	O	O
Nylon	G	G	G	E	P	P
Nylon Spandex	P	P	G	E	P	P
Polyester Fabric	G	G	G	E	P	P
Polyurethane Foam	O	O	G	G	E	P
Rayon	P	G	G	G	P	G
Silk	P	P	G	G	F	F
Styrofoam	O	O	O	O	O	O
Vinyl	O	O	O	O	P	P
Wool	O	O	O	O	P	P

O = Does not bond.
P = Poor bond: Bond fails with first laundering or dry cleaning.
F = Fair bond: Materials stay bonded for up to five launderings or dry cleanings.
G = Good bond: Materials stay bonded for up to fourteen launderings or dry cleanings.
E = Excellent: Bond appears permanent.

Hot-Melt Pellets

Description *Pellets* are crystalline chips approximately one-quarter inch in diameter, devised for use in automatic applicators, primarily by large manufacturers of clothing and other textile goods. Pellets are not especially practical in costume shops. Use is best limited for decorative texturing, in which case the pellets could be mixed with another adhesive, paint, or coating, then brushed or trowled onto a surface.

We did not test this material because of its impracticability.

Where to Find Manufacturers of hot-melt products.

Sizes 50 lb. - 300 lb.

Hot-Melt Powders

Description *Hot-melt powder* is used primarily in the garment industry for fusing low-cost garment parts like interfacing, appliqués, and certain linings. It is more difficult to control than either glue sticks or web and is impractical for use in the costume shop. Powder, like other hot melts, is often made from polyester or polyamide and is highly hazardous. We do not recommend its use.

We also did not test this material because of its impracticability.

Some Brands Hot Stitch Glue, Aleene's; Platamid Hot Melt, Rilsan Corp.; Polyamide Powder, Bostik Inc.; White Stuff, Uncommon Conglomerates.

Where to Find Manufacturers.

Sizes White Stuff: 1 lb. - 250 lb.
Others: 250 lb.

Jewelry Adhesives

Brands Tested	Manufacturers
Bond Rhinestone Adhesive #916	Bond Adhesives Company
Gem-Tac	Beacon Chemical Company
Jewel-Glue	Ridlen Adhesives, Inc.
Jewel-It	Aleene's (Division of Artis, Inc.)

Examples of Use Adhere jewelry and small decorative items to fabric and nontextile costumes.

Description *Jewelry adhesives* come in small, easy-to-use containers and are available at most fabric stores. They are designed to attach small nonporous surfaces to other porous or nonporous materials and are thin and syrupy in viscosity. Bond Rhinestone Adhesive is solvent-based. Gem-Tac, Jewel-Glue and Jewel-It are slightly different formulations of polyvinyl acetate (white glue) and are water-based.

These are not the only adhesives that bond jewels to fabrics. Among the many adhesives that work well for this purpose are cyanoacrylates (super glues) and

Phlexglu (a polyvinyl acetate, or white glue). Phlexglu bonded to all the materials we tested, and the bond remained through more than fifteen washings and cleanings. Hot-melt glue sticks will also adhere ornaments.

When selecting the proper adhesive for bonding jewelry onto other surfaces, check to see which adhesives will bond to both surfaces. Rhinestones are usually backed by natural or colored aluminum. Modern sequins can be made from acetate, Mylar, vinyl, or other materials. Vintage sequins are usually cellulose or metal. Inexpensive "paste" jewelry is either glass or acrylic; distinguish between the two by comparing weights— glass is the heavier. Some adhesives can affect the powdered aluminum backing on rhinestones. Of all the jewelry adhesives tested, Ridlen's Jewel-Glue was the only one that remained bonded to metal after both fifteen launderings and fifteen dry cleanings. Test first.

Stones and sequins with an adhesive backing may be quickly bonded to fabric. M. Frankel and Sons and Jehlor Fantasy Fabrics carry such jewelry.

How to Use Squeeze from the tube directly onto the "jewel" and press the jewel onto the fabric or other surface. Or squeeze onto a small dish and brush or swab onto the surface. Allow one hour drying time before wearing.

When gluing sequins to fabric, apply plenty of glue; press the sequin into the glue, making sure that a glob of glue comes up through the sequin's center hole. When dry, the glue will form a protrusion through the hole, holding the sequin in place.

The tested materials that withstood solvents best were adhered with Bond Rhinestone Adhesive and Ridlen's Jewel-Glue. Refer to the chart for details and specific fabrics.

Solvent for Cleanup Bond Rhinestone Adhesive: acetone.

All others: soap and water.

Precautions Take care to confine the adhesive only to areas of material being bonded, for it will stain fabric.

Health and Safety All adhesives should be used in a ventilated area; with Bond, take additional fire precautions for it contains acetone.

Some Untested Brands Solvent-based: Jewelry and More, Creatively Yours; Victory 1991, Bond Adhesives Company; G-S Hypo-tube Cement, Germanow-Simon.

Water-based: Jewel & Fabric Glue, Jurgen; Jewel Glue, Plaid Enterprises.

Where to Find Jewelry findings stores, hobby and craft stores, fabric stores.

Sizes 1¼-oz. - 8-oz. tubes or squeeze bottles.

JEWELRY ADHESIVES **LAUNDER** DRY-CLEAN

Surface	Bond Rhinestone Adhesive #916		Gem-Tac		Jewel-Glue		Jewel-it	
Acetate Fabric	P	F	F	F	F	G	P	P
Acetate Sheeting	P	P	E	F	E	E	P	P
Acrylic Fabric	P	P	E	G	F	P	F	P
Acrylic Sheeting	E	P	E	E	E	E	P	P
Cotton	G	F	E	F	E	E	P	F
Glass	E	F	E	E	E	E	P	P
Leather	F	P	E	F	E	E	P	P
Linen	G	P	G	G	G	E	G	P
Metal	F	P	F	G	E	E	F	P
Mylar	P	P	E	G	E	E	P	P
Nylon	F	P	F	P	F	E	P	P
Nylon Spandex	G	P	E	G	E	E	E	F
Polyester Fabric	F	F	G	P	F	E	P	P
Polyurethane Foam	E	P	E	G	E	E	G	P
Rayon	E	P	E	F	F	E	G	P
Silk	P	P	E	F	F	E	P	F
Styrofoam	P	P	F	F	E	P	E	P
Vinyl	E	P	E	F	E	E	E	P
Wool	F	P	E	G	E	E	G	P

0 = Does not bond.
P = Poor bond: Bond fails with first laundering or dry cleaning.
F = Fair bond: Materials stay bonded for up to five launderings or dry cleanings.
G = Good: bond Materials stay bonded for up to fourteen launderings or dry cleanings.
E = Excellent: Bond appears permanent.

Latex

Brands Tested	Manufacturers
Liquid Latex	Alcone Company Inc.
A-R #74 Flexible Latex Molding Compound	A-R Products, Inc.
A-R #280 Latex	A-R Products, Inc.
L-200 Latex	Cementex Corporation

Examples of Use
- Adhere latex sheeting and cast latex to itself and to other materials.
- Create other stretchable bonds.

Use latex only on porous surfaces and rubber, since it does not adhere well to nonporous surfaces. Latex, used as an adhesive, works well when high flexibility is required. It is also used for mask making, where the molded forms can be strengthened with pieces of open weave knit cloth that are dipped into or brushed with latex. Latex can also be used for coating and texturing fabrics. See page 90 of the Coatings section for coating with latex.

Description *Latex* is liquid natural rubber from rubber plants in a dispersion, most frequently of ammonia and water. (A-R #74 does not contain ammonia.) Though manufactured for casting and mold making, liquid latex also serves well as an adhesive and as a coating. Latex is especially useful when maximum stretch is required on items that will not undergo many launderings or dry cleanings.

How to Use Latex is strongest when applied to both surfaces, as a contact cement. Apply with brush or spatula. The bond will occur within about two minutes of application.

Solvent for Cleanup Acetone.

Precautions Over time, latex yellows and rots from oxidation.

Health and Safety The vapors from ammonia are harmful to skin, eyes, and lungs. Use adequate ventilation and gloves. Do not mix ammonia or substances containing ammonia with any products that contain bleach, as such combinations create highly toxic gases.

Recent studies have shown that 1 percent of the population is allergic to latex and 15 percent of those who work with latex suffer allergies. Latex allergies can be serious, with reactions ranging from skin discoloration to fatal anaphylactic shock. Testing for latex allergies is available at hospital laboratories.

Some Untested Brands The following manufacturers and distributors are among many who carry latex for casting and molding: A-R Products, Cementex Corp., Chicago Latex Co., Mydrin, Inc., and Pink House Studios.

Where to Find Manufacturers and distributors.

Sizes 1 qt. - 50 gal.

LATEX **LAUNDER** DRY-CLEAN

Surface	Alcone		A-R 74		A-R 280		L-200	
Acetate Fabric	P	P	P	P	F	P	O	O
Acetate Sheeting	P	P	P	P	P	P	O	O
Acrylic Fabric	F	P	E	P	G	P	O	O
Acrylic Sheeting	P	P	P	P	P	P	O	O
Cotton	E	P	E	P	G	F	E	E
Glass	P	F	P	P	P	F	O	O
Leather	P	P	F	P	E	F	O	O
Linen	P	P	F	P	F	P	P	E
Metal	P	P	F	F	P	F	P	P
Mylar	P	P	P	P	P	P	O	O
Nylon	P	P	P	P	P	P	O	O
Nylon Spandex	F	P	G	P	E	F	E	E
Polyester Fabric	G	P	G	P	G	P	O	E
Polyurethane Foam	E	P	F	P	E	P	E	E
Rayon	P	P	F	P	G	P	E	E
Silk	P	P	G	P	G	F	E	P
Styrofoam	P	P	E	P	G	P	O	P
Vinyl	P	P	G	P	G	F	O	P
Wool	E	P	G	P	G	P	E	E

O = Does not bond.
P = Poor bond: Bond fails with first laundering or dry cleaning.
F = Fair bond: Materials stay bonded for up to five launderings or dry cleanings.
G = Good bond: Materials stay bonded for up to fourteen launderings or dry cleanings.
E = Excellent: Bond appears permanent.

Miscellaneous Plastic Cements

Brands Tested	Manufacturers
Bond 527	Bond Adhesives Company
Duco Cement	E.I. Du Pont de Nemours and Company, Inc.
Duro Household Cement	Loctite Corporation
Fastbond 48-NF Foam Adhesive	3M Company
Scotch-Grip Industrial Adhesive 4475	3M Company
Velcro Adhesive	Velcro USA Inc.

Examples of Use

- Use to glue plastic sheets and small plastic pieces—those ordinarily "hard-to-glue" materials.
- Fill gaps and smooth uneven surfaces on plastic.
- Create jewel-like beads by dropping the thicker adhesives onto fabric.
- Build a base for holding thin vertical attachments, like plastic rods onto head-dresses.

Use when bonding plastic to plastic or to other materials. Plastics that cannot be bonded with these adhesives include polyethylene, polypropylene, and some forms of polyvinyl chloride. It may be necessary to contact the manufacturer before using plastic cements with materials not mentioned here.

The thicker adhesives can be dripped onto fabric or costumes to create jewel-like decorations.

Description

This is a wide category of adhesives that are manufactured primarily for bonding plastics to plastics. According to manufacturers' information, these adhesives are composed of different resins and proprietary "unspecified polymers." They are usually clear in color. This category contains adhesives that are usually highly toxic and flammable.

When applied to small surface areas, plastic adhesives dry quickly. Applied to large areas, they dry more slowly and often shrink during the drying process. This group of adhesives is solvent-based, except for 3M 48-NF, which is water-based and, therefore, safer to use. For more information on bonding other specific plastics, see pages 244-245 of the the Plastic Sheetings section.

Bond 527: Multipurpose cement; excellent for glass and metal; clear; medium syrup; tube; cures in one-half to twenty-four hours, depending on substrate; very stiff; stains fabric; unspecified polymer.

Duco Cement: Specific to glass, metal, leather; excellent for acetate sheet; clear; medium syrup; twenty-four hour cure; nitrocellulose.

Duro Household Cement: Clear, flexible, water resistant; specific to wood, china, metal, leather, rubber, porcelain, and most plastics; resistant to oil and gasoline; two- to three-hour cure; medium viscosity.

Fastbond 48-NF Foam Adhesive: Designed for bonding flexible latex and polyurethane foam; tan syrup; does not bond rigid, nonporous surfaces; synthetic elastomer; water-based.

Scotch-Grip Industrial Adhesive 4475: Specific to bonding rigid surfaces like ABS, PVC acrylic, and vinyl to themselves and to metal, ceramics, and glass; clear; medium viscosity.

Velcro Adhesive: Intended to bond Velcro to rigid surfaces; medium viscosity; clear.

How to Use

First, carefully clean the surfaces being bonded. Apply the adhesive with a brush, putty knife, or directly from the tube to one or both surfaces, according to package directions. Most plastic cements will bond more strongly if the adhesive is applied to both surfaces, though package directions specify recommendations for application. Let the surface stand until tacky and then press together.

Solvent for Cleanup

Acetone or mineral spirits. Read package directions or technical-data sheets for correct solvent to use.

Health and Safety

Use with a good ventilation system or respirator. Wear gloves and goggles if necessary, as this group of adhesives is highly toxic. Keep away from flame, food, and drink.

Some Untested Brands

3M Company (Scotch-Grip 4213-NF is water dispersed, and 1099 is popular among many costumers); Industrial Polychemical Service Corporation, Inc. (IPS); Weld-on, Loctite Corp.; Ross Adhesives.

Where to Find

Duco, Bond, and Duro: Home-improvement and hardware stores

Velcro: Fabric stores

Weld-on: Plastics' suppliers

3M: Manufacturer and distributors.

Sizes

1½ oz. - 16 oz.

MISCELLANEOUS PLASTIC CEMENTS LAUNDER DRY-CLEAN

Surface	Bond 527		Duco Cement		Duro Household Cement		Fast-bond 48-NF		Scotch-Grip 1099		Scotch-Grip 4475		Velcro Adhesive	
Acetate Fabric	E	G†	P	G	G	P	G	G	G	G	P	P	E	P†
Acetate Sheeting	E	E†	E	G	G	E	P	P	P	F	G	E	E*	P†
Acrylic Fabric	G	G†	E	E	E	E	G	G	E	E	E	E	E**	P†
Acrylic Sheeting	G	P†	F	F	P	P	P	E	O	O	P	P	G	P†
Cotton	E	E†	E	E	E	E	G	E	F	F	F	E	E**	P†
Glass	E	F†	P	P	P	P	O	O	P	F	P	G	P	P†
Leather	E	E†	G	F	G	E	P	G	P	F	E	F	G	P†
Linen	G	F†	E	E	G	E	G	G	F	F	G	F	F	P†
Metal	P	E†	E	E	G	E	P	E	E	G	E	E	P	P†
Mylar	P	G†	P	F	G	G	P	F††	P	F	F*	E	P	P†
Nylon	E	E†	E	G	E	P	G	P†	F	F	P	F	E**	P†
Nylon Spandex	E	E†	E	G	E	G	G	G	F	F	E	E	F	P†
Polyester Fabric	P	E†	E	G	E	G	G	G	F	P	E	E	P**	P†
Polyurethane Foam	E	E†	E	E	E	F	G	F	E	O	G	E	P	P†
Rayon	E	E†	E	E	E	E	E	G	F	P	E	E	P	P†
Silk	E	E†	E*	E	E	E	G	F	F	O	E	E	P**	P†
Styrofoam	P	P†	P	P	F	P	G	F††	P	O	F	P††	P	P†
Vinyl	E	G†	P	F	E	E	G	G	F	P	E	E	E	P†
Wool	P	G†	E	P	E	E	G	G	F	P	E	E	G	P†

0 = Does not bond.
P = Poor bond: Bond fails with first laundering or dry cleaning.
F = Fair bond: Materials stay bonded for up to five launderings or dry cleanings.
G = Good bond: Materials stay bonded for up to fourteen launderings or dry cleanings.
E = Excellent: Bond appears permanent.

Note: Plastic cements often stiffen fabrics.
* Surface disfigures.
** Adhesive stains.
† Adhesive remains sticky.
†† Surface disintigrates.

Polyvinyl Acetate (PVA/PVAc—White Glue)

Brands Tested	Manufacturers
Craft and Hobby Glue	Macklenburg-Duncan
Elmer's Glue-All	Elmer's Products, Inc.
Phlexglu	Spectra Dynamics Products
Quick N' Tacky	Delta Technical Coatings, Inc.
Sobo	Delta Technical Coatings, Inc.

Examples of Use

- Bond most nonporous items such as sequins and beads to both porous and nonporous surfaces of costumes, millinery, and other accessories.
- Stiffen or size fabrics with white glue instead of with regular sizing.
- Stiffen fabrics into primitive pleated costumes. See page 93.
- Coat fabrics—see PVA/White Glue under Coatings pages 92-94.
- Mix with powdered pigment or paint for decorative effects or coating. See page 93.
- Use for papier-mâché instead of old-fashioned wheat paste.

White glue in pots is brushed onto a traditional Chinese costume. White glues are found in costume shops around the world.

Use on fabrics, leather, smooth plastics, metal, glass, and other slick surfaces. Though white glues create a bond to many nonporous surfaces (like metal and Mylar), it is advisable to use other adhesives for those materials in a situation when physical stress is a factor. With all surfaces tested, white glue created an initial bond; however, there is considerable variation in the bonds after dry cleaning and laundering, as noted in the charts at the end of this section.

Description

Polyvinyl acetate (white glue), one of the most popular adhesives, is found in most costume shops around the world. White when wet, it dries clear and colorless. Different manufacturers offer white glue in various viscosities. Though white glues can be thinned with water, just a small amount of water greatly weakens the bond. Some experts recommend never thinning under any circumstances.

Polyvinyl acetate bonds to porous substances, such as fabric and leather, as well as to many nonporous surfaces with bonds that are fairly flexible. Flexibility varies from one brand to another, but this can be increased with additives when required. Because white glue is a water emulsion, most brands seldom survive long immersion in water, though in most cases they withstand some dry cleaning. White glue is one of the safest adhesives to use and is commonly available in easy-to-use tubes, squeeze bottles, and standard bottles.

How to Use Apply with brush, squeeze bottle, or knife, coating one or both surfaces. For surfaces less porous than textiles, a weight or clamp should be used. Setting time is approximately twenty to thirty minutes, and high-strength bonds usually develop in less than twenty-four hours. If increased flexibility is required, add a plasticizer, such as Phlexglu Plasticizer, to any brand of PVA. For heavier consistency, add thickeners, such as Cab-O-Sil, and stir well. (Cab-O-Sil Silica Powder, from the Cabot Corporation, is a thickener used with many casting materials.) Thickeners and plasticizers decrease transparency to a translucence.

Solvent for Cleanup Water.

Precautions PVA stiffens slightly some fabrics and will also discolor thin textiles when seepage occurs. Over time, and if left to air exposure, all white glues will turn yellow.

Since PVAs are water soluble, most do not withstand laundering nearly as well as dry cleaning. Phlexglu is unique among those we tested in that it withstands at least fifteen dry cleanings and launderings.

Health and Safety Although PVA glues are essentially nontoxic, some contain very small amounts of free, unreacted vinyl acetate, and therefore they may not be suitable for use by children.

PVA adhesive, or white glue, can bond and coat paper and cloth appliqués onto costumes. Care must be taken in choosing the correct adhesives when laundering and dry cleaning are considerations.

DESIGN: THE AUTHOR FOR *LAND OF THE DRAGON* AT THE UNIVERSITY OF CALIFORNIA, LOS ANGELES. PHOTO: JOHN CAUBLE.

Some Untested Brands Crafts' size: 481 Tacky (extra thick), Bond Adhesives Company; Metylan Stanfix, Ross Adhesives; Velverette, Delta Technical Coatings, Inc.; White Glue, Aleene's; White Glue, Ross Adhesives.

Industrial size: 3M and Swift Adhesives are two of many manufacturers.

Where to Find Except for Phlexglu, the smaller sizes are at hardware, hobby, home-improvement stores, and drugstores. Phlexglu and large quantities of the others are available from their manufacturers.

Sizes 2 oz. (Delta and other crafts' glues) to 50 gal. (Phlexglu and other glues from industrial glue manufacturers).

POLYVINYL ACETATE (PVA/PVAc)(WHITE GLUE) LAUNDER DRY-CLEAN

Surface	Craft and Hobby Glue		Elmer's Glue-All		Phlexglu		Quick N' Tacky		Sobo	
Acetate Fabric	P	E	F	G	E	E	F	E	F	G
Acetate Sheeting	G*	F*	F*	G*	E*	E*	P*	E*	G*	E*
Acrylic Fabric	P	F	F	F	E	E	P	E	G	G
Acrylic Sheeting	G	P	F	P	E	E	P	E	F	P
Cotton	F	E	F	F	E	E	P	E	E	E
Glass	E	E	E	E	E	E	P	F	G	E
Leather	P	E	F	G	E	E	P	G	F	E
Linen	P	E	F	G	E	E	P	E	F	G
Metal	E	E	E	E	E	E	E	E	E	E
Mylar	P	F	F	E	E	E	P	E	F	G
Nylon	F	F*	P	E	E	E	F	E	F	F
Nylon Spandex	P	F	F	F	E	E	F	E	F	F
Polyester Fabric	P	F	F	F	E	E	G	E	F	F
Polyurethane Foam	F	F*	F	F	E	E	G	E	P	F
Rayon	F	E	F	F	E	E	P	E	P	E
Silk	P	E	F	F	E	E	P	E	E	G
Styrofoam	E	P	G	P	E	E	F	P	E	P
Vinyl	G	F	F	F	E	E	F	E	P	P
Wool	F	E	E	F	E	E	E	E	P	P

0 = Does not bond.
P = Poor bond: Bond fails with first laundering or dry cleaning.
F = Fair bond: Materials stay bonded for up to five launderings or dry cleanings.
G = Good bond: Materials stay bonded for up to fourteen launderings or dry cleanings.
E = Excellent: Bond appears permanent.

Note: Polyvinyl acetate stiffens fabrics slightly.
* Surface becomes brittle.

Rubber Cements

Brands Tested	Manufacturers
3M High Strength Adhesive 90	3M Company
3M High Tack 76	3m Company
3M Super 77 Spray Adhesive	3m Company
Barge All-Purpose Cement	Pierce & Stevens Chemical Corporation
Household Goop	Eclectic Products, Inc.
Press-in-Place Caulk	3M Company
Scotch-Grip 30-NF	3M Company
Scotch-Grip Rubber and Gasket Adhesive 847	3M Company
Scotch-Weld Urethane Adhesive 3549	3M Company
Stabond C-148, 836, U-148, V-36	Stabond Corporation
W/290 H Witcobond	Witco Corporation
Urethane Bond	Conap, Inc.

Examples of Use

- Repair shoes and other leather items.
- Create an especially flexible bond of plastics and fabrics.
- Bond natural and synthetic rubber.
- Bond polyurethane flexible foam (insulation and upholstery types).
- Bond metal and glass.

Use on fabrics, plastics, rubber, and most other surfaces where flexibility is important. Do not use solvent-based rubber cements to bond Styrofoam, which dissolves from the solvents. Styrofoam can only be bonded with water-based rubber cements.

Description

All rubber cements are one part, meaning that they contain some kind of solvent that must evaporate before a good bond will occur. Some rubber cements are *contact* types: Adhesive is placed on each of the two surfaces to be bonded, allowed to dry, and when the two coated and dried surfaces are joined, a strong bond is instantly created. *Noncontact* adhesives are referred to as *open-time* adhesives: These bond after the applied cement has dried to become tacky to the touch; the parts are then joined, and the bond develops slowly as the solvent continues to evaporate and the cement to dry. A bond made with noncontact cement is slower to develop high strength, but allows extra time to reposition the parts being bonded.

Rubber cements include *chloroprene rubber* (Neoprene), *nitrile, styrene-butadiene rubber* (SBR), *polypolyurethane rubber*, and *polybutane*. When bonding any of these materials to themselves, the best results are achieved by using an adhesive with the same ingredients, i.e., to bond Neoprene to Neoprene, use a Neoprene-based adhesive. Viscosities of rubber cements vary from a thin to a thick syrup. Color ranges from clear to brown, often darkening with age and oxidation. Packaging is usually tube or can, with brush application the most common. Some of these adhesives, like 3M's 76 and 77, are packaged in spray cans.

This group of cements must not be confused with the rubber cements like Best Test and LePages that are meant for bonding paper and other light-weight materials.

Rubber cement is ideal for shoe repair and is the adhesive of choice by professional shoemakers.

Popular with costumers because of their flexibility, rubber-based adhesives are especially effective for bonding leather, rubber, and fabrics. Generally, rubber cements are not recommended for bonding rigid plastics. When bonding polyurethane foam, use 3M 76, 77, 847, 1357, 30-NF, Stabond G-304, or Barge Cement. Rubber cements adhere initially to most surfaces and are generally washable, but dry only at low temperatures because all adhesives are thermoplastic. Because most rubber adhesives will not withstand dry cleaning solvents, dry cleaning is not recommended. The water-based rubber cements are especially recommended for use when possible because they are less toxic to the health of the worker and to the environment. Unfortunately, water-based rubber cements dry more slowly.

Rubber-cement spray can be used for laminating polyurethane foam to itself and to other materials.

Solvent-Based Rubber Cements

3M High Strength Adhesive 90 (spray): One-surface bond recommended for polyethylene and polypropylene; works well on other synthetic materials; aerosol can; styrene-butadiene rubber (SBR).

3M High Tack 76 (spray): One-surface bond for natural and synthetic rubber foams (will dissolve styrofoam) and recommended for synthetic and natural fabrics; up to ten minutes for open bonding, up to 60 minutes open time for contact bonding; resists high temperatures; packaged in aerosol can; SBR.

3M Press-In-Place Caulk: Very thick, pale gray, rolled molded coil; press in place where bulk is required; polybutane.

3M Super 77 Spray Adhesive: Contact cement; bonding range fifteen to thirty minutes; spray lightly on both surfaces for strongest bond; use only on lightweight materials; aerosol can; SBR.

Barge All Purpose Cement: Especially good for shoe repair; may be used for fabrics, leather, natural and synthetic rubber foams, and some other plastics; tan color; contact adhesive; SBR.

Devcon Rubber Adhesive: Amber color; medium viscosity; withstands laundering excellently and hence excellent for fabrics; comes in convenient three-ounce tubes; Neoprene.

Household Goop: Thick; white; bonds to most surfaces; withstands most laundering; squeeze from tube; SBR.

Scotch-Grip Rubber and Gasket Adhesive 847: Referred to in East Coast shops as brown glue; heavy viscosity; brown color; brush or flow; bonding range up to fifteen minutes; flexible, oil resistant; nitrile.

Scotch-Weld Urethane Adhesive 3549: Brown, two-part, thick and rigid; do not use on flexible materials; cures at room-temperature or with heat; up to four hours work time; 3532 is the same formulation, but fast-curing and up to thirty minutes work time; 3535 is very fast-curing with up to twenty minutes work time; polyurethane.

Stabond 836: Thin syrup of black color; withstands laundering well on all fabrics except acrylics; cannot be dry-cleaned; Neoprene.

Stabond C-148: Tan color; withstands most laundering; nitrile; acetone solvent.

Stabond U-148: Clear medium syrup; high strength on rigid natural and synthetic rubbers, acetate, acrylic, vinyl, ABS; contact adhesive; polyurethane.

Stabond V-36: Range of colors; medium syrup; brush application; bonds and coats well on flexible materials; highly flammable; nitrile.

Urethane Bond: One part; clear and thick; tube application; designed for ceramics, but makes a flexible bond on fabrics; polyurethane.

Water-Based Rubber Cements

Fastbond 30-NF: Neutral or green color; strong bond; contact adhesive; bonding time can be up to four hours; adhesive may be dried with a hair dryer to speed drying time; available in convenient quarts; Neoprene.

W/290 H Witcobond: Thin; two part adhesive; needs addition of a thickener; industrial size containers; polyurethane.

How to Use   Except for the adhesives specified as contact adhesives, apply to one or both surfaces to be bonded. Follow directions when listed on the container. In any case, contact bonding, or applying the adhesives to both surfaces, creates a stronger bond.

Clothespins hold pieces together while rubber cement is curing.
PHOTO: CORNELIUS SKATES

When applying to only one surface, allow the adhesive to become "tacky" and then press together. For contact bonding, apply the adhesive, or cement, to both surfaces and allow it to dry; the dry cement will stick to itself.

For an even stronger bond, use solvent reactivation technique, allowing a longer drying time and then wetting the adhesive with its solvent and bringing the two surfaces together. The application of pressure adds to the adhesion, and in some cases heat will add even more strength.

Solvent for Cleanup   Water-based adhesives: soap and water.

3M's 76, 77, 847,1357, 4693, Press-in-Place Caulk; Barge; Goop; and Stabond G-304: benzine or paint thinner.

All other adhesives listed in this category: acetone or other ketones.

Precautions   Only in a few cases will rubber cements stiffen fabric. Stains occur when rubber-based adhesives are used on thin fabrics, and discoloration sometimes occurs over long periods of time.

Dry cleaning results were negative with most adhesives we tested, while many were launderable on specific surfaces.

Health and Safety   Take personal safety precautions for skin protection. Use the water-based products whenever possible, and avoid breathing vapors from the solvent-based products, either by working in a well-ventilated area or wearing a respirator. Keep away from heat, food, and drink.

Headdress of plastic screening is decorated with expanded polyure-thane, shells, and Mylar, bonded by latex and rubber cement. Liquid latex protectively coats the entire surface.

DESIGN: JACK EDWARDS FOR ORION IN *A MIDSUMMER NIGHT'S DREAM* AT THE GUTHRIE THEATRE, MINNEAPOLIS.

Always get MSDSs on rubber cements. The most common rubber-cement solvent, n-hexane, is one of the most potent neurotoxins known. It can cause a disease similar to multiple sclerosis on repeated exposure. Rubber cements containing hexane are much less toxic.

Only use spray products in spray booths or other suitable local exhaust systems. Respiratory protection can be used, but will not protect others in the shop. The respirator must be approved for paint, lacquer, and enamel mists or be a combination of an organic vapor cartridge and mist prefilter.

Some Untested Brands   Water-based: Copydex Adhesive, Henkel Home Improvement & Adhesive Products (UK); Water-Based Urethane Adhesive, Uncommon Conglomerates,

Solvent-based: Most major adhesive manufacturers have a line of rubber cements. The 3M Company, Bond Adhesives Company, Eclectic Products, and Stabond have many cements in addition to those listed.

Where to Find   Barge: shoe repair and leather suppliers.
3M products: 3M distributors.
Stabond: manufacturer.
Most others: hardware stores and plastics suppliers.

Sizes   Barge: 2 - 4 oz.
Devcon: 3 oz.
Spray cans: approx. 16 - 20 oz.

Stabond: 1 pt. - 55 gal.

3M's Fastbond 30 NF, Scotch-Grip 847, Scotch-Grip 1099: several oz. - 5 gal.

3M Press-In-Place Caulk: 5/16" by 22".

Urethane Bond: 1 oz.

All others available only in 5 or more gal.

RUBBER CEMENTS (SOLVENT BASED)   LAUNDER   DRY-CLEAN

Surface	3M Press-in-Place Caulk		Barge All-Purpose Cement		Devcon Rubber Adhesive		Household Goop		Scotch-Grip 847	
Acetate Fabric	P	P	G	P	E	F	E	P	E	E
Acetate Sheeting	E	E	E	E	G	G	E	E	G	O
Acrylic Fabric	P	P	E *	F	G	F	E	F	E	E
Acrylic Sheeting	E	P	E	P	E	E	E	E	E	P
Cotton	F	P	E *	P	P	P	E	F	P	P
Glass	E	E	G	P	G	P	E	E	E	P
Leather	F	P	E	P	G	F	E	P	G	P
Linen	F	P	E	P	F	P	G	F	P	E
Metal	E	P	E	F	E	G	E	E	P	O
Mylar	E	E	E	G	P	P	E	E	P	F
Nylon	E	P	E	P	E	F	E	F	P	F
Nylon Spandex	G	P	E	P	P	P	E	F	P	P
Polyester Fabric	P	F	E	P	E	P	E	P	G	F
Polyurethane Foam	F	P	E	P	E	P	E	F	E	P
Rayon	G	P	E	P	G	P	E	F	P	P
Silk	P	P	E	P	E	P	E	P	E	P
Styrofoam	E	P	P	P	P	P	F	F	G	P
Vinyl	E	P	E	P	G	F	E	F	E	P
Wool	F	P	E	P	P	E	E	F	P	P

O = Does not bond.

P = Poor bond: Bond fails with first laundering or dry cleaning.

F = Fair bond: Materials stay bonded for up to five launderings or dry cleanings.

G = Good bond: Materials stay bonded for up to fourteen launderings or dry cleanings.

E = Excellent: Bond appears permanent.

*Surface yellows.

RUBBER CEMENTS (SOLVENT-BASED) **LAUNDER** DRY-CLEAN

Surface	Scotchweld 3549 A/B		Stabond 836		Stabond C-148		Stabond U-148		Stabond V-36		Urethane Bond	
Acetate Fabric	F*	F*	E	F	E	P	E	E	G	G	F*	F*
Acetate Sheeting	P*	P*	E	P	F	P	E	G	G	G	F	E
Acrylic Fabric	E*	E*	F	P	F	F	P	P	F	F	F	P
Acrylic Sheeting	E*	E*	E	P	E	E	E	P	P	P	F	P
Cotton	F*	P*	E	P	F	P	P	P	P	P	F	F
Glass	F*	P*	P	P	E	E	P	P	E	E	F	P
Leather	F*	F*	E	P	P	P	G	P	P	P	F	F
Linen	F*	P*	E	P	F	P	P	P	P	P	F*	F*
Metal	E*	E*	E	P	E	E	P	F	P	F	F	F
Mylar	P*	F*	E	P	G	F	P	G	G	G	P	F
Nylon	F*	P*	E	P	F	P	F	P	G	G	F*	F
Nylon Spandex	E*	P*	E	P	F	P	P	P	P	P	F	F
Polyester Fabric	F*	P*	E	P	E	F	P	P	E	E	F*	F*
Polyurethane Foam	F*	P*	E	P	E	F	F	P	E	E	F	F
Rayon	F*	P*	E	P	E	P	P	P	P	P	F*	F*
Silk	F*	P*	E	P	P	P	G	P	P	P	P	F
Styrofoam	F*	P*	F	P	0	0	P	P	P	P	0	P
Vinyl	F*	P*	E	F	E	F	E	E	P	P	F	F
Wool	F*	P*	E	P	F	F	P	P	P	P	F	F

0 = Does not bond.
P = Poor bond: Bond fails with first laundering or dry cleaning.
F = Fair bond: Materials stay bonded for up to five launderings or dry cleanings.
G = Good bond: Materials stay bonded for up to fourteen launderings or dry cleanings.
E = Excellent: Bond appears permanent.

Note: These rubber cements may stiffen some fabrics.
* Surface stains.

RUBBER CEMENTS (WATER-BASED) **LAUNDER** DRY-CLEAN

Surface	Scotch-Grip 30 NF		W/290 H Witcobond	
Acetate Fabric	E	E	G	G
Acetate Sheeting	E	P	P	F
Acrylic Fabric	E	E	G	F
Acrylic Sheeting	E	P	E	P
Cotton	E	E	G	P
Glass	E	P	E	E
Leather	E	E	G	G
Linen	E	E	G	G
Metal	E	E	E	E
Mylar	E	G	F	F
Nylon	E	G	E	G
Nylon Spandex	E	E	F	F
Polyester Fabric	P	P	F	F
Polyurethane Foam	E	P	G	E
Rayon	E	E	E	G
Silk	E	E	F	F
Styrofoam	E	P	E	P
Vinyl	E	E	F	F
Wool	E	E	F	F

O = Does not bond.
P = Poor bond: Bond fails with first laundering or dry cleaning.
F = Fair bond: Materials stay bonded for up to five launderings or dry cleanings.
G = Good bond: Materials stay bonded for up to fourteen launderings or dry cleanings.
E = Excellent: Bond appears permanent.

RUBBER CEMENT SPRAY ADHESIVE **LAUNDER** DRY-CLEAN

Surface	3M 76		3M 77		3M 90	
Acetate Fabric	G	P	P	P	F	F
Acetate Sheeting	E	G	P	P	G	F
Acrylic Fabric	G	F	E	P	F	F
Acrylic Sheeting	E	E	P	F	F	P
Cotton	G	F	F	F	F	F
Glass	P	P	P	P	F	F
Leather	P	P	F	P	F	F
Linen	F	P	F	P	F	F
Metal	E	P	E	F	E	F
Mylar	G	P	F	P	F	F
Nylon	F	P	F	P	F	F
Nylon Spandex	P	P	P	P	F	F
Polyester Fabric	F	P	G	P	F	F
Polyurethane Foam	F	P	F	P	F	F
Rayon	E	P	P	P	F	F
Silk	G	P	F	P	E	F
Styrofoam	F	P	F	P	F	F
Vinyl	G	P	G	P	F	F
Wool	F	P	P	P	P	F

0 = Does not bond.
P = Poor bond: Bond fails with first laundering or dry cleaning.
F = Fair bond: Materials stay bonded for up to five launderings or dry cleanings.
G = Good bond: Materials stay bonded for up to fourteen launderings or dry cleanings.
E = Excellent: Bond appears permanent.

Silicone Sealants

Brands Tested	Manufacturers
732 Multi-Purpose Sealant	Dow Corning
Permatex Form-A-Gasket 6	Permatex Division of Loctite Corporation
Household Glue and Seal II	General Electric, Silicone Products Division
Seal and Gasket Silicone II	General Electric, Silicone Products Division

Examples of Use
- Create relief designs by squeezing directly from the tube.
- Build up a thick mass to create a base for applying dimensional objects to a costume.

Silicone sealant is especially effective for bonding glass. Because glass is so brittle, it breaks less easily when cushioned with a flexible adhesive. On other materials, use where flexibility and body are desirable and on pieces that do not need dry cleaning. Among the different brands there is great variety in withstanding laundering and dry cleaning.

Description
Commercially prepared as industrial sealants for caulking and weatherproofing, *silicone sealant* can also be used for adhesive and decorative purposes by costumers. It successfully bonds to most metals, rubbers, and plastics. Silicone is colorless, blue, or white and highly flexible. It often withstands water but is generally not resistant to dry cleaning fluid or other solvents. It is usually packaged in tubes or caulking guns.

How to Use
Silicone caulking and sealants are in tubes and may be squeezed into place, or they may be spread with a knife or spatula. Some silicones are available in large caulking guns. Others are sold as solid pellets that can be inserted into hot-melt resin applicators. (See Hot-Melt Resin section page 48.) Silicones are of heavy viscosity and cannot be thinned.

Solvent for Cleanup
Acetone.

Precautions
In a few cases silicone sealant discolors and stiffens fabrics.

Health and Safety
Use with extreme caution. Wear a respirator, goggles, and skin covering. The solvents used in silicone cause release of vapors that are strong irritants to the eyes, nervous system, and respiratory tract.

Some Untested Brands
Clear Caulking, Hercules; Colourseal, Evo-Stick (UK); Kwik Seal, DAP, Inc.

Where to Find
Hardware stores, drugstores, and home-improvement centers.

Sizes
1½ oz. - 2.8 oz

SILICONE SEALANT   **LAUNDER** DRY-CLEAN

Surface	732 Multi-Purpose		Form-a Gasket 6		Household Glue & Seal II		Seal & Gasket Silicon II	
Acetate Fabric	F	F	E	E	F	P	P	P
Acetate Sheeting	P	P	P	P	G	F	F	E
Acrylic Fabric	G	F	P	P	E	E	G	E
Acrylic Sheeting	G	E	P	P	E	E	E	E
Cotton	G	F	E	P	G	F	G	F
Glass	E	E	E	P	P	F	F	P
Leather	G	G	P	P	E	G	P	P
Linen	F	F	P	P	F	P	G	F
Metal	P	P	P	E	E	E	E	E
Mylar	F	P	P	P	P	P	F	F
Nylon	F	P	E	P	P	P	P	P
Nylon Spandex	F	F	E	P	P	P	E	E
Polyester Fabric	P	F	E	E	G	F	G	F
Polyurethane Foam	G	G	E	P	E	E	E	E
Rayon	G	F	E	E	E	F	P	F
Silk	F	P	E	E	G	F	G	F
Styrofoam	E	P	E	F	E	G	E	E
Vinyl	P	P	E	P	F	F	P	P
Wool	P	F	E	F	E	E	E	F

O = Does not bond.
P = Poor bond: Bond fails with first laundering or dry cleaning.
F = Fair bond: Materials stay bonded for up to five launderings or dry cleanings.
G = Good bond: Materials stay bonded for up to fourteen launderings or dry cleanings.
E = Excellent: Bond appears permanent.

Note: Household Glue and Seal II may stiffen and discolor many fabrics.

Tapes, Double-Sided

Brands Tested	Manufacturers
Scotch Adhesive Transfer Tape 924	3M Company
Se-lin Tape	Gaylord Brothers

Examples of Use

- Use as an adhesive cut-out for applying solid or sprinkled-on motifs.
- Apply rhinestones, jewels, and small decorations.
- Repair quickly various kinds of costume pieces.
- Cover belts and belt buckles with delicate or hard-to-sew fabrics.

Use when decorating fabric. Create motifs of glitter and flocking in an allover pattern to a costume. Cirque du Soleil uses it for creating allover patterns in small areas and for stripes on long pieces, including metallic stripes on stretchy trouser legs.

For quick repairs, it will temporarily hold loose soles on shoes, mend loose hems, or aid in other catastrophes. On costume parts receiving stress, it is best to replace the quick repairs with sewing.

Description

This is the thin, transparent, *double-sided tape* that is sold sandwiched between two layers of paper or on a roll adhering to one layer of paper. The tape from 3M is most often used for packaging and for bonding paper items, while Se-lin Tape is marketed for holding costume, prop, and art pieces. Se-lin Tape is available both as a two-way and a four-way stretch tape. It is strong, and adheres to most surfaces through hand laundering. Se-lin Tape is available through the distributors of Jean Teton Creations' products, where it is often referred to as "Jean Teton Double-Sided Sticky Tape."

To use double-sided tape for adhering glitter, first place the tape cut-out onto the fabric, leaving a layer of the paper coating intact.

Then peel off the paper coating and sprinkle glitter on top of the double-sided tape.

How to Use Se-lin Tape can be used to create motifs textured by glitter, flocking, or another sprinkle-on material. First cut out the motif pattern from the tape. Peel off one layer of protective coating. Place the motif onto fabric or costume and rub it well into place. Peel off the top side of the backing and sprinkle it with a decorative texture.

This tape has enough flexibility to be compatible with most fabrics. However, when working with knit and spandex fabrics, first stretch out the fabric and secure it by pins onto a work surface. Then apply the tape motifs. This technique can be used to apply stripes and large motifs to spandex knit.

Double-sided tape can also be used to apply rhinestones and other very small applied pieces. Cut the tape into small patches, apply to backs of rhinestones and small appliqués, and push firmly onto the costume surface.

For applying small decorations, such tapes bond well on areas that are free from friction and contact, and this should be considered when decorative effects are added.

Precautions Hand-launder and air-dry only. Do not dry-clean.

Some Other Brands 3M Company has a full line of double-sided tapes.

Where to Find Scotch Adhesive Tape: Hardware stores and 3M distributors.
Se-Lin Tape: Manufacturer.

Distributor: Mendel's and Far Out Fabrics,
San Francisco.

Sizes Scotch Tape: ½" and ¾" × 1296".
Jean Teton Se-Lin Tape: 2-way stretch: 2" × 36"; 4-way stretch: 4" × 36".

TAPES, DOUBLE-SIDED **LAUNDER** DRY-CLEAN

Surface	Jean Teton Double-Sided Tape		Scotch Adhesive Transfer Tape	
Acetate Fabric	E	P	E	P
Acetate Sheeting	E	P	E	P
Acrylic Fabric	E	E	O	P
Acrylic Sheeting	P	P	P	P
Cotton	P	P	P	P
Glass	E	P	O	P
Leather	G	P	F	P
Linen	E	P	E	P
Metal	E	P	O	P
Mylar	E	P	O	P
Nylon	E	P	E	P
Nylon Spandex	E	P	F	P
Polyester Fabric	E	E	O	P
Polyurethane Foam	P	P	O	P
Rayon	P	P	F	P
Silk	E	P	E	P
Styrofoam	E	P	O	P
Vinyl	E	P	F	P
Wool	E	P	O	P

O = Does not bond.
P = Poor bond: Bond fails with first laundering or dry cleaning.
F = Fair bond: Materials stay bonded for up to five launderings or dry cleanings.
G = Good bond: Materials stay bonded for up to fourteen launderings or dry cleanings.
E = Excellent: Bond appears permanent. Note: Scotch tape wrinkles and bunches laundered fabric.

Tapes Especially Formulated for Fabrics

Brands Tested	Manufacturers
Res Q Tape	Seams Great Corporation
Wonder Tape	W. H. Collins, Inc.

Examples of Use
- Patch torn costumes.
- Repair rips and tears in an emergency.
- Substitute for basting.
- Hem and adjust costumes having short-term use.

These tapes serve well for quick and emergency repairs and as a substitute for hand basting. Some tapes must be ironed on; these are actually hot-melt-resin backed strips of fabrics and are more permanent than the others.

Description These *cloth-backed* and *plastic-backed tape adhesives* are sold primarily to home sewers. Because they are flexible, they can be an aid in both home and commercial sewing.

How to Use Apply like any other tape. When basting prior to sewing, place the tape next to, not on, the stitching line so that the needle will not become gummy.

Apply tape for basting prior to machine stitching. Note that tape must be clear from the hem's edge.

Precautions These tapes do not dry-clean or wash, so they are not advisable for permanent bonds.

Solvent for Cleanup Water and/or hydrocarbon solvents.

Some Untested Brands Cloth Tape, Dritz.

Where to Find Fabric stores.

Sizes ¾" × 360" (Wonder Tape)

¾" × 180" (Res Q Tape)

TAPES ESPECIALLY FORMULATED FOR FABRICS   **LAUNDER** DRY-CLEAN

Surface	Res Q Tape		Wonder Tape	
Acetate Fabric	P	P	P	P
Acetate Sheeting	P	P	P	P
Acrylic Fabric	P	P	P	P
Acrylic Sheeting	P	P	P	P
Cotton	P	P	P	P
Glass	P	P	P	P
Leather	P	P	P	P
Linen	P	P	P	P
Metal	P	P	P	P
Mylar	P	P	P	P
Nylon	P	P	P	P
Nylon Spandex	P	P	P	P
Polyester Fabric	P	P	P	P
Polyurethane Foam	P	P	P	P
Rayon	P	P	P	P
Silk	P	P	P	P
Styrofoam	P	P	P	P
Vinyl	P	P	P	P
Wool	P	P	P	P

O = Does not bond.
P = Poor bond: Bond fails with first laundering or dry cleaning.
F = Fair bond: Materials stay bonded for up to five launderings or dry cleanings.
G = Good bond: Materials stay bonded for up to fourteen launderings or dry cleanings.
E = Excellent: Bond appears permanent.

Vinyl Adhesives

Brands Tested	Manufacturers
Bond 634	Bond Adhesives Company
Duro Vinyl Adhesive	Loctite Corporation
Scotch-Grip 2262 A/B	3M Company
Weld-on 1001	Industrial Polychemical Service Corporation Inc. (IPS)

Examples of Use

- Patch torn vinyl pieces.
- Bond vinyl to itself and to other materials for maximum flexibility and maximum strength.

These adhesives are acceptable for bonding vinyl to itself and to other materials. Different brands will bond different fabrics and surfaces. Maximum strength is developed between two hours and seven days after application, depending on the specific adhesives.

Description

Vinyl cements of synthetic resin-base adhesives in a solvent blend are formulated for bonding vinyl to itself and to other surfaces, for they have been designed to bond vinyl without plasticizing (softening) the vinyl. They are clear or pale amber in color, generally of syrupy consistency, of varying viscosities, and remain flexible after bonding. Vinyl cements are most commonly available in cans and tubes. Scotch-Grip 2262 is a two-part product, while the others are one-part.

How to Use

Apply from tube using stiff brush or knife. Weld-on and Scotch-Grip should be applied on both surfaces being joined.

The drying time varies with the individual adhesives as well as with the physical characteristics of the surfaces. Thickly applied adhesives will dry and cure more slowly because the solvent must escape before cure begins.

Solvent for Cleanup

Scotch-Grip: Methyl ethyl ketone or Scotch-Grip Brand Solvent No. 3.

Others: Acetone.

Precautions

Vinyl adhesives will dissolve on many surfaces when laundered or dry-cleaned. Since they are runny, they often seep through loosely woven textiles, causing stains.

Health and Safety

Use safety measures—a good ventilation system, or a respirator—because of high toxicity.

Some Untested Brands

Instant Vinyl, W. H. Collins Victory Vinyl Repair Kit, Bond Adhesives Company

Where to Find

Hardware and home-improvement stores, and distributors.

Sizes

1 oz. - 4 oz.

VINYL ADHESIVES LAUNDER DRY-CLEAN

Surface	Bond 634		Duro Vinyl Adhesive		Scotch-Grip 2262		Weld-on 1001	
Acetate Fabric	F	F	G	P	P	F	P	F
Acetate Sheeting	P	P	P	P	P	E	P	P
Acrylic Fabric	P	P*	P	P	P	F	F	P
Acrylic Sheeting	E	P	P	P	E	E	P	P
Cotton	E	F	P	P	P	F	P	P
Glass	P	F	P	P	E	F	P	P
Leather	P	F	P	P	P	P	P	P
Linen	P	E	P	P	P	F	E	F
Metal	P	F	P	P	E	E	E	E
Mylar	P	F	P	P	P	P	F	F
Nylon	E	F	P	P	P	G	P	F
Nylon Spandex	E	P**	P	P	G	F	G	F
Polyester Fabric	E	F	P	P	P	F	P	F
Polyurethane Foam	F	P	P	P	P	P	E	G
Rayon	E	E	P	P	P	F	P	P
Silk	E	E	P	P	E	F	G	P
Styrofoam	F	P	P	P	P	P	G	P
Vinyl	E	E	P	P	E	P	G	P
Wool	E	E	P	P	P	F	P	P

O = Does not bond.
P = Poor bond: Bond fails with first laundering or dry cleaning.
F = Fair bond: Materials stay bonded for up to five launderings or dry cleanings.
G = Good bond: Materials stay bonded for up to fourteen launderings or dry cleanings.
E = Excellent: Bond appears permanent.

* Surface dissolves.
** Surface stiffens.

Coatings

Coatings offer exciting possibilities for surface modification, decoration, and protection. Coatings can seal, change texture, fill gaps in porous surfaces, provide smooth contours, and add weight, density, rigidity or flexibility.

Many of the materials discussed in other sections of this book, especially adhesives and casting materials, also work effectively as coatings. Latex, polyester resin, silicone sealant, and polyvinyl acetate (white glue) all protect and modify surfaces as well as bond them. And, conversely, most of the coatings covered in this section can also be used for some bonding purposes as well. However, the bond of coatings is generally not as strong as that of actual adhesives.

Coatings in this section are limited mostly to those that designers and costume craftspersons have adapted for fabric modification. The coatings discussed here also have practical application for nontextiles, and some of those nontextile applications are listed in each section. Coatings that have been developed expressly for plastics, metals, and other materials are innumerable; therefore, many of the coatings included in this section have already proven practical for fabric costumes.

Like adhesives, coatings work through surface attachment. They either attach mechanically, by locking into grooves or cracks in a surface, or chemically, by molecular attraction. Coatings are water-based or solvent-based. Water-based coatings are those materials that can be dissolved in water, such as acrylics, and polyvinyl acetates.

As with adhesives, colorants, and metallizers, we have tested all the coatings listed at the top of each section on eighteen different surfaces. The coatings that adhered to the surfaces were divided in half. Each was laundered and dry-cleaned up to fifteen times. The charts accompanying each section list the results. It is important to keep in mind that variations in each material can affect a material's compatibility with most coatings. For instance, the thickness, openness, stretchability, texture, and surface treatment may cause results different from those listed in the charts. Adhesion of most substances is affected by heat and humidity as well as by the thickness of the applied coating. Coatings that are not extremely flexible will crack when applied to solid flexible surfaces such as leather, vinyl, and most plastic films.

Working Methods Coatings are usually applied much as are paints, with a brush or other painting implement. Some coatings, however, like thick acrylic gels are more effectively applied by trowel or spatula. Others, like a thinned solution of white glue, require that the material being coated be dipped into the coating.

Most coatings can be colored, thereby combining two processes. Paint may be added to the coating for color; in that case it is imperative that the paint be compatible with the base of the coating; i.e., water-based acrylic paint and universal colors are compatible with water-based coatings. Pigments compatible with individual coatings can also be added.

Coatings can create textures. Costumers add materials as various as glitter, seeds, sand, and pickling spices to create exciting and novel surfaces. Such additional materials can be stirred into the coatings before their application, or they can be sprinkled or placed onto the surface, and then the surface can be coated for protection. This is a wonderful area for experimenting with novel and other-worldly looks.

For health and safety, use water-based coatings whenever a choice can be made. The advantages of using water-based substances are lower cost and less toxicity. Water-based substances are less likely to catch fire, more easily dry-cleaned, and have a wider range of viscosity. Solvent-based materials are more water-resistant (more easily laundered), dry within a wide range of time, and adhere better to metal and other nonporous surfaces.

The disadvantage of water-based materials is their poor resistance to water. They shrink, soften fabrics, and dry slowly. Solvent-based materials have poor flame resistance, poor resistance to dry cleaning solvents, are hazards to health and the environment, and require health and safety equipment when being worked with.

Health and Safety   Precautions for specific products are listed individually in the following pages of this section. Use a water-based coating whenever it is possible. When working with solvent-based coatings, follow these measures for safety.

- Work in a well ventilated space or wear the correct type of respirator.

- Wear work gloves for hand protection and avoid contact with skin.

- Keep away from stoves and heating elements.

- Use spray products only in spray booths or other appropriate local exhaust systems. Respiratory protection can be used, but will not protect other workers from excessive amounts of solvent vapors created during the spray process. The respirator must be approved for paint, lacquer, and enamel mists or be a combination of an organic vapor cartridge and mist pre-filter for solvent-containing products.

- If water-based materials are sprayed, use a respirator with a dust/mist filter. With water-based materials, check the MSDS and call the manufacturer to be sure that the material does not also contain significant amounts of solvents.

- *Do not smoke or use near flames, and keep away from food and drink.*

Acrylic Gel

Brands Tested	Manufacturers
Createx Clear Ply Adhesive Coating	ColorCraft, Ltd.
Liquitex Acrylic Gel Medium	Binney & Smith Inc.
Polymer Medium	Golden Artist Colors, Inc.
Sculpt or Coat	Sculptural Arts Coating, Inc.

Examples of Use

- •Change original surface or texture of a fabric or other material.
- •Add weight to costumes.
- •Use as a transfer medium for monoprinting.
- •Seal plastic foams with a skinlike quality.
- •Glaze slick surfaces to simulate metal and glass.
- •Laminate onto fragile materials to increase their durability.
- •Mix with paint and other colorants for a thicker or smoother consistency.

Use as a coating to change the fabric's hand, its surface, or as a protective coating. The gel can be used over polyurethane rigid foam sculpture, masks, and accessories to form a skinlike protective sealant.

Sculpt or Coat is mixed with paper pulp and water extruded through a pastry tube to create the vine motif on this breast plate. When finished, Sculpt or Coat is thinned with water and applied as a glaze on the entire piece.

DESIGN: JULIAN CHEEK FOR HIPPOLYTA IN *A MIDSUMMER NIGHT'S DREAM* AT THE UNIVERSITY OF NORTH CAROLINA AT GREENSBORO. PHOTO: PATRICK STRAIN.

Dip foam, open-weave fabrics, and feathers into the gel to form new textures. These can impart an other-worldly texture to familiar fabrics. At the Pacific Conservatory of Performing Arts in Santa Maria, California, Pat Handrych used this technique for forming fish fins. See Fabric Modification on page 411 for an example of use on futuristic costumes in *Off on a Tangerine*.

Sculpt or Coat is thicker and more flexible than the other acrylic gels. Julian Cheek, Costume Shop Director at the University of North Carolina, finds many uses for it. He squeezes it from a pastry tube into raised motifs on fabrics, armor, and headdresses. He uses it to mold and coat jewelry and laminates it onto feathers and other delicate materials for increased durability. He also brushes it onto fabrics and dips fabric into it when he wants to create a sculptured-looking costume, as for the Commandatore in *Don Giovanni*, and mixes it with glitter, bronzing powder, latex paint, acrylic paint, and dye.

Description   *Acrylic gel* medium is a transparent, highly viscous liquid that is available in either a matte or shiny texture. Some brands offer gels in several viscosities, with different drying times and in sundry textures—such as sandy and gritty. Acrylic gel medium is white, but becomes transparent when dry. Many brands of gels are marketed by manufacturers of artists' paints as media for changing the viscosity, clarity, surface quality, texture, and adhesion of acrylic paints. Sculpt or Coat is marketed for texturing theatrical props, costumes, and scenery. Costumers can use acrylic gels to add texture, dimensional ornamentation, and stiffness to fabric and other surfaces. Acrylic gel can also function as an adhesive.

How to Use   To modify the surface of or add weight to a costume, apply with a brush or other hand-painting tool. Use straight from the container or thin with water. Apply with any kind of painting technique—sponge, brush, hands, spatula, etc.—except spray. Sculpt or Coat, which is thick, can also be squeezed from a pastry tube right onto fabric or on nonporous costume pieces, such as armor.

Different textural effects can be created while the coating is still drying by working the still-moist surface with an instrument such as a comb, brush, screen, etc.

Add water-soluble colorants, pigments, or texturing materials either to the mixture or apply them afterwards.

Sculpt or Coat is thick enough to cast as well as coat and is an easy material for molding jewelry and decorative items.

Drying time is short with acrylic media. Keep a water jar handy for rinsing brushes immediately.

Solvent for Cleanup   Soap and water.

Precautions   Acrylic gel medium stiffens fabric. If machine laundered or dry-cleaned, most acrylic gels soften and stick to themselves. Careful hand washing or spot cleaning are recommended. For this reason, no charts have been included in this section.

Health and Safety   Gel medium is relatively safe, but wear gloves to avoid direct contact with the skin and eyes which can cause irritation. Some media contain very small amounts of formaldehyde and ammonia, which can affect some people. For protection against formaldehyde fumes, use a formaldehyde respirator; for protection from ammonia vapors, use an ammonia respirator.

Some Other Brands   Artist Color Gel Medium, Rotring; Gel Medium, Windsor & Newton, Inc.

Where to Find   ColorCraft: manufacturer.

Liquitex, Golden, and other artists' brands: art supply stores.

Sculpt or Coat: manufacturer or theatrical suppliers.

Sizes   1 pt. - 1 gal.

Crackle Surface Media

Brands Tested	Manufacturers
Crackle and Age It	Bond Adhesives Company
Folk Art Crackle Medium	Plaid Enterprises

Examples of Use
- Use on nonfabric costume pieces that are to appear old and weathered.
- Coat the media onto antiquated armor or other molded costume pieces.

Description *Crackle surface* media, originally formulated for antiquing furniture and frames, is excellent for creating an aged and crackled look on surfaces that are both porous and hard, including plaster, primed metal, and primed plastics. It is not effective on most fabrics. Bond's product is tan and thick and composed of PVA (the ingredient found in most white glues). Plaid's clear liquid contains silicates and resins. Both are in a water solution.

One half of a purse is distressed by a coat of crackle surface medium, then followed by a layer of thick acrylic paint.

PHOTO: RICHARD S. BAILEY.

How to Use Apply a thick coat to a painted or plain surface and allow to dry for one to four hours. Apply a coat of acrylic water-based paint. The thicker the coating, the more extensive will be the crackling. Bond suggests mixing their glue stick with pigment for the top coat. Allow to dry, and the crackling will begin. If a mistake occurs during the top-coating process, quickly wipe off and begin again.

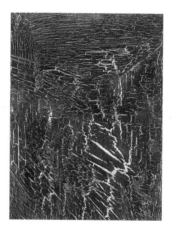

A piece of low-temperature-setting thermoplastic sheeting is coated first with a layer of crackle surface medium and then a layer of thick acrylic paint.

Solvent for Cleanup Water.

Precautions Crackle surface media is not recommended for fabrics, and laundering or dry cleaning are rarely applicable.

Health and Safety Avoid contact with eyes. These products are generally nontoxic and harmless, but the plasticizer can cause eye or skin irritation if direct contact occurs.

Some Other Brands Aleene's Mosaic Crackle; Aleene's Product of Duncan Enterprises.

Where to Find Small sizes: hobby shops, home-improvement centers, and fabric stores.
Large sizes: manufacturers.

Sizes Folk Art: 2 oz., 4 oz., and 8 oz.
Crackle and Age It: 4 oz., 8 oz. 1 qt., 1 gal., 55 gal.

Fabric Stiffeners

Brands Tested	Manufacturers
Aleene's Fabric and Draping Liquid	Aleene's Product of Duncan Enterprises
Get Set	Bond Adhesives Company

Examples of Use

- Stiffen a too-soft but otherwise desirable fabric.
- Stiffen trims, laces, and ribbons.
- Revive cloth and straw hats.
- Dip fabrics to be cut and shaped for flower petals and leaves.
- Use with fabric pieces for papier-mâché.
- Create sculptural effects with fabric and other soft materials.

Use on fabric instead of sizing or starch, or use to stiffen accessories and trimmings when extra body, rigidity, and stiffness are desirable. Fabric stiffeners can also create rigid sculpture from cloth.

Description

Fabric stiffeners are liquid synthetic substitutes for starch and sizing and similar to white glue. Made from an emulsion of acrylic resin and vinyl acetate, fabric stiffeners can be thinned with water or used undiluted, depending upon the desired degree of stiffness. Fabric stiffeners were originally developed for home crafts and for custom-made window shades, but they have many other uses for costumers. Other substances, such as acrylic mediums and white glues can also be used to stiffen fabrics.

Fabric texture can be altered by an application of fabric stiffener.
PHOTO: RICHARD S. BAILEY.

How to Use

First, test material to be stiffened and decide if water should be added to soften the fabric stiffener. Up to 50 percent water may be added without destroying the integrity of the stiffener. Pour stiffener (and water if desired) into a bowl or large vessel.

Costume parts like lace ruffles can be stiffened by fabric stiffener when rigidity is desired.
PHOTO: RICHARD S. BAILEY.

Add fabric and squeeze it, if possible, to allow the stiffener to penetrate. Remove the fabric and wring out excess liquid, remembering that less squeezing results in stiffer fabric.

To dry fabric, hang or lay it flat on wax paper. The stiffener can be colored by adding acrylic paint to the liquid before using, or it may be painted afterwards with acrylic paint.

Solvent for Cleanup

Thin with water. Clean with detergent and water before curing takes place.

Precautions

With Aleene's product, thin cotton becomes bubbled and wrinkled upon application and remains in that condition through dry cleaning. Smooth plastics, like vinyl, may be left with a dull film.

Fabric stiffeners disappear from most surfaces in laundering.

Health and Safety Fabric stiffeners can irritate the skin if used over a prolonged period. Protect hands with gloves.

Where to Find Fabric stores, craft and hobby shops, home-decorator departments.

Sizes 4 oz.- 1 gal.

FABRIC STIFFENERS	LAUNDER	DRY-CLEAN		
Surface	Aleene's		Get Set	
Acetate Fabric	G	E	E	E
Acetate Sheeting	P	E	P	F
Acrylic Fabric	E	E	E	E
Acrylic Sheeting	F	F	P	E
Cotton	G	E *	F	E
Glass	F	F	P	P
Leather	E	E	P	P
Linen	E	E	E	E
Metal	F	F	P	P
Mylar	P	P	P	P
Nylon	P	E	P	F
Nylon Spandex	P	E	E	F
Polyester Fabric	G	E	F	P
Polyurethane Foam	P	F	P	P
Rayon	E	E	E	E
Silk	P	E	E	E
Styrofoam	F	F	P	P
Vinyl	F	G	P	P
Wool	G	E	F	F

O = Does not bond.
P = Poor bond: Bond fails with first laundering or dry cleaning.
F = Fair bond: Materials stay bonded for up to five launderings or dry cleanings.
G = Good bond: Materials stay bonded for up to fourteen launderings or dry cleanings.
E = Excellent: Bond appears permanent.

* Surface puckers.

Gesso

Brand Names	Manufacturers
Gesso	The Art Store
Gesso	Golden Artist Colors, Inc.
Gesso	Liquitex

Examples of Use
- Create a thick, textured coating on a nonporous or porous surface.
- Smooth out rough or uneven surfaces on nontextile pieces.
- Build up a crusty layer of gesso mixed with acrylic paint to simulate mud or other debris on porous or nonporous materials.
- Use gesso to build up thickness on vacuum-formed armor and other solid items. Some costumers make armor of sized felt which they cover with first a coat of gesso and then an overcoat of acrylic paint.

Description
Gesso has been used traditionally by oil painters to prepare and size canvases or boards before painting. Most modern gesso is a mixture of plaster and adhesive, and modern gessoes incorporate an acrylic emulsion as the adhesive. Gesso comes in white and a limited range of colors, and it can be colored easily with acrylic paint or universal pigments.

How to Use
Spread on with brush or spatula. Apply one thick coat for a rough surface; lay on several thin coats to leave a smooth surface. When applying the gesso in thinner coats, mix with either plain acrylic emulsion or white glue and water. Do not thin only with water, for the gesso will tend to adhere poorly and crack.

On dense surfaces, gesso dries in minutes, but on fabric or other porous surfaces, drying takes longer. Gesso can be textured by working into it while still damp; a hard, dried surface can be smoothed with an electric sander.

Solvent for Cleanup
Soap and water while still wet.

Precautions
Use gesso when laundering and dry cleaning are not required, for gesso survives immersion only a limited number of times.

Health and Safety
Gesso is relatively safe, but wear gloves because direct contact with the skin and eyes can cause irritation. Some gessoes contain very small amounts of formaldehyde and ammonia, which can affect some people. For formaldehyde protection, use a formaldehyde respirator; for protection from ammonia vapors, use an ammonia respirator.

Some Other Brands
Gesso, Modern Masters Custom Paint and Chemical Co.; Gesso, Lascaux.

Where to Find
Artists' supply stores.

Sizes
4 oz. - 10 gal.

Larger quantities are available by special order.

GESSO   **LAUNDER** DRY-CLEAN

Surface	Art Store		Golden		Liquitex	
Acetate Fabric	G	G	G	E	G	G
Acetate Sheeting	G	P	E	P	E	G
Acrylic Fabric	G	F	G	E	G	E
Acrylic Sheeting	G	P	E	P	E	P
Cotton	G	F	F	E	G	E
Glass	F	P	P	P	P	P
Leather	G	P	G	G	E**	P**
Linen	F	G	G	G	G	G
Metal	G	P	E	G	G	P
Mylar	G	P	G*	F	F	F
Nylon	F	F	G	F	G	P
Nylon Spandex	G	G	G	G	O	O
Polyester Fabric	F	G	G	E	F	E
Polyurethane Foam	G	G	G	E	E	G
Rayon	G	G	G	E	G	E
Silk	G	G	G	E	G	E
Styrofoam	G	F	G	P	E	P
Vinyl	G**	P**	G**	P**	G**	P**
Wool	F	P	G	E	G	G

O = Does not bond.
P = Poor bond: Bond fails with first laundering or dry cleaning.
F = Fair bond: Materials stay bonded for up to five launderings or dry cleanings.
G = Good bond: Materials stay bonded for up to fourteen launderings or dry cleanings.
E = Excellent: Bond appears permanent.

* Coating cracks.
** Surface curls.

Latex

Brands Tested	Manufacturers
A-R #74 Flexible Latex Molding Compound	A-R Products, Inc.
A-R #280 Latex	A-R Products, Inc.
L-200 Latex	Cementex Corporation
Liquid Latex	Alcone Company Inc.

Examples of Use

- Coat fabric for texturizing.
- Protect and coat flexible surfaces.

Use only on porous surfaces and rubber, for latex does not adhere well to nonporous surfaces. For a production of *The Orestia* at the Shaubuhne in Berlin, Moidelle Bikel coated the costumes of the Furies with latex to achieve a reptilian look. She dipped thin cotton-knit fabric into a vessel of black pigmented latex, then sewed the latex-coated fabric to fitted bodysuits. Knit sculptured appendages were also coated with the latex and sewn to the costumes. Texture can be added to latex skin, as used for coating an alien costume for a Kokanee Beer commercial. Both of these costumes are described in Part Three.

Surrealist effects have been achieved by coating fabrics; in the *Batman* films of 1989 and the '90s, Batman's capes were latex spray-coated for texture and weight. Costumes for *Parsifal* at the Frankfurt Opera in Germany are of heavy cotton fabric, brush-coated with alternating layers of latex and torn paper. Descriptions of these two costumes are also in Part Three.

Description

Latex is liquid natural rubber from rubber plants in a dispersion, usually of ammonia and water. A-R #74 does not contain ammonia. Though manufactured for casting and mold making, liquid latex also serves well as a coating and adhesive. For use in casting, see pages 210-213 of Casting Materials; for use as an adhesive, see pages 56-57 of Adhesives.

How to Use

Latex can be brushed or troweled onto a surface, with a number of coats layered on to build up the desired texture. Allow several minutes of drying time between coats. Latex can also be placed into a vessel and fabric can be dipped into it.

To pigment latex, use special pigment available through distributors.

To bond latex-coated surfaces, use more liquid latex.

Solvent for Cleanup

Acetone.

Precautions

Latex does not withstand dry cleaning solvents and can be laundered only on a few fabrics.

Health and Safety

The vapors from ammonia are harmful to skin, eyes, and lungs. Use adequate ventilation and gloves. Do not mix ammonia or substances containing ammonia with any products that contain bleach, for these combinations create highly toxic gases.

Recent studies have shown that 1 percent of the population is allergic to latex and that 15 percent of those who work with latex develop allergies. Latex allergies can be serious, with reactions ranging from skin discoloration to fatal anaphylactic shock. Testing for latex allergies is available at hospital laboratories.

Some Other Manufacturers Burman Industries, Inc., Chicago Latex Co., Mydrin, Inc.

Where to Find Manufacturers and distributors.

Sizes 1 qt. - 50 gal

LATEX	LAUNDER	DRY-CLEAN						
Surface	**A-R 74**		**A-R 280**		**Alcone**		**L-200**	
Acetate Fabric	G	P	G	P	E	P	O	O
Acetate Sheeting	P	P	P	P	P	P	O	O
Acrylic Fabric	E	E	E	P	E	P	E	P
Acrylic Sheeting	P	P*	P	P*	P	P	O	O
Cotton	E	P	E	P	E	P	E	P
Glass	P	P	P	P	P	P	O	O
Leather	F	P	F	P	P	P	O	O
Linen	E	E	G	P	E	E	E	P
Metal	P	P	P	P	P	P	O	P
Mylar	P	P	P	P	P	P	O	O
Nylon	G	P	F	P	E	E	O	O
Nylon Spandex	E	P	E	F	P	P	E	P
Polyester Fabric	E	E	E	F	E	E	E	F
Polyurethane Foam	E	P	G	F	F	P	E	F
Rayon	E	E	E	P	E	P	E	P
Silk	E	P	E	P	E	P	O	O
Styrofoam	P	P	P	P	P	P*	O	O
Vinyl	P	P	P	P	P	P	O	O
Wool	E	E	E	F	P	P	E	F

O = Does not bond.
P = Poor bond: Bond fails with first laundering or dry cleaning.
F = Fair bond: Materials stay bonded for up to five launderings or dry cleanings.
G = Good bond: Materials stay bonded for up to fourteen launderings or dry cleanings.
E = Excellent: Bond appears permanent.

Note: Latex sometimes sticks to itself in machine laundering and dry cleaning.
* Latex dissolved.

Polyvinyl Acetate PVA/PVAc — (White Glue)

Brands Tested	Manufacturers
Craft and Hobby Glue	Macklenburg-Duncan
Elmer's Glue-All	Elmer's Products, Inc.
Phlexglu	Spectra Dynamics Products
Quick N' Tacky	Delta Technical Coatings, Inc.
Sobo	Delta Technical Coatings, Inc.

Examples of Use

• Strengthen latex, leather, and other flexible molded material for masks and accessories.

• Crinkle-texture fabric.

• Form primitive pleats.

• Protect impermanent surfaces like nonpermanent paints, glitters, and texturing materials.

• Size fabrics.

Use on fabrics, leather, smooth plastics, metal, glass, and other slick and porous surfaces for texturing. Mix it with thickening powders, like Cab-O-Sil, for thick textures.

PVA can also be used with cloth or paper in mâché work. See the Papier-Mâché section on pages 221-225.

PVA can be mixed with powdered pigment or painted to use as a colored coating.

Masking tape can be wrapped round the tip of a squeeze bottle to draw or to create a fine line.

In Berlin's Komische Oper, PVA was used with a paper cone for producing "drawn" dimensional motifs, as a substitute for embroidery.

With all the surfaces tested, excepting metals, white glue created an initial bond; however, in laundering and dry cleaning, surfaces tend to adhere to themselves and each other. For this reason, there are no charts included in this section.

Description

Polyvinyl acetate (white glue), one of the most popular adhesives, is found in costume shops around the world. Though white when wet, it dries to be clear and colorless. White glues widely vary in their resistance to water and dry cleaning solvents. They also vary in flexibility and viscosity. Among the brands we tested, we found that Phlexglu is by far the most flexible as well as the most permanent. White glues are excellent coating materials as well as adhesives.

How to Use

Apply with brush, squeeze bottle, or knife, coating one or both surfaces. Setting time is approximately twenty to thirty minutes. If increased flexibility is required, add

Phlexglu Plasticizer to any brand of PVA. For heavier consistency, add thickeners such as Cab-O-Sil and stir well.

These products will decrease transparency to a translucence.

To use for strengthening other materials, paint the glue inside, outside, or both. The applied glue will create a shiny surface.

To texture fabrics, dip fabric into a thinned-out pail of glue, or brush the glue onto the fabric. Crinkle the fabric desired amount, place on polyethylene or Teflon sheet, and allow to dry.

To form primitive, crinkly broomstick pleats, place PVA into a pail and thin with water. Submerge the fabric in the solution. Remove it and fold the fabric into pleats, securing the pleats through basting. This method will form stiff yet permanent pleats that can usually be dry-cleaned. Refer to the following chart for which glues withstand dry cleaning on specific fabrics. For more information on pleating, see Pleating with Adhesives in Part Three.

To size fabrics, use either the brush or the dip method.

At the Komische Oper in Berlin, surface effects are created with PVA mixed with vinyl powder and applied with a spatula.
DESIGN: COURTESY KOMISCHE OPER, BERLIN.

To paint or draw with PVA, add paint, glitter, or bronzing powder. Either paint with a brush or other traditional painting implement or place into a squeeze bottle, syringe, or cone and then draw. Make a cone by rolling up a piece of vellum, Mylar, or plastic coated paper into a cone shape, leaving an opening at one end. The modified PVA will be squeezed through this opening to the desired line. A squeeze bottle can also be modified to create a finer line by wrapping masking tape around its tip.

Solvent for Cleanup Water.

Precautions Over time, and if exposed to air, all white glues will yellow.

Though many white glues retain a bond with fabric through laundering and dry cleaning, the glues may soften and then fasten in an undesirable way to themselves and to other items in the machine.

Health and Safety PVA is generally nontoxic and harmless to the user, but the plasticizer, though nontoxic, can cause eye or skin irritation if direct contact occurs. When using powdered thickeners like Cab-O-Sil or colorants like pigments, be sure to wear a particle mask for protection.

Precaution: When using Cab-O-Sil and similar lightweight powders, wear a protective mask to avoid inhalation. Cab-O-Sil is amorphous silica and though the degree of its toxicity is arguable, it can stay in the lungs for life!

Some Other Brands   Crafts' size: 481 Tacky (extra thick), Bond Adhesives Company; Metlyn Stanfix, Ross Adhesives; Velvette, Delta Technical Coatings, Inc; White Glue, Bond Adhesives Company; White Glue, Aleene's Product of Duncan Enterprises; White Glue, Ross Adhesives.

Industrial size: 3M Company and Swift Adhesives are two of many manufacturers.

Where to Find   Except for Phlexglu, the smaller sizes are at hardware, hobby, home-improvement stores, and drugstores.

Phlexglu and large quantities of the others are available from the manufacturer.

Sizes   2 oz. (Delta and other crafts' glues) to 50 gal. (Phlexglu and other glues from industrial glue manufacturers).

Cab-O-Sil: 10 lb. minimum order. 4-oz. samples also availabe.

Synthetic-Rubber Coatings

Brands Tested	Manufacturers
Polyshield	Aervoe Pacific Company, Inc.
Plasti Dip	PDI Inc.
Vulcabond V-36	Stabond Corporation

Examples of Use
- Modify fabrics for a heavy, thick, rubbery quality.
- Use for waterproofing.
- Cover metals and fragile surfaces for protection against scratches and weathering.
- Form a skin over open-cell, reticulated, foams.
- Use to provide a solid exterior over foam products or to protect metals and other hard surfaces.

Description   *Synthetic-rubber coatings* like Plasti Dip are usually marketed as coatings for metal and plastic tools, but we found that they are also convenient for coating costume fabrics. All come in a wide range of colors as well as in a colorless transparency. These rubber coatings are solvent-based and not soluble in water.

Plasti Dip and Polyshield, both polyvinyl chlorides (PVC), are obtainable in most hardware stores where they are sold to coat handles of tools for easier gripping. Vulcabond, a nitrile, is marketed as a general coating and is available through the manufacturer. Hardware and paint stores also carry other brands that are specified for coating tool handles and equipment.

How to Use   Make sure that surfaces are clean and free of oils and dust. To improve adhesion on metal and other slick surfaces, sand the surface and prime with a metal primer. (PDI has a special Primer.) Spray, dip, or brush onto a surface. For spraying, first dilute 20 to 50 percent with the thinner made or recommended by the manufacturer. Wait the recommended period of time between additional coats.

For dipping, use without thinning, or thin with recommended thinners up to 30 percent. Allow the recommended time period of thirty minutes to four hours between each dipping. Allow about four hours to dry. These products should not be used on nonskinned foam.

Solvent for Cleanup   Toluene, naphtha, or Plasti Dip Thinner.

Precautions   Store in temperatures between 60° and 80°F.

Health and Safety   When working with synthetic-rubber coatings, do so only in a local exhaust system or with a respirator. For prolonged and heavy use, wear protective goggles and gloves. Keep away from open flames, cigarettes, and electrical equipment.

Some Other Brands   Vinyl Strippable Protective Coatings, Sprayon Products Industrial Supply.

Where to Find   Hardware stores.

Sizes   14.5 oz.

SYNTHETIC-RUBBER COATINGS **LAUNDER** DRY-CLEAN

Surface	Plasti Dip		Polyshield		Vulcabond	
Acetate Fabric	E	P	E	P	F	G
Acetate Sheeting	E	P	E	P	F	G
Acrylic Fabric	E	P	E	F	F	P
Acrylic Sheeting	E	P	E	P**	P	P
Cotton	E	P	E	F	P	P
Glass	P	P	P	P	E	E
Leather	F*	P	E	F	P	P
Linen	E	P	E	F	P	P
Metal	F	P	E	P	E	F
Mylar	E*	P	E	P	G	F
Nylon	E	P	E	F	G	F
Nylon Spandex	E†	P	E	F	P	P
Polyester Fabric	E	P	E	F	E	E
Polyurethane Foam	E	P	E	P	E	E
Rayon	E	P	E	F	P	P
Silk	E	P	E	F	P	P
Styrofoam	E	P	E	P**	P	P
Vinyl	F*	P †	F	P	P	P
Wool	E	P	E	F	P	P

0 = Does not bond.
P = Poor bond: Bond fails with first laundering or dry cleaning.
F = Fair bond: Materials stay bonded for up to five launderings or dry cleanings.
G = Good bond: Materials stay bonded for up to fourteen launderings or dry cleanings.
E = Excellent: Bond appears permanent.

Note: Color from Polyshield bleeds.
* Coating peels.
** Material dissolves.
† Material curls.

Varnish

Brands Tested	Manufacturers
A-1 Urethane Varnish	A-1 Paint & Varnish Company
Heirloom Satin Varnish	McCloskey (Division of the Kalspar Corporation)
Varathane	The Flecto Company, Inc.

Examples of Use

- Coat fabrics and other surfaces for protection and stiffening.
- Dip soft materials to mold them into stiffly sculptured ornamental shapes.

Use polyurethane (urethane) varnish for transforming bits of acrylic fleece and other soft objects into feathers, spiky hair, and other decorations.

Some costumers brush varnish over shoes to give longer life to thin leathered shoes that otherwise would last only a few performances. Polyurethane varnish imparts good surface hardness and scuff resistance.

Description

Varnish is a tough film, usually for protecting floors and other wooden surfaces. Most brands offer a choice of gloss, semigloss, and matte. Varnishes have traditionally been manufactured with an oil base, though today a polyurethane base, in either water or solvent solution, is available. Polyurethane varnish can produce unusual costume effects.

Other commercial uses are for outdoor maintenance coatings and patent leather finishes.

How to Use

Brush the varnish over a surface, or dip a soft object into a container of varnish and allow to air dry.

Acrylic-pile fabric is soft and malleable before being dipped into varnish.
PHOTO: RICHARD S. BAILEY.

To make stiff-haired wigs, start with a piece of long, furred acrylic fabric. Cut the backing into 1" × ¼" strips. Take care not to cut through to any of the pile. Dip the acrylic fleece strip into the varnish and lay to dry on a polyethylene surface formed to mold the fleece into the desired shape.

Solvent for Cleanup

Mineral spirits or paint thinner.

Health and Safety

Work in a well-ventilated area or wear a respirator.

Acrylic-pile fabric becomes stiff and spiky after being dipped into varnish and air dried.
PHOTO: RICHARD S. BAILEY.

Where to Find

Hardware and paint stores.

Sizes

1 pt. - 1 gal.

VARNISH   **LAUNDER** DRY-CLEAN

Surface	A-1		Heirloom		Varathane	
Acetate Fabric	E	E	E	E	E	E
Acetate Sheeting	F**	P**	E**	P**	F	P
Acrylic Fabric	E	E	E	E	E	E
Acrylic Sheeting	G	P	E	P**	P	P
Cotton	E	E	E	E	E	E
Glass	F	P	P	P	P	P
Leather	G	P	E	F	E	E
Linen	E*	E*	E*	E*	E*	E*
Metal	P**	P**	P	P	P	P
Mylar	F**	P**	G	G	P	F
Nylon	E	P	E	E	E	E
Nylon Spandex	E*	E*	E*	E*	E*	E*
Polyester Fabric	E	E	E	E	E	E
Polyurethane Foam	E	E	E	E	E	E
Rayon	E	E	E	E	E	E
Silk	E	E	E	E	E	E
Styrofoam	E	G	E	F	F	F
Vinyl	E**	P**	F**	P**	G**	F**
Wool	E	E	E	E	E	E

O = Does not bond.
P = Poor bond: Bond fails with first laundering or dry cleaning.
F = Fair bond: Materials stay bonded for up to five launderings or dry cleanings.
G - Good bond: Materials stay bonded for up to fourteen launderings or dry cleanings.
E = Excellent: Bond appears permanent.

* Surface becomes brittle.
** Surface remains sticky.

Waterproofing

Brands Tested	Manufacturers
Scotchguard	3M Company
Weather Guard	CSL. Inc.

Examples of Use

- Waterproof costumes that may become wet on stage.
- Protect fabrics against greasy spills.

Use on items that need protection from grease and water spills. One can protects eighteen to twenty-two square feet (two to three average size modern dresses).

Weather Guard and other water repellents made for leather are useful for protecting items made from natural and imitation leather.

Description

Waterproofing products are composed of a clear resin in a hydrocarbon solvent and come as thin liquid, packaged in spray cans for consumer use. They do not change the look or feel of the fabric.

How to Use

First, test fabric for colorfastness by clipping a sample from a hem or seam of the completed garment. Then, spray the fabric or garment until wet, while holding the can vertically six inches from the fabric. Overlap the sprayed areas, spraying with a slow, sweeping motion until the waterproofing solution is evenly applied. Allow three hours drying time before wearing. Then test for water resistance by dripping a few drops of water onto the treated surface. If the water drops form beads, the waterproofed fabric is ready to use. If not, spray a second coat.

Dry-clean rather than wash. Because repeated and extensive wettings on most fabrics eventually dissolve the protector, it is necessary to recoat the fabric occasionally. Test the extent of water-proofing by dropping water on the surface to see if beads are formed.

Solvent for Cleanup

Soap and water, immediately, before cure sets in.

Precautions

On most fabrics, waterproofing begins to dissipate by the second immersion in both laundry and dry cleaning.

Waterproofers made especially for fabric, like Scotchgard, should not be used on leather, vinyl, clear plastic, or imitation suede. Test before using on other materials.

Health and Safety

Spray in a ventilated area, wearing a protective mask, and avoid breathing vapors and mists. Use it away from flames, heat sources, and electrical equipment (e.g., a non-explosion-proof ventilation fan).

Some Other Brands

Meltonian Water and Stain Protector, Magid Corporation; Rain Guard Water Repellent, Dorfman Pacific; Tectron Fabric Protector, Blue Magic Products, Inc.; Water and Stain Protector, Water Repellent Shield, Cadillac Shoe Products, Inc.

Where to Find

Paint, shoe repair, and fabric stores.

Sizes   Scotchguard: 16 oz.

Weather Guard: 5.5 oz.

WATERPROOFING	**LAUNDER** DRY-CLEAN			
Surface	**Scotchguard**		**Weather Guard**	
Acetate Fabric	F	F	P	P
Acetate Sheeting	P	P	P	P
Acrylic Fabric	F	F	P	P
Acrylic Sheeting	P	P	P	P
Cotton	F	F	P	P
Glass	P	P	P	P
Leather	P	F	P	F
Linen	F	F	P	P
Metal	P	P	P	P
Mylar	P	P	P	P
Nylon	F	G	P	P
Nylon Spandex	F	F	P	P
Polyester Fabric	G	G	P	F
Polyurethane Foam	F	F	P	F
Rayon	F	F	P	P
Silk	F	F	P	P
Styrofoam	G	P	P	P
Vinyl	F	F	P	F
Wool	F	F	P	P

0 = Does not bond.
P = Poor bond: Bond fails with first laundering or dry cleaning.
F = Fair bond: Materials stay bonded for up to five launderings or dry cleanings.
G = Good bond: Materials stay bonded for up to fourteen launderings or dry cleanings.
E = Excellent: Bond appears permanent.

Colorants

Paints and inks are usually composed of two parts: a pigment and a vehicle, or base. Pigments are *coloring agents*, usually in the form of fine powders, derived from natural sources—plants, animal, or minerals—or synthesized from chemicals. When the colorant is a dye, the pigment is often available as powder, or already combined with additives such as mordants. Paints, inks, glazes, and stains are almost always suspended in a vehicle. Vehicles allow the paints to flow and are solvents or water, often including binders and additives, like stabilizers, preservatives, plasticizers, antioxidants, and fillers. Some of the solvents used with pigments are ketones and petroleum-derived hydrocarbons. Binders are usually polymer emulsions (like acrylic), oils, or casein.

In this section we will be discussing paints, inks, stains, glazes, pastel crayon, and some dyes. Textile dyes are covered thoroughly in other sources, especially in Deborah Dryden's *Fabric Painting and Dyeing for the Theatre*, which contains superb and thorough information for the costumer. The dyes described in this book are not traditionally designated for textile use. Most of the coloring agents discussed here form a bond with the surface of the fabric. Dyes, on the other hand, penetrate and form chemical reactions with the interior fibers of the fabric.

Before altering the surface of any fabric, it is important to know its fiber content, since different fibers accept colorants differently. For example, some paints adhere to all types of fibers and will withstand laundering and dry cleaning; other paints may remain adhered to only a few fibers during cleaning and to another few fibers during laundering.

Some fabrics are coated with finishes during manufacture. Finishes affect the manner in which the fabric accepts any kind of coating or coloring. Finishes do not welcome surface treatment and vary in their longevity, just as do fabrics, in the extent to which they resist stains and water. Other finishes are sometimes added to enhance the appearance of fabrics in the salesroom and, for this reason, washable fabrics should be laundered, when possible, before treating.

When treating a fabric, some considerations are the pile of a fabric, whether it is thick or thin, soft or stiff, matte or shiny. The technique with which to apply paint or any other colorant is important. For instance, if there is no access to a steamer, dry heat-set colorants must be used. Always test the colorant on a fabric to learn both its effect on that fabric as well as how the color may change once it has dried on the fabric selected.

Paint for fabric differs from paint for other surfaces. Because fabric is flexible, textile colorants usually contain plasticizers; and because fabrics are usually subjected to water or dry cleaning solvents, fabric paints are usually made with binders resistant to water and solvents.

Dyes

Dyes are organic chemical compounds of either natural or synthetic origin. The late nineteenth-century development of coal tar as a base for dyestuff allowed the development of numerous strongly colored dyes, and today almost all dyes are synthetic. Some dyes form a chemical bond, unlike paints, and actually change fibers of the fabric, rather than sit on its surface. Dyes do not usually affect the fabric hand, or tactile quality. Dyes are specific to certain fibers, except for union dyes, like Rit and Tintex, which have a limited affinity for most fibers. Dyes generally are used in vat dyeing, but they can also be sprayed or thickened with certain pastes and used like paints.

Inks

Inks are intended for drawing, writing, or painting. Ink can be a fluid, a semifluid, or a paste containing pigment. Drawing ink is usually called India ink and consists of pigment that is finely dispersed in a solution along with wetting agents and preservative.

The traditional binder used in India or drawing ink is a combination of shellac and borax. Writing ink is somewhat thicker and can be composed of a variety of solvents. Oil is the most common. Writing ink is generally less permanent than drawing ink. Regular printing ink is usually even thicker, but it is not of concern here. Silk-screen ink, however, is used by many costume painters. Textile and silk-screen ink is quite thick, and sometimes even referred to as paint. Water-base textile inks (like Deka and Versatex inks) are actually dyes and will not affect the hand of a given fabric. Water-based textile inks have the advantage of brilliant color and are an excellent medium for airbrushing.

Marking pens are normally used on paper, and they are useful to costumers as well for drawing on fabrics. The inks in markers can be solvent or water-based. Solvent-based colors are usually more lasting and should be used in work that is designed to last longer. Most water-based inks dissolve washing and dry cleaning.

Paints

Paints are composed of pigment powders that are dispersed in a medium or binder. The medium preserves suspension and allows the paint to be applied to a surface. The pigments are derived from either natural sources like vegetables or from synthetic sources. Paints both color and protect surfaces through close adhesion between a surface and a medium. In paints, the binder is usually opaque and firm, often adding stiffness to soft and pliable materials like textiles. With increased developments in modern chemistry, however, more paints that do not stiffen are available. Chemists are developing the very qualities so important to costume painters.

Some of the various media used for binders are synthetic plastics like acrylic, vinyl, and synthetic rubbers, while more traditional paints use oil. In most cases, the paints that have proved the most successful on fabrics are those with an acrylic base, and are found among textile paints, house paints, scenic paints, and easel artists' paints. A number of mediums can be added to acrylic paint to affect the finish as well as the viscosity, and these include matte and gloss mediums and gels.

In this section of the book, paints are categorized according to their known use; examples are scenic paints, easel artists' paints, etc. The emphasis is on paints that are less traditional, since excellent material on textile paints is readily available in several references listed in the bibliography.

Pastels and Crayons

Pastel sticks formulated for textile use are in an oil base, similar to artists' oil pastels and somewhat softer than crayons.

Three types of crayons available today for textile work are *transfer* crayons, *iron-fixed* crayons, and *steam-based* crayons. Composed of wax and pigments, textile crayons closely resemble children's coloring crayons. Transfer crayons may be applied successfully only on synthetic fabrics or synthetic blends. Iron-fixed crayons are, as their name suggests, set by the heat of the iron after coloring. Steam-fixed crayons are to be used either alone, like ordinary coloring crayons, or in combination with resist dyes. With the latter, the crayon melts into the fabric, forming an outline barrier to enclose a painted interior design.

Stains and Glazes

Stains are comprised of transparent pigment in a solution with oil, alcohol, or water. *Glaze* is a term usually applied to stains manufactured specifically for glass and certain other products. Wood stains are generally in oil, for oil does not affect wood grain as do water and alcohol. Glass stains, or glazes, are often in a solvent like toluol. Hydrocarbon solvents like toluol are highly toxic and should be used only with great caution.

The stains and glazes recommended for use on costumes are not to be confused with the stains, glazes, and enamels that are applied only to ceramic, metal, and glass work and which require kiln firing.

The colorants discussed in this section are organized by the categories Dyes, Inks, Paints, Pastels and Crayons, and Stains and Glazes. Within each of these categories, the products are listed alphabetically.

Working Methods   Techniques for using paints, inks, and other colorants with textiles are as various as those who use them and have been beautifully covered in the following books: *Fabric Painting and Dyeing for the Theatre* by Deborah M. Dryden; *Everything You Ever Wanted to Know About Fabric Painting* by Jill Kennedy and Jane Varrall; *Surface Design for Fabric* by Richard M. Proctor and Jennifer F. Lew; *Fabric Painting Made Easy* by Nancy Ward.

To successfully use the colorants discussed in this section, we recommend following specific product package instructions. It is important always to wash launderable textiles before applying color. Washing removes sizing and other finishes that may inhibit a maximum reaction between the textile and coloring substance. Setting usually requires an iron, a dryer, or a steam cabinet—whichever is recommended or appropriate for the specific colorant.

In testing these products, we have approximated normal costume-care conditions. Two sets of samples of each product were subjected to as many as fifteen dry cleanings and launderings. Samples were washed in warm water with ordinary laundry detergent and dried for thirty minutes in a warm dryer. Dry-cleaned samples were submitted to commercial dry cleaning establishments that used perchlorethylene cleaning solvent in a standard dry cleaning machine. At least one day was allowed between each wash and cleaning to simulate a real situation.

We found that different colors of the same products sometimes react differently to laundering and dry cleaning. For instance, three colors of the same brand of ink may last through different numbers of launderings. One may even alter or stiffen the hand of the fabric more or less than the others. To list all of these differences is impractical; every single color or each product would have to be tested. Where these differences occurred in our testing, we listed them in the charts as a range, for example, P-G, G-E, etc. In addition, different individuals apply the same products differently. For example, one painter may apply paint more thickly, or use less heat than another. Paints and coatings that are not extremely flexible will crack when applied to solid flexible surfaces such as leather, vinyl, and most plastic films.

Finally, differences in the quality of fabric, the openness of its weave, and other variables in its structure will affect the lasting quality of any applied substance.

Health and Safety   Some pigments contain lead and should be avoided. These are chrome green, chrome yellow, flake white, and Naples yellow. Lead is no longer found in consumer wall paints, though some auto, boat, artists' and industrial paints, and metal primer may contain lead.

Inorganic pigments commonly contain toxic or carcinogenic metals such as lead, chrome, manganese, cobalt, cadmium, and so on. Many natural and synthetic organic pigments are based on known carcinogens such as anthrazuinone and enzidine. Some synthetic organic pigments also contain highly toxic impurities such as polychlorinated biphenyls (PCBs) and dioxins. Most pigments have never actually been studied for long-term toxicity and legally can be labeled nontoxic even when they are related to known carcinogens. (Chemicals in the United States are innocent until proven guilty!)

Users of paints and pigments often will not even be able to determine the identity of the pigments in their products. There is no law requiring manufacturers to disclose pigment, and many are mislabeled or given such meaningless names as "Navy Blue" or "Wine." For these reasons, it is wise to treat all pigments as toxic.

For safety in working, follow these rules:

- For protection, procure MSDSs for coloring agents.
- If there is a choice between water-based and solvent-based products, choose those that are water-based.
- Use colorants that are premixed in order to avoid powdered pigments, which are harmful to inhale.
- Do not drink, eat, or smoke in the work area.
- Do not use the same equipment and utensils for both food and colorants.
- Use the proper type of respirator mask. Spraying water-based products requires a respirator with a dust-mist filter. Solvent-based products require the use of an organic vapor cartridge along with a spray prefilter; the cartridge and the filter may be combined and sold as a paint, lacquer, or enamel-mist cartridge.
- Use gloves or barrier creams to protect hands, and wear protective clothing. Wear goggles when working with corrosive chemicals.
- Before using solvent-based products, read the section in this book on safety measures for working with solvents.

Dyes

Leather Dye

Brands Tested	Manufacturers
Angelus Brand Leather Dye	Angelus Shoe Polish Company
Fiebing's Leather Dye	Fiebing Company, Inc.

Examples of Use

- Dye all leathers except for suede and synthetic leathers.
- Paint motifs and decorations onto specific fabrics.
- Mix with shellac to use as French enamel varnish (FEV).

These dyes are excellent for painting strongly colored, transparent, vibrant patterns and textures on both leather and fabrics.

Description

Leather dyes are transparent, formulated for dying leather, and are a compound of pigment in a denatured ethyl alcohol and carbitol solution. They are available in many vibrant colors.

How to Use

Use transparent leather dye on leather shoes, bags, belts, etc. as well as on fabrics.

First clean and prepare with a *deglazer* (manufactured by dye manufacturers).

Paint with a brush, spray, or applicator. A small applicator is supplied by the manufacturers. Both these finishes are excellent for hand-painting motifs and decorations on leather and fabrics. Heat-setting is not required.

Solvent for Thinning and Cleanup

Alcohol, followed by soap and water.

Precautions

Use Fiebing's on fabrics that will be washed, but not on cotton, and only on some synthetics that will be dry-cleaned. Angelus does not sustain its bond on as many surfaces when laundered and dry-cleaned.

Leather dyes do not stay bonded to most fabrics after cleaning and laundering. Read the following charts and test before using when cleaning could be a factor.

Health and Safety

Keep away from flames, wear a respirator, and use in an open or well-ventilated area. Obtain MSDSs to identify the solvents they contain and choose the right kind of protective gloves.

Some Other Brands

Color-Lac, L-C-I; Lincoln Shoe Dressing, John Lincoln Co.; Miracle Colour-Up, CSL Inc.

Where to Find

Shoe-repair and leather-supply stores.

Sizes

4 oz. - 8 oz.

LEATHER DYES   **LAUNDER** DRY-CLEAN

Surface	Angelus		Fiebing's	
Acetate Fabric	G	F	G	F
Acetate Sheeting	G	G	F	P
Acrylic Fabric	F	G	F	F
Acrylic Sheeting	G	P	F	P
Cotton	F	F	F	F
Glass	P	P	P	P
Leather	F	F	E	F
Linen	G	G	F	F
Metal	P	P	P	P
Mylar	F	F	G	P
Nylon	G	F	F	P
Nylon Spandex	E	F	F	G
Polyester Fabric	F	F	F	F
Polyurethane Foam	F	F	E	G
Rayon	F	G	F	F
Silk	F*	F *	F *	P*
Styrofoam	F	P	P	P
Vinyl	G	F	G	P
Wool	F	F	F	P

0 = Does not bond.
P = Poor bond: Bond fails with first laundering or dry cleaning.
F = Fair bond: Materials stay bonded for up to five launderings or dry cleanings.
G = Good bond: Materials stay bonded for up to fourteen launderings or dry cleanings.
E = Excellent: Bond appears permanent.

Note: Colors of leather dyes sometimes change after application to textiles.
* Surface stiffens.

Vinyl Spray Dye for Fabric

Brand Tested	Manufacturers
Fab Spray for Fabric	Zynolite Products co.

Examples of Use
- Apply a thin dye coat of color onto fabrics or other surfaces.
- Distress costumes.
- Modify fabrics to add dimension and depth.

Use when time is a factor. Since the chemicals composing Fab Spray are dangerous, it is best to use another, more innocuous dye or paint that can be sprayed from a Pre-Val sprayer or airbrush.

Fab Spray for Fabrics is especially suited for coloring launderable garments of polyester or acrylic fibers.

Description *Fab Spray* is packaged in an aerosol can and is the only dye in this category that we have found available on the retail market. A transparent color sits on top of a surface, unlike other dyes that penetrate the fibers. Fab Spray is composed of a vinyl resin base in a methyl ethyl ketone (MEK) solvent. Colors are limited.

The fabric spray bonds to all fabrics and causes some stiffening. It launders and dry-cleans on many that we have tested. The targeted market for Fab Spray is upholstery.

How to Use Hold fabric vertically, either on a dress form or tacked to a wall. Keep spray can upright and at least two feet from the fabric. Press nozzle and spray with sweeping strokes that overlap the edges of the fabric.

Solvent for Cleanup Acetone.

Precautions Fab Spray causes slight stiffening on fabrics.

Health and Safety MEK, an ingredient of Fab Spray is toxic and dangerous to humans. Use only with good ventilation, a respirator, gloves, and goggles or spray in a local exhaust system such as a spray booth.

Where to Find Paint stores.

Sizes 12 oz.

VINYL SPRAY DYE FOR FABRIC   **LAUNDER** DRY-CLEAN

Surface	Fab Spray	
Acetate Fabric	G	G
Acetate Sheeting	P-G	P-F
Acrylic Fabric	G	F-G
Acrylic Sheeting	G-E	P
Cotton	F	F
Glass	P	P
Leather	E	F
Linen	G	P
Metal	P	P
Mylar	P-G	P
Nylon	P-G	G-F
Nylon Spandex	G	F
Polyester Fabric	G	F
Polyurethane Foam	F	F
Rayon	F	P
Silk	F	P
Styrofoam	F	P
Vinyl	G	F-E
Wool	P	P

0 = Does not bond.
P = Poor bond: Bond fails with first laundering or dry cleaning.
F = Fair bond: Materials stay bonded for up to five launderings or dry cleanings.
G = Good bond: Materials stay bonded for up to fourteen launderings or dry cleanings.
E = Excellent: Bond appears permanent.

Note: Vinyl spray dye causes surfaces to stiffen slightly.

Inks

Artists' Inks

Brands Tested	Manufacturers
FW Acrylic Artists Ink (Waterproof)	Steig Products
Higgens Waterproof Drawing Ink	Faber-Castell
Luma Inks	Steig Products
Pelikan A (Waterproof)	Pelikan A. G.

Examples of Use
- Strain and spray where an intense color is desired.
- Draw or stencil small- to medium-size motifs.
- Use on stiff and medium-hand fabrics when stiffening the fabric is not a problem.

Description These are the familiar *artists' inks* for drawing and lettering, used with fountain and dip pens or artists' brushes. Waterproof India inks are made with intense dyes and are carried in a shellac solution or in a water base with an acrylic additive. The solution varies slightly with the type of ink. Coloring costumes with India ink is an expensive technique compared with most others. Luma Inks are often used in painting with a watercolor technique while the three other inks are more commonly used for drawing and lettering.

How to Use Use with brush, dropper, pen, etc., as when drawing or writing on paper. The inks are meant for the comparatively smooth surface of paper, and they do not flow as easily on more textured fabrics.

Solvent for Thinning and Cleanup For thinning, use distilled water. For cleanup, use alcohol or detergent and water.

Precautions India inks stiffen most fabrics and sometimes cause streaks. They are especially difficult to brush onto deeply textured or porous fabrics.

Both Higgens and Pelikan inks are water-based, and the waterproofing is more successful on paper, lasting on fabrics through only several immersions at best.

FW Ink bonds fairly well to many fabrics through dry cleaning, though the color bleeds on some. It remained well only on cotton through laundering.

Health and Safety If painting a large area or spraying, use only with good ventilation, a respirator, gloves, and goggles, or spray in a local exhaust system such as a spray booth.

Some Other Brands Koh-I-Noor, Koh-I-Noor; Rotring Art Pen Ink, Rotring GmbH.

Both Higgens and Pelikan have extensive lines of inks.

Where to Find Art supply stores and stationery stores.

Sizes 1 oz.

ARTISTS' INKS   **LAUNDER** DRY-CLEAN

Surface	FW Acrylic Artists Ink		Higgens Waterproof		Luma Inks		Pelikan A	
Acetate Fabric	G	E	P-F	F-G	F	E	G	E
Acetate Sheeting	E	P	P	P	F*	F	P	F
Acrylic Fabric	G	G	P-F	F	G	E	G	E
Acrylic Sheeting	G	P	P	P	F*	P	F	P
Cotton	E	E	P	P-G	G	E	G	E
Glass	F	P	P	P	F*	P	P	F
Leather	F	F	P	P	P	F	P	F
Linen	G	E	P	P	G	F	G	E
Metal	P	F	P	P	G	P	P	P
Mylar	G	P	P	P	E*	P	P	F
Nylon	G	P	P	P	F	F	P	F
Nylon Spandex	G	G	P	P	P	P	P	P
Polyester Fabric	F	G	P	F	G	E	F	E
Polyurethane Foam	G	F	P	P	F	F**	F-G	F
Rayon	G	E	P	F-G	E	P	F	E
Silk	G	G	P	P-F	F	G	F	E
Styrofoam	F	F	P	P	F	P	P-E	P
Vinyl	F	F	P	P	F	P	O	O
Wool	F	F	P	P	G	F	F	P

O = Does not bond.
P = Poor bond: Bond fails with first laundering or dry cleaning.
F = Fair bond: Materials stay bonded for up to five launderings or dry cleanings.
G = Good bond: Materials stay bonded for up to fourteen launderings or dry cleanings.
E = Excellent: Bond appears permanent.

* Colorant cracks or chips.
** Colorant dulls.

Ballpoint Pens

Brands Tested	Manufacturers
Bic Accountant	Bic USA
Lindy	Lindy Manufacturing Company
Papermate	Write Brothers
Pentel	Pentel Company, Ltd.

Examples of Use
- Draw fine linear patterns.
- Outline areas to fill in with other paints or dyes.

Use as border designs, textural patterns, or small motifs on fabrics that will not be laundered or dry-cleaned. Ballpoint ink adheres to porous surfaces like paper, leather, and fabrics but does not remain on most slick surfaces.

Description *Ballpoint pens* are the commonly used writing pens, familiar to all. Their ink is composed of pigment dispersed in either an oil or water solution.

How to Use Write or draw on fabric as on paper, being sure to keep the fabric on a horizontal base. Ballpoint pens create a thin line that is discernible only at a close distance.

Solvent for Cleanup Paint thinner, spot cleaners, or send out for dry cleaning.

Precautions Ballpoint pens do not withstand well washing or dry cleaning.

Some Other Brands Eastman, Eastman Corp.; Pilot, Pilot Corp.

Where to Find Stationery stores and drugstores.

BALLPOINT PENS   **LAUNDER** DRY-CLEAN

Surface	Bic Accountant		Lindy		Paper Mate		Pentel	
Acetate Fabric	F	P	G	P	O	G	P	P
Acetate Sheeting	0	0	0	0	0	0	0	0
Acrylic Fabric	F	G	F	G	F-G	G	P	P
Acrylic Sheeting	0	0	0	0	0	0	0	0
Cotton	P	P	F	P	F	E	P	P
Glass	0	0	0	0	0	0	0	0
Leather	G	F	F	P	F	P	P	P
Linen	P	P	F	P	F	G	P	E
Metal	0	P	P	P	P	P	0	0
Mylar	0	P	F	P	P	P	0	0
Nylon	F	F	F	P	F	P	P	P
Nylon Spandex	P	P	P	P	F	G	P	G
Polyester Fabric	F	P	F	F	F	G	P	P
Polyurethane Foam	P	P	P	P	F	P	P	P
Rayon	F	P	F	P	F	E	F	P
Silk	F	F	F	P	F	G	F	P
Styrofoam	P	P	P	P	P	P	P	P
Vinyl	F	F	F	P	F	P	P	E
Wool	P	P	F	P	F	P	F	P

0 = Does not bond.
P = Poor bond: Bond fails with first laundering or dry cleaning.
F = Fair bond: Materials stay bonded for up to five launderings or dry cleanings.
G = Good bond: Materials stay bonded for up to fourteen launderings or dry cleanings.
E = Excellent: Bond appears permanent.

Felt-Tip Marking Pens

Brands Tested	Manufacturers
Design Art Marker	Eberhard Faber Incorporated
Dylon Color Fun	Dylon International, Ltd.
Magic Marker	Berel Corporation
Marvy Fabric Marker	Uchida Corporation
Seta Scrib	Pébéo industries
Sharpie Fine Point Permanent Marker	Sanford Corporation

Examples of Use
- Draw decorative linear motifs and stripes on costumes that need little or no dry cleaning.
- Use when speed is necessary and when time-consuming color mixing must be avoided.

Colored markers are most effective on those fabrics and soft plastics requiring neither laundering nor dry cleaning, with the exception of Seta Scrib. Sharpie is available in only six colors, while other brands are available in a broad spectrum of colors.

Information on metallic markers can be found on pages 164-165.

Description   *Felt-tip markers* are basically metal tubes containing an ink-saturated quarter-of-an-inch felt strip that protrudes as a nib. They are available with permanent (hydrocarbon solvent) or water-soluble inks. Those markers we tested were made with a hydrocarbon solvent, though there are others that are water soluble and created specifically for marking on fabric.

Felt-tip markers are commonly used by illustrators and layout artists for quick drawing. They are also excellent for quick costume sketches, although they will fade over time if left in a light room.

Seta Scrib, Dylon, and Marvy brand markers are designed for use on fabric, and hold up better after laundering and cleaning than do the others.

How to Use   Use for simple drawing. Markers are a fast and easy-to-use tool because they have a broad sturdy nib and dry on contact. Before drawing on soft or thin fabrics, prepare a wooden frame to hold the fabric firmly in position for drawing. The frame should be the width of the fabric, and the length as long as necessary to secure the fabric. Stretch and carefully thumbtack or staple the outer edges of the fabric.

Solvent for Cleanup   Odorless paint thinner will clean most markers. For the correct solvents for specific markers, obtain MSDSs to learn the solvents used in the markers. Select one of the least toxic and use it. Try not to use solvents with threshold limit values (TLVs) of 100 or less than 100 parts per million. Of those solvents most likely to be in markers, ethyl alcohol is the safest. Refer to the Solvents section on pages 417-423 of the appendix to learn about solvents and to the specific charts for TLV information.

Precautions Test results varied among the other four brands, showing that certain brands will begin to fade around the 10th laundering or cleaning, though almost all fade by the 15th immersion.

Health and Safety Use in a well-ventilated area; these are highly toxic. Wear a respirator when working with marking pens over a long period. To select the proper respirator, consult MSDSs, for many different solvents are used in various combinations in markers.

Some Other Brands Art markers: Ad Marker, Chartpak; CPG International Design Art Marker, Faber-Castell Corp.; Pantone, Pantone, Inc.; Prismacolor, Berol Corp.

Fabric markers: Speedball Fabric Painters, Hunt Mfg. Co.

Where to Find Art stores, stationery stores and drugstores.
Fabric markers are also available at fiber-arts stores.

Sizes 3" - 5" length, approximately ¾" diameter.

FELT-TIP MARKING PENS FOR ART WORK   **LAUNDER** DRY-CLEAN

Surface	Design Art Marker		Magic Marker		Sharpie	
Acetate Fabric	G	F	F	F	G	P
Acetate Sheeting	O	O	G	P	F	P
Acrylic Fabric	G	F	G	F	G	P
Acrylic Sheeting	O	O	E	P	F	P
Cotton	F	F	G	F	F	P
Glass	O	O	F	P	P	P
Leather	F	F	E	F	P	P
Linen	G	F	F	P	P	P
Metal	O	O	G	P	F	P
Mylar	O	O	F	P	F	P
Nylon	G	P	F	P	G	P
Nylon Spandex	F	P	G	P	G	P
Polyester Fabric	G	P	P	P	G	P
Polyurethane Foam	E	P	F	P	E	E
Rayon	F	P	F	P	F	P
Silk	F	P	F	F	F	P
Styrofoam	E	E	G	P	F	P
Vinyl	E	G	G	P	E	P
Wool	F	P	F	P	F	P

O = Does not bond.
P = Poor bond: Bond fails with first laundering or dry cleaning.
F = Fair bond: Materials stay bonded for up to five launderings or dry cleanings.
G = Good bond: Materials stay bonded for up to fourteen launderings or dry cleanings.
E = Excellent: Bond appears permanent.

Note: These inks bleed somewhat in laundering.

FELT-TIP MARKING PENS FOR FABRIC **LAUNDER** DRY-CLEAN

Surface	Dylon Color Fun		Marvy Fabric Marker		Seta Scrib	
Acetate Fabric	G	F	E	F	F	F
Acetate Sheeting	P	P	P	P	P	P
Acrylic Fabric	P	P	G	G	G	F
Acrylic Sheeting	P	F	P	P	P	P
Cotton	F	F	E	G	G	G
Glass	P	P	O	O	P	P
Leather	P*	E*	P	P	G	P
Linen	F	F	G	G	G	G
Metal	P	P	P	P	P	P
Mylar	P	P	P	P	P	P
Nylon	F	P-F	P-F	P-F	G	F-G
Nylon Spandex	F	E	P-F	F-G	F	F-G
Polyester Fabric	F	F	G-E	F	F	F
Polyurethane Foam	F-G	F	F	P	F	P
Rayon	F	F	G	G	F	F
Silk	F-G	G	G	G-E	F	F
Styrofoam	G	P	G	P	F	P
Vinyl	F	P **	F	P	F	P
Wool	F	G	F	F	F	P

O = Does not bond.
P = Poor bond: Bond fails with first laundering or dry cleaning.
F = Fair bond: Materials stay bonded for up to five launderings or dry cleanings.
G = Good bond: Materials stay bonded for up to fourteen launderings or dry cleanings.
E = Excellent: Bond appears permanent.

* Surface stiffens.
** Colorant splotches.

Textile Ink In Water Solution

Brands Tested	Manufacturers
Peintex	Sennelier Paris
Versatex Airbrush Ink for Fabrics	Siphon Art

Examples of Use
- Airbrush texture, color modulate, and shadow.
- Brush, or line paint images onto textiles; the color is brilliant and will not stiffen fabrics.
- Paint motifs, images, shadow, aging, and all kinds of color effects.

Description   *Textile inks in water solution* are medium-thin viscosity inks that have been especially formulated for translucency. The airbrush inks for fabrics are not the same as regular airbrush inks. Peintex ink is best used for airbrushing, for it bleeds when brushed onto fabrics.

How to Use   Versatex ink is already prefiltered, but it is advisable to filter it again before airbrushing by straining it through a cheesecloth. Apply the ink according to package directions. Set it by heat, with either an iron or a clothes dryer.

Peintex fabric ink can be airbrushed, stenciled, brushed, or printed. Set it with a hot iron or clothes dryer.

Solvent for Cleanup   Water or alcohol.

Precautions   Store in the refrigerator. Airbrush textile ink may not adhere if it is stored incorrectly.

Use with caution on woolens and synthetics because the inks require heat setting, which could be damaging to the fibers.

Versatex inks color initially and will withstand dry cleaning or laundering on natural fibers, polyester, and nylon, but they will not last well on nylon spandex.

Peintex bonds initially to all fabrics but withstands laundering only on acrylic fiber. Peintex lasts through dry cleaning on most fabrics.

Health and Safety   Use only with good ventilation, a respirator, gloves, and goggles, or spray in a local exhaust system such as a spray booth.

Some Other Brands   Createx Transparent Airbrush Colors; PROfab Textile Inks; Rocco Airbrush Ink.

Where to Find   Art stores and fiber-art stores.

Sizes   4 oz. and 16 oz.

TEXTILE INK IN WATER SOLUTION   **LAUNDER**   DRY-CLEAN

Surface	Peintex		Versatex Airbrush Ink	
Acetate Fabric	G	G	F	F
Acetate Sheeting	P	P	P	P
Acrylic Fabric	E	G	F	F
Acrylic Sheeting	O	P	P	P
Cotton	G	E	E	E
Glass	P	P	P	P
Leather	G	G	F	F
Linen	G	G	E	E
Metal	P	P	P	P
Mylar	P	P	P	P
Nylon	F	F	E	E
Nylon Spandex	G	G	G	G
Polyester Fabric	G	G	E	E
Polyurethane Foam	G	F	P	P
Rayon	G	F	E	E
Silk	G	G	E	E
Styrofoam	F	F	P	P
Vinyl	G	G	P	P
Wool	G	E	E	E

O = Does not bond.
P = Poor bond: Bond fails with first laundering or dry cleaning.
F = Fair bond: Materials stay bonded for up to five launderings or dry cleanings.
G = Good bond: Materials stay bonded for up to fourteen launderings or dry cleanings.
E = Excellent: Bond appears permanent.

Note: Peintex bleeds when brushed onto surface and is possibly best used for airbrushing.

Paints

Acrylic Paint for Leather, Vinyl and Plastic

Brands Tested	Manufacturers
Magix Shoe Color Spray	Kiwi Brands Inc.
Nu-Life Color Spray	Magic Corporation

Examples of Use
- Color leather, vinyl, fabric, and flexible surfaces, such as shoes, accessories and other costume pieces.
- Shadow, highlight, color modulate, and distress fabric pieces that do not require dry cleaning.

Description   The highly flexible paints from Kiwi Brands Inc. and the Magic Corporation are used widely at shoe repair shops for coloring genuine and synthetic leather shoes and handbags. Also known as *shoe makeup*, they are bottled and available for both spray and brush-on coating. Because the paint sits on top of the surface, it cannot produce the beauty of well-cured leather. But these paints in spray cans can add color quickly to fabric costumes. The paint surface will be glossy when applied to a smooth surface. Two sizes of spray containers are available, with a wider range of colors available in the smaller containers.

How to Use   When coloring leather, prepare the surface by cleaning with acetone or a leather preparer (packaged by all three brands), wiping with a wet cloth to remove dirt, grease, or any previous coating. To color shoes, first stuff the shoe with crumpled paper and mask the soles with masking tape. (Later the edge of the soles may be repainted with a special shoe-sole coloring made for that purpose.) Spray or brush a thin coat on the shoes. Allow the paint to dry thoroughly and apply again. (Two coats are usually necessary to cover completely and smoothly.) If the paint is sprayed on too thickly, or if drying time is not adequate, the paint will soon crack.

Additional spray-on colors can be mixed by using an even lighter coating of spray paint. When one thin coating is sprayed on top of another, the undercoat will show through, creating the effect of a new color combination.

When spraying on fabric and other porous materials, secure the fabric vertically; paint can only be sprayed when the can is held upright. Place already constructed costumes onto dress forms. Always start the spray beyond the edge of the garment, spraying evenly across the surface to beyond the opposite edge. Use as small a stroke as possible to avoid clogging the spray nozzle. After spraying, clean the sprayer by turning the can upside down and pressing the nozzle until the spray stops.

Solvent for Cleanup Acetone.

Precautions These sprays will slightly stiffen many fabrics, including acetate, wool, acrylic, cotton, and nylon, as well as polyurethane foam. Although the paints leave a satin finish on leather and leather substitutes, on porous surfaces like fabrics they produce a dull finish and will suppress the gloss of satiny surfaces. Spandex loses some of its elasticity. Protect the surrounding area with plenty of masking.

Different colors react differently in laundering. On any costumes that may be laundered, be sure to test each individual color on the specific fabric in use.

Use only on garments that are not intended to be dry-cleaned. In most instances the paint will survive a few laundering cycles.

Health and Safety Use only with good ventilation, a respirator, gloves, and goggles, or spray in a local exhaust system such as a spray booth. The solvents and pigments in this paint are among the most toxic of substances.

Some Other Brands Spray Application: Prism Color Spray, CSL Inc.; CSL Miracle Colour Up. Brush Application: Starlight Paints.

Where to Find Shoe-repair shops and leather suppliers.

Sizes 5 oz. and 12 oz.

ACRYLIC PAINT FOR LEATHER VINYL AND PLASTIC **LAUNDER** DRY-CLEAN

Surface	Magix		Nu-Life	
Acetate Fabric	F-G*	P*	F-G*	F*
Acetate Sheeting	F-E*	P	F-E	P
Acrylic Fabric	F-G	P	E*	P*
Acrylic Sheeting	E	P	E	P
Cotton	P*	P*	G-E*	F*
Glass	P	P	P	P
Leather	F-E	P	F-E	P
Linen	P-G*	P*	G-E	E
Metal	P-G	P	F-G	P
Mylar	P-G	P	F-G	P
Nylon	P-G*	P*	G-E*	P*
Nylon Spandex	P	P	G-E	F
Polyester Fabric	P-G	P	G-E**	F⁰
Polyurethane Foam	P-F*	P*	P-F*	P*
Rayon	P-F*	P*	G-E	F
Silk	F-G*	P*	G-E	P
Styrofoam	P	P †	P	P †
Vinyl	F-G	P	F-G	P
Wool	P	P	F-G	F

0 = Does not bond.
P = Poor bond: Bond fails with first laundering or dry cleaning.
F = Fair bond: Materials stay bonded for up to five launderings or dry cleanings.
G = Good bond: Materials stay bonded for up to fourteen launderings or dry cleanings.
E = Excellent: Bond appears permanent.

* Surface stiffens.
** Colorant bleeds.
† Surface dissolves.

Airbrush-Formulated Textile Paint

Brands Tested	Manufacturers
Badger Air Tex Fabric Paint	Decart, Inc.
Deka Permanent Air Fabric Paint	Decart, Inc.

Examples of Use

- Lay a thin layer of color over fabric.
- Create decorative motifs.
- Texture and add depth to folds.
- Paint through a stencil.
- Age costumes and accessories.

Airbrushing works well when painting details and drawing designs and motifs as well as when texturing and distressing.

Description   *Airbrush-formulated paints* are thin viscosity water-soluble fabric paints so formulated that they may be applied with an airbrush. Finely ground pigments are carried in an acrylic and water solution that does not clog the airbrush as other paints do. Because these paints are specifically designed for textiles, they do not stiffen the fabrics.

Other types of paints can be airbrushed if diluted first with water and then strained carefully through cheesecloth. Silk paints, more than others, clog the nozzle of the airbrush.

How to Use   Airbrush-formulated paints are thin and may be thinned further for easier control or more transparency. Though specifically formulated for an airbrush sprayer, they can also be applied with an ordinary paintbrush. Because they are paints, they are opaque. Even after thinning, they do not reach the degree of transparency or translucency of dyes.

Unitards are airbrushed with DekaSilk paint, creating a smooth color transition. Headdress/masks are of plaster bandages cast in clay molds, their surfaces smoothed with spackle, and painted with artists' acrylic paints.

DESIGN: JENNIFER LANGEBERG FOR THE REDWOOD EMPIRE ICE ARENA.
PHOTO: KEN SCIALLO.

Solvent for Thinning and Cleanup   For thinning, use water. For cleanup, soap and water.

Precautions   Cover surrounding area well. Clean up immediately, for these fabric paints may color the surrounding area permanently.

Airbrush paints bond well to natural fabrics, polyester, and nylon and retain their original brilliance and flexibility through at least fifteen launderings and dry cleanings. Badger will bond to acetate and acrylic, though it does not remain on polyester when laundered.

Health and Safety   Use only with good ventilation, a respirator, gloves, and goggles, or spray in a local exhaust system such as a spray booth.

Some Other Brands Createx Airbrush Paint, ColorCraft, Ltd.; Jürek Professional Airbrush Colours, Medea Airbrush Products.

Where to Find Art stores and textile art stores.

Sizes Badger: 1 oz.
Deka: 8 oz. and 1 qt.

AIRBRUSH-FORMULATED TEXTILE PAINT   **LAUNDER**   DRY-CLEAN

Surface	Deka		Badger	
Acetate Fabric	G	G	G	G
Acetate Sheeting	P	P	P	P
Acrylic Fabric	G	G	G	F
Acrylic Sheeting	P	P	P	E
Cotton	E	E	E	E
Glass	P	P	P	P
Leather	G	G	F	G
Linen	E	E	E	E
Metal	P	P	P	P
Mylar	E	P	P	P
Nylon	F	E	E	E
Nylon Spandex	F	F	F	F
Polyester Fabric	E	P	E	P
Polyurethane Foam	P	P	P	P
Rayon	E	E	E	E
Silk	E	E	E	E
Styrofoam	P	P	P	P
Vinyl	P	P	P	P
Wool	E	E	E	E

O = Does not bond.
P = Poor bond: Bond fails with first laundering or dry cleaning.
F = Fair bond: Materials stay bonded for up to five launderings or dry cleanings.
G = Good bond: Materials stay bonded for up to fourteen launderings or dry cleanings.
E = Excellent: Bond appears permanent.

Artists' Acrylic Paints

Brands Tested	Manufacturers
Artist Color Opaque Acrylic	Rotring
Artists' Acrylic Colours	Windsor & Newton, Inc.
Liquid Acrylic Colours	Windsor & Newton, Inc.
Liquitex	Binney & Smith Inc.

Examples of Use

- Paint motifs onto fabric and most other surfaces.

- Add depth to folds of fabric with either a brush or sprayer.

Use on almost all surfaces for both large and small motifs and when stiffening of fabric is not a factor. Use on materials that will not be submerged in water. With spandex, acrylic offers the advantage, unlike most other paints, of stretching somewhat with the fabric.

Fluid acrylic paint, sold in jars, is particularly suitable for airbrushing.

Description

Acrylic paints are composed of pigment, water, and acrylic polymer and dry into a hard, clear film. Acrylic artists' paints are designed for use by easel painters. They are similar to oil paints in viscosity, though they dry much more quickly. Oil paints take weeks to dry, while acrylics dry in minutes. Some well-known painters who prefer acrylics are David Hockney and Frank Stella.

We tested both thick acrylic paints in tubes and the more fluid acrylic paint in jars. Results differed between the two viscosities.

How to Use

Apply by brush, airbrush, other sprayers, printing implements, or stencil to most surfaces. The most suitable brushes for applying acrylics are those used by oil painters—stiff bristle brushes of either synthetic or natural hog hair. The paints can be mixed with water for thinning or with a matte or gloss medium, giving a smoother consistency and a matte or glossy surface finish. The paints are made translucent with a gel medium. They can be airbrushed by thinning with water and passing through a cheesecloth strainer before spraying. Many costumers use them for stenciling designs; though convenient for stenciling, acrylics dry too quickly for silk-screening and may gum

The motif on this velveteen tabard is outlined by stitching, then completed with Liquitex artists' acrylic paint.

DESIGN AND ARTISTRY: JIMMY WAUFORD FOR *ARIODANTE* AT THE UNIVERSITY OF WASHINGTON SCHOOL OF DRAMA.
PHOTO: JOSIE GARDNER.

up the screen. Be sure to keep a water container in which to immerse painting tools immediately after use.

Certain additives will affect the properties of acrylics. Golden Paints makes an Acrylic Flow Release that increases the paint's slackness and flow. Golden's GAC 200 Acrylic Polymer for Stiffening Fabrics is a fabric-stiffener additive. GAC 900 Acrylic Polymer for Clothing Artists is an additive that produces softness and laundering stability to regular paint.

In many cases, we found that during laundry or dry cleaning the paint may rewet and then stick to itself, sometimes even peeling away from the fabric.

Apply in thin coatings for better adherence.

Solvent for Thinning and Cleanup Water for thinning, and soap and water for cleanup.

Precautions These paints may stiffen fabrics, especially cotton, linen, nylon spandex, polyester, and rayon, and will peel if applied thickly. They do not bond to most vinyls and will crack when applied to vinyl, leather, and other flexible solid surfaces. Any spilled acrylic artists' paint must be cleaned up immediately to avoid permanent staining.

Colors bond differently. If dry cleaning or laundering is a consideration, first test the individual colors on the appropriate fabric.

Health and Safety Artists' acrylic paints are of low toxicity, but their pigments are the same toxic pigments found in oils and watercolors. Some of the manufacturers of these paints will identify their pigments.

Some Other Brands Cryla Artists' Acrylic Colors, Rowney; Finity, and Galeria, Windsor & Newton, Inc.; Golden Artists Colors, Golden Artist Colors, Inc.; Prima Acrylic Colors, Martin F. Weber Company; Sun Burst Colors, American Art Clay Co., Inc.

Where to Find Art stores.

Sizes 2-oz., 4-oz., 8-oz., and 16-oz. tubes.

Black and white are available in 1-gal. cans.

ARTISTS' ACRYLIC PAINT IN TUBES   **LAUNDER**   DRY-CLEAN

Surface	Liquitex		Windsor & Newton	
Acetate Fabric	E	E	F-E	F
Acetate Sheeting	F	P	F-E	P
Acrylic Fabric	E	E	F-G	P
Acrylic Sheeting	E	P	F-E	P
Cotton	E	E*	G	G-E
Glass	P	P	F	P
Leather	P	P*	E	P
Linen	E	E	F-E	F-G
Metal	E	P	F	P
Mylar	E	P	P	P
Nylon	E	E	F	P
Nylon Spandex	F-E	G	G-E	F
Polyester Fabric	E	E	E	E
Polyurethane Foam	E	E	G	F
Rayon	E	E	E**	E**
Silk	E	E	E	E
Styrofoam	G-E	P	E	P
Vinyl	E	P	E	P
Wool	F-G	E	E	E

0 = Does not bond.
P = Poor bond: Bond fails with first laundering or dry cleaning.
F = Fair bond: Materials stay bonded for up to five launderings or dry cleanings.
G - Good bond: Materials stay bonded for up to fourteen launderings or dry cleanings
E = Excellent: Bond appears permanent.
Note: Artists' acrylic paints stiffen fabrics.

* Colorant becomes dull.
** Colorant sticks to itself in dryer and in dry cleaning machine and then peels off of the fabric.

ARTISTS' FLUID ACRYLIC PAINT IN JARS   **LAUNDER** DRY-CLEAN

Surface	Rotring Fluid Acrylic		Windsor & Newton Liquid Acrylic Colours	
Acetate Fabric	P-G	G	P	F-G
Acetate Sheeting	P	P-F	P	F-E
Acrylic Fabric	G	G	P	F-G
Acrylic Sheeting	P	P	P	P
Cotton	P-G	G	P	F-E
Glass	P	P	P	G-G
Leather	P	P-F	P	F
Linen	P-G	F	P	F-E
Metal	P	P	P	F-E
Mylar	P	F	P	F
Nylon	P-F	F	P	F
Nylon Spandex	P-F	G	P	G-E
Polyester Fabric	P-F	G	P	F-G
Polyurethane Foam	F-G	P-F	P	F
Rayon	P-G	G	P	F-E
Silk	P-F	F	P	F-E
Styrofoam	P-F	P	P	P
Vinyl	P-G	P-G	P	F
Wool	P-G	P-F	P	F

O = Does not bond.
P = Poor bond: Bond fails with first laundering or dry cleaning.
F = Fair bond: Materials stay bonded for up to five launderings or dry cleanings.
G = Good bond: Materials stay bonded for up to fourteen launderings or dry cleanings.
E = Excellent: Bond appears permanent.

Note: Rotring Fluid Acrylic bleeds on most surfaces during laundering and dry cleaning.
Artists' acrylic paints stiffen fabrics.

Flexible Paint In Squeeze Bottles

Brands Tested	Manufacturers
Polymark (Iridescent, Glow, Glitter, Shiny, Sparkling)	Polymark Product of Duncan Enterprises
Tulip (Crystals, Glitter, Pearl, Iridescent, Puffy, and Slick)	Tulip Product of Duncan Enterprises

Examples of Use

- Dot onto costumes for a jeweled, beaded, or sequined effect.
- Highlight and emphasize an existing motif or drawing.
- Paint motifs onto fabric and other surfaces.
- Use for stripes, edging, lettering, and other linear patterns.

For *Jacques Brel . . .* , in Los Angeles's Back Alley Theatre, glitter was dotted onto costumes to create highlights.

Designer John Brandt used puff pens to emphasize motifs that otherwise would have been lost when playing in a large house for *Strike up the Band* at Los Angeles's Dorothy Chandler Pavilion. The allover pattern of an entire dress was outlined with puff paint, yet this did not destroy the delicacy of the design. Brandt, a freelance costume designer with many years in fashion design and who headed UCLA's costume shop in the Department of Theatre for many years, says that the dress needed the dimension of the puff paint to give it life.

Description

Flexible paint in squeeze bottles comes in different textures. The containers are shaped with a thin spout that allows painting one-quarter-inch lines.

Duncan Iridescent Scribbles Dimensional Fabric & Craft Paint, an iridescent paint, highlights the woven fabric pattern on this vest. Tiny opalescent sequins are added to the wet paint.

DESIGN AND ARTISTRY: KAREN LEDGER FOR *POSTCARD FROM MOROCCO* AT THE UNIVERSITY OF WASHINGTON SCHOOL OF DRAMA. PHOTO: JOSIE GARDNER.

The various textures come from a metallic glitter pen that is formed from finely ground glitter mixed with a transparent medium and include a wet-look (Slick); a fluorescent, glow-in-the-dark; and an iridescent, changeable color paint. These different textures are available in flat paint, and some as puff paint. The puff paint, which leaves a slight dimensionality, must be expanded by heat, and it does not work well on thin, soft textiles that pucker easily.

Dimensional and textured paints are stocked in most art-supply and fabric stores. They are popular among the general public for drawing slogans and patterns on T-shirts. Unfortunately, paint packaged this way is fairly expensive, but the same types of paints are available in special-order quantities from these and other manufacturers and can be placed in empty squeeze bottles or handmade cones to achieve the same effect.

How to Use Squeeze the bottle while drawing a linear pattern. To cover a wide area, squeeze a small amount onto a palette or jar and spread with brush or fingers. Masking tape can be wound around the point of the container to narrow the line width. No fixing is required with these paints, although heat is required to "puff" the puff paint.

Solvent for Cleanup Soap and water.

Precautions Recommended shelf life for these paints is one year.

Health and Safety The health hazards can vary. Obtain MSDSs and treat the pigments as toxic.

Some Other Brands Deka-Flair and Deka-Fun, Decart, Inc.; Delta Swell Stuff, Delta Technical Coatings, Inc.; Dimensional Fabric Paint, Binney & Smith Inc.; Scribbles Product of Duncan Enterprises.

Where to Find Art stores and manufacturers.

Sizes 1 oz., 2 oz., and 4 oz.

Free-form glitter lines can easily be drawn onto fabric by squeezing the glitter paint container.

FLEXIBLE PAINT IN PLASTIC SQUEEZE BOTTLES   **LAUNDER** DRY-CLEAN

Surface	Polymark		Tulip	
Acetate Fabric	F-G	G-E	E	E
Acetate Sheeting	F-G	F-E	E	E
Acrylic Fabric	G *	E *	E	E
Acrylic Sheeting	G-E	P-E	E	E
Cotton	G-E *	E *	E	E
Glass	P	E	E	E
Leather	E	F-E	E	E
Linen	E	E	E	E
Metal	E	F-E	E	E
Mylar	F	F	E	E
Nylon	P	P	E	E
Nylon Spandex	F	F-E**	E	E
Polyester Fabric	G-E *	E *	E	E
Polyurethane Foam	G	F	E	E
Rayon	G *	E *	E	E
Silk	E	E	E	E
Styrofoam	G	G	E	E
Vinyl	G	F-E	E	E
Wool	G *	E *	E	E

O = Does not bond.
P = Poor bond: Bond fails with first laundering or dry cleaning.
F = Fair bond: Materials stay bonded for up to five launderings or dry cleanings.
G = Good bond: Materials stay bonded for up to fourteen launderings or dry cleanings.
E = Excellent: Bond appears permanent.

* Colorant cracks or chips.
** Colorant bleeds.

Latex Spray Paint

Brand Names	Manufacturers
Pactra Latex Plus	Pactra Industries, Inc.

Examples of Use

- Spray thinly to coat fabric to create texturing and shadows.
- Use to distress costumes that will not be immersed in water or dry cleaning solvent.

Latex Plus is easy to use, is reportedly less toxic than other latexes, and dries quickly.

Description *Latex spray paint* is a gloss enamel, formulated to paint metal, as a rust stopper, as well as to paint wood, rigid plastics, glass, and pottery. It also is supple enough to spray onto fabrics without stiffening them.

How to Use Paint only on clean surfaces, painted, unpainted, or smoothly varnished, or on clean fabric. Apply several thick coats to create a smooth surface. For best results, both store and use within a 70° to 90°F temperature range.

Solvent for Cleanup Soap and water.

Precautions Use protective measures throughout the surrounding area.

Use on fabrics and surfaces that do not require dry cleaning or laundering. In our testing, the only immersed material that held Latex Plus was leather, which was dry-cleaned. When applied as solid coatings to leather, vinyl, and other flexible solid surfaces, latex spray paints may crack.

Health and Safety Spray in an open space, wearing gloves and a protective respirator. Keep away from flames and cigarettes.

Where to Find Paint stores and hobby shops.

Sizes 12 oz.

LATEX SPRAY PAINT   **LAUNDER** DRY-CLEAN

Surface	Pactra Spray Paint	
Acetate Fabric	F	F
Acetate Sheeting	P	P
Acrylic Fabric	P	P
Acrylic Sheeting	F	F
Cotton	P	P
Glass	P	P
Leather	G	G
Linen	P	P
Metal	P	P
Mylar	P	P
Nylon	P	P
Nylon Spandex	P	P
Polyester Fabric	P	P
Polyurethane Foam	P	P
Rayon	P	F
Silk	F	F
Styrofoam	P	P
Vinyl	P	P
Wool	P	P

O = Does not bond.
P = Poor bond: Bond fails with first laundering or dry cleaning.
F = Fair bond: Materials stay bonded for up to five launderings or dry cleanings.
G = Good bond: Materials stay bonded for up to fourteen launderings or dry cleanings.
E = Excellent: Bond appears permanent.

Luminous Paints: Phosphorescent and Fluorescent Colors

Brands Tested	Manufacturers
Deka Permanent Fabric Fluorescent Paint	Decart, Inc.
Fluorescent Neon Acrylic Paint	Palmer Paint Products, Inc.

Examples of Use

• Use for glow-in-the-dark effects on both porous and nonporous materials.

• Create fluorescent effects (when seen by UV light) on porous and nonporous materials.

For some luminous effects, reflective material, described in the Plastic Sheetings on pages 286-287, may be a practicable substitute for paints.

Description

These are two categories of paints that have unique qualities which cause specific kinds of luminescence. *Fluorescent* colors glow only when illuminated by ultraviolet (UV) or "black" light. Deka Permanent Fabric Fluorescent Paint and Palmer's Fluorescent Neon Acrylic Paint are in this category.

Phosphorescent colors contain phosphoric acid, causing them to transfer light after exposure to and removal from incandescent lights. Each of these paints adheres differently after washing and drying. Glow-in-the-Dark Pens are phosphorescent. Phosphorescent paints, such as these, stiffen fabrics.

Retroreflective ink is also sometimes used for luminous effects. However, retroreflective ink is only available in gray and can be purchased from the 3M Company. For example, in the film of *The Wiz*, the Flying Monkeys' costumes were decorated with 3M's reflective ink.

How to Use

Apply paint with the same techniques used for applying any kind of paint. Thinning and dilution will lessen the quality of luminescence.

Solvent for Cleanup

Use soap and water before the paint has a chance to cure.

Precautions

Use where the stiffness is not a factor, and use only flexible paints on leather, vinyl, and other flexible solid surfaces.

Health and Safety

Health hazards vary. Obtain MSDSs and treat the pigments as toxic.

Some Other Brands

Fluorescent paints: Cloud Cover, Cerulean Blue; Createx Fluorescent Textile Colors.

Phosphorescent paints: Glow-in-the-Dark Fabric Paint, Sax Arts and Crafts.

Reflective Ink: 3M Company 8010 Reflective Ink (Reflective ink is used for nighttime visibility of signs. See pages 286-287 for description of reflective materials.)

Where to Find

Art, hobby, and fiber-arts stores.

Sizes

Deka: 1 oz. - 1 gal.
Palmer: 1/13 oz. - 2 oz.
Tulip: 1 oz. and 2 oz.

LUMINOUS PAINT   **LAUNDER** DRY-CLEAN

Surface	Deka Flourescent Paint		Flourescent Neon Acrylic Paint	
Acetate Fabric	E	E	F	G
Acetate Sheeting	P	P	E	F
Acrylic Fabric	E	E	E	E
Acrylic Sheeting	P	P	E	P
Cotton	E	E	F	G
Glass	P	P	P	P
Leather	F	P	E	F
Linen	E	E	E	E
Metal	P	P	E	P
Mylar	P	E	G	P
Nylon	E	E	G	F
Nylon Spandex	F	F	G	E
Polyester Fabric	E	E	G	G
Polyurethane Foam	P	E	F	P
Rayon	E	E	E	G
Silk	E	E	E	G
Styrofoam	P	P	G	P
Vinyl	P	P	E	F
Wool	E	E	E	P

0 = Does not bond.
P = Poor bond: Bond fails with first laundering or dry cleaning.
F = Fair bond: Materials stay bonded for up to five launderings or dry cleanings.
G = Good bond: Materials stay bonded for up to fourteen launderings or dry cleanings.
E = Excellent: Bond appears permanent.

Note: Of the two luminous paints tested, only Deka did not stiffen fabrics.

PAX Paint

Brands Tested	Manufacturer
Pros-Aide Prosthetic Adhesive mixed with Liquitex	A.D.M. Tronics Unlimited, Inc.
Acrylic Paint	Binney & Smith Inc., Inc.

Examples of Use
- Paint stretchy materials and objects where flexibility is important.

Description
PAX paint is mixed by the user. It is a mixture of fairly equal parts of Pros-Aide type-B prosthetic adhesive and acrylic paint. Type-B adhesive is an acrylic emulsion. Although there are other brands of type-B adhesive, they are primarily used in medical practice, and the price is prohibitive for those using it as a paint additive. We tested with Liquitex paint, though other acrylic paints are also available.

PAX paint is most frequently used for painting latex, polyurethane, Neoprene, and other flexible materials. Many of the costumes described in Part Three are painted with PAX paint.

We tested PAX on the same nineteen surfaces on which the other colorants were tested and found that it adheres well to all.

How to Use
Mix adhesive and a liquid acrylic paint in fairly equal amounts. The more acrylic paint used, the more opaque will be the PAX mixture. The adhesive provides the flexibility and bonding power, while the paint supplies the color. Apply with brush or other painting tool.

Some nonporous surfaces remain tacky after application and require powdering.

Pros-Aide may also be used as a primer. Paint it directly onto the surface and then coat it with the acrylic paint, rather than mixing the two together.

Solvent for Cleanup
Makeup remover.

Health and Safety
Makeup adhesives are fairly safe, since they have been formulated for use on the skin.

Where to Find
Pros-Aide adhesive: Manufacturer and makeup suppliers.

Acrylic paint: Artists' supply stores.

Sizes
Makeup adhesives: 2 oz. - 55 gal.

Acrylic paint: 1 oz. - 1 gal.

PAX PAINT   **LAUNDER** DRY-CLEAN

Surface	Pros-Aide and Liquid Acrylic Paint	
Acetate Fabric	E†	E†
Acetate Sheeting	G	P
Acrylic Fabric	E	E*
Acrylic Sheeting	E†	P†
Cotton	E	E
Glass	F	P
Leather	F†	P†
Linen	E	G
Metal	G	P
Mylar	F†	P†
Nylon	E	E
Nylon Spandex	E	E
Polyester Fabric	E	E*
Polyurethane Foam	E	F
Rayon	E	E*
Silk	E	G
Styrofoam	E	G
Vinyl	E†	G**†
Wool	E	E

O = Does not bond.
P = Poor bond: Bond fails with first laundering or dry cleaning.
F = Fair bond: Materials stay bonded for up to five launderings or dry cleanings.
G = Good bond: Materials stay bonded for up to fourteen launderings or dry cleanings.
E = Excellent: Bond appears permanent.

* Colorant bleeds.
** Material curls.
† Colorant remains sticky.

Polyurethane Paint

Brands Tested	Manufacturers
Aqualyte	Zynolyte Products Company
Skin-Flex Paint	BJB Enterprises, Inc.

Examples of Use
- Paint stretchy materials and objects.
- Paint polyurethane solid and foam pieces.
- Protect polyurethane surfaces.

Use only where stretch is important. Though polyurethane paint could be used on nylon spandex, it is preferable, for health and safety, to use a thickened dye paste or another paint.

Description   *Polyurethane paint* is the most flexible of all paints. It is ideal for painting on rubbers, polyurethane sheeting, and stretchy fabrics. Skin-Flex Paint has a 700 percent elongation and is recommended for fabrics, latex, and foamed and unfoamed polyurethane. Skin-Flex Paint is solvent-based. Aqualyte, from Zynolyte, is an aerosol spray product and is water-based.

Polyurethane paints are hazardous and should be used only when no other paint is satisfactory.

How to Use   Aqualyte: Place fabric, costume, or object on a vertical plane. Hold spray can in a vertical position, about two feet from the fabric. Spray in long sweeping strokes that overlap each other and overlap the edges of the fabric.

Skin-Flex: Add Skin-Flex Pigments, also from BJB, to this clear coating to achieve appropriate color. Prime with Skin-Flex II or III Primer for better adhesion when painting polyurethane surfaces. Add Skin-Flex Thinner for smooth application. When airbrushing, add more thinner and strain through cheesecloth into airbrush unit. Apply in very thin coats. This paint is available in gloss, semigloss, and flat finishes.

Solvent for Cleanup   Aqualyte: soap and water; Skin-Flex: Skin-Flex Thinner.

Health and Safety   Use only with local ventilation or supplied-air respirators. Wear goggles, gloves, and protective clothing. Polyurethane paint contains isocyanates. Keep away from heat, electrical apparatus, sparks, and flame.

For working with the Skin-Flex Primer, use an organic vapor respirator and impermeable gloves. Keep away from water, strong bases, alcohols, metal compounds, and surface active agents.

Where to Find   Aqualyte: paint stores; Skin-Flex: Burman Industries Inc. (distributor for BJB Enterprises, Inc. products).

Sizes   Aqualyte: 12 oz.; Skin-Flex: 1 qt. and 1 gal.

POLYURETHANE PAINT   **LAUNDER**   DRY-CLEAN

Surface	Aqualyte		Skin-Flex Paint	
Acetate Fabric	P-G	E	E	E
Acetate Sheeting	P-E	G	E	P
Acrylic Fabric	P-G	F	E	E
Acrylic Sheeting	P-G	P	E	P
Cotton	G	E	E	G
Glass	P	P	F	P
Leather	E	E	F	P
Linen	E	E	E	E
Metal	P	P	F	P
Mylar	P	E	E	G *
Nylon	P	F	E	E
Nylon Spandex	G	E	E	E
Polyester Fabric	G	E	E	E
Polyurethane Foam	G	E	F ††	E
Rayon	P	F	E	E
Silk	P	F	E	E
Styrofoam	E	P	O **	O **
Vinyl	F-G	P	E ‡	E †
Wool	P	G-E	E	E

O = Does not bond.
P = Poor bond: Bond fails with first laundering or dry cleaning.
F = Fair bond: Materials stay bonded for up to five launderings or dry cleanings.
G = Good bond: Materials stay bonded for up to fourteen launderings or dry cleanings.
E = Excellent: Bond appears permanent.

* Surface becomes brittle.
** Material dissolves.
† Material curls.
†† Colorant cracks or chips.
‡ Colorant remains sticky.

Scenic Paints

Brands Tested	Manufacturers
Iddings Deep Colors	Rosco Laboratories, Inc.
Off-Broadway paint	Rosco Laboratories, Inc.
Super-Saturated Rosco Paint	Rosco Laboratories, Inc.

Examples of Use
- Thin down for spray coating onto fabric.
- Paint motifs and decorations on fabrics that do not need to remain soft and pliable.

Scenic paints stiffen the hand of fabric; therefore they should be used on stiff surfaces or they should be thinned with water. Once thinned with water, scenic paints are suitable for a light spray coating.

Description *Scenic paints* are available in a wide range of colors. They are the consistency of thick paste and require thinning with water. Iddings paints are composed of soy casein, while Off-Broadway is a vinyl-acrylic paint, and the Super-Saturated paint has an acrylic base. All three are in a water solution.

How to Use Thin to a desired viscosity. Paint with brush, stencil, or strain for use with a sprayer or airbrush.

Off-Broadway paint must be applied over an undercoat or a primer when painted on a slick, nontextile surface. For use on fabric, paint it only onto costumes not requiring laundering or dry cleaning.

Solvent for Cleanup Water, only while still wet.

Precautions Do not try to heat set, for the dryer or iron may cause the paint to become sticky or to crack. To keep brushes from hardening, keep a jar of water close by.

Iddings adhered to all of our testing surfaces and lasted indefinitely through launderings, though it did not last on all fabrics through fifteen dry cleanings. To launder any fabric painted with Iddings, hand wash and drip dry only, because Iddings softens with any immersion longer than a few minutes and becomes sticky from high heat. Scenic paints may crack when painted on surfaces leather and vinyl.

Health and Safety Manufacturers of these paints do not identify their pigments.

Some Other Brands Acrylic: Acrylic Scenic Paint, Oleson; Artistic Acrylic Colors, Cal Western Paints, Inc.; Casein: Gothic Casein Fresco Colors, Gothic Ltd.; Para Casein Paint, Alcone Co. Inc. Vinyl Acrylic: Artist's Choice Paints, Sculptural Arts Coating, Inc.; Varabond, Mann Bros.

Where to Find Suppliers of scenic materials.

Sizes 1-gal. cans for all colors but white and black, which are available in 5-gal. cans. The two Rosco brands are also available in test kits, comprised of 2-oz. jars.

SCENIC PAINT **LAUNDER** DRY-CLEAN

Surface	Iddings		Off-Broadway		Supersatured Rosco	
Acetate Fabric	P-F	G	F-E	P-F	E	P
Acetate Sheeting	O-F	O-P	F-G **	P	E	P
Acrylic Fabric	P-F	G	G-E	P-F	E	P
Acrylic Sheeting	O-P	O-P	P *	P	E	P
Cotton	F	G	F-G	P-F	E †	P
Glass	P	P-F	P	P	P-F	P
Leather	P	G	F-E	F	F-E	P
Linen	P-F	G-E	F-G	P-F	E	P
Metal	P	P-F	P-E **	P-E	F-F	P
Mylar	P	P	P-G	P	G	P
Nylon	F	G	P-E	P-F	E	P
Nylon Spandex	P	G	F-G	P	E	P
Polyester Fabric	F	G	F-E	P-F	E	P
Polyurethane Foam	P-F	G †	F-E	P	E	P
Rayon	F	G	F-E	F	E	P
Silk	F	G	F-E *	P-F *	E †	P
Styrofoam	F	F	G-E	P	E	P
Vinyl	P-F	O-P	P-G	P	E	P
Wool	F	G	P-F	P-F	E †	P

O = Does not bond.
P = Poor bond: Bond fails with first laundering or dry cleaning.
F = Fair bond: Materials stay bonded for up to five launderings or dry cleanings.
G = Good bond: Materials stay bonded for up to fourteen launderings or dry cleanings.
E = Excellent: Bond appears permanent.

* Surface becomes brittle.
** Colorant splotches.
† Colorant bleeds.

Textile Paints

Brands Tested	Manufacturers
Color Fun Fabric Paint	Dylon International Ltd.
Createx Transparent Colors	ColorCraft, Ltd.
Createx Pearlescent Colors	ColorCraft, Ltd.
Createx Poster/Fabric Colors	Colorcraft, Ltd.
Deka Permanent Fabric Paint	DeCart
Elbetex	LeFranc & Bourgeois
Texticolor	Sennelier
Versatex Textile Paint	Siphon Art

Examples of Use

- Paint large and small patterns on textile, leather, or plastics with most implements including brush, sponge, stencil, and silk screen.
- Use the thicker paints, like Createx, for silk-screening and stenciling, and the thinner paints, like Texticolor, for airbrushing.

Description *Textile paints* are medium- to thick-viscosity liquid paints especially formulated to allow fabrics to retain their original flexibility. The brands listed here have different formulas. Some are thicker, and most adhere differently to specific materials. The textile paints containing a sizable quantity of acrylic bond best to most surfaces.

How to Use All these paints can be thinned with water, though adding water reduces brilliance of color. Extenders can also be added to increase flow and smoothness of stroke. Before painting a fabric, make a test on a small sample of the same fabric. Colors sometimes change when they dry and after heat setting.

Apply with brush, airbrush, or other painting tools. When airbrushing, these paints must be thinned; however, there are other special inks made specifically for airbrushing on fabrics. The initial bond to all the surfaces is excellent, though not all withstand dry cleaning and laundering.

Heat-set according to manufacturer's directions. Textile paints generally require dry heat-setting with either an iron or in a clothes dryer. When using an iron to heat-set, place a thin cloth or a piece of paper between the iron and the paint and press for about two minutes. For setting in a clothes dryer, allow thirty minutes drying time. All but the pearlescent paints can be heat-set in a dryer.

To create a strong coverage on nonporous surfaces, prime first with a coating, such as Createx Clear Ply Adhesive Coating. After the paint has dried, apply another layer of coating as a sealer. The pearlescent colors show effectively only on smooth surfaces, like satin, and become dull when applied to matte surfaces.

Solvent for Cleanup Water, but only while the paint is still wet.

Precautions   Wait at least two weeks after painting before washing or cleaning.

The recommended storage time is up to six months.

Pearlescent paint does not hold up in a hot dryer or dry cleaning machine. To clean, hand wash carefully, then lay flat or hang to air dry.

Only a few of the paints lasted well on spandex, probably because the fabric stretches while the paint does not.

Health and Safety   For personal safety, keep an exhaust fan at an open window to avoid inhaling the small amounts of ammonia, formaldehyde, and possible solvents that are released during drying. Some of these paints contain small amounts of solvents.

For airbrushing, use only with good ventilation, a respirator, gloves, and goggles, or spray in a local exhaust system such as a spray booth.

Some Other Brands   Cloud Cover, Cerulean Blue, Ltd.; Jacquard Textile Color, Rupert, Gibbon & Spider Inc.; Rowney Screen and Fabric Printing Color, George T. Rowney and Co.

Where to Find   Manufacturers, art, fiber-art, and fabric stores.

Sizes   1 oz. - 1 gal

TEXTILE PAINTS   **LAUNDER**   DRY-CLEAN

Surface	Color Fun		Createx Pearlescent		Createx Poster/Fabric		Createx Transparent		Deka Permanent		Elbetex		Texticolor		Versatex	
Acetate Fabric	F-G	P-F	P	P	F	P	E	E	G	G-E	E	E	G	E*	E	E
Acetate Sheeting	P	P	P	F	P	P	P	P	P**	P**	P	P	P	P	P-E	P-F
Acrylic Fabric	F	P	F	F	G*	P	E	E	G*	E*	E	E	E	E	E	E
Acrylic Sheeting	G	G	P	P	P	P	P	P	F	P	P	P	P	P	P†	P
Cotton	G	G-E	P	G-E	E*	E	E	E	E	E	E	E	E	E	E	E
Glass	P	F	P	P	P	P	P	P	P	P	P	P	P	F	P	F-G
Leather	F	F	F-E	G-E	F	F	E	E	F	F	P	P	F	F	E	E
Linen	G	G	F	F	E*	E	E	E	G	E	E	P	E	E	E	E
Metal	P	P	F	P	P	P	P	P	P	P	P	P	P	P	P	P-F
Mylar	P	P	P	P	P	P	P	P	F**	P**	P	P	P	P	P	G-E
Nylon	F	F	P	F	E	E	E	E	F	F	P	P	P	P	E	E
Nylon Spandex	F	F	F-E*	P*	P	F	E	E	E	E	P	P	P	P	E	E
Polyester Fabric	G	G	P	F	E	E	E	E	E*	E*	G	E	E	E	E	E
Polyurethane Foam	F	G-E	F	F	P*	P	P	P	F	E	F	F	G	G	P-F	E
Rayon	G	G	P	F	E*	E	E	E	G	E	G	E	E	E	E	E
Silk	G	G	P	F	E*	E	E	E	F-G	E	F	E	P	E	E	E
Styrofoam	E	P	P	P	P	P	P	P	F	P	G	P	F	P	F	P
Vinyl	P	P	P	P	P	P	P	P	F-E	F-E	P	P	P	P	G	P
Wool	F	F	P	P	E	E	E	E	G	E	G	F	G	G	E	E

O = Does not bond.
P = Poor bond: Bond fails with first laundering or dry cleaning.
F = Fair bond: Materials stay bonded for up to five launderings or dry cleanings.
G = Good bond: Materials stay bonded for up to fourteen launderings or dry cleanings.
E = Excellent: Bond appears permanent.

Note: Createx Pearlescent sticks together in dryer and then peels off its surface. Hand laundering and air drying are recommended.
* Surface stiffens.
** Colorant streaks.
† Surface dissolves.

Pastels and Crayons

Crayons for Fabric

Brands Tested	Manufacturers
Crayola Craft Fabric Crayons	Binney and Smith
Crayola Transfer Crayons	Binney and Smith

Examples of Use
- Use where a crayon drawing style is preferred.
- Use when children and novice workers are decorating costumes.
- Draw or mono-print one-of-a-kind designs on fabric and other surfaces.

Use when a crayon is more convenient than paint or when a crayon-style motif is appropriate. Crayons are usually easier for working on projects with children, as long as the crayons are not heated and not ironed, because then toxic gases may be released.

Description *Crayons for fabric* are made to color all types of fabric with the same look on fabric as on paper. Some fabric crayons are steam-fixed and others are iron-fixed. Both are fade-resistant and machine washable after heat fixing, but they cannot be dry-cleaned.

When using transfer crayons, the design is colored onto a paper and then heat-transferred onto fabric. Transfer crayons are most successful on nylon fabric, and the crayons do not maintain their brilliance on most other materials after washing and dry cleaning. It is important to test before using transfer crayons, because the colors appear differently on paper.

How to Use With Crayola Craft Fabric Crayons, draw a design directly onto fabric and heat set according to package directions. Some brands are set by steam and others by iron.

When using transfer crayons, draw the design onto any kind of paper. Place the design face up on an ironing board. Place the fabric on top of the paper and iron on the wrong side of the fabric for at least five minutes.

Solvent for Cleanup Paint thinner.

Precautions Crayons for fabric do not launder or dry-clean well on most surfaces.

Health and Safety When heated, crayons and wax release highly toxic gases such as formaldehyde and acetaldehyde. These are irritating and damaging to the respiratory tract, sometimes developing into bronchitis and chemical pneumonia, and possibly cancer.

Projects with heating and melting crayons should not be used with children under age thirteen. Both wax and pigments are hazardous. Heated wax emits toxic gases into the air, and heated pigments emit toxic chemicals. When children are older, they can use melted crayons with proper ventilation.

For personal protection, set irons at lowest possible settings and use next to a table-level window exhaust fan, a slot-hood table, or in a local exhaust system.

Where to Find   Fiber-art and art supply stores.

Sizes   Packages of twelve crayons.

CRAYONS FOR FABRICS	**LAUNDER** DRY-CLEAN			
Surface	**Crayola Craft Fabric Crayons**		**Crayola Transfer Crayons**	
Acetate Fabric	F	P	F	F
Acetate Sheeting	F	P	P	P
Acrylic Fabric	P	P	P	P
Acrylic Sheeting	P	P	P	P
Cotton	P	P	F	P
Glass	P	P	P	P
Leather	P	P	P	P
Linen	F	P	F	G
Metal	P	P	P	P
Mylar	P	P	P	P
Nylon	F	P	F	G
Nylon Spandex	P	P	F	F
Polyester Fabric	P	P	F	F
Polyurethane Foam	F	P	P	P
Rayon	P	P	G	G
Silk	F	P	G *	G *
Styrofoam	F	P	P	P
Vinyl	F	P	P	P
Wool	P	P	P	P

O = Does not bond.
P = Poor bond: Bond fails with first laundering or dry cleaning.
F = Fair bond: Materials stay bonded for up to five launderings or dry cleanings.
G = Good bond: Materials stay bonded for up to fourteen launderings or dry cleanings.
E = Excellent: Bond appears permanent.

* Surface crinkles

Pastel Sticks for Fabric

Brands Tested	Manufacturers
Pentel Fabric Fun	Pentel Company, Ltd.

Examples of Use
- Draw motifs on fabric.
- Make allover patterns, particularly those with a hand-drawn effect.
- Use when a crayon drawing style is desired.
- Use when children and inexperienced people are decorating.

Use for any size motif or allover patterning, especially when soft edges and soft colors are desirable. This medium is easier to handle than are paint and brush, which makes them particularly suited for use by nonartist students, and work may be done quickly.

Description These are pastel sticks in an oil base, similar to both artists' pastel sticks and soft crayons. They come in a variety of bright colors, and have the same character as regular pastels and crayons. Pastel sticks for fabric bond well to laundered fabric, unlike regular artists' pastels, which cannot be submerged in water.

How to Use Stretch or stabilize fabric or garment, then draw with pastel stick on the surface as with any crayon. Wait two to three weeks before wearing to allow the color to set completely. Fabric Fun must be heat set for permanence with an iron at a high setting. Because of the high heat required, Fabric Fun cannot be set permanently on nylon, leather, foam, or sheet plastic.

Solvent for Cleanup Paint thinner.

Precautions Pentel Fabric Fun lasts indefinitely through launderings, but it does not dry-clean on any surfaces.

Health and Safety Use only pastels with a wax binder. Dusty pastels release pigments that may be inhaled.

Where to Find Art and fabric stores.

Sizes 4"-long by ½"-diameter sticks.

PASTELS STICKS FOR FABRICS   **LAUNDER** DRY-CLEAN

Surface	Pentel Fabric Fun	
Acetate Fabric	E	P
Acetate Sheeting	E	P
Acrylic Fabric	E	P
Acrylic Sheeting	P	P
Cotton	E	P
Glass	P	P
Leather	P	P
Linen	E	P
Metal	E	P
Mylar	P	P
Nylon	P	P
Nylon Spandex	P	P
Polyester Fabric	E	P
Polyurethane Foam	P	P
Rayon	E	P
Silk	E	P
Styrofoam	P	P
Vinyl	E	P
Wool	E	P

O = Does not bond.
P = Poor bond: Bond fails with first laundering or dry cleaning.
F = Fair bond: Materials stay bonded for up to five launderings or dry cleanings.
G = Good bond: Materials stay bonded for up to fourteen launderings or dry cleanings.
E = Excellent: Bond appears permanent.

Photocopying

Examples of Use

- Mono-print, or transfer, an already printed image from one surface onto another surface.
- Use when only one image is required; especially successful for reproducing photographic images.

To make repeat patterns or multiple images, it is necessary to make as many photocopies as there will be final images.

Alan Armstrong used photocopies as the motifs of his design for *The Illusion* at Santa Fe Stages, which featured black and white drawings of prominent historical figures on the costume fabric.

Description

Photocopying is successful on almost all materials. An image is selected, printed onto transfer paper, and then transferred onto another surface. This method is usually performed at photocopy shops to place images onto T-shirts.

Enlargements of photocopied images outlined with black felt-tip marker are placed onto transfer paper, then ironed onto this velvet robe.

DESIGN: ALAN ARMSTRONG FOR ALCANDRE, PLAYED BY CHARLES ANTALOSKY, IN *THE ILLUSION* AT SANTA FE STAGES.
PHOTO: COURTESY OF SANTA FE STAGES.

Reduced photocopied images are collaged to a costume sketch, which is then photocopied and painted.

DRAWING: ALAN ARMSTRONG FOR *THE ILLUSION* AT SANTA FE STAGES.

How to Use   Select a printed image from any source and photo-print onto transfer paper by means of either a heat-transfer press or a clothing iron set to 375°F. Heat-transfer presses produce more reliable images because of their high temperature and pressure. Using a clothes iron offers less reliable results. Once on the transfer paper, move the image onto the desired surface with either the heat-press machine or an iron.

Transfer paper is available at photocopy shops but can also be purchased from silk-screen suppliers for a lower price.

For this method, first find an image, and heat-transfer it onto transfer paper with the heat-transfer press. Then stretch it over the table of the press, and heat press the image from the transfer paper onto the fabric. When done by professional T-shirt shops, this process costs approximately $15 a print.

There are also products available that are made especially for the purpose of transferring. These products are available at art and hobby shops.

Another method, devised by Marjorie Croner and explained in detail in her book *Fabric Photos*, uses iron-on mending fabric (available at fabric stores) and a hot iron. Her technique is to press the mending fabric onto a paper photocopy, peel away the mending fabric that has picked up a reverse of the printed image, and then iron the mending fabric image onto the cloth.

When Alan Armstrong used photocopies of existing images for his designs in *The Illusion*, he followed this technique: The drawings were first enlarged on the photocopy machine, then the drawing lines were reinforced with black marker. The drawings were then photocopied onto transfer paper and each was cut to its outermost edge. The fabric was laid onto an ironing board, where two people worked together—one ironing and the other quickly peeling the transfer paper from the fabric. The process took approximately one-and-a-half to three minutes per picture. When the transferring was completed, marking pen lines again strengthened the drawings. Armstrong applied the same photocopy technique to his costume sketch, only this time he decreased the size of the drawings before photocopying.

Solvent for Cleanup   Soap and water.

Precautions   Hand washing and line drying are recommended.

Health and Safety   This is a safe process.

Where to Find   Photocopy shops and distributors, silk-screen supply distributors.

Sizes   Usually 8"× 10" or 11" × 17".

PHOTOCOPYING   **LAUNDER** DRY-CLEAN

Surface	Photocopying	
Acetate Fabric	E	E
Acetate Sheeting	E	P
Acrylic Fabric	G	F
Acrylic Sheeting	O	P
Cotton	F	G
Glass	P	P
Leather	G	E
Linen	E	G
Metal	O	O
Mylar	F	F
Nylon	G	E
Nylon Spandex	E	E
Polyester Fabric	E	E
Polyurethane Foam	F	P
Rayon	F	F
Silk	E	F
Styrofoam	O	O
Vinyl	E	P
Wool	F	F

O = Does not bond.
P = Poor bond: Bond fails with first laundering or dry cleaning.
F = Fair bond: Materials stay bonded for up to five launderings or dry cleanings.
G = Good bond: Materials stay bonded for up to fourteen launderings or dry cleanings.
E = Excellent: Bond appears permanent.

Stains

French Enamel Varnish

A colorant mixed by the user

Examples of Use
- Create an antique look with deep colors over metallics.
- Give an iridescent illusion with a light spray of a contrasting color.
- Age rich-looking fabric or other costume materials.

Use when transparent, brilliant, shiny, or reflective coloring is desired. This varnish is especially effective on metallic accessories and metallic fabrics, and when overdying with a color to obtain depth and richness. Use on fabrics not requiring cleaning or washing.

Description *French enamel varnish* is a transparent mixture of a binder (shellac), a thinner or solvent (usually alcohol), and pigment or alcohol-soluble dye. The shellac allows FEV to bond to most porous and nonporous surfaces. It is particularly effective for antiquing armor, accessories, jewelry, and similar pieces.

Painting French enamel varnish onto fabric stiffens the fabric and it does not withstand dry cleaning or laundering particularly well.

How to Use The formula consists of four parts denatured alcohol, one part shellac, and a colorant of either leather dye, aniline dye or India ink. The colorant should be sufficient to create the desired intensity.

Mix thoroughly, varying proportions if desired. Varying the proportions affects flexibility, transparency, and intensity. Brush or spray onto fabric. FEV does not require heat setting.

Apply by brush, spray, or with stencil.

Solvent for Cleanup Alcohol.

Precautions Do not dry-clean, launder, or iron. FEV used on soft fabrics will cause stiffening.

Health and Safety Use in an open or ventilated work area; wear respirator, gloves, goggles and protective clothing. Store FEV, solvents, and shellac in a sealed container in a metal cabinet reserved for flammables.

Where to Find Alcohol: Hardware stores.

Shellac: Hardware and paint stores.

Colorants: Art stores, dye distributors, and shoe repair suppliers.

FRENCH ENAMEL VARNISH   **LAUNDER** DRY-CLEAN

Surface	Cova Leather Dye and Shellac	
Acetate Fabric	P	F
Acetate Sheeting	0	0
Acrylic Fabric	P	F
Acrylic Sheeting	0	0
Cotton	P	P
Glass	0	0
Leather	P	P
Linen	P	P
Metal	0	0
Mylar	P	P
Nylon	P	P
Nylon Spandex	P	P
Polyester Fabric	P	F
Polyurethane Foam	P	F
Rayon	P	F
Silk	P	F
Styrofoam	0	0
Vinyl	P	P
Wool	P	P

0 = Does not bond.
P = Poor bond: Bond fails with first laundering or dry cleaning.
F = Fair bond: Materials stay bonded for up to five launderings or dry cleanings.
G = Good bond: Materials stay bonded for up to fourteen launderings or dry cleanings.
E = Excellent: Bond appears permanent.

Note: FEV causes fabrics to stiffen.

Glass Stain

Brands Tested	Manufacturers
Glass Stain	Stain Glass Products
Great Glass Stain	Plaid Enterprises

Examples of Use
- Color jewelry and other glassy items.
- Glaze surfaces of costume pieces that do not requiring cleaning.

Glass stain creates beautiful translucent effects on stiff, slick-surfaced fabrics. This product may be laundered several times on most fabrics, though brands differ in their lasting qualities.

Description *Glass stains and glazes* are shiny, translucent, thin liquids formulated for staining glass and other hard surfaces. On fabric, they leave a stiff, transparent glaze. These compounds of butyl cellulose and toluene are used mostly by glass crafters for simulating stained glass. For costume use, be sure to get the glass stains that do not require kiln firing.

How to Use Simply brush onto a clean surface.

Solvent for Cleanup Paint thinner or consult manufacturer and MSDS.

Precautions Glass stain stiffens fabrics. To stain or glaze fabrics, it is usually preferable to use French enamel varnish, which stiffens the fabric less and retains bonds through laundering. In laundering glass stain, the color may disappear, but the stiffness will remain. If glass stains are used on stretch fabric, the fabric will lose elasticity.

Health and Safety Glass stains are toxic. Use only with good ventilation, a respirator, goggles, and gloves, or spray in a local exhaust system such as a spray booth.

Where to Find Art-supply stores, and hobby and crafts shops.

Sizes ½ - 2 oz.

GLASS STAIN **LAUNDER** DRY-CLEAN

Surface	Glass Stain		Great Glass Stain	
Acetate Fabric	P	P	P	P
Acetate Sheeting	F	P	F-G	P
Acrylic Fabric	G	P	E	P
Acrylic Sheeting	F	P	F-G	P
Cotton	F	P	F	P
Glass	P	P	P	P
Leather	G	P	F-G	P
Linen	F *	P *	F *	P *
Metal	P	P	P	P
Mylar	P	P	P-F	P
Nylon	F	P	F	P
Nylon Spandex	F	P	F	P
Polyester Fabric	G	P	F-G	P
Polyurethane Foam	F *	P *	F-G *	P *
Rayon	F	P	F	P
Silk	G	P	F-G	P
Styrofoam	P	P	P	P
Vinyl	F *	P *	F *	P *
Wool	G	P	F-G	P

0 = Does not bond.
P = Poor bond: Bond fails with first laundering or dry cleaning.
F = Fair bond: Materials stay bonded for up to five launderings or dry cleanings.
G = Good bond: Materials stay bonded for up to fourteen launderings or dry cleanings.
E = Excellent: Bond appears permanent.

Note: Glass stains stiffen fabrics.
* Colorant splotches.

Wood Stain

Brands Tested	Manufacturers
Deft Safe & Easy Biodegradable Wood Stain	Deft, Inc.
Heirloom Wood Stain - Interior	McCloskey, Division of the Valspar Corporation
Minwax Wood Finish	The thompson Minwax company
Varathane Diamond Wood Stain	The Flecto Company, Inc.

Examples of Use
- Distress costumes of both textiles and other materials.
- Color glaze for depth and dimension.
- Paint transparent motifs.

Wood stains are effective distressing agents. They can be used on almost any surface; however, they stiffen fabrics, and they cannot be dry-cleaned or laundered on all.

Description *Wood stains and finishes* are a fairly thin viscosity stain that can be used like French enamel varnish or like glazes for transparent and translucent effects on all kinds of surfaces. Colors are limited to natural woods and are especially suitable for distressing. Although wood stains bond initially to most surfaces, in most cases they do not withstand dry cleaning.

How to Use Brush, roll, or thin with appropriate solvent and spray onto surfaces. As with any brands, read the labels to learn the appropriate solvent, for solvents vary among brands.

Solvent for Cleanup Deft and Varathane: soap and water. Minwax: mineral spirits or paint thinner.

Precautions These products do not launder or dry-clean well in most instances.

Health and Safety Use adequate ventilation or work in local exhaust (see the Health and Safety on page 16 in Part One) with both types of products. When working with stains, also use goggles, ventilator, and protective gloves, and keep away from open flames and food.

Though Deft includes "Safe & Easy" in its name, it is not as safe as the name indicates, for it contains glycol ethers, which have extremely low threshold-limit values and are highly dangerous to our health.

Where to Find Paint stores and home-improvement stores.

Sizes ½ pt. - 1 gal.

WOOD STAIN **LAUNDER** DRY-CLEAN

Surface	Deft		Heirloom		Minwax		Varathane	
Acetate Fabric	P	G	E	G	F	G	G	F
Acetate Sheeting	P	G **	E	P	F	F	P	P **
Acrylic Fabric	P	G *	E	E	F	F *	G	F
Acrylic Sheeting	P	F	E	P	F	P	P	P
Cotton	P	G *	E	G	F *	F *	E	F
Glass	P	P	G	P	P	P	P	P
Leather	G	P	E	P	P	F	F	F
Linen	G	G	E	G	F *	F	E	P
Metal	P	F	E	P	F	F	P	P
Mylar	P	F	G	P	P	F	P	P
Nylon	P	F	E	G	F	F *	G	F
Nylon Spandex	P	G *	E	G	F *	G *	G	P
Polyester Fabric	P	G	E	G	P	P	E	F
Polyurethane Foam	P	F	E	P	P	F	G	P
Rayon	F *	P	E	E	F *	F *	G	F
Silk	P	E *	E	G	P *	F	G	F
Styrofoam	P	E **	E	P	F	P	E	P **
Vinyl	P	P	E	P	P	P	G	P
Wool	P	P	E	G	P	P	G	F

O = Does not bond.
P = Poor bond: Bond fails with first laundering or dry cleaning.
F = Fair bond: Materials stay bonded for up to five launderings or dry cleanings.
G = Good bond: Materials stay bonded for up to fourteen launderings or dry cleanings.
E = Excellent: Bond appears permanent.

Note: Wood stains streak on most non-porous surfaces.
*   Colorant bleeds.
** Surface dissolves.

Metallizers

Finding ways to create imitation metal is a common problem in costuming, and with so many different and varied ways to do so, the subject deserves extensive discussion. In this case, we tested most all the methods in this section by laundering and dry cleaning nineteen different treated materials (the same nineteen materials tested throughout this reference for paints, coatings, and adhesives). We did not test metallic finishes on additional plastics.

Most metallic finishes are of aluminum that has been colored with pigment. The pigment is sometimes lost during laundering and dry cleaning; color is lost as the metallic coatings return to their natural aluminum color. With some finishes, the metallic sheen becomes dull during washing or dry cleaning.

The techniques included here for metallizing range from applying simple and inexpensive bronzing powder in a binder to more sophisticated and costly approaches, such as gold leafing and vacuum plating.

Working Methods For all methods, follow instructions carefully. Even though two products may fall into the same generic category, formulas vary between brands, and working techniques from one craftsperson to another may differ slightly.

When metallizing designs on fabrics, we suggest using hard, nonabsorbent fabrics that are closely woven and hard-surfaced. Soft fabrics, like fleecy woolens, chiffons, and many knits, absorb moisture from the metallizer, taking on the color but not the shininess of metal; furthermore, soft surfaces resist rubbed or brushed-on substances. The most successful finishes sit on top of the fabric surface. These include metallic foils, thick glitter paint, and metallic hot-melt glue.

Dense, nonporous, nontextile surfaces, such as acrylic and Mylar sheeting, take metallic finishes well. Most paint, foils, leafs, and other materials can look convincingly metallic when applied with care to such surfaces.

Paint and coatings that are not extremely flexible will crack when applied to flexible solid surfaces such as leather, vinyl, and most plastic films.

Health and Safety Obtain MSDSs on all materials. Metallic aluminum powders, long suspected of contributing to Alzheimer's and other chronic diseases, are part of most metallic finishes. Working with powders can damage lungs, eyes, and skin. Metal powders are absorbed into the skin or respiratory system and can damage blood, kidneys, lungs, and brain. Buddy Ebson lost the role of the Tin Man in the original film of *The Wizard of Oz* because of a serious lung reaction to aluminum powder.

Many metal powders including aluminum are fire and explosion hazards. When dust gets in the air it can be easily ignited. In fact, metal powders are major ingredients in fireworks.

- Do not rub on metal powders and compounds with bare skin. When package directions advise rubbing a compound with bare hands or fingers, use instead a soft cloth or thick cloth gloves.
- Do not blow metal powders, like bronzing powders, into the air.
- When solvents are part of a compound, work with a good ventilation system like those described in the *Health and Safety* section in Part One.
- *Do not eat, drink, or smoke near hazardous materials.*

Bronzing Powder and Glitter Mixed with Adhesives

White Glue Brands Tested	Manufacturers
Elmer's Glue-All	Borden, Inc.
Phlexglu	Spectra Dynamics Products
Sobo	Delta Technical Coatings, Inc.
Rubber Cements Brands Tested	**Manufacturers**
Household Goop	Eclectic Products Inc.
Barge All-Purpose Cement	Pierce and Stevens Chemical Corporation

Examples of Use
- Embellish motifs.
- Accent folds in fabric or high points on hard surfaces.
- Mix with various binders to form paint.

Use for creating flat or dimensional motifs and decorations on all kinds of surfaces in place of metallic fabric paint. Also use for accenting metallic or rich surfaces and creating motifs, especially on costumes not to be dry-cleaned. For highlighting plate armor for *Hamlet*, see page 300, and for use with double-sided tape, see pages 74-75.

Description Bronzing powder and glitter are usually made from colored aluminum, and used primarily in the crafts industries. Bronzing powder in a flexible binder—coating, glue, or paint—produces a good paint for metallizing costumes. Tested were several adhesives and paint binders that have proved to be satisfactory coatings for fabrics as well as for other surfaces.

Bronzing powder can be mixed with water-soluble white glues (see PVA in the Adhesives section); rubber cements (see Rubber Cement in the Adhesives section); or other adhesives and coatings to produce metallic paint. White glues and rubber cements are flexible and well suited to fabrics and other pliable surfaces.

Repeated laundering and dry cleaning cause the mixture of bronzing powder and adhesive to lose its luster, though glitter mixed with adhesive retains its luster. For adherence of other types of binders to surfaces, refer to the appropriate pages in the Adhesives, Coatings, or Colorants sections.

How to Use Mix the bronzing powder or glitter into an adhesive or binder in a ratio dependent upon the desired effect. A water-soluble adhesive/binder will appear whitish when mixed with any PVA glue or acrylic emulsion, though it will dry to be fairly clear with a metallic look. The mixture can be applied by brush or spatula. Dimensional motifs can be created if the powder/glitter mixture is thick enough, or the mixture can be thickened with Cab-O-Sil and squeezed though a pastry gun.

When using the above method, Doreen Johnson of the Guthrie Theatre mixes bronzing powder with the thinner and flexible low-crock Pro Chem binder, available through silk-screen suppliers. She usually finish-coats the metallic coating with a layer of sealer from Angelus Leather Dye.

Bronzing powder may also be applied to surfaces painted with adhesives, coatings, and colorants by sprinkling on while the surface is still tacky. To produce an even surface, sprinkle the powder through a sieve. Sprinkled in this manner on the outer folds of rich or metallic fabrics, bronzing powder can increase the opulence of a fabric. Rubbed over armor and hard "metal" objects, the powder causes an illusion of increased depth.

Another way of creating a metallic-looking fabric is to apply bronzing powder or glitter over net. First, choose a net in a color compatible with the desired gold effect. Apply PVA by brush, then gently sprinkle the powder or glitter through a sieve and onto the net. Stretch the net, shake off the excess, and the net is ready to use either alone or layered over opaque fabric.

Troweling bronzing powder mixed with rubber cement creates a believable metallic finish for armor or jewelry and can also be used for creating metallic designs on fabric. This method, from the Deutsche Oper in Berlin, allows some flexibility and resembles dull steel or other metals:

• First presize felt or other heavy, dense fabric with white glue or other sizing. When dry, apply with a trowel a mixture of metallic powder and rubber cement to the fabric. Smooth the surface by brushing with acetone. When the mixture is dry, iron the felt or fabric until shiny. *Use ventilation for this method. The heated acetone will release hazardous dust into the air.*

• The second method from the Deutsche Oper results in a stiffer, newer looking metal. First size the fabric armor and allow to dry. Then mix bronzing powder with rubber cement into a paste. Apply the paste with a trowel and allow to dry out completely, usually overnight. With a metal object, such as a spoon or knife, buff the "metal" until it shines.

To impart a particularly rich effect over drawn dimensional patterns, first draw the pattern with a container filled with pearlescent, dimensional paint or with thickened, dimensional white glue. A plastic squeeze bottle or a parchment cone works. While the surface is still tacky, sprinkle on bronzing powder. This lasts well through dry cleaning, if a compatible glue and paint are chosen. We tested by mixing both glitter and powder with Phlexglu and Tulip Pearlescent Paint on cotton velvet.

Natural colored lace was dyed black and shaped, then painted with Aleene's Flexible Stretchable Fabric Glue thinned with acetone and applied with a small paint roller. Next, gold bronzing powder was applied, then small particles of glitter were sprinkled on the wet glue mixture.

DESIGN: GAIL MCKEE FOR *THE MISANTHROPE* AT THE UNIVERSITY OF WASHINGTON SCHOOL OF DRAMA. ARTISTRY AND PHOTO: JOSIE GARDNER.

For creating small metallic motifs, bronzing powder, as well as glitter, can be applied to double-stick tape. Cirque du Soleil uses double-sided tape, such as Se-Lin from Jean Teton, when decorating costumes that do not require dry cleaning. First, cut the tape to the shape of the motif. Pull off the underneath, clear covering, and place the tape itself onto the costume, rubbing it into place. Pull off the top, brown-paper coating. Sprinkle bronzing powder or glitter onto the motif. With this method, the glitter motif can look like part of the fabric itself.

Solvent for Cleanup With water-soluble adhesives and binders, use soap and water while the mixture is still wet. With rubber cement, use the solvent recommended on the label or literature from the rubber-cement container.

Precautions Successful washing and dry cleaning depend upon the choice of adhesive or binder. Refer to the charts that follow to see which are most suitable for individual fabrics and how change may occur with dry cleaning. With white glues, bronzing powder loses its luster after six to ten launderings or dry cleanings.

Health and Safety When using bronzing powder or glitter, wear a particle mask to avoid inhaling the metal. Do not apply bronzing powder by blowing, for metallic particles dispersed in the air are a health hazard. Keep sources of ignition, such as cigarettes, away from the metallic powders.

With the glues, follow precautions specific to the glue being used and always work in a ventilated area.

Where to Find Craft and hobby shops and distributors.

Sizes 1 oz. - 1 pt.

Glitter Paint

Brands Tested	Manufacturers
Createx Colors Glitter Paint	ColorCraft, Ltd.
Glitter Fabric Paint	Tulip Product of Duncan Enterprises
Puffy Glitter Paint	Polymark Product of Duncan Enterprises

Examples of Use

- Paint for jeweled, beaded, and sequined effects.
- Highlight and emphasize existing motifs.
- Create motifs.
- Use for stripes, dots, edging, lettering, etc.

Glitter paint can be used for the same effects as the previously discussed mixture of bronzing powder and glitter mixed with an adhesive. Glitter paint is effective for creating flat or dimensional motifs and decorations on all kinds of surfaces and for accenting metallic or rich surfaces and creating motifs.

Definition These *glitter paints* come in squeeze bottles and tubes, making them easy to apply directly onto a surface as dots, lines, and small patterns. The puff paint, after application, needs heating with an iron or dryer in order to rise into a relief design.

Like other flexible paints in squeeze bottles, most glitter paints are sold in art-supply and fabric stores. ColorCraft products, however, are only available through their manufacturer. For large quantities, buy direct from any of these manufacturers. The large containers of paint can be transferred into empty squeeze bottles or handmade cones.

How to Use Draw a pattern or motif at the same time as squeezing the bottle or tube. For wider coverage, use the paint from a palette or jar, applying with brush, trowel, or fingers. These paints do not need heat fixing, though heat is necessary for "puffy" paint to become dimensional.

Solvent for Cleanup Soap and water.

Precautions Recommended shelf life is one year.

Health and Safety Health hazards can vary. Obtain MSDSs and treat the pigments as toxic.

Some Other Brands Scribbles 3-Dimensional Craft and Fabric Paint Glittering, Scribbles Product of Duncan Enterprises.

Where to Find Art stores, fabric stores, and manufacturers.

Sizes ½-, 1-, 2-, and 4-oz. tubes and bottles.

GLITTER PAINT   **LAUNDER** DRY-CLEAN

Surface	Createx		Polymark		Tulip	
Acetate Fabric	P	P	G	G	E	E
Acetate Sheeting	P	P	G	G-E	E	E
Acrylic Fabric	G *	P	G	G-E	E	E
Acrylic Sheeting	P	P	G	G-E	E	E
Cotton	F	P	E	G-E	E	E
Glass	P	P	P	G	E	E
Leather	P	P	E	E	E	E
Linen	P	P	E	G	E	E
Metal	P	P	E	G	E	E
Mylar	F	P	F	G	E	E
Nylon	P	P	P	P	E	E
Nylon Spandex	F	P	G	G	E	E
Polyester Fabric	G	P	E	G	E	E
Polyurethane Foam	F	P	E	F	E	E
Rayon	F	P	G	G	E	E
Silk	P	P	G	E	E	E
Styrofoam	F	P	E	P	P	P
Vinyl	P	P	G	G	E	E
Wool	F	P	G	E	E	E

O = Does not bond.
P = Poor bond: Bond fails with first laundering or dry cleaning.
F = Fair bond: Materials stay bonded for up to five launderings or dry cleanings.
G = Good bond: Materials stay bonded for up to fourteen launderings or dry cleanings.
E = Excellent: Bond appears permanent.

Note: Polymark bleeds in washing machine.
* Surface stiffens.

Metallic Felt-Tip Marking Pens

Brand Names	Manufacturers
DecoColor Opaque Paint Marker	Marvy, Uchida of America, Corp.
Pilot Metallic Markers	Pilot

Examples of Use
- Draw small, linear, metallic patterns onto all kinds of firm surfaces, whether textile or nontextile.

Description   *Felt-tip markers* are basically metal tubes containing an ink-saturated quarter-of-an-inch felt strip that protrudes as a nib. Metallic marking pens contain opaque paint, rather than the usual transparent ink found in other markers. The metallic colors available in most brands of markers are gold, copper, and silver. Those we have tested are made not only for painting on textiles, but are also fine for illustration and graphic design. We have found that they may be used in a variety of ways and that felt-tip markers are in most cases able to withstand many launderings.

How to Use   Use as any marking pens are used, for drawing lines and filling in small areas. Be sure to shake well before using and press firmly while drawing.

Solvent for Cleanup   To select the correct solvents for specific markers, obtain MSDSs to learn which solvents are found in the markers. Select the least toxic. Try not to use solvents with threshold limit values (TLVs) of 100 or less than 100 ppm. Of those solvents most likely to be in markers, ethyl alcohol is the safest. Refer to the charts in the Solvent section of the appendix to learn the TLVs of solvents.

Precautions   Do not use on soft plastics. Be sure to cover tightly.

Health and Safety   Use in a well-ventilated area, for many markers are highly toxic. If good ventilation is not possible when using marking pens for a prolonged period, wear a respirator. To select the proper respirator, consult MSDSs, for many different solvents are used in various combinations in markers.

Some Other Brands   Niji Metallic Marker.

Where to Find   Art supply stores and craft and hobby shops.

Sizes   6" long by ½" to ¾" diameter.

METALLIC FELT-TIP MARKING PENS LAUNDER DRY-CLEAN

Surface	DecoColor		Pilot	
Acetate Fabric	F	P	E	F
Acetate Sheeting	F	P	E	P
Acrylic Fabric	F	P	E	F
Acrylic Sheeting	E	P	E	P
Cotton	P	P	E	P
Glass	P	P	P	P
Leather	P	P	E	P
Linen	P	P	E	P
Metal	E	P	E	P
Mylar	F	P	G	P
Nylon	F	P	E	P
Nylon Spandex	F	P	E	F
Polyester Fabric	P	P	E	P
Polyurethane Foam	F	P	G	P
Rayon	P	P	E	P
Silk	F	P	E	P
Styrofoam	G	P	G	P
Vinyl	P	P	P	P
Wool	P	P	G	P

O = Does not bond.
P = Poor bond: Bond fails with first laundering or dry cleaning.
F = Fair bond: Materials stay bonded for up to five launderings or dry cleanings.
G = Good bond: Materials stay bonded for up to fourteen launderings or dry cleanings.
E = Excellent: Bond appears permanent.

Metallic Foil

Brand Names	Manufacturers
Fashion Foil	Jones Tones Inc.
Liquid Beads Press & Peel Foil	Plaid Enterprises, Inc.

Examples of Use
• Use for metallic motifs on fabrics and other surfaces.

Metallic foil simulates rich Gothic and Renaissance damasks successfully and is excellent for embellishing futuristic costumes. Metallic foil can be used for quick antiquing effects and even for coating large surfaces.

Description
Heat-transfer *metallic foil* sheets are sold in a wide range of metallic colors that are protectively coated by a layer of Mylar and are manufactured with an adhesive backing made specifically for applying the foil on particular surfaces. Less costly and more easily handled than gold leaf, heat-transfer metallic foil may be heat set with a heat-transfer press, or—with limited success—a hand iron. Some costume shops use a heat-transfer press to embellish costumes with rich allover designs of metallic foil. Heat-transfer presses are available from silk-screen suppliers and distributors of foils. The cost ranges from approximately $1,200 to $2,600.

Adhesive-Set Foil

How to Use
Use only the adhesive designated for companion use, and use only on fabrics to be laundered, not those to be dry-cleaned as follows:

1. Protect underside of fabric with Teflon or cardboard.

2. Adhere fabric to board with pins or tape to ensure its flatness.

3. Squeeze the adhesive onto fabric in the shape of motif. Press the foil into place. When using Plaid's product, brush on Plaid's sealer.

4. Let the garment dry in a flat position.

Heat-Set Foil

How to Use
With a heat-press machine, follow this technique:

1. Set the machine temperature to 350°F and the pressure on medium to heavy.

2. Protect the inside of the garment with a piece of release paper, Mylar, or Teflon.

3. Cut the foil to size and place over the motif with the dull side down. Holding dull side down, place the foil onto the garment.

4. Press for approximately twenty to twenty-five seconds, or the time recommended by manufacturer. When cooled, pull off the transparent top coating.

Solvent for Cleanup
To clean up the adhesive, use soap and water before it dries.

Precautions Manufacturers specify laundering in cool or lukewarm water, and hanging to dry, not machine drying. Even so, most of the foil will flake off after several launderings, though foil laminated with a heat-press machine has a somewhat longer life expectancy. Though manufacturers warn against dry cleaning foil-decorated costumes, our testing showed that Liquid Beads foil dry-cleaned well.

Some Other Brands For Fabrics: Becca Industries

For Use with a Heat-Press Machine: Roll Leaf, Admiral Coated Products, Inc.; EZ Foil, Dry Print Foils, Inc.

Health and Safety Work with ventilation when using the adhesive as it contains a small amount of formaldehyde (0.1 %).

Where to Find Silk-screen and textile-arts supply stores and craft and hobby shops.

Sizes Sheets 12" × 12" and 12" × 20" Rolls 12" × 200'

Transfer metallic foil sheets are also sold in a kit in conjunction with a special adhesive at craft stores. The foils we tested are those sold for decorating fabrics and were packaged in a kit with an accompanying adhesive. Their manufacturers and distributors are listed at the end of this section. Results on the following chart are from tests of foils applied with their accompanying adhesives.

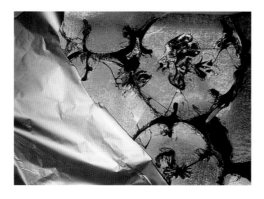

The foil can be applied to fabric through a stencil, using a hot iron or a heat-transfer machine.
PHOTO: CORNELIUS SKATES.

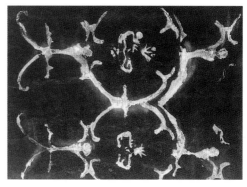

A stencil and sheet of hot-stamp foil are used to achieve this metallic pattern.
PHOTO: CORNELIUS SKATES.

METALLIC FOIL   **LAUNDER** DRY-CLEAN

Surface	Fashion Foil		Liquid Beads	
Acetate Fabric	P	F	G	E
Acetate Sheeting	P	P	F	E
Acrylic Fabric	P	P	G	E
Acrylic Sheeting	F	P	P	E
Cotton	P	P	G	E
Glass	P	P	O	O
Leather	P	P	G	E
Linen	F	P	F	E
Metal	P	P	O	O
Mylar	P	P	P	P
Nylon	P	P	G	E
Nylon Spandex	P	F	E	E
Polyester Fabric	P	P	G	E
Polyurethane Foam	P	P	G	E
Rayon	F	P	G	E
Silk	F	F	F	E
Styrofoam	P	P	F	F
Vinyl	P	P	G	G
Wool	F	F	G	E

O = Does not bond.
P = Poor bond: Bond fails with first laundering or dry cleaning.
F = Fair bond: Materials stay bonded for up to five launderings or dry cleanings.
G = Good bond: Materials stay bonded for up to fourteen launderings or dry cleanings.
E = Excellent: Bond appears permanent.

Note: Metallic foil on fabric may be successfully hand laundered and air dried.

Hot-stamp foil applied by a heat-transfer machine creates the appearance of a Renaissance metallic damask fabric.

DESIGN: ANN HOD-WARD FOR *RICHARD II* AT THE GUTHRIE THEATRE. PHOTO: RICHARD DANIEL.

Metallic Hot-Melt Glue Sticks

Brand Names	Manufacturers
Uni-Stick	Tecnocraft, Division of Uniplast, Inc.

Examples of Use
- Create 3-D metallic decorations.
- Bond and decorate simultaneously.
- Cast jewelry and small metallic-looking decorations.

Use for dimensional decorations on costumes that do not require laundering. Trimming armor edges and creating relief decorations on fabrics are two useful applications of metallic hot glue. Like several other adhesives, hot-melt glue sticks can also simulate beads in small areas.

Description   *Hot-glue sticks* in metallic colors provide a simple way of decorating costumes. Uni-Sticks are of colored ethyl vinyl acetate (EVA) with added coloring and glitter. Uni-Sticks can be used as high- or low-temperature glue and are sold in crafts stores along with a compatible gun.

At this writing, Tecnocraft is the only known manufacturer offering metallic hot-glue sticks.

How to Use   Use in a compatible standard-size low- or high-temperature glue gun—Tecnocraft also makes guns.

First, draw the desired pattern on the costume piece and apply the hot glue.

For casting into molds to create jewelry, see pages 208-210 of Casting.

Solvent for Cleanup   For cleanup, simply peel and scrape the cooled glue from the working surface.

Hot-melt Uni-Stiks dry-clean well, but will not survive laundering.

Precautions   Store in a cool, dry area.

Health and Safety   Work with ventilation and eye protection. Wear gloves and long sleeves to protect from burning. Hot-molten material that touches the skin will cause burns. At high temperatures, fumes may irritate the eyes, throat, and nose. Overexposure can cause redness, tearing, and itching in the eyes. If molten material contacts the skin or eyes, immediately flush or immerse affected area in large amounts of cold water; do not attempt to peel the material from the skin. For large jobs, use an organic vapor cartridge.

The odor from normal usage (not from overheating) is from the volatilization of chemicals called plasticizers. Most manufacturers do not identify plasticizers on MSDSs, nor do they refer to them as "nontoxic." Most plasticizers have not been studied for long-term hazards, though many are chemically related to known toxic and/or carcinogenic substances. Until more is known, it is wise to use ventilation with hot glue.

Where to Find   Hobby and crafts stores.

Sizes   5/16" and 1/2" diameter by 4" long, in packages of 6, 12, 30 and 72.

METALLLIC HOT-MELT GLUE STICKS   **LAUNDER** DRY-CLEAN

Surface	Uni-Stick	
Acetate Fabric	E	E
Acetate Sheeting	G	G
Acrylic Fabric	E	E
Acrylic Sheeting	F	G
Cotton	E	E
Glass	G	E
Leather	G	E
Linen	F	E
Metal	E	E
Mylar	F	G
Nylon	E	E
Nylon Spandex	G	E
Polyester Fabric	E	E
Polyurethane Foam	G	E
Rayon	G	E
Silk	G	E
Styrofoam	G	E
Vinyl	F	G
Wool	G	E

O = Does not bond.
P = Poor bond: Bond fails with first laundering or dry cleaning.
F = Fair bond: Materials stay bonded for up to five launderings or dry cleanings.
G = Good bond: Materials stay bonded for up to fourteen launderings or dry cleanings.
E = Excellent: Bond appears permanent.

Metallic Leaf

Brand Names	Manufacturers
Easy Leaf	MaDaNa Manufacturing Company
Metallic Leaf	Old World Art

Examples of Use
- Simulate embroidery and woven patterns on fabric.
- Create metallic appearance on large or small areas.

Metallic leaf is best applied only on small areas and only as highlights or to create antiquing effects on larger surfaces. Metallic leaf is difficult to affix and when an entire sheet is applied, it usually leaves a crackled effect, which can also give an antique and otherwise attractive look.

Description *Metallic leaf* comes in small squares of thin metal foil. Leaf can be made of actual precious metals, like gold, silver, and copper; but because of cost, metallic leaf is usually an imitation of a precious metal, formulated by mixing color into aluminum powder and pressing the mix onto a thin foil. Real metal leaf comes in four-inch-square sheets, and imitation metal leaf is in five-and-a-half-inch squares. Gold leaf has been in use for centuries, mostly on artworks and furnishings. The metallic leaves tested for this book are imitation metal leaf.

Metallic leaf is applied with adhesive bonding. Manufacturers of metallic leaf also manufacture adhesives and sealers. Old World's adhesive is solvent-based, while Easy Leaf's is water-based. Other adhesives such as Phlexglu, Japan gold size, and shellac also bond metal leaf.

How to Use Begin by brushing a coat of adhesive evenly onto the desired surface. The brushed surface must be smooth and without puddles. As it dries, the adhesive becomes colorless and transparent. After about an hour, the adhesive should be dry enough to work, though drying time varies depending on individual surfaces. Do not let the adhesive dry out completely, or it will not be sufficiently tacky to bond the leaf.

With clean, dry hands, apply a sheet of leaf to the surface. When the surface is completely covered, smooth with a brush or soft implement. Leaves may be overlapped, for surplus pieces can be brushed off. If small gaps appear, fill them with small pieces of leaf. Buff gently with cheesecloth.

After the leaf is applied, seal the applied surface over all with a coat of sealer for protection against scratching and tarnishing. Old World has its own sealer, which can be brushed on, though white glues also seal metal leaf. Wait approximately two hours before covering with a second coat and before handling.

For a smoother appearance, apply the leaf to a surface already covered by metallic paint. For an antiqued effect, apply the leaf over a suitable base coat like sienna, venetian red, or black. When choosing a base coat, use a color that will enhance the metal leaf color.

Solvent for Cleanup   Detergent and water.

Health and Safety   The adhesive and sealer are flammable and harmful if swallowed. Use in a well-ventilated area, for exposure to the vapors may cause nausea, headache, confusion, instability, irritation of the eyes or chest, as well as birth defects. Do not use near heat or flames, and do not use if pregnant.

Where to Find   Art stores and hobby and craft shops.

Sizes   5 ½"-square sheets in packages of twenty-five or five hundred.

METALLIC LEAF	LAUNDER	DRY-CLEAN		
Surface	Easy Leaf		Metallic Leaf	
Acetate Fabric	P	P	G	P
Acetate Sheeting	P	P	E	P
Acrylic Fabric	P	P	F	P
Acrylic Sheeting	P	P	E	P
Cotton	P	P	P	P
Glass	P	P	F	F
Leather	P	P	F	F
Linen	P	P	G	F
Metal	P	P	E	F
Mylar	P	P	E	P
Nylon	P	P	E	F
Nylon Spandex	O	O	O	O
Polyester Fabric	P	P	F	P
Polyurethane Foam	P	P	E	P
Rayon	P	P	F	P
Silk	P	P	P	P
Styrofoam	O	O	O	O
Vinyl	P	P	E	P
Wool	P	P	F	F

O = Does not bond.
P = Poor bond: Bond fails with first laundering or dry cleaning.
F = Fair bond: Materials stay bonded for up to five launderings or dry cleanings.
G = Good bond: Materials stay bonded for up to fourteen launderings or dry cleanings.
E = Excellent: Bond appears permanent.

Metallic Textile Paint

Brands Tested	Manufacturers
Jacquard	Rupert, Gibbon and Spider, Inc.
Metallic Fabric Paint	Liquitex, Division of Binney & Smith Inc., Inc.
Permanent Fabric Paint	Decart, Inc.

Examples of Use
- Decorate with motifs on fabric or other surfaces.
- Highlight folds and raised ornamentation on fabrics.
- Create antiquing effects.

Paint or apply judiciously over fabric for metallic effects or over other surfaces for a metallic, antique, or worn, appearance.

Description These are thick, opaque, flexible water-based paints that dry-clean well. *Metallic textile paints* are available in plastic squeeze bottles and in jars. They work well on fabric, but do not cover other surfaces as successfully.

How to Use Paints in plastic squeeze bottles can be easily squeezed onto any surface. Paint from jars can be spread with a soft brush, stamped, stenciled, and silk-screened. To use with airbrush, thin with water. These paints are water soluble and should be heat set with an iron or by thirty minutes in the dryer.

Solvent for Cleanup Soap and water, immediately after using.

Precautions Do not use on water-repellent fabric.

Health and Safety For personal safety, keep an exhaust fan at an open window to avoid inhaling the small amounts of ammonia, formaldehyde, and possible solvents that are released during drying. Some of these paints contain small amounts of solvents. See precautions for working with metallizers in the beginning of this section.

Some Other Brands Createx Metallic Colors, ColorCraft, Ltd.; Deka Permanent Fabric Paint, Decart Inc.; Lumiere Fabric Paints, Cerulean Blue, Ltd.

Where to Find Artists' supply and fabric-arts supply stores.

Sizes Decart: 1 oz. - 1 gal.

Liquitex: 1.25 oz.

METALLIC TEXTILE PAINT   **LAUNDER** DRY-CLEAN

Surface	Jacquard		Metallic		Permanent	
Acetate Fabric	E	G	E	E	G	E
Acetate Sheeting	F	P	F	G	F	G
Acrylic Fabric	E	G	F	E	G	E
Acrylic Sheeting	F	P	F	G	F	G
Cotton	E	F	E	E	E	E
Glass	P	P	F	G	P	F
Leather	F	P	G	E	G	E
Linen	G	G	E	E	E	E
Metal	F	P	F	F	F	G
Mylar	P	P	P	F	P	F
Nylon	E	G	E	E	E	E
Nylon Spandex	G	G	G	E	G	E
Polyester Fabric	E	G	E	E	G	E
Polyurethane Foam	E	P	F	G	G	G
Rayon	E	G	E	E	E	E
Silk	E	G	G	E	E	E
Styrofoam	G	P	F	E	F	G
Vinyl	G	P	P	E	P	P
Wool	E	G	E	E	G	E

0 = Does not bond.
P = Poor bond: Bond fails with first laundering or dry cleaning.
F = Fair bond: Materials stay bonded for up to five launderings or dry cleanings.
G = Good bond: Materials stay bonded for up to fourteen launderings or dry cleanings.
E = Excellent: Bond appears permanent.

Metallic Waxes

Brands Tested	Manufacturers
Rub 'N Buff	American Art Clay Company, Inc.
Treasure Gold	Plaid Enterprises

Examples of Use
- Rub on top of decorative dimensional pieces for highlighting.
- Antique jewelry, etc.
- Create small motifs and decorations on preexisting surfaces.

Use for highlights on armor and large metallic accessories. Or use alone over smaller pieces like jewelry or applied pieces. As applied decoration, it is most successful on smooth surfaced, substantial fabrics.

Description *Metallic waxes* are compounded from wax, metallic powders, and selected pigments and are packaged in tubes or jars. Used in the decorating and antiquing fields, they can be applied on almost all surfaces as well as on surfaces already painted. Metallic waxes come in a variety of different metallic colors.

How to Use The manufacturers recommend fingertip application, which is more successful and less wasteful than other methods, though expect fingers to be covered with metallic wax and for your body to absorb unhealthful quantities of wax, metal, and pigments. The wax can also be applied with cheesecloth, chamois, a dry, firm, short-haired bristle brush; or it can be applied wearing latex surgical gloves. The wax dries in a few seconds. Nonporous treated materials dry more slowly than porous fabrics. Buff with a soft cloth for a glowing metallic surface.

Rub 'N Buff creates the highlights on this Neoprene mask.

DESIGN AND CONSTRUCTION: JULIAN CHEEK FOR *A MIDSUMMER NIGHT'S DREAM* AT THE UNIVERSITY OF NORTH CAROLINA AT GREENSBORO. PHOTO: PATRICK STRAIN.

Metallic waxes can also be brushed over larger surfaces with a brush first dampened with paint solvent. First, dip the brush into the solvent, and paint the solvent onto the surface; then rub the wax over that surface. Or the brush can be coated with paint solvent, dipped into the metallic wax, and painted over a surface. These techniques will result in a thinner and more even coating. Pieces coated with the combination of metallic wax with a solvent cannot be dry-cleaned. Sturdy fabrics are easier to work with, although it is difficult to create a smooth surface on almost any fabric.

Solvent for Cleanup Paint thinner or mineral spirits.

Precautions Do not dry-clean if the metallic wax has been thinned with a solvent. During laundering, the metallic surface loses some of its sheen.

Health and Safety   Rub-on metallics are combustible and must not be used or stored near heat or flame. Work with a rubbing instrument, rather than bare fingers, for these waxes contain metal and pigments that can be hazardous. Follow precautions for solvent use.

Some Other Brands   Mini-Luster Rub-On, Crafts Products, Inc.; Sculpey Metallic Daubing Paint, Polyform Products Inc.

Where to Find   Hobby and craft stores.

Sizes   Rub 'n Buff: ½ fluid oz. tube.

Treasure Gold: 24-oz. jars.

METALLIC WAXES	LAUNDER	DRY-CLEAN		
Surface	**Rub 'n Buff**		**Treasure Gold**	
Acetate Fabric	P	E	P	P
Acetate Sheeting	G	E	G	P
Acrylic Fabric	G	E	F	P
Acrylic Sheeting	G	E	G	P
Cotton	G	P	P	P
Glass	F	G	P	P
Leather	F	F	P	P
Linen	G	G	P	P
Metal	G	G	P	P
Mylar	G	G	P	P
Nylon	G	F	P	P
Nylon Spandex	G	G	P	P
Polyester Fabric	G	F	P	P
Polyurethane Foam	G	F	P	P
Rayon	G	F	P	P
Silk	G	F	P	P
Styrofoam	F	P	F	P
Vinyl	F	P	P	P
Wool	G	G	P	P

O = Does not bond.
P = Poor bond: Bond fails with first laundering or dry cleaning.
F = Fair bond: Materials stay bonded for up to five launderings or dry cleanings.
G = Good bond: Materials stay bonded for up to fourteen launderings or dry cleanings.
E = Excellent: Bond appears permanent.

Patina Antiquing Kit

Brand tested	Manufacturers
Patina Antiquing Kit	Modern Options, Inc.

Examples of Use   Create a real patina surface on metal or other surfaces. Patina Antiquing can create interesting results on armor and jewelry pieces.

On some textiles, this process will leave a dull antiqued patina that will fare well through several or more immersions of dry cleaning or laundering. The substances in this kit adhere best to thick materials on which a mechanical bonding can occur.

Description   *The Patina Antiquing Kit* is a nine-part kit made specifically for creating patina surfaces on metal. The nine parts include Metal Master cleaner, a patina solution, Primo Primer and Sealer, Copper Topper to modify the surfaces of metals that are not receptive to a patina, four bristle brushes, two foam brushes, latex gloves, a sponge, and an emery cloth. Testing showed that the Modern Options Patina Antiquing Kit also works well on textile surfaces.

Modern Options, Inc. produces twelve patina color finishes.

How to Use   To coat actual pieces of copper, brass, or bronze, remove all dirt and grease from the surface to be covered. Then cover with the Metal Master cleaner. Cover the surface of the item with Metal Master, either by brushing with a bristle brush or by soaking.

Materials from Modern Options applied over metal produce the patina on this headdress.

DESIGN: DEBORAH NADOOLMAN FOR *THE WAITING ROOM* AT THE MARK TAPER FORUM, LOS ANGELES. PHOTO: CRAIG SCHWARTZ/JAY THOMPSON.

Coat the prepared item with the patina, and a dull film will appear. After this coat is dry, apply a second coat. More coats may be required for a darker finish, though too many coats applied too quickly may flake. After three to four days, the Sealer should be applied to prevent further oxidation.

For coating other metal surfaces, seal the surface with a base coat of sealer and possibly a primer. Apply Copper Topper to the primed surface. After curing (see instructions), apply a second coat. Brush on Patina Green to this surface and allow three to four days for curing, before applying a light sealing coat.

Solvent for Cleanup Detergent and water before curing.

Precautions Heavy coats of sealer may leave an undesirable sheen, and incorrect drying times may cause flaking or spotting. Experiment before using.

Store in tightly closed, original containers at room temperature.

Health and Safety Obtain the MSDS for the kit. The label does not identify the exact composition of the patinas, but many are known to contain highly toxic metals such as antimony, lead, selenium, and tellurium. These metals may be in the form of sulfides, which are in a solution containing acids such as hydrochloric and hydrofluoric acid. When in contact with metal, the acids generate smelly and highly toxic emissions such as hydrogen sulfite, hydrogen selenide, and tellurium chloride gases.

When using more than a few drops of patina, work in exhaust ventilation. Wear the protective gloves that are included in the kit, chemical splash goggles and other protective clothing while applying these solutions. Work in local ventilation. Do not mix these substances with any other chemicals. Keep away from children, cooking utensils, and food. Dispose properly of the empty containers in accordance with local regulations.

Some Other Brands Patina-It, A-West. Antiquing and patina kits are available from the following manufacturers: Bibo Palmas, Creative Craftsmen, JAX Chemical Co. Inc., MC Canfield, Novacan Industries.

Where to Find Home-decorating shops or manufacturers.

Sizes Kit contains 4 oz. each of Patina Green, Copper Topper, Primo Primer and Sealer, and 2 oz. of Metal Master.

PATINA ANTIQUING KIT **LAUNDER** DRY-CLEAN

Surface	Patina Antiquing Kit	
Acetate Fabric	G	E
Acetate Sheeting	G	G
Acrylic Fabric	F	G
Acrylic Sheeting	F	G
Cotton	F	G
Glass	E	G
Leather	G	E
Linen	G	E
Metal	E	E
Mylar	F	G
Nylon	F	G
Nylon Spandex	G	G
Polyester Fabric	F	G
Polyurethane Foam	G	E
Rayon	G	E
Silk	F	G
Styrofoam	G	E
Vinyl	F	F
Wool	G	E

0 = Does not bond.
P = Poor bond: Bond fails with first laundering or dry cleaning.
F = Fair bond: Materials stay bonded for up to five launderings or dry cleanings.
G = Good bond: Materials stay bonded for up to fourteen launderings or dry cleanings.
E = Excellent: Bond appears permanent.

Sequin and Micro Transfers

Brand Names	Manufacturers
Sequin Transfers	Jeweltrim, Inc.

Examples of Use
- Substitute for sewn sequins.
- Produce a smooth metallic surface on fabric costumes that are seen from a distance.

Iron-on sequins are quicker and less costly than sewn sequins, but can be discovered in a close-up. Sequin and micro transfers are a good solution to metallizing stretch fabric, since they cover only in spots. Used in small areas on costumes seen from a distance, they give the appearance of a metal surface. They were successfully used in *Starlight Express* on nylon-spandex fabric. (See the *Starlight Express* costume description in Part Three.)

Description The *sequins* and *micros* are actually circles of colored Mylar glued to a backing, with an adhesive on the underside and a metallic surface on the top. The sequin sheets are of round, regularly spaced sequins, while the micros are irregular in shape and spaced onto the backing in a random pattern. The top surface is bonded to a wide strip of transparent Mylar film. The heat and pressure of an iron causes the underside of the sequin to bond to another surface. Iron-on sequins come on a 15-inch width of Mylar sheet.

How to Use These sequins are easier to apply to a flat piece of fabric than to finished garments, for an iron may not be able to reach the crevices and mold to the curves of a garment. Cut out the sequined film to the desired shape. Lay the fabric on an ironing board or padded table. Then place the film over the fabric and iron with pressure with a medium-heat dry iron.

Where to Find U. S. Distributor: Fred Frankel and Sons, Inc.

Sizes Widths of 15" with a minimum order of $25.

SEQUINS AND MICRO TRANSFERS   **LAUNDER** DRY-CLEAN

Surface	Sequin Transfers	
Acetate Fabric	F	G
Acetate Sheeting	P	F
Acrylic Fabric	E	E
Acrylic Sheeting	P	P
Cotton	E	E
Glass	P	E
Leather	F	F
Linen	E	E
Metal	F	G
Mylar	P	F
Nylon	P	F
Nylon Spandex	E	E
Polyester Fabric	F	G
Polyurethane Foam	O	O
Rayon	E	G
Silk	E	E
Styrofoam	E	P
Vinyl	F	F
Wool	E	E

O = Does not bond.
P = Poor bond: Bond fails with first laundering or dry cleaning.
F = Fair bond: Materials stay bonded for up to five launderings or dry cleanings.
G = Good bond: Materials stay bonded for up to fourteen launderings or dry cleanings.
E = Excellent: Bond appears permanent.

Note: Hand washing is advisable for Sequin Transfers.

Vacuum Plating

Examples of Use

•Impart a shiny metallic surface to a plastic, metal, or other nonporous surface.

This expensive technique is justified when the costume manufacturer must supply durable costumes for a long run—for feature films, and long-running stage productions. Those costumers making items for commercials, walk-around costumes, and those to be seen in close-up viewing—when a convincing metallic surface is needed—also use vacuum plating when the budget is large.

For an example of vacuum-plated costumes, see the description of armor made for the film *Masters of the Universe* in Part Two.

Description

Vacuum plating is a process by which a thin bright film of metal is deposited on an already formed plastic surface in a high vacuum. The usual metal film is of aluminum, though others can also be used. Small clips are attached both to the metal to be deposited and to an electrically heated filament. When electric energy is applied to the filament, the clips melt and form a coating. Vaporization from increased energy causes plating of the product. The coating thickness is about five millionths of an inch. When color other than that of natural aluminum is desired, the colors are included in a final finishing coat of lacquer.

Vacuum plating over cast polystyrene creates convincingly realistic metallic effects, such as on this popular style of fringe.

DESIGN: BILL HARGATE FOR THE BARBARA MANDRELL AND THE MANDRELL SISTERS TELEVISION SERIES. PHOTO: ROBERT W. ZENTIS.

In large cities, vacuum platers will perform the type of work needed by theatrical costumers. Vacuum-plating companies do not specialize in theatrical work, but can usually fit it in between other types of jobs.

Metallic finishes on films and sheets are produced in this manner, as are many of the electronic and decorative fixtures seen daily. Commonly used items that are generally vacuum-plated include doorknobs, hinges, lamp parts, eyeglass frames, and decorative pieces on automobiles.

How to Use

Vacuum plating is done by specialists in professional vacuum-plating companies.

Precautions

Disadvantages of vacuum plating are its price and its high shine. For film, the shine is so high that the surface must usually be sprayed with dulling spray.

Be careful not to nick or scrape plated items, for the repair will require another plating procedure.

Where to Find

Yellow pages under "Vacuum Plating."

Sizes

Up to 72" x 18".

Materials for Forming Costumes

Making a Life Cast

Some of the costumes described in Part Three are body-hugging garments, based on life casts. Some of these are for the full body and others are only for the head. The costumes in this book built from life casts are identified as such. Careful preparation is especially important when building a body-hugging outfit, such as that worn by Batman in the *Batman* films, or by Sirod in the film *Masters of the Universe*, costumes described in this book. To build these costumes, a life cast was required, and in constructing similar costumes, the costume maker or mold maker will face the challenge of creating a life cast of the performer who is to wear the costume.

Making a life cast requires skilled experience and complete cooperation by three to four required mold makers and physical endurance and great patience from the performer, who must remain absolutely motionless for minimum of fifteen minutes (when the head is being cast) to an hour or more (for casting the body). Therefore, creating a life cast also represents a substantial investment in time for all concerned. Obviously, life casts should not be attempted unless at least one or two experienced persons are on hand.

Before anyone inexperienced in the process becomes involved in attempting to create a life cast, books should be studied and/or available videos viewed (some of both are listed in the bibliography), and he or she should work as an assistant to a mold maker experienced in life-casting. Costumes that were built from life casts and which are described in this book are identified as such, giving the reader a variety of situations requiring the life cast.

Following is the method used by many sculptors and special effects studios for building head and body casts.

The Head Cast

1. Three sculptors are preferable working together to create the head cast, for speed is essential. The performer's head will be completely encased during this process, which can take as little as fifteen minutes if the sculptors work efficiently. The performer should be sitting upright in a chair, as relaxed as possible, and remain absolutely motionless, communicating only through pre-planned hand gestures.

2. First, cover the hair with a latex bald cap, such as the kind sold by makeup suppliers. Trace the hair-

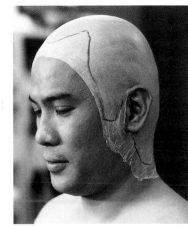

The latex bald cap is fitted to the performer with the hair line traced onto in with an indelible marker.

line onto it with an indelible marker; the marker ink will later transfer to the mold's interior.

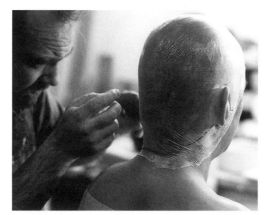

Morticians' wax may be placed behind the ears.

Saving the nose for last, spread the alginate carefully with a small implement.

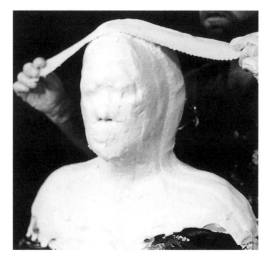

Plaster bandages are now applied over the alginate.

3. For easier removal of the cast, some sculptors place mortician's wax behind the ears, so that the finished plaster ear will be thicker at the undercut behind and less likely to break. Place some wax on the eyebrows and cotton in the ears.

4. Place about four cups of dental alginate in a mixing bowl. Pour over it the amount of water specified by the manufacturer, and mix, preferably with an electric mixer at high speed.

5. Two people should apply the alginate to the back and ears, while one applies the alginate to the face. Spread the mixture by hand, working from top to bottom (gravity causes the alginate to drip), and press the mixture, both firmly and gently, against the face to avoid air bubbles. To slow the setting process, use cool water.

6. Take care to prevent the alginate from flowing into the nose. Save the nose for last, spreading the alginate carefully around the nostrils with an implement like a small brush or a tongue depressor.

7. For extra adhesion, some mold makers cover the area from the forehead down and over the mouth with thin terry-cloth or surgical cotton. This will prevent the alginate from separating and allow the plaster bandages to adhere properly.

8. After the alginate has gelled, apply the plaster bandages, using precut strips of bandages approximately six inches wide and twelve to twenty-four inches in length and other strips cut to about two by six inches. Start at the front of the head with a

twenty-four inch strip; place it in water, following manufacturer's directions; remove and squeeze out most of the water. The plaster bandages will create a temporary mother mold that supports the alginate.

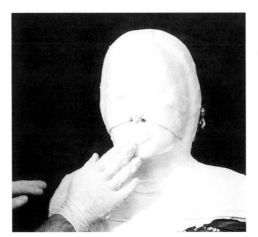

The plaster bandages cover the head except for the nostrils.

9. Apply a median ridge along the edge of the front of the cast, which will extend from the center top of the head, in front of the ears, and down the side of the neck. Start the median ridge by creating a thick strip at the edge of the cast with a thicker layer of bandage. Place this bandage at the edge of the plaster cast and fold it over lengthwise to double its thickness. Reinforce the area around the strips with an additional layer of plaster.

10. Cover the rest of the front of the head up to the median strip, continuing to overlap onto the ridge forming the lip. Apply petroleum jelly to the front edge of the mold as a release agent to prevent the front and back plaster mold pieces from sticking together. Lay an overlapping strip of bandage next to these edges, making sure that the plaster strips conform, and create a lip where the front and back halves will meet.

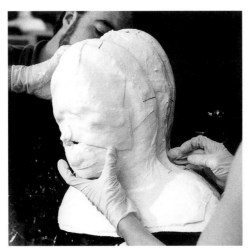

When the mold is dry, separate the front and back molds and carefully lift the front away.

PROCESS COURTESY OF
STICKS AND STONES.

11. Now cover the back of the head in the same manner as the front, making sure to overlap onto the front half that forms the lip.

12. When the back is dry, in about three to eight minutes, separate the front portion of the cast from the back and carefully lift it away from the alginate-covered head.

13. Using a spatula or butter knife, slice the alginate open down the back of the head; some mold makers start at the neck and work upward to the crown while placing a finger between the model and the alginate for guidance. Then with the performer's head leaning down and forward, gently pull it away from the head and ears. Now pull off the complete cast. The alginate and plaster will stay joined in the front due to the terrycloth or surgical cotton. Place the back half together with the front using more strips of plaster bandages.

14. Fill the nostril holes with water-based clay or alginate or mortician's wax, being careful not to distort the nose. (Mortician's wax is available at Pink House Studios and Burman Industries.) Cover the nostril holes with a plaster bandage. Test the front and back pieces together for fit, making sure that the lip touches together all the way around, and firmly wrap the two pieces together with plaster bandages. If the alginate pulls away from the plaster mother mold, use a dab of wet plaster or cyanoacrylate to hold it in place, then reach inside to be sure that the alginate is placed correctly.

15. The plaster positive mold can now be cast from the negative mold, and because the negative mold is of alginate, a release agent will not be necessary.

The Full-Body Cast

To make the full-body cast, three or four sculptors should work together. This process takes between one and four hours, depending on the number of sculptors and their level of skill. Because the performer assumes one position without moving for at least an hour, it is important to make conditions as comfortable as possible. And since communication may be necessary, decide on a set of simple signals that do not involve body movement.

1. The first step is to build a support system for the performer's arms. Onto a piece of plywood, approximately four by four feet, glue a one-inch-thick expanded polystyrene sheet, such as Styrofoam, the same size as the plywood. The foam provides both insulation and firmer support. Attach to the foam and plywood two vertical beams—two by twos or a comparably sized pipe the length of the performer's hand height—positioned at the performer's hand placement.

2. Also have ready prepared armatures that will support the front and back mold pieces as they are pulled from the body. Later, the armatures serve as supports throughout the casting process. Build the armatures from wooden one-by-ones, as "H"s with two crossbars. The height should reach the shoulders and the width should span the outside of the arms.

3. Make the body cast from alginate or plaster bandages. Alginate, the more expensive, imparts more detail and is preferable for making molds for costumes that are viewed close-up. Plaster bandages are less expensive, lightweight, set up quickly, and are satisfactory for molds for costumes viewed at some distance where detail is unimportant. Some mold makers, however, prefer to use plaster of Paris because it holds more detail than the bandages and is less expensive than alginate.

4. When using plaster bandages, first cover the performer's body with a release agent, such as petroleum jelly or cold cream, or dress the performer in a spandex bodysuit and coat it with spray-on vegetable oil. Then have the performer assume the position best suited to the needs of the costume.

5. With alginate, apply in the same manner as described for making a cast of the head. If plaster bandages are to be used, start applying the bandages as one layer to the front half of the body. An alternative method is to apply the bandages two at a time; the two layers should be stacked and set up in advance. Be sure to overlap the bandages when applying them with either method.

6. When this first layer of either alginate or plaster bandages is set, add a second, reinforcing layer of plaster bandages to the front of the body. Dip the plaster bandages in water and apply directly over the first layer.

7. Before casting the back, create a ridge, as described for making the head cast, to the edges of the front piece so that the front and back can be taken off the body separately.

8. Place the armatures next to the figure, and quickly attach the armatures with plaster bandages.

9. Remove the mold from the model, being careful not to twist it. The armature should help prevent any twist.

10. Coat the interior of the plaster mold with a release agent, such as petroleum jelly or green soap, and create the positive form by pouring in the casting material, usually plaster of Paris or Ultracal. Some mod makers prefer to cast in fiberglass filled with ridgid urethane foam.

11. When the casting material is hardened, the original, negative mold may be peeled off, leaving a positive cast of the figure. The head can be cast separately and attached to the body with plaster bandages.

Hands and feet may be cast by quickly dipping correctly positioned hands and feet into a tub of alginate. One should practice this procedure a few times so the mold will turn out correctly. These pieces can also be attached to the body with plaster bandages.

Sources for other methods of making life casts can be found in the bibliography.

Casting Plastics

The word *plastic* means pliable and formable. We also use *plastic* to identify synthetic materials; however, the term actually applies to all substances that are soft during formation and moldable, but that eventually solidify. At some point in their manufacture, all plastics are truly *plastic*, either as liquids or as solid sheets, pellets, or tubing, and are pliant enough to be formed and molded.

The Society of Plastics Engineers defines *plastics* as a large and varied group of materials that consist of or contain, as an essential ingredient, a substance of high molecular weight which, while solid in the finished state, at some stage of its manufacture is soft enough to be formed into various shapes—most usually through the application (either singly or together) of heat and pressure.

The range of synthetic plastic formulations is wide, and the same plastic may appear as many varieties. For example, polyester may be a liquid resin, a paint ingredient, a textile fiber, a surfboard, a transparent film, or something else. Some plastics are widely known by popular brand names, though the same plastic may be manufactured under many other brands. Plexiglas, from Rohm and Haas Company, is just one brand name for acrylic plastic. In our everyday lives, we are surrounded by cast plastic objects, from toothbrushes to armchairs, shoes, jewelry, and rain ponchos.

Plastics are divided into two groups: *thermoplastics* and *thermosetting plastics*. *Thermoplastics* soften when exposed to heat and harden after cooling. This forming process may be repeated indefinitely with thermoplastic materials. The liquid resins of the thermoplastic group require specialized conditions for forming cast objects and are more suited to forming thousands of copies, as in industrial manufacture. *Thermosetting plastics*, or *thermosets*, are changed by the chemical process of cross-linking, which is caused by the action of a catalyst, into a solid form. Once formed, thermosets will not return to the original liquid state, because the molecular structure has been altered permanently, though they may soften at temperatures above 350°F.

Most of the plastics discussed in this section are thermosetting resins because most of the casting plastics used for making theatrical costumes and props are thermosets. Costumers most commonly use cast plastics for making objects like space suits, armor, helmets, jewelry, and decorative appliqués. Many of today's casting and forming techniques originated in the makeup field. Innovative makeup artists like Dick Smith, Stan Winston, and Rob Burman, when creating facial prosthetic pieces, carried those methods over to making body parts and masks, and they and others adapted those techniques to create puppets and props, which led to the development of many of the unusual modern costume effects.

Listed below are the principal groups of liquid casting resins included in this section and which are most used by theatrical costume and properties craftspersons. Brand names are not included in most sections because there are far too many to list.

Thermoplastics	Acrylic
	Ethyl Vinyl Acetate (Hot-melt glue sticks)
	Polyamides (Hot-melt glue sticks)
	Polyester
	Vinyl
Thermosetting Plastics	Chloroprene Rubber (Neoprene)
	Epoxy
	Modified Glass Fiber Reinforced Gypsum System
	Polyester (Cross-linked with styrene)
	Polyurethane
	Silicone

Foaming Plastics	Polyurethane
Miscellaneous Materials	Latex (Natural Rubber)
	Latex Foam
	Papier-mâché

Working Methods Mold making and casting with plastics are complex and specialized crafts that require extensive skill and technical knowledge that is much too complex and specific to be covered here. Only basic techniques for dealing with one-part molds along with an overview of various casting methods are covered in this section. The remainder of this section serves as a guide for selecting the appropriate materials. For more complete and advanced techniques, consult the following references: Thurston James's *Casting and Molding for the Theatre*; Tom Savinis's *Grand Illusions*, and Time-Life's *Working with Plastics*. Instructive videotapes are available; particularly helpful are the series from Burman Foam Products, Inc., *The Videoguide to Special Makeup Effects*, and Ball Consulting's *Mold Making and Casting*, which serve as guides to general casting and molding. Reading books and watching videos will supplement hands-on experience, but the costumer will learn the most by taking workshops and classes, apprenticing, and through trial and error.

Health and Safety Almost all of the materials discussed in this section are hazardous—both to the body and to the environment. Thus, it is important to take the correct precautions while using these materials; be sure to read carefully the MSDSs. The safety measures outlined below are only general. Specifics for each type of material are included in the individual sections of this category.

- Look for the least toxic products. Compare brands by requesting and reading technical product literature and MSDSs.

- Work in a well-ventilated workspace, provided with either a local exhaust system, such as a spray booth, or work next to a window outfitted with an exhaust fan. Neither respirator cartridges or respiratory-system protectors guard against emissions from heated plastics.

- Use the correct kind of work gloves. Ask glove manufacturers which ones provide the most effective protection against the specific materials being used. Skin-barrier creams are not adequate.

- Use ventilation or wear the appropriate respirator to guard against particular toxic vapors from solvent-based products.

- When working with powders or dusts, such as plaster, alginate and moulage, wear a dust mask to avoid lung irritation.

- When working with a fairly large quantity of materials, be sure to wear protective clothing.

- Wear gloves and try not to get plastics or solvents on the skin. If that happens, clean skin first with acetone, and then wash well with warm water and soap. Immediately replace the oils of the skin with a good emollient cream. Acetone, if left on the skin, leaves the skin open to absorption by other chemicals. When using acetone, keep it away from flames and heat.

- Take care not to mix catalysts and promoters or accelerators together, and do not mix materials in amounts other than those specified by the manufacturers. Explosions and decomposition can easily occur.

- Supply the work area with an ABC-rated, dry-powder fire extinguisher.

- Follow instructions carefully. If ingredients are not mixed exactly, safety hazards as well as an unsuccessful casting will occur.

- *Do not smoke or use near flames or lit cigarettes, and keep away from food and drinks.*

Mold Making Plastic materials can be cast in molds that are flexible or rigid, handmade or machine-made, and which have been crafted from a variety of materials, i.e., metal, plaster, wood, sand, synthetic rubber, and vinyl. Metal molds, the strongest rigid molds, are used by industry to turn out hundreds of duplicates; metal molds may be used to produce the multiples required by corporate theme parks such as Disneyland.

The costumer needs far fewer duplicates. But the costumer must consider the shape of the form to be duplicated and decide whether a one-part or a multiple-part mold will be required and whether the type of mold selected should be rigid or flexible. Only the simplest of forms can be made with a one-part mold; examples of such forms are breastplates of armor, masks, or a warrior's shield.

More complex spherical forms, such as complete heads, a full helmet, a small, round bead, or forms that include undercuts, such as dragon heads or a rose in full bloom, require multiple-part molds. Undercuts are indentations or projections that may lock a form into a mold, preventing its release. In mask making, the undersides of ears and curls are undercuts. Casting a form with a number of undercuts may also require that the multiple-part mold be of flexible material, for undercuts make removal of the cast piece difficult, while a flexible mold ensures easier removal.

Molds are either *negative* (cavities *into* which a casting material is placed) or *positive* (forms *over* which material is placed). Into negative molds, liquid plastic is poured, or successive layers of plastic are laid—and often layered with an inserted reinforcing material. Onto positive molds, plastic materials can be sprayed, brushed, laminated, or layered.

In any case, the first stage of the work of casting is to select a model or form (also called a pattern or master) to be duplicated. The easiest model to work from will be made of nonporous materials. Porous models must be sealed before using. A model can be found and used as is, or it can be sculpted. Many mold makers prefer using an oil- or wax-based plasticine clay to sculpt the original model.

Rigid Molds *Rigid molds* are most often made from plaster of Paris (or casting plaster), Hydrocal, and number 1 pottery plaster. Plaster of Paris is inexpensive, easy to work with, and is ready to use in less than a half hour. Hydrocal is actually a gypsum cement and harder than plaster of Paris. Its strength allows it to retain intricate detail and withstand more repeated use. Unlike plaster of Paris, Hydrocal accepts pressure and is suitable for heat-cured molds. Number 1 pottery plaster is highly absorbent and the preferred material for absorption casting (also called slip casting), which requires that the mold absorb liquid, allowing the cast piece to set. Plaster bandages, actually produced for medical casts, are one of the most popular mold materials.

Rigid molds can also be of materials like metal or polyester resin with fiberglass. Metal molds, as mentioned above, are commonly used in industry because they are strong and last a long time. But for most costume shops, metal molds are impractical for the fewer number of duplications required. If a large number of duplications are necessary a master can be sent to a professional molding company for either injection or compression molding. For information on metal molds, see *Plastics Designs and Materials* by Sylvia Katz or *Industrial Plastics* by Ronald J. and David T. Baird.

Methods of Making Rigid Molds

To keep the work surface clean, cover it with a polyethylene sheet, which is resistant to almost all materials. To keep the mixing bowl and stirring implements clean, coat

Making a clay model and its one-piece plaster of Paris negative mold are the beginning stages for many casting processes.

SCULPTURE: MAKEUP & EFFECTS LABS INC.
PHOTO: ROBERT W. ZENTIS

them with a light film of kerosene or petroleum jelly before use. (Petroleum jelly, like Vaseline, is much safer than kerosene.) When cleaning up, rinse the tools in a bucket of water before the plaster hardens and never pour cleanup plaster into a sink, drain, or toilet. The plaster will harden and plug up the plumbing.

For a *one-part mold*, prepare the model by resting it face up on a wooden block that is at least one inch larger on all sides. Secure the model onto the working surface with plasticine clay, shaping and smoothing the clay from the model onto the base. Secure the model by blocking up the bottom of an open container like a vinyl pail, or creating a box by building up four walls of plasticine at the edge of the wooden base. The plasticine walls should be one inch thick, and a minimum of one inch higher than the highest point of the model. Brush the model, its base, and the interior walls of the box or container with a light coating of a parting agent, such as petroleum jelly.

To make a *plaster mold*, use a flat-bottomed plastic dishpan or mixing bowl, and mix the plaster into the water at a ratio of roughly two parts plaster to one part water. Sift the plaster into the pan by hand, distributing it evenly, until an island of dry plaster and almost no exposed water is left on the surface of the pan. After three to four minutes, stir the plaster mixture until it is smooth and without lumps. The mixture should be thick, but pourable. Pour the plaster into the container, up to the top. Allow to cure overnight, and the next day remove the plasticine walls, then lift the model from the wooden base. Remove the model by loosening the mold with a gentle bending and twisting action. It may also be necessary to place it on a flat surface and wedge fingers or a tool between the model and mold for removal.

Plaster, Hydrocal, and pottery plaster molds can be strengthened by adding hemp fiber, burlap, or wire screening. Chemical additives, like an acrylic latex cement hardener, can also be used. To control the rate of thickening, use warm water, which speeds hardening. Plaster will also harden faster if it is stirred for a ong time. Adding vinegar to the mix retards hardening which is desireable when adding detail, such as in building thin walls around facial features.

Never use stored plaster without first testing it, for if it has been stored in a damp or humid atmosphere, it absorbs moisture and will not harden properly.

Before casting each piece, check the mold interior surface for flaws. Use paint thinner and scrape the plaster with a knife to remove any release agent, then fill or rebuild any damaged areas with spackling compound or a small amount of thick plaster. If necessary, smooth out any surface

A hot-air, or heat gun is used for drying the clay master.
SCULPTURE: MAKEUP & EFFECTS LABS, INC.PHOTO: ROBERT W. ZENTIS.

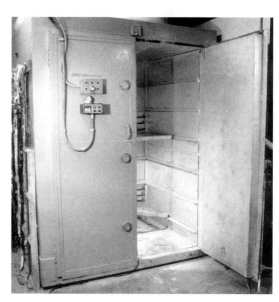

The curing process is being accelerated by placing the mold in a large industrial oven like this one or in a smaller industrial oven.
PHOTO: ROBERT W. ZENTIS.

roughness with fine steel wool. Cracks and breaks in the cured mold can be repaired with white glue. After pouring, wait for eight to ten hours before removing the casting. Freshly poured plaster retains some water in its crystals and will continue to gain strength for another five to seven days as the water evaporates from the casting. The curing process can be accelerated by placing the mold in a 150°F oven for twelve to twenty-four hours, depending on the size of the casting. After curing, coat the mold with several layers of shellac, lacquer, varnish, or white glue, which work as sealants, making the mold smooth and nonabsorbent.

Polyester resin and *fiberglass* mold making follows the same process as used for casting these materials.

Flexible Molds   *Flexible molds* are similar to rigid molds, but are made with different materials. Flexible molds bend when they are removed from the model, thus preserving intricate forms and details. A mold for one-time use can be from alginate, but those for reuse are usually made of natural and synthetic rubbers.

Flexible mold compounds are most frequently made of silicone rubber, natural latex rubber, polyurethane rubber, vinyl, alginate, or moulage. The correct consistency of a properly mixed compound will differ according to its ingredient material, and the compound will remain at pouring consistency for ninety seconds to twenty minutes, depending upon the ingredients chosen. To protect the mold compound from moisture, use metal, glass, or plastic utensils and containers. Wooden utensils and disposable paper contain moisture and may prevent the compound from fully curing. For these same reasons, plasticine clay should be used if sculpting the original. When the mold is complete, apply a light coat of mold release, wrap in waterproof covering, and store in a cool, dark, and dry place.

Flexible molds are less apt to chip than are molds of plaster or stone. Thin molds of flexible materials are more pliable. and thick molds are stronger and more rigid.

Silicone rubber compounds create the most satisfactory flexible molds. Though expensive, they capture fine detail, and require no release agent. They are room-temperature vulcanizing (RTV), and do not all have to be heated in an oven, though some may be, which allows the resin casting to cure completely in a shorter time. Any oven used for plastics must not also be used for food. The oven should be vented to the outside and be fitted with a range or other hood system. The silicone peels easily off of the model and is flexible enough to use for designs containing deep undercuts. Silicone rubber is tough, tear resistant, resilient, and long-lasting. It withstands temperatures elevated to the melting point of many resins.

Silicones and other resins emit dangerous fumes when heated. Silicone rubber is considerably more expensive than latex and some other flexible mold materials. Costs can be cut by reinforcing with a stretch fabric and casting thin molds into plaster shells, as discussed below.

Typically, the silicone is mixed in a ratio of ten parts silicone to one part catalyst. Stir thoroughly until the mixture is uniform in color. Spoon out a thin coating of the mixture onto the model. Allow to set for about an hour. Add another coating of the silicone mixture and allow to set, again for about an hour. Add additional coatings depending upon the size of the object to be cast. The mold will cure in about twelve hours. Costume craftspersons add a filler to extend the volume of the silicone economically. Cab-O-Sil and ground silicone rubber are the most effective fillers and, as with all materials, should be used according to package instructions. Use discretion when choosing a filler, for most are hazardous to the health since particles from the air can enter the lungs. All fillers reduce elasticity and in excess amounts cause brittleness.

Latex sold for casting and mold making is liquid rubber to which ammonia and other ingredients have been added. When forming the mold, coat the model with liquid soap or aerosol silicone mold release, not an oil or grease. If the model contains cutout areas, those areas should first be filled with plasticine so that the latex may be later removed. Then coat the model with the liquid rubber by dipping it into a container of latex or by brushing or carefully pouring the latex over the model surface. Check carefully for small air bubbles and eliminate them by dabbing with a brush.

Dry the latex by air, hair dryer, or a low-heat oven. Air drying will take at least eight hours. Give the latex-coated object a second coating, and perhaps a third and fourth, depending upon the size of the object and the viscosity of the latex.

After it is completely cured, which will take several days, remove the model from the latex. When cured, latex produces a flexible skin that can be peeled off in one piece. Undercuts are not as much of a problem when forming latex molds as they are with other materials.

Vinyl is another excellent flexible material, though it can be used only if the casting material can withstand 350°F. Hot-melt vinyl may be purchased either as a sheeting or a liquid. It is melted at 350°F, then poured over the master. When the vinyl is cool, it pulls away easily from the object inside and leaves a good image. Vinyl also contains a natural release agent. Vinyl is especially hazardous, however, because of the vinyl chloride fumes and because of the danger of working with such high heat.

Polyurethane RTV is prepared by combining two components: the resin and a catalyst. The chemical reaction causes the mixture to set in six hours, with another ten hours at room temperature necessary for complete curing. It is important to weigh the two components with an accurate scale, for a small error can change the consistency of the mold. If it is too soft, it may tear; and if too hard, it can crack. Brands will vary, so the manufacturer's instructions must be followed carefully. Polyurethane molds always require release agents.

Alginate, derived from algae and favored by dentists for casting dental pieces, is most frequently used for casting prosthetics (body parts), life masks, and intricate designs. It is flexible, fast-setting, and self-releasing. It will not adhere to any material, not even itself. With a complex pattern, only one casting may be possible, for alginate is soft and fragile and may require cutting from the mold. It is easy to use and available as a powder to be mixed with water.

When forming a mold, pour the alginate into a container approximately one inch larger than the model. Mix cold water into alginate powder in ratios prescribed by the product directions. Then stir with a spatula or electric mixer until thick but pourable, about forty-five seconds. If it becomes too thick to pour, more water must be added. Since solidification takes only one-and-a-half to three minutes, the work must be done quickly. To slow the set time, add ice water in the mixing process, or use a prosthetic grade cream (PCG) like that manufactured by the Teledyne-Getz Co., which with its special additive can slow the set-up time to sixteen minutes.

Quickly insert the model, wait until the material has set up, and remove the alginate mold from the box. Then very gently remove the model from the flexible mold. As alginate molds are moist, they must not be used with casting materials that do not cure when in the presence of water, and they must be used quickly, for alginates shrink and distort when left standing.

Moulage is a flexible impression product that is thermoplastic, so it may be resculpted and revised. Also an alginate material, it is derived from moist and shredded seaweed. To prepare for mold-making, heat in a double boiler until melted, then brush onto the model while still hot. A release agent is not necessary. Where moulage is used for a living subject, it should first be cooled. Since moulage is not strong, it needs to be reinforced, either by laying it into a *mother mold*, or plaster jacket, or inserting one or more layers of cheesecloth, to retain the desired shape.

Moulage is excellent for casting small, detailed objects made from casting materials that are compatible with water. Like alginate, moulage molds usually have only a one-time use, and they shrink and distort if left standing.

Plasticine oil- or wax-based clay forms a simple shallow flexible mold for one-time use. First, coat the model with a release agent, and then push a thick slab of plasticine into it. Press the plasticine firmly into the details. When the details are satisfactory, carefully remove the model from the plasticine. Lay this mold flat, and cast a duplicate of the model by the above methods.

A plasticine clay mold can be used immediately and without curing, but it will serve for only one casting because it must be stretched out of shape to remove the casting.

Supporting a Thin Flexible Mold If the flexible mold is thin, or if thin sections in a mold are supporting a heavy casting, those sections must be supported by building a *plaster jacket,* or *mother mold,* around the flexible mold. Plaster bandaging is the most recommended material for making plaster jackets. When using a jacket, it is best to avoid extreme undercuts.

Casting

Several of the plastics discussed in this section—including polyester, epoxy, polyurethane, and silicone—are comprised of two or several components which always include the resin itself and its hardener. Other components can be fillers, foaming agents, and hardeners. When using multiple component systems, careful measuring and thorough mixing are essential. Take care not to introduce moisture or air bubbles into the mixture.

Follow product directions exactly. The same chemical may be formulated differently by different manufacturers. Measure resins by weight and hardeners by the drop. Proportions of the two depend on the desired characteristics. The higher the proportion of hardener, the shorter the curing time and the more brittle the casting. To adjust proportions, mix several test batches and choose the one that produces the best combinations of properties.

As with all casting compounds, it is important to avoid making air bubbles. Always pour the ingredients slowly down the side of the mixing container and mix gently. Use only utensils and containers that are clean, dry, and without wax coatings. Water and wax coatings can contaminate the resin.

The best hand-stirring utensil for small batches is a narrow metal kitchen spatula or a flat wooden stick. Resins can also be mixed by electric mixers—Jiffy brand has the highest recommendation—which should be set at a very slow speed. When mixing, always pour the hardener into the resin, following specific instructions for each kind of casting compound.

A Solid Casting in a Flexible Mold

To make a solid casting in a flexible mold, prepare a mold as described above. Make sure that the mold is covered with a mold release, or parting agent, so that the cured cast form will separate easily. Different molding and casting materials require different kinds of release and parting agents. The most common mold-release agents for this phase are polyvinyl alcohol (PVA), silicone spray, and petroleum jelly. First brush on one coat of the release agent, allow it to dry thoroughly, and then brush on a second coat. For any hard-to-reach details or undercuts, pour a small amount of release into the mold, swish it around, and pour out the excess.

Mix the casting materials together, following instructions. Work slowly to avoid air bubbles. Rotate and tap several times to allow air bubbles to escape. Set the mold aside and allow the casting to cure. It is cured when the resin residue in the mixing container is no longer tacky and when a firmly pressed finger does not leave an impression. Then peel the cast material from the mold. Clean the mold as described above before commencing with the next casting.

Hollow Casting in a Rigid Mold

Begin by applying mold release except when using a molding or casting material that does not require one. Spread it over the interior, stopping one-eighth-inch short of its edge. This one-eighth-inch space allows the casting material to grip the edges of the mold pieces when curing, thus reducing shrinkage along the seams.

Coat the mold with the casting material, spreading it evenly with a small brush. The number of coats applied will differ depending on the type of material being cast. Large objects may require thicker casting than small objects. Layers of reinforcing material may be added between coats of casting to strengthen large pieces.

When the casting is ready, gently pull it away, separating the mold from the casting. After the casting is removed, clean the mold by first removing surface imperfections with rasps and small woodworking tools to carve and shave away imperfections. Large defects can be restored with patches of resin sculpted into place with a wood tool, small chisel, or utility knife.

If the mold is unstable and irregular in shape, add wads of clay to the outer bottom side of the mold or place the mold into a container of sand. After the cured casting is released, it can be finished by cutting away unwanted pieces, sanding away rough spots, and polishing.

Mold Releases

Most mold materials require a *release*, or *parting*, agent to prevent the casting material from adhering to the mold's interior. Others release casting material naturally as a result of their composition or because they contain water, which releases certain materials. Some mold materials that require no release agent are alginate, hot-melt rubber, and silicone-casting rubber.

Slip-casting materials, like Neoprene and latex, which are absorption cast in a plaster mold, do not require a release agent. Other materials that do not stick to moist surfaces are polyethylene, polypropylene, and most hot-melt glues. These materials work well in damp plaster molds. To dampen a plaster mold, soak the mold in water for several minutes.

Petroleum jelly, green soap, liquid dishwasher detergent, and wax are effective parting agents for Celastic, papier-mâché, and gypsum products, like plaster. Green soap can be properly prepared by chipping the soap and placing it into hot water until melted.

Polyvinyl alcohol is an effective parting agent for most epoxies, polyester resins, and polyurethanes. As it is sprayed or brushed into a mold, the alcohol evaporates, leaving a coating of vinyl. This process is repeated several times to ensure a proper release.

Thin sheetings—like Mylar, polyethylene film, or aluminum foil—can also serve as release agents if loss of detail is not a factor.

Manufacturers' directions usually include recommendations on the proper release agents. For more information and an excellent chart on release agents, see Thurston James's *The Prop Builder's Molding & Casting Handbook*.

Bonding

These casting plastics can be bonded to themselves with the liquid form of the plastics or with specific adhesives. For information on bonding, see the recommendations in each individual section.

Coloring

Colorants for liquid plastics are available at most plastics suppliers. To achieve transparencies, colorants are added during the molding process while the plastic is still in a liquid state. Some plastics can be colored only with specific kinds of pigments, dyes, and paints. When adding color, drop in a small amount at a time to both resin and hardener until each is the desired color, then pour the hardener into the resin. For opaque painting after completion of curing, follow the specific recommendations for each plastic material. Before using colorants, be sure to obtain and refer to their MSDSs.

Acrylic

Some Manufacturers

Imperial Chemical Industries Ltd. (ICI), UK

Long Dental Manufacturing Company

Rohm and Haas Company

Examples of Use
- Make glasslike jewelry and ornamental attachments.
- Create inflexible animal body parts like teeth and claws.
- Use for jewelry, animal teeth, and special glasslike pieces that will be seen close up.

Acrylic casting is more appropriate for film than for the theatre, where audience viewing distance allows designers to choose more practical materials.

Description
Acrylic is not commonly used by costumers because it is expensive and difficult to work with. However, in the commercial manufacture of synthetic glass, it is the most frequently used plastic material. Acrylic is lightweight, clear, and sparkling. Its surface is softer than that of epoxy, similar to that of aluminum. Casting acrylic is complex and difficult, and because of the complexity of working with it, most artists and craftspeople use liquid acrylic only when they must have its specific glasslike effects. Acrylic can be polished to a high shine.

Like other resins, acrylic is obtainable as a two-part system in liquid form accompanied by a separate hardener. Acrifix 90 by Rohm and Haas Company and Tensol No. 7 by I. C. I. both work well as casting materials for items that must appear glassy.

For dentistry, acrylic comes in powder form with liquid binder and catalyst. This form of acrylic is an opaque material and is ideal for casting pieces such as teeth and nails. Available colors are off-whites and pinks. Opaque dental acrylic is easier to use than the pourable, clear acrylic, and the user need not be as exacting as when working with clear, liquid acrylic.

Other forms of acrylic are more accessible to the costumer; for example, acrylic in sheet plastic is fairly simple to form. As a base for a wide range of paints, acrylic is in general use today, and acrylic-based adhesives bond to many surfaces. Items on the commercial market made from acrylic are jewelry, dental plates and teeth, eyeglass lenses, watch and clock faces, drinking vessels and dishes.

How to Use   The opaque dental acrylics involve mixing together a liquid monomer and a powder polymer. Neither material needs to be weighed or measured as when working with the clear, pourable mixtures. Add liquid acrylic to the powder until the powder is just covered with liquid, then stir to wet all the particles. More liquid gives lower viscosity and a longer working time, and less liquid gives a thicker viscosity with a shorter working time. Because the powders are almost always pigmented, one need not mix in pigments, which can cause trapped air bubbles.

All acrylics are copolymers composed of acrylic acid, methyacrylic acid, esters of these acids (e.g., methyl-acrylate) or acrylonitrile. Before working with acrylics, learn which resin is being used to assure it will be satisfactory for the purpose and to become familiar with the health hazards. The acrylic least hazardous to health is methyl methacrylate. The following is a synopsis of the process followed when working with clear, liquid acrylics.

The preferred mold material is room-temperature-vulcanizing (RTV) silicone for multiple flexible molds. Flexible molds for one-time use can be alginate. Polyethylene is also suitable and is readily available in many preformed objects (ice cube trays, small kitchen utensils and containers, etc.). For rigid molds, dental stone is an ideal material, while glass and steel also work well and are easily obtainable in preformed goods.

First mix the catalyst, bleach, and pigment together, following strictly the manufacturer's directions. Then add the acrylic resin, stir well for a minimum of two minutes, and pour the mixture into the mold.

When casting acrylic or any other resins, the thicker the casting, the less catalyst is needed. There is not as much heat buildup for acrylic during the curing period as there is when curing polyester, though some contraction takes place. Air bubbles tend to stay in the mixture unless the following process is followed carefully, or unless the air can be removed in a vacuum chamber. Limited access to vacuum chambers is one of the problems of working with acrylic, though several vacuum dental devices are available for molds of small dimensions (e.g., teeth).

Castings over three quarters of an inch generate a lot of heat and often need to be cured in a mold immersed in cold water. If the resin cures at temperatures over 130°F, bubbles usually form as the resin evaporates. Before actually casting acrylic, test some small pieces to learn the process. Use an immersion-type bayonet thermometer or a glass-stem thermometer wrapped in aluminum foil to better control the formation of air bubbles. If bubbles still form when curing is below 130°F, decrease the catalyst by 0.5 percent.

If the heat during curing rises over 160°F, quickly immerse the mold in ice cold water, which will reduce the curing action and stop the formation of bubbles. If the top of the form is tacky and not curing, cover with detergent (in the ratio of nine parts water to one part detergent). Pour a layer of the detergent mixture one-quarter-of-an-inch thick over the acrylic. The resin may take several hours to harden. Once it is hard, pour off the detergent and clean and dry the acrylic's surface. If no heat has been generated during the curing process, a brownish cast may develop. Heat finishing or annealing will cause it to disappear. (Annealing is a process of slow heating and cooling down that increases toughness.) Discoloration may also occur if the catalyst is old.

Bond acrylic to itself with methylene chloride using the *solvent bonding* technique (see page 244.) Sometimes, 1,1,1-trichloroethane can also be used. Ethylene dichloride is sold for this purpose, but it is extremely toxic. A formula for a modified solvent gluing system, recommended by the Rohm and Haas Company, is as follows:

Methylene chloride	60%
Methyl methacrylate monomer stabilized	40%
1/2 strength peroxide catalyst	2.4 grams per pint

Cast acrylic pieces can be bonded with any of the *adhesives* mentioned in the section on acrylic sheeting as well as with the same acrylic mixture used for the casting.

Color with resin pigment during the mixing process. Use the pigment judiciously in small amounts and follow manufacturer's specific instructions. Acrylic is marketed in a wide range of off-whites and pinks.

Solvent for Cleanup Methyline chloride or methyl methacrylate, followed by soap and water.

Precautions Acrylic in a liquid state is highly volatile. Be sure to cover it carefully before storing.

Health and Safety Most acrylics are highly volatile and are toxic due to inhalation and absorption through the skin. Choose an acrylic containing methyl methacrylate, with a higher threshold limit value (TLV), rather than one with methyl acrylate, ethyl acrylate, acrylonitirile, n-butyl acrylate, or acrylic acid. Methylene chloride, a common ingredient in many resins systems, metabolizes to carbon monoxide in the blood and is a suspect carcinogen.

Cast in local ventilation or with respiratory protection appropriate for the particular resin. Wear goggles, gloves, and long sleeves.

Where to Find Plastics supply stores, dental suppliers, medical suppliers, special-effects distributors.

Chloroprene Rubber (Neoprene)

Manufacturer Chicago Latex Products

Examples of Use
- Cast flexible or semiflexible costume pieces, like armor and jewelry.
- Create fantasy headdresses.

Neoprene has been used successfully for casting masks, armor, and reptile skin. Jane Clugston, costume maker and sculptor in Oregon, prefers Neoprene over other liquid casting materials, especially when many duplications are required. Thurston James, prop maker, prefers Neoprene over most other materials for casting and has used it for creating masks. In the *Armor* section of Part Three (pages 297-298) is a description of armor made with cast Neoprene.

Description   Neoprene was the first of the synthetic rubbers to be manufactured in large scale and is among the densest of this family of materials. It is a water-based material and is excellent for casting shells or hollow pieces. It is used much as is natural rubber latex, though Neoprene has a shorter curing time and is harder.

Neoprene is both firm and flexible. Neoprene's strength is comparable to that of natural rubber, and Neoprene is also resistant to flame, oxidation, and aging. On the negative side, Neoprene in its latex state is thinner than natural rubber and thus more difficult to control. It is too toxic for use except with a local exhaust system, and it is more expensive than natural rubber latex.

Though Neoprene is not widely used among costume makers, it has proven effective for creating decorative items and costume accessories. Neoprene requires a more careful working process than do some other casting materials. Those who use it find general-purpose Neoprene the most suitable for costume- and prop making. It is popular with puppeteers for making both body parts and clothing accessories. Commercially, Neoprene is used for such varied products as wet suits, gaskets, flooring, and oil pipelines.

At the date of this writing, 1998, Chicago Latex Products is the only company selling it in nonindustrial quantities.

How to Use   Use in a similar manner to natural rubber latex.

The mold should be of plaster of Paris or Hydrocal. Use either no release agent or a small amount of talc. Release agents like petroleum jelly clog the pores of the mold, preventing the escape of the liquid from the Neoprene.

Performance masks, like these, are easily cast from Neoprene.

DESIGN, CONSTRUCTION, AND PHOTO: THURSTON JAMES.

The most common *casting* technique is slip casting. Pour liquid Neoprene up to the brim of a plaster mold. In one to three hours, depending on the manufacturer's directions, when the walls of the casting begin to reach the desired thickness, pour off the excess liquid. (Setting time depends more on absorption qualities of the mold and on the specific product being used than on weather conditions, and may take between two and five hours.) The finished shell will be no more than one-quarter-inch thick. Allow about ten to twelve hours for curing before pulling the cast piece from the mold.

Neoprene shrinks during curing, making it easier to pull from the mold, though possibly causing costume-fitting problems.

Paints for Neoprene can be acrylic as well as some others. Neoprene has some flexibility but does not stretch.

Bonding Neoprene to itself or other materials can occur during casting, or the Neoprene latex can be used to adhere other objects to the cast Neoprene afterwards. Adhesives made with cyanoacrylate, Neoprene, and other synthetic rubbers bond Neoprene both to itself and to other materials. See the pages 37-38 of Adhesives.

Solvent for Cleanup Soap and water.

Precautions Be aware of the tendency of Neoprene to shrink to avoid fitting problems with costumes.

Liquid Neoprene evaporates quickly and must be stored in an airtight container. Do not buy more than needed, since Neoprene has a short shelf life of only about a year.

Health and Safety Use protective clothing, gloves, and goggles. Use an air-supplied respirator and work only in local exhaust ventilation, such as a spray booth, for exposure to Neoprene vapors can be very dangerous. Contact with eyes can cause irreversible damage. Contact with the skin requires immediate washing with soap and water. If there is contact with clothing, immediately remove and launder it. Take care to follow all label directions and MSDSs.

Where to Find Manufacturer

Epoxy

Some Manufacturers The Dow Chemical Company

Hexcel Corporation

Reichhold Chemicals, Inc.

Rezollin, Inc.

Shell Chemical Company

Examples of Use •Cast metallic-looking jewelry and decorative items.

•Form rigid accessories like armor, headdresses, and weapons.

•Produce animal parts like shells, heads, and other body pieces.

•Make molds.

When making jewelry and other rigid accessories, start with a flexible mold like polyethylene or silicone. To add embedments (other items such a glass, stones, or wood), make the articles in three pours with the embedments added between pours. The first pour is of clear resin, catalyzed at six to eight drops per ounce.

Thick epoxy can be filled with metal powders like colored aluminum bronzing powder and then shaped like clay to create small jewel-like and decorative forms. Other objects, like glass and beads, may be pressed into the plastic before it hardens.

Description   *Epoxies* are among the easiest-to-use casting plastics. They color easily, cure at room temperature, and are fairly resistant to environmental changes. Epoxies can be rigid, flexible, fast-curing, slow-curing, and modified by additives to meet a variety of requirements; after the resins are cured, they are unaffected by most chemicals. Epoxies have great adhesive properties and can hold more filler and reinforcements than other resins. The pure resin is transparent, though modifications from hardeners and other common additives cause them to be opaque, with a color varying from pale amber to golden brown. Epoxies cure well without application of external heat, have low shrinkage during cure, and good stability. Epoxies are also electrical insulators; epoxies do not conduct electricity, so they can be used to advantage with electric appliances. Several formulations of resin and hardeners are available for achieving different effects.

How to Use   There are many brands of epoxies and catalysts, and each has its own mixing ratios and specific features. They vary from those with lower exothermic (self-generated heat) curing to those requiring oven curing, with different shrinkage, different colors, different time spans for curing, and varying sensitivities to curing agents. Epoxies can be laminated with fiberglass and set up with gel coats.

Materials   Resin and curing agent are the most essential materials. Fillers, stabilizer, color, and other additives are options.

Equipment   Mixing bowls such as metal containers, plastic (polyethylene) bowls, paper cups; stirring implements such as tongue depressors, thin metal spatulas, wooden sticks, and spoons; measuring spoons of aluminum, glass, or ceramic.

Process   If a thickener, usually a hydrated or fumed silica like Cab-O-Sil, is used, it should be the first element mixed into the resin. Add a small amount at a time, stirring between each addition.

Next, add the correct amount of curing agent. There are several curing agents used with epoxy, some that cure at room temperature, and others that are cured at elevated temperatures. Consult with the manufacturer as well as a safety specialist to chose the best epoxy and best curing agent for the job. Many manufacturers specify dropping the catalyst into the resin one drop at a time. The proportion of catalyst to resin varies with brands, and manufacturer's formulas should be followed carefully. Thoroughly stir the correct amount of the catalyst into the mixture until the ingredients are smoothly dispersed. Casting must begin immediately, and work must be done fairly quickly, for the pot-life (length of time the mixture remains in liquid form) is from twenty-five minutes to an hour, depending upon the size of the mixture and how much catalyst it contains. Too much catalyst can cause resins to heat and begin to burn spontaneously.

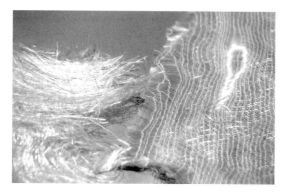

Fiberglass mat, on left, or fiberglass woven cloth, on right, commonly reinforce epoxy or polyester resin in making molds and costume pieces.
PHOTO: ROBERT W. ZENTIS.

Fiberglass is good for reinforcing epoxy and is available as cloth, mat, roving, or small, chopped pieces. Using fiberglass and fillers minimizes shrinkage. Fiberglass cloth is made of woven glass fibers. Mat is pressed, chopped fiberglass pieces. Roving is made from glass fibers formed into soft ropelike strands.

The type of cloth that is sold for boat making and repairing is satisfactory for making sizable costume pieces. It does not usually disappear completely in the casting, but instead will be seen as a cloudy pattern. A type of fiberglass called *surfacing cloth* or *mat* is the only type available that disappears completely in the resin and completely transparent. Use it like any other cloth and cut it with scissors, though the cloth will dull scissors blades.

First, let the resin stand until all bubbles disappear. Then dip the mat into the resin or brush the resin into the flat mat. In a few minutes, the resin will completely saturate the fibers, and the fiberglass will become transparent or translucent. Be sure all areas of the fiberglass are completely saturated to eliminate the occurrence of white patches.

Allow time for the resin to saturate the fibers. To prevent air bubbles, pour the resin into one place in the mold. If resin is poured into several places at one time, the intermingling pools of resin will entrap air bubbles.

Laminating fiberglass can be done with either a negative or positive mold. In either case, the mold should be of a flexible material like polyurethane or silicone, because a flexible mold can be pulled away. To form the epoxy and fiberglass over a positive mold, make the mold from materials that can be dismantled after casting. Almost anything, from chicken wire to cardboard, is usable, as long as it is covered with a release agent. For easy removal, remove the reinforced cast resin while it is still in the gel stage, yet formed enough to hold its shape. If time lapses before removing the casting, the cast will stick to the mold.

Beginning with a gel coat before making the fiberglass lamination gives the surface of the casting a smoother texture and covers the pattern of the fibers. Colored thixotropic resin may be applied to the prepared mold before the fiberglass is laid in. Gel coats are vapor barriers for liquids and weeping due to the fiberglass "wicking" action. When using a wax mold release, gel coats are not needed. Instead, coat the wax with a polyvinyl alcohol release agent (PVA). Gel coats should be from .010 to .020-inch thick. Any thicker, and they may crack the surface later.

Purchase either a colored gel coat or mix color into a thixotropic resin catalyzed with a 2 percent catalyst and brush it over the release agent. Clean the brush in acetone or lacquer thinner, then wash with water and detergent.

To prevent the gel from running, add a powdered filler like calcium carbonate or silica. Use such fillers carefully because they retard the curing of the resin. In about thirty minutes, the gel coat sets and is ready for application of laminating resin. Test the gel coat with your finger for dryness and then proceed to laminate the resin. All work must be done quickly since the pot-life is only about fifteen minutes. Gel coats can be applied with brush, spatula, or spray gun. Spray guns are made especially for mixing the correct proportions of resin and catalyst while spraying.

When casting with epoxy or polyester resin and fiberglass, first brush on the gel coat. Then, add fiberglass mat or cloth. The fiberglass can be either dipped into resin or laid on top of the gel coat and brushed with resin.

Next, lay in a second fiberglass cloth, adding to it another coat of resin.

PROCESS: COURTESY OF MAKEUP & EFFECTS LAB INC.

Material and Thickness	Resin per Sq. Ft.
Gel coat, .010" to .20"	½ to 1 oz.
Finishing mat, .010" to .030"	1 to 2 oz.
2 oz. glass cloth, .003"	1 oz.
10 oz. glass cloth, .013"	3 to 4 oz.
¾ oz. chopped strand mat	2 to 4 oz.
1½ oz. chopped strand mat	4 to 6 oz.
3 oz. chopped strand mat	8 to 10 oz.

Use epoxy adhesive to bond epoxy to itself and to other materials.

To color, special pigments that are available as transparent, opaque, and translucent can be mixed into the resin. These colors are either powders or liquid concentrates. Usually a very small amount of pigment will supply intense color. When adding the color, first place the pigment into the resin, and then add the catalyst. When coloring a resin and putty mix, first combine the putty and resin, next add the pigment, and then the cream hardener. Add small amounts at a time, stirring between each.

Paint also can be brushed or sprayed on after curing. Acrylic and enamel paints as well as lacquer adhere well to epoxy.

To add filler, such as powdered metals, follow the same sequence as for adding pigments.

To use epoxy putty, pour the resin into the putty, then add the cream hardener that is supplied with the putty.

The release agent for epoxy is silicone.

Solvent for Cleanup First, clean equipment with acetone or paint thinner, then wash well with warm water and detergent. A pre-soak or surfactant can also be used before the epoxy cures to remove epoxy from clothing and work surfaces. After curing, epoxy is resistant to all solvents.

Precautions Air inhibits the curing process, and drafts can interfere with proper curing. Adding too much curing agent can cause the resin to heat and burn.

Cover liquid materials with aluminum foil or polyester film in a container that will lock in the vapors. Store uncured resin in a secure container in a cool and dry enclosure.

Resins are difficult to remove from clothing and other items. If resins are accidentally spilled, clean up immediately.

Health and Safety It is important to choose carefully the safest epoxy. Those that contain dimethylaniline are too toxic for use. Amines, the safest curing agents, are often sensitizing and toxic. It is wise to consult with a safety specialist, listed in Resources on pages 353-356, when selecting an epoxy. MSDSs are especially needed when working with epoxies because there are so many chemicals that can be present in them. Some epoxies are much more toxic than others.

Liquid epoxies are likely to contain glycidyl ethers that are absorbed rapidly through the skin and are harmful to reproductive functions. In addition, they are narcotic, irritating, and damaging to the liver and blood. They also penetrate many types of chemical gloves without altering the gloves' appearance. Ask the glove manufacturer for the proper type.

Use local exhaust ventilation. If that is not possible, use a respirator with organic vapor/ammonia cartridges if amine-curing agents are present. Consult MSDSs for recommendations about which kind of respirator to wear. If the curing agent is an amine and if large amounts of epoxy are being used, the respirator should be a combination ammonia/amine cartridge.

Place curing resin into a separate environment where it will not affect workers. Fifty percent of workers exposed to epoxy resin systems have developed epoxy allergies.

Keep resins off the skin. If liquid resins do touch the skin, remove with acetone, wash with soap and water, and immediately replace oils of the skin with a good emollient cream.

If *cured* resin is on the skin, solvents won't help much. Rub baby oil around the resin and try peeling. After one day, it will peel off more easily.

Fiberglass is a strong irritant to eyes and lungs, and its sharp fibers easily penetrate the skin, causing dermatitis in some persons. After using fiberglass, store it in a closed container and immediately clean the work area. Use a vacuum cleaner and a damp rag on all surfaces to clear up all small particles.

Work in local exhaust ventilation. Keep fiberglass, epoxy resin, and additives away from food.

Where to Find   Plastic supply stores, hobby and crafts shops and distributors.

Distributors of epoxies include:

Carl F. Miller Company

Erskine-Johns Company

Hastings Plastics

Polytek Development Corporation

Hot-Melt Glue (Polyamide or Ethyl Vinyl Acetate)

Some Manufacturers   3M Company

Bostik Inc.

Stanley Fastening Systems

Uniplast, Incorporated

Examples of Use
- Cast jewelry, gems, and small decorative pieces, such as belt buckles.
- Form small and moderate-size hard-surfaced accessories.
- Apply as decorative trimmings.

Description   *Hot-glue sticks* are generally made of either ethylene vinyl acetate (EVA) or polyamide—both thermoplastics. When used for casting, we have found no differences among brands. Natural colors of glue sticks range from clear through milky white to brown. The products from Bostick and 3M are in natural color and melt only at high temperatures, whereas Uni-Sticks from Uniplast are available in a wide range of colors (including metallics) and are manufactured to accommodate both high and low temperatures. The hot-glue gun melts hot glues to liquid, and air exposure induces fast drying.

Commercially, hot-glue sticks are used for assembling electronic parts and packaging.

How to Use   The ejection of a glue pellet or stick through a special gun causes the glue to melt. The melted glue adheres to one or more substrates and then gels after brief exposure to air. Application temperature for most hot glues is 220 to 400°F. Be sure to have the right size gun and temperature for specific glue pellets.

Use a plaster mold, according to instructions in the beginning of this section. Immerse the plaster mold in a container of water for a minute (the water acts as a release agent), thus preventing the hot glue from adhering to the plaster. One dip into water should last for three castings.

Other materials that can serve for molds are metal, glass, and room-temperature vulcanizing (RTV) silicone. For a release agent, use petroleum jelly or silicone gel. Do not use polyethylene or polypropylene as molds with hot-melt glue, for they will melt from the heat.

Cast the hot glue by shooting the glue from the glue gun into the mold. Allow about five minutes for cooling, and then remove the glue. The glue sticks must be of a suitable size and used in a hand-held, portable applicator. To use any low-temperature-setting glue pellets, purchase a low-temperature glue gun, available at hobby shops.

Sculpting can also be accomplished without a mold by ejecting the glue onto a flat surface. Choose a resistant plastic surface, like Teflon, and shoot one or more layers of the glue to build a form. Or, to apply a hot-glue decoration to a surface, choose a surface that is not resistant to the glue, preferably one that is textured, which will provide good mechanical adhesion. Some costume makers shoot small dots of hot glue onto a costume surface as a substitute for jewels.

Bond dry finished pieces to the same or to other materials with more hot glue.

Though color can be added with acrylic paint, the finished product has a tendency to chip. For added protection, seal with a coat of acrylic sealer. Leather dye can add translucent color to hot-glue castings. Or use the Uni-Stiks, which are already colored.

Solvent for Cleanup For cleaning up, simply peel and scrape the cooled glue from the working surface.

Precautions Store in a cool, dry area.

Health and Safety Work with ventilation and eye protection. Wear gloves and long sleeves for protection from burning. Hot-molten material that touches the skin will cause burns. At high temperatures, fumes may irritate the eyes, throat, and nose. Overexposure can cause redness, tearing, and itching in the eyes. If molten material contacts the skin or eyes, immediately flush or immerse affected area in large amounts of cold water, and do not attempt to peel the material from the skin. For large jobs, use a respirator with an organic vapor cartridge.

The odor from normal use (not from overheating) is from the volatilization of chemicals called *plasticizers*. Most manufacturers do not identify plasticizers on MSDSs. Most plasticizers have not been studied for long-term hazards, though many are chemically related to known toxic and/or carcinogenic substances. Until more is known, it is wise to have good ventilation when working with hot glue.

Where to Find Hobby and crafts stores, plastic supply stores, hardware stores, manufacturers and distributors.

Sizes 5/16" to 1" diameter, 2" to 8" length, in quantities of six sticks through 11 lb.

Latex

Some Manufacturers A - R Products, Inc.

Cementex Latex Company, Inc.

Chicago Latex Products.

Mydrin, Inc.

Examples of Use
- Form body parts on fantasy and animal costumes.
- Construct pliable headdresses and fantasy items.
- Create molds.
- Mold articles that may or may not require flexibility, like jewelry pieces.

Latex is the material of choice for pieces requiring some degree of flexibility, such as oversize shoes, or body parts and masks, as well as for more pliable items. Latex can also be used for armor, headdresses, and detailed cast objects.

Description The term *latex* can refer to either natural or synthetic rubber in its liquid form. In its original application, *latex* was the name for the milk of the rubber tree, though the term can also apply to an aqueous suspension of either natural rubber or the synthetic rubbers. *Elastomer* refers to substances that are rubber-like. Usually when costume and prop makers use the term *latex*, they are referring to natural rubber. Natural rubber looks like milk and smells of ammonia; however, when the liquid evaporates or dries, the rubber particles cohere to form a tough, pale amber mass. Manufacturers usually add ammonia to natural rubber as a preservative. Since ammonia is volatile, it quickly evaporates from the cast article.

Liquid latex, a thermosetting substance, is available in a variety of forms: casting latex, balloon latex, and foaming latex. Slip or casting latex is the most commonly used, and it is usually prevulcanized for the best elongation and return memory. Casting and molding latex compounds can be either one-part or two-part systems. Cementex L-200, for example, must be used with #64 hardener. Latex is meant to be brushed or slip cast and can be tinted to any shade with colors. Filler may be added to build up density and rigidity, though it reduces the natural elasticity of latex. Aside from molding and casting, latex will make a strong skin on polyurethane foams.

Balloon rubber is a latex for casting into thin rubber sheets with the slip-casting method (see how to use on page 211). Pure gum latex is an unfilled pure gum rubber that air dries to a tough elastic coating. It is not suitable for casting most costume items, but it is excellent for making inflatable bladders by casting it into thin sheets.

The advantages of natural latex over its imitations are its flexibility and thickness as well as an economical price. Besides these advantages as a casting material, latex is an effective adhesive and coating material. (See *Adhesives* and *Coatings* sections.) The popular latex-based paints are made with one of the synthetic rubbers, SBR, rather than natural latex.

The disadvantages of latex are its fragility—it usually needs reinforcement—and its brief life span: latex deteriorates more quickly than other materials, especially if used as a mold.

When measuring latex, the hardness of a latex-finished product is measured numerically, with 10 as a soft rubber and 40 as a hard rubber.

How to Use   Molds for casting latex are usually of Ultracal, plaster of Paris, dental alginate, or dental die stone. (Dental die stones are available at dental supply stores.) Ultracal 30 is highly recommended by many mold makers. Keep the plaster molds warm and dry to promote maximum absorption and evaporation of the liquid from the rubber.

Release agents are not necessary; however, dusting the plaster mold with talc will help separate the latex from its mold.

Cast the latex by the *slip*, or *absorption* method, pouring it gently—to avoid air bubbles—and filling the mold. Let this cast latex stand about fifteen minutes until sufficient deposit and an effective thickness is formed. Pour off the excess liquid and reserve it to use in later work. The piece may be removed in eight to twelve hours. The time can be less if the drying is hastened by heat from a hair dryer or oven. Curing may take several days. The thickness of the casting depends upon the size of the finished piece; a small piece of jewelry may need only about one eighth of an inch, while a piece of armor will require more. Latex pieces are usually no more than an about 1/8 to 1/4-inch thick. Latex filler can be added as a hardener when casting latex into a negative mold. Expect shrinkage of about 5 percent. The thicker the casting, the greater the shrinkage.

To reinforce the latex for longer-lasting, sturdier items, add one or several layers of fabric during the casting process. When adding fabric, brush layers of the latex into the mold, allowing about a day curing time between each added layer. Cheesecloth is a preferred fabric, though a firmer open-weave fabric is preferable when extra strength is needed, or a fabric like cotton spandex would offer flexibility.

When reinforcing the latex, start by just covering the inside of the mold with latex; then add a layer of cloth. The cloth can be in one piece for a fairly flat low-relief casting, or cut pieces can be patched together if the mold is extremely dimensional. With a stiff brush, push the cloth into the latex. Then add another layer of cloth, and push in as before. Allow some of the cloth to exceed the mold, providing firmness and a means for attaching other pieces.

Liquid latex can also be used to create latex sheeting. Start by working on a table covered with your desired texture. Glass or smooth acrylic are best for producing a smooth surface. Other textures can be produced by using already textured nonabsorbent sheetings for a work surface. Place casting latex into a sprayer or air gun, first straining it through a chemical strainer. Smoothly spray several coats of latex, allowing each to dry completely before spraying the next coat.

This sheet can be used as is, or it can be self-laminated to another material. For the capes worn by Batman in the Bob Ringwood-designed *Batman* films of 1989 and the 90s, fabric was laid into three coats of latex sheeting that had been sprayed over the same size gores of leather-textured upholstery vinyl. See *Batman* in Part Three.

Bond it with liquid-casting latex, prosthetic adhesive type B (like Pros-Aide), or a latex-based adhesive (like Copydex from Henkel, Great Britain).

Color can be introduced in the casting stage, or it can be applied after the piece has set. Latex should be painted with flexible paint, or a flexible primer should be added before painting. For items with a high degree of flexibility, mix rubber cement with acrylic paint, or use a polyurethane-based paint, or mix up a blend of PAX paint. PAX paint is a mix of equal amounts of PA-B (prosthetic adhesive, type B) and acrylic tube paint. Acrylic paint matte medium can be added to dull the surface. For relatively nonflexible items, mix latex into the paint to increase the paint's flexibility, or prime the latex with prosthetic adhesive or rubber cement before painting. Priming with rubber cement may leave the surface somewhat sticky.

To color the latex before casting, add a small amount of universal pigment or colors specifically designed for latex to the liquid latex. Use universal tints to create pale colors. The pigments from Sandoz are most successful for producing strong colors, even including a deep black. Add the Sandoz pigment at the ratio of 3 grams pigment to 150 grams of latex.

Solvent for Cleanup Soap and water.

Precautions When using a spray gun with latex, do not leave liquid latex in the sprayer for any length of time and always clean out the sprayer completely. Otherwise, latex particles will jam the sprayer.

Health and Safety The vapors from ammonia and probably also formaldehyde are present and are harmful to skin, eyes, and lungs. Use adequate ventilation and gloves. Do not mix ammonia or substances containing ammonia with any products that contain bleach, for such combinations create highly toxic gases.

Recent studies have shown that 1 percent of the general population is allergic to latex, and about 15 percent of those who work with latex develop latex allergies. Latex allergies can be serious, with reactions ranging from skin rashes to fatal anaphylactic shock. Testing for latex allergies is available at hospital laboratories.

Wear gloves and either a respiratory mask or work in a well-ventilated area. For large jobs, use a respirator with an ammonia cartridge.

Where to Find Manufacturers and distributors.

Alcone Co.

A-R Latex Co.

Davis Dental Supply

Don Post Makeup Studios

Burman Industries

Hastings Plastics

Joe Blasco Makeup Center

Pink House Studios.

Latex Foam

Some Manufacturers

A-R Products, Inc.

Burman Industries Inc.

Cementex Company, Inc.

GM Foam, Inc.

Sherman Foam (UK).

Examples of Use

- Form body parts on walk-around and specialty costumes.
- Create pliable headdresses, armor, and fantasy items.
- Build masks and prosthetic appliances.
- Shape skin for human characters and creatures.

Latex flexible foam is especially popular in the theatre when prosthetic facial additions are needed. About 99 percent of the appliances are of latex foam. Because it is so difficult to work with, flexible foam is not as popular with costumers, who have found substitutes such as Neoprene and polyurethane both easier and more durable as casting plastics. But natural latex is a less hazardous material, which is an important advantage. A successful example of latex foam use for an entire costume is the Batman costume, found in Part Three. Also in Part Three are some examples of latex foam used for costumes for the Butchered Cow and the Topiary Lion.

Description

In the preceding section is a description of latex that describes as well foam latex. *Foam latex* is created by whipping a mixture of natural gum latex and ammonia. To this is added a foaming agent, which is whipped in at high speed and which causes frothing. A sulfuric, or sulfur-based, curing agent vulcanizes the mixture and gives strength, elasticity, and memory. Finally, a fourth component, a gelling agent, solidifies the foam.

The gelling of foam latex is affected by humidity, barometric pressure, temperature, mixing time, and the amount of ammonia in the mixture. For that reason, making and working with latex foam requires experimentation and patience. Even experts hold their breath.

Running is the term that refers to making foam latex and to the amount of time necessary to mix the components. Batch size refers to the amount of foam being made. Batches are based on 150 grams of latex base. A one-gallon kit of foam latex makes approximately twenty-five batches. Kits are available from manufacturers and distributors.

The mix needs to be refined to get an even cell structure in the foam. This stage is done with either a Whirlpool (formerly Hobart) Kitchen Aid mixer on a number 1 speed or on a classic Sunbeam Mix Master on number 4 and number 2 speeds, which free oversize air bubbles and ammonia. With too much ammonia, the latex will not gel.

Foam latex has the advantage of being lightweight, flexible, economical, and safer to use than synthetic rubbers. Disadvantages are its fragility and the shrinkage and discoloration that occur with oxidation.

The above is offered only as an overview and a warning on working with latex foam. For more complete instructions on the use of latex foam, see Donna Drexler's *Foam Latex Survival Manual*, available through Burman Industries, Inc., or the video *The Special Makeup Effects Artist's Guide to Using GM Foam*, produced and distributed by GM Foam Inc. Both emphasize the importance of taking copious notes on every step of production and at each stage of the process.

How to Use   Molds for casting foam latex are best made from high-density stones like Ultracal #30 or dental die stone, fiberglass with polyester or epoxy, and some silicones. Be sure that stone molds are mixed properly and that they are free from moisture; and oven bake them immediately after fabrication at 175° to 200°F for at least eight hours. Otherwise, the heat will cause defects that affect the casting. When casting foam latex, it is necessary to use both a negative and a positive (or core) mold.

A special release agent is a necessity. Take care to brush the separator evenly and totally with a soft bristle brush. Any excess must be removed, preferably by careful sponging, for too much separator can cause defects in the finished latex piece.

When mixing, follow carefully the manufacturer's instructions, for methods vary. Runs should be logged to record speed, time, and cumulative time. Logging is easiest if it is done on a graph.

During the mixing stage, the foaming process is affected by air temperature. Temperatures below 70°F can inhibit the foaming of large volumes, and special additives may be needed. These are available through foam distributors.

Cast by injecting or pouring the mixture into the mold. Follow manufacturer's instructions for baking time and bake at approximately 175° to 200°F, depending upon the type of foam. Overbaking can dry out the mold and the foam.

When removing molds from the oven, wrap them in towels to avoid cracking. Open the molds slowly while they are still warm and before the foam has a chance to stick to a cooled surface. Pry open with two one-inch chisels or two screwdrivers. Powder the mold with talc or baby powder as cast pieces are being removed to prevent the edges from sticking to themselves, and gently pull out the casting.

Coloring can be added to the batch of foam during the final mixing, or refining, stage, or it can be added to the gelling agent before mixing. Use no more than two or three drops of universal tints or latex pigment. Adding any more pigment will affect the quality of the foam. Paints that can be applied after casting are the same as those used with unfoamed latex. Use either polyurethane-based paint or add a flexible primer like a prosthetic adhesive type B or rubber cement before painting, or mix one of these adhesives into acrylic paint. Blends of rubber cement, and acrylic paint remain sticky, but those with prosthetic adhesives (PAX paint) dry well.

Adhesives that bond well are type B-prosthetic adhesives and latex adhesive, like Copydex (from Henkel, Great Britain), and liquid latex itself.

Solvent for Cleanup Water.

Precautions Do not dry-clean items made from this material.

Health and Safety The vapors from ammonia, and possibly formaldehyde, are present and are harmful to skin, eyes, and lungs. Use adequate ventilation and gloves. Do not mix ammonia or substances containing ammonia with any products that contain bleach, for such combinations create highly toxic gases.

Recent studies have shown that 1 percent of the general population is allergic to latex, and about 15 percent of those who work with latex develop allergies. Latex allergies can be serious, with reactions ranging from skin rashes to fatal anaphylactic shock. Testing for latex allergies is available at hospital laboratories.

Wear gloves and wear either a respiratory mask or work in a well-ventilated area.

Where to Find Manufacturers and distributors.
Distributors include:
Alcone Co.
Complexions International, Ltd. (Ontario, Canada)
Davis Dental Supply
Don Post Makeup Studios
Joe Blasco Makeup Center.

Casting in Foam Latex

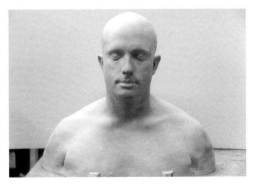

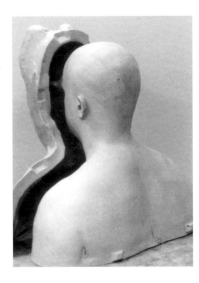

The following are stages of casting in foam latex. This example of foam latex casting is for a facial mask, cast in a plaster of Paris mold taken from a life cast. (Life casts are explained on pages 184-188)

The life cast is surrounded by its plaster of Paris mold.

The latex core mold (inner positive mold) is surrounded by the plaster of Paris mold. The latex foam is inserted through the sprue opening.)

Latex foam is most easily mixed in electric mixers..

Latex is poured into a large syringe, then carefully injected into the sprue, or opening, of the latex mold.

The mold is baked in a small industrial oven. Baking time and temperature vary with the type of foam.

PROCESS: COURTESY OF GM FOAM. PHOTOS: ROBERT W. ZENTIS.

Low-Temperature-Setting Thermoplastic Pellets

Some Brands	Manufacturers
Adapt-it	UnNatural Resources
Aquapellets	Smith & Nephew Rolyan Inc.
Friendly Plastic	American Art Clay Company, Inc.

Examples of Use
- Create small ornaments and jewelry.
- Patch torn rigid costume parts.
- Bonding to rigid costume parts.
- Form teeth and claws on animal or monster costumes.

Mask makers sometimes use thermoplastic pellets for making animal teeth, since the cast pellets look like enamel.

Definition *Low-temperature-setting thermoplastic polyester pellets* are made from a nontoxic form of water-soluble polyester that can become soft and castable by softening in hot water. Adapt-it is marketed for theatrical costume and prop making and is akin to Protoplast, also from UnNatural Resources. Aquapellets from Smith & Nephew are available as an orthopedic casting material. Friendly Plastic pellets are available at craft and hobby shops. All of these brands are naturally pale colored, opaque, and easy to paint. They bond to fabric, leather, wood, paper, and many other plastics. A disadvantage is the fairly high price, limiting use to fairly small objects.

Adapt-It and Aquapellets

How to Use To mold Adapt-it and Aquapellets, soften in hot water of 160° to 180°F for about one minute. The pellets will become transparent, sticky, and putty-like.

As soon as the material becomes clear, lift it out of the water with a wooden implement. Allow it to cool for about ten to thirty seconds. By that time it can be worked like clay, with bare hands, but will remain soft and pliable for only several minutes. Unlike clay, it dries to a hard and durable surface. It can be free-formed or cast into a mold.

Color can be added during the boiling process with union dyes, like Rit or Tintex. After forming, the material can be painted with acrylic paints.

Bond by reheating or by adding more melted pellets to the already formed substance.

Solvent for Cleanup Soap and water.

Precautions Store out of direct sunlight, away from open flames and sources of heat in a cool, dry environment.

Where to Find Manufacturers and distributors.

Distributors include:

Douglas and Sturgess

Pink House Studios

Alcone Company.

Sizes 1, 3, 25, and 50 lb.

Friendly Plastic

How to Use Heat water to about 140°F. The manufacturer recommends using an electric skillet for temperature control. Hot water can also be poured into a heat-resistant bowl (not aluminum). As the water in the bowl cools, more hot water can be added. Add a few drops of cooking oil to the water container to prevent the plastic from sticking to it. Add the pellets to the hot water, and let them set for about thirty to sixty seconds, or until they become transparent. Use an implement to remove the pellets.

When the plastic is cool enough to handle, sculpt with hands or press the warm pellets into a mold. Use any type of implement for a tool. After a design is complete, place the material into cold water to set. The cold water will set the plastic as well as turn it opaque. If embedments, such as jewels or sequins, are included, they should be added while the material is still soft.

Friendly Plastic is thermoplastic and can be resoftened.

Bond with itself by melting more pellets to use as a mass, or heat and melt the plastic and press pieces together.

Color with acrylic paint, model paint, permanent ink markers, or acrylic enamel paint markers. American Art Clay Co. recommends using their Spray 'n Seal protective coating after painting.

Solvent for Cleanup Soap and water.

Precautions Friendly Plastic adheres to fingernail polish, acrylic, aluminum, Styrofoam, and PVC. It will soften or melt under exposure to direct sunlight or other high heat. Keep away from direct sunlight, open flames, and sources of heat. Store in a cool, dry environment.

Where to Find Manufacturer.

Hobby and craft stores.

Theatrical suppliers and distributors.

Sizes 4.4 oz., 28 oz., 25 lb.

Modified Glass Fiber Reinforced Gypsum System

Brand Name	Main Distributor
Forton MG	Ball Consulting, Ltd.

Examples of Use
- Shape animal body parts.
- Make small armor pieces.
- Create small headdresses.
- Cast ornaments, like jewelry.
- Form molds and shell, or mother, molds.

Use in place of fiberglass-reinforced epoxy or polyester or as a substitute for rigid polyurethane. Forton MG can be employed in a wide variety of rigid-cast costume pieces, though it may be too heavy for large headdresses or full breastplates since it is 20 percent heavier than polyester and fiberglass.

Description
The *modified glass fiber reinforced gypsum system* is a new water-based substitute for fiberglass-reinforced polyester or epoxy. It is a four-component casting system and mixture of proprietary formulations. The ingredients are VF-812 (a water-based, cross-linking acrylic resin with a formaldehyde preservative), FGR-95 (gypsum), MF-415 dry resin (melamine), and a 10-76 hardener (ammonium chloride). The ingredients of this system are completely specialized, and there are no substitutes. This modified gypsum system is completely opaque, with a shrinkage of less than 1 percent. Curing takes between twenty-four and forty-eight hours.

Compared with more traditional materials, the modified glass reinforced gypsum system (Forton MG) is cheaper than resins, kinder to the environment, and imparts a mild, pleasant odor. Easier to work with than resins, it takes less time to complete a casting. Forton MG is about 20 percent heavier than the polyester fiberglass combination.

Currently, Forton MG is used for mold cases, statuary, and props. Its original application was in architectural façades as a substitute for fiberglass and for steel-reinforced cement.

Forton MG is available in kits from suppliers listed on page 220; however, Ball Consulting and only a few distributors are currently offering fairly small kits.

Instructions for using Forton MG are available through Ball Consulting's video as well as through brochures available with the system.

How to Use
Molds can be of any material that best suits the design or the piece. Release agents are the same as those used with plaster of Paris. (See page 195.)

To cast, first weigh the VF-812 liquid. Weigh the gypsum with the resin and hardener together, adding additional fillers and powders. Add the dry materials into the liquid, and mix thoroughly for one to two minutes. Extra water may be added if additional powders thicken the mix too much.

For pour casting, pour the mix slowly over the edge of the mixing container to prevent air bubbles from forming.

When brushing the mix into a mold for a hollow casting, be sure to eliminate all bubbles. The thickness of a hollow casting when using fiberglass is about one-eighth to one-half inch. A thickening agent, such as Cab-O-Sil, can be added for a smooth gel coat. Without an accelerator, pieces can usually be released from the mold after an hour.

An accelerator of aluminum sulfate can be added if desired. Mix, by weight, one-part aluminum sulfate to ten parts of water. The ratio is one tablespoon of accelerator to ten pounds of gypsum. The use of an accelerator allows the casting to be removed from the mold before curing.

Reinforce with fiberglass, jute, cheesecloth, or other absorbent open-weave, natural-fiber fabric. Chopped fiberglass strand works well when cast into the mold.

Bond with itself by using the material before it hardens. It will bond to most other materials as well.

To color, add either dry pigment or predispersed acrylic type pigment to the VF-812 liquid before mixing, though the absolute color cannot be determined until after drying. First test on a sample of MG; it usually dries lighter. It can be painted with acrylic paint after completing. Very convincing metallic finishes can be obtained by adding metal powders to the VF-812. Ball recommends their bronzing powders of -325 mesh.

Solvent for Cleanup	Water.
Precautions	Forton MG will degenerate if allowed to stand in water for any length of time and will harden on any tools that are left in a water container.
Health and Safety	Forton MG is not especially toxic, but a National Institute of Health and Safety (NIOSH) approved dust mask is necessary when weighing and mixing any powders. People who are sensitive to formaldehyde may need ventilation.
Where to Find	Manufacturer and distributors.
	Distributors include:
	Ball Consulting, Ltd.
	Composite Materials, Inc.
	Pink House Studios
	Polytek Development Corporation.
Sizes	5-gal. kit (about $200) plus gypsum
	1-gal. starter kit at Pink House, Polytek, and Ball Consulting, Ltd.

Papier-Mâché

Some Brands	Manufacturers
Claycrete	American Art Clay Co., Inc.
Celluclay	Activa Products

Examples of Use

- Model any hard-surfaced costume piece, such as armor, jewelry, fantasy head dresses.

- Cover, texture, and decorate already-made objects.

Jewelry pieces may be made from the paper combined with carpenters' glue and/or acrylic polymers. Using these binders is especially good for turning out forms with metallic-like firmness.

Armor can be made successfully with any of these materials; however, cloth by itself or in combination with papers is more durable than paper alone.

Papier-mâché is used for covering, decorating, or otherwise altering the surfaces of ready-made objects. Tissue paper and similar lightweight papers can be crumpled and crimped, then applied in a textural or decorative manner. Tools can be used to dig into soft tissue paper to form relief and dimensional designs.

Description

Combining *papier-mâché* with either synthetic or natural binders offers unlimited possibilities. A variety of papers—including newspaper, bond paper, and tissue paper—can be used for mâché work. When a more flexible, yet stronger medium is required, cloth can be substituted for paper or layered with paper in combinations. Packaged premixed paper pulps with various adhesives are also available. Making papier-mâché requires soaking pieces of paper or cloth in a plastic medium and overlapping them until they fuse into a hard mass or skin.

Papier-mâché is discussed here because, like all plastics, it can be molded when wet and will then dry to a rigid form. Papier-mâché has played a major role in the long history of theatre and of theatre costuming. It also plays, an important role in theatre today. In most parts of Asia, where tradition is important and budgets more restricted than in the West, papier-mâché is the main component of masks and of most rigid costume pieces. In China and India, it is the material of choice for traditional masks and large headdresses. Because working with papier-mâché is more

This papier-mâché Chinese dragon head is decorated with glued fringes.

economical and safer than forming plastic, it is a particularly popular crafts material in schools.

In Mexico and Italy, papier-mâché is popular as a material with which to create finely crafted art objects and colorful sculptures of all sizes.

How to Use   ## Types of Paper

Tissue paper is best for making small papier-mâché objects like jewelry and delicate decorations. Tissue is torn into small strips and the piece formed by casting on either positive or negative molds. For a smooth surface, paper should be torn, not cut, because the resulting fibrous overhang from tearing creates a soft edge that blends easily into a surface. Tissue paper can also be used to texture-coat by unevenly layering or crumpling it on top of a surface.

Newspaper is for making less-detailed objects. Newspaper can be torn into small strips for casting or covering, or it can be crumpled and twisted to form substantial freely formed textural pieces.

Heavy paper, like brown wrapping paper and art papers, will form hard stiff pieces and serve as underlayers. When choosing papers, use only papers that have some porosity.

This Mexican papier-mâché mask is embellished with a beard of acrylic-pile fabric glued in place.

Hard paper and most coated paper do not absorb enough water to be usable. Heavy paper alone is more difficult to control and less flexible than are the thinner newsprint and tissue paper. When using these as an underlayer, work from heavy up to lighter weights—heavy paper as the bottom layer, newspaper for the middle, tissue paper on the top finishing layer.

Instant papier-mâché is a commercial product available in hobby and craft stores. It is composed of shredded paper reduced to a fine powder and mixed with a bonding medium. The addition of water, mixed in and thoroughly kneaded, turns the compound into a claylike substance. This can be mixed by spoon in a bowl (best to use a polyethylene bowl for easy removal of the mâché) or directly in its plastic bag. The mix is ready to use in about fifteen minutes. Drying at room temperature takes several days, varying, of course, with the size of the piece. Though manufacturers recommend oven drying at 150°F, it is best not to force-dry it at any higher temperature, since high heats can cause it to crack or shrink.

After forming, papier-mâché can be sanded, sawed, drilled, or sliced. It can be covered with gesso to impart a smooth and workable surface. From this material, small decorations that are self-bonding can be made, or small pieces such as jewelry can be sculpted by casting or modeling with fingers or small tools. Instant papier-mâché will bond to almost all surfaces except to plastics, which require adhesives.

Cloth lends a strength and stability not available from paper because of the strength of the woven structure of cloth. Natural fibers work the best because they are porous and hold more liquid than do synthetic fibers. For maximum pliability and easier shaping from cloth, cut the cloth into bias pieces.

Cloth, when combined with flexible media like white glues and acrylic, is more elastic than paper because of its innate softness and pliability; however, it can become as rigid as paper when combined with a more rigid bonding medium, such as epoxy.

Cloth layers can be cast in combination with paper layers to have the advantages of both media. Large pieces of cloth can also be used to sculpt elaborate folds on garments with immobile, sculptural drapery.

Binders

Wheat paste is a combination of wheat flour and water. Working with wheat paste is a traditional and inexpensive method, but one that produces less sturdy results than the more modern media. To make wheat paste, mix the flour with enough water to form a thick soup of paste.

Wallpaper paste is another traditional medium for papier-mâché work. Wallpaper paste is formulated for adhering wallpaper, is easy to mix, and fairly inexpensive. Follow package directions; generally, wallpaper paste is also mixed to a thick soup consistency. When selecting wallpaper paste, chose one that is specifically sold for using with crafts because standard wallpaper paste often contains large amounts of pesticides and fungicides.

Carpenter's glue can be used with paper or cloth. It has more body and strength than the pastes. It is made in the double boiler. First boil water in a bucket or large saucepan, then place an empty bucket or saucepan into the boiling water, and add glue granules or a block of glue. Stir the glue until melted. Use the melted glue either straight or thin it with water. For stronger bonding power and higher saturation, use it unthinned and hot.

White glues are probably the most common papier-mâché mediums in use today because of their strength and flexibility. Because they need no mixing (except for optional thinning), they are easier to use than wheat or wallpaper paste, and they are more pliable; however, they are also more costly.

Acrylic media, such as acrylic-paint media, gesso, acrylic-based coatings, and other PVAs are also effective binders for papier-mâché, and they, like white glues, are premixed, strong, flexible, and can be thinned with water.

Molds

Molds can be negative or positive and of practically any material. If a ready-made, fully-dimensional object is chosen for use as a positive mold, either the object will need to be flexible, or the casting will have to be cut off the mold in two pieces, and then mâchéd together. If the mold is of porous material, a release agent, such as petroleum jelly, will be necessary.

Armatures

Wire, chicken wire, cane, or wood can be made into a *framework* or *armature*, then covered with paper or cloth-mâché for building large headdresses. Using papier-mâché in this manner has been practiced for centuries for theatrical as well as for other designs.

Styrofoam and polyurethane rigid foam provide lightweight and workable cores on which to build items that appear solid. Both Styrofoam and polyurethane foam bond to the above-mentioned glues, except for carpenters' glue, which must be used hot and could melt these plastic foams.

Paints

Paints that will bond to and color papier-mâché are those meant for paper. Tempera, acrylic, other polymers, casein paint, and oil-based paints all serve well.

Tempera, coated with a transparent surface, is inexpensive and fast-drying, but if painted too thickly, it will crack and chip.

Acrylic paint, like the other polymers, also dries quickly and is less apt to crack or chip, though it is more expensive.

Casein paint handles similarly to tempera, but is of better quality and less liable to crack or chip; however, it is not as readily available as are the other paints.

Oil paint can lend rich and even textural effects, but it needs an experienced hand to apply it with artistry and takes about a week to dry. Dry pigment powder can be mixed with any of the adhesive media or can be mixed with the final coating. Paints can be applied at several stages. Like dry pigment, ready-made paint can be mixed into the glues. If this choice is made, be sure that the paint and glue are compatible. Paint can also be mixed with the final coating. Adding paint in this manner will save time and create a feeling of depth, but the color will also be pale, not vibrant, in hue.

Coatings

Gesso will strengthen, harden, and provide a solid paintable surface before painting. Gesso should be applied with a brush and then sanded when dry.

Other coatings, like artists' varnish, household varnish, clear enamels, and acrylic liquid coatings both protect and finish off the surface. Artists' varnishes for coating oil paintings, available in jars at artists' supply stores, take over a day to dry. For quicker drying and for less sheen, use household varnishes or acrylic coatings. Acrylic coatings and clear enamels come in spray cans and dry in minutes. Shellac can be used to create an even more durable surface and can be applied to the dried papier-mâché before painting.

Techniques

- Prepare torn paper pieces by soaking them overnight in a container of water. Drain off the water. Dilute the glue or paste medium with one part water, and into it dip the paper pieces. Apply these to the surface of the positive or negative mold, overlapping all pieces of paper while working. The layering may start with the heavier paper for the first layers, then tissue paper for the top and final layers. The number of layers depends upon the finish size of the cast. Three to seven layers is usually sufficient. When the layering is complete and dry, brush over it a thick coat of acrylic medium or varnish. Allow it to dry, then sand the surface for smoothness.

- Tear strips of paper or cut strips of cloth into small sections. Pour glue or paste into a bowl and dilute with water if desired. Dip the paper or cloth, one strip at a time into the medium, apply in an overlapping manner, and smooth out by brush. Cloth can be used for bottom layers, and thinner cloth or tissue paper for finishing. Allow to dry. If the piece is to be rigid, cover with gesso. Add decorations, then apply varnish or another clear coating.

- Pour instant mâché in a bowl, gradually add water, and slowly stir with a spoon or fork until the mixture feels clay-like. Wear a dust mask while handling these powders. Do not mix with hands, which could cause dry pockets to form. Let stand for fifteen to twenty minutes before use. After drying, sand and gesso the surface for smoothness. Paint and decorate. Finish with a protective coating.

Solvent for Cleanup Solvent chosen depends upon the binders used. Refer to package directions.

Precautions Instant papier-mâché is of varying shades of gray, for it usually contains ground ink-bearing magazines.

Health and Safety Instant papier-mâché should be used with good ventilation or a toxic dust mask during mixing and sanding in order to inhibit inhaling the dust. Furthermore, the papers and ground magazines for instant mâché usually contain toxic materials, such as fillers made from potentially toxic ingredients, and inks containing lead or other toxic pigments. Some papier-mâché powders may be made with asbestos-contaminated talcs. Instant papier-mâché is not a safe material for working with children.

The methods with paper or cloth strips dipped into a binder should cause no problems.

Where to Find Carpenter's glues: paint and scenic supply stores.

Wheat and wallpaper paste: paint stores.

Instant papier-mâché: craft and hobby shops.

Polyester

Polyester resin and fiberglass with inserted grasses form this mask.

DESIGN AND SCULPTURE: FRED NIHDA.

Some Manufacturers

American Cyanamid Company

Polytek Development Corporation

Reichhold Chemicals, Inc.

United States Rubber Company.

Examples of Use

- Cast jewelry.
- Construct animal parts like shells, heads, and other body pieces.
- Craft hard accessories like armor, headdresses, and weapons.

Many special effects studios use polyester for mold-making, such as for the full bodysuits described in Part Three for *Batman* and *Running Man*.

Description

Polyesters are the least expensive, the most versatile, and the easiest to use of the liquid plastics. Similar to epoxies, they are catalyzed by MEK color easily, cure at room temperature, can be either rigid or semiflexible, fast- or slow-curing, resist most chemicals, are easily modified by additives, and are generally unaffected by environmental changes. Unlike epoxy, they shrink more than most resins but are fairly economical. Polyesters are usually available as clear and white formulas and cure to a translucent amber. They are preferred for casting translucent- and opaque-looking materials. For added strength, they are, like epoxy, often reinforced with fiberglass or other fibrous substances. Specialty type polyesters can be made with some additional properties of light stability as well as resistance to water, heat, and flame.

How to Use

Polyester techniques are similar to those of epoxy. Refer to Epoxy on pages 203-208, modifying working processes: according to manufacturers' instructions.

Using fiberglass and other fillers will minimize polyester shrinkage. Shrinkage produced when creating solid castings can be compensated for by introducing more resin. For hollow casting, in which resins are painted into the mold sections, shrinkage can be controlled by using a resin that contains polyester putty.

When making jewelry, start with a flexible mold like polyethylene or silicone. If embedments (other small items such a glass, stones, or wood) are to be added, make the jewelry in three pours, with the embedments added between pours. The first pour is of clear resin, catalyzed at six to eight drops per ounce.

Solvent for Cleanup

Be sure that all the MEK has evaporated before cleaning the equipment. To clean, first use acetone, then wash well with warm water and detergent. A presoak or surfactant like Amway L.O.C., Shout, or Zout can also be used before curing to remove polyester from clothing and work surfaces. If the polyester is cured, nothing will remove it.

Precautions Humid air inhibits the curing process, and drafts can interfere with correct curing.

Resins are difficult to remove from clothing and other items. If some resin spills accidentally, clean it up immediately.

Keep all pours covered with aluminum foil, plastic film, or in a tightly closed container to contain the fumes. Store in a cool and dry enclosure.

Health and Safety Place curing polyester resin into a separate environment where it will not affect workers. The resin gives off styrene vapors, which are suspect carcinogens. They are also narcotic, irritating, and damaging to the liver and blood.

Never use acetone to cleanup MEK or any other form of peroxide. The combination of the two chemicals is explosive.

Keep resins off the skin. If liquid resins do touch skin, remove with acetone, wash with soap and water, and immediately replace oils of the skin with a good emollient cream.

If cured hard resin is on the skin, solvents are not much help. Rub baby oil around the resin and try peeling. After one day, it will peel off more easily.

Fiberglass is a strong irritant to eyes and lungs, with sharp fibers that easily penetrate skin, sometimes causing dermatitis. Keep fiberglass, polyester resin, and additives away from food. After using fiberglass, store it in a closed container and immediately clean the work area. Use a vacuum cleaner and a damp rag on all surfaces to clear up all small particles.

Wear gloves, protective clothing, and an organic-vapor respiratory mask. Work in local-exhaust ventilation. Place curing resin into a separate environment where it will not affect workers.

Where to Find Plastics' suppliers, hobby and craft shops.

Distributors include:

Cementex Latex Corporation

Hastings Plastics

Polyurethane Foam

Some Manufacturers

BJB Enterprises, Inc.

Cementex Company Inc.

Devcon Corp.

Vagabond Corp.

Zeller International Ltd.

Examples of Use

- Create otherworldly headdresses.
- Make lightweight decorations.
- Cast heads and accessories for character and animal costumes.
- Build a positive mold for casting.

Rigid foam can be used as a substitute for wirework when forming large headdresses and other fantasy accessories. See page 317 for an example of a headdress from *The Tempest*.

Polyurethane foam can change the quality of a fabric. Create thick textural fabrics by laminating the foam to the underside of thin-textured fabrics, or use it to texture the exterior, as seen in *Aliens* on pages 340-341.

Flexible foam is often used for body-padding pieces, soft sculptured body parts, and costume pieces. Armor worn in the 1989 and '90s films of *Batman*, armor in the film *The Terminator*, the mermaid tail from the film *Splash*, and padding from *Death Becomes Her* were all cast from polyurethane foam. In Part Three is a description of the *Batman* armor.

Dancers in the film *The Super Mario Brothers* wore revealing costumes made from cast polyurethane foam. The process is described on page 229.

Description

Polyurethane, or *urethane*, *foam* is lightweight and can be either rigid or flexible. It can be poured directly onto a surface, or it can be cast into a negative mold. Polyurethane foam is available in two-part and three-part ratio systems, which in some cases can be varied to produce different degrees of flexibility or rigidity. Other variations such as demold time, viscosity, setting time, impact-resistance, weight, strength, hardness, surface qualities, and density of pores can be selected by the user. In its rigid form, it is the most commonly used plastic for casting foamed objects. In its flexible form, it is stronger than latex foam.

Some types of polyurethane foam are blown with water and are less toxic to use, such as BJB's TC-351 and Zeller's E.Z. Plastic.

Polyurethane foam can be purchased packaged in a ready-to-use system that releases the two elements at one time through a nozzle. It also can be purchased in a spray can that premixes the two elements.

Industrially, some popular uses of rigid polyurethane foam are boat flotation systems, furniture parts, and packaging. The flexible foam is most commonly used for furniture padding and filtration systems.

How to Use For molds that are flexible, silicone RTV rubber is preferable since polyurethane sticks to all other materials. With silicone there is a clear release. For rigid molds, use plaster. Before using a plaster mold, carefully dust the mold interior with talc or brush in a thin layer of liquid latex and allow eight hours drying time. All other mold materials require a release agent like polyethylene, petroleum jelly, mineral oil, or a paste wax, such as carnauba wax. Polyurethane foam bonds to everything except polyethylene.

Cast by mixing the liquid reactive components of the foam formulation together, following carefully manufacturer's instructions, or use a two-part spray system. Mix with a Jiffy Mixer blade in an electric drill at 2000 to 3000 RPM, or hand mix with a clean and dry wooden or metal spatula. After thirty to forty seconds, a slight change in volume indicates the start of the chemical action. The mixture will heat up, darken, and start foaming. At this point, withdraw the mixer, and pour the foam into place. The two parts can be poured into a closed or open mold, or onto a surface. Within seconds, the mix starts to foam and rise. It will flow around the mold cavity, filling all spaces, while clinging to all the walls. The foam sets up in approximately three to five minutes, though internal curing takes from thirty minutes to several hours.

While the foam is setting, do not touch or move it in any way. Forming polyurethane foam is much like cake baking, and any movement completely destroys the process.

Most foams, except for the very flexible, create their own skin upon curing. Others need the addition of a special skin coat of either a rubber or polyurethane for protection.

Additives to produce textures in flexible foam can be as varied as pickling spices, metal gaskets, yarn, and pieces of Mylar.

Bond any parts of both rigid and flexible polyurethanes to themselves with special polyurethane adhesives, such as BJB's TC 89 Primer. For bonding flexible polyurethane foams to other materials, use polyurethane adhesives or contact cement. See the charts in the adhesives section of this book for more detailed recommendations.

Color the foam during the mixing stage with dry pigments, casein paint, or acrylic paints. If liquid paints are mixed in, the foam will be spongier as well as less pure in color after it is set.

For flexible items, paint the finished surface with polyurethane-based paint, such as those from BJB and Zeller. On nonflexible surfaces, acrylic or casein paints will adhere. For transparency on finished surfaces, use stains such as wood stain, glass stain, French enamel varnish, and shoe dyes. Metallize with graphite or bronzing powder by sprinkling on top of the setting surface.

Following is the process used to create dancer's costumes for *The Super Mario Brothers:* Before casting, the mold was brushed with metallic powder and the foam was colored with pigment to give the polyurethane a metallic appearance. During casting, an armature wire was inserted into the foam to stabilize the shape of the foam for a tight fit onto the dancers. The polyurethane pieces were secured to the dancers' skin with a type-A prosthetic adhesive. Cloth G-strings and vacuum-formed bra cups (lined with soft, napped fabric) were worn underneath the polyurethane pieces. Costumes were designed by Joseph Porro and built by Makeup & Effects Laboratories (MEL) in Los Angeles.

A store mannequin is used to form the clay sculpture for a snake that wil surround the performer's torso.

The finished costume contains an armature wire inserted into the foam in order to create a close fit. It is secured to the dancer's skin with a type-A prosthetic adhesive.

DESIGN: JOSEPH PORRO FOR *THE SUPER MARIO BROTHERS*. PHOTOS: COURTESY OF MAKEUP & EFFECTS LAB INC.

Solvent for Cleanup   Acetone, naphtha, or paint thinner are good solvents for polyurethane foam, but only while the foam is in a liquid state.

Precautions   Cover all containers tightly, for moisture from the air will cause polyurethane to cure. Cure time of polyurethane is inhibited if it is used with clays containing sulfur, like Roma Plastilena. To prevent such inhibition, first coat the clay with a sealer coat of acrylic spray.

Polyurethane should be fireproofed after casting, or purchased in a fire-retardant form, as polyurethane is an especially dangerous material. It contains an explosive fluorocarbon that volatilizes quickly at room temperatures. Polyurethane is flammable and, when aflame, will emit hydrogen cyanide, carbon monoxide, isocyanate, and other highly toxic gases.

Health and Safety   Polyurethanes are made from a class of chemicals called *isocyanates* or *diisocyanates* and during use emit gasses in what is called *off-gassing*. Off-gassing from polyurethane takes a minimum of twenty-four hours, and if the polyurethane is not mixed properly, it may emit dangerous gases for years.

If there is no ventilation, an air-supplied respirator, attached to a compressed air cylinder, is required since no respirator cartridges have been approved for use with polyurethane. These air compressors are usually available for rent from an environmental product's rental company. (Lab Safety Supply in Jamesville, Wisconsin, is one company that rents such equipment.) Obviously, no one should work in the shop until the resin is through off-gassing. Working with polyurethanes can cause *isocyanate asthma*. This asthma can severely limit one's life. Severe respiratory reactions to polyurethanes during casting has also caused a number of deaths.

Of the forty-three diisocyanates in use, only about four are regulated. Some manufacturers take advantage of this by using those that are unregulated and calling their proudest "safe." Even though MSDSs may say "no industrial standards apply" or "nontoxic," polymer chemists know that all isocyanates have the same toxic effects on the body.

Take all precautions to avoid contact with skin, eyes, or clothing. Be sure to use goggles. Work with disposable clothing, gloves, and headgear, and dispose of all equipment immediately after completing the job. Use disposable utensils and containers because any remaining polyurethane will continue to volatilize dangerous vapors into the air. When possible, use water-based polyurethanes, which are somewhat safer.

Where to Find Manufacturers and distributors.

Distributors include:

Burman Industries Inc.

Hastings Plastics

Pink House Studios

Vagabond Corp.

Polyurethane RTV

Some Manufacturers BJB Enterprises, Inc.

Cementex Company, Inc.

Devcon Corporation

Smooth-On, Inc.

Zeller International Ltd.

Examples of Use
- Form animal and human body parts.
- Create rigid and semirigid costume forms.
- Cast beads and small decorative pieces.
- Produce low-relief ornamentation.
- Make molds for casting.

Polyurethane RTV is excelent for objects requiring detail. Use polyurethane RTV when time is a factor—for polyurethanes set up very quickly. Both rigid and flexible polyurethanes are popular for animal parts, ornaments, and armor.

See descriptions of cast polyurethane RTV for the *Robot* in Anheuser-Busch's King Cobra Malt Liquor commercial on page 391 and for the *Batman* costume on page 396.

Description   *Room-temperature-vulcanizing (RTV) polyurethane*, or *urethane*, is a thermosetting material with a wide range of qualities. Polyurethanes can be brushed or poured; their consistency can be hard and rigid to soft and flexible to gelatinous; and their clarity can be opaque through water-clear. Surface quality extends from matte through shiny. Hardening time varies from four minutes to twenty-four hours. They are lightweight and extremely pliable, with some polyurethanes elongating up to 700 percent. Ideal for casting low-relief forms, they permit excellent duplication of detail, though in not as absolute a replication as silicone RTV. Polyurethanes are available in two-part and three-part systems. Polyurethanes have low viscosity, as well as higher tensile strength than any other known rubber. They adhere readily to a wide range of materials and require an adequate mold release. Finished rigid-polyurethane castings can be drilled, sanded, cut, and threaded.

Comparatively, polyurethanes cost more than natural latex but less than silicone. They are less flexible and tear more easily than silicone and are safer to work with than polyester or epoxy resins. It is important to keep polyurethanes away from moisture, which interferes with the curing process.

Commercially, polyurethanes are widely used for furniture components, sculpture replications, picture frames, and toys. They are extremely popular for costume and prop craftspeople.

How to Use   To find the proper polyurethane for a particular use, first consider the following variables: flexibility, color, method of application, working time, demold time, strength, viscosity, and softness.

Molds for casting polyurethane RTV are most successfully made with silicone when flexible molds are needed. In casting over forty pieces, a barrier coat of a special alcohol-based lacquer will protect the silicone mold from the polyurethane material. Instructions for preparing silicone and a barrier coat are provided by the manufacturers.

Prepare the mold according to the manufacturer's specific directions. Then mix the barrier coat and its thinner in equal parts. Spray a thin coating of this mixture into the mold at fifty parts per square inch (PSI). If too much coating is sprayed, the cast piece may not dry completely and will have surface flaws. Allow about three minutes for the coating to dry.

For rigid molds, use plaster only if the plaster mold is freshly cast. To be successful with polyurethanes, the plaster must be smooth-surfaced, fresh, and dry. Seal the mold with two light coats of lacquer, then use polyvinyl alcohol (PVA) as a release agent for each casting. Use paste wax to coat the dried PVA, and buff it well.

Other moldmaking materials include latex, polyethylene, polyurethane, and fiberglass-reinforced polyester or epoxy. With these materials, use a release agent like liquid or paste wax, or use silicone packaged in an aerosol container. After removing the cast piece from the mold, remove all wax from the casting before applying any kind of coatings or finishings.

Casting methods often require mixing equal amounts of several components. Some polyurethanes are to be mixed according to weight and others by volume. Mixing directions vary with the manufacturer and the type of polyurethane and are given on the product labels. Directions must be followed carefully, for incorrect mixing will impair casting. Manufacturers recommend mixing with a Jiffy Mixer for best results, though it is important to watch for the formation of air bubbles. Jiffy brand Mixers are available through distributors of polyurethanes.

Pour the mixed polyurethane into the mold, being careful not to disturb or move it once the resins begin gelling. As it sets, the cast piece should lose its rubbery feel and be ready for release. Leaving the polyurethane in the mold longer than the specified time will make release difficult and shorten the life of the mold. The finished piece should be placed on a paper, wood, or plastic surface. Do not place it on metal, for this causes unequal cooling.

Bond to itself and to other materials with adhesives designed for polyurethane and sold by distributors, or use either a polyurethane-based adhesive or a flexible cyanoacrylate.

Color can be introduced during the casting stage, or it can be applied after the piece has set. To place pigment into the polyurethane before casting, use special dry pigments or liquid tints available from polyurethane manufacturers. Do not use universal colors or dyes designed for use with latex. Prime polyurethane before applying paint. Use special polyurethane primers, like Skin-Flex by BJB, distributed by Burman Industries, or A-Prime made by Zeller. Paint rigid objects with acrylic paint or enamel, but use only special flexible paints on flexible objects. Flexible polyurethane paints are also available through Burman Industries.

Solvent for Cleanup Acetone, paint thinner, or mineral spirits.

Precautions Cover all containers tightly, for moisture from the air will cause polyurethane to cure.

Cure time of polyurethane is inhibited if it is used with clay molds containing sulfur, like Roma Plastilena. To prevent such inhibition, first coat the clay with a sealer coat of acrylic spray.

Polyurethane should be fireproofed after casting or purchased in a fire retardant form, because polyurethane is an especially dangerous material. It contains flourocarbon, an explosive that volatilizes quickly at room temperatures.

Polyurethane is flammable and, when aflame, will emit isocyanates and other highly toxic gases.

Health and Safety Polyurethanes are made from a class of chemicals called *isocyanates* or *diisocyanates*. If there is no ventilation, an air-supplied respirator, attached to a compressed air cylinder, is required since no respirator cartridges have been approved for use with polyurethane. These air compressors are usually available for rent from an environmental product's rental company. (Lab Safety Supply in Jamesville, Wisconsin, is one company that rents such equipment.) Obviously, no one should work in the shop until the resin is through off-gassing. Working with polyurethanes can cause *isocyanate asthma*. This asthma can severely limit one's life. Severe respiratory reactions to polyurethanes during casting has also caused a number of deaths.

Of the forty-three diisocyanates in use, only about four are regulated. Some manufacturers take advantage of this by using those that are not regulated and then calling their products "safe." Even though MSDSs may say "no industrial standards apply" or "nontoxic," everyone in this field knows that all isocyanates have the same toxic effect on the body.

Take all precautions to avoid contact with skin, eyes, or clothing. Be sure to use goggles. It is preferable to work with disposable clothing, gloves, and headgear, and throw out all equipment immediately after completing the job. Use disposable utensils and containers because any remaining polyurethane will continue to volatilize dangerous vapors into the air.

Where to Find Manufacturers and distributors.

Manufacturers and distributors include:

A-R Products, Inc.

Burman Industries, Inc.

Pink House Studios

Vagabond Corporation

Walco Materials Group.

Silicone Rubber

Some Manufacturers

BJB Enterprises, Inc.

Circle K Products, Inc.

Loctite Corporation

Polytek Development Corporation

Rhône-Poulenc Chimie

Shin-Etsu Silicones of America, Inc.

Examples of Use
- Make flexible molds.
- Create pliable costume parts.
- Make fleshlike pieces.

Silicone rubber is the preferred material for long-lasting, flexible pieces for molding and casting. It is especially good for reproducing pieces on which detail is important. For an example of silicone rubber as a material for a stretchable pregnancy padding, see pages 331-332.

Description

Silicone rubber is an easy-to-work-with two-component system that cures at room temperature. Furthermore, it is durable and flexible, with high tear strength. Silicone rubbers are resistant to water and weathering and do not bond to most other materials. Other characteristics of silicones: resistance to heat, oxidation, water, and weathering; can be recycled; stretches up to 300 percent; does not break down easily, except in the presence of a hydrocarbon solvent (like paint thinner); and has minimal shrinkage. All silicones are stable at temperatures of 500°F and above, as well as flexible at temperatures below 100°F.

RTV silicone rubber will not cure in the presence of sulfur-based clay. Other disadvantages of RTV silicone are the high price and a tendency to deteriorate in the presence of polyurethane, rubber cement, and ketones (MEK and acetone).

Commercially, silicone is mainly used for electrical switch parts, heating parts, and textile finishes—especially water-repellent finishes.

A popular RTV silicone used by Los Angeles special effects' costume and prop makers is Loctite's 1065.

How to Use

Undercuts are possible with RTV silicone rubber because of the high degree of flexibility.

When molding and casting with RTV silicone rubber, no mold-release agent is necessary because silicone does not stick to anything except itself. When casting silicone into a silicone mold, obtain a special mold-release manufactured for this purpose.

When mixing, the measurements must be precise by weight or by volume. The main variable is the type of curing agent being used. Directions for mixing vary with the manufacturer and the type of silicone and are given on the product labels. Directions must be followed carefully, for incorrect mixing will impair the casting. Because of silicone's flexibility, objects and molds may require fabric reinforcement. Curing requires from twenty-four to forty-eight hours, but it can be shortened by placing the mold in an oven at 150° to 212°F, with temperature and time varying according to the manufacturer.

To color silicone, add dry pigment during mixing, or paint while it is still wet with special silicone paints, like those made by Dow Chemical Co., or make a paint by mixing pigment with the silicone.

For bonding, use silicone which has not set to bond the substance to itself. It does not bond at all to other materials.

Solvent for Cleaup Silicone casting and molding material does not stick to other surfaces and can easily be lifted off.

Health and Safety Avoid skin and eye contact and work in a well-ventilated area. Use protective gloves. The catalyst causes irreversible damage if splashed into the eyes, so wear goggles. When working with those silicones that release acid, wear a respirator with an acid-gas cartridge. For others, read carefully MSDSs for respirator recommendations. Wash hands, arms, and face thoroughly after working with silicone.

Some silicones include organic peroxides in their curing agents. MSDSs may not so identify them, but only list curing agents as "trade secrets." The vapors of organic peroxides may cause eye and respiratory irritation. Vapors from organic peroxides also react with oxygen in the air to form explosive chemicals. It is important to dispose of such materials regularly. If peroxides are unopened, dispose of them after six months and, if opened, after three. Never mix with acetone or other solvents, for such combinations are explosive. Always store them in a cool area, away from each other, and away from other combustible materials.

Where to Find Manufacturers, plastics' suppliers and distributors, craft and hobby shops.

Distributors include:

A-R Products Inc.

Burman Industries

Hastings Plastics

Pink House Studios

Walco Corporation.

Vinyl (Polyvinyl Chloride/PVC)

Some Manufacturers

Dow Chemical Company

Flexible Products Company

Marchem Corporation

Polytek Development Corporation

Examples of Use

- Develop soft, molded costume pieces.
- Create masks.
- Produce decorative strands and veinlike pieces.
- Make molds.

In creating a sea wasp costume for *Mantis*, a TV series, Makeup and Effects Laboratories (MEL) devised a realistic look using vinyl. Multicolored veins of vinyl were created by dropping small amounts of hot vinyl into cold water. The resulting reaction caused the vinyl to coagulate into thin strands. The veins were subsequently enclosed by RTV silicone layers.

Description

Vinyl plastics constitute one of the most varied groups of plastics, though polyvinyl chloride (PVC) is the only vinyl included here. PVC is the most used plastic material in the world, for it is low in cost, resistant to chemicals, and strong. Yet casting with vinyls has never been popular among theatre craftspersons because most vinyls are fairly dangerous to work with. They are set by high heat and emit toxic, carcinogenic fumes, vinyl chloride gas, and phosgene.

PVC comes in multiple-part systems of resin, plasticizer, and stabilizer which must be mixed together, or which can be purchased premixed. The premixed PVC is sold in two different forms. One is a plastisol, or liquid suspension, and the other is sold as chunks or shreds that can be heated to liquid form. PVC can be heated in an electric oven. Advantages of vinyls are their low prices and strength. Vinyls are resistant to most chemicals and, therefore, can forge a strong bond with a limited number of materials.

As a flexible mold material, PVC is not as flexible nor does it reproduce details as well as RTV silicone. However, it sets up quickly and serves other purposes satisfactorily.

In familiar commercial items, vinyls form floor tiles, shower curtains, toys, bottles, and flexible tubing.

How to Use

Molds of plaster or silicone are most commonly used with vinyl. When employing a plaster mold, allow the mold to age for two weeks before using it with PVC. Otherwise, excess moisture in the plaster will cause bubbles in the casting.

Release agents are not needed with silicone molds, but plaster molds must be flooded with linseed oil to prevent the vinyl from bonding to the casting.

Vinyl is available either premixed as a liquid, or in solid chunks, or shredded pieces. Mix vinyl according to instructions. Prepare the correct heating equipment and implements.

Mix with spatula or electric drill. Some manufacturers of vinyl products use an electric drill with mixing blades permanently positioned over the stove or hot plate. To avoid dangerous mishaps, never leave the heating vinyl unattended.

Vinyl heats best in an electric turkey roaster. A small amount of eight cups or less can be heated in a carousel microwave for four to six minutes. (Do not use the same turkey roaster or microwave for food that is to be eaten.) When removing the vinyl from a microwave, be sure to mix it well.

Vinyl is a difficult and dangerous material to use. The above directions are general and meant as a preliminary guide only. Formulas vary among brands. Be sure to obtain complete directions from the manufacturer, and follow them carefully.

When casting, pour the mixture carefully into the mold. The vinyl sets in about 45 minutes, though it takes at least another hour for the inside of the casting to cool down from the 350°F temperature.

Be sure to clean the surface with acetone before applying adhesives or paints.

Bonding is successful with most vinyl adhesives. The Oatey Company manufactures both flexible and rigid PVC solvent adhesives, and special PVC glues are available through distributors of PVC.

PVC coloring can be added by the manufacturer before purchase to use with premixed liquid vinyl. Pigment can be added by first mixing it into a small vinyl suspension then adding to the complete mixture. To paint it, first apply a spray adhesive for priming. Acrylic paints bond to an adhesive primer.

Solvent for Cleanup Acetone, MEK, and industrial-grade isopropyl alcohol.

Precautions Be careful of the high temperature, which could cause hazardous leaks or spills.

Health and Safety Overheating PVC releases carcinogenic and poisonous toxic vapors. Use a forced air-ventilation system, a respirator, leather gloves, and a leather apron. Have a fire extinguisher close by.

Where to Find Plastics manufacturers and suppliers.

Plastic Sheetings

This section deals with the plastic sheetings that are available mainly from plastics suppliers and manufacturers. Discussed are foamed plastic sheetings, plastic sheetings especially manufactured for theatrical costume and prop industries, and plastic sheeting formed for other industries. In this section, plastic film is considered a sheeting, for the difference between film and sheeting is arbitrary. Nylon sheeting and acetate sheeting are not discussed here, for they are rarely used to fabricate costume pieces. Tubing and a few other forms of solid plastics are included.

Plastic substances are pliable and formable. All plastic materials fall into one of two main groups: *thermosetting plastics* or *thermoplastics*. Most of the materials discussed in this category are thermoplastics, which are available in solid form, ready for cutting and forming.

Thermoplastics are so named because they can be formed and reformed, bent and twisted into complex shapes many times over when heated. Each time they are reheated, they regain their pliancy. They also have the tendency to return to their original shape; this is called *memory*. For example, an acrylic tube previously bent will remember to straighten when reheated to its softening point. Heat sources can be kitchen-type ovens, industrial ovens, vacuum-formers, turkey roasters, heating strips, and heat guns. (Ovens used for food preparation should not be used for heating plastics.)

Thermosetting plastics, or *thermosets*, can be molded into a form only once; the form is then solidified through a chemical process. Heat decomposes thermosetting plastics, and though they will always soften at temperatures above 350°F, they cannot be reformed after the original shaping. Thermosetting plastics are available as sheets, rods, foams, and other shapes, which can be cut and bonded, though not heat formed. Molding and casting thermosetting resins are discussed in a preceding section.

The material on the following pages is brief and general. It is important to procure complete literature from individual manufacturers or distributors and study their specifications before selecting from among the many varieties of each type of plastic, or before proceeding with exacting techniques such as vacuum-forming.

The materials in this section of the book are organized as follows: *Flexible Plastic Foam Sheetings, Flexible Plastic Sheetings, Rigid Plastic Foam Sheetings, Rigid Plastic Sheetings,* and *Textiles*. Within each category, types of products are listed alphabetically.

Below are the types of sheetings covered in this section. All of these can be useful to the costumer.

Thermoplastics Discussed	Some Brand Names
Acrylic	Plexiglas, Lucite, Perspex
Acrylonitrile-Butadiene Styrene (ABS)	Cadco ABS, Royalite, SP 900's
Acrylic-Polyvinyl Chloride	Kydex, Royalite
Polycarbonate	Lexan, Merlon, Tuffak
Polyester	Friendly Plastic, Hexcelite, Mylar, Orthoplast, Polyform, Veriform
Polyethylene	Cadco, Plastazote,
Polyethylene, expanded (foam)	Ethafoam, Minicel, Plastazote
Polyolefin, spunbonded	Tyvek
Polystyrene	Catalin, Lustron
Polystyrene, expanded (foam)	Dyplast, Styrofoam
Vinyl	Naugahyde
Vinyl, expanded (foam)	Sintra
Thermosets Discussed	**Some Brand Names**
Chloroprene Rubber	Neoprene
Polyurethane, expanded (foam)	Foamall, SIF (Scott), Vibrathane
Also Discussed	**Some Brand Names**
Beaded mesh	Dimensional Bedazzers, Metalite
Latex natural rubber sheet	Dental Dam, Four D Latex Rubber
Silicone treated fabric	Scotchlite reflective material
Thermoset-treated fabric	Solvoset

Working Methods

Forming with Heat

Many thermoplastics become pliable when heated to temperatures between 250° and 300°F. The exact temperature for heatforming a specific plastic should always be checked with the manufacturer's specifications: Heating a plastic at too high a temperature can cause bubbling, scorching, and irreversible structural changes; heating at too low a temperature can cause crazing (fine cracks on the surface of the plastic). At the correct temperature, thermoplastics can be bent into new shapes. They must be shaped quickly, for once heated, thermoplastics cool rapidly, and when cool, the plastic is frozen into place. Cooling time depends upon the type of plastic as well as the thickness and size of the sheet.

Kitchen ovens can be used for forming some thermoplastics, but caution must be taken—plastic fumes are toxic, and temperature controls and air circulation in kitchen ovens are not dependable. Because of the residue of toxic fumes, any kitchen-type oven used for plastic formation should, obviously, not be used for food preparation. If a kitchen oven is to be used, place the plastic sheeting on a soft cloth-covered cookie tin or on a piece of fiberglass mat. Laying the plastic on racks will heat the plastic unevenly and deform it. Work with thick cotton gloves and have ready a cloth on which to set the plastic.

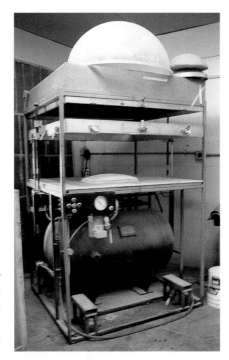

A large vacuum-former can be used for making large costume pieces from plastic sheetings.
PHOTO: ROBERT W. ZENTIS.

Vacuum-formers have been used successfully by costume and prop workshops since before World War I. When vacuum-forming, a plastic sheet is held in a frame, or vacuum press, and heat is applied until the plastic is soft and pliable. A vacuum is applied through small holes in the mold cavity, and the atmospheric pressure forces the softened sheet against the surface of the mold. When the plastic is cooled and solid, it will retain the shape of the mold.

Straight vacuum-forming involves placing a negative mold directly underneath the framed plastic sheet. *Drape* forming uses a positive mold under the plastic sheet. Straight vacuum-forming is more successful with heavier sheeting that is molded to a relatively shallow form, not requiring an exactly consistent thickness. Drape forming is more useful with thinner sheeting and for creating deeper forms or for producing surfaces needing a more consistent thickness.

For costume-making purposes, molds for vacuum-forming are often made of rigid polyurethane foam (green foam), plaster, and reinforced epoxy or polyester. Frequently, a model is made from a soft material, like an oil-based clay, which is then cast over with reinforced epoxy or polyester to make a strong and long-lasting positive mold. To avoid melting the clay with heat, use special types of oil- or wax-based plasticine clay, such as VanAken Modeling Clay and Roma Plastilina. You can also freeze the clay before it is put in the oven, or coat the clay model with either epoxy and fiberglass or polyester and fiberglass, or with a thin layer of vacuum-formed, thin-

A small vacuum-former is useful for creating smaller objects.
PHOTO: ROBERT W. ZENTIS

plastic sheeting. Other materials that can be used for models include wood, cast aluminum, and found objects. Both polyurethane foam and oil-base clay will melt at the oven's high temperature and will need to be scraped out of the vacuum-formed piece if used.

1 heater

2 clamp

3 plastic sheeting

4 mold

5 vacuum

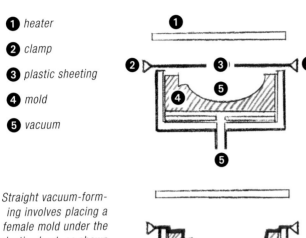

Straight vacuum-form-
ing involves placing a
female mold under the
plastic sheet, as shown
in this cross section of
a vacuum-former.

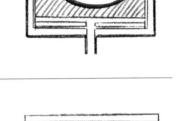

Drape-forming uses a
male mold under the
plastic sheet, as shown
in this cross section of
a vacuum-former.

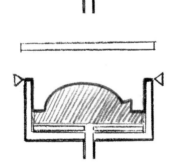

Vacuum-formers are costly to buy, but shops have built their own economically—at a cost of a few hundred to several thousand dollars. Thurston James, in *The Prop Builder's Molding and Casting Handbook*, devotes twelve pages to instruction on building a vacuum-former. Thelma Newman, in *Plastics as an Art Form*, describes a method of creating a vacuum-forming apparatus suitable for small objects from a vacuum cleaner and self-made wooden boxes. Complete information about both these books can be found in the *Bibliography*.

Many workshops send a design and its pattern to a business specializing in vacuum-forming. Most large cities have vacuum-forming shops. In New York, costume workshops often send special designs to Costume Armour, Inc., and in Los Angeles, shops most frequently use Prop Masters Incorporated. Sign makers often have vacuum-formers and are another resource for the costumer. Some costume shops even purchase miniature vacuum-formers, built by toy manufacturers, in order to produce very small decorative items like jewels.

Plastic sheetings typically thermoformed include butyrate, ABS, polycarbonate, polyethylene, polystyrene, acrylic, and vinyl. These sheetings are available in a variety of thicknesses, opacities, and textures.

For further information on vacuum-forming, refer to Thurston James's *The Prop Builder's Molding and Casting Handbook*, Thelma Newman's *Plastics as an Art Form*, or Nicholas Rourkes's *Crafts in Plastics*, all listed in the *Bibliography*.

Heat guns, also known as *hot-air blowers*, operate much like hair blow dryers, though at far higher temperatures, sending a concentrated stream of hot air through a blower fan and the nozzle. Temperatures range from 150° to 1,000° F; only the lower temperatures are appropriate for plastic forming. Heat

Standard heat guns, ranging in temperature range from 150° to 1,000°, are useful tools for melting plastics.

guns are manufactured for fabricating both metals and plastics as well as for setting adhesives, castings, coatings, and other chemicals. Some heat guns supply cool as well as hot air.

Heat guns can be used for melting the edges of thermoplastics when bonding them to like surfaces. Heat guns are also handy for melting thermoplastic sheeting before hand-draping it over molds in a free-form style. Finally, heat guns can be used for laminating and heat-sealing.

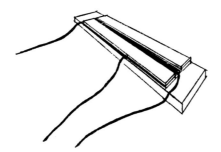

Strip heaters can be assembled from kits available at most plastic suppliers.

Strip heaters offer the easiest method for heat bending solid thermoplastics and can produce a clean straight bend. The plastic is heated only along a straight line in a localized strip limited to the long narrow shape of the heater, which usually consists of a heating element a half-inch wide by thirty-six inches long embedded in a metal and wood base. Strip heaters are available at plastic sheeting suppliers. Those wishing to make their own strip heaters will find them fairly simple to construct by following the instructions in Time-Life's *Working With Plastics*.

When using the strip heater, heat plastic sheeting less than ¼ inch in thickness only on one side, making sure that the plastic is one-sixteenth inch away from the heating element. Sheets over ¼ inch thick should be heated on both sides, either by heating on each side of the plastic or by turning the sheeting from side to side while working. When the plastic has been heated, bend it to the desired angle and hold it until cool.

When forming angles, place the plastic into a jig or other support while it cools, using rubber bands or weights to hold it in place. The plastic bends evenly only if it has been sufficiently heated. If it is bent before reaching the proper temperature, crazing, or small cracks, will occur. If it is overheated, the plastic will melt and form bulges.

The strip heating method is especially effective with acrylic. Because acrylic scratches easily, remove the protective paper covering only from the surface area that is to be heated.

Heating with hot sand is a method used to bend pipes or tubes. First, warm the sand in a saucepan on a kitchen burner or hot plate. Stir the sand to assure an even temperature of at least 300°F throughout, occasionally dipping the end of the plastic pipe into the sand to test for pliability of the pipe. When the pipe becomes easily pliable, cap one end with aluminum foil or with a polyvinyl chloride (PVC) cap. Very carefully and quickly, pour the sand into the top end of the pipe through a funnel, and cap the top end. The sand will cool during the transfer, and care must be taken not to spill the hot sand. As soon as it is flexible, bend the pipe by gloved hand or around a form. When the pipe is cool, remove the caps, empty out the sand, and clean out with a water hose. To shorten the setting time, cool with water. This method is well suited to working with PVC. Work with caution, for it is easy to be burned when working with hot sand.

Opticians use hot sand, heated in a saucepan or skillet, to heat and soften eyeglass frames. They dip the frames in the hot sand to soften the plastic and remove the lenses. In Part Three is an example of the hot-sand method as used in making a pair of wings. See page 336.

Bonding

Thermoplastics may be bonded by several different methods: with *solvents*, with *adhesives*, or by *heat*. Upon request, manufacturers will supply recommendations for bonding as well as for coloring.

Solvent bonding is a method that uses a solution to dissolve the surface of plastic. When two treated pieces are placed together, the dissolved plastics intermingle and bond as the solvent evaporates. Solvents and solvent cements are easy to use and produce strong and integral joints. Solvent bonding is the preferred method for thermoplastics and will not work at all with thermosetting plastics.

Soak cementing. Pour solvent in pan to approximately 1/16th inch. Place wires or brads under the sheet and hold for about 30 seconds or until the edge is softened.

Solvent bonding includes dope cementing, capillary cementing, and soak cementing methods. Dope cementing is mixing a solvent with pieces of the same plastic as that which is being cemented. Dope cementing has a high viscosity and will fill gaps easily and with little shrinkage. With capillary cementing, an appropriate solvent is applied with a brush or eyedropper to both edges to be joined. The parts are held together with light pressure until the edges are bonded. Soak cementing requires soaking one of the edges to be joined in the appropriate solvent for one-half to eight minutes, depending on the solvent, the plastic sheet, and the desired bond strength. Drain the excess liquid from the edge, and then place the two sheeting edges together, holding one-half to one minute. Place in a jig or clamp for ten to thirty minutes, and allow another eight to twenty-four hours before using.

Adhesive bonding uses materials that stick to the surface of other materials. When bonding smooth-surface plastics, first remove all dirt and grease, then sand the edges to be bonded. Many plastics are difficult to join with adhesives, making solvent-bonding generally more successful. Adhesive-bonding is the *only* bonding method possible for thermosetting plastics and expanded, or foamed, plastics. Epoxy, polyester, and silicone are best bonded with epoxy or certain rubber and plastic cements specially formulated for their use. Contact cements are preferable for most foamed plastics, while white glue is most suited for Styrofoam.

Applied heat also bonds by dissolving the edges of the plastic. The edges can be pressed together until joined and cooled. Two plastics that must be joined this way are polyethylene and polypropylene. Heat guns work well for heat bonding.

An ordinary *household iron* can provide heat for bonding. First, insulate the worktable from the heat with a sheet of cardboard or Teflon. If working with cardboard, wrap the plastic sheeting in between two sheets of silicone-coated paper to avoid bonding the plastic to the cardboard. The bottom layer of silicone paper will be needed only if the iron has a nonstick Teflon coating. Before working with the actual plastics, experiment with some scraps to learn the correct temperature setting and length of time needed to create a bond. In order to create a straight seam, make a template from a piece of wood, attach it to the worktable on top of the plastic sheeting, and use it to guide the iron.

Be sure to follow safety guidelines when working with solvents and adhesives. Work in a well-ventilated area wearing gloves, and avoid extended skin contact. Avoid open flames and cigarettes. Never use chemicals after drinking alcohol, for these solvents and fumes are dangerous to work with and require a clear head.

Cutting

Sawing with power saws, such as jigsaws, band saws, circular saws, or saber saws, is the quickest way to cut both rigid solid sheeting and rigid foam. A high-blade setting on any of the table saws makes the cleanest cut with the least likelihood of chipping and kickback; however, the greater open profile of the blade demands extra caution when sawing. Band saws need either wood-cutting or metal-cutting skip-tooth blades with at least ten teeth per inch. Leave in place any protective sheeting before cutting, and cover unprotected sheeting with cardboard or heavy wrapping paper, which is bonded in place with white glue or masking tape. Coat the saw blade with soap to prevent paper pieces from clogging the saw blade. Specifics for using band saws and circular saws with each kind of plastic are included in the listing for that plastic.

Because plastics quickly dull saw blades, it is wise to have an assortment of blades reserved for this purpose. The best blades, and the most expensive, are carbide blades, manufactured for band, circular, and table saws. Regular wood-cutting blades will clog, melt the plastic, and quickly wear out. For more on saw blades, see Time-Life's *Working with Plastics* or other more detailed industrial plastics' references.

Among the smaller power tools, the jigsaw and the portable saber saw are most versatile and will cut all types of plastics in straight lines as well as into bevels, curves, and intricate patterns.

Hacksaws also cut plastic, though less efficiently than power saws. They work well on rigid sheeting over one-eighth inch and on rigid tubing. The sheeting or tubing should be firmly clamped into place on the workbench, and the saw should be held at a 90-degree angle to the material.

Scissors and *tin snips* will cut flexible foams as well as all of the films and thinner plastic sheetings mentioned in this section. Scissors used for cutting plastics should not also be used for cutting textiles, for plastics will dull them.

Breaking is an easy method for evenly dividing rigid plastics of up to a quarter of an inch into straight lines. If the plastic is covered with a protective paper coating, cut right through. Mark the line on the paper or plastic, and lay a steel square along the line, clamping it if it is too large to control. Score the line repeatedly with a plastic draw knife, utility knife, or mat knife, cutting about halfway through the plastic. Lay the plastic on a table with the scored line at the table edge, or lay the scored line over a three-quarter-inch inch dowel, cut side up. Use one hand to brace the wide part of the sheet and press down with the other, shaping the sheet into two parts. This method can also be used with rigid tubing and rods.

Cutting with a *razor blade*, *paper cutter*, or *tin snips* works well on thin sheets of rigid foam, less than a half-inch thick. Razor blades will also work on flexible foams.

Carving with an *electric carving knife* works for rigid foams and thick flexible foams. Electric carving knives are excellent tools for cutting curves and intricate shapes as well as straight lines.

Commercial foam cutters are similar in shape to carving knives, but consist of two long blades that move in opposite directions. The blades are attached to a flat base that adds stability to the process. Take special care when using these cutters—they easily cause burnings. Foam cutters are available through internet sources such as Superior Fomebords Corperation and Crown North America. Instructions for making foam cutters can be found on the internet under *Poorman's Hot Wire Foam Cutter.*

Observing safety precautions is essential when using power tools. Do not work alone, even if you are familiar with the tool. Follow manufacturers' directions exactly and specifically. Learn how to hold plastic sheeting correctly, since it grabs easily and could cause the hand to slip.

Plastic dust will seriously irritate eyes and lungs. Use great care when cutting plastic with tools that make dust and loose particulate matter. Small chips darting into the air can injure the eyes and face. Wear goggles, a protective face mask, protective clothing, and gloves, and inspect edges which could be a hazard if they are sharp and uneven.

Coloring

Sheet plastics can be colored with dyes, paints, and other coloring agents, though many, like acrylics, are already available in colors. Plastics are colored just as are textiles, though many have surfaces resistant to almost all chemicals and oils. Dip-dyeing, brushing, spraying, rubbing with a cloth, or using an eye dropper are all possible coloring methods. The specific colorant for each method is listed within the description of each sheeting. Plastics manufacturers recommend specific colorants for their products; however, many of those recommended are only available in large industrial quantities.

Dyes are available at plastic-supply companies as either powders or solutions. Before dyeing, be sure all sanding, polishing, and cleaning is complete. If the surface is not clean, the dye or paint may not bond. Most stains can be removed with detergent and water; acrylic cleans well with isopropyl alcohol. Do not use ketones and hydrocarbons, like acetone, lacquer thinner, and paint thinner, for cleaning most plastics; they can cause crazing. After cleaning, handle the plastic using lint-free cloths because fingerprints can mar the surface.

Test the color on a scrap of the same material, as when textile dyeing, both to test the color itself and to discover the immersion time necessary for obtaining the desired color. For pastel colors, mix in thinners or dye toners.

Cold-dip dyes are for acrylics and acetates, with three minutes the average time in the dye bath. Tints of colors can be obtained with a quick dip, and dark colors with a longer time in the dye bath. After dyeing, rinse the plastic in clean cold water and dry with a clean soft cloth.

Hot-dip dyes are concentrated liquids, usually mixed with one part of the dye to ten parts of water. Brands vary, so always look for manufacturers' directions. Hot-dip dye is heated to 190°F before the plastic is immersed. Immersion time ranges from a second up to one minute, depending upon the depth of color desired. After dyeing, rinse the piece in cold water. Some plastics may be deformed by so high a temperature. Thin acetates should be colored at 165°F. Never heat paint or other materials that may contain lead.

Paints as well as lacquers affect and change the surface texture. For this reason, dyes are usually the coloring agents of choice. Please consult the appropriate sections of this book for finding the compatible selection of paints. Clear plastics, such as acrylic, can be effectively painted from the rear side, allowing the color to show through without destroying the surface qualities.

Health and Safety   Since plastic dust is dangerous to the respiratory system, the following cautionary measures should be followed when cutting:

- Always wear safety goggles and a dust mask to protect against fine dust.
- Be sure that any power tools are fitted with guards.

- If you are using an oven or a strip heater to form sheet plastics, do not leave it unattended. Check the oven's accuracy with a thermometer.

- Do not heat plastic near an open flame, or allow it to touch the heat source.

- Be sure to protect your hands with thick protective cloth gloves.

- Supply your work area with an ABC-rated, dry-powder fire extinguisher.

- To avoid danger from heat, adhesive, or solvent fumes, wear a respirator *and* work in a well-ventilated area, and avoid contact with skin. Remember, there is no respirator cartridge to protect against emissions from heating plastics. Ventilation is always needed when working with plastics.

- *Do not smoke or use plastic sheeting near flames, and keep away from food.*

Flexible Plastic Foam Sheetings

Expanded Polyethylene

Some Brands	Manufacturers/Distributors
Ethafoam	Dow Chemical Co.
Minicel L-200, 300, 400	Voltek
Plastazote	BXL plastics limited (London area)
Polyethylene Foam	Allied Plastics

Examples of Use

- Fabricate bodies and heads of animal and character costumes requiring exceptional durability.

- Form armor and thick semiflexible garments and accessories.

- Make trimmings on heavyweight and rigid garments.

- Pad body parts.

This semirigid foam sheeting is extensively used for the bodies of walk-around and character costumes. It is soft enough to provide flexibility for the wearer, while at the same time maintaining a solid form. Ventilation holes can be cut with a circular-drill bit or with an awl. Polyethylene foam has served as the basis for an assortment of costumes representing animals, dancing peanuts, and golf balls.

Polyethylene can be used decoratively or when a firm padding is needed.

Polyethylene rod is commonly used for interior structures, or armatures, of walk-around costumes. Decoratively, it can embellish helmets, armor, and outer-space costumes. For an example of decoration, see the *Space Suits* section on page 393.

Description   This *polyethylene-foam sheeting* preferred by costume and prop craftspeople is of high density, yet is flexible and strong. It has excellent heat-forming capabilities, and is practical for shallow pieces. Usually manufactured as white, but available in other colors, it is easy to paint and coat. One of its early notable uses was on the London stage: the life-size chess pieces of the original production of *Chess* were made of expanded polyethylene.

Ethafoam by Dow is stiffer than the other listed foam sheetings and is covered by a waxy coating. Ethafoam rod, a standard among costumers, is flexible, strong, and sometimes used for decorative effects. Besides Ethafoam rod's popularity for decoration, it is often used to construct flexible armatures.

Commercially, polyethylene foam is commonly used for padding, gaskets, and insulation. Plastazote brand is used in the medical field for casts, splints, and packaging delicate instruments, though it is equally suitable for costume use.

How to Use   Many shops shape polyethylene-foam sheeting with a cutting and gluing technique. Cut with razor blade, mat knife, or scissors. Shops with vacuum-formers can take advantage of polyethylene's thermoforming capabilities and form the sheeting in an oven.

Heat-forming requires temperatures between 325° to 425°F. Vacuum-formers, kitchen-type ovens, heat guns, and wands may all be used for molding polyethylene foams. Heat the sheeting very gradually and evenly, for it conducts heat internally at a very slow rate. Because of its thickness, polyethylene foam does not cast well into deeply volumed forms, and unwanted folds will result.

Bonding works well with thick-bodied adhesives such as PVAs (white glues). When bonding polyethylene foam to itself, cut the pieces to exact shape, bevel edges when curved forms are desired, butt them together, and hold for about a minute or until set. To cover polyethylene foam with fabric, use either solvent or water-based rubber contact cement. (Barge, Scotch-Grip 1099, and Fastbond NF-30 are the favored rubber cements among those costumers interviewed.) Costumes made with this material are usually neither laundered nor dry-cleaned, so the choice of adhesives is fairly free.

When bonding or coloring Ethafoam brand, first prepare the coated surface by either lightly scuffing with a fine sandpaper or wiping with mild dishwashing detergent and water.

 Polyethylene sheeting can be colored by applying acrylic artists' or scenic paint, though these do not necessarily promise longevity, since polyethylene is more flexible than regular acrylic paint. When painting polyethylene rod, it is necessary first to prime it, using either a rubber-based adhesive, like 3M 77, or a latex adhesive like Pros-Aide. For opacity, use acrylic-based scenic or artists' paints, such as those used on The Thing from a Marvel Comics commercial and the True Value Boy walk-around, both described in Part Three.

Coat unpainted foam sheeting with a flexible white glue (like Phlexglu), as in the costumes from the film *Caddy Shack II* described on page 382, with polyester resin, or with liquid polyurethane resin. (Burman Industries' WC575 is transparent, non-yellowing, and works well for this purpose.)

Health and Safety The precautions that should be followed are listed in the introductory on pages 247-248.

Where to Find Plastic supply stores and distributors.
Distributors include:
Foamex Products, Inc.
Compac Industries
Duraco.

Sizes Sheeting: 1/8" - 4" thick.
Rod: 1/2" - 3" diameter.

Expanded Polyurethane (Urethane Foam)

Polyurethane is a thermosetting plastic—in other words, it cannot be reformed after it is once shaped by heat. Flexible polyurethane foam is like foamed natural rubber—soft and spongy. In fact, it was developed as a rubber substitute, and there are many who still refer to it as *foam rubber*. There are two basic types of flexible polyurethane foam that costumers use, and they will be defined and treated separately, for though they can be used interchangeably, they also have characteristics that are sufficiently different to reserve each for a different purpose.

Reticulated Insulation Foam (Scott Foam)

Some Brands	Manufacturers/Distributors
SIF (formerly Scott Foam)	Foamex Products, Inc.

Examples of Use
- Create the shells of soft-structured animal and character costumes.
- Use for padding suits and for padding actual garments.
- Make oversize headpieces and other garments requiring soft structure.

Polyurethane insulation foam is ideal for padded and highly structured costumes and is the favored material for this purpose among many costume craftspersons.

For building padding, see the *Padding Suit* section on pages 327-332. For using foam as the structure for bodies of animals and character costumes, see various examples in Part Three.

Polyurethane can be used for stylized wigs, crowns, and large structural pieces. Because of its strength and body, it eliminates the need for buckram or other interior stiffeners. Although not considered usable for fine millinery, this material is appropriate for low-budget productions.

Description *Reticulated insulation foam*, commonly referred to as *Scott Foam*, is a patented flexible, open-pored, plastic foam produced from an ester type of polyurethane. The structure is heat-formed to create a strong network between cells. The composition is one of thin strands that occupy 3 percent of the space, leaving 97 percent empty space. Its variety of texture—from coarse to soft—is attributable to its number of pores per linear inch (ppi), ranging from 10 ppi, coarse, to 100 ppi, soft. Those known to costumers are in the 10 ppi to 30 ppi range. Though it comes in colors, most costumers and prop makers use the charcoal gray, the most commonly available color. Lighter colors darken and yellow with light, while the dark gray is unaffected by light. Reticulated foam is stable, and is known to last for more than five years. It is completely launderable, with the ability to withstand intermittent temperatures up to 250°F. It is not adversely affected by cleaning solvents and so may be dry-cleaned.

Industrially, it is most often used for filtration systems. It is found in air conditioners, furnaces, and noise suppressors, as well as rug underlays, gaskets, paintbrush applicators, and powder puffs.

How to Use   Reticulated foam can be easily cut, nailed, stapled, sewn, glued, and grommeted.

Cutting the thinner foam sheet is most easily done with scissors or razor blades, though the thicker foams can be cut with an electric carving knife or a commercial foam cutter. A method advised by some is to lay the foam on top of a metal, glass, or tough plastic sheet, and then cut it with a razor blade. To cut with a band saw, use a metal cutting blade of no more than fourteen teeth per inch at a slow speed. Note that polyurethane will dull the saw blade.

Polyurethane reticulated foam can be easily formed into costume pieces such as this helmet.
FABRICATION: JANET HARPER.

Bonding any kind of urethane foam to itself is most satisfactory with synthetic rubber adhesives. Barge Cement, Stabond 846, Devcon's Rubber Adhesive, and 3M's Fastbond 48-NF (water-based) are popular among costumers for bonding the foam to itself and to fabrics. Epoxies and rubber cements like Barge and polyurethane adhesives work well for bonding to metal and reinforced plastics. Epoxies and contact rubber cements are the preferred adhesives for cementing to reinforced plastics (typically epoxy or polyester resin reinforced with fiberglass). Most of the rubber cements and epoxies will last well through laundering, though not through dry cleaning. Refer to the charts in the adhesives section on pages 42 and 68-71.

When bonding foam to itself, cut out pieces to the exact shape, with no overlap, apply the adhesive, and butt the edges together. For reinforcement, apply liquid latex onto the seam lines. Polyurethane foam can also be sewn by hand or machine. The most durable methods of fastening are gluing pieces together, or sandwiching them inside of two fabric layers and seaming the fabric just outside the edges of the foam.

Coloring is successful with either artists' acrylic paints or acrylic-based scenic paints such as Iddings Deep Colors.

Precautions   Softer foams are shorter lived than the denser.

Health and Safety   Polyurethane has a low melting point and must be kept away from heat and flame. In using it with adhesives, solvents, and colorants, follow the safety precautions outlined on earlier pages.

Where to Find   Plastic-foam distributors. Foamex can supply a vendor list.

Sizes   Pores per inch: 10, 20, 25, 30, 45, 60, 80, 100.

1/8" - 2" thick.

40" - 52" wide.

Upholstery Foam

Some Brands	Manufacturers
Foamall	Woodall Industries, Inc.
Vibrathane	United States Rubber Company

Usually sold by generic name

Examples of Use
- Make padding for padding suits and pad actual garments for short-time use.
- Fabricate oversize garments and pieces requiring a soft structure.
- Produce mock-ups for garments to be built out of sturdier foam.

Many costumers, when confronted with the challenge of building long-lasting padded costumes, construct a mock-up from the less expensive upholstery foam, then use reticulated insulation foam for the actual costume. Though upholstery foam can be used just as is insulation foam, its use is best limited to the short term.

Description   *Polyurethane upholstery* foam was the first substitute for natural foam rubber; in fact, many still refer to it by that name. Polyurethane upholstery foam has been used for many years for padding costumes, but it does not have the stability of the newer, reticulated foams and will degenerate upon exposure to light. Usually sold in white, it is sometimes available in other colors. It is much less expensive than the reticulated foam, and it is just as easy to work with.

In industry, this type of foam is commonly used for furniture, automobile seats, and rug padding as well as toys and household sponges.

How to Use   Cutting upholstery foam requires the same implements as those for cutting reticulated foam: Use scissors, razor blades, electric carving knives, or commercial foam cutters.

Bonding methods are also the same as those for reticulated foam. Please refer to page 251. However, this foam should not be sewn by machine. The foam can tear easily along the sewing-machine-made perforations, and hand-sewing is tenuous. Many costumers successfully encase the foam between two sewn layers of fabric.

Coloring polyurethane upholstery foam is possible with a wide range of dyes, paints, inks, and stains. It can be dyed with union dyes, like Rit and Tintex, in a machine. Acrylic-based paints, artists' acrylic paint, and Iddings Scenic Paint last well through laundering, though we have found only the Tulip brand paints to last through dry cleaning. For transparent and translucent coloring, Pelikan brand inks and Fiebing's Shoe Dyes last well.

Health and Safety Same as for insulation foam. Please refer to the page 251.

Where to Find Fabric stores, upholstery suppliers, and some plastic-supply shops.

Sizes 48" wide by 1/8", ¼", ½", 1" thick, and blocks that can be cut to size.

Polyvinyl Chloride, Expanded ("Sintra")

Some Brands	Manufacturers
Sintra	Allucabond Technologies, Inc.

Other makes are sold generically

Examples of Use
- Form hard surfaced costumes like armor, headdresses, and wings.
- Create armatures.

Use when flexibility, strength, and light weight are important. For using Sintra to build a pair of wings, see pages 335-337.

Description *Sintra* is a moderately expanded polyvinyl chloride (PVC) with half the density of normal PVC. It is tougher, more flexible, and has greater impact resistance than some of the other traditional thermoplastic sheetings. Sintra has high chemical resistance, is lighter weight than most solid plastics, and is available in eight colors and many thicknesses. It can be nailed, screwed, heat-formed, and coated. Some industrial applications are for indoor and outdoor signs and as a substitute for foamcore in making models and displays.

How to Use Cutting the thinner sheets of Sintra is easily done with a utility or mat knife. To cut thicker sheets, use a band saw with a skip tooth or wood blade at a low to medium speed. High-speed cutting can melt Sintra. When cutting, watch for debris collection, which could jam the blade.

Heat-forming Sintra can be done with vacuum-former or with any other heat-forming process. It has a low-temperature melting point of 300°F.

A bonding agent for successful solvent bonding is tetrahydrofuron (THF). To bond with adhesives, use cyanoacrylate adhesives or vinyl cements such as Weld-on 10 or 3M Scotch-Grip 1099. Hot-glue pellets can be used, but only judiciously, for the high heat can disfigure the Sintra.

Coloring Sintra should be preceded by an undercoat of auto-body primer or plastic primer. Sintra then can be painted with acrylic paint. Metallic finishes look especially good on Sintra.

Precautions Sintra has a low melting point. Do not submit temperatures over 300°F and avoid high-speed cutting equipment that could melt the material.

Health and Safety	Same as for insulation foam. See page 250.
Where to Find	Plastics distributors.
Sizes	1 mm. - 19 mm.

Flexible Plastic Sheetings

Chloroprene Rubber (Neoprene)

Some Brands	Manufacturers
Neoprene	E. I. Du Pont de Nemours and Company

Examples of Use

- Add shoe soles.

- Fabricate semirigid and fairly flexible outer-space, futuristic, and animal costumes and accessories.

Shoe soles can be easily added in the costume shop by cutting Neoprene to shape and contact cementing it with any of the above adhesives. It is convenient to keep a few yards in stock, for most theatrical productions require the quietness of rubber-soled shoes.

Space suits can gain a protective look through the use of synthetic rubber floor matting or Neoprene yard goods. (See *Space Suits* in Part Three for an inventive use of Neoprene floor matting.) Thin Neoprene film is similar to natural-latex film, though less stretchy, and is mostly suitable for thin garments that can be glued.

Description   *Chloroprene*, commonly known by the brand name *Neoprene* is a thermosetting plastic and the first rubber to be synthesized. Other synthetic rubbers are silicone, SBR, and nitrile, but of this group, Neoprene is the most available and practical because it is long-lasting, flame-resistant, and moderately priced. As high-density foamed sheeting, it is a practical material for costumers and craftspersons. As a thin, unfoamed sheet, it is similar to natural rubber, though opaque, thicker, and not as elastic. It is naturally pale in color, though usually marketed in black since exposure to light causes the lighter hues to discolor. Further advantages are that it is longer lasting than other synthetic rubbers, and it is more resistant to burning than most other plastics. Expanded or foamed, Neoprene is also available, laminated to jersey.

In industry, it is found in soling, gaskets, and auto tires as well as in waterproof floor-matting material generally available on the retail market, though not all floor mats are Neoprene. Foamed Neoprene is also used for waterproof divers' suits and as a protective sheet coating. Synthetic rubbers like Neoprene have far overtaken the use of natural rubbers.

How to Use   Cutting chloroprene sheeting cleanly depends upon its thickness and density. For most applications, a mat knife or electrical knife is suitable.

Fabric-covered Neoprene sheeting forms the headdress, shoulder pieces, and appliqués on these lizard costumes. The headdresses are formed from cast plastic bandages covered with Neoprene; the shoulder pieces are machine sewn, and appliqués are glued onto the unitards with shoemaker's rubber cement.

DESIGN: JENNIFER LANGEBERG FOR COSTUMES WORN AT THE REDWOOD EMPIRE ICE ARENA.
PHOTO: KEN SCIALLO.

In bonding, use either solvent-bonding or adhesive-bonding. For solvent-bonding, use a ketone, such as acetone.

Adhesive bonding is most successful with Neoprene-based and other synthetic rubber-based adhesives, such as Barge, Scotchgrip 2141 and Stabond 836.

For coloring Neoprene, some of the paints that bond to it without chipping are polyurethane-based paint, rubber-cement paint, and type B makeup adhesive mixed with acrylic paint (PAX paint described on page 212). Other paints will bond initially, but, being inflexible after a short while they may chip on a flexible surface.

Solvent for Cleanup   For cleaning up adhesives, use acetone; for cleaning after painting, use the solvent appropriate for that paint. When using acetone, keep in mind that it is a solvent for Neoprene and must be used judiciously.

Health and Safety   Use precautions for adhesives and paints as outlined in the introductory material to working with plastic sheeting on pages 247-248.

Where to Find   As rubber matting: auto-accessory stores.

Neoprene sheeting: shoemakers' supply stores and rubber-sheeting distributors.

Sizes   Usually 36" wide.

1/32" - 2" thick.

Latex

Some Brands	Manufacturers
Dental Dam	Coltene Whaledent Inc.
Latex Rubber Sheet	Four D Rubber Company Ltd., UK

Examples of Use
- Build garments and garment parts with high flexibility and smooth texture.
- Make flexible hinges to attach latex sheet to itself and other materials.

Costumes designed for the futuristic film *Space Hunter* were made by covering nylon-spandex leotards with latex sheeting that had been bonded with 3M's 77 spray. Both spandex and latex were garnished with cutouts and embellished with found objects of junkyard scrap and plastic tubing. Julie Weiss designed the costumes, which were built by J & M Costumers, Inc.

Other latex-sheeting costumes, as well as fashions, have been built by Syren in Los Angeles. The costumes have been used for a number of films—including Catwoman from *Batman Returns*—and worn by stars like Roseanne and Madonna. See the description of Catwoman's costume on pages 365-366.

Thin latex has been used for translucent wings that actually stretch as well as for magical garments like the Batman cape, though a thicker latex was used for the Time Lord cape worn in a television commercial, both described in Part Three.

Small squares of Dental Dam can serve as reinforcements and hinges. They can make bladders hidden inside costumes. Where designs demand growth or pulsating movement, air bladders can be attached to hoses ending as small air pumps in an actor's hand. This technique has been used in monster movies to create a deep, threatening breathing pattern. In *Off on a Tangerine*, a large latex bladder was used to simulate a speedy on-stage pregnancy in the leading lady. For those interested in bladder making, there are excellent instructions to be found in Vincent J.-R. Kehoe's *Special Makeup Effects*.

Description Natural *latex* rubber has the flexibility of plastic and may also be molded. Costumers needing a thin sheet material with extreme flexibility will find natural-latex sheet to be the perfect material: It stretches to 400 percent of its unstretched form. Four D Latex Rubber Company's sheeting is available in thirty colors as well as many thicknesses. The sheeting from the Hygienic Corporation, when purchased from a distributor, is available in only three neutral colors; however, if a minimum of five hundred yards is purchased from the manufacturer, colors can be customized.

To store latex rubber, powder it with talc to keep it dry, then place in a dry, dark closet; latex rubber is affected adversely by dampness, ozone, and ultraviolet light. It is also possible to make your own thin latex sheet; see description in Casting Materials on page 212.

Commercially, thin latex is used in balloons, medical appliances, and fabric coatings. Dentists use it in small squares to dam up saliva that is flooding ongoing dental work.

Latex is also available in foam sheeting, which has a short life and is therefore seldom used. Costumers prefer synthetic foams because they last longer.

How to Use Cut with scissors. This material is too stretchy to cut evenly with a mat knife.

Bond rather than sew. Bonding is stronger, less visible, and does not perforate latex with needle holes, which quickly become larger and tear. Adhesives that have proved the most satisfactory in bonding latex to itself are liquid latex or rubber-based contact cements like 3M 77, Barge, 3M's Scotch-Grip 847, Bostick 3851 and 4602, and Copydex (a latex-based adhesive made by Henkel Ltd. and sold in Great Britain). Bostick 4602, which is available in Great Britain, is also recommended by Four D Rubber Co. Ltd.

Latex will adhere to most fabrics with rubber-base cements. When bonding to metals, use cyanoacrylate or epoxy. Note that rigid adhesives like epoxy and cyanoacrylate will cause the latex to become rigid.

In bonding, as in sewing, seams should be lapped approximately one-quarter inch to avoid buckling.

To sew latex sheet, use a Teflon presser foot and a Teflon-coated thin needle; however, sew latex only where the costume fits loosely, where it will not tear at the seams, and when the costume is to be viewed at such a distance that seams are not visible to the audience—unless the design specifies otherwise.

Color with polyurethane elastomer-based paint to retain the greatest flexibility. Other paints with a lesser degree of flexibility are rubber cement paint or a mixture of latex and acrylic paint. Other paints will leave the latex stiff and finally chip off. If using the less flexible paints, prime the latex first with Phlexglu or rubber cement, though rubber cement will add a permanent tackiness. Keep the paint thin to avoid a buildup that could interfere with flexibility.

To protect latex against deterioration from oxidation, coat it with a flexible paint or coating.

Precautions   Rubber is flammable and should be kept away from flames and lit cigarettes. Store in a cool area, away from heat, humidity, and strong light. Protect rubber from oils, solvents, and grease, which will destroy it.

Health and Safety   Recent studies have shown that 1 percent of the population is allergic to latex, and about 15 percent of those who work with latex suffer allergies. Latex allergies can be serious, with reactions ranging from skin rashes to fatal anaphylactic shock. Testing for latex allergies is available at hospital laboratories. When working with latex, wear gloves and wear either a respiratory mask or work in a well-ventilated area.

Where to Find   Dental and medical suppliers.

Rubber-sheeting distributors.

Distributors:

Canal Rubber Supply Company, NY

VWR Scientific, Bridgeport, NJ

McMaster & Carr, LA area.

Davis Dental Supply, LA area

(Manufacturers of latex-sheeting require large minimum orders.)

Sizes   Coltene Whaledent Inc.: Boxed squares, 5" × 5" and 7"× 7" sheeting, 42" wide .006" to .040" thick.

Four D Rubber Co.: Sheeting, 92 cm wide and 15/18 mm through between 76 and 89 mm thick.

Polyester

Polyester resins can be either thermoplastic or thermosetting plastics. Among the thermoplastics are the popular transparent film Mylar and the easy-to-use Friendly Plastic. Most of the low-temperature thermoplastics discussed on pages 276-279 contain polyester. The thermosetting polyesters that are used for casting are discussed on pages 217-218.

Polyester Film (Mylar)

Some Brands	Manufacturers
Mylar	E.I. Du Pont de Nemours and Company
Cadco	Cadillac Plastic and Chemical Company
Scotchpack	3M Company

Examples of Use

- Make decorative and jeweled effects.
- Create outer-space, futuristic, and fantasy clothing.
- Construct fish and reptile scales.
- Produce stays or stiff interlining.
- Use as a release film when casting.

Use polyester film where transparency, flexibility, and durability are important. Iridescent rainbow Mylar has been used effectively for wings, reptile and fish scales (See *Fantasy Creatures* in Part Three.), as well as for insect shells. (See also *Animals* in Part Three.) As an appliqué on cloth garments, it lends an elusive and shimmery appearance.

In designing the many-layered Elizabethan ruffs in *The Revenger's Tragedy* at Stratford on Avon, designer Michael Levine encased rainbow Mylar in nylon organza.

Polyester film is useful for thin stays, belt interfacing, cap visors, and rigid interior forms.

Description

Polyester film is a thermoplastic, with characteristics of heat resistance, strength, flexibility, and durability. As a transparent film, it is available in a range of thin to medium weights in both shiny and matte surfaces. Translucent sheeting comes in heavier gauges, also in shiny and matte surfaces. Mylar film is available in a wide variety of colors as well as in metallic finishes and rainbow, or iridescent, colors. Aging causes neither yellowing or brittleness. It can be bonded, laminated, metalized, painted, and coated. It is unaffected by water, oils, and most aromatic hydrocarbons. Costumers commonly use it for decorative purposes, but polyester film also serves well for interior stiffenings or interfacings.

Many modern sequins and paillettes are formed from polyester film. It is sometimes used as a release agent in casting from a mold or from a flat surface. Some of its industrial functions are as a protective coating, transparent tape, decals, and shrink-wrap packaging. Mylar strips are also used to form apparel stays for corsetry. Metallized polyester film cut into thin strips combines with textile fibers to form metallic yarns and lamé fabrics.

Polyester film is manufactured with a range of specific characteristics including thickness, clarity, brilliance, and resistances.

How to Use   Cutting polyester film can be done simply with ordinary scissors, a scoring knife, or a mat knife. Thicker sheets of unreinforced polyester are best cut with a metal or carbide-tipped blade of eight to ten teeth per inch at a high speed, with the blade projecting about three inches above the surface of the table.

Heat-forming in vacuum-formers is with temperatures ranging from 450° to 500°F. For maximum forming with any heat-forming technique, first moisten the polyester film with benzyl alcohol solvent.

Bonding is most successful with plastics' adhesives, such as 3M 90 spray or 3M 4693. The latter is available only in large quantities from 3M distributors, though 3M 90 is sold retail in smaller sizes. Sobo Glue, Phlexglu, and Barge Cement adhere well through washing and dry cleaning. Because polyester film is tough and does not tear, it can also be sewn, either by hand or by machine, if the stitches are spaced widely enough to resist weakening the material.

Polyester film is the usual material for pailettes.
DESIGN: BILL HARGATE.
PHOTO: ROBERT W. ZENTIS.

Sewing with finely spaced stitches creates perforations and consequent tearing. Some costumers avoid perforating polyester film by encasing it in net fabric. Otherwise, sew only on polyester film with large stitches, a thin needle, and only on areas where there is no stress.

Coloring is possible with a variety of media. For opaque color on items requiring water immersion or laundering, Pactra Spray Paint, Iddings Scenic Paint, Deka Permanent Textile Paint, Liquitex Acrylic Artists' Colors, and shoe color-coatings create a good bond. Articles made of polyester film that need dry cleaning cannot be painted, though those that will not be immersed in either water or cleaning solvents can be painted with all the paints that we have tested. For transparent effects on articles to be washed, use Fiebing's Leather Dye, and for pieces to be neither laundered nor dry-cleaned, use almost any of the transparent media included in this book.

As a release agent, it is particularly effective on flat surfaces, and, because of its chemical resistance, most substances will separate easily.

Solvent for Cleanup   When using adhesives and colorants with polyester film, check the charts in this book for the most effective solvents.

Health and Safety   There are no precautions for using polyester film alone. Used with solvents, however, the usual precautions need to be followed.

Where to Find   Plastic-supply stores, display stores, and some hobby shops.

Sizes   Width: up to 55".

Thicknesses: .0075" - .001" .

Friendly Plastic

Some Brands	Manufacturers
Friendly Plastic	American Art Clay company

Examples of Use
- Create jewelry.
- Make ornaments applied to armor and rigid headdresses.
- Fashion facial features, teeth, and fingernails on character and animal costumes.
- Join or hinge other materials together.
- Form joints on sculpture armatures.

Use for metallic-looking jewelry, like earrings and brooches, as well as for ornaments. As it is heavier and more rigid than most fabrics, it will affect the hand of soft and lightweight textiles. Friendly Plastic is effective as decoration on armor and other rigid pieces. Because of its shininess and durability, many costume craftspersons form items such as animal teeth and claws with it.

Friendly Plastic bonds well to acrylic, polyester, glass, most metals, and some fabrics (test before using), while adding strength and durability to the joints.

Use Friendly Plastic for creating small pieces when under close time restrictions.

Description   *Friendly Plastic* is a low-temperature polyester that can be formed in hot water or in an oven. Manufactured for the crafts' trade, it is easy to use, and it sets up quickly, in a process similar to that of many of the low-temperature thermoplastics which are discussed in the Low-Temperature-Setting Thermoplastic Sheetings section. It has a shiny, opaque surface and, like polyester in general, it is tough. Friendly Plastic is available in a wide variety of colors as well as in metallics.

How to Use   Cut with paper scissors or razor blade.

Heat form through the hot-water method for creating free-form shapes. The manufacturer recommends using an electric skillet in order to have temperature control. If using other implements, check the water temperature with a cooking thermometer for best results. Heat water to approximately 140°F, add one or two drops of cooking oil to prevent sticking, and dip in a piece of Friendly Plastic. For nonmetallics, remove in about thirty seconds; for metallics, remove sooner to retain the metallic brilliance. Shape into a desired form with hands or any kind of forming implement. Texture can be added with ordinary items like kitchen knives and hardware. Place under cool water to set.

Friendly Plastic can also be formed by heating it in a 225°F oven to produce designs of layered plastic. The Friendly Plastic pieces can be cut into shapes, layered one on top of the other, and set onto a flat metal surface, like aluminum foil or a cookie tin. Bake for two to three-and-a-half minutes for the pieces to melt together. The longer the pieces are left in the oven, the flatter the surfaces will become. Remove from oven, add further texture of decoration, and place into cold water for three to five seconds.

Since Friendly Plastic is a thermoplastic, it can be resoftened and reshaped, and decorative pieces may be embedded while the material is soft.

To make a hinge or fastening strip, first soften, then quickly apply to the two parts to be fastened.

Bond Friendly Plastic to itself and other materials merely by melting it with heat or hot water or use E-6000, an adhesive distributed by Leisure Crafts.

Color with glass stains, leather dye, and acrylic paints; however, Friendly Plastic is already available in many colors.

Precautions Do not leave stove or oven unattended while working.

Where to Find Craft and hobby stores.

Sizes 1½ × 3"

1½ × 7"

4 × 7" (available in fewer colors than the first two sizes)

Polyethylene Sheet and Film

Some Brands	Manufacturers/Distributors
Plastazote	BXL Plastics Limited (London area)
Cadco	Cadillac Plastic and Chemical Company

Usually sold by generic name.

Examples of Use
- Shape rigid costume pieces like animal heads, armor, and props.
- Construct found-object costumes from plastic garbage bags and other polyethylene ready-made objects.
- Make space suits, raincoats, and futuristic clothing.
- Waterproof garments.
- Protect a work area.

Polyethylene can be a useful material for shiny, plastic looking and waterproof costumes. Because it possesses high electrical-insulation properties, it may also be useful when such protection is necessary. It is, however, a solid, nonporous material and can be extremely uncomfortable and unhealthy to wear unless aerated with punched holes or used in combination with other "breathable" materials.

It also is effective for costumes with a found-object theme. In the film *The Wiz*, Michael Jackson, as the Scarecrow, wore polyethylene garbage bags for trousers. Polyethylene sheeting and garbage bags have been fashioned for camp costumes in many theatrical productions.

Thicker polyethylene can be an excellent material for rigidly molded costume pieces that require no painting.

For the Guthrie Theatre's production of *Merton of the Movies*, the millinery department created straw boaters for a scene in which waterproof straw hats were needed. First, the polyethylene film was cut into strips. The strips were then braided, sewn together into straw boater shapes, and coated with Phlexglu for stiffness and protection.

Definition   *Polyethylene* is naturally white and waxy, with a smooth texture. It is tough at low temperatures and is resistant to most chemicals such as paints and adhesives. As a film, it is available in many colors, and also manufactured in black, which leaves it impervious to the effects of sunlight. Because it is resistant to most chemicals, bonding is most frequently done by heat. Polyethylene has excellent thermoforming capabilities and is often used in vacuum-forming, at a comparatively low cost.

Polyethylene is also formed into tubes that are available in most plastic supply houses. The tubes are in demand for hospital and laboratory work.

Industry uses the film for coverings, garbage bags, and temporary shelters, and the thicker, extruded plastic is commonly used for freezer containers, squeeze bottles, and medical prosthetics. Sometimes called polythene, and a member of the polyolefin family, polyethylene is the most popular of all plastics for industrial use.

How to Use   Cutting polyethylene film is easy with ordinary scissors. To cut the thicker sheet, use a band saw with a skip-tooth wood blade of four to six teeth to the inch.

Heat-forming is successful because polyethylene can be molded at temperatures of 325° to 425°F in a vacuum-former or an oven. It is not as elastic as some of the other sheetings discussed in this section and is best used only for those forms with fairly shallow structures.

Bonding is only successful with a few adhesives. The 3M Company recommends their 3748, 3764, and 3796 hot melts as well as 4693 and 4910-NF Scotch-Grip Adhesives. Uncommon Conglomerates makes Ole-Bond to bond polyethylene both to itself and to most other surfaces.

Polyethylene sheeting is used as the fabric for this futuristic-looking robe.

DESIGN: ELINOR KLEIBER FOR *LEAR* AT THE KOMISCHE OPER, BERLIN. PHOTO: ARVID LAGENPUSCH.

Most craftspersons bond polyethylene to itself or other materials with a soldering iron or the type of heat sealer used in food packaging.

Coloring polyethylene sheet with a permanent color was not possible before 1995 because of polyethylene's high resistance to chemical substances. Now, with technological advances, a primer has been developed for bonding colorants to polyethylene. As with bonding, the Ole-bond adhesive primer works as a primer for painting. After the primer is dry, apply acrylic or enamel paint. Other methods will provide only temporary coloring. Flexible sprayed pigments, like Fab Spray or inks, should be applied as light mists, for if sprayed as solid coatings, they will crack. Floral paints and shoe colorings form a slight mechanical bond, but eventually peel off. If the paint is applied as a normal smooth coating, it will result in crazing. To improve adhesion, rubber-cement spray, like 3M 77 can be used as a primer before painting.

Health and Safety If using adhesives or paints with polyethylene film, follow the usual safety precautions. Always have adequate ventilation and protective covering in working with plastic sheeting and heat.

Where to Find Plastic-supply stores and building trade suppliers. Bags and found objects are usual items at grocery and hardware stores. Tubing can also be found at medical suppliers.

Sizes .020"- 3" thick.

Usually 48" and 96" wide.

Vinyl

Some Brands	Manufacturers/Distributors
Naugahyde	Uniroyal Engineered Products
Expanded Vinyls	Alexander and Co., Inc.
Expanded Vinyls	Leathertouch

Usually available by generic name

Examples of Use
- Use as a leather substitute.
- Create futuristic and outer-space costumes.
- Simulate reptile and fish textures.

By itself, vinyl sheeting can be credible as leather, but adjacent to real leather it looks synthetic and flat. To modify the "flat" appearance of any vinyl, texture it with spray, sponge, or brush, which will modify and deepen its synthetic look.

Alan Armstrong used polyurethane foam-backed vinyl to produce an elegant, rich effect on a costume for Claudius in the Alabama Shakespeare Festival's *Hamlet*. The method is described below under How to Use.

Description The type of supple *vinyl* sheeting available in fabric and auto-upholstery shops is a form of polyvinyl chloride (PVC). Such vinyl can be purchased either as a laminate (with a polyester or nylon fabric knit backing) or as a nonlaminated sheet. Vinyl is sold in a variety of textures and colors, and in its nonlaminated form it is also available in opaque or transparent, or with adhesive backing.

This rich-looking costume is created from vinyl sheeting coated with Phlexglu, hot-melt glue, metallic leaf, orange shellac, and glitter.

DESIGN: ALAN ARMSTRONG FOR CLAUDIUS IN *HAMLET* AT THE ALABAMA SHAKESPEARE FESTIVAL. PHOTO: ASF/SCARBROOK.

The headdresses and jewelry pieces are formed from vinyl sheeting highlighted with mirror Mylar and acrylic jewels, edged with hot-melt glue, and painted with artists' acrylic paint.

DESIGN AND PHOTOS: JENNIFER LANGEBERG FOR THE 1996 OLYMPICS OPENING CEREMONY.

In the costume shop, vinyl-coated fabric is frequently used, especially as a substitute for leather. In industry, the fabric-backed vinyl is used primarily for furniture and automobile upholstery, while nonlaminated vinyl sheeting is found in shower curtains, toys, and simulated leather coverings.

Vinyl (PVC) tubing is another useful material for costuming. Commonly available for medical and chemical purposes, it is found at most plastics' suppliers.

How to Use Cut with scissors.

Heat-form with vacuum-former, standard oven, heat gun, clothes iron, or hair dryer.

Floor matting can be cut and assembled into garments, such as this laced-together vest.

DESIGN: JOHN BLOOMFIELD FOR THE FILM *WATERWORLD*. PHOTO: RICHARD J. BAILEY.

Bond with either solvents or adhesives. On those vinyls we tested, we recommend the following: solvent-bond with tetrahydrafuran; adhesive-bond with flexible adhesives like vinyl cements and fabric-formulated glues for costumes requiring limited washing and cleaning. On garments to be dry-cleaned and laundered, many adhesives—including Phlexglu, high-quality cyanoacrylates, Bond 634, and Stabond U-148—adhere well to most vinyls.

Sew by hand or machine. In either case, use heavy-duty needles and sturdy thread.

For color that is transparent, we found Fiebing's Leather Dye to be successful on costumes to be laundered, but not dry-cleaned. We recommend using any of the other leather dyes if the costumes are not to be washed or cleaned. For opaque effects, use acrylic-based paints. For spray painting, use leather spray paints such as Nu Life or Magix for garments requiring only limited laundering, and no dry cleaning. Fab Spray, a translucent spray dye, held up well through both laundering and dry cleaning on the vinyls tested.

Transparent sheeting heat-set to fabric by ironing lends an unusual texture to a skirt.

DESIGN: ELINOR KLEIBER FOR *LEAR* AT THE KOMISCHE OPER, BERLIN.

To add dimensional texture to vinyl sheet, use a heat-bonding technique: The bonding could be to another, but flat, sheet of vinyl or of fabric, though fabric will form only a weak, temporary bond with the vinyl. With a clothes iron or a soldering gun, adhere folds of vinyl to the fabric or sheeting. Or, crumple the vinyl into folds, lay the flat sheeting (protectively covered by fabric) or the cotton fabric over the vinyl, and press the heating implement over the fabric. The bond will be weak, but sufficient to hold the crumpled sheet in place before edge-stitching the two layers together.

Following is the process for making a foam-backed vinyl costume for Claudius in *Hamlet* at the Alabama Shakespeare Festival. Alan Armstrong purchased white foam-backed vinyl and, using Rit, dyed it black. He brushed the black vinyl topping with Phlexglu and then applied gold and copper synthetic leaf. Hot-melt glue was drizzled randomly over the leaf. Once dry, the surface was painted with two coats of orange shellac. Finely grained glitter was sprinkled onto the wet shellac. Chunks of this material were cut and applied to a base of fabric, some by sewing and others by gluing.

Do not use ketones (like lacquer thinner and acetone) with vinyl, for they can alter the surface texture.

Health and Safety Use the appropriate precautions for vinyl adhesives and for acrylic spray paints, both listed in the *Adhesives* section.

Where to Find Laminated vinyl: fabric stores, upholstery and auto-upholstery shops.

Nonlaminated vinyl: plastics suppliers and distributors.

Sizes Usually 45" wide.

Rigid Plastic Foam Sheetings

Expanded Polystyrene (Styrofoam)

Some Brands	Manufacturers
Styrofoam	Dow Chemical Company
Expanded polystyrene	Foam Pack Industries
Expanded polystyrene	Permafoam, Inc.

Usually sold by generic name

Examples of Use
- Sculpt into positive molds for making many costume items.
- Carved headdresses and accessories for short-term productions.
- Cut and carve into printing blocks.

Styrofoam is brittle and breaks easily; therefore, use it for ornamental pieces that will receive only limited use. In a short-term production, it is practical for costume parts such as headdresses, masks, and props.

Like polyurethane rigid foam, expanded polystyrene makes effective printing blocks.

Description *Expanded polystyrene*, commonly known by one of its brand names—*Styrofoam*—is a familiar material to most craftspeople as a white or pale-blue rigid sponge. It is readily available in sheets, balls, cones, blocks, and pellets; it is inexpensive and easy to carve, bond, and paint, and is excellent for carving into a model for a primary positive mold.

Outside the theatre, its commercial uses include packaging, disposable food containers, and insulation.

How to Use

To cut, use a knife, single-edged razor blade, band saw, electric carving knife, foam cutter, or hot wire cutter. Hot wire cutters cut polystyrene with the most accuracy and are the professional model makers' tool of choice. Heated implements, such as electric soldering irons, also work well because expanded polystyrene melts easily. Precautions must be taken when using high-heat tools like hot wire cutters and soldering irons, because heat causes Styrofoam to produce toxic cyanide fumes. When cutting with a band saw, use a metal cutting blade with ten to eighteen teeth per inch.

To bond polystyrene foam, use water-based polyvinyl acetate glues, Sobo, Elmers, Phlexglu, etc., for best results when bonding expanded polystyrene to itself and to fabric. Use epoxy and polyurethane adhesives when bonding to metal and reinforced plastics. Be careful when using other adhesives because their solvents can dissolve the polystyrene. With the above adhesives, use the contact method of bonding by applying the adhesive to each surface, allowing the water to evaporate, then pressing the two surfaces together. These rigid foam surfaces dry slowly because they are impervious to air.

To color, paint with water-based acrylic paints, like artists' acrylics or scenic paints.

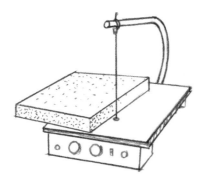

A table-size electric hot wire cutter for cutting expanded styrene can be purchased or assembled.

For a protective coating, any of the following materials will work: Foam Coat (Rosco Products), plaster (not plaster of Paris, but a home-decorating plaster), polyester putty, any of the white glues, Sculpt or Coat, acrylic-based gesso or acrylic painters' media. Thick coatings, like plaster and polyester putty, both protect the styrofoam and create a surface that welcomes interesting textural effects.

When making a printing block, draw a design onto a one-inch piece of Styrofoam with an ordinary utensil like a kitchen knife, nail, pencil, or stick. Or burn in a design with an electric burning implement like a soldering iron or a wood-burning tool. If acrylic paint is used for printing, it will be necessary to slow the drying time by adding glycol. If the polystyrene foam is to be coated with polyester, first prime the Styrofoam with a barrier coat of plaster.

Precautions

Protect the Syrofoam from dissolving, and do not use solvent-based adhesives, paints, or coatings. Protect it from burning by keeping it away from heat sources.

Health and Safety

When cutting and sanding, wear a face mask to avoid the small dust particles.

Where to Find

Hobby shops, plastic-supply stores, and building suppliers.

Sizes

Sheets: ½" - 2" thick.

Blocks: variable sizes.

Expanded Polyurethane, Polyurethane Rigid Foam (Green Foam)

Some Brands	Manufacturers/Distributors
Trymer	Dow Chemicals
Designer Foam	Stro-Fab, Inc.

Usually sold generically

Examples of Use

- Create positive molds for cold-forming and thermoforming.
- Fashion into small carved decorative items.
- Sculpt into forms for covered headdress parts.
- Carve into blocks for printing on fabric.

The most common use by costumers for this material is in sculpting positive molds for heat-forming. Usually in a block, it is the preferred substance for vacuum-forming molds for pieces that will have only one pull. Many who use it for vacuum-forming recommend coating it well with epoxy resin and fiberglass before using in a vacuum-former.

Description

Most commonly known as *green foam*, *rigid polyurethane foam* resembles styrofoam, yet differs in density and chemical compatibility. It is also less brittle and easier to cut. Rigid polyurethane foam is available as sheets, slabs, and blocks. Its most common commercial use is as roofing insulation.

How to Use

When cutting, use a razor blade, knife, electric knife, hot wire cutter, electric saw or a good-quality hand-operated cross-cut saw. To cut with a band saw, use any type of fine-toothed blade. Sculpting can be done by carving or by adding and adhering pieces with glue or pins. It should not be heat-cut, and if it must be burned with hot tools like an electric knife, hot wire cutter, or electric saw, great care must be taken because it is extremely toxic.

For bonding, the best results are with polyurethane and epoxy adhesives; however, since polyurethane foam is brittle and not strong, the area next to the glue joint may break away. The drying time for bonding polyurethane foam with adhesives is longer than usual because the foam is not porous; this prevents the circulating air from evaporating the adhesives' solvents. No recommendations are made here for dry cleaning and washing, for this is rarely required for rigid foams, though polyurethane foam is resistant to most solvents.

To apply coloring, use water-based paints, preferably acrylics.

Coating is recommended for most applications of polyurethane foam because of its brittleness. For a simple protective coating, Phlexglu, Sculpt or Coat, and thickened polyester or epoxy resin can be satisfactory. For a sturdy coating, use polyester or epoxy resin reinforced with fiberglass (see Epoxy in the Casting Materials section on pages 203-208). For coating a polyurethane-foam positive mold to use in heat-forming, use reinforced epoxy resin; it will withstand a higher temperature than does polyester.

As a replacement for a wood or linoleum block, rigid foam is easy to use for printing motifs onto fabrics and other surfaces. The designs can be cut into the foam with gouges and kitchen knives, coated with acrylic paint, and stamped onto a surface. The polyurethane can be coated with a layer of PVA (white glue) or epoxy for a smoother surface.

Health and Safety Try to avoid using heat methods for cutting or carving, for the fumes from polyurethane are highly toxic. When sawing polyurethane, the dust particles are light in weight and fill the air, making particle masks a necessity.

Where to Find Hobby shops, craft stores, plastics' suppliers, and insulation suppliers.

Sizes Blocks, sheets, and slabs of variable sizes.

Rigid Plastic Sheetings

Acrylic

Some Brands	Manufacturers/Distributors
Plexiglas	Rohm and Haas Company
Lucite	E.I. Du Pont de Nemours and Company
Perspex	Imperial Chemical Industries Ltd. (I.C.I.). UK

Examples of Use
- Make clear or colored glasslike jewelry and gems.
- Create transparent crowns and unusual transparent rigid body pieces.
- Use prefabricated large domes for outer-space helmets.
- Apply prefabricated small domes and curbed forms for eyes and facial features to novelty costumes.

Use acrylic sheet for rigid and transparent costume pieces. It creates a *Star Wars* outer-space look, especially on such pieces as helmets, epaulettes, and armor. See the section on Space Suits in Part Three.

Jewelers have been using acrylic for years to produce imitation transparent gems and glass. Clear and sparkling, it does not have quite the shine of glass, though it is lighter in weight, less expensive, and a close substitute. For some of the magnificent possibilities of acrylic jewelry, see *Plastics for Jewelry* by Harry Hollander, listed in the Bibliography.

Description *Acrylic* is a thermoplastic synthetic resin, which may reheated and reformed as often as desired. It is especially known for its crystal-like clarity and remarkably durable surface. Costume craftspersons who use acrylic prefer the extruded and the cast sheet form. Of the two types of acrylic sheet, the extruded type is easier to vacuum-form into intricate shapes; unfortunately, the extruded type does not have the special clarity that is found in the cast sheet, which is also more commonly available. Although the cast sheet is clearer, it is tougher and more difficult to form.

Acrylic is manufactured as both shrunk and unshrunk sheeting. Either one can be purchased as resistant to heat, crazing, and fire. Although unshrunk acrylic shrinks when heat formed (about 2 percent in length and width and 4 percent in thickness), this small shrinkage is not usually a problem for the user. Unshrunk acrylic is also less expensive.

In its transparent form, acrylic is so clear that it transmits most of the light reaching it. It is also available as translucent sheeting in a wide range of colors and textures. Acrylic is sold in other forms besides sheeting, such as tubing, rod, and geometric shapes.

Acrylic scratches easily and should be stored in its masking paper until ready to use. The protective paper should remain on the acrylic until handling is complete, to avoid scratches or other disfiguring marks.

Acrylic is seen daily in windows, display cases, lamps, jewelry, medical equipment, and lighted signs.

How to Use The machining qualities of acrylic sheet are excellent, and its shelf life is indefinite.

Cutting requires a band saw fitted with a metal blade of five to seven teeth per inch or a table saw with a hollow ground blade of three to four teeth per inch.

Heat-forming acrylic requires a strip heater, heat gun, an oven, or a vacuum-former. If the sheeting is over one-eighth inch thick, a heat source should be placed on either side of it. A strip heater works on thin pieces of acrylic. First place the acrylic, cut to the desired contours, over the strip heater, bracing it properly. When the surface begins to ripple, the sheet should be soft enough to bend. Place it on a support during the brief cooling period of one to two minutes.

Acrylic also forms well with a heat gun. Wear protective gloves when bending the acrylic into shape. A second person may work the gun while the first person molds in a free-form method, bending the acrylic over a mold, table, or other object as the heat softens it. Multiple curves may be formed by bending one curve at a time. Work must be done quickly, for acrylic heats rapidly. Avoid placing acrylic on a surface that might be scarred. As soon as the acrylic is the desired shape, cool with cold water for faster curing.

When using an oven or a vacuum-former, place the acrylic sheet over a mold of a rigid material such as plaster of Paris, wood, or metal. (Any oven used for plastics should not also be used for food.) Insert it into an oven of the temperature specified by the manufacturer's instruction for the specific type and thickness of acrylic. Forming temperatures for acrylic range from approximately 240° to 360°F, though extruded plastics should not be heated to as high a temperature as cast sheets. It is wise to experiment with scrap before forming the actual piece.

The temperatures for heat-forming thick plastics are lower than those needed for thin plastics, for thick stock cools very slowly. Sometimes the molds should be preheated up to 150°F to prevent the mold from chilling the plastic sheet. To avoid surface imperfections after casting, thick plastics may need to be preheated above the forming temperature and allowed to cool for a few seconds before molding. Acrylic and other clear plastics such as polycarbonate absorb water in storage and require precuring at about 180°F for 12 or more hours to avoid blistering during the forming process. Experiment with scrap before forming the actual piece. Care must be taken not to heat it to its melting point, for like all transparent plastics, acrylic may fog and lose its transparency. Do not force the acrylic once it starts to cool.

Bond with either solvent-bonding or adhesive-bonding techniques. Solvents that dissolve acrylic are ketones, acetone, ethyl acetate, ethylene dichloride, toluene, and lacquer thinner.

These solvents can be used in the capillary, soak-cementing, and dope-cementing methods. Soak- and dope-cementing are described on page 244. Capillary cementing is described in the introductory material of Plastic Sheetings on page 35.

Solvent-cements such as methylene dichloride are available at any plastic-supply company. The introduction to this section advises on the use of solvents.

Solvent Cements for Bonding Acrylic to Itself

Cadco PS-30 (Cadillac Plastic)	low viscosity	slow-setting
Cadco SC-125 (Cadillac Plastic)	low viscosity	fast-setting
Cement II (Rohm and Haas)	high viscosity	slow-setting
Weld-on 3 (IPS)	low viscosity	very fast-setting
Weld-on 4 (IPS)	low viscosity	moderately fast-setting
Weld-on 16 (IPS)	high viscosity	quick -setting

Adhesives for Bonding Acrylic to Most Other Materials

Most cyanoacrylates*	low to high viscosity	quick-setting
Scotch-Grip 4475	medium viscosity	medium-setting
Weld-on 10, 2 part cement	high viscosity	quick-setting

When bonding acrylic to metal, glass, and wood, use epoxy cement or the appropriate cyanoacrylate (superglue).

Annealing is a method for firmly stabilizing the cast piece, but it is not generally used by many theatrical craftspersons. For some information on annealing procedures, see a reference such as Thelma Newman's *Plastics as an Art Form*.

Colorants are available either as powders or solutions. Since brands vary in their chemistry, follow carefully the instructions that accompany your dye. Paints are successful on acrylic if the surface is first wiped clean and then dried well. Sanding imparts "tooth," or a rough texture, that will allow stronger adhesion. Acrylic paints, oil-based paints, and lacquers all bond well to acrylic and leave the acrylic opaque. For transparent effects, mix polyester resin with dye and catalyst, following manufacturer's directions, or use transparent lacquers and brush or spray them onto the surface of the acrylic casting.

Precautions Paper-coated plastic sheetings may be stored for a long time. After being stored at an extremely hot temperature, the protective paper may stick tenaciously to the surface. To remove, use mineral spirits or special solvents sold for this purpose.

If transparent acrylic is not removed from heat before reaching the melting point, it will lose its transparency. Acrylic must be formed just as it softens and is beginning to melt.

Health and Safety When heated, most acrylics are highly volatile and are toxic by inhalation and absorption through the skin. Methylene chloride, a common ingredient in many acrylic-resin systems, metabolizes into carbon monoxide in the blood and is a suspect carcinogen.

Work in local ventilation or with appropriate respiratory protection. Wear goggles, gloves, and long sleeves.

Where to Find Plastic-supply stores and distributors.

Perspex is available through J. B. Henriques, Inc. in Great Britain as well as through some U.S. distributors.

Sizes 0.030" - 4" thick.

Acrylic-Polyvinyl Chloride (Kydex)

Some Brands	Manufacturers
Kydex	Kleerdex Company
SP 500	Spartech Corporation
Royalite Acrylic PVC	Uniroyal Chemical Company Inc.

Examples of Use
- Construct dimensional armor.
- Make transparent helmets and other accessories.
- Form facial features for animal and character costumes.

Use on armor, helmets, headdresses, jewelry, etc., that have sculptural relief. Acrylic-polyvinyl chloride (PVC) is satisfactory for all vacuum-formable objects, but because it is more costly, it is often reserved for those costume parts that are more difficult to form from other, less expensive, plastic sheetings. Acrylic PVC is popularly used for outer-space and other-worldly costume pieces.

In Part Three are examples of how Kydex was used in costumes for *Disney's Beauty and the Beast* and *Starlight Express*.

Description   *Acrylic-polyvinyl chloride* is commonly known among costumers and special-effects artists by the popular brand name *Kydex*, though it is manufactured by other companies under their individual brand names. It is among the most rigid, tough, and resilient of thermoforming materials and is especially useful for creating forms with depth. It is an alloy, combining the outstanding features of acrylic and polyvinyl chloride (PVC). Acrylic PVC also has the highest chemical resistance of all thermoplastics. Commercially, acrylic PVC is used for housing such appliances as computers, venting grills, orthopedic braces, and wallcoverings. Costume makers use it to create rigid costume pieces that must withstand long or hard wear. For this purpose, the most popular form of this sheet is one with a leathery matte surface on one side and a smooth shiny surface on the other. Acrylic PVC is manufactured only as sheets, but in a variety of textures, and with a variety of special features, one of which is flame-retardancy. The flame-retardant sheets are, however, extremely expensive. Acrylic PVC is manufactured in thirty-three colors as well as five textures in opaque sheeting.

How to Use   Acrylic-polyvinyl chloride is easy to cut and tool by machine, and it especially lends itself to forming molded structures with depth.

Cutting straight lines is best accomplished with a circular saw. For thin gauges, use a plywood cutting blade with a taper-ground rim; and for thicker gauges, use a carbide-tipped blade with square and advance tooth, both of six to eight teeth per inch. For cutting curves, use a band saw with a standard metal-cutting blade of eight to 14 teeth per inch.

Kydex acrylic-polyvinyl chloride sheeting was vacuum-formed to create this helmet.
CONSTRUCTION: RICHARD TAUTKUS.

Heat-forming requires temperatures of 350° to 390°F through vacuum-formers, ordinary kitchen ovens, heat guns, etc. For deep draws, the temperature should be in the upper ranges of 365° to 390°F. Higher temperatures cause degradation of the material. Acrylic PVC can be easily molded because of its excellent plasticity.

Bonding is with either solvent or adhesive techniques.

Solvent bonding with acrylic PVC is most successful with a 50:50 ratio of tetrahydrafuron (THF) and methyl ethyl ketone (MEK). THF can be used alone, but when it is used alone, the adhesion is weaker than when in combination with MEK. Stronger bonds can be obtained by adding

10 percent acrylic PVC shavings to the THF before adding the 50 percent MEK. See page 244 for dope-cementing techniques.

For adhesive-bonding acrylic PVC to itself and to most other plastics, the Kleerdex Company, manufacturers of Kydex, suggests using Welding Gel, a viscous tetrahydrofuron-based adhesive available from the Sealtek Company in Milton, Wisconsin. IPS recommends their Weld-on 10, 66, and 1784. Other adhesives that are recommended for forming strong bonds with acrylic PVC to itself and to other materials are cyanoacrylates (superglues), and two-part polyurethane adhesives, such as Ciba's Urethane 5774 adhesive. Weld-on's 1001 is suggested for bonding to metals as well as to many other plastics.

Mechanical fasteners, such as rivets and screws, can also be successfully attached to acrylic PVC because of its strength.

Coloring agents recommended by the Kleerdex Co. are The Sherwin-Williams Company's polyurethane-based paints Polane +, Polane T, and Polane T+.

Health and Safety   When heat-molding and working with solvents, allow adequate ventilation, or wear a ventilator mask and goggles. Wear padded gloves to avoid burning. Do not leave containers open, and avoid extended skin contact with solvents and adhesives. See the introduction to this section for more complete safety information.

Where to Find   Plastic-supply stores.

Sizes   .028" to .250" thick.

Acrylonitrile-Butadiene Styrene (ABS)

Some Brands	Manufacturers
Cadco ABS	Cadillac Plastic and Chemical Company
Kralastic	Naugatuck Chemical Division
Royalite	Uniroyal
SP 900 series	Spartech Corporation

Usually sold by generic name

Examples of Use   Form articles subjected to tough or rough use, like armor and helmets worn in scenes of actual combat, where resilience and strength are required.

Description   *ABS is an alloy of styrene rubber, butadiene, and acrylic, a combination that produces both high-impact strength and resilience. One of the most economical of thermoplastic materials, ABS is glossy, opaque, and especially tough. Light tan is its natural color, though many other colors are available. ABS is resistant to impact, scratching, and to most chemicals, and is sold as sheets, rods, and tubes. It is commonly found in household items such as molded chairs, plumbing pipes, luggage, and appliance housings. The specific characteristics of different grades dictate specific uses; a fire-retardant grade, for instance, has obvious advantages.*

How to Use ABS can be cut, drilled, and bonded.

Heat form at a temperature of 300° to 350°F by heating in a vacuum-former, a standard oven, or with a heat gun.

For cutting with a band saw, use a skip-tooth wood blade with five to seven teeth per inch. To cut with a table saw, use a combination blade with four to six teeth per inch.

Bonding is possible with either solvents or adhesives. For maximum adhesion when bonding, prepare the surface by sanding. When bonding ABS to itself with solvents, use methyl ethyl ketone (MEK). Dope-cement by cutting the plastic chips into MEK.

For adhesive bonding when joining ABS to itself, the recommended adhesives include cyanoacrylates, Weld-on ABS Glue, and Oatey Company's ABS solvent cements. Bond ABS to reinforced plastics (such as those strengthened with fiberglass) and to fabrics with many of the solvent-based synthetic rubber adhesives and ABS primer cement. For bonding ABS to reinforced plastics, use Weld-on 10. To bond ABS to fabric, use Weld-on 1784 (medium viscosity), or 1909 (more viscous), both of which are clear of color. To bond ABS to rubbers, glass, and metals, use cyanoacrylates or epoxy. To bond ABS to expanded (foamed) polystyrene and polyurethane, use PVA or Phlexglu. These adhesives can be hazardous to health and should be used with care. Please see appropriate health and safety sections.

For coloring, use acrylic, polyurethane, or silicone-based paint (like Krylon's silicone paint). To avoid painting ABS, purchase colored sheets, available in a wide range of colors.

To obtain a secure mechanical bond with paint or adhesive, be sure to prepare the surface by sanding.

Health and Safety *Do not handle ABS near cigarettes, flames, or food.*

Where to Find Plastics suppliers and distributors.

Sizes .062" - 4" thick.

Low-Temperature-Setting Thermoplastic Sheetings

Some Brands	Main Distributors
Altra-Form	UnNatural Resources, Inc.
Aquaplast	Smith & Nephew Rolyan Inc. EBI
Ezeform	Smith & Nephew Rolyan Inc. EBI
Fabric-Form	UnNatural Resources, Inc.
Hexcelite	AOA, Division of Biomet Corp.
Orthoplast	Johnson & Johnson Orthopaedics
Orthoplast II	Johnson & Johnson Orthopaedics
Polyflex	Smith & Nephew Rolyan Inc. EBI
Polyform	Smith & Nephew Rolyan Inc. EBI
Protoplast	UnNatural Resources, Inc.
Vara-Form	UnNatural Resources, Inc.
X-Lite	Smith & Nephew Rolyan Inc. EBI

Examples of Use

- Make masks.

- Form jewelry.

- Sculpt armor, headdresses, and other solid costume pieces and accessories.

Use where time, weight, and easy working procedures are a priority. The use of these products is particularly suited to shops without vacuum-formers.

These materials are used widely for armor, masks, jewelry, headpieces, and props. For examples of low-temperature-setting thermoplastics used for headpieces, see Headdresses in Part Three. For a description of backpacks made for *Disney's Beauty and the Beast*, see Kitchen Utensils, Tableware and Furnishings also in Part Three.

Any of these products are useful for patching costume pieces molded from other materials.

Description

These *low-temperature-setting thermoplastics* are available as solid sheetings and as fabric mesh impregnated by plastic. They are easily formable by hand after softening with either hot water or hot air. Also lightweight, durable, and nontoxic, these sheetings are quick, easy, and safe to work with whether molding, dyeing, painting, or bonding. Though all share these qualities, they differ in weight, texture, and thickness. Memory (the tendency of thermoplastics to return to their original shape after reheating) and working processes vary. Costumers and craftspeople who use them extensively often prefer them as a substitute for vacuum-forming plastics. Smith & Nephew and UnNatural Resources provide variations on the above materials and materials in addition to those listed above.

These low-temperature-setting thermoplastics were originally created for the aerospace and medical industries, with the products by AOA, Johnson & Johnson, and Smith & Nephew marketed mainly for orthopedic cast-making. UnNatural

Resources' products are marketed for theatrical design and model-making. Smith & Nephew is a large medical supplier with many more products that could be of interest to the theatrical costumer. Both Smith & Nephew and UnNatural Resources have brochures and easy-to-follow instruction sheets that come with their products. Smith & Nephew also makes Aquatubes, a thermoplastic tubing that works well for making armatures and hinging.

Altra-Form and Fabric-Form, fabric-reinforced thermoplastics, come with either a shiny or a matte surface in a variety of weights. Fabric-Form is a polyethylene-impregnated woven cloth available in white, gray, or pale blue in two different weights. Altra-Form is naturally gray and opaque and well suited for hard costume pieces and accessories.

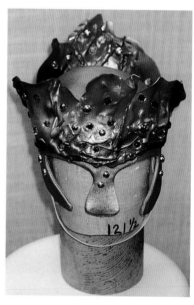

Lightweight head-dresses of Polyform low-temperature-set-ting thermoplastic sheet are quickly and easily created.

DESIGN: JENNIFER LANGEBERG FOR PRINCESS CRUISE LINE. CONSTRUCTION AND PHOTO: CONSTANCE IOLCUVAR CO.

Aquaplast, Orthoplast, and Protoplast are solid, nonreinforced, plastic sheetings, suitable for armor and sizable costume pieces. All are manufactured in smooth or perforated sheets, with Aquaplast in five choices of perforations. Aquaplast is available in many colors, as either coated or uncoated sheets, and with variations in hardness and stretch. These products have excellent memory.

Ezeform, Polyform, and Polyflex come from Smith & Nephew. Excellent for reproducing small detail, these three sheetings have limited memory. Ezeform has stretchability, is uncoated, and comes both solid and perforated. Polyform has a high degree of stretchability and is coated. Polyflex has excellent strength and rigidity, moderate stretch, and is coated. All three come in one-eighth-inch thickness, three colors, and a choice of perforated or plain sheet.

Hexcelite, Vara-Form, and X-Lite are large, mesh plastic-impregnated fabrics. Available in two weights, they are excellent for armatures and open-weave masks.

How to Use   To cut the thinner materials, use a pair of shears or utility knife. Cut the heavier sheet with a low-speed table saw with a skip-tooth blade.

To heat form, immerse material into water of 140° to 180°F, or soften it in a hot-air oven. An electric frying pan is recommended for water-softening. To spot heat, use a heat gun, hair dryer, or hot water. Temperature usually depends upon thickness and density of the selected sheeting. Remove the sheet from hot water or heat source as soon as the material is visibly softening. (When soft, the material becomes transparent.) This stage varies from thirty seconds to approximately one minute. Drain and form by hand or apply to a mold. The material may be applied as one uncut sheet, or it may be applied in a series of patches and layered like papier-maché.

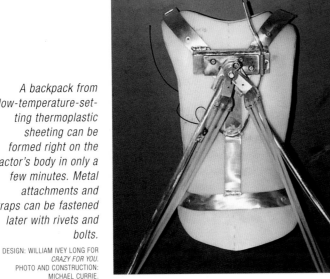

A backpack from low-temperature-setting thermoplastic sheeting can be formed right on the actor's body in only a few minutes. Metal attachments and straps can be fastened later with rivets and bolts.

DESIGN: WILLIAM IVEY LONG FOR *CRAZY FOR YOU*. PHOTO AND CONSTRUCTION: MICHAEL CURRIE.

Working time is about three minutes. To extend the working time, add extra heat (spraying or sponging with hot water, or heating with a hair dryer or heat lamp). Allow several minutes for setting. After about ten minutes, the material becomes rigid, with a maximum strength developing in thirty minutes or less. In order to decrease setting time, dip the material in cold water, rub with crushed ice, or spray with cold water within an aerosol sprayer.

Methods for bonding these sheets to themselves or to other materials depends upon whether the sheets are coated. If uncoated, apply the sheeting directly to the other bonding surface while it is still wet, or reheat one surface and press together with the other, for these sheets stick to any material while soft. If coated, remove the coating and bond as above, or use an adhesive. Both epoxy and hot-melt glues are recommended.

To color with dye, merely add a union dye, like Rit, into the hot water, or paint with acrylic, enamel, oil, or alkyd paint after the material has hardened. The sheetings from Smith & Nephew come in many colors. Metallic paints and bronzing powder mixtures are particularly effective.

Before painting the coated materials, treat with a solvent that strips off the surface coating, like that from Smith & Nephew. After painting, seal the paint with spray varnish.

Where to Find   Distributors include:

Alcone Co. Inc.

AOA, Division of Biomet Corp.

Douglas and Sturgess

Johnson & Johnson Orthopaedics

Smith & Nephew Roylan Inc. EBI.

Sizes   Hexcelite and X-Lite: 2", 3", 4", and 6" wide in 2-yd. rolls.

Varaform: 50" wide yardage.

Others: 18" × 24" to 24" × 60".

Polycarbonate (Lexan)

Some Brands	Manufacturers
Lexan	General Electric Company
Merlon	Mobay Chemical corporation
Tuffak	Rohm and Haas Company

Examples of Use
- Form heads and features for animal, character and walk-around costumes.
- Construct armor, helmets, etc.
- Make strong and rigid costume pieces.
- Create jewelry.

Polycarbonate is most useful for items that are meant for tough and heavy wear. The walk-around and character costumes meant to be worn daily for at least a year often contain important elements fabricated from polycarbonate. To learn how Lexan polycarbonate was used for futuristic looking Las Vegas costumes, see Showgirls' Starburst Tails in Part Three.

Description   *Polycarbonate* is best known to costumers through the popular brand *Lexan*. It is one of the toughest plastics in the thermoplastic category. It comes in sheet form, ready to use for molding and other machining and fabricating techniques. Though somewhat similar to acrylic, polycarbonate is tougher, more resilient, more costly, and more easily scratched. In its natural form, it is water-clear, as transparent as glass and acrylic. However, the clear polycarbonate yellows with long exposure to ultraviolet light and, as mentioned, scratches easily; some forms of polycarbonate have been stabilized to inhibit these disadvantages. Polycarbonate is also available in a variety of opaque colors, and accepts most paints and coloring agents. A high melting point of 500°F makes it useful where high temperatures may be present, and polycarbonate is heat- and flame-resistant. As with other plastic sheetings, additives and modifiers create a range of sheetings with specific enhancements, including bullet-proof sheet. In its thin gauges, it is soft and flexible, but because of the softness, it cannot be buffed.

Common uses are for helmets, bulletproof glass, protective face masks, sunglasses lenses, and shoe heels. Some jewelers specializing in plastics have created particularly beautiful pieces from Lexan. In commercial uses, polycarbonate is found in coffeepots, air conditioners, and window panes. It is obtainable in several varieties of texture, clarity, and colors.

How to Use   Cutting recommendations for a band saw are a metal blade with ten to eighteen teeth per inch. For cutting with a table saw, use a hollow ground blade with four to six teeth per inch.

Heat-forming should be preceded by overnight drying in an oven at a temperature of 120°F. To form in a vacuum-former, temperature should be at 440° to 500°F. Strip-heaters heated to 315°F are ideal for bending polycarbonate. Forming is easiest and works best when the heaters are placed at both sides of the polycarbonate sheet.

Bonding can be with either solvents or adhesives, but bonding is successful only on polycarbonate that has been both cleaned and sanded. To clean, use methyl or isopropyl alcohol. Sand with an emery cloth to abrade lightly, thus allowing a mechanical, as well as a chemical, bond.

Solvent bonding can best be accomplished with two hazardous substances and should therefore be avoided. Methylene dichloride (MDC) is a highly hazardous substance, and General Electric, the manufacturer of Lexan, recommends using MDC alone, or, for an absolutely clear bond, adding a small amount—no more than 10 percent—of glacial acetic acid, also an unsafe substance, to the equally hazardous MDC. If solvent bonding is necessary, bond with just enough solvent to wet the joints; any excess will increase the set time and destroy the sheeting finish. Hold parts firmly together until dry.

For adhesive bonding of polycarbonate to itself, make a dope cement using methylene chloride thickened with polycarbonate chips. Because of personal safety, it is preferable to use glue. Glues that bond polycarbonate to itself are polyurethanes (two-part highly viscous polyurethane adhesives are strongest) and Weld-on's 4, 16, and 55, and hot-melt glues specific for plastics' bonding. For adhering it to reinforced plastics (like fiberglass-filled epoxy or polyester), use synthetic-rubber adhesives. When cementing to metal, use epoxy cement or Weld-on 10.

Colorings for polycarbonate are silk-screen ink with a polyester base, enamel-based paint, flexible vinyl paint, lacquer-base translucent ink, and inks manufactured for outdoor signs. General Electric, manufacturer of Lexan, recommends Wyandotte Paint Products Company's Gripflex Paints, FR-2 series or GF-2 series for spray or FR-1 or GF-1 series for screen, though these paints are only available in large quantities and through the manufacturer.

Solvent for Cleanup   Use terahydrofuran for cleaning up bonding substances. To remove paint, ink, or dye, use the same solvents that are in the paint, ink, or dye. For removal of labels, stickers, etc., use kerosene, naphtha, or petroleum spirits. Do not use gasoline.

Health and Safety Use protective ventilator masks, goggles (usually made of polycarbonate), and gloves, and work in a well-ventilated area when using heat, adhesives, or solvents. Consult glove manufacturers about permeability of gloves in the presence of some solvents. *Do not smoke or eat while working.*

Where to Find Plastic-supply stores and distributors.

Sizes .010" - .250" thick.

Sheets for the thinner range are 28" × 60".

Sheets for the thicker range are 40" × 72 ".

Polystyrene

Some Brands	Manufacturers/Distributors
Catalin Styrene	Catalin Corporation of America
Lustron	Monsanto Company
Cadco	Cadillac Plastic and Chemical Company

Usually sold by generic name

Examples of Use
- Construct rigid costume pieces: headdresses, armor, masks, and accessories.
- Use as a permanent covering on a polyurethane, Styrofoam, or plasticine clay model for vacuum-forming.

Polystyrene sheeting is probably the sheeting most commonly used for costume armor, helmets, and other accessories that can be vacuum-formed because it is inexpensive and easy to work with.

Bubble-wrap polystyrene film can be cut into decorative pieces to use on costume parts that receive gentle wear in short-term productions.

Description *Polystyrene*, or *styrene*, is a crystal clear or opaque thermoplastic resin with the properties of rigidity, smoothness, and easy formability. It is available in rods, sheets, and tubing. It colors well, often producing outstanding results with transparent, translucent, and opaque colorants. A disadvantage is its tendency towards brittleness. Pieces that receive much handling will need to be reinforced. Another disadvantage is its retention of static electricity, which causes pieces to pick up and retain dust. Polystyrene becomes yellow and brittle with age when its uncoated surface is exposed to light. Compared to many other sheet plastics, it is low in cost. Aside from molded costume parts, it is commonly seen in refrigerator and automobile-interior pieces.

Polystyrene is also manufactured as a medium- and high-impact product, obtained by blending polystyrene with an additive. In its high-impact form, it is either translucent or opaque white and requires a more lengthy bonding time.

As film, polystyrene can be printed, thermoformed, vacuum-formed, and pressure-formed. Polystyrene film is used commercially in packaging and is well known in its bubble-wrap form.

How to Use   When cutting thinner gauges, use scissors, a draw knife, or an electric knife. With an electric knife, be careful not to pause during cutting, for the plastic may be heated past its melting point and melt the edges producing toxic vapors that are dangerous to inhale. For the thicker polystyrene, use an electric knife or a saw. Band sawing should be done with a metal blade of ten to eighteen teeth per inch at speeds varying between two and three thousand feet per minute.

Heat-forming qualities of polystyrene sheeting are excellent. It is easily formed at temperatures ranging from 430° to 450°F. Vacuum-forming is frequently used and successful. Forming by ordinary oven and hot-air gun are also common.

Bonding techniques include solvent-bonding and adhesive-bonding.

Solvent-bonding can be done with methyl ethyl ketone (MEK). Methylene chloride is recommended by manufacturers, but should be avoided because it is extremely hazardous. For solvent-bonding technique see page 244.

Vacuum-formed poly-styrene sheet is commonly used for armor pieces because it is inexpensive and easy to work with.

CONSTRUCTION: MAKEUP & EFFECTS LAB INC. PHOTO: ROBERT W. ZENTIS.

Adhesive-bonding of polystyrene to itself can be done with Weld-on's styrene adhesives, 40 or 52/4052, or with 3M's 1099, 4475, or 4693. With the use of hot-melt glue sticks, Hysol's Formula 1946 produces a strong yet rough bond. To adhere polystyrene to reinforced plastics (those containing fiberglass), use epoxy cement; for bonding to metal, use cyanoacrylate (superglue). For bonding to acrylic and other plastics, consult with 3M or Weld-on, who manufacture and distribute a variety of specialized adhesives for plastics. Weld-on products are available from many plastics' distributors, and 3M products are available in small quantities through distributors.

Coloring can be done either before or after forming. Dyes, inks, metallic powders, and acrylic paint all bond to polystyrene, though for stronger adhesion, abrade the surface before painting. When painting the polystyrene surface before heat-forming, the paint must be applied in thin coatings so it will not become gummy during heating. Overheating discolors painted surfaces, so remove the piece from the oven as soon as the polystyrene corners have softened.

Solvent for Cleanup   MEK and methylene chloride.

Health and Safety   When molding by heat, use ventilation or respirators to protect the lungs and respiratory system, goggles to avoid hazards from fumes, and padded cotton gloves to avoid burns. When working with solvents and adhesives, always work in a well-ventilated area, preferably outdoors or in local-exhaust ventilation, or wear goggles and a respirator. Do not leave containers open and avoid extended skin contact with the solvents and cements. Never use these substances after drinking alcoholic beverages, or near an open flame or food.

Where to Find Plastic supply shops and distributors.

Distributors include:

Christler Distributors, NY

Cadillac Plastics and Chemical Company

Sizes .001" - .500" sheets. (Thinner gauges are usually sold as rolls.)

Textiles

Beaded Mesh

Some Brands	Manufacturers
Dimensional Bedazzlers	Lumured
Meta-Lites	UnNatural Resources, Inc.

Examples of Use
- Use for chain-mail armor.
- Drape into soft-plastic surfaced garments.
- Sew or glue cutout pieces into appliqués.
- Use for lightweight chain mail, and for fantasy, metallic, and plastic-looking garments and accessories.

Description *Beaded mesh* can be sewn or glued to itself or to other surfaces to give the look of metal chain mail, jeweled or sequined fabric, or scales. It comes in small, one-eighth to one-quarter inch, slightly raised, round and square beads and tiles that are laminated to pliable polyester net. The beads are of cellulose acetate and can be washed or dry-cleaned, except for those with a metallic finish, which can be only washed. They should not be placed in a dryer. With an order of large enough quantity, the manufacturers will custom-apply the beads to other fabrics.

Beaded mesh has been made into purses for the retail market, and the purses have the look of 1940s beaded bags.

A soldier's hood created from plastic-beaded mesh appears metallic when seen from a distance.

DESIGN AND CONSTRUCTION: JOHN BRANDT FOR *MACBETH* AT THE UNIVERSITY OF CALIFORNIA, LOS ANGELES.
PHOTO: ROBERT W. ZENTIS.

How to Use Cut with scissors.

Bond with an adhesive compatible to both polyester and the other surface being bonded.

Sew by hand. Machine-sewing is incompatible with these small pieces of plastic that can break needles.

Color with acrylic paint, though the paint can easily chip. The material comes in so many colors that painting may not be necessary.

Precautions Rubbing this material against itself causes the beads to fall off the mesh. Do not use beaded mesh at underarm or other areas that are susceptible to abrasion.

Where to Find Lumured: from manufacturer
UnNatural Resources: from manufacturer or distributors
Distributors include:
Alcone Company
Norcostco

Sizes Half sheets: 9" × 34".
Full sheets: 18" × 34".

Polyolefin, Spunbonded (Paper Cloth)

Some Brands	Manufacturers
Tyvek	E.I. Du Pont and de Nemours and Company

Examples of Use
- Fashion into disposable costumes.
- Form items resembling paper.

Description *Tyvek* is the brand name for E.I. du Pont's durable sheet products that look like paper, yet are stronger. Sometimes referred to as *paper fabric*, Tyvek is manufactured from high-density polyethylene fibers. It is strong, lightweight, smooth, opaque, and resistant to water and to tearing. Although similar to nonwoven fabrics like Pellon, Tyvek is much tougher and nonpliable. It can be cut, sewn, glued, and colored. It is produced in both hard and soft structures, with thicknesses varying from that of thin to thick paper. It is also available in several textures, including one with pin-size perforations for air permeability.

For a short period in the 1960s, a material resembling paper Tyvek was used in the manufacture of disposable clothing. Because it is strong and waterproof, commercial uses for Tyvek include packaging (sturdy mailing envelopes), protective industrial garments for house painters, nuclear plant, and hospital workers, and protective covers for buildings under construction.

According to E I. du Pont, the types of Tyvek with the most suitable properties for costume making are 1422R, 1443R 1445A, and 1622E.

How to Use   Cutting is done simply with scissors or a razor blade.

Heat-forming is possible to a small extent. Since Tyvek is thermoplastic, it can be distorted by temperatures above 175°F, and it can be blocked or shaped with a household iron.

Bonding Tyvek to itself is successful with heat lamination. The following adhesives tested successfully on type R and D Tyvek: water-based Phelxglu, 3M's Fastbond 30NF, and Fast Frame Trade Grade cyanoacrylate (superglue) from Uncommon Conglomerates. All three of these adhesives withstood dry cleaning tests. 30NF and the cyanoacrylate also held up well in laundering. Phlexglu held up in laundering only on type R. For more adhesives information, contact E I. du Pont for the *Adhesive Suppliers for Tyvek* brochure.

Sewing can be by hand or machine. For machine sewing, use the minimum number of stitches per inch and a small needle to avoid making perforations that might be easily torn.

Coloring is successful only on certain types of Tyvek. Those that more readily accept colorants are identified by a number with a D, R, or E suffix. Alcohol-soluble dyes impart stronger color than do the standard union or fiber-specific dyes, which only leave pale tints. (An alcohol-soluble binder such as clear nitrocellulose lacquer or alcohol-soluble polyamide is recommended.) E. I. du Pont has compiled a list of recommended dyes. For stronger colors, use lacquer-based or solvent-based polyurethane-screen process inks and paints such as latex enamel. Avoid inks and paints containing a high amount of mineral spirits.

In our testing for type D, we found that for opaque coloring, Liquitex acrylic paint is excellent, withstanding laundering and dry cleaning. Tests for transparent color proved Deka transparent dyes and Magix spray dye to bond well through either kind of immersion. On type R, Liquitex paint faded after ten washings, and Magix spray did not dry-clean well.

Solvent-based polyurethane silk-screen inks are the colorant recommended by E. I. du Pont for coloring apparel made of 1422-1433R; these are successful for costumes needing dry cleaning or washing. When dyeing or painting Tyvek, allow more drying time than usually allowed with fabrics because Tyvek is non-absorbent.

Tyvek can be special ordered in twenty-five custom colors.

Precautions   Tyvek can be weakened by hydrocarbons, oils, and ketones.

Where to Find   Some distributors:
Fibermark Inc.
Cadillac Plastics and Chemical Company.

Sizes   White: 60" wide.
Colors: 30" - 50" wide.

Retroreflective Fabric

Some Brands	Manufacturers
3m Scotchlite Reflective Material	3M Company

Examples of Use

- Create costumes that reflect light even more brightly than white.
- Apply decorations that reflect strongly.

3M Scotchlite Reflective Material has been effectively used for costumes having especially brilliant effects. In the 1978 film *Superman*, the hero's antagonists wore jumpsuits of silver 3M Scotchlite Reflective Material, lending the figures an unworldly brilliance. Michael Jackson, in his 1984 Victory Tour, wore an orange 3M Scotchlite Reflective Material jumpsuit, designed by Ted Shell. Adhesive-backed 3M Scotchlite Reflective Material has been used in costumes made by the experimental J & M Costumers in several instances: for the "Globies," mascots of the Harlem Globe Trotters, costumes were striped with 3M Scotchlite Reflective Material; for a marching band, uniforms were decorated with musical notes of reflective material that radiated light in an unusually dramatic way, more brightly than white material; and for an outer-space movie, an alien's costume was decorated with reflective material fringe that imparted an eerie glow.

Description

A *retroreflective* surface is one that reflects the brilliance of the light back to the source of the light. One type of reflective material contains wide-angle lenses which are packed together and bonded to a durable backing that can be fabric or adhesive. The lenses reflect a brilliant light up to five hundred times brighter than white, but the reflection can be seen only from a point directly behind the light source. For this reason, a retroreflective surface is more suitable for film than for live theatre.

Some commercial examples of its applications are found on safety vests, highway markers, firemen's coats, and the stripes taped onto cyclists' clothing and running gear. Colors for most materials are limited to red-orange, lime-yellow, silver, gray, and white. High-gloss products include red, yellow, blue, green, white, orange, fluorescent red-orange and fluorescent lime-yellow.

3M Scotchlite Reflective Material is available in a variety of forms: as yard goods, solid and multicolor trims, heat-transfer films, and high-gloss products, and some are backed with fabric or adhesives.

How to Use

Cutting can be by scissors or razor blade.

Bonding retroreflective material to itself and to other materials is easily done by using the adhesive-backed material. Adhesives that bond and survive both laundering and dry cleaning are cyanoacrylates (we tested with Fast Frame from Uncommon Conglomerates), though expect stiffening from this type of adhesive. The 3M Company's Fastbond 48-NF survives laundering well, but it only lasts through several dry cleanings.

Sewing by machine should be with no more than twelve stitches per inch with a stitching line at least a half inch from the fabric's edge. Teflon-coated needles are best for sewing with 3M Scotchlite Reflective Material.

Coloring is successful using Deka Transparent Inks for transparency and artists' acrylic paints for opacity. Both survive laundering and dry cleaning. Contact the 3M Personal Safety Products Department for recommendations on screen-print inks.

Precautions Store in a cool, dry area and use within one to two years of purchase, depending on product. To keep 3M Scotchlite Reflective Material flat and unwrinkled, suspend it horizontally from a pipe or rod though the core of the packing tube or keep the rolls in their original shipping cartons.

3M Scotchlite Reflective Material may be cleaned with a damp cloth: Wipe with warm water and mild detergent and rinse thoroughly. Dry with a soft cloth or air dry.

For laundering and dry cleaning recommendations, see the 3M technical data sheet for individual product care and maintenance.

Where to Find Manufacturer:
3M Personal Safety Products Department, 3M Safety and Security System Division.
Distributors:
Head Lites Corporation
Iron Horse Safety Specialties
M.L. Kishigo Manufacturing Company
Safe Reflections, Inc.
Safety Effects
Safety Flag Company of America

Sizes ½" - 50" rolls
Custom-slit widths are available.
½" - 12" is available in 100 yd. rolls.
Over 12" is available in 50 yd. rolls.
$500 minimum through manufacturer. Minimum order varies with distributors.

Thermoset-Treated Fabric

Some Brands	Manufacturer/Distributor
Solvoset	Alcone Company

Examples of Use • Create rigid pieces like headdresses and armor.
• Produce jewelry and metallic-looking accessories.

Solvoset is available in three weights. Use the lightweight for small objects and for draping. The medium weight is recommended for masks, headpieces, and medium-size accessories, and the heavyweight is preferable for larger pieces like armor.

Description   *Solvoset*, formulated in 1991, is the Alcone Company's replacement for Celastic, and is a woven cotton fabric impregnated with a thermosetting plastic; the exact plastic is a proprietary secret. Advantages over the now unavailable Celastic are many. It is safer than Celastic, for Solvoset will dissolve in acetone instead of methyl ethyl ketone (MEK); it easily bonds to itself, and it forms more easily than Celastic. It is also less flexible, less absorbent, and has a longer drying period.

How to Use   Cutting is simply done with scissors. Use either paper scissors or heavyweight shears.

Form Solvoset by dipping it into acetone and then draping it over a positive mold or into a negative mold. Shallow forms can be made either from an uncut sheet or from cut or torn strips. Alcone recommends using aluminum foil as a release agent.

Wearing protective gloves, dip the pieces into acetone for a minute, remove the fabric, and hold it flat in both hands. Knead the piece of Solvoset to loosen its weave. Then return it to the acetone a second time, moving it from the acetone onto the mold. Do not allow it to touch itself, for it will bond to itself and be difficult to work with. Use as many layers as necessary to build up a form. Remove the Solvoset as soon as it is dry and can hold its shape.

Solvoset has a longer drying time than Celastic. The drying time depends on the humidity and on the size of the casting. The thinner sheeting activates and dries relatively quickly, while the heavy sheet takes a much longer time to activate and dry. To hasten the drying time, be sure to remove the aluminum-foil release agent so that air can penetrate the weave and, if possible, use a forced air dryer.

Bonding is easily done by laying Solvoset onto itself while one surface is still wet. To bond, simply lay up thin patching strips of acetone-soaked Solvoset.

Coloring can be achieved with almost any type of paint, but can be applied only after the piece is thoroughly dry. If paint is applied while it is still damp, it will prevent the air from drying the Solveset, and, as a consequence, the Solvoset may never dry.

Solvent for Cleanup   Acetone.

Health and Safety   Wear protective rubber gloves, for the softened plastic will adhere to unprotected skin. Acetone must be handled under the usual safety precautions of ventilation, protective clothing, and respirator. Pay special attention to fire protection as acetone is extremely flammable.

Where to Find   Alcone Company

Theatrical-supply distributors.

Sizes   Light weight: 20" × 60" (sold as linear yardage).

Medium weight: 20" × 46" (sold as sheets).

Heavy weight: 20" × 57" (sold as sheets).

PART THREE

Applications

Many of the world's finest costume designers and craftspeople are creating costumes and costume parts with plastic materials. Bob Ringwood uses latex foam to build body-armor suits for *Batman*; Dominique Le Mieux makes feathers from thermoplastic boning and fabric for Cirque du Soleil; Ann Hould-Ward invented the "Bead Vac" process to embellish costumes featured in *Disney's Beauty and the Beast*.

A few costume pieces created from more traditional materials—costume pieces not mentioned in other resources—are discussed in this section. In all cases, proven methods for creating unusual costumes and accessories and recommendations for the most suitable materials are here set out.

Most of the materials and equipment for creating these specialty costumes have been discussed earlier in the book. Since some materials may be less available than others, and not all costume makers have vacuum-formers and table saws, it is possible to substitute materials and modify the construction methods suggested here. If this section does not offer ideas that meet your needs specifically, perhaps by learning about the work of others you will be inspired to develop your own methods and approaches.

In this section, Costume Pieces and Accessories includes individual pieces such as jewelry, padding, headdresses, and armor. Specialty and Special Effects Costumes are complete costumes for such disparate characters as drag queens, superheroes, or walk-around bears who advertise the Bimbo Bakery. Surface Effects discusses distressing, embroidery, and surface modification. All can be achieved with more facility by learning about the experience of the designers, craftspeople, and technicians who have made this book possible.

Cost is almost always a concern. One *Batman* costume can cost as much as a Porsche. The average costume for Cirque du Soleil must outlast three hundred performances and can cost as much as a few thousand dollars to produce; these exquisite custom-made garments must also survive the rigors of complex acrobatic movements and daily laundering. On the other hand, the average costume for a few performances of Shakespeare's *Henry IV* at the University of Evansville, Indiana, may cost only a few dollars. Between these extremes lies a wide range of choices for today's costumer. Certainly, it is more economical to build one costume that will last throughout the production run rather than to build many costumes with shorter life spans. However, the restrictions of a tight budget sometimes force a clever designer or costumer to come up with wonderfully inventive solutions. Such was the case with Lizzy Gardiner, who designed *The Adventures of Priscilla, Queen of the Desert*, which you will read about in this part of the book.

Many of the costumes described here are extraordinary—elegant and powerful. Most of the people who made them are well aware of the hazards of working with sheet plastics, plastic resins, and solvents. Sawing and grinding sheet plastics emit lung-irritating powders into the air. Paints and solvents discharge dangerous fumes. Before you start using the following techniques and materials, take care to read MSDSs, follow manufacturers' instructions, and pay attention to the safety precautions outlined in the individual materials descriptions in this book. Finally, please read carefully the Health and Safety section on pages 13-24 as well.

Costume Pieces and Accessories

Armor

Chain Mail

Aluminum Wire

In Cirque du Soleil's *Alegría*, the Strong Man wore a handsome handmade chain-mail tunic. Using the authentic centuries-old method, DNA 69, a workshop in Montreal, linked wire rings together to become one piece of cloth.

To make your own piece of chain mail, buy a length of aluminum wire of the desired gauge or, preferably, buy anodized wire premade links from DNA 69. The wire should be anodized so it does not tarnish and turn the wearer black. However, if discoloration will not be a factor, use the nonanodized wire. Form the wire into links around a metal rod with a diameter the size of the inside of the finished links. The degree of pliability of the finished mail is directly proportional to the inside diameter of the links—the larger the inside diameter, the more pliable the mail.

To make links, carefully wind a length of wire around the rod until the rod is covered entirely. The wound wire must be absolutely smooth.

Pull this spiraled wire off the rod. Using a jeweler's saw, carefully cut it vertically into individual links.

Open the links slightly, and place each one inside four others until a metal cloth is formed. Many linking patterns are possible; however, this particular linking pattern was chosen for the Cirque du Soleil since it is the most flexible.

Metal cloth made in this manner allows enough flexibility for the mail to stretch like jersey with the wearer. The mail should fit the wearer closely for a good appearance, but stretch for maximum movement.

Metal rings make authentic chain mail. Surround one ring with two rings per side and link together as pictured. (Diagram shows front and top linkage.) Add intermediate links, and repeat the process until a fabric of the desired size is achieved.

PROCESS AND DRAWING: DNA 69.

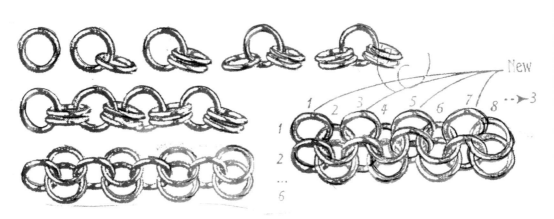

Latex ⚠   Another method of forming chain mail is to cast liquid latex into a mold of knit chain mail. The following is the method used by Rodney Gordon in making headdresses for the Ninja Turtles at the Universal Studios Tour:

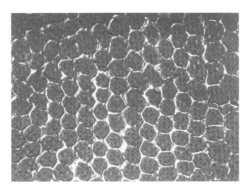

Liquid latex reinforced with cloth can be cast into a plaster mold of a knit chain-mail pattern to create costume pieces.
DESIGN: ANN HOULD-WARD FOR *RICHARD II* AT THE GUTHRIE THEATRE, MINNEAPOLIS.

An 18-inch square of chain mail was knit from string. The knit square was coated with a sealer to impart the necessary nonporous surface—use white glue or acrylic coating. Next, a release agent was applied—use silicone or petroleum jelly. Thick layers of casting plaster were brushed over the knit mail to create a plastic mold. (See Rigid Molds in the Casting Materials section on pages 191-193.)

Subsequent copies of chain mail were cast in latex with a lightweight, loosely woven cloth embedded between layers of latex. Because the latex pieces contained embedded cloth, they could be cut to shape and sewn together like yardage. After assembly, the chain-mail pieces were primed with rubber cement and painted with acrylic paint.

⚠ THIS SUBSTANCE OR PROCEDURE MAY BE HAZARDOUS TO HEALTH AND SHOULD BE USED WITH CARE. PLEASE READ THE APPROPRIATE HEALTH AND SAFETY SECTION.

Rodney Gordon has a costume shop in Manhattan specializing in costume accessories. He has constructed pieces for many Broadway productions.

Doreen Johnson, costume craftsperson at the Guthrie Theatre in Minneapolis, also used this method in making the chain-mail armor for the Shakespeare *Histories* in 1991.

Metal Mesh   Metal-ring mesh, originally developed for making butcher's aprons and the safety gloves for shark-diving suits, makes an authentic appearing chain-mail armor. Costume makers all over the western world, from Los Angeles Center Theatre Group to studios in Italy and England, have found this material to look as realistic as actual chain mail. Ferrani Studios in Rome dressed Jane Fonda in it for the feature film *Barbarella*, and Tina Turner wore a metal ring mesh dress in the film *Mad Max*. Metal mesh also serves as an elegant contemporary evening fabric.

To fashion any garment from mesh, use metal shears to cut pieces (without seam allowance) to shape. Butt the edges together and lace the pieces together with thin, soft-aluminum wire.

Metal mesh, used primarily for modern protective clothing, looks like actual chain mail.
PHOTO: RICHARD S. BAILEY.

Metal mesh is available in the United States from Whiting and Davis in New York, who also manufacture a wide variety of brass and aluminum meshes, exciting glamour fabrics that have been seen on the covers of *Vogue* and *Cosmopolitan*.

Plastic-Beaded Mesh

Plastic-beaded mesh is actually small pieces of acetate bonded to a polymer textile mesh. From a distance, this material resembles chain mail. It comes in a variety of colors: silver, dull steel, and dull gold. Cut out pattern pieces with seam allowances. This material must be hand-sewn. After the pieces have been sewn, spray the garment lightly with a matte spray paint to camouflage the shiny plastic look. This metallic-looking mesh is available from Douglas & Sturgess Corp. and from Lumered Plastics.

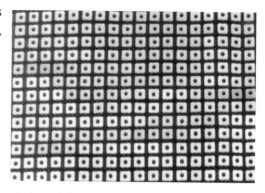

A sheet of plastic-beaded mesh, created from small pieces of acetate backed by a textile mesh, is used for chain-mail garments.
PHOTO: RICHARD S. BAILEY.

For the low-budget production, found objects can be remarkably effective.

(Found objects are ready-made, available articles like safety pins, bottle tops, and electronic gadgets that can be assembled into an artwork.) When Patty McCrory at the University of Evansville, in Indiana, was faced with dressing an army of medieval soldiers for *Richard III*, she used found materials.

Start with a fitted tunic of heavy dark muslin or another heavy cotton fabric. Pin a horizontal row of two inches of safety pins near the top of the tunic. Pin succeeding rows to the above row and to the cotton tunic, with head to tail of each pin. Using Phlexglu, solder each joint together (this to avoid accidental opening of the pins). When all the pins are in place, lightly spray paint the "armor" with black leather or acrylic spray paint for a dull and more realistic iron appearance.

Safety pins are pinned in horizontal rows onto a fabric tunic to give the illusion of chain mail.
DESIGN AND PHOTO: PATTY MCCRORY FOR *RICHARD III* AT THE UNIVERSITY OF EVANSVILLE, INDIANA. CONSTRUCTION: JEAN TERIO.

String, Graphite, and White Glue (or Polyvinyl Acetate Coating)

Traditionally in the theatre, costume chain mail has been manufactured by knitting it from string, using large knitting needles. Patterns for an ordinary tunic and close-fitting trousers can be adapted by the knitter.

After the garment has been knitted, rub the loops with graphite, then coat with white glue for both sheen and protection. Or dry brush with metallic paint or bronzing powder mixed with a clear coating such as white glue. Or mix

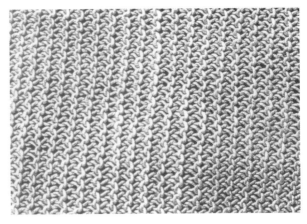

String, knitted into a chain-mail pattern, coated with graphite and glue and distressed with spray paint, is a traditional method of making theatrical chain mail.
COSTUME: COURTESY OF WESTERN COSTUME COMPANY.
PHOTO: RICHARD S. BAILEY.

graphite and shellac and paint onto the string and eliminate the coating. To flatten and produce a more realistic appearance of the garment after applying any of these coatings, take a hot iron and either rub or pound it onto the coated string.

Washers Over Fabric or Leather

First sew and fit a cloth or leather tunic snugly. Apply metal washers, overlapping one row on top of another. The washers can be bonded together with a rubber cement ⚠ like Barge All-Purpose Cement or 3M Scotch-Grip 1099, or they can be sewn in place with a strong nylon cord. If sewn, sew only the top of the washer; this allows flexibility. When bonding with adhesives, allow less overlap than when sewing the washers, but make sure the garment remains flexible.

When Alan Armstrong designed this type of armor for the Louisiana Shakespeare Festival's *Macbeth*, it was bonded together with Barge Cement.

Metal washers can be glued with rubber cement or sewn with nylon cord to a cloth or leather tunic to simulate the appearance of chain mail.
DESIGN: ALAN ARMSTRONG FOR *MACBETH* AT THE ALABAMA SHAKESPEARE FESTIVAL. PHOTO: COURTESY OF THE ALABAMA SHAKESPEARE FESTIVAL.

Plate Armor

Armor Ready-Made Costume shops can build armor from molds if they have a vacuum-former, which can be expensive. On the other hand, armor made with the vacuum-forming process is readily available by mail order from Costume Armor in New York (See Appendix VII.). These white, molded plastic pieces, usually polystyrene, come in a wide variety of periods and styles and require only fitting and trimming and the attachment of fasteners.

Because the polystyrene is fairly thin, the costumer will often need to reinforce vacuum-formed armor for long-running productions. Reinforcing can best be done by cutting leather or a heavy fabric into rectangles and applying the rectangles to the interior with an overlapping papier-mâché technique.

The armor can also be strengthened by decorating the outside of the polystyrene with leather cutouts. Any of the following techniques strengthen the polystyrene:

- Cut out rectangles of metallic-surfaced vinyl. Overlap and bond them with a vinyl cement ⚠ like Weld-on 1001.
- Cut out precisely fitted shapes from vinyl or leather and laminate to the preformed armor with the same adhesive.

The following are decorating techniques that have been used:

- With Barge or other thick rubber cement, adhere aluminum washers or other hardware to the armor in patterns or selective motifs.
- Add pieces of heavy lace and adhere with adhesive. Brush the surface with white glue or other adhesive to stiffen and create a smooth surface suitable for painting.
- Glue on cord to form scrolls, stripes, or other linear decoration. Coat with a sealant, such as white glue or Sculpt or Coat described on page 83, to size and smooth the surface in preparation for painting.

Cast Neoprene (Chloroprene Rubber) ⚠ When armor is needed for a large number of soldiers, multiples may be made from the same mold. Jane Clugston recommends the following method:

1. Fashion from clay a breastplate, back plate, and epaulettes in the style of the design and in one or several sizes, depending upon the range of actors' sizes.

2. Coat the mold with a separator, such as soap or silicone spray ⚠, to aid in separation.

3. Then make a plaster mold by covering the clay form with about four inches of plaster of Paris. Remove the clay from the plaster mold in about eight hours.

4. When the plaster is completely dry (in about five days), remove the clay from the mold. The molds are now ready to use.

5. When using *Neoprene*, Clugston casts with the slip-molding technique. First pour liquid Neoprene into the mold. Let the Neoprene sit about one-and-a-half hours, or until a skin develops next to the plaster mold. Pour out the excess liquid. The

⚠ THIS SUBSTANCE OR PROCEDURE MAY BE HAZARDOUS TO HEALTH AND SHOULD BE USED WITH CARE. PLEASE READ THE APPROPRIATE HEALTH AND SAFETY SECTION.

Neoprene can be cast easily in forming breast plates.

DESIGN AND PHOTO: COURTESY OF BALLETMET FOR THE RAT KING IN *THE NUTCRACKER BALLET* AT BALLETMET, COLUMBUS, OHIO.

finished cast piece of armor will remain in the mold. The cast piece will be about one-quarter-inch thick.

6. Paint the armor with acrylic metallic paint. Brush on and then wipe off a layer of French enamel varnish ⚠ for a more antique look or to add more depth. The dense, smooth surface of Neoprene will resemble that of metal.

7. Belt strap ends can now be riveted onto the armor for fastenings.

Neoprene shrinks, and the thicker the casting, the more the shrinkage. Armor should be cast at least one size larger than the piece required as finished.

Jane Clugston used this technique for casting the armor for the Rat King and his troupes in *The Nutcracker*, performed at Ballet Met in Columbus, Ohio, in 1993. Clugston works out of her studio in Portland, Oregon, where she makes costume pieces for theatres throughout the United States.

Industrial Felt, Soap, and Graphite

Industrial felt sized with PVA, textured with soap, and painted is a safe and durable method for making armor. Lace and other embellishments may be added for decoration.

DESIGN: LEWIS BROWN FOR DR. PANGLOSS IN *CANDIDE* AT THE AHMANSON THEATRE, LOS ANGELES. PHOTO: JAY THOMPSON, ©1995.

Industrial felt has been widely used for a number of years to create armor and other metallic looking pieces. It is inexpensive, fairly durable, and safer to work with than many plastics. The following is one method of creating felt armor:

1. Place the industrial felt over a form matching the desired final form of the armor. This could be of plasticine clay. Drape and cut the felt to approximate the desired shape. Take the felt off the form and cover the form with a plastic sheet. Soak the felt by placing into a solution of one part water to two parts PVA (or white glue). Place the wet felt over the form, stretch, and hand press to shape. Allow the felt to dry thoroughly.

2. Rub a moist bar of strong industrial soap onto the surface, and iron the soaped felt heavily with an industrial iron.

3. If texture or low-relief shallow decorations are part of the design, glue or attach them onto the armor at this time. Decorations may be of heavy lace, cast latex, vacuum-formed plastic sheeting, braids, and other appliqué materials.

4. The armor may be made to appear metallic by using one of the following methods. This first method was used to create the armor pictured, constructed by Carol DeMarti and worn in *Candide* at the Ahmanson Theatre, Los Angeles.

   a) Paint with metallic acrylic artists' paints.

   b) Brush over the paint a glaze of bronzing powder mixed with acrylic gel medium.

   c) Spatter with metallic automobile lacquer.

This second method of metallizing is from London's National Theatre:

   a) Rub graphite powder on the felt.

   b) Brush on one or two coatings of PVA (white glue) or acrylic gel coating to add shine and protection, and then paint.

After painting is completed, attach hinges, straps, and buckles with rivets.

Molded Polystyrene Sheet ⚠

Fantasy armor based on a specific period may be heat-molded in a free-form manner, without using an actual armor mold. The following method, used at Alterion Studios near Los Angeles, requires two experienced costume makers;

1. Develop a paper pattern of the general desired shape.

2. Cut polystyrene sheet from the pattern.

3. Use a heat gun to soften the polystyrene and immediately start bending it into the desired form, keeping the heat gun directed on the armor piece.

4. Shape sculptural and decorative elements by placing the polystyrene over table corners, screwdriver handles, wooden blocks, etc., still using the heating gun.

5. Trim off excess edges of polystyrene.

6. Sand the surface with sandpaper, use a paint primer spray, and then spray with the appropriate color of acrylic paint.

7. Add interior reinforcements (see above) and fastenings.

See page 282 of the Polystyrene section for recommendations on adhesives.

Polyethylene Foam and Leather

A thicker armor can be made by covering molded polyethylene foam sheeting (like Voltek's Minicel L-200) with leather or other material. The foam sheeting, which will serve as the form, may be shaped in one of two ways.

Polyethylene foam sheeting, of any desired thickness, can be cut to approximate the shape of the armor piece desired, then placed on a mold and set in a vacuum-former. After the piece has been taken out of the oven, it can be trimmed for an exact fit. See

⚠ THIS SUBSTANCE OR PROCEDURE MAY BE HAZARDOUS TO HEALTH AND SHOULD BE USED WITH CARE. PLEASE READ THE APPROPRIATE HEALTH AND SAFETY SECTION.

Polyethylene-foam sheeting cut to shape and glued together is covered by leather to form this plate armor.

DESIGN: GABRIEL BERRY FOR *ANGELS IN AMERICA* AT THE MARK TAPER FORUM, LOS ANGELES. PHOTO: JAY THOMPSON.

Plastic Sheetings on page 265 for an explanation of vacuum-forming technique.

Alternatively, the foam sheet can be cut into pieces of exact shape and size, much as one would cut the patterned pieces for a fitted cloth garment. If the edges of the foam have been cut carefully, they may be butted together and glued with a rubber contact cement. ⚠ The foam form is then placed on a mannequin. To cover the form, cut leather to the approximate shape and dip in water until soaked. Place the leather over the foam sheeting form and stretch and mold it until it is smooth. Adhere the leather within several inches of the edges on both the outer and inner sides with a thick coating of Barge or another rubber cement.

This second technique, used on armor designed by Gabriel Berry and constructed by Jeff Shoenberg at the costume shop of the Los Angeles Center Theatre Group, was used to create the armor for Angels in America.

Polyurethane Foam and Vinyl Sheeting

Alan Armstrong, who has designed costumes for the Mark Taper Forum, Santa Fe Stages, Alabama Shakespeare Festival, and the Repertory Theatre of St. Louis and is a professor at the University of California at Los Angeles, designed armor for the Alabama Shakespeare Festival's production of *Hamlet* using one-half-inch polyurethane-flexible-foam sheeting. Because the costumes were constructed to last, the shop chose reticulated, ventilation foam; for a short run, less expensive upholstery foam would be adequate.

The foam was cut to shape using fitted, curved pieces to create depth, with no seam allowance, but with edges beveled to fit smoothly. The edges were glued with rubber cement ⚠ (preferably 3M Scotch-Grip 1099) and then butted.

Laminated vinyl yard goods were cut with a two-inch fold-over allowance and then bonded to the armor surface with the same kind of adhesive. The extra two inches were folded inside and glued.

Gold leaf was glued unevenly on top of the vinyl (using Duro Household Cement) to produce an antique look. Next, glitter was sprinkled over the gold leaf while the sizing was still tacky. When dry, the entire surface was covered with orange shellac.

Polyurethane-foam sheeting covered by vinyl sheeting is decorated with gold leaf, glitter, and shellac for this armor.

DESIGN : ALAN ARMSTRONG FOR *HAMLET* AT THE AT THE ALABAMA SHAKESPEARE FESTIVAL. PHOTO: COURTESY OF THE ALABAMA SHAKESPEARE FESTIVAL.

Rubber Gasket Waste

Rubber-gasket waste is an effective and inexpensive method for creating armor.

DESIGN AND PHOTO:
PATTI MCCRORY FOR *RICHARD II*
AT THE UNIVERSITY OF
EVANSVILLE, INDIANA.

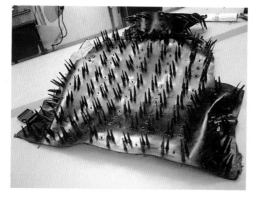

University budgets often require extra creativity from their designers, who many times must search for alternative inexpensive materials. Patty McCrory, costume designer and faculty member at the University of Evansville, Indiana, when constricted by a small budget for *Richard II*, was able to costume the medieval army with scraps of synthetic rubber obtained from a local gasket maker.

This scrap rubber was one-sixteenth-inch thick, shiny, flexible, strong, reminiscent of floor matting, and easily cut with scissors. A heavy cotton cuirass-shaped doublet was sewn, fitted, lined, and dyed black. The gasket rubber was adhered to the finished doublet with a heavy rubber cement ⚠. The rubber was sprayed with leather spray paint. (Both Magix or Nulife leather paint adhere well to rubber while providing flexibility.)

Vacuum-formed Polystyrene, ⚠ Cast Polyurethane, ⚠ and Metal

A variety of sophisticated techniques were necessary to create this handsome piece of armor worn by Sirod in the feature film *Masters of the Universe*. The design for this specific costume was by Bill Stout: Julie Weiss was the overall designer, and the workmanship was by Makeup & Effects Labs (MEL) in Hollywood.

⚠ THIS SUBSTANCE OR PROCEDURE
MAY BE HAZARDOUS TO HEALTH
AND SHOULD BE USED WITH CARE.
PLEASE READ THE APPROPRIATE
HEALTH AND SAFETY SECTION.

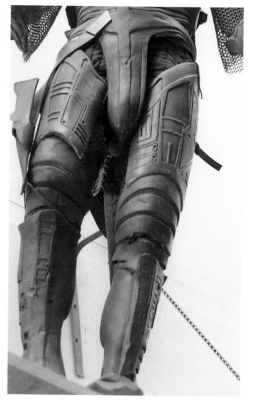

A plasticine-clay model was sculpted over a life-cast for the first stage of creating this sophisticated suit of armor. Styrene sheet and flexible polyurethane form the completed armor. Vacuum metallizing imparts a realistic finish.

DESIGN: BILL STOUT. PHOTO:
MAKEUP AND EFFECTS LAB INC.

1. Using a life cast for the base, model all pieces in a plasticine clay.

2. Form Hydrocal negative molds from the clay models of the upper breastplates and back plates as well as the glove and thigh pieces (see Casting Plastics section on pages 190-193).

3. Vacuum-form the above pieces from polystyrene sheet.

4. Use the clay models for the stomach pieces, cod piece, gauntlet cuffs, and epaulettes to form silicone molds. Cast the silicone molds following the manufacturer's directions. Form polyester and fiberglass mother molds to hold the more flexible silicone molds. (See Casting Plastics.)

5. Cast flexible polyurethane (MEL used products from BJB) from the silicone molds. For the epaulettes, back the polyurethane with power net for extra strength.

6. Metallize all pieces by vacuum metallizing at a specializing company, or metallize them in-house with a less-expensive method. See Metallizing section on page 183 for information on processes.

7. Link metal rings together to form the pieces of chain mail. Then join the armor pieces with additional metal links.

8. Form the helmet by first modeling in clay, then creating a polyester-resin and fiberglass mold, as with the body pieces. Cast in polystyrene by vacuum-forming.

9. Make decorations of cast Neoprene.

Collars

Elizabethan Collars

Millinery Wire and Acrylic Sheeting

Millinery wire is useful for creating large collars. Though not strong enough for enormous Mardi Gras and Las Vegas costume pieces and headdresses, this wire is easier to manage and does not require the special knowledge or materials necessary for joining heavier wire. Susan Rheame, designer at the Alabama Shakespeare Festival, and craftsperson Peg Brady created large collars from millinery wire for *A Midsummer Night's Dream*. Heavy-weight millinery wire is cut to the desired circles' circumferences with additional wire strips cut as radii between the outer circle and the circle of the wearer's neck size. Thin millinery wire is wrapped at each joining, then all pieces are wrapped with bias strips of fabric, providing both decoration as well as protection from any projecting wire ends.

Millinery wire covered with acrylic-plastic sheeting was used to create an Elizabethan collar for A Midsummer Night's Dream

CONSTRUCTION & PHOTO: PEG BRADY.

△ THIS SUBSTANCE OR PROCEDURE MAY BE HAZARDOUS TO HEALTH AND SHOULD BE USED WITH CARE. PLEASE READ THE APPROPRIATE HEALTH AND SAFETY SECTION.

For the petal shapes on the pictured collar, fine millinery wire was bent to the shape of each petal, then covered with cutouts of acrylic-plastic sheeting, the sheeting hand-sewn in place, then lightly coated with spray paint. △

Wirework with soldered joints forms the structure for a Mardi Gras collar.

Large wire-work Mardi Gras collar spans many feet in height and width.

DESIGN AND PHOTO: ANTHONY COLUMBO OF ARTISTIC CREATIONS.

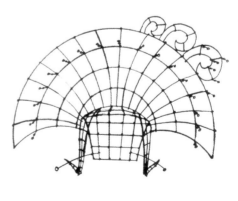

Mardi Gras Collars

Soldered Wire At the New Orleans Mardi Gras, a collar is an oversize neckpiece that can extend several feet on either side of the body, reaching as much as nine feet in height and width. Carried on the neck alone, the weight of these collars would be unmanageable, but supported by backpacks, or wire structures around the upper torso, they are safe and fairly comfortable.

Because the bulk of the collar supports could distort the figure, the collars are worn over the gown or tunic and are camouflaged with fabric and decorations. Anthony and Shirley Columbo work together at their Artistic Creations shop just outside of New Orleans. Anthony is responsible for the armature and structure of the costume pieces, and Shirley does the decorating. Anthony normally commences work by freely shaping a wire armature according to the design of a costume sketch. (Some costumers make a paper template or enlarge the original sketch to use as a pattern for the armature.)

The most difficult part of creating the collars is determining a correct balance. The weight of the collar must be distributed evenly from front to back as well as from side to side. A piece extending high over the head tends to pull the wearer off balance and may require lead weights for counterbalancing. These problems are solved during the fittings.

One or two fittings are usual. The first is made after the armature is completed. At that time, additional bracing pieces may be added, the armature bent to conform to the torso, and the collar adjusted for balance.

Anthony Columbo first measures the wearer from shoulder to shoulder across the back. For large and heavy collars, he also measures from neck to waist.

He uses 14-gauge smooth, galvanized steel wire to build the basic structure of the armature with its bracing harness and 16-gauge for additional decorative pieces. The solder he uses is resin-core 60/40.

After curving one length of wire for each outer edge of the collar, he bends the wire to the shape of the collar design, soldering the joints. For collars that require bracing, he adds wires to form a waist-length harness. Next, he places horizontal and vertical supporting wire between the collar edges at five-inch intervals. These wires, which are soldered at each joint, support the basic shape and provide a base for the decorative pieces and feather-holders which will be added later.

To create the feather holders, Anthony cuts five-inch lengths of 167-gauge wire. Working freehand, he twists a half-inch diameter loop at one end of the wire. Three-quarters of an inch away from the first loop, he fashions a second half-inch loop. The wire piece is then soldered into position onto the armature by the remaining two-inch stem.

The decorations are constructed into the desired designs from number 16 wire, which is bent and soldered before being attached to the armature. The collar is then ready for first fitting.

If the collar is especially large or heavy, Anthony creates additional bracing. Two parallel rows of wire about two inches apart encircle the waist and chest, hooking at center back. The hooks and fastening rings are fashioned from number 16 wire. At this time, additional weights may be added to the armature to correct the balance.

Shirley Columbo cuts rayon satin to cover the armature, allowing sufficient excess to fit between its decorations and plume holders. She allows at least a half-inch overlap for piecing as well as a half inch to overlap the edge of the armature. Both sides of the structure are covered with satin fabric.

Next, she sponges the back of the satin with white glue (preferably Sobo). Placing the still-wet fabric over the wire armature, she cuts edges of a half-inch overlap, clipping or rolling them over the wire edge. Glue adheres the fabric to the wire, while the satin contracts and tightens during the drying.

Velvet pieces are cut similarly to fit the satin. The satin covering is brushed with white glue and then covered with the velvet. The same process is repeated to cover the decorative pieces.

Seams and edges are decorated with braid, sequins, or rhinestones. Shirley dots rhinestones as required by the design. The average Columbo collar is spotted with 700 rhinestones in sizes 20 and 30.

Caution: Solders are mixtures of various metals that melt at relatively low temperatures. As they melt, metal fumes become airborne; therefore solder containing highly toxic metals like lead, antimony, or cadmium should be assiduously avoided. Fortunately, there are many suitable solders on the market that are free of these metals.

Resin-cored solders also release resin decomposition gases and vapors that are toxic and cause allergies. Acid-core solders emit corrosive gases and vapors. Ventilation is required for all soldering operations.

Showgirl Collars

Brazed Wire Joe Venturini, wire and metal sculptor in Hollywood, makes giant collars for Las Vegas revues, commercials, and other theatrical productions; he also creates his own fine art and commercial metal and wire sculpture. When building collars, he uses spring-steel music wire, preferring it

Wire-work with brazed joints forms the structure for a large collar by Joe Venturini.

to other metals because of its resilience. Though springy at the outset, the spring steel loses some of its flexibility after it has been heated and cut into small pieces.

When making his giant collars, Venturini finds that the first step is to have a paper pattern made from the designer's sketch. This is either provided by the designer, or it is made by the wireworker.

The paper pattern gives both dimensions and size. First, the pattern is laid flat and pinned to the worktable, where it serves as the guide for cutting and bending the wire. Venturini finds it best to work with an assistant, who helps to hold the wire away from the table when necessary, though Venturini also holds the wire in place with weights. To attach the wire pieces to each other, Venturini prefers a #110 brazing rod for general work and a #.091 for the more delicate work. After heating a brazing rod with an oxy-acetylene welding torch, he injects it into a #1 blue Peterson flux. This cleans the rod. Then he pushes the hot rod onto the piano wire, which melts the wire and adheres it to the other pieces of metal.

Shoulder harnesses that hold the collars in place are usually formed from a wire about 30 inches long, which is bent twice at the center to make a two-inch squared-off end. The wire is bent back towards its origin at the back of the harness. A central wire and several cross wires are cut and soldered into place for reinforcement. All the wires are then covered. When completed, the collars can be decorated in many ways: fabric and foam are often the basis over which are laid feathers and jewels.

For the Miss Universe Pageant of 1991, Venturini fashioned wirework crescent-shaped collars. Pete Menefee, costume designer, adorned the collars with balloons, producing costumes with unique and expansive theatricality.

Among the many shows with brazed collars made by Venturini are those seen at Las Vegas's Riviera, Flamingo, and MGM hotels, as well as in shows for The Radio City Music Hall's Rockettes.

Caution: Brazing rods are composed of various metals that become airborne during use. Fluxes usually contain acids or fluoride compounds that are highly hazardous to inhale. Thorough training and good ventilation are required when using gas-torch (acetylene, propane, etc.) brazing.

Welding is a highly hazardous craft that should be attempted only by persons with adequate training. Many OSHA regulations, fire laws, and environmental rules apply to welding. Many of these regulations and laws incorporate the standards of the American Welding Society (AWS), the American National Standards Institute (ANSI), and the National Fire Protection Association (NFPA). People unfamiliar with these standards are advised not to weld.

Welding cannot be done legally in most costume shops because the regulations require either an enclosed welding booth or removal of all combustible materials (e.g., wood, cloth, paper) within thirty-five feet of the welding activity.

Headddresses

Crowns

Felt Industrial, or rug, felt has long been a traditional material for building basic crown shapes. Start with a correct base to build over, such as the lower part of a hat block or clay sculpted to shape. Make a pattern and then cut out two or more layers of felt, determining the exact shapes over the base. Then soak the layered felt in white glue, or PVA, and allow to dry over the base.

One method is to paint the crown with a mixture of white glue and bronzing powder, adhering decorations such as metallic-filigree jewelry and metal chain with a thick layer of more white glue.

Another method is to paint the felt with metallic or nonmetallic colored paint. Use the metallic paint for a "new" look and the nonmetallic paint for an "antique" appearance. Lay over the painted

Industrial felt, hot-melt glue, and acrylic paint form this crown made by Rodney Gordon.

DESIGN: SANTO LOQUASTO FOR KEVIN KLINE AS *RICHARD III* IN THE NEW YORK SHAKESPEARE FESTIVAL PRODUCTION. CONSTRUCTION AND PHOTO; RODNEY GORDON.

felt a thin layer of silk-screen metallic-foil adhesive, and then the metallic foil. For decorations, apply pieces such as stones and jewelry, or draw on lines of hot-melt glue and then rub them with bronzing powder. Both these methods are from the Guthrie Theatre in Minneapolis, used on crowns made for Shakespeare's *Histories*.

Buckram Buckram also serves as a solid base for building a crown. Use one or two layers depending on the size of the crown and the durability requirements.

Cut out the buckram crown shape and sew millinery wire around the edges. For a complex silhouette, sew by hand, though machine sewing is satisfactory for a more simple shape. Extra durability may be added by brushing the buckram with a coating such as PVA or polyester resin. ⚠ After building this basic form, there are many methods for embellishment. The following are two methods used by New York costume craftsperson Rodney Gordon.

⚠ THIS SUBSTANCE OR PROCEDURE MAY BE HAZARDOUS TO HEALTH AND SHOULD BE USED WITH CARE. PLEASE READ THE APPROPRIATE HEALTH AND SAFETY SECTION.

First, paint the crown with gold acrylic paint. Cut out a piece of gold net from the crown pattern. Pin the net into place, then use hot-melt glue ⚠ to draw a ridge around the crown's edges, to both decorate the crown and secure the net. Decorate the crown by adding glass or plastic jewels, bonded by either more hot-melt glue or by epoxy cement⚠.

Cast Latex For a highly dimensional piece, casting latex can be successfully used. First, trace the original crown pattern onto a piece of heavy paper. Sculpt over that shape with oil-based clay. Using the clay form to create a plaster mold, proceed to cast latex from it. After the latex is dry, bond it to the buckram crown with rubber cement. Add latex to dark brown acrylic paint and brush onto the crown. Spray paint ⚠ with gold acrylic paint, and then add further embellishment such as gold leaf, painted jewels, etc.

Kydex⚠, Acrylic, Cork, and Wire

This jeweled headpiece was constructed by Rodney Gordon and worn in *Madame Butterfly* in a joint production of the Houston, Dallas, and Miami Opera Companies. The headpiece was made from an ingenuous assortment of unlikely materials.

1. A wire, shaped to fit over the head, was extended about six inches horizontally on either side of the head. Kydex acrylic-polyvinyl chloride sheeting was cut to fit it, then drilled with small holes and laced to the six-inch wire extensions.

Kydex acrylic-polyvinyl chloride sheeting, acrylic, cork, and wire are the materials forming this crown.

DESIGN: ALLEN CHARLES KLIEN FOR *MADAME BUTTERFLY*, A JOINT PRODUCTION OF THE DALLAS/MIAMI OPERA COMPANIES. CONSTRUCTION AND PHOTO: RODNEY GORDON.

2. From each hole was suspended another wire that was covered, from the top down, with plastic beads, then large cork beads, and finally acrylic-tube beads (as those in beaded curtains). On the curved center pieces, additional wires held small plastic flowers.

3. After assembly, the entire piece was sprayed with gold acrylic paint ⚠, individual pieces were painted with fake gold leaf, and French enamel varnish (FEV) ⚠ was added for richness.

Note: Kydex is the trade name for the Kleerdex Company's acrylic-polyvinyl chloride and is the brand commonly used by costume and prop makers.

There are endless other plastic materials and methods that can be utilized for crown making. Following are a few of them.

Low-Temperature-Setting Thermoplastic Sheeting

Thermoplastic sheetings, like the products from UnNatural Resources and Smith & Nephew Roylan, can be easily molded over a sculpted form made from clay, hard foam, or almost any material that can be assembled to simulate a crown. Follow the directions in the Jewelry section on pages 325-326 or in the manufacturer's brochure, paint with acrylic paint, and use more of the material itself to adhere decorations.

Polystyrene or Other High-Temperature-Setting Thermoplastic Sheeting

First sculpt the appropriate crown shape from either oil-based clay or polyurethane rigid foam to use as a positive mold. Then cast a plastic sheeting over it and form in a vacuum-former ⚠. See the section on plastic sheetings for more information on this process as well as the correct plastics to use. Be sure to follow manufacturer's instructions and use only the recommended adhesives, paints, and coatings for any embellishments, for many plastics resist some of these substances. If the plastic is thin, the crown structure may be strengthened by bonding felt or soft polyurethane foam to the interior.

Polyurethane Foam

Cut out a crown shape, butt the ends together to form the circle, and bond those ends with strong rubber cement ⚠. After producing this basic shape, paint it directly with acrylic spray or laminate it to another material and then paint it. Any decorations added directly to the foam should by bonded with a rubber cement. Either upholstery foam or ventilation foam can be used. Upholstery foam is less expensive and faster to deteriorate, while ventilating foam is more costly but longer lasting.

Vinyl Sheeting and Polyethylene Foam

For the *Once Upon The Brothers Grimm* TV Special, Bill Hargate created a silver crown using a one-quarter-inch sheet of polyethylene foam (like Minicel L-200) and two layers of cloth-backed, pebble-textured vinyl sheeting.

Polyethylene-foam sheeting is covered with textured silver vinyl and decorated with lurex cording and felt-tip marking pen to create this crown.

DESIGN: BILL HARGATE FOR *ONCE UPON THE BROTHERS GRIMM.* PHOTO: ROBERT W. ZENTIS.

1. Cut out the foam to the desired crown shape. Cut the two vinyl layers into shapes slightly larger but without points. Cut strips of millinery wire to the height of the foam crown points.

2. Lay the cutout foam flat on a table, placing a wire strip to rise vertically to each point. Rubber cement ⚠ the wires into place with a length of cloth tape. (Hargate uses Barge All-Purpose Cement.) Allow to dry.

3. Butt and glue the crown ends together to form a circle.

4. Apply a layer of vinyl to the crown's interior, rubber-cement it, then trim to the shape of the foam. Apply the other vinyl layer to the crown's exterior, cement, and trim.

5. Edge the crown with lurex cording, rubber-cemented into place. Add shade and dimension by drawing with black marking pen.

Drag-Queen Headdresses

Gaffer's Tape, Rodent Wire, and Found Objects

The headdresses worn in *The Adventures of Priscilla, Queen of the Desert* were designed and made on a minuscule budget by innovative Oscar-winning designer Lizzy Gardiner. She followed the methods used by real Australian drag queens, who prefer making their headdress bases with black gaffer's tape and rodent wire. Rodent wire, a screening with holes smaller than that of chicken wire, is available at hardware and building stores in the United States as aviary wire. Because the wire is metal, the process is painful, but, according to those who use this technique, the success of the process makes the pain worth the effect.

⚠ THIS SUBSTANCE OR PROCEDURE MAY BE HAZARDOUS TO HEALTH AND SHOULD BE USED WITH CARE. PLEASE READ THE APPROPRIATE HEALTH AND SAFETY SECTION.

Skullcap

1. From two layers of rodent or aviary wire, cut shapes just larger than the wearer's head. Lay them over the head; press and mold them to fit snugly. Using wire shears, cut to fit around the ears, then carefully cut the entire edge to fit over the hairline.

2. While the wire is still on his head, cover the entire surface with black gaffer's tape until there is a clean, smooth shape of the individual's skull.

3. Remove the cap and add extra tape around the ears. Add tape to line the interior to prevent inordinate piercing. If the design requires some skull to be visible, glue on a flesh-colored bathing cap.

4. Sculpted polystyrene foam can be added as the base for large headdresses. Starting with a block of polystyrene, shape it to fit using an electric carving knife. Glue it to the skullcap with shoe cement ⚠ (like Barge). Then cover it with a layer of extra-strong gaffer's tape. This adds the strength needed for longevity.

5. On top of this structure, attach the actual headdress elements: flowers, feathers, found objects, etc. by gluing them into place.

In *Priscilla*, enormous problems occurred because of the desert heat. The heat melted the glue from the headdresses while the actors were wearing them. Hardly anything was durable enough to withstand the pressures of a low-budget film shot in the Australian desert.

Plastic Tubing

Narrow, blue, plastic tubing from an electrical-supply shop decorated one outrageous headdress. In this case the covering material was applied directly to the taped skullcap.

1. Cut strips of tubing individually, and carefully lay them into place. Cut the first strip, place a line of hot glue on the skullcap and press the tubing into place. Keep repeating the process until the cap is covered.

2. Curling each length of tubing independently. Glue them together with hot-melt glue, one by one, until the curl is complete, and then glue the entire curl to the rest of the headdress.

Lipstick Cases and Feathers

Lipstick cases, each of a different color, were fitted with their pink plastic-display-lipstick shapes projecting forward and glued in place. The cases were arranged in a crescent shape, rimming the front of the headdress. Feathers top the headdress. The stems are wired then attached to thin wires that pierce the gaffer's tape and wind around the top layer of the interior rodent wire.

Flower Headdress

Polyester Resin⚠, Latex⚠, Millinery Net, and Other Fabrics

These seemingly simple headdresses from *The Will Rogers' Follies* were constructed from a variety of materials and methods. The materials include casting latex, buckram, polyurethane floor varnish ⚠, polyester resin, nylon net, Bridal Adhesive ⚠ and acrylic paint. The methods used by Rodney Gordon in his New York workshop included casting, sewing, coating, and bonding. To create a similar design, follow these steps.

1. Make or buy a buckram form and strengthen it with a coating of polyurethane floor coating. It will be clear and fast-drying.

2. Cover a suitable-size head form with plastic wrap, then use an oil-based clay, like Roma Plastalina, to sculpt over the form a hat in the shape of a large sepal. Use the clay form to cast a negative plaster mold. After making the mold, clean it out well. To cast the latex sepal hat form, slush mold the casting latex by pouring the liquid latex into the plaster mold. (Be sure to follow the manufacturer's directions carefully when casting with latex.) Allow the latex to cure about one hour to form a skin and then pour out the excess liquid. After the latex is set and removed from the mold, paint the outer surfaces with acrylic paint mixed with liquid latex.

A variety of materials make up this Sunflower headdress worn in Will Rogers' Follies.

The polyurethane-coated buckram form can be seen from this side view.

DESIGN: WILLA KIM FOR THE ORIGINAL BROADWAY PRODUCTION OF *WILL RODGERS' FOLLIES*. CONSTRUCTION AND PHOTO: RODNEY GORDON.

3. Cut flower-petal shapes from a heavy millinery type of nylon net and brush Bridal Adhesive around their edges to prevent fraying. These pieces will serve as interlinings. Cut petal shapes from desired fabrics, allowing for a small seam. Stitch pairs together, trim, and press. Cover both sides of the net interlining pieces with this petal fabric.

4. Sew layers of the petals onto the edges of the buckram head form, and then glue the cast latex sepal in place with either a rubber-based contact cement △ (like Barge) or liquid latex.

△ THIS SUBSTANCE OR PROCEDURE MAY BE HAZARDOUS TO HEALTH AND SHOULD BE USED WITH CARE. PLEASE READ THE APPROPRIATE HEALTH AND SAFETY SECTION.

Will Rogers' Follies costumes were designed by Willa Kim.

Multiple Headdresses

Cast Neoprene △

Jane Clugston, innovative sculptor and costume and prop maker, finds Neoprene (chloroprene rubber) casting excellent for making multiple as well as one-of-a-kind headdresses and costume prop pieces. For *Antony and Cleopatra* at the Oregon Shakespeare Festival, she used this method to create a headdress for Cleopatra.

1. Using a Styrofoam head-block for a base. Sculpt from clay the model for the head-dress. Clugston prefers water-based potters' clay.

2. Spray a release agent like silicone spray ⚠ over the clay. Build, on top of the clay model, a plaster of Paris mold about one-inch thick. The mold made by Clugston was comprised of two sections.

3. After about eight hours, pull the Styrofoam block away from the plaster mold and clay model, tearing the Styrofoam if necessary. Remove all clay from the molds.

4. Now the Neoprene can be cast, using the slip-casting technique. Start by pouring liquid Neoprene into the mold. After at least an hour, or when a wall develops next to the plaster, pour out excess liquid. The remaining Neoprene, about one-eighth-inch thick, will form the headdress.

5. Spray or brush on acrylic paint. For Cleopatra's headdress, Clugston first sprayed a coat of gold acrylic paint ⚠, then followed with gold leaf, and concluded with a sprayed coat of French enamel varnish ⚠. (See French Enamel Varnish on page 152.)

Vacuum-Formed Polystyrene ⚠

A way of quickly creating multiples of almost anything is through the vacuum-form process. Even top hats can be vacuum-formed. When molded in polystyrene and covered with velour or other thick fabric or with flocking, they look as convincing as if painstakingly blocked from felt.

Vacuum-formed polystyrene is a material of choice for creating multiples, such as this top hat.

COURTESY: BILL HARGATE.
PHOTO: ROBERT W. ZENTIS.

1. To create molded traditional hats, make a mold from an actual hat by filling it with plaster.

2. When the plaster is dry, set the filled hat in the vacuum-former and form over it the polystyrene or other thermoplastic sheet.

3. Cut out the selected hat fabric.

4. Sandpaper the plastic, cover it with adhesive, and carefully apply the fabric.

Vacuum-Formed Polystyrene ⚠, Silk Rouleaux, Vinyl Rods, and Polyurethane Foam

For the circus scene in *Batman Forever*, Bob Ringwood designed vacuum-formed, black, shiny legionnaires' helmets. The helmets are decorated with high feathery crests of dyed silk rouleaux, or tubes of fabric, which can be especially sewn by a custom-pleating and stitching company.

1. Cut tubing into strips twice the length of the desired crest.

2. Fold them in half, then clip the fold with a double-tipped shoelace ending (available at fasteners' suppliers).

3. Ombré-dye them into multicolored stripes. First, prepare dye pots with black, yellow, red, and green and bring them to a boil. Dip groups of rouleaux together into

water, then into the pots of color. If the colors just come together, they will bleed slightly, forming soft, ombréed stripes.

4. Insert both ends of the rouleaux into thin vinyl rods half the length of each folded rouleaux. This should cause each one to stand up like a feather.

5. Next, cut out curved crest shapes from one-quarter-inch Scott, or SIF black poly-urethane insulation foam. Glue the stiffened, ombré-dyed silk rouleaux in place with hot-melt glue ⚠.

6. Glue the interior curve of the foam crests in place onto each helmet. Hot-glue each into place onto the helmets. Actors wearing these headdresses are dressed in matching colored harem costumes.

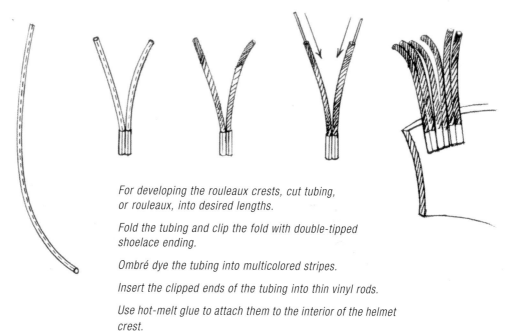

For developing the rouleaux crests, cut tubing, or rouleaux, into desired lengths.

Fold the tubing and clip the fold with double-tipped shoelace ending.

Ombré dye the tubing into multicolored stripes.

Insert the clipped ends of the tubing into thin vinyl rods.

Use hot-melt glue to attach them to the interior of the helmet crest.

Oversize Headdresses

Helmets to Support Large Headdresses

Michael Curry Design and Sculptural Engineering studio in Oregon designs and makes costume and prop pieces that are shipped all over the United States, supplying venues such as Disneyland, Las Vegas nightclubs, and Broadway theatres. Some productions with costumes made by Curry Design are the recent Broadway production of *Crazy for You* and The 1996 Olympics' opening ceremony.

Because the pieces are shipped by plane, Curry Design must take into consideration the variables of weights and the freezing temperatures of high altitudes when designing and selecting costume materials. Freezing temperatures can destroy some glue bonds and other substances.

The following describes how Curry Design creates the large sculptural headdresses for Las Vegas showgirls and for opera singers. The latter cannot use chin straps, for they would interfere with voice production. These types of headdresses are made specifically for one individual and are not interchangeable.

Epoxy ⚠, Carbon-Graphite Cloth, and a Plastic Bag

This first method requires vacuum-bagging, which is low-tech and uncomplicated, although it requires a vacuum pump costing about $800.

1. Start with a plaster cast of the wearer's head. Seal the plaster with beeswax by melting a flat sheet of beeswax and placing it over the cast. The beeswax will seal the plaster and make the headdress slightly larger.

2. Place a fitted felt cap over the plaster cast. Brush on a layer of epoxy and laminate on it two layers of fiberglass or carbon-graphite cloth. Then place a plastic bag over all.

3. Attach the plastic bag to a vacuum pump. The vacuum will suck the plastic bag tightly to the underlayers of the epoxy, fiberglass, or graphite, and to the felt skull-cap, eliminating all air and creating a thin, firmly finished piece.

The key to making lightweight laminates is to use 40 percent resin and 60 percent fiber. Vacuum-bagging is the only method to achieve this weight, for the vacuum wicks off the heavy resin that is in excess of this ratio.

Felt, Polyester Resin, and Carbon-Graphite Cloth or Fiberglass

From Michael Curry come yet more methods for making the helmets that carry large headdresses. Fit a felt cap onto the wearer or wearer's cast. For strength and rigidity, lay up fiber cloth and polyester ⚠ or vinylester ⚠ resin over the felt cap. Curry prefers vinylester over polyester because it is less volatile, less toxic, and less flammable, yet costs about the same and can be worked by the same methods as those used on polyester. Most suppliers of polyester also supply vinylester.

Helmet Liners

To make headdresses with a large inner circumference that fit closely on a wearer's head, it is often necessary to insert a liner that fits the head. Such liners can have metal or foam extensions reaching to the walls of the outer headdress. Some welding-helmet companies manufacture a good, crank-down welding-helmet liner. In the back of the inside of the helmet is a crank. To adjust it to the size of the wearer's cranium, just reach inside and give the crank a small twist. This liner can be adjusted to several wearers. Such helmet liners cost only a few dollars.

Polyethylene or Ethyl-Vinyl-Acetate Foam Sheeting

This is another method from the Michael Curry Design and Sculptural Engineering studios for creating a helmet base that carries large, ornamental headdresses. These helmets lock onto the head, and are especially good for walk-around characters. Polyethylene foam sheeting, such as the Minicel L-200 type from Voltek or ethyl vinyl acetate foam sheeting *(EVA)*, serve as the base material. Curry prefers EVA because it has more strength. Since foam sheeting is resilient, it is comfortable and adaptable for costumes that must be exchanged between actors. Helmets of a nonfoam plastic sheeting, like thermoplastic polyester or polystyrene, can never be exchanged because they do not have the flexibility needed to fit more than one head.

1. Start by patterning a skullcap from a one-half-inch or three-quarter-inch foam sheet. Make it very tight around and below the cranium, so that it grasps the lower part of the back of the head. Butt the edges together, gluing with 3M's Scotch-Grip 847 (brown glue) ⚠ or a similar rubber cement.

2. For reinforcements, make two EVA or polyethylene-foam headbands, about one-inch wide, one going from front to back, and the other from side to side. Glue in place with rubber cement.

Low-Temperature-Setting-Thermoplastic Sheeting

This type of headdress is one of the best for holding attachments and for gripping the head.

1. First, place a bald cap on the wearer's head, or atomize the hair with water, and place Saran Wrap or another plastic film over head and hair, or over a plaster cast of the head.

2. Next, from low-temperature-setting thermoplastic sheeting perforated with one-eighth-inch holes, cut a rectangle slightly larger than the head size. Dip it into hot water and, while it is cooling, drape over the head. Fit past the hemisphere, widest across the temples, between the ears. Press closely around the hemisphere to the bottom of the cranium, or the undercut of the skull, being careful not to stretch too much. (Stretching thins the thermoplastic and weakens it.) Fitting the cap closely eliminates the need for chin straps.

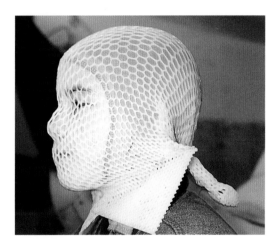

Low-temperature-setting thermoplastic sheeting forms a snug-fitting supportive cap.

3. Cut a two-inch vertical slice in the bottom edge of the back of the cap, enlarging into a dart, which is then spanned with a piece of elastic. This makes the cap slightly smaller than its original size, creating a tension that holds the headdress more securely.

4. The one-eighth-inch holes allow for mechanical attachment—for sewing, riveting, or other methods—of

A cap of low-temperature-setting thermoplastic sheeting is fitted with structural metal

⚠ THIS SUBSTANCE OR PROCEDURE MAY BE HAZARDOUS TO HEALTH AND SHOULD BE USED WITH CARE. PLEASE READ THE APPROPRIATE HEALTH AND SAFETY SECTION.

Low-temperature-setting thermoplastic sheeting forms the foundation for these large, elaborate headdresses.

DESIGN: WILLIAM IVEY LONG FOR THE ORIGINAL BROADWAY PRODUCTION OF *CRAZY FOR YOU.* CONSTRUCTION AND PHOTO: MICHAEL CURRY.

securing decorative pieces. (Pieces must be securely attached to withstand the rocking and shifting of the head.) To color the thermoplastic, add dye to the hot water in which the plastic is being softened. A disperse dye or union dye like Rit or Tintex works well.

5. Placing the cap onto the head for the first time can be a difficult moment, but once the cap slips into place, it will fit perfectly.

6. Headdresses supporting elaborate ornamentation will require additional strengthening. Over the original cap, made from the thermoplastic rectangle with one-eighth-inch holes, place a sheet of solid thermoplastic, about three inches square. Lay this across the top of the head, and on top of it place a three-inch-square contoured aluminum plate. The aluminum can be contoured by forging, or heating and hammering into shape. Pieces that ornament the headdress are then welded onto the aluminum. The tall headdresses worn by Las Vegas showgirls balance beautifully on such a foundation. Headdresses for showgirls who are not required to speak or sing, can be further secured with a chinstrap.

For information on thermoplastic sheeting, see the Low-Temperature-Setting Thermoplastic Sheeting section on page 276-279.

Headddress Structures

Foam Insulation Spray ⚠

To make large airy headdresses without using wirework, follow this novel solution offered by freelance craftsperson Peg Brady, who used polyurethane ⚠ foam insulation spray to create a lightweight, oversize form.

1. Take a plastic bicycle helmet and cut off any extruding brim pieces.

2. Spray the entire helmet with three to six inches of insulation foam.

3. With an electric knife (or a sharp kitchen knife), carve the foam-covered helmet into a smooth rounded form and spray it with acrylic paint.

4. Select the objects that will decorate the head-piece. Squeeze hot glue onto the ends of the decorative pieces and poke them into the foam. In this case, Christmas-tree ornaments served the purpose beautifully.

Polyurethane-foam insulation spray forms the foundation of this headddress.

DESIGN: ALAN ARMSTRONG FOR *THE TEMPEST* AT THE ALABAMA SHAKESPEARE FESTIVAL. PHOTO: SCARSBROOK/ASF.

Headdresses made by this method were worn by the Goddesses in *The Tempest*, which was designed by Alan Armstrong for the Alabama Shakespeare Festival in 1988.

Foam Sheeting

To quickly fabricate hats that do not require closeup viewing, durability, or long-term wear, take foam sheeting, like polyurethane and polyethylene. Use one-quarter-inch sheeting for smaller headdresses and one-half for the larger.

Begin with a paper pattern, taping edges together to test the fit. Then cut out the sheeting with the fitted paper pattern for the inside wall of the headdress. Because of the thickness of the foam, the outer wall of the headdress will be somewhat larger. Bevel the edges to obtain a smooth fit.

Glue all edges together with rubber contact cement ⚠.

Hats and headdresses made with this techniques can be colored with dye—polyurethane, but not polyethylene, dyes easily with union dyes like Rit Dye—or the headdresses can be spray painted ⚠. Large projecting pieces like brims can be stiffened with buckram, which can be glued in place before painting to match.

Polyethylene foam with rubber-cemented seams is the material for this bonnet.

DESIGN: BILL HARGATE FOR THE *ONCE UPON A BROTHERS GRIMM* TV SPECIAL. PHOTO: ROBERT W. ZENTIS.

⚠ THIS SUBSTANCE OR PROCEDURE MAY BE HAZARDOUS TO HEALTH AND SHOULD BE USED WITH CARE. PLEASE READ THE APPROPRIATE HEALTH AND SAFETY SECTION.

Wirework Joe Venturini is a specialist in making frames that serve as the basis for large headdresses, such as those worn in Las Vegas revues and designed by such notables as Bob Mackie and Pete Menefee.

Some designers present a pattern to delineate size and shape, and others present the sketch, from which Venturini develops the pattern. Venturini prefers to work in his self-invented brazing method. (Brazing is a process of soldering metal using a hard solder and a high melting point.)

Venturini works with music wire, which is a type of spring steel, usually using #.110 for the heaviest part of the structure, #.091 for medium-size work, and #.0625 for the more delicate. He prefers music wire over other wires because it has resilience and is less likely to split apart at the joint if it is accidentally dropped or hit. Some of the wire's springy quality disappears when it is heated by the acetylene torch or when it is cut into the short lengths that make up a costume piece. The more lengths required, the less springy the final piece. For brazing rod, he chooses the size compatible with the size of the smallest wire. He always uses a flux. (Flux is a substance applied to the surfaces being joined that is used to facilitate the flow of solder while soldering and brazing.)

Polyurethane reticulated insulation foam with rubber-cemented seams forms this bonnet.
DESIGN: BILL HARGATE FOR THE *ONCE UPON A BROTHERS GRIMM* TV SPECIAL. PHOTO: ROBERT W. ZENTIS.

A wirework structure is the basis for many large headdresses.
WIREWORK AND PHOTO: JOE VENTURINI.

1. Bend the wire into a curved base that will fit the wearer's head. This can be either a crescent, a cloverleaf, or another shape. Fill it with cross-wires to stabilize it. This is the foundation that later will be hand-stitched to a firm skullcap.

2. Lay the headdress pattern on a worktable, and cut and bend the wire to the pattern's shape. If the design is for a symmetrical headdress, turn the pattern over and take many measurements.

3. Cover a piece of wood with thin brass or steel sheeting for a worktable. First draw the design on the brass, then shape the wire over the drawing, heating it with the torch. Join the wire together and stabilize it by adhering it to the brass tabletop by means of short pieces of brazing rod. Later, remove the metal structure from the

brass tabletop by heating it and removing the small pieces of brazing rod with pliers.

4. Start with the outer edges of the form of the design. Fill across the silhouette with bars or struts for supports to strengthen the headdress. The number and spacing of these supports will depend upon the size and shape of the headdress. Some pieces can be worked flat on a table and be held by weights.

5. In working on large pieces, Venturini advises that it is necessary to have an assistant hold the structure steady for the next steps.

6. Heat one end of the brazing rod with an acetylene torch and then dip the rod into the flux. Push the hot-fluxed rod into a joining of the piano wires, causing the rod to melt around the wires and bond them. Continue working in this way until all the pieces are joined.

7. For feather-holder rings, apply metal washers with the same technique.

8. Weld the headpiece to the curved base. Test it for balance, and equalize it if necessary with extra pieces of wire.

For *Batman Returns*, Venturini worked with designer and costume craftsperson Ted Shell. For some of the headdresses, the wirework was left bare and uncovered, creating airy structures depicting both Big Ben and The Eiffel Tower.

For the Renaissance Bride from Bob Mackie's Originals collection, Venturini created a bridal headdress from wire loops attached to a wire crescent shape, which was worn atop a bridal veil. He formed the wire into loops that were welded together. The loops were then covered by hand-beaded gold banding decorated with gold bugle beads and rhinestones.

This wirework headdress is covered with hand-beaded gold banding and decorated by gold bugle beads.

DESIGN: BOB MACKIE FOR THE RENAISSANCE BRIDE FROM BOB MACKIE'S ORIGINALS COLLECTION AS PART OF A WEDDING ENSEMBLE.
WIREWORK AND PHOTO: JOE VENTURINI.

A wire structure is prepared as the basis for the headdress.

The wire structure is covered with dyed polyurethane foam.

DESIGN: PETE MENEFEE FOR RAG DOLL DANCERS IN A CHRISTMAS REVUE AT THE RADIO CITY MUSIC HALL. WIREWORK AND PHOTO: JOE VENTURINI.

The red festive headdresses designed by Pete Menefee, worn by Rag Doll dancers in a Radio City Music Hall revue were made by first welding metal wire into a diamond shape reinforced by both vertical and horizontal lengths of supporting wire. The diamond is welded to a cloverleaf shape, which is sewn to a buckram cap. The cap is covered in red fabric and decorated with red-dyed strips of polyurethane foam that are overlapped into a draped turban shape. The metal-wire form supports more strips of the dyed foam, which are looped at the top and then sewn to the diamond shape and to each other.

Venturini did the wirework for a large crab headdress designed by Pete Menefee and worn by a showgirl in Las Vegas's Riviera Hotel *Splash* revue. Here Venturini created a wire sculpture, according to the designer's specifications. An assistant helped hold the large and difficult piano wire form as he assembled it. The legs and pinchers were left loose, and fastened by tape hinges to maintain a spring action.

This headdress is so large it requires additional support from the shoulders. The shoulder-support wirework covers a two-and-a-half-inch-wide area, curving over the shoulders for about eight inches in the front and eight inches in the back. It is covered with fabric matching the costume and attached to small strips of webbing to keep it in place. Both wire and webbing are kept as small as possible, since the showgirl's costume is fairly brief.

Nylon spandex covers the wire for this Show-girl's crab headdress worn in the Splash revue at the Mirage Resorts in Las Vegas.

DESIGN: PETE MENEFEE WIREWORK: JOE VENTURINI. CONSTRUCTION AND PHOTO: JUDY CORBETT.

In this set of costumes, Venturini worked with Judy Corbett of J & M Costumes who covered the crab's body and legs with nylon spandex. The fabric is stretched, sewn in place, and decorated with metallic gold textural shapes of fabrics and scattered rhinestones, both glued ⚠ in place.

Caution: Brazing rods are composed of various metals that become airborne during use. Fluxes usually contain acids or fluoride compounds that are highly hazardous to inhale. Thorough training and good ventilation are required when using gas (acetylene, propane, etc.) torch brazing.

Welding is a highly hazardous craft that should only be attempted by persons with adequate training. Many OSHA regulations, fire laws, and environmental rules apply to welding. Many of these regulations and laws incorporate the standards of the American Welding Society (AWS), the American National Standards Institute (ANSI), and the National Fire Protection Association (NFPA). People unfamiliar with these standards are advised not to weld.

Welding cannot be done legally in most costume shops because the regulations require either an enclosed welding booth or removal of all combustible materials (e.g., wood, cloth, paper) within thirty-five feet of the welding activity.

Jewelry

Latex Casting latex can be molded to create lightweight jewelry. A mold is taken from existing jewelry, jewelry pieces, or from created jewelry designed in clay. Latex-casting requires special expertise. (See a good reference such as Thurston James' *The Prop Builder's Molding and Casting Handbook* for mold-making methods.) A mold made from plaster does not require a parting agent and is preferable.

1. Pour latex into the mold. After about fifteen minutes, when the latex has begun to set, pour out the still-liquid latex.

2. For reinforcement, add a layer of cheesecloth or other fabric large enough to extend beyond the edges of the mold. Use a brush to push it into an even shape. When this first layer of latex is dry, pour in more latex, and add another piece of cheesecloth. Add more latex. The amount of buildup of cloth and latex depends upon the size of the jewelry piece.

3. Instead of cheesecloth, power net (a strong elastic net fabric) can be added. The power net which strengthens the latex while allowing it to retain its flexibility is particularly well suited to dance costumes. Whether to use cheesecloth or power net and the amount used depends upon the purpose of the pieces and how much strengthening is required.

4. When the molds are set and after the latex pieces are removed from the molds, they can be painted. Because paint does not adhere well to latex, an adhesive must be applied as primer before applying the paint, or an additive must be mixed into the paint. An excellent primer is Pros-Aide, a prosthetic makeup adhesive, sold specifically to adhere makeup to latex prosthetics to the skin. Another favored primer is rubber cement ⚠, like 3M 77 spray. As an alternative to using a primer,

△ THIS SUBSTANCE OR PROCEDURE MAY BE HAZARDOUS TO HEALTH AND SHOULD BE USED WITH CARE. PLEASE READ THE APPROPRIATE HEALTH AND SAFETY SECTION.

add latex to acrylic paint as a binder in the ratio of one-part latex to two-parts paint. If the mixture needs thinning, use ammonia ⚠.

5. Paint with acrylic paint.

6. The latex pieces can be embellished with beads and other jewelry and bonded in place with latex, rubber cement, or hot-melt glue ⚠. The cast latex pieces can also be intermingled with jewelry pieces made from other materials.

Examples of Cast-Latex Jewelry

Cast latex sewn onto power net forms the jewelry and metallic adornment for this costume.

DESIGN: THEONI ALDRIDGE FOR JOHAN RENVALL DANCING THE ROLE OF THE *GOLDEN IDOL* IN *LA BAYADERE* IN THE AMERICAN BALLET THEATRE'S 1980 PRODUCTION. CONSTRUCTION: JANET HARPER AND THE BARBARA MATERA COSTUME SHOP. PHOTO: KENN DUNCAN ©1980.

For the 1978 American Ballet Theatre production of *La Bayadere*, all the jeweled pieces were of made of cast latex ⚠. Power net was embedded in the latex during the casting process. The molded pieces were sprayed with gold acrylic paint, gilded with gold leaf, painted with French enamel varnish (FEV) ⚠, and sewn onto a body garment of power net. The headdress was of fabric decorated with both cast latex and metal pieces sewn in place. The designs were by Theoni Aldridge with jewelry construction by Janet Harper. The latex pieces were sewn to the power net at the Barbara Matera Costume Shop.

A heavy looking necklace created for the production of *Gianni Schicci* at the Dallas Opera was made from a combination of cast-latex pieces, wooden drapery rings, and glass beads strung together on a heavy jewelry cord. The pieces were painted first with dark brown acrylic paint, then coated with a mix of millinery lacquer ⚠ and bronzing powder. The design was by Peter J. Hall and the construction by Rodney Gordon.

Another necklace designed by Peter J. Hall and built by Rodney Gordon was of cast-latex pieces painted with dark acrylic paint coated with millinery lacquer and bronzing powder. The pieces were decorated with metal settings and glass stones and bonded with Barge All-Purpose Cement ⚠.

For the Strongman in Cirque du Soleil's *Alegría*, latex ⚠ forms the large medallion on the front of a leather belt. In order to make the medallion, a model

Wooden rings, glass beads, and cast latex pieces form this necklace.

DESIGN: PETER J. HALL FOR *GIANNI SCHICCI* AT THE DALLAS OPERA. CONSTRUCTION AND PHOTO: RODNEY GORDON.

was sculpted from a plasticine clay. From the clay a negative plaster mold was made. Soft liquid latex was poured into the plaster mold (for processes, read about latex in the Casting Plastics section on pages 210-213). The medallion was painted with acrylic paint and bronzing powder was brushed on and then wiped off for an antique look.

This medallion could be adhered with a rubber contact cement to the wide leather belt. The Cirque du Soleil shop placed a functional buckle underneath the medallion.

Micro-Crystalline Wax ⚠ and Wood

The production style of Shakespeare's *Henry V* at the University of Evansville, Indiana, in 1993, was primitive and barbaric. Costumes and set emphasized an organic, rough-hewn look. To achieve this in the clothing design, the jewelry and many of the costume accessories were carved out of plywood, and then coated with a chocolate-brown layer of micro-crystalline. Local newspapers compared the effect to that of "old iron."

This pendant of wood is coated with drips of micro-crystalline wax.
DESIGN AND PHOTO: PATTI MCCRORY FOR *HENRY V* AT THE UNIVERSITY OF EVANSVILLE, INDIANA.

The wax, micro-crystalline, was originally developed for the lost-wax process, a method most often used in casting jewelry and small metal sculptures. For this production, designer Patti McCrory, working with Michelle Goodman and Kraig Brown, carved the form of the jewelry from wood and dripped the heavy dark-brown wax over the surface, where it ran like drippings from a melting candle. They then brushed it lightly with a metallic fabric paint ⚠.

Wax is hazardous when heated, emitting decomposition which emits toxic gases into the air. These gases can irritate and damage respiratory tracts, causing a breakdown of the respiratory system, bronchitis and chemical pneumonia when exposed to large amounts or to repeated small amounts. No respirator cartridge is effective against these emissions, and ventilation is required.

Chloroprene Rubber (Neoprene) ⚠ and Latex

When Ted Shell was faced with the challenge of designing and constructing some 240 costumes for the Lost Boys in the feature film *Hook*, he wanted to decorate the costumes with natural and organic items, such as seashells, chicken bones, bamboo stalks, coconut shells, and gourds. Since these natural objects are too fragile and too brittle to withstand sewing or hard use, it was necessary to make life-size replications.

1. Shell collected originals of these items, including four sizes of chicken bones, a wide assortment of seashells, sand dollars, and several sizes of bamboo stalks and shards. These were the positives for the molds.

2. Plaster molds were used for the uncomplicated shapes, and silicone RTV (room-temperature vulcanizing silicone rubber) was used where flexibility was required, allowing complex pieces with extensions and undercuts to be pulled easily out of

⚠ THIS SUBSTANCE OR PROCEDURE MAY BE HAZARDOUS TO HEALTH AND SHOULD BE USED WITH CARE. PLEASE READ THE APPROPRIATE HEALTH AND SAFETY SECTION.

the molds (see the Casting Plastics section on pages 188-189). The forms were then cast variously from Neoprene rubber and from latex.

3. All the cast objects were painted with water-based vinyl-acrylic scenic paint. Layers of thin lacquer ⚠ were painted to simulate the depth and texture of the natural shell or organic object.

4. Bone and shell forms were drilled with holes and sewn with heavy cord underneath garments. Leaf decorations made from cloth leaves, and purchased vinyl plastic leaves were hand-sewn to the costumes.

5. The actors wore the Neoprene forms, while the stuntmen wore the latex forms. The latex allowed softness and flexibility and accommodated acrobatic activity. The garments to which the forms were attached were made of textured natural fabrics, such as silk shantung, raw silk, and soft-textured cottons.

For some of the headpieces, actual gourds were used. To make them fit the actors' heads, the costume shop lined the gourds with fiberglass and polyester resin ⚠, which gave durability. The gourds were then adhered to fitted caps formed from Scott insulating foam covered by cheesecloth dipped in latex.

The shop worked for six months on these exciting and extraordinarily inventive costumes. The 26 actors each required two costumes, the 187 stuntmen each one, while Ruffio, the leader of the Lost Boys, needed six sets of the same costume.

Shell was the designer for the Lost Boys, but the overall costume design for *Hook* was by Bob Ringwood.

Resins ⚠   Prepare a mold using methods discussed in the Casting Materials section. Almost all small containers and nonporous materials around the home or shop may be used to create regular, symmetrical forms. Coat the container with a release agent, line with Mylar or aluminum foil, or use a clean glass receptacle. Resins can also be cast directly onto a sheet of wax paper, aluminum foil, or glass for making less regular shapes.

Epoxy-resin auto-body filler was used to cast this necklace.

DESIGN: THE AUTHOR FOR *MEG* AT THE DEPARTMENT OF THEATRE ARTS, UNIVERSITY OF CALIFORNIA, LOS ANGELES. CONSTRUCTION: ROBERT SECRIST. PHOTO: THURSTON JAMES.

Polyester is a resin with a shiny, transparent jeweled appearance and is easy to use. Epoxy, though opaque, is equally easy to work with. Acrylics yield the most transparency, yet are very difficult to cast. Small jewelry pieces may also be cast from certain adhesives, like cyanoacrylate (superglue) and hot glue, squeezed directly out of a dropper or a glue gun. Following are some general steps for casting resin jewelry; however, for specific information, refer to the applicable sections of this book or to a specialized reference book on resin-casting.

1. Mix casting resin with a catalyst, following mixing directions, and pour into the mold or drip onto a flat surface. Add coloring or embed small items such as seeds, string, sequins, etc., while the resin is setting.

2. For making strung pieces of jewelry, such as beads, insert glitter, stones, and objects of your choice while the resin is still workable and uncured.

3. Allow adequate time for the resin to cure. Refer to the manufacturer's directions, since curing time varies with different products and brands. After curing, remove it from the mold. If a shiny appearance is desirable, sand and polish the surface.

4. Either glue it directly to a surface using a thick-bodied adhesive such as hot glue, or adhere a jewelry backing such as earring findings or a brooch pin. Refer to the casting section of this book for compatibility of adhesives with surfaces.

After casting transparent gems, such as with polyester resin, bond to Mylar or other metallic-looking backing for additional shine.

Preformed Plastics

Many plastics are available in sheet, rods, spheres, tubes, and other shapes in an assortment of sizes. Thicknesses of formed plastic may be cut into jewelry shapes for mounting or drilling, or the shape can be left intact, as in a flat plane, circle, etc., or it can be heat-formed and bent.

Preformed plastics like acrylic can be sliced, cut, carved, and polished. Pieces such as acrylic rings, spheres, and cubes can be adhered together by simply brushing ethylene dichloride ⚠ (a solvent for acrylic) on opposing surfaces. Jewelry pieces can be made by laminating several different colors of the plastic to form a block; or other materials, such as paper, cloth, dried flowers, and thin jeweled pieces can be laminated between two sheets of transparent plastic.

Preformed-acrylic pieces can be cut and assembled into jewelry.
PHOTO: RICHARD S. BAILEY.

Once joined, acrylic forms can be carved with cutting and grinding instruments. Pieces cut from acrylic sheets can be formed by heating them in an oven of about 275°F, over a heating strip, or with a heat gun. With gloved hands, pieces can be shaped in free-form, or they can be formed around a positive or negative mold. When attaching acrylic jewels to other surfaces, epoxy cements ⚠ are recommended.

Thermoplastic Sheeting

Low-temperature-setting thermoplastic sheetings, like those from UnNatural Resources, Smith & Nephew Roylan, and Friendly Plastics, lend themselves to quick jewelry-making. Simply cut the sheeting into small shapes, dissolve in hot water (170° to 220° F), and twist or fold into a jewelry or bead design. While the material is still tacky, almost any other substance will stick to it, so it is not necessary to use an adhesive to apply earring findings, brooch pins, etc. For making beads, wrap strips around themselves, leaving open the spaces that become the holes for stringing.

⚠ THIS SUBSTANCE OR PROCEDURE MAY BE HAZARDOUS TO HEALTH AND SHOULD BE USED WITH CARE. PLEASE READ THE APPROPRIATE HEALTH AND SAFETY SECTION.

Alternatively, wrap the strips around a string for making items like necklaces. Acrylic paint, various lacquers, glitter, etc., can be used for coloring and further decoration. For more information on these materials, see Low-Temperature-Setting Thermoplastic Sheetings on page 274 and Friendly Plastics on page 218.

Vinyl and Mylar Sheetings With Polyester Resin ⚠

Another, more complex, method of making jewelry comes from Lauryn Cone, a jeweler who incorporates jeweled pieces into theatrical garb and designs jewelry for Frasconi Jewelers in San Francisco.

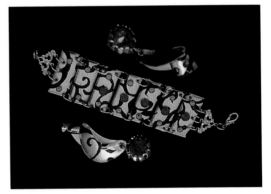

Sheetings of vinyl and Mylar are combined with polyester resin to form this jewelry.
DESIGN: LAURYN CONE.

1. Cone laminates adhesive-coated metallic-Mylar sheets to thick (20 mil) vinyl sheeting, and then cuts out the desired shapes. Next, she coats both sides of the pieces with polyester resin.

2. Cone mixes metallic powders into epoxy adhesive ⚠, which she uses to bond the jewels into place. For jewels, Cone prefers Austrian crystal, though an acrylic gem could substitute.

Vinyl Six-Pack Soft Drink Can Holders

Even so simple a found object as vinyl six-pack can holders can be used in costuming! For a production of Schiller's *Mary Stuart* at the Guthrie Theatre, Annette Garceau, looking for novel and cost-saving materials, used these vinyl rings to create jewelry settings. She cut the circles apart, crushed and crunched each ring into an individual wad, and spaced the wads as though to bake cookies on a cookie tin. The tin of vinyl cookies was placed in an oven at a low-temperature setting. The vinyl pieces melted into themselves. She then colored each wad with red nail polish. Next she sewed a large pearl in the center of each wad, and sewed each wad with its pearl onto Mary Stuart's gown. The effect was one of an unusual richness—at no expense.

Melted vinyl six-pack holders form jeweled decoration on this costume.
DESIGN: JANE GREENWOOD FOR *MARY STUART* AT THE GUTHRIE THEATRE.

Any of the above methods can be combined together effectively, or hand-designed jewelry can be joined with preformed and purchased items. Ideas and materials for jewelry are endless, and jewelry is relatively simple to create, for decorative elements rarely require the structural strength needed in practical costume pieces.

Padding Suits

Polyurethane Foam and Polyester Batting

Padding suits are much-used costumes, especially by theatre departments in schools and universities where younger and smaller actors must often portray older and heavier individuals. Padding suits add muscle, fat, pregnancy, deformities, cartoon exaggerations, and age. When designing and making the suit for a specific actor, be sure that the padded masses are consistent with the actor's own physicality. The final product should present a flow of the actor's own body into his newly acquired physique.

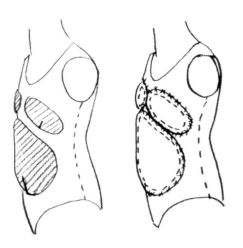

Polyurethane foam sheeting shapes are placed onto leotard to form body padding.

Polyester batting is placed over the polyurethane-foam pieces before the entire leotard is covered with spandex.

It is usual to build padding suits onto nylon leotards, either purchased or custom-made. The most frequently used padding material is polyurethane foam. Because of its durability, most shops prefer reticulated insulation foam (such as Scott Foam) rather than upholstery foam. Insulation foam is available in a number of densities—pores per inch (ppi) and thicknesses. A density of 30 ppi and thicknesses of one-half inch and one inch are most commonly used for creating body padding. Padding suits that cover large areas of the body require ventilation. See Keeping Actors Safe and Healthy in the Appendix.

Other supplies are polyester bat-sheeting (used to form a smooth cover over the foam), rubber-based contact cement,* like Barge, as well as sewing materials. A second leotard will be needed to cover the first, padded leotard. This second leotard will often be custom-made.

1. Plan on a small-scale paper diagram before working with the actual materials. Start by fitting the actor in a leotard, and customize the padding to the individual body. Use tailor's chalk to map the areas to be padded.

2. Place the leotard on a mannequin.

3. Make a paper pattern to approximate closely the desired three-dimensional shape for each needed pad.

4. Cut each polyurethane pad to the size of the paper pattern and place against the leotard, starting with the smallest piece next to the body, and grading upwards towards the outer form.

5. If form-fitting is required, cut darts into the pad. For most shapes, bevel the borders of each pad to create a natural smoothness.

⚠ THIS SUBSTANCE OR PROCEDURE MAY BE HAZARDOUS TO HEALTH AND SHOULD BE USED WITH CARE. PLEASE READ THE APPROPRIATE HEALTH AND SAFETY SECTION.

6. Butt the dart edges with rubber cement, and hand-sew with large diagonal stitches.

7. Hand-sew the bottom pad to the leotard with large, loose cross-stitches. Tight stitches constrain stretchability.

8. Use adhesive bonding to secure the pads to one another to create smooth maximum joining. The top pad should be both cemented to the pad underneath it and sewn to the leotard.

9. Cut the covering polyester layer—also darted and eased to an inch beyond the foam. Laminate the two materials with rubber cement or padding stitches to eliminate shifting. Hand-sew the edges as before.

10. Cover the padded leotard with the second, slightly larger, leotard. Sew the two together at the neck, arm, and leg openings.

11. If the padding covers only a small area on the leotard, you can avoid adding a complete leotard, and instead use only smaller matching pieces of fabric over the padded areas for the final covering.

12. This suit can only be washed. Either hand-wash or short-cycle machine-wash in warm water. Dry cleaning will destroy the bond of the rubber cement.

As an alternative to a padding suit that must be laundered, one that will withstand dry cleaning can be constructed by following this method:

1. Cut out all pieces of foam as above. Additionally, for each piece of foam, cut out two pieces of nylon tricot or another thin and flexible fabric, adding a seam allowance to fit over each piece of foam.

2. Encase each piece of foam padding within the two layers of fabric. Sew the edges of the fabric to the leotard instead of using adhesives, thus allowing the padding suit to be dry-cleaned.

Fabric is cut and sewn to shape and boning strategically stitched to the fabric to achieve this "bird-like" silhouette.

Thermoplastic Boning Another method of creating voluptuous bodies was used by the Cirque du Soleil in *Alegría* for the characters of The Old Birds. Instead of adding foam to shape the body, "pouter pigeon" chests were created by adding plastic stays to shaped, woven-cotton undergarments.

1. Cut and drape paper-pattern pieces over a dress form, taping the seams together to develop a voluptuous chest shape.

2. Make paper patterns from the draped pieces and cut from cotton duck.

3. Add enough boning strips to form and support the desired body shape. The Cirque du Soleil costume shop prefers to use a boning that maintains a round form but does not crease if bent.

4. Use this shape either as a separate padding piece, or stitch it to the inside of the costume.

Seed For producing bodies with soft, jiggly areas of fat, a longtime favorite filler is birdseed. Birdseed used as stuffing produces the weight and just the right amount of movement to be realistic.

A method for producing lighter-weight fat areas is to combine the birdseed with either Styrofoam pellets or polyester pillow stuffing.

When using birdseed, be careful to store the costume pieces in a dry area to prevent the seeds from sprouting!

Complete Body Suit

Foamed Latex ⚠ This technique comes from SFX studio in Hollywood. It is more complex than the above padding methods, and requires an oven and the necessary skill to work with foamed latex; however, for flexibility and detail, it is a superb method.

Clay sculpture forms the model for a latex bodysuit.

The foamed-latex body-suit, locked into a spandex covering, is completed.

CONSTRUCTION AND PHOTO: XFX.

1. Sculpt in clay the desired body shape. The sculpture needs to be in an erect stance, similar to a dress or tailoring form—at a later stage, a negative mold of the sculpture will be placed over it.

2. Make a multiple-part plaster mold from the sculpture.

⚠ THIS SUBSTANCE OR PROCEDURE MAY BE HAZARDOUS TO HEALTH AND SHOULD BE USED WITH CARE. PLEASE READ THE APPROPRIATE HEALTH AND SAFETY SECTION.

3. Then, tailor a spandex bodysuit to fit the actor. Place on the appropriate size dress form. Tape, using gaffer's tape, over the zipper. Position and close the plaster mold over the bodysuit and dress form.

4. Prepare foamed latex, cast the latex into the open space between the two "bodies," and bake. The foam will seep into the fabric, locking the two together.

Muscle Suits

Polyurethane Foam and Spandex

In the 1994 *Sigfried & Roy* show at The Mirage Resorts in Las Vegas, the Acolytes are strong men with muscles so large that their musculature had to be manufactured in this manner:

1. High-necked long sleeved, unitards are used for the body base that is covered by layers of polyurethane insulation foam. The foam is first cut into individual muscle shapes, each one made of several graded layers.

2. Hand-sew the smallest layer into place, with the following layers each glued onto the layer below it, using 3M's Scotch-Grip 847 or a similar rubber contact cement ⚠. For the top layer, hand-sew large cross-stitches and glue it in place.

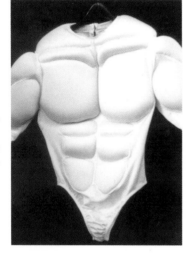

A sculpted polyurethane-foam muscle suit is covered by hand-stitched spandex pieces.

DESIGN, CONSTRUCTION, AND PHOTO: CHIP'S CREATIONS.

3. Fit each dancer individually for correct adjustment of the muscles to his own body.

4. Cover the muscled leotard with another, larger leotard. This second leotard is hand-quilted to the padded under-leotard, a technique that emphasizes the exaggerated anatomy.

5. For further emphasis, paint shadows under the musculature with silk-screen paint.

These costumes for the *Sigfried & Roy* show were designed by John Napier and constructed by Parsons-Meares Ltd. in New York.

Silicone Gel and Spandex

In the feature film *Dune*, with costumes designed by Bob Ringwood, Kenneth Macmillan's costume was so heavily padded with silicone muscles that it was necessary to wheel him around in an A-frame support during all of the shooting time.

1. The base part of his padding was built from a heavy, fitted spandex bodysuit of Zeta, a heavy spandex from Germany. Muscles were individually cut out of Zeta, made into an additional body layer, and then sewn onto the first spandex suit. In cutting the muscles, the muscular shapes were cut large enough to form a third dimension by adding extra inches all around. The muscles project away from the bodysuit to form an empty pocket.

2. Inject dense silicone caulking gel through a large syringe between the two layers; as it sets, a soft, jelly-like fatness will form. Due to gravity, the silicone will fall to the bottom, giving a natural look to the fat and its movement. Though some silicone may seep through, this may work to advantage. In *Dune*, the seepage was caught by MacMillan's pink rubber corset.

For *Dune*, the corset was made of colostomy-bag rubber, purchased from a medical supplier. Over this, Macmillan, playing an alien, wore a harness that allowed him to be flown.

Pregnancy Padding

Polyester Batting, Spandex, and Birdseed

For Boston's Huntington Theatre production of *A Streetcar Named Desire*, designed by Erin Quigley, the character of Stella required two stages of pregnancy padding. The first, indicating two months of pregnancy, and the second, showing eight months, were both worn underneath thin, clinging, silk slips. Denise Wallace, the costume shop supervisor, devised a method of padding that would be smooth and natural, without the bumps and bulges that are seen in normal padding. Wallace built the padding onto one-piece body-slimmers— lingerie pieces readily available in retail shops.

Pregnancy padding is sewn with "honeycomb" stitch .

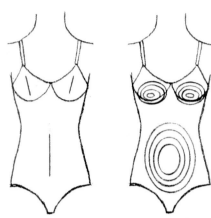

Padded areas are slit for insertion of birdseed-or rice-filled bags. These slits require either zipper or snaps s[...] that the seeds or rice can be removed for laundering.

Shaped batting is applied to a body-slimmer with a "honeycomb" stitch.

PROCESS: DENISE WALLACE FOR *A STREETCAR NAMED DESIRE* AT THE HUNTINGTON THEATRE, BOSTON.

1. Pad the bra by building an opening into the bra lining, then sewing, one by one, five thin, graduated layers of crescent-shaped polyester sheet-batting, placing the larger shapes away from the body and the smaller shapes towards the body. The thin layers are created by peeling away the thin sections that make up the polyester batting. They are darted and eased as needed and sewn together with padding stitches.

2. Place the body-slimmer onto a dress form and start padding the abdominal area. First, cut teardrop-shaped segments of split polyester-batting, building up from small to large. There are only a few such layers of batting in the earlier pregnancy padding, and thirty in the late pregnancy piece.

3. Sew these together with a "honeycomb" stitch, a stitch invented by Wallace to create this pregnancy padding, similar to a herring bone or padding stitch. The thin layers are darted and eased as needed. Any darts are cut out and butted together to avoid unnatural bumps.

4. Towards the bottom of the padding pieces, place nylon-spandex bags filled with birdseed to impart the slight movement that enhances the natural quality of an artificial pregnancy. The bags are zipped or snapped into place to be removed for laundering.

⚠ THIS SUBSTANCE OR PROCEDURE MAY BE HAZARDOUS TO HEALTH AND SHOULD BE USED WITH CARE. PLEASE READ THE APPROPRIATE HEALTH AND SAFETY SECTION.

5. The actress will probably have to be fitted several times to ensure that the padding looks like a natural pregnant body.

When the padding suit is complete, cover the piece with power net of fine spandex to smooth out the form.

Silicone and Cast Polyurethane Foam
Cast plastics may also be used to build a pregnancy suit. Rob Burman of Sticks and Stones near Los Angeles is a sculptor well versed in the use of casting plastics. Burman devised this method to create a whole-term pregnancy padding:

1. Make a temporary negative life cast of the wearer's body from alginate.

2. Then, from the inside of the alginate mold, make a plaster positive cast. Later, it will become the "core," used within the finished mold.

3. Use water-based clay to build up the pregnancy form on top of the plaster cast.

4. Build a fiberglass and polyester ⚠ negative mold over the newly-shaped clay pregnancy form. Open the mold and clean out thoroughly, removing all remains of the clay.

5. Into this new mold, slush-cast silicone ⚠ to one-half-inch thick. Lay the first fiberglass and polyester casting into this form as a plug—there should be a space of at least several inches between the two fiberglass forms—and inject two-part expandable polyurethane foam ⚠. The polyurethane foam will fit to the wearer's own body and provide a natural soft movement. As the months go by, extra padding of upholstery foam sheeting can be added near the body, stretching out the silicone to a greater dimension.

This padding is so realistic that these pieces were worn by a woman who used the pregnancy pieces in real life and convinced others that she was actually pregnant!

Voluptuous Breasts

Rubber Balloons
Following are two methods employed to create breasts from balloons that are worn by drag queens. The first is Lizzie Gardiner's technique from the feature film *The Adventures of Priscilla, Queen of the Desert.*

1. Blow up dozens of balloons to approximately twice the intended breast size. Leave them for two days to stretch them out.

2. After forty-eight hours, let the air out of the balloons, and fill about half full with water. There should be less water than the original amount of air, allowing the rubber to shrink up and become like skin texture.

3. Place the water-filled balloons onto the actor, who is wearing the correct-size bra.

4. If the filming takes place in a warm studio or outside in warm sunshine (*Priscilla* was shot in the hot Australian desert), the balloons will not last long. They expand away from the body and then burst. For *Priscilla*, the water-filled balloons were kept in a portable ice box to prevent them from heating too quickly.

The second process is from Doug Spesert of Los Angeles, who designed and made costumes for a Drag Queen Halloween Ball.

1. Using two balloons per breast, place one inside of the other. Blow them up to the desired size of the breasts. Pour about two tablespoons of hot tap water into the bottom of the inner balloon.

2. Into the inner balloon, insert a funnel and pour in an entire packet of unflavored gelatin. Swirl or shake it until it seems mixed.

3. Place the set of balloons under a faucet and fill with warm water until the balloons reach the correct size. Swirl again and tie tightly.

4. Place the balloons, tie-side down, in the refrigerator until the gelatin has set. The gelatin will impart a lifelike movement to the breasts.

Showgirls' Starburst Tails

Silvered Polycarbonate and Mirrored Acrylic

Enter the Night, a revue at Las Vegas's Stardust Hotel, was designed by Bill Hargate, who has designed for many TV series (*Murphy Brown*, *Barbara Mandrell and the Mandrell Sisters*, *The Mary Tyler Moore Hour*, etc.), as well as for film, legitimate theatre, individual performers, and other Las Vegas revues. Hargate has his own union workshop and popular rental house in Hollywood.

Hargate created striking starburst tails for the showgirls, using silver-coated Lexan polycarbonate. Finding the most suitable materials required much time-consuming experimentation, for these starbursts had to be unbreakable, resilient, lightweight, shiny, and transparent. Further experimentation was necessary to find adhesives that would adhere the polycarbonate to itself, and the rhinestone decorations to the polycarbonate. Following is the method Hargate used:

Lexan polycarbonate rods make up this giant tail.

DESIGN: BILL HARGATE FOR *ENTER THE NIGHT* AT THE STARDUST HOTEL IN LAS VEGAS. PHOTO: IAN VAUGHAN.

⚠ THIS SUBSTANCE OR PROCEDURE MAY BE HAZARDOUS TO HEALTH AND SHOULD BE USED WITH CARE. PLEASE READ THE APPROPRIATE HEALTH AND SAFETY SECTION.

1. All the pieces of polycarbonate rod and all the mirrored acrylic pieces were cut to the proper lengths. Small holes were drilled into the acrylic, and the mirrored acrylic pieces were sewn to G-strings.

2. Polycarbonate circles eight inches in diameter were cut. Some performers needed two circles, some three, depending upon the individual's costume. The circles were attached to the metal backpacks, and holes were drilled to accommodate attachment bolts.

3. A pattern for each tail was laid down onto a flat surface. Over the pattern, at the center of the tail's radius, was placed one polycarbonate circle. Next, the ends of the rods were arranged onto it. Some of the designs required a second layering of rods and a circle. The rods were adhered to the circle with polycarbonate adhesive. (Let's Grip by General Electric and Weld-on 4 by IPS are specific to polycarbonate ⚠.) The top layer of the rods was coated with more adhesive, and the second circle was pressed into place.

4. The Lexan was then dotted with a low-temperature hot glue ⚠, and a rhinestone was placed onto each dot.

5. Backpacks of iron wire were used to hold the tails in place. Both sides of the wire were covered with buckram. The body sides of the wire were covered with rubber padding, then the entire backpacks were encased in nude spandex. Rhinestones were sewn to the spandex to camouflage any fabric left uncovered. To the top corners and bottom corners of the backpacks, loops of webbing were attached to fit around the shoulders and underarms.

6. The Lexan circles were then bolted to the metal backpacks.

Each of the showgirls had a differently-shaped circular tail. These pieces were lightweight and moved with an impressive swaying motion. Dancers in the same number wore short skirts fashioned of the same materials.

Wings

Celastic ⚠ and Acrylic Sheet

The ethereal-looking *wings* in the Los Angeles production of Tony Kushner's *Angels in America* were designed by Jeff Shoenberg and devised by Sasha McMullen at the Los Angeles Center Theatre Group Costume Shop. These wings were actually sturdy and practical appendages. This is the process McMullen devised for creating them:

1. For the upper part of the wings, McMullen used cardboard, both as a pattern and then for a positive mold. She scored and bent the cardboard to achieve a three-dimensional accordion form, then placed aluminum foil over the cardboard as a separator between the cardboard and the Celastic, which would be laid on next.

2. Four pieces of Celastic, two pieces per wing, were cut to approximate shape, dipped into acetone ⚠, and laid over the aluminum foil and cardboard. After these were dry, the pieces were trimmed to an exact shape.

3. Next, the pieces were coated with liquid latex ⚠ for additional thickness. When dry, they were colored first by a spray coating ⚠ of gray Flex Stone paint, followed

by a coat of silver latex paint. The Flex Stone added an uneven texture to the silver paint.

4. To create the feathers, McMullen used thin acrylic sheeting, some opaque and some transparent. The feathers were cut to simple shapes, with just one or two notches for a suggestion of feathers, and then they were painted. The white acrylic feathers were spray painted in the same manner as the wings' upper piece. However, on the transparent feathers, McMullen created a stencil by using a utility knife to cut away a design suggestive of feather veining from the bonded protective paper that comes with acrylic sheets. After spraying with silver paint and peeling away the paper, the veins and a few swirly lines remained, imparting a lovely feathery look.

5. The upper-wing pieces and the base of the feathers were coated with a clear contact cement ⚠. When all pieces became tacky, layers of overlapping feathers were sandwiched between the upper-wing pieces. For extra security, rivets were added along these overlapping edges after the adhesive was dry.

6. The harnessing was made from webbing padded with one-half inch polyurethane foam, attached to a form-fitting acrylic sheet back piece that had been molded onto the actual back of the actress playing the Angel. The wings were made mobile through four hinges formed from Celastic strips, self-adhered, and riveted to the acrylic back piece. For further mobility, four springs were fastened from the back of the wings to the back piece, with nylon cord wending its way through the feathers. The ending, tied to a nylon ring, allowed the actress to manipulate the wings easily.

Though Celastic in this form is no longer available, the same procedure could be followed using low-temperature-setting thermoplastic sheetings and Solveset.

Polyvinyl Chloride Foam Sheeting and PVC Tubing

These wings were made for a production of *Mad Forest* at The University of California at Los Angeles from Sintra, a lightweight expanded, or foamed, polyvinyl chloride (PVC) sheeting, lighter for its dimensions than other sheetings with similar properties. Feathers are alike though they vary in length and width. There are forty-three feathers per wing, with a minimal overlap at the top of each feather. *PVC* pipe, of three-quarter-inch outer diameter, is used for the structure, creating a finished overall span of about fifteen feet and a total weight of fifteen pounds. In this production, the wings were flown down from the beam to the actor on stage, who put them on in view of the audience. This is the method used by Rob Secrist, prop maker, and Cheri Trotter, designer:

1. Form a pattern from heavy pattern paper. With a mat knife, score midway through the back side of the center of each feather. Fold at each scoring line at about a 30-degree angle. Sew through the wings with needle and heavy thread, to both secure and determine spacing of the feathers.

Sintra expanded-poly-vinyl sheeting is used to create these wings.

2. Cut out the wings from Sintra, following the paper pattern. Draw the vertical center on the back side of each feather. Then score the back of each with a draw knife (a knife made especially for scoring plastic sheet and available at plastic suppliers). For the most accurate cut, inscribe the plastic feather two times.

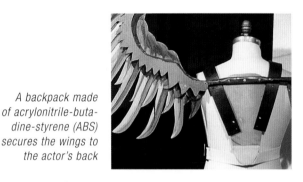

A backpack made of acrylonitrile-buta-dine-styrene (ABS) secures the wings to the actor's back

3. Next, carefully fold the feather along the newly inscribed line to an angle of about 60 degrees. This prefolding increases the rigidity of the feather piece by a factor of several times.

4. While holding each feather at an angle, drip cyanoacrylate adhesive, tetrahydrofuron adhesive ⚠ or solvent from a needle bottle into the fold. The solvent holds the plastic feathers in stable rigid shapes.

5. Starting with an eight-foot PVC pipe, cut the pipe in half and use a heat gun to shape it to the desired form for the top of the wings. Saw off any extra pipe.

6. Glue the feathers, overlapping minimally, to the pipe and to each other with cyanoacrylate or tetrahydrofuran.

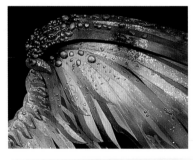

Hot-melt glue drops and glitter add sparkle to the feathers.

DESIGN: CHERI TROTTER FOR *MAD FOREST*, AT THE DEPARTMENT OF THEATER ARTS, UNIVERSITY OF CALIFORNIA, LOS ANGELES. CONSTRUCTION: ROBERT SECRIST. PHOTO: ROBERT ZENTIS.

7. Prime the feathers and the pipe with auto-body primer, and then spray both with gold-enamel spray paint ⚠—the enamel has a more glossy, metallic look than acrylic paint.

8. While the paint is still wet, sprinkle on some gold glitter.

9. When the paint and glitter are dry, brush on brown acrylic paint to add dimension. Add more glitter on top of this coat of paint.

10. Apply some jewels—either use rhinestones, or make your own jewels from hot-melt glue stick drippings ⚠, and apply them to the wings with drops of hot glue.

The armor that holds these feathers is actually a breastplate and back plate connected by a two-inch strapping over the shoulders, and similar to a backpack. A rigid plastic rectangle (the choice was acrylonitrile-butadiene styrene, or ABS) at the shoulder-blade area contains shaped "pockets" that hold the PVC tubing. The breastplate is ABS sheeting vacuum-formed over a mold created from polystyrene armor that Secrist filled with plaster. The straps are aluminum strips bent on a vice and padded with one-inch foam sheeting. (Sechrist used Minicel L-200 polyethylene foam.) The foam sheeting is cemented to the metal and the ABS with hot-melt glue. Pop rivets hold these pieces together.

Spandex, Latex ⚠ and Wire

At Alterian Studios, just outside of Los Angeles, a pair of large, mechanized demon wings were of wire, nylon spandex, and natural-rubber casting latex. Because of their latex-covered, nylon-spandex skins, they stretch approximately two times over their original size. To create these wings, craftspeople at Alterian invented this method:

1. Measure the desired vertical height of the wings at their highest point and cut wire to that length.

2. Cover each wire with two forms resembling bones. Make these by padding the wire to shape with cotton batting, then covering the batting with a sewn cotton spandex sheath. Brush the sheet with casting latex, then hand-form it into bone shape. Bond the ends of the bones together with dental acrylic ⚠.

3. For the skin, or body, of the wings, cut nylon spandex to shape and hand-sew it to the "bones." Lay this entire piece flat and secure over a smooth surface and spray coat ⚠ it with colored liquid latex.

4. Glaze over the entire wings with a diluted flexible paint, like a polyurethane-based ⚠ paint, for an interesting textural effect.

5. Mount the wings on a back brace and harness and then mechanize. Tony Gardiner, head of Alterian Studios, advises that base-drum harnesses, which are manufactured for marching bands and orthopedic back braces are ideal as Backpacks for harnessing wings and other costume parts that need to sit on a wearer's back. Such bases are readily available through suppliers.

Window Screening and Duck Feathers

For *The Mutant*, a multimedia performance art show in Los Angeles, these wings were worn by a boy who passed through puberty to become an angel instead of a man. His life passage required several pairs of wings, graduating in size from a few feathers spirit-gummed to his shoulders, to four-inch-wide wings, to wings several sizes larger, and finally to a pair of wings approximately thirty inches in width. The larger sets of wings were created similarly, and the final pair had to be resistant to water. The actor swam under water in a pool to give the illusion of being suspended in the air.

⚠ THIS SUBSTANCE OR PROCEDURE MAY BE HAZARDOUS TO HEALTH AND SHOULD BE USED WITH CARE. PLEASE READ THE APPROPRIATE HEALTH AND SAFETY SECTION.

1. For the larger sets of wings, first create the frames by bending heavy aluminum wire into wing shapes. Cut short lengths for struts, and adhere them with epoxy putty ⚠. Bend these frames to a convex form. Cut aluminum window-screening

into pieces sufficient to create dimension and convexity. Sew these together with polyester thread and then sew them onto the frame of the wings. Reinforce with the epoxy ⚠.

Aluminum window screening and duck feathers are attached by silicone caulking for this large pair of wings.

Medium-size wings are also created from screening and feathers attached by caulking.

DESIGN: THE AUTHOR FOR MULTI-MEDIA PRODUCTION *THE MUTANT*. PHOTO: ROBERT W. ZENTIS.

2. No special preparation is required for the feathers that cover the smaller sets of wings. However, for the final and largest set, special precautions must be taken if the wings are to be waterproof. For such feathers, poke two holes through the stem of each duck feather to allow a mechanical as well as a chemical adhesion. Use a silicone sealant or caulking from a caulking gun ⚠ to adhere feathers to all of the wings. Place the feathers in overlapping rows on both the front and the back sides of the screening base.

3. For the final decorative touches on the two largest sets of wings, silicone caulking is used to glue on a few peacock feathers, rainbow Mylar confetti, and scattered rhinestones.

4. To secure the wings to the wearer, make small harnesses from nylon webbing and disguise the webbing with small feathers.

5. The two pairs of smaller wings can be held in place with surgical cement.

Wire, Vinyl Sheeting, and Acrylic Sheeting

These "Wings of Peace," designed and built by freelance designer Donna May, were featured in a production of *Marisal* at Bridgewater State College in Massachusetts. Following is her method:

1. Build a frame of plastic-coated, three-ply twisted blue guide wire to correspond with the outer silhouette of the wings. Use two lengths of wire doubled and twisted together.

2. Form about six horizontal cross-pieces with 16- and 18-gauge aluminum wire, twisting them into place onto the guide wire. Use the 16-gauge for the shorter cross-pieces and the 18-guage for the longer.

3. Using clear vinyl sheeting, two yards of lightweight and two yards of heavyweight, slice the sheeting into strips of about two and one-half inches wide by the length of the vinyl. Crumple the sheeting and hot-melt glue ⚠ it to the inside of the existing wire wing frames.

4. Break a sheet of acrylic mirror (such as Plexiglas) into small shards. Shards may be from about one-half-inch squares to about one inch by three inches. Hot glue them onto the vinyl, adding extra glue around the sharp edges for protection.

5. Using a heat gun or a hot hair dryer, melt and soften the vinyl to change the texture as well as to flatten it.

For the same production May created "The Wings of War":

1. Create a basic shape from fencing wire, with three inch-square openings, and cover with heavyweight, clear vinyl sheeting.

2. Cut out the appropriate newspaper headlines and collage them with white glue on top of the vinyl sheet. In this case, the appropriate headlines were those of violence and war.

3. Border the outer edge of the wings with flexible aluminum-covered insulation tubing, starting with a twenty-eight foot piece of four-inch diameter tubing. Cut the tubing in half, one half per wing. Shred the aluminum surface, crush the tubing, then attach this disheveled piece to the edge of the wings with pieces of wire. May chose 18-gauge aluminum wire, cut into two-inch pieces. Add pieces of silver pipe cleaners to give the allusion of barbed wire.

This production required the two pairs of wings to be interchangeable in the harness. The harness was built according to this method:

1. For the shoulder straps, cut one inch strips of polyurethane upholstery foam, two and one-half inches wide by eighteen-inches long. Cover them with muslin or other cotton fabric.

2. For the chest strap, use heavyweight one and one-half-inch-wide belting. Connect the belting to the foam with machine-stitching. Secure the harness onto the actor by attaching with ties or hooks.

3. Use a metal strip two-inches wide by about one-eigth-inch thick, cut to an eleven-inch length. Drill two sets of two holes about three inches from each end.

4. Drill corresponding holes in two metal tubes, one inch in diameter by about six inches long. Bolt the tubes onto the metal strip.

5. Into the metal strip, drill two sets of four holes about one-half-inch and two-inches from its ends. Attach the ends of the cloth-covered foam straps to the metal strip by sewing through these holes.

⚠ THIS SUBSTANCE OR PROCEDURE MAY BE HAZARDOUS TO HEALTH AND SHOULD BE USED WITH CARE. PLEASE READ THE APPROPRIATE HEALTH AND SAFETY SECTION.

6. Sew the belting onto the other end of the cloth-covered foam.

7. To remove and insert the two pair of wings, attach aluminum rods to the inner border of the wings that can be inserted into the tubes.

Specialty and Special-Effects Costumes

Aliens

Insulation Foam, Latex, Pickling Spice

This endearing monster Alien costume, created by Ted Shell was constructed for a Kokanee Beer commercial. The monster body is made of reticulated polyurethane insulation foam ⚠ (one-inch thickness at thirty pores per inch). The body is then texture-coated with pickling spice, oatmeal, and garbanzo beans mixed into liquid latex ⚠ to create an unearthly skin. These are the steps that were followed:

1. Mock up a bodysuit costume, which will resemble huge padded coveralls, from polyurethane upholstery foam. When the pattern is perfected, follow it to cut out the insulation foam

2. Cut out all parts and butt edges together, gluing with a rubber cement, ⚠ such as Barge.

3. Sculpt hands and feet from rigid polyurethane foam, and cast them from polyurethane flexible foam ⚠. Similar appendages can be made by patterning, cutting, and gluing polyethylene-foam sheeting. (Shell used Volteck's Minicel L-200.)

Polyurethane insulation foam sheeting was used for fabricating this alien costume.

DRAWING AND DESIGN: TED SHELL FOR A *KOKANEE BEER* COMMERCIAL. PHOTO: COURTESY OF KOKANEE BEER.

4.   The monster's head, which is vacuum-formed, projects almost a foot above the actor's head.

5.   Both body and head are coated with liquid latex (Shell prefers Hastings brand) and painted into three-dimensional skin folds. While the latex is still wet, work into it the garbanzo beans (for warts), *pickling spice*, and oatmeal. When the first latex coat is dry, apply a second coat. This second coat may contain color. (Use either universal pigments or pigments available through latex manufacturers.)

6.   Spray the entire body with a primer, such as 3M's Super 77 Spray Adhesive ⚠, which adheres the paint to the latex. Brush coat with acrylic paint, using color variations to achieve additional texturing and depth.

This costume has electronic eyes and mouth; lights and movement are also added.

Costumes like this one that cover large areas of the body require ventilation. See *Keeping Actors Safe and Healthy* in the Appendix.

Latex Sheeting, Latex Adhesive, Casting Latex

For the *Tattooed Alien Fighters from Beverly Hills*, a children's TV series beginning in 1994, Andy Wilkes built the Aliens' costumes as designed by Marizio Bizarri from latex sheeting. The two female and two male costumes started as asymmetrical, one-sleeved unitards. Each of the four wears a different, yet coordinated, design. One girl has a crop-top with bicycle pants, and the other Aliens wear individualized short unitards. Here are the steps for building these costumes:

1.   The basic costumes are each cut directly from paper patterns a size smaller than the actors. Seams are overlapped a quarter inch and bonded with a latex or rubber-based adhesive ⚠. (Use Copydex, 3M Scotch-Grip 847, or Bostick 3851.)

2.   Vertical stripes are set into the costumes and sewn into place. Do not place horizontal stripes into latex; the stitching does not stretch, and the material will bulge and restrict movement.

3.   Zippers are top-stitched into the back neck of the costumes.

To age the costumes, distress by coating with a combination of a latex adhesive, casting latex ⚠, and acrylic pigment. This mixture is stippled onto the costumes, and while still wet, oatmeal, rice, cornflakes, and tissue paper are added for texture.

For more details on working with latex, see *Catwoman* on page 365 and Latex Sheeting on page 212.

⚠ THIS SUBSTANCE OR PROCEDURE MAY BE HAZARDOUS TO HEALTH AND SHOULD BE USED WITH CARE. PLEASE READ THE APPROPRIATE HEALTH AND SAFETY SECTION.

Birds

Here are many different methods for creating birds, though these are not the only methods available. Such methods are as infinite as the imagination of the designer and costume maker.

Eagle Headdress and Wings

Buckram, Polyester Resin, Acrylic-Polyvinyl Chloride, Enamel Paint and Acrylic Paint

The eagle headdress and wings for *Phantom of the Opera* were based on polystyrene foam positive molds and sculpted by Rodney Gordon. He then built the costume pieces following this method:

Layered buckram coated with polyester resin, vacuum-formed Kydex, paints, and various metallic finishes were used to create this eagle costume.

DESIGN: MARIA BJORNSON FOR *PHANTOM OF THE OPERA*, ORIGINAL BROADWAY PRODUCTION. CONSTRUCTION AND PHOTO: RODNEY GORDON.

Head

1. Cut or tear buckram into squares of workable size, about three by three inches. Dip them in water and patch them over the sculpted form, overlapping the pieces. Apply three or four layers, depending on the intended bulk of the finished piece. When the buckram is dry, slit it up the back, and remove it from the styrofoam mold.

2. Rough up the beak with sandpaper in order to give it a contrasting texture.

3. Cut holes in the center of the eyes as well as at points widely spaced for both visibility and ventilation.

4. From cut and creased buckram, form the feathers. Coat them with polyesterresin ⚠ for durability and a smooth metallic texture. Sew the feathers in place.

5. Apply several coats of different paints to the head and to the feathers. First, spray ⚠ with a dark-brown spray enamel. When the enamel paint is dry, brush over it with gold acrylic paint. For some highlights, glaze selected spots with a gold bronzing powder mixed with acrylic paint ⚠.

Wings

1. To produce the wings, carve a model from polystyrene foam.

2. Vacuum-form Kydex acrylic-polyvinyl-chloride sheet plastic ⚠ over the positive styrofoam mold.

3. Make additional feathers from buckram coated with polyester resin. Poke holes into the Kydex, and attach the feathers by sewing through the holes.

4. Paint the wings with acrylic-based paint, following the directions for painting the head. If the paint is to adhere, the Kydex must be first primed with a polyurethane ⚠ adhesive or painted with a polyurethane-based paint.

Old Birds

Thermoplastic Boning and Silk Fabrics

The voluptuous bodies of The Old Birds in Cirque du Soleil's *Alegría* were shaped by thermoplastic boning. Instead of adding foam for shaping, "pouter pigeon" chests and large thighs were created by adding stays to shaped cotton-duck undergarments.

Bodies

1. Cut and drape paper-pattern pieces over a dress form, taping the seams together to develop a voluptuous chest shape.

2. Make patterns from the draped pieces and cut from cotton duck.

3. Add enough boning strips to form and support the desired body shape. The Cirque du Soleil costume shop prefers Desira Plast ⚠, a thermoplastic boning that maintains a round form but does not crease when bent. Form the boning into the desired curves with a heat gun.

4. For the female birds, add large-size shaped pockets at breast level. Form separate breast shapes, using the above method, and place the breasts into the pockets. With this method, the costume piece can be cleaned or washed without destroying the breast form.

5. Use this newly formed shaping either as a separate padding piece, or stitch it to the inside of the costume.

Thighs

Create short trousers in the shape of large thighs. Cut, sew, and heat-form Desira Plast boning to the desired shapes.

For launderability, these thigh pieces are constructed separately and not sewn into the outer costume.

Tails

1. Make feathers by cutting tapered strips of the costume fabric into segments of one inch to two inches in width and about twenty inches in length. Plan on one to three layers per feather.

2. Cut a strip of boning to a matching length.

3. Using a heat gun, curve the boning to the desired shape.

4. Combine the boning with the fabric layers, and machine-stitch together down the center of the boning. Fray the fabric edges.

5. The outer layers of The Old Bird costumes are luxuriant silk satins and brocades decorated by lace, gilt braid, and rhinestones.

⚠ THIS SUBSTANCE OR PROCEDURE MAY BE HAZARDOUS TO HEALTH AND SHOULD BE USED WITH CARE. PLEASE READ THE APPROPRIATE HEALTH AND SAFETY SECTION.

Young Birds

Thermoplastic Boning and Nylon Organza

In *Alegría*, Cirque du Soleil's 1994 production, magical costumes were designed by Dominique Lemieux. Many of the acrobats, tumblers, and clowns were birds, and two beautiful little girls, performing on the high wire, were costumed as bluebirds. Soft, silky feathers were attached to the undersides of their arms, and when they raised their arms, wings spread magically.

When designing and building circus performers' and dancers' costumes, weight and safety are the first concern. Substitutes must often be found for materials that are fine for other productions. Thus, feathers reinforced with wires can be dangerous for performing acrobats and tumblers. To make the lightweight wings of the bluebirds, the designer combined nylon organza layers with Desira Plast boning. To produce the look of soft, feathered birds, the Cirque du Soleil costume shop used this method:

Wings
1. Cut nylon organza fabric of various blues and greens into strips, tapering from one inch to two inches wide and about twenty-four inches long. Plan on three to four layers for each feather.

2. Cut a matching length of boning, and heat it with a heat gun until it curves or curls.

3. Sandwich the boning between the layers of fabric, and machine-stitch down the center.

4. Fray the edges of the fabric to create a soft, feathery texture.

5. Sew cloth pads with large snaps onto the bottom back of the wings, with corresponding snaps on the back shoulders of the costumes.

Bodies
1. Make a pair of high-waisted, empire-level, nylon-spandex tights. Dye the tights a golden yellow.

2. With blue chenille yarn, hand-crochet a wide netting, and affix the netting from waist to ankle over the dyed tights.

3. Cut a length of blue-velvet spandex large enough for bodice and wide sleeves. Paint it with a feather design.

4. Make the bodice and arms of the blue-velvet spandex backed with a golden-color spandex matching that of the legs. Cut the blue-velvet spandex more than twice the measurement of the performer's underbust measurement. Cut the golden spandex to fit. Stitch both layers of fabrics together and onto the empire-waistline tights, holding the blue velvet loosely enough to form pleats. Use a zigzag stitch

with one-inch intervals. Keep the blue velvet loose so that once stitched in place, pleats are created. After the stitching is completed, cut the velvet to fit.

5. When the velvet bodice and sleeves are complete, slash them to reveal the golden-yellow spandex underlayer.

6. Crochet blue-chenille bands to be worn around the performers' necks and to be added to the bottom of the blue-velvet empire bodices. Sew thin bands around the necklines of the unitards.

Headdress
1. Create many feathers in the same manner as the wings.

2. Make skullcaps by shaping an easy-to-use thermoforming material, like those described in the Low-Temperature-Setting Thermoplastics section on page 276, over a head shape. Cover with more painted blue-velvet spandex.

3. Hand-sew the feathers—real and cloth—to the top and back of the skullcaps.

4. To finish the headdresses, find ready-made plastic hollow balls about 3 inches in diameter. Paint with golden-yellow acrylic paint, slice in half, punch holes around the edges, and sew to either side of the skullcaps.

Insects

Bee

ABS, Polyurethane Foam, and Polyethylene Foam

"Sting" is a bee, the mascot and the walk-around costume for the Nevada Pro Sports' indoor football team.

Shafton Inc. costume workshop manufactured Sting. The head is made of vacuum-formed acrylonitrile-butadiene styrene (ABS), and the body is of polyurethane insulation foam and Voltek's Minicel L-200 polyethylene foam. To make a similar bee's head, follow this process:

Head
1. Carve a head from rigid polyurethane green foam. Cut it in half for a two-part negative mold and vacuum-form in ABS, leaving an overlap of about one inch. Cut out the eye sockets and the mouth, then bond the two parts together with acrylic cement ⚠ (see Acrylic Cement section), and smooth out the surface with sandpaper.

2. Shape the eyes from another piece of polyurethane rigid foam (green foam), and vacuum-form ⚠ over it with smoked acrylic sheet. With hot glue ⚠, bond the acrylic eye shapes to the inside of the ABS eye sockets. Paint to the desired colors with acrylic paint.

Polyurethane foam, polyethylene foam, ABS, and spandex are the materials for this bee costume.
DESIGN: SHAFTON, INC. FOR "STING," THE BEE MASCOT FOR THE NEVADA PRO SPORTS. PHOTO: SHAFTON, INC.

⚠ THIS SUBSTANCE OR PROCEDURE MAY BE HAZARDOUS TO HEALTH AND SHOULD BE USED WITH CARE. PLEASE READ THE APPROPRIATE HEALTH AND SAFETY SECTION.

3. Place sturdy black net inside the mouth area, and bond it with hot glue.

4. Cover the head with stripes of nylon napped fabric, such as Tempo ⚠, bonded in place with spray-on rubber cement ⚠, like 3M's 99. Tempo Display Loop Fabric, a 100 percent soft-napped nylon-knit fabric with a polyester core, available in forty colors, can be purchased through Lockfast Inc., manufacturer.

5. For antennas, cover springs with tubes of spandex, making sure the supporting base can be hidden underneath the Tempo.

6. Add spandex-covered one-half-inch foam for the neck, hot-glued into place. Place matching large snaps on the bottom of this neck piece and on the inside of the bee body.

Body 1. Make a mock-up of the design from polyurethane upholstery foam, using about four vertical-shaped pieces to create the correct form.

2. For the top half of the body, from shoulders to waist, cut out one-inch insulation foam of thirty pores per inch (ppi) with no seam allowance. Enclose each section in an envelope of nylon marquisette that includes an added one-inch seam allowance, and sew the seams together so the foam fits tightly. Add extra pieces of foam to the shoulders.

3. For the waist to hip area, shape Minicel L-200 pieces with no added seam allowance. Encase each in marquisette, and stitch together as before.

4. Cover with napped fabric, rubber-cemented into place.

5. Add a zipper to the center back.

For the legs, use tights dyed to match.

Sting's shoes are made of L-200 polyethylene foam, vacuum-formed. (They could also be cut and bent to the desired shape, then butted and glued together.) They are lined with soft one-inch upholstery foam. The gloves are of one-quarter-inch insulation foam covered with spandex.

Hydrosect

Nylon Spandex, Polyester Batting, Polycarbonate Sheet, and Polyurethane Upholstery Foam

For the Hydrosect fantasy insect costume in the children's television series, *Masked Rider*, Total Fabrication built costumes based on the original Japanese designs for television. Because the insects were aliens, fantasy prevailed. The desired end result was to be one of interesting colors and wrinkled texture. The structure of the costume was based on a nylon-spandex unitard. Following is the method:

1. Sculpt the basic insect shape by layering a sheet of polyester batting onto the unitard, gluing and sewing it into place. For an adhesive, use a shoemaker's rubber cement ⚠.

2. In areas where extra volume is desired, add polyurethane upholstery foam, sewing and gluing it into place.

3. Drape a pattern over this new form. Then cut it out of a nylon spandex.

4. Paint the spandex on a flat work surface, using a flexible fabric paint, like Createx.

5. Glue the spandex over the padded, sculpted unitard.

6. Build a wide, high-standing collar of polyethylene-foam sheeting, laminate it to painted spandex, and sew it to the body.

7. Add tail and spine of polyurethane foam covered with painted spandex.

8. Build the winged headdress using a batter's helmet for the base. Then follow this process:

9. Build an antenna-like structure from one-inch-square stock aluminum to support the wings.

10. Affix the structure to the helmet by bolting the pieces to holes drilled into the helmet. Pad the inside of the helmet for comfort and a closer fit.

11. Sculpt the new headdress with upholstery foam. Cover with painted spandex.

12. Make wings that will attach to the headdress. Cut to shape a very thin sheet of polycarbonate, like Lexan. Paint veins with glass-leading paint and spray on a window frost paint. To the top of the wings, attach a thin piece of aluminum with pop rivets.

13. Since these wings are operated by the wearer, it is necessary to build both a harness and operating cords. The harness aids in securing the equilibrium of the headdress, for weight shifts from the wings could otherwise throw the actress off balance.

14. The harness is made from two-inch-wide nylon webbing. Build it to go over the shoulders and across the chest like suspenders, and add another strap around the waist. Attach nylon rings to the shoulders of the harness and also to the outside of the helmet, between the helmet and the foam. Then attach nylon cord, carrying it from the actress's hands, through the shoulder rings, the helmet rings, and up to the top side of the wings. Now the actress can control the wings with the cords.

△ THIS SUBSTANCE OR PROCEDURE MAY BE HAZARDOUS TO HEALTH AND SHOULD BE USED WITH CARE. PLEASE READ THE APPROPRIATE HEALTH AND SAFETY SECTION.

Hands and Feet

1. Build the feet over canvas slippers. Cover them with thin polyurethane foam sheeting, and spray-coat △ them with acrylic paint and a protective coating like PVA, vinyl △, or polyurethane △.

2. For the hands, use cotton gloves. Cover the outer palm with foam sheeting. Paint and spray coat, as with the feet.

Iridescent Insects

Rainbow Mylar on Polyform Helmets

When Sasha McMullen crafted the unusual plastic headdresses designed by Carol Brolowski for the actor-size *insects'* headdresses for the feature film *Honey, I Shrunk the Kids*, she followed this process:

1. Working over a positive mold, she shaped the basic helmet-headdress shapes from Polyform sheeting ⚠. Polyform is a low-temperature-setting-polyethylene-saturated fabric which is softened for molding by heating in hot water.

2. She then brushed Phlexglu over the surface and pressed into it small pieces of rainbow Mylar ⚠, a thin iridescent polyester film that changes from pink to green. See Polyester Film on page 258.

3. For color variety, she left some of the headdresses in the original color of rainbow Mylar, which is in a range of pinks and greens; however, when other colors were desired, she added acrylic paint to the Phlexglu before applying it.

4. After the Mylar pieces were in place and dry, she used a heat gun over the surface to shrink portions of the Mylar into a more organically uneven and rippling surface.

Mammals

Bear

Polyurethane Insulation Foam, Polyethylene Foam, and Acrylic Fabric

For the Bimbo Bakery in Mexico City, Chip's Character Creations Inc. developed a walk-around bear costume of Minicel L-200 polyethylene foam (from Voltek) and SIF polyurethane insulation foam (formerly Scott Foam). Chip Wickett, art director, has named this type of costume a "built-down" character costume because the costume is kept "down" (small) in size, permitting the actor wearing it to look out of the hat. This costume is built according to the method that Wickett uses for many of the costumes he creates.

A bear mascot is fabricated from polyurethane insulation foam, polyethylene foam, and acrylic-pile fabric.

A "built down" costume allows the performer to see through the headdress.

DESIGN AND PHOTO: CHIP WICKETT FOR THE BIMBO BAKERY IN MEXICO CITY. THE BEAR IS A REGISTERED TRADEMARK OF CENTRAL IMPULSORA, S.A.

1. Make a pattern from one-inch upholstery foam. Then, cut an eight-piece pear shaped body from one-inch-thick, thirty-pounds-per-inch (ppi) insulation foam. From these foam pieces, make a muslin pattern and set aside for later. Adjust foam pieces to fit closely together. Do not add an allowance for seaming or overlap, and bevel-cut the edges.

2. Spread an adhesive on both surfaces of the one-inch edge. Allow it to become tacky and press together. Reinforce the seams with hand-sewing, and insert a zippered placket in the neck back.

3. Cut spring steel strips two inches larger than several bands around the exterior circumferences, encase them in cloth tape, and glue into place with a rubber-based contact cement for reinforcement and strength. For an adhesive, Wickett prefers 3M's nontoxic, water-based Fastbond 30-NF.

A "pod," fabricated from polyurethane foam sheeting, is used as the basis for many walk-around costumes. This pod has a yoke of fabric and a lower body of glued and sewn foam. Two bands of spring steel covered with twill tape encircle the form.

4. From the muslin pattern, cut and sew Tempo soft-napped nylon-knit fabric for the furry body cover. Add one-inch seam allowances. Cut and sew shapes for the arms, which are unlined and unstructured. Add an industrial zipper at the back neckline to allow for easy laundering.

The paws are mittens of the same pile fabric, with Tempo sewn onto the palm area.

The apron is sewn from a substantial cotton-polyester blend poplin.

Feet For the shoes, cut one-inch polyethylene foam to the desired shape and butt the edges together, using a rubber contact adhesive, such as the 30-NF. Line the interior with one inch polyurethane foam, glued together, and make the soles from one-quarter-inch thick, dense Neoprene-foam sheeting, bonded with rubber contact adhesive.

Head 1. Using upholstery foam, make a pattern for a head so that the top of the head will be open and sit on the wearer's shoulders. Adjust it to fit the wearer. Cut out the shape first from muslin and then from one-inch Minicel L-200 polyethylene foam, and bond the foam pieces together with rubber contact cement.

2. Use the muslin pattern for a cloth covering, leaving open spaces for the ears, eyes, nose, and mouth. Stitch the covering together and fit over the head.

3. Cover the mouth and tongue with the acrylic pile fabric. Add plastic window screen to mouth interior to supply ventilation.

4. For the eyes, vacuum-form shapes from clear-plastic sheeting (such as acrylic-polyvinyl-chloride Kydex or polystyrene). Glue in place with thick cement. Cut one-quarter-inch polyethylene foam for lashes and rims around the eyes, spray with acrylic paint ⚠, and cement into place. Cover the nose with the fabric. (Chip's Character Creations uses Tempo.)

5. After the coverings for these features are glued into place, the head fabric can be adjusted and also glued.

6. The hat is also of foam covered with fabric.

⚠ THIS SUBSTANCE OR PROCEDURE MAY BE HAZARDOUS TO HEALTH AND SHOULD BE USED WITH CARE. PLEASE READ THE APPROPRIATE HEALTH AND SAFETY SECTION.

Cut a square opening in the bottom of the hat and insert a plastic screen so the actor can see without being seen, then paint it with acrylic spray paint. Wickett usually places a small, battery-run fan inside the hat for ventilation.

Wickett used a similar method of construction for the walk-around costume for the Tru-Value Store chain. The paper bag worn by the character is of polyethylene foam, and the foods are constructed of polyurethane insulation foam. Both are spray painted with acrylic paint ⚠.

Cow

Polyurethane Foam Sheeting, Latex Sheeting, Latex Foam, ⚠ and Aluminum Strips

In *Dead Heat,* an entire butcher shop comes to life. One piece of meat, a slaughtered cow, is an actual costume with an actor inside. And since the cow had no head, the actor's head is inside the neck of the cow. Todd Masters, who built the creature for XFX, made this costume over a restructuring of the human form by first building an aluminum skeleton. When creating lifelike animal costumes such as this one, it is necessary for the designer and craftspeople to be familiar with the animal's anatomy. Here is a synopsis of the process for making this costume:

1. Begin by building a life cast (see pages 184-188) of the actor's body with the actor on all fours and his arms supported by stilts. Then lengthen his arm span to the proper "leg" length of the cow. From the life cast, make a sculpture from epoxy ⚠ and fiberglass.

2. Use that sculpture as the base for the cow's skeleton and, later, for its body. First, build around the sculpture and aluminum frame that simulates the skeletal structure of a cow. Add foot-size extension for the front feet and build a long extension for the neck. The actor will additionally wear aluminum stilts strapped to his arms, extending them, like front legs, to the length of the actor's actual legs.

3. Attach aluminum braces to attachments that fit strategic areas of the actor. Make the attachment rings of vacuum-formed Kydex and polyethylene foam ⚠. These are placed onto the actor and permit him to move the animal's skeleton as he moves his own.

4. To form the outer shell of the cow's body, first cut pattern pieces from paper, draping and fitting them over the skeleton. Then cut the pieces from polyurethane foam, with no seam allowance. Butt them together, adhering them with rubber cement ⚠. Use coarse open-celled insulation foam for the bottom of the feet, bonding to the polyurethane with rubber cement.

5. To create a feeling of loose skin layers, bridge across the bony areas and joints with latex sheet and polyurethane insulation foam, bonded in place with liquid latex.

6. Fill in the top of the neck cavity with latex and hot-melt vinyl ⚠.

7. The entire costume is painted with rubber-cement paint ⚠ applied by airbrush and paintbrush.

Gorilla

Insulation Foam, Spandex, and Natural Hair

Big Foot, the hairy primate and title character from the film *Big Foot*, looks remarkably like a real ape. In reality, he is an actor in a costume built by Makeup & Effects Laboratories, Inc. (MEL) in North Hollywood. This is the technique the costume makers developed:

Body

1. With heavyweight black spandex, build a custom bodysuit that reaches from neck to ankles. Place this bodysuit onto a legged mannequin the size of the actor.

2. Create large, well-developed muscle groups from polyurethane reticulated insulation foam sheeting, such as SIF foam from Foamex. Layer the foam in two or three layers, depending upon the size of the muscles. Miter the foam pieces, placing small muscle shapes under the large shapes, and bond them to each other with Barge or another

The actor playing Big Foot uses a battery-operated fan to cool off between takes.

rubber contact cement ⚠. Stitch the edges of the first, smaller layer to the bodysuit, making sure not to lose much of the spandex's stretch.

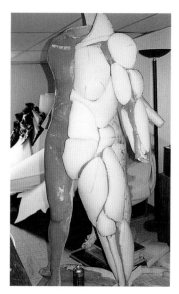

A mannequin is built to the size of the actor. One half is draped with a polyurethane upholstery foam mock-up to determine the sizes of the muscle groups.

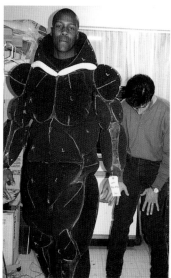

The actor is fitted in a nylon-spandex unitard with the actual muscle groups of insulation foam sheeting pinned in place.

In a second fitting, spandex coverings are pinned around the already attached foam muscle groups.

DESIGN AND PHOTOS: MAKEUP & EFFECTS LAB INC. FOR THE FILM BIG FOOT.

⚠ THIS SUBSTANCE OR PROCEDURE MAY BE HAZARDOUS TO HEALTH AND SHOULD BE USED WITH CARE. PLEASE READ THE APPROPRIATE HEALTH AND SAFETY SECTION.

3. Cut pieces of spandex slightly larger than each muscle group and hand-stitch them over the padding and to the suit while the suit is still on the mannequin.

4. Using the pattern for the spandex covering, cut the same shapes from hair fabric. Cover the entire suit with the hair fabric, hand-sewing it in place. MEL had hair fabric custom-blended by National Hair Technologies.

Head

1. Cast the head and feet from latex foam ⚠. Begin by making a life cast (see page 00) of the actor's head with alginate. From the negative alginate mold, cast the head shape from Ultracal. On top of the plaster head shape, use plasticine clay to sculpt an ape head and ape feet. Make the negative mold from silicone ⚠ in order to retain the lifelike detail, and use the plaster head shape for the inside core while casting the latex.

2. The teeth can be cast from dental acrylic ⚠ to look as lifelike as possible. Eye holes, which are left vacant for the actor to see through, also serve as the ape's deeply set eyes.

3. The sides and back of the head are covered, as is the body, with the same blended hair.

Feet

Feet are cast from foam latex, using a plasticine clay model and a silicone mold in the same manner as for the head. The soles are of rubber, bonded to the cast feet by shoemaker's rubber cement.

Lions

Fiberglass, Epoxy, Urethane Foam, Pile Fabric, Foamed Latex, and Cat Whiskers

The lion, "Aslan," of the BBC-produced *Chronicles of Narnia* was designed and constructed by Vin Burnham at her shop in London. Ms. Burnham started building props at Covent Garden as a teenager and today is considered one of the world's foremost special-effects costume designer/builders. Among her many creations are the original Batman costume for the 1989 film of the same name, which was designed by Bob Ringwood. Her Shredder costume for *Teenage Mutant Ninja Turtles II* and a Mermaid costume for a Peroni Beer commercial are dicussed here.

Research for construction of Aslan (Aslan means "lion" in Turkish) began at Longleat Park in London, a game reserve holding lions and tigers; but a stuffed lion was also studied, as were lions in a zoo. In the *Chronicles of Narnia*, Aslan represents Christ, and his appearance therefore must include a benign aspect. Although Aslan represents a real lion, the costume, as constructed, could not be totally realistic but had to be adapted to accommodate the physicality of the working performers.

Construction began by making life casts of the two performers who would be inside of Aslan. To make the life casts, the performers assumed the positions they would take inside the constructed costume, standing on the balls of their feet, wearing blocked-up, carved, solid-rubber shoes.

From the life casts, backpacks were made from carbon fiberglass-reinforced epoxy ⚠, for in one episode the lion would have to fly with two children sitting on his back. Harnesses were attached to the backpacks.

Niki Lyons, one of Burnham's team who specializes in building skeletons and muscles, built a lion skeleton over the life-cast backpacks. Nylon rods were chosen for the spine because of their strength and flexibility. Hanging from the spine was the rib cage of cut pieces of seven-millimeter nylon sheeting. The spine and rib cage were fastened primarily with riveting.

The leg bones were mostly of nylon rod and sheeting, with some added bits of tubing. Rods were of different diameters, depending upon the size of actual bones. Riveting was used for most of the fastenings. Over the nylon skeleton, Lyons built muscles (large muscle groups) that were hand-clipped from reticulated foam sheeting; each muscle was covered with nylon spandex and then elasticated, like ligaments, at the ends, so that the muscles could slide over each other. Muscles were suspended and tensioned with different weights of spandex and elastic. For example, the shoulder blades had to move with the front legs, so they were connected to permit the muscles to spring back. Attachments were a mixture: some were sewn into holes drilled through the nylon bones, and others were riveted.

Shoes blocked up on solid-rubber heels were worn to lift the performers' own heels off the ground. The paws were fabricated from polyurethane reticulated insulation foam, with the pads on the bottom of the feet sculpted and cast of hard black latex. The pads had to be strong and durable because most of the action was to take place at outdoor locations throughout three years of filming.

The skin was made of a stretch-knit pile car-seat covering, with pile fabric about one-half-inch thick. The chosen pile was not so fluffy that it appeared to be a toy. For realistic color variation, the pile was airbrushed. Before shooting, the costumers spritzed the fur with water to give it a sleek, realistic look. Fastenings were concealed on the insides of the legs and deep in the fur through the center of the belly.

The head was sculpted from clay by Burnham. The mouth was set in a half-open position, so it would both open and close in a believable and realistic manner. The eyes were also sculpted to be half-open. This way, the animatronic designer, Tim Rose, could make the eyelids open and close completely.

The clay head was sculpted over a welded armature, then molded and cast in plaster. Multiple sections of fiberglass negative molds were taken as the molds for latex-foam injection casting. The foam casting was done by another expert, Aaron Sherman, a popular marketer of latex foam in England. A core, which is the animal's skull—the head without the foam—was created by Tim Rose, who lay the thickness of the clay inside the mold to determine the thickness of the latex foam. Rose, who would mechanize the lion's head, cast in clay the muscle forms around the skull into the open space inside and then made up the core from fiberglass-reinforced epoxy. Rose

⚠ THIS SUBSTANCE OR PROCEDURE MAY BE HAZARDOUS TO HEALTH AND SHOULD BE USED WITH CARE. PLEASE READ THE APPROPRIATE HEALTH AND SAFETY SECTION.

determined where the variations of the latex's thicknesses should be laid. Very often the sculptor makes this determination, but Rose always cores his own molds, ensuring that the mechanized controls will be set precisely.

To insert the eyes, Rose cut a corresponding area into the skull. The size of the eyeballs presented a challenge. If the eyes were too small, the visage would appear mean-looking; if the eyes were too large, Burnham would have a caricature on her hands. The eyes were made of acrylic by Nissels, a manufacturer of human false eyes, and were painted by experts.

The eyes were a focal point, and it was important that they appear neither doe-like nor piercing. Ideally, two sets of eyes would have been constructed: mean eyes for harsh scenes and soft eyes for kindly scenes. The eyes were about 45 millimeters in diameter, of solid acrylic, with a high-gloss finish, and nearly round. They were placed on universal joints, allowing them to move not just back and forth, but in every direction. Rose also made brass eyelids, onto which the foam was fixed.

The mouth interior included a latex-foam tongue and acrylic teeth sculpted by Alli Eynon, using real lion's teeth as models. It was crucial that the teeth not prevent the mouth from closing. The mold maker, Paul James, molded and cast the teeth and gums in one piece, using dental acrylic ⚠ by first pouring the ivory tooth color and then the pink acrylic to color the gums.

Whiskers were quills from several sources: coque feathers, which were stripped down and punched; pig bristle; and real cat whiskers (courtesy of Burnham's own cat, Jimini, whose whiskers fell out from time to time).

Facial hair was made of predyed yak and goat hair and flocked by Alli Eynon at the studio with a machine that was designed to flock pieces one-half-inch long. Aslan's hair was white under the eyes and changed color on his head as it blended into his mane. The beard, adhered by #355 makeup prosthetic adhesive, was from a knotted piece of horsehair. His mane was a combination of yak hair, gathered nylon net, and gold thread.

The jaw opened and closed, the nose wrinkled up when the muzzle lifted, baring the teeth, and the head was rigged to the spine for rotation. The actress Alisa Berk, who is an expert at playing animals and was positioned inside the lion's front, held the head with closed hands and also pulled various ringed levers, much like a puppeteer, to operate Aslan's movements. Rose operated the animatronics with radio control, and William Todd Jones, who performed at the back of the body, operated the tail.

**Latex Foam ⚠,
Aluminum Strips,
Polyurethane Foam
Sheeting, and
Imitation Foliage**

In the film, *The Shining*, topiary hedge animals come to life. The movement for most of the animals is computer-generated, but one—a lion—moves because the costume is worn by an actor. The skeleton for this topiary lion is built over a restructuring of the human form, with the mobile-articulated features of the lion's head operated by remote control. Thorough anatomical research is a preliminary necessity when building such realistic animals. XFX, who built this lion, followed techniques similar to those used for building the butchered cow costume, described earlier.

The topiary lion is built of aluminum strips, latex foam, and polyurethane foam sheeting, and covered with imitation foliage.

DESIGN: MILENA CANONERA FOR THE FILM *THE SHINING*. PHOTO: XFX.

1. With the actor on all fours and arms supported by stilts, build a life cast. Use that cast to make a sculpture of the actor from epoxy ⚠ and fiberglass.

2. Build around the sculpture an aluminum frame to simulate a lion's skeleton. For the front feet, add foot-size extensions and another extension for the neck. Later, the actor's arms will be extended to leg length by strapped-on stilts.

3. Aluminum braces must be attached to extend between the skeleton and actor. Onto the braces are fitted rings that encircle the actor and permit him to move the lion's skeleton as he moves his own.

4. The outer shell of the body is fabricated from polyurethane flexible foam. First drape and fit pattern pieces over the skeleton. Then cut shapes from the foam, mitering, then butting and gluing into place. Use coarse open-celled reticulated insulation foam to build the feet, and bond it with rubber cement ⚠.

5. Use a high-necked, long-sleeved unitard to fit onto the original fiberglass and epoxy sculpture. Place over it the animal skeleton and outer body. Through an opening in the rear end, fill the cavity between the unitard and the animal body with casting foam latex. This will help to achieve added realism.

6. Next, for a topiary lion, add the foliage that will cover the lion's entire body and head.

For *The Shining*, XFX purchased six-inch flats of simulated boxweed from Autograph Foliage, a manufacturer of plastic plants in California. The flats were secured to the lion's body with 24-gauge galvanized wire.

Or, for a furry lion, acrylic-hair fabric can be cut to shape and rubber-cemented to the lion's body.

⚠ THIS SUBSTANCE OR PROCEDURE MAY BE HAZARDOUS TO HEALTH AND SHOULD BE USED WITH CARE. PLEASE READ THE APPROPRIATE HEALTH AND SAFETY SECTION.

Polyethylene Insulation Foam, Acrylic Fur Cloth, and Yak Hair

For this lion costume, fabricated by Shafton, Inc., polyethylene foam and acrylic fur cloth were the principal materials. First, the polyethylene was cut and glued together into a form to cover the actor. Next, acrylic fur was cut and sewn together and glued to the polyethylene. Yak hair was then added to create the mane. For more details on Shafton's construction techniques, see pages 358 - 359 for Bullwinkle® the moose.

This lion costume is fabricated from polyethylene foam and covered with acrylic fur cloth and yak hair.

DESIGN: SHAFTON, INC. FOR THE SADDLEBACK CHURCH IN MISSION VIEJO, CALIFORNIA.

Monkey

Polyurethane Insulation Foam, Polyethylene Foam, and Nylon Fleece Fabric

In Seoul, Korea, the Farmland Parade featured various species of animals. Included was a Monkey, whose costume was designed by John Ramirez and built by Chip Wickett of Chip's Character Creations Inc. The techniques for building the monkey costume were similar to those for building the bear costume described earlier and also designed by Wickett. In this case, only the head was structured, while the other costume pieces were of unlined cloth.

The specific materials employed for the head were L-200 polyethylene foam, reticulated polyurethane insulation foam (Scott, or SIF), and fleece fabric, materials favored by this shop.

Body

Foam sheetings covered by acrylic fleece form this monkey costume.

1. Wickett starts his costumes by first making patterns for body pieces and heads from one-inch upholstery foam. After the pattern is established, he cuts the actual pieces from one-inch-thick, thirty-pound-per-inch (ppi) insulation foam. From these foam pieces, he makes his pattern pieces. The pattern pieces are set aside for cutting out the fur body and the clothing.

2. Wickett bevel-cuts the edges of the actual foam pieces, then spreads adhesive on both surfaces of the one-inch edges. The edges are allowed to become tacky and then pressed together. (Wickett prefers nonhazardous water-based rubber cements.) He reinforces the seams with hand-sewing.

3. Following the muslin pattern, he cuts out the furry body cover from the acrylic-fleece fabric and sews it up. Next, he cuts and sews the arms,

which are unlined and unstructured. An industrial zipper is inserted at the back neckline to allow for easy laundering.

Feet For the shoes, Wickett cuts one-inch Minicel L-200 polyethylene foam (from Voltek) to the desired shape and cements the edges together. He lines the interior by gluing in one-inch polyurethane foam. For soles, dense Neoprene-foam sheeting is bonded with rubber contact adhesive.

Head
1. Using upholstery foam, he makes a pattern for a head and hat. He adjusts the pieces to fit, cutting out the shape first from muslin, and then from one-inch polyethylene foam, and bonds the foam pieces together with rubber contact cement.

2. The muslin pattern is used to make the pile or fur covering, leaving open spaces for the ears, eyes, nose, and mouth. The covering is stitched together and fit over the head.

3. Tempo fabric covers the mouth and tongue. Plastic window screen is placed in the mouth's interior, supplying ventilation.

4. For the eyes, shapes are vacuum-formed from clear-plastic sheeting (such as Kydex or polystyrene) and glued in place with thick cement. One-quarter-inch polyethylene foam is cut for lashes and rims around the eyes, sprayed with acrylic paint, and cemented into place. The nose is covered with Tempo napped-nylon fabric.

5. After the coverings for these features are glued into place, the head and hat fabrics are adjusted and glued.

Carefully shaped pieces of polyethylene foam are glued together to form a monkey head.

DESIGN: JOHN RAMIREZ FOR THE FARMLAND PARADE IN SOEUL, KOREA.
PHOTOS AND CONSTRUCTION: CHIP WICKETT.

6. The crown was of Minicel L-200 polyethylene foam, coated with fluorescent paint and glazed with gold-colored metallic foil.

7. All fabrics for the clothing were dyed with fluorescent dyes. The jacket motifs were silk-screened with fluorescent paint, and the decorative appliqué circles were sewn on. Three-fingered gloves were sewn from fabric-backed vinyl.

Moose

Polyurethane Foam, Polyethylene Foam, and Marquisette

The familiar character of Bullwinkle® was made at Shafton Inc. in North Hollywood by the following method:

Body

1. Make a mock-up of the costume by draping a dress form with eight long strips of one-inch-thick polyurethane upholstery foam. (Some of the strips may need to be as much as two feet wide.) These long strips will be used to form the body, which is in the shape of a pod. (Pod is the common term for an understructure of a constructed body. See illustration in the Bear section on page 349.)

Bullwinkle®, the moose, is fabricated from foam sheetings encased in marquisette, with fur and clothing from a brushed-nylon fabric.

DESIGN: SHAFTON, INC. FOR BULLWINKLE COPYRIGHT© 1993 BY UNIVERSAL CITY STUDIOS, INC. COURTESY OF MCA PUBLISHING RIGHTS, A DIVISION OF MCA INC. ALL RIGHTS RESERVED. PHOTO: SHAFTON, INC.

2. Basing the body on the adjusted pattern mock-up, cut the eight pattern pieces from one-inch, thirty pound-per-inch (ppi) insulation foam. Then cut pairs of each pattern piece from nylon marquisette fabric, so that each piece of foam is matched with a pair of nylon marquisette pieces. Sandwich the foam between the matching pieces of marquisette. Stitch the marquisette to the foam as close to the edge as possible, then stitch all pieces so that the vertical seams form the pod that will enclose the actor's body.

3. Tempo, a nylon-napped fabric, will be made into an outer suit that will cover the pod body. Follow the original pattern to cut from the acrylic fabric the outer suit, adding the necessary seam allowances. Stitch the Tempo pieces together and adjust as necessary. The outer suit will remain separate from the pod and will be easier to maintain and clean.

4. Sleeves may be kept with the pod or built separately, and the choice of method depends on the costume maker. The final sleeve will have an undersleeve of quarter-inch-thick insulation foam, which will be covered with napped fabric.

Head

1. The head is a separate piece. As with the body, use one-inch polyethylene foam to make a mock-up. Use as many sections of the one-inch foam as is necessary to prepare for shaping the unusual facial contours. When the mock-up is completely adjusted, use it for a pattern. With the pattern as your guide, cut the headpieces out of polyethylene-foam sheet (L-200 is used by Shafton), spread all edges with rubber cement ⚠ (Shafton uses water-based, nontoxic rubber cement), and butt edges together.

2. For the eyes and nostrils, use precast shapes of ABS, which can be bought at a train model shop. Cut vision holes in the neck, for this is where the actors' eyes will be located.

3. Cut out antler shapes from Minicel L-300 (a denser polyethylene foam), and pierce aluminum wire through the core of each antler base for greater stability. Glue the antlers onto the head with rubber cement.

4. Cover the head with the Tempo fabric cemented into place, and paint the eyes, nostrils, and antlers as desired with acrylic paint. Cover the vision holes in the neck with heavy net painted the same color as the fabric.

Hands and Feet Gauntlets are one-quarter-inch foam covered with Tempo.

Feet are cut from one-inch L-200, which is shaped and glued, interlined with insulation foam, lined with Spandex, and covered with napped fabric.

Legs The legs consist of purchased tights, with protective built-in pockets at the knees containing pads of shapes cut from polyethylene foam.

Reptiles

Dinosaurs

Cast Latex Foam Stan Winston Studios worked for over two years making both the giant dinosaur puppets and the smaller "raptor" costumes for the feature film *Jurassic Park*. The dinosaurs were life-size, while the raptor costumes were somewhat larger than man-size and fitted to the actor who "worked" the costume.

1. A plaster life cast was made of each actor playing a raptor. The actor assumed the bent position of his role, with his feet functioning as the creature's knees. (See the instructions for making a life cast on pages 184-188.)

2. To make the plaster cast, the actor put on a spandex leotard covered with petroleum jelly (like Vaseline), which worked as a release agent. The Vaseline-covered leotard was covered with wet plaster bandages, forming what would become a negative mold.

3. Taking the plaster that had been removed from the body, epoxy resin* and fiberglass were cast. The epoxy and fiberglass became the base over which was shaped a clay form with scales carved into the surface.

4. New molds made from epoxy resin and fiberglass were cast over the clay sculpture. When these new molds were removed, their interiors were filled with several inches of liquid-foam latex. For specific information on latex foam casting, refer to Donna Drexler's *Foam Latex Survival Manual* or GE Foam's videotape.

⚠ THIS SUBSTANCE OR PROCEDURE MAY BE HAZARDOUS TO HEALTH AND SHOULD BE USED WITH CARE. PLEASE READ THE APPROPRIATE HEALTH AND SAFETY SECTION.

5. After the latex foam was set, it was removed from the mold. The interior of the latex foam was lined with a layer of segments of sheet graphite. Strips of cotton

canvas were added to hinge the graphite segments, and the canvas was bonded into place with rubber contact cement.

6. Also included in the back section of the costume was a backpack containing the electronics that directed the raptor's movements.

7. All raptor costumes and dinosaurs were painted with flexible paint. Those characters that would get wet were sealed with silicone sealant ⚠.

Desert Tortoise

Nylon Spandex and Cyanoacrylate ⚠

Tony Gardener, of Alterian Studios near Los Angeles, made this realistic *desert-tortoise* costume with spandex and cyanoacrylate adhesive.

1. Paper patterns were made according to the size of the arms and legs of the actor wearing the costume.

2. Nylon-spandex limbs were cut out. These are three times longer than the actor's actual limbs, to allow ample fabric for folds and wrinkles.

3. The oversize fabric pieces were sewn into tubes and placed onto a mannequin, with the extra fabric wrinkled and folded into place.

4. Cyanoacrylate was dripped over approximately one half of the surface, fixing the folds and producing the uneven reptilian texture.

5. A tortoise shell was then sculpted to form the model, and a mold was made of plaster of Paris. The shell was then cast, textured, painted, and colored.

Lizards

Liquid Latex ⚠ Over Cotton Jersey

These costumes for Berlin's Schaubühne Theatre were designed in 1982 by Moidelle Bickel for *The Orestia*. Bickel, known internationally as the designer of the feature film *Queen Margot*, was then the staff designer for the Schaubühne. During the Schaubünhe's customary several-month rehearsal, Bickel had the opportunity to experiment with different costume forms and respond to the actors' input. These are the steps taken when making these costumes:

1. First, body-fitting coveralls were made of heavy woven cotton and covered with a layer of cotton jersey.

2. The cotton jersey was painted with several thick coats of liquid latex.

3. Cotton batting was dipped into liquid latex, laid onto the latex-covered jersey and molded into smooth, distorted forms.

4. To create the sharklike appendages and the scaly spines that run down the back of the actors, polyurethane foam sheeting was cut and glued (with rubber cement ⚠) to shape, covered with additional coats of liquid latex, and then latex-bonded to the body garments.

5. Both body and appendages were painted with black latex-based scenic paint.

Quilted Spandex and Textile Paint

Peg Brady used a different method to create lizardlike costumes for a production of Seascape at the Krannart Center of the University of Illinois. She based her designs on custom-built spandex unitards. Back sections of the unitards were quilted, and the long tubes of double-layered spandex that made the tails were reinforced with self-cased spring-steel coils. The spring steel created both three-dimensionality and lifelike movements. The quilted texture allowed the tails to blend smoothly into the reptiles' backs. Airbrushed Deka brand textile paints ⚠ were used to create color variation and luminosity.

Snake

Nylon-Spandex Painted With Glitter Paint and Deka Airbrush Ink

Snake costumes from paint and ink on nylon spandex were worn by dancers portraying snakes at an extravagant Middle Eastern theme industrial show and party in Palm Springs, California.

1. Dancers were fitted into individually custom constructed high-neck tightly hooded nylon-spandex unitards.

2. Each leotard was dyed a different pastel color and then placed on a plastic-covered legged dress form.

3. Scale shapes in vertical snakelike patterns were painted with Deka Airbrush Ink ⚠; the scale outlines were intensified and highlights were drawn with glitter paint.

4. Before each wearing, the costumes were sprayed with glitter hair spray ⚠ for additional sheen. The glitter spray comes off through wearing and touching, though the dyes, inks, and paints remain through the repeated launderings necessary for dance costumes.

Sea Life

Octo-Man

Polyurethane Foam, Bailing Wire, and Casting Latex ⚠

For the 1995 television series *Tattooed Teenage Alien Fighters from Beverly Hills*, frightening creatures such as Octo-man, Snake-man, and Dino-Man were all built similarly from polyurethane foam. This is the method used by Rob Burman at Sticks and Stones to create the costume for the Octo-Man.

Body

1. Place a spandex unitard onto a body form. Construct the octopus body on top of it, gluing ⚠ pieces onto the unitard.

2. Cut a paper pattern for the entire body—torso, arms, and legs—working over a dress form to determine size and shape. Cut out the desired shape from polyurethane foam. To make the extra rolls of skin, cut out extra pieces, bevel the edges to force the foam into the rolling forms. For a costume with short-term use, upholstery foam is adequate, but if the costume is meant to last over a period of time, use insulation foam of thirty ppi.

⚠ THIS SUBSTANCE OR PROCEDURE MAY BE HAZARDOUS TO HEALTH AND SHOULD BE USED WITH CARE. PLEASE READ THE APPROPRIATE HEALTH AND SAFETY SECTION.

Polyurethane foam sheeting, cast polyure-thane, bailing wire, and casting latex make up this creature.

The head is cast from polyurethane; features are sculpted and added later.

DESIGN: MARIZIO BIZZARI FOR TATTOOED TEENAGE ALIEN FIGHTERS FROM BEVERLY HILLS. PHOTO: ROB BURMAN.

Tentacles of polyurethane foam sheeting wrapped over wire are placed onto the body before painting.

3.   Butt edges together and adhere rubber cement—like Barge All-Purpose Cement—to both edges. Allow them to dry to a tacky state, and press together.

4.   Spray with a cobwebbing solution ⚠, like BJB'S SC 89, to smooth the grainy texture of the foam.

5.   Paint liquid casting latex over the entire surface for further texture and strength. The latex can be applied by either brush or sponge.

6.   Paint with rubber cement mixed with acrylic paint.

7.   Finish the feet with soles made from cast latex, reinforced with burlap, and glued with rubber contact cement.

Head 1. Sculpt the desired head shape from clay. Do not include the tentacles in this piece of sculpture.

2. Create a one-part plaster mold from the clay sculpture. Depending upon the design, two or more part molds may be required.

3. Coat the inside of the mold with liquid latex—either by painting, slushing, or absorption skinning method—to create a "skin" for the finished mask.

4. Cast two-part flexible polyurethane foam ⚠ into the plaster cast, filling it completely. Then trim the foam out of the center to make room for the actor's head. A core could be used to create a hollow space, but it would have to be incorporated into the original sculpture and made to fit the final mold.

5. Make suction cups of varying sizes in the same manner as the head. These will be used later to cover the octopus's tentacles.

6. Eye shapes can be made from smoked acrylic hemispheres cut down to size.

7. Sculpt the tusks in clay, create silicone molds ⚠, and then cast them from rigid material, like TC-806, a rigid polyurethane foam ⚠ from Burman Industries.

Tentacles

1. Cut 16-gauge bailing wire to desired lengths. Fold back one of the ends for actor's safety.

2. Cover with tapered strips of polyurethane foam sheet, wrapped firmly around the wire and then glued together.

3. Make additional tentacles without wire. By varying the structure of the tentacles in this way, some will have mobility, and others will be more rigid.

4. Glue suction cups to tentacles, then glue the tentacles to the headpiece, texturing and painting them following the same method used on the body.

Sea Creatures

Nylon Spandex, Polyurethane Foam, and Pearlescent Paint

In the performance piece *See Below Middle Sea*, at Taper, Too, Los Angeles, sea creatures were featured. Their essence found visual representation in custom-built nylon-spandex unitards dyed to silvery gray. Separate polyurethane-foam protective knee and elbow pads were covered with matching spandex. To mimic the usual patterning of many species of fish, the belly, or front, side of the unitards was airbrushed and stippled with pearlescent white textile paint; the top, or back, side of the unitards were airbrushed and then stippled with a brilliant range of ombréed colors.

Sprayed dye and stippled opalescent paint give a suggestion of sea creatures.

DESIGN: THE AUTHOR FOR THE PERFORMANCE PIECE *SEE BELOW MIDDLE SEA* AT TAPER, TOO, LOS ANGELES. PHOTO: JAY THOMPSON.

⚠ THIS SUBSTANCE OR PROCEDURE MAY BE HAZARDOUS TO HEALTH AND SHOULD BE USED WITH CARE. PLEASE READ THE APPROPRIATE HEALTH AND SAFETY SECTION.

Drag Queens

Upholstery Foam, Balloons, and Polystyrene Foam

For *The Adventures of Priscilla, Queen of the Desert*, costume designer Lizzy Gardiner had the opportunity to prove the old adage that necessity is indeed the mother of invention. "I love the fact that you can do things without much budget," says Gardiner. Costumes were sewn by prison "lifers" (men condemned to a life in prison), headdresses built from cast-off Barbie Dolls and empty lipstick cases, and costume parts traded with real-life drag queens. Gardiner found creative solutions to creating dozens of costumes on an extremely restrictive budget. Part of her design process was to enter into the spirit of being a resourceful drag queen. Some drag queens are lucky enough to afford the bounteous curves available through shops like Frederick's of Hollywood; however, most drag queens in Australia create their own female curves. To costume the transvestite played by Terrence Stamp, Gardiner padded him "head to toe," with various padding pieces on different parts of his body according to the necessities of scene and costume. This was the process she followed:

Body padding
1. From polyurethane upholstery foam, create body pieces for the thighs, hips, and any other sections needing added curves, with the exception of the breasts—they are made from another material. Using an electric kitchen knife—the type used for ordinary meat carving—for each area to be padded, shape the interior side of the foam pieces with concave curves to fit snugly to the wearer's body, and shape the outer portion to resemble female curves.

2. Several fittings may be necessary to ensure that the foam pieces fit snugly and blend into the actor's body realistically.

3. Purchase a long-line "body shaper" that fits from bra line through midthigh.

4. As the actor dresses, hold each piece in place while the "body shaper" is carefully pulled on over the pieces.

5. Keep the padding pieces separate from the "body shaper" to achieve a tight fit and easy launderability.

Breasts
For *Priscilla*, Gardiner found that prosthetic breasts are not as natural as the look needed for the film. Since the texture, flexibility, and movement of natural breasts was required, Gardiner and her crew experimented with all kinds of materials. After dozens of tries with lentils, rice, and various other small objects, Gardiner and her crew found that the most natural look could be obtained with water-filled balloons. The method they used can be found in the Padding Suits section on page 00.

Shoes
Gardiner found it necessary to make all the shoes worn by the three drag queens. Shoes were platform wedgies and made according to this special invention, which worked beautifully:

1. First cut out dense polystyrene foam in the form of a wedge. Insert a steel rod through the polystyrene into the heel sections for strengthening.

2. Cut out dense Neoprene-sole-rubber sheet to the approximate shape of the sole. Glue in place with a rubber-contact shoe cement $\triangle$ (like Barge).

3. Cover the insole and outside of the wedge with colored-vinyl sheet or fabric, bonding it in place with the same shoe cement. Attach plastic and fabric straps by sewing and gluing to the covered wedge. For one costume, the straps were of actual thong sandals drilled with three holes at each end and then sewn to the shoe.

Dresses Dresses were made of all types of materials; but the most unique was the costume composed of thong sandals. The sandals were among the many found-object costume parts. To make a similar costume, drill a hole at both ends of each sandal. Then add links, ala 1960s fashion designer Paco Rabanne, or use a cord, to attach them to each other.

Headdresses In the film there are wigs galore, some purchased and others obtained by making trades with actual drag queens. Some of the marvelously inventive headdresses are from glued together piles of found objects—Barbie Dolls, baby dolls, doll shoes, and doll limbs, as well as mirrors, lipstick cases and plastic flowers (found in the garbage of a defunct mortuary). The outrageous combinations of materials create bulk, though the details are mostly lost on the film audience. More about the specific headdress method is on pages 307-321.

Fantasy Creatures

Catwoman

Latex Sheeting and Latex Foam ⚠ The slinky Catwoman costume worn in the film Batman Returns was designed by Bob Ringwood and made by Andy Wilkes. Wilkes presently works out of Syren, his custom-design studio and retail store in Hollywood, where he both designs and produces sleek and sexy clothing from latex sheeting. Some of his most famous customers are Madonna, Roseanne, and Cher. Wilkes finds that latex clothing and unitards actually flatter, since they pull in and distribute equally those parts of the body that most women try to hide.

This famous costume worn by Michelle Pfeiffer was made from .014" black latex sheeting and cut directly from a paper pattern into the actual latex. Wilkes always works in this method, for there is no other material with the same amount of stretch (400 percent); thus, to make a mock-up from another material would be a waste of time. To make the costume, he followed this procedure:

1. Cut out the latex unitard, working one size smaller than the actor's measurements if the actor is of average proportions. For larger wearers, use dimensions two sizes smaller. Allow for quarter-inch seams. Overlap, then bond the seams with a latex-based adhesive ⚠ like Bostik 3851 or Copydex (a latex cement from Great Britain). Use only glue; do not sew, to join the seams.

2. Dress the actor in the suit, waiting about twenty minutes before starting the fitting. During this time, the latex will warm up, become flexible, and stretch to adjust to the actor's body. Then fit the suit and mark with a china-marker pencil for notations. If it does not fit perfectly, start over. Keep making and fitting new suits until you have created an exact fit—Wilkes made eighteen versions of Catwoman's unitard before he had the perfect fit!

⚠ THIS SUBSTANCE OR PROCEDURE MAY BE HAZARDOUS TO HEALTH AND SHOULD BE USED WITH CARE. PLEASE READ THE APPROPRIATE HEALTH AND SAFETY SECTION.

3. Finish off edges by coating with the same adhesive and folding them under about a quarter of an inch.

4. Polish the latex surface with automobile wax.

Catwoman's unitard appears to be stitched together with large cord. Since it undergoes several stages of disintegration, different techniques were used to achieve the look of the stitching. In her first costumes, white millinery elastic was laced through slits cut into the latex. An additional strip of latex was glued underneath for reinforcement. For her final costume, the torn pieces were held by stitching composed of strips of cast pieces on which lacing was placed across the open seams, in a manner similar to that on her headdress described below. These cast pieces were camouflaged by feathered edges that would blend into the unitard. They were painted and finally bonded to the costume with the glue.

Headdress

1. Make a life cast of the actress's head, using alginate. It will be a temporary negative cast for performing the following step.

2. Make a plaster positive cast from the inside of alginate cast. It will be the "core" used later, when casting within the finished mold. Using the plaster for the model, make a silicone ⚠ negative mold and then an epoxy ⚠ and fiberglass positive, taking care to make it as smooth as possible.

3. Onto the plaster head, sculpt the hood shape with a hard oil-base clay like Roma Plastilina #F4. Add ears and any other dimensional features with the same clay.

4. From this new clay sculpture, make a silicone negative mold. Then open it and clean thoroughly.

5. Cast the actual piece from dense, black-pigmented foam latex ⚠. Use the original epoxy and fiberglass as a core inside the silicone negative mold. The core will enable the headpiece to fit closely, while the negative forms the design.

6. Next, paint the stitching white. Ninety percent of the stitching in *Batman Returns* was sculpted directly into the original head sculpture or it was applied as thin-edged appliqués glued to the costume. They would only be stitched with actual thread in areas to be broken open and frayed.

7. When the paint is dry, rub the mask with silicone fluid to create a brilliant shine.

Corset

Catwoman's corset, made at the Warner Brothers Studio costume shop, was manufactured of latex bonded to a boned-felt structure .

Accessories

The high boots were custom-made from leather, and the gloves were sewn from vinyl.

The latex unitard was made in sixty-three doubles, to be worn both by Pfeiffer as well as her three stunt women. Before getting dressed in latex clothing, it is advisable for the actor to rub down with talcum powder so that the garment will slide on smoothly.

Mermaids

Polyurethane Reticulated Foam, Silicone ⚠, and Stretch Velour

A mermaid was designed and made by Vin Burnham of London for an Italian Peroni beer commercial. Costumes like this one, that must float in the water, present special problems. In addition, this particular costume was to look realistic and sleek, unlike a pantomime or caricature. Because the costume required both positive and negative buoyancy, the materials had to be of an exact weight. They could not lift the mermaid above the surface of the water, or could they drag her to the bottom. Scott, or SIF, reticulated polyurethane insulation foam was the perfect material to fulfill all these requirements. Since glues and all other materials had to be impervious to salt water, silicone ⚠ caulking was the chosen bonding agent. There were only two weeks within which to build the costume, and using materials that could be assembled quickly was a necessity—certainly, there was no time to make castings.

The mermaid tail, like all costumes created by Vin Burnham, began with a life cast of the model playing the mermaid, as well as a life cast of her stuntwoman. For the life cast, it was necessary to make the performers' feet as vertical and pointed as possible, so the performers wore the highest heels that could be found. Ideally, their feet would have been on point.

To make the tail, nylon spandex was fitted over the life cast. Then a sheet of reticulated polyurethane foam was draped, glued ⚠, and with scissors carefully shaped into a fishtail shape. All was covered with another layer of spandex. A zipper was hand-sewn down the back, so the performer could get into the tail, much as one wiggles into a sleeping bag, with a final skin of stretch velvet "scales" pulled over the tail to conceal the zipper.

Hiding the knees and the heels are the most difficult tasks when creating a mermaid costume. To achieve this camouflage, Burnham and her team made a leg brace out of sheet nylon that extended past the performers' feet for another eighteen inches, at which point it splayed out into a finned shape. The brace, which prevented the performers from bending their knees, started in the middle of the thighs. It was fashioned from a flexible and strong nylon sheet, about ten millimeters thick.

For the fin, a membrane three-feet wide was sculpted over the nylon and cast in clear silicone ⚠, then attached to the nylon with silicone sealer. The joint had to be seamless if it were to be invisible. The membrane was afterwards painted with oil paint. The buoyancy and mobility of the fin was tested in a swimming pool in London, and the tail was tested in the Jacuzzi of Michael Portelly, the director.

For the outer covering of the tail, Zeta four-way stretch velvet (Zeta spandex is available from Zeta Trikotagenfabrik in Germany. See appendix for address.)was dyed and then screen-printed. The velvet skins stretched sufficiently to be pulled over the spandex-covered foam tail, eliminating the need for opening or fasteners.

For color and pattern, Burnham found her inspiration at Harrod's meat and seafood department, where she purchased beautiful goldfish tinged with pink. She chose to

⚠ THIS SUBSTANCE OR PROCEDURE MAY BE HAZARDOUS TO HEALTH AND SHOULD BE USED WITH CARE. PLEASE READ THE APPROPRIATE HEALTH AND SAFETY SECTION.

relate the tail color to the golden color of the beer, with the tail golden around the front, and blending at the back into a vivid red that matched the red color of the spine.

Silk screens were created of a fish-scale pattern that gradated from large to small, with the smaller scales placed at the bottom. Nicola Killeen, who printed the costume, used a discharge-printing method, so the scales were outlined in white, emphasizing a realistic, reflective quality. The scales were then highlighted with strategically placed bits of iron-on clear, iridescent sequins to give an overall fishlike shimmer. Four such skins were created for the tail—one for closeups, one for stunts, and two for spares. Iron-on sequins are available in the United States from Fred Frankel and Sons. See page 181 for more information.

The mermaid's actual tail began at her hips, where the scales blended into her flesh tones. To keep the tail in place, silicone waistbands were made, then glued to the stretch velvet. The makeup designer used waterproof prosthetic adhesive to glue the silicone bands to her body.

Two latex-foam starfish formed the bra. The starfish were cast directly from real starfish and later painted with PAX paint, then were adhered to the mermaid with the same #355 prosthetic adhesive as that used with the silicone waistbands.

Dressing the mermaids brought yet another problem. In this case, the stunt mermaid started dressing while lying down on the floor of a room at five A.M. so that by seven A.M. she would be completely dressed and ready to be lifted onto a stretcher by four men. When the location for the shot was reached, the performer and the stretcher were placed into a small boat, and the mermaid was then tipped off the stretcher and into the water. The performer wore a snorkel under water and was passed supplementary air; this allowed her to remove her mask and work under water for about 16 seconds at a time.

There were worries about the sun and salt fading the costume, so after shooting, the tail was removed immediately using #355 prosthetic-adhesive solvent (made by Dow Corning but now discontinued) to remove the glue from the waistband. The tail was then placed immediately under a shower to remove the salt water, which otherwise would have quickly rotted the fabric.

Spandex and Mylar In making the mermaid tail for the *Splash* revue at the Mirage Resorts in Las Vegas, Judy Corbett of J & M Costumes used materials that could be worn underwater, and still emerge looking beautiful. To create such a tail, try following her method:

1. Start by fitting a heavy nylon-spandex shape close to the body, from the waist to below the feet.

2. Cut scales from patterned Mylar film, iridescent sheer-nylon fabric, and colored sequin fabric.

3. Sandwich between the sheer nylon some scales of the sequined fabric and some of the Mylar pieces. Sew around the edges with a narrow overlock stitch.

4. Pin the scales to the tail piece, closely overlapping them, and gradating them in size from large at the top to small towards the end of the tail. Hand-sew them in place with heavy nylon thread, making sure to stretch the spandex while sewing.

5. Fins can be from knife-pleated iridescent nylon organza.

6. The *Splash* revue at the the Mirage Resorts in Las Vegas was designed by Pete Menefee, costume designer for many revues, musicals, and television productions.

Spandex, Organza, and Hot-Melt Web Film

To build a mermaid costume that will not be submerged in water, Judy Corbett used this method:

1. Plain nylon four-way-stretch spandex was tightly fitted over the actress's lower torso and legs to create the basic tail.

2. Scales were cut from two-inch squares of nylon organza, sequin cloth, and lurex metallic fabric. The sequin cloth was sandwiched between two layers of organza, with an additional layer of hot-melt film placed between the back of the sequin cloth and one organza layer. These pieces were ironed for stability, and then all layers were overlocked together.

3. Gold and silver "lastex" fabric was used for more scales. It was overdyed with colors that softened and harmonized with the other fabrics, and then cut out in the same scale shapes. Hot-melt film (like Wonder Web) was cut to the same shapes and sandwiched between two layers of lastex. The three layers were pressed, then overlocked.

4. The scales were sewn onto the tail in a close pattern, overlapping as real scales do.

Bob Mackie was the designer of this tail, worn in a photograph for a *Town and Country* magazine article in 1990 and in the Academy Award ceremony of 1991, by a chorus member.

The Orc

Nylon Spandex, Polyethylene Foam, and Urethane Upholstery Foam

Though the Orc is a fantasy monster, the look of a real, lifelike creature was desirable. This costume was built over a custom-made spandex unitard, with the unitard serving as the base for realistic, well-developed muscles sculpted of polyurethane upholstery foam.

Body

1. Pattern each muscle group and cut the forms from polyurethane foam sheeting. Bevel-cut and carve the edges of the foam, so the pieces representing each muscle group bulge outwards as they are glued to the spandex. Leave the interior of each piece hollow; no filling is required. For articulation, leave the insides of the joints free of foam.

⚠ THIS SUBSTANCE OR PROCEDURE MAY BE HAZARDOUS TO HEALTH AND SHOULD BE USED WITH CARE. PLEASE READ THE APPROPRIATE HEALTH AND SAFETY SECTION.

2. Use an all-purpose shoemaker's cement ⚠, like Barge All-Purpose Cement, to bond the edges of the muscle forms to the spandex and to each other.

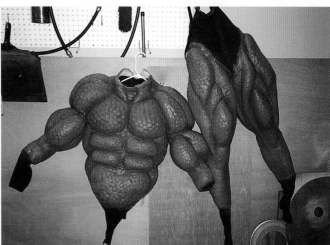

Foam muscles are adhered to the fitted nylon unitard.

Scale texture is burnt into the foam with a soldering iron.

The separate body pieces after texturing are coated with a flexible, colored coating.

The pieces are assembled before painting.

The Orc's head is fabricated from polyurethane foam sheeting.

DESIGN, CONSTRUCTION AND
PHOTOS: TOTAL FABRICATION.

3. Fill in gaps between the muscles with silicone sealant.

4. When the muscles are completed, draw an over-all scale pattern onto the muscular form with a soldering iron.

5. Pattern to shape a covering for the entire muscular form, using as few seams as possible, and placing the seams in hidden areas. Cut out the pattern pieces from quarter-inch polyurethane upholstery foam. Brush the same cement over the muscular form, including inside the burned-out scale outlines.

6. Place the quarter-inch foam sheeting on top of the form, and rub it in place thoroughly and carefully. Now the subtle scale outlines will project a more realistic look.

7. Spray the entire costume with a flexible, colored coating of polyurethane ⚠, latex ⚠, or vinyl ⚠.

Head To build the Orc's headdress, follow this method:

1. The headpiece is based on a baseball batter's helmet. Pad the inside of the helmet with polyurethane upholstery foam sheeting to fit the actor's head. Build up the actual head shape with polyethylene flexible foam sheeting, like Minicel L-200 or Plastazote. Glue it into place with shoemaker's rubber cement. Burn in a scale texture, cover with quarter-inch polyurethane foam and paint, as with the body.

2. The large horns are hollow. Pattern and cut them from polyethylene foam. Butt and glue the edges together, then fill the inside with a polyurethane foam spray, sprayed into the cavity.

3. Small horns and teeth are carved from polyethylene foam and sanded. Coat them with a protective coating, like polyurethane ⚠ or PVA, paint with acrylic, and then finish coat with epoxy resin ⚠.

4. The eyes are solid acrylic hemispheres, available at most plastics' supply shops. First, make a circle the same diameter as the hemisphere on a piece of paper. Draw and color the pupil and the iris. Coat with a quick-drying epoxy cement ⚠ and bond to the acrylic hemisphere. The thickness and shape of the acrylic will magnify the eye and cause it to "follow" the perceiver.

Additional body parts for the "Orc" are made in the following manner:

Hands and Feet
1. Hands are slip cast latex gloves ⚠. The fingernails are shaped from pieces of Friendly Plastic.

2. For the feet, purchase snow boots, cover with acrylic-fur fabric and suede by patterning and then glueing to the boots, including the bottom of the sole. Over the sole, glue a new sole from half-inch dense chloroprene (Neoprene) or other synthetic rubber sheeting.

3. Clothing worn by the Orc is limited to a breastplate and back plate of Minicel L-200 polyethylene armor. Pattern and cut to shape. Butt the edges, gluing them with shoemaker's cement. With a multipupose hand tool, gouge the surface until it looks like worn metal.

Polyethylene foam, polyurethane upholstery foam, and nylon spandex are the principal materials fabricating the Orc costume.

⚠ THIS SUBSTANCE OR PROCEDURE MAY BE HAZARDOUS TO HEALTH AND SHOULD BE USED WITH CARE. PLEASE READ THE APPROPRIATE HEALTH AND SAFETY SECTION.

Spray with metallic acrylic paint. Age with dark-brown or black spray paint, and coat with a clear protective coating.

The "Orc" was designed and built by Ken Hall after the CD-ROM character and was built at Total Fabrication, his North Hollywood workshop, as a walk-around promotional costume.

The Thing

Polyethylene Foam, Acrylonitrile-Butadiene styrene Sheeting (ABS), and Nylon Spandex

The Thing, a walk-around character from Marvel Comics, resembles a gigantic and animated explosion of red sandstone. The body comprises two layers of polyethylene, the under layer is smooth, and the outer layer is a pieced and cracked covering. Both body layers were vacuum-formed ⚠ from Voltek's Minicel L-200 polyethylene-foam sheeting and were constructed at Shafton Inc. in North Hollywood according to the following method:

Body

1. Using polyethylene foam sheeting, cut out two layers to the shape of the costume. Use the first layer to form the smooth silhouette or underbody of the costume. Cut the second layer into the outer shards, or cracked pieces.

Spandex over polyethylene foam give the illusion of sandstone for The Thing.

THE THING™ ©1996, MARVEL CHARACTERS, INC. ALL RIGHTS RESERVED AND USED WITH PERMISSION ONLY.

2. Cover each piece of both layers with predyed spandex and stitch all of the pieces together into the correct formation, the underlayer into one piece and the outer, cracked pieces into another.

3. After all pieces are assembled, line the underbody with cotton tricot fabric, sewn into place.

4. Cut eight pieces of stretch-mesh fabric into curved, diamond-shaped gussets, approximately six by twenty-four inches. When gluing the elbow and knee joints together, insert at the joint a diamond gusset of stretch mesh fabric, which will serve as a hinge. Stitch the arms and legs to the torso, again adding the stretch mesh hinges.

5. Darken the interior spaces, or cracks, between the shards with air brushed Pantone Inks ⚠ to emphasize shadows and give dimension.

Head

1. Carve a block of polyurethane rigid foam to a desired head shape, measuring carefully to ensure symmetry. Projecting ears and rock-head features can be secured with straight dressmakers' pins. Slice the shaped head in half from ear to ear, place

in the vacuum-former, and mold from #093 ABS sheeting, being sure to allow an extra one-and-a-half inches for overlap. Glue the two parts together with Weld-On ABS glue ⚠.

2. Cover all seams with one-inch-wide thermoplastic sheet, such as Thermoform.

3. Spray paint* with acrylic lacquer, first a base coat to match the spandex body, and then a spatter coat with one or two more colors of Pantone Ink for the stonelike texture. Draw cracks with Sharpie pen.

4. Insert a welding helmet headband for support, since the head will project above the head of the wearer and will need additional support. Metal rods will need to be extended from inside the head structure for about two inches to the metal headband.

5. Cover the mouth from the inside with black rigid netting and hot-glue ⚠ in place. Follow the same process for the eyes, using brass-colored netting, and painting with blue, black, and white acrylic paint.

6. Cut one-inch slits in the top of the head for ventilation.

7. The neck is of flexible three-quarter-inch polyurethane foam, covered by *nylon spandex*, and hot-glued into place. The bottom edge is finished by a painted flexible vinyl tube that forms a ridge to sit on the actor's shoulders. The ridge holds snaps that attach to the torso piece.

Feet   Feet are of L-200 polyethylene foam, flexible upholstery foam, and chloroprene rubber (Neoprene) sheeting, and assembled as follows:

1. The foot shape is of molded and glued L-200 foam, cushioned with flexible upholstery foam, which is glued into place. The entire interior is lined with matching nylon spandex, with a few inches of spandex remaining above the shoe top to better camouflage the actor within. The flexible foam interior allows actors with different foot sizes to fit into these shoes.

2. The cracks and shards are created by adhering separate covered and painted polyethylene foam pieces, following the same method as with the body. All pieces are both glued and hand-sewn.

3. Shoe soles are of half-inch Neoprene shoe soling, both glued (with Barge All-Purpose Cement ⚠) and stitched into place.

4. Large snaps are sewn to the spandex shoe lining to secure the feet to the body.

⚠ THIS SUBSTANCE OR PROCEDURE MAY BE HAZARDOUS TO HEALTH AND SHOULD BE USED WITH CARE. PLEASE READ THE APPROPRIATE HEALTH AND SAFETY SECTION.

This process can be hazardous to health and should be used with care. Please see appropriate *Health and Safety* section.

Trolls

Polyurethane Insulation Foam, Polyethylene Foam, and Spandex

Troll costumes for the 1994 *Sigfried & Roy* show in Las Vegas were designed by John Napier (who, in this case, was also responsible for the total design, direction, and concept of the show). Construction was by Parsons-Meares Ltd. Each troll wore different garb, though all were constructed similarly.

Bodies

1. Onto each fitted spandex leotard and tights ensemble was built a different deformity. The deformities—unusual humps and bumps—were made from different types of foam, sculpted into shape, enclosed in fabric cases, and sewn on. The type of foam, from soft polyurethane insulation foam to more rigid high-density polyethylene, was selected according to the individual deformity. Additionally, clumps of "hair" from frayed fibers of iridescent nylon organza were inserted at strategic spots on the leotard and tights.

2. The altered leotards and tights were covered by a second set encompassing the new deformity and cut out in places matching up with the "hair" clumps. Some trolls had tails created from a combination of hard and soft articulated foam pieces attached to a layer of fabric that served both to unite and hinge them. They, too, were covered with matching spandex. Spines worn by some of the trolls were made of leather.

Clothing

Clothing covering these bodies were separate garments specifically designed to allow for the individual deformity. Many of the garments were given extra body and form by being constructed of fabric quilted over thin foam padding.

Because these costumes were built as layers of individual items, they were completely launderable. They were built to last for twelve performances per week for over four years.

Humanoids

Acolytes

Polyurethane Insulation Foam, Spandex, and Silk Screen Paint

The Acolytes in the 1994 *Sigfried & Roy* show, at The Mirage Resorts in Las Vegas, are muscle men with exceptionally large muscles, built of layers of Scott polyurethane insulation foam applied in anatomical shapes onto spandex leotards.

Body

1. The first, and smallest, layer of the foam was hand-sewn in place, and the additional graded layers glued △ and layered onto the others (using 3M Scotch-Grip 847, or brown glue). The foam layers were sculpted with scissors to closely resemble specific muscle groups. The top layer was both glued and hand-sewn in place with large cross-stitches. Each dancer was individually fitted for correct adjustment of the muscles to his own body.

2. The muscled leotard is covered by another, larger leotard, which was shaped by draping spandex over the first, padded leotard. The muscle outlines were quilted by hand through all layers of leotards and padding to emphasize the exaggerated anatomy. For emphasis, the musculature outlines were shadowed with silk-screen paint. Additional painted motifs went on the back of each unitard, giving each dancer a different type of cat design.

Clothing   1. These muscled dancers wore Near Eastern style trousers, each made of a different rich fabric, decorated by panels of fabric quilted over one-quarter inch polyurethane insulation foam. Their vests are also interlined with thin foam, covered with rich fabrics, and decorated with heavy grommets and studs.

2. The cod pieces, of thicker insulation foam, were again covered with fabric and metal pieces. Spandex-covered foam gauntlets with studs over the knuckles left the fingers free.

Hair   Wigs of yak hair were streaked with paint, blending in and matching the makeup.

Boots   Boots of leather were decorated with the same elements used on the other costume pieces.

The Amazon Army

Kydex, Spandex, Iron-on Sequins, and Insulation Foam   Costumes for the Amazon Army in the Las Vegas *Siegfried & Roy* show, designed by William Ivey Long, were built at the Parsons-Meares, Ltd. in New York and at Costume Armour Inc. in upper New York state. The two costume shops worked together in this manner to costume 40 female dancers.

Armor   1. Paper mock-ups of the hard armor were created at Parsons-Meares, Ltd. The mock-ups were sent to Costume Armour, Inc., where Nino Novelino sculpted copies of the shapes with a plasticine clay. From the clay, he made more permanent molds that would withstand many pulls from the vacuum-forming ⚠ oven. Using Kydex (acrylic-polyvinyl chloride), Novelino vacuum-formed the front leg pieces. He then placed gold Mylar over the Kydex and vacuum-formed the same shapes a second time. The backs of the leg pieces were made of elastic-covered gold fabric for flexibility in dancing, and elastic strips held the backs and fronts together.

2. The entire leg pieces were hung from G-strings which had a hard vacuum-formed Kydex shape, both in the front and the back. Large snaps were strategically placed to attach the G-string to the unitard, keeping it in place on the dancing body. G-strings were held in place with gold-covered elastic.

3. Bra cups were also vacuum-formed and held in place with the gold straps.

4. The softer shoulder pieces were made of a high-density polyurethane insulation foam. The foam was cut to shape, then covered with nylon spandex that was prelaminated with iron-on sequins.

⚠ THIS SUBSTANCE OR PROCEDURE MAY BE HAZARDOUS TO HEALTH AND SHOULD BE USED WITH CARE. PLEASE READ THE APPROPRIATE HEALTH AND SAFETY SECTION.

5. The dancers also wore unitards covered by iron-on sequins. Large snaps were sewn onto match with the G-strings and bra cups to prevent their shifting.

6. All vacuum-formed pieces were primed with auto-body primer and then spray painted ⚠ with gold-metallic acrylic paint

Headdresses Headdresses were made by covering a gold-colored spandex fitted hood with a removable vacuum-formed Kydex helmet. Soft upholstery foam was glued ⚠ to the inside of the helmet, fitting it snugly to the dancer's head.

The Evil Queen in this same production wears a coiled snake bra, also constructed from vacuum-formed Kydex.

Dolls

Polyethylene Foam Sheeting and Polyurethane Coating ⚠ For a series of Duracell Battery commercials, XFX studios, under the direction of Steve Johnson, created the Putterman family, a group of costumes that gave the actors the appearance of dolls. The costumes were especially effective because just the right combination of materials and articulated puppet-like joints were put together.

1. Make paper patterns and cut them out of polyethylene foam sheeting. Butt the edges and glue the foam with a rubber cement.*

2. Pinch together the parts of the clothing that would be naturally folded or wrinkled—inside elbows, backs of knees, etc. Secure the wrinkles by gluing a piece of fabric tape or webbing several-inches wide over these areas in the interior of the costumes.

3. Make these costumes with front or back openings and sleeveless, with the sleeves as separate units. To the sleeve tops, glue a harness made of wide elastic straps that go across the actor's back and chest, using Velcro strips for attachments. The actor will put the sleeves on last.

4. Inside the armscye of the bodice or shirt, place a piece of curved, hard plastic—like polystyrene sheeting—that will hold the armscye shape around the actor's shoulders.

5. The actor will first put on the sleeve-harness piece and over it the bodice or shirt.

6. A dresser will then fit the sleeves into the sockets and connect the elastic strips together with the Velcro. Inside the bodice or shirt, the Velcro and elastic strips work together to form tension and to swivel between the sleeves.

7. For male characters, pattern the trousers, and cut from polyurethane foam. Glue a zipper along the entire crotch seam—from front waist to back waist—bonding the zipper in place with a rubber cement; again XFX used Krayton. Use Velcro (glued into place) to attach the trousers to the waistband.

8. Spray paint with acrylic paint ⚠, and then coat with polyurethane casting resin ⚠. The polyurethane used for these costumes was especially formulated by BJB Enterprises, Inc. to have a longer working time. XFX added Cab-O-Sil as a thick-

ener, to prevent runs and drips. The polyurethane coating offers protection and flexibility as well as a shiny, smooth, overall "plastic" appearance.

Man About Town

Heat-Transfer Printing

Joey Krebs, performance and conceptual artist in Los Angeles, believes in wearing his politics literally on his sleeve. His self-designed performance suit blends many art styles and represents a new kind of designed lifestyle, une mode de vivre.

Based on styles of the 1950s, Krebs's suit is of white woven polyester fabric, printed by a heat-transfer printing process. The suit was both printed and sewn in Seoul, Korea. Printing was done by the New Light Manufacturing Company. Following is the method:

1. Krebs and his assistant selected photographs of contemporary works of art. They re-photographed these photographs which were processed by a one-hour photo shop into three-by-five-inch prints.

2. The photos were cut out into the desired sizes and shapes and pasted up on eleven-by-seventeen-inch paper. The paste-up sheets were then photographed. Ten copies of each of the pages were printed onto eleven-by-seventeen-inch paper.

3. New Light Manufacturing Company transferred each of the photographs onto an iron-on transfer paper (available at many silk-screen supply shops) with a heat-press (also available at silk-screen shops).

4. This step can also be completed by using an iron set as hot as possible on dry heat without burning the paper. Cover the bottom of the iron with a flat plate to avoid transfer of its holes pattern. Use pressure and hold the iron on each area to be transferred for about twenty seconds. Do not slide the iron.

5. New Light next transferred the transfer-paper image with the use of a heat-transfer press to the uncut piece of polyester yardage.

6. For a costume maker lacking a heat-transfer press, it is possible to use an iron and the same techniques as above. If doing this work with an iron, re-iron the entire surface to set better the printed colors.

Heat-transferred contemporary art works embellish this 100% polyester performance-art suit.
DESIGN: JOEY KREBS. PHOTO: FRAGWURDIG.

⚠ THIS SUBSTANCE OR PROCEDURE MAY BE HAZARDOUS TO HEALTH AND SHOULD BE USED WITH CARE. PLEASE READ THE APPROPRIATE HEALTH AND SAFETY SECTION.

7. After the printing was completed, the suit was sewn at a Seoul tailoring shop. This method is most successful on 100 percent polyester fabric, and somewhat less successful on other synthetic fabric or fabric containing at least a 50 percent blend of polyester. This method is also most favorable on white fabric. The colored inks are invisible on dark fabric and not usually brilliant on pale colors, since the ink is not opaque.

Professor Gizmo

Polyurethane Insulation Foam and Polyethylene Foam Sheetings

Professor Gizmo, from Cincinnati, wears costume and mask by Chip Wickett of Chip's Character Creations, manufactured much as was the Bimbo Bear costume described on earlier pages. Professor Gizmo, portrayed by Paul Adams of Paul Adams Productions in Cincinnati, performs for children in live shows and in TV shows on science and the environment.

The specific materials employed were Minicel L-200 and Scott (substitute with SIF) insulation foam, both especially favored by this shop.

Body

Two types of foam sheeting form the body of this character costume.

DESIGN AND CONSTRUCTION: CHIP'S CHARACTER CREATIONS FOR A PROMOTIONAL COSTUME WORN BY PROFESSOR GIZMO FOR PAUL ADAMS PRODUCTIONS IN CINCINNATI, OHIO. PHOTO: COURTESY OF PAUL ADAMS.

1. Wickett starts his costumes by making patterns for body pieces and heads from one-inch upholstery foam. After the pattern is established, he cuts the actual pieces from one-inch-thick, thirty pounds-per-inch (ppi) reticulated insulation foam. From these foam pieces, he makes pattern pieces that are set aside for cutting out the body fabric and clothing pieces.

2. Wickett bevel-cuts the edges of the actual foam pieces, then spreads adhesive on both surfaces of the one-inch edge, allowing the adhesives to become tacky before pressing together. (Wickett's choice in adhesives is nonhazardous water-based rubber cements.) He reinforces the seams with hand-sewing, and, when necessary, inserts a zippered placket in the neck back.

3. From the muslin pattern, he cuts and sews the fabric for the clothing or body cover. Next, shapes for the unlined and unstructured arms and legs are cut and sewn. An industrial zipper is usually inserted at the back neckline to allow for easy laundering.

Feet

For the shoes, Chip cuts one-inch Minicel L-200 polyethylene foam (from Voltek) to the desired shape and cements the edges together. He lines the interior by gluing in one-inch polyurethane foam. For soles, dense Neoprene foam sheeting is bonded with rubber contact cement.

Head
1. Using upholstery foam, he makes a pattern for a head and hat. He adjusts the pieces to fit, cutting the shape out first from muslin and then from one-inch polyethylene foam, finally bonding the foam pieces together with rubber contact cement.

2. The muslin pattern is used to make the cloth head-covering, leaving open spaces for the ears, eyes, nose, and mouth. The covering is stitched together and fit over the head structure.

3. For Professor Gizmo, one-quarter-inch polyethylene foam was used for hair and whiskers and cemented into place. His eyeglasses are from aluminum sheeting, cut to shape and buffed. The chin is a separate piece of fabricated foam sheet, covered with fabric, and secured by an elastic strap stretched around his ears.

The Riddler

Hologrammed Fabric, LEDs, and Spandex
Designed by Bob Ringwood and manufactured at Warner Brothers, the character of The Riddler from *Batman Forever* goes through a series of personality transformations that necessitate a large number of costume changes. His costumes evolve to match his character, as he metamorphosizes from a weird computer nerd wearing multicolored garb into a bizarre and heartless hooligan wearing bright green and black with an allover design of question-mark motifs. He wears several bodysuits made of Zeta, an especially strong spandex fabric from Germany; other costumes are highly tailored suits. The question marks on all suits are in colors and textures that contrast with the costume fabric and increase the dimensionality of the costumes. These motifs of flocking, glitter, and rhinestones were manufactured by several specialty firms.

For The Riddler's glitter-covered tailored suits, the first step was to make a muslin mock-up of the suit and place it onto a tailoring form. Ringwood then gathered dozens of paper question marks, in a variety of sizes, positioned them onto the suit, and drew the placement of each onto the muslin. The muslin suit was next removed from the form, taken apart, and used for the suit pattern itself as well as for the arrangement of the question marks. Both the tailored suits and the spandex bodysuits were sewn together before the motifs were applied.

Question marks, designed by Ringwood, were cut out with both metal dies and by computers. Several resources created and cut out the special fabrics that were used. Jean Teton Creations, of San Francisco, which makes a wide variety of custom-decorated fabrics and other materials including many in spandex, furnished green hologrammed motifs that imparted a special gleam and depth. A Los Angeles manufacturer contributed question marks of flocking and of glitter, which added more dimension and richness, and also supplied heat-transfer paper cut to the same question-mark shapes. These ready-made cut-outs were pressed onto the costumes using a heat-transfer press—popular among T-shirt decorators and available at many silk-screen supply shops. (This press has a temperature control and imparts more weight and pressure than a regular iron.) The different appliqués were then applied on top of the heat seal paper with the same machine but with varying heat settings to accommodate the various motif materials. Precise timing was an important factor in such an operation.

For the final touch, variegated green rhinestone question marks were heat sealed on top of the already rich pattern, with additional jewels from Jeweltrim in New York which supplies rhinestones ready for heat-setting onto fabrics, dotted throughout. In one of his scenes, The Riddler's lunacy is accentuated by a costume further embellished by flashing light-emitting diodes (LEDs).

For his finale, The Riddler wore a white outfit with an Elvis design, made from spandex covered with hologram glitter and embellished with clear rhinestone jeweled question marks.

When applying motifs to The Riddler's spandex costumes, the costumes were first stretched onto a board cut to the size and shape of the actor. The costume crew created a Teflon-covered, folding, hinged board. The Teflon prevents the board from bonding to the appliqués, and the hinges allow the pattern to insert easily inside a sewn unitard.

Time Lord Of The Future

Latex Sheeting and Latex Liquid ⚠

For a television commercial made for Lamot Lager, Andy Wilkes of Syren, in Los Angeles, built a costume of a latex-sheeting fitted bodysuit and a heavy, ¼-inch gauge, latex enveloping cape for the body-builder who played the role. The bodysuit was made as described later for Catwoman, and the dramatic cape was simply cut as a partial circle. The garments were aged according to the following method:

1. Place the garment on a tailoring form.

2. Fill bottles with pigmented casting latex and check that there is a very small opening in the top of each.

3. Place two or three metal lighting stands next to the garment. Onto each stand, clamp one of the bottles with a "C" clamp. The liquid will slowly empty over the costumes, creating an organic-looking multicolored distressing, suggestive of melting—and in this instance—the melting away of time.

The Valu Kid

The Valu Kid is a promotional walk-around costume made by Chip's creations, using fabrication techniques similar to those for building Professor Gizmo (described above) and the Bimbo Bakery Bear (described on page 348-350).

Inanimate Objects

Bottle

Acrylonitrile-Butadiene ⚠ Styrene (ABS) or Polyethylene Foam Sheeting and Aluminum Strips

This de-greaser bottle was vacuum-formed from ABS, although it could have been easily vacuum-formed from polyethylene foam sheeting.

The advantage of both ABS and polyethylene over insulation foam is that these materials can be heat formed. Using insulation foam will produce a lighter weight costume, more comfortable to wear over a long period of time, but one requiring an inner support system of aluminum strips to strengthen it. Following is the method used to vacuum-form a bottle such as this:

1. Use polyurethane rigid "green" foam to carve an entire bottle form. Cut the foam into pieces that will be of appropriate casting shapes and sizes. Vacuum-form from sheet material, allowing at least a one-inch overlap for adhering by adhesive bonding. (The recommended adhesive for ABS is Weld-on ABS Glue ⚠.)

2. Pop-rivet one-inch metal rings to the interior of the bottle at shoulder level. Attach an adjustable harness to these rings.

3. Fit the foam-plastic bottle, with its attached harness, onto an actor, to determine placement of the eye holes. Draw the holes at this time; then remove the bottle and carefully cut out the holes. Glue appropriate size and color of net inside the eye spaces, using rubber cement ⚠, or hot glue ⚠.

4. Paint the bottle with acrylic paint. To make the graphics, either cut out letters from adhesive-

Polyethylene and polyurethane foams are used to create The Valu Kid walk-around promotional costume.

DESIGN BY CHIP WICKETT FOR THE VALUE KID™, THE MASCOT FOR VALU PLUS FOOD WAREHOUSE AND TOP VALU MARKETS AND REGISTERED UNDER THE K.V. MART CO. PHOTO: CHIP WICKETT.

This walk-around bottle costume is formed from vacuum-formed ABS.

DESIGN AND CONSTRUCTION: SHAFTON, INC. FOR THE SMART AND FINAL IRIS COMPANY. PHOTO: COURTESY OF THE SMART AND FINAL IRIS COMPANY.

⚠ THIS SUBSTANCE OR PROCEDURE MAY BE HAZARDOUS TO HEALTH AND SHOULD BE USED WITH CARE. PLEASE READ THE APPROPRIATE HEALTH AND SAFETY SECTION.

backed vinyl, from vinyl adhered with vinyl cement, or paint through a stencil with either acrylic-paint or lacquer.

A leotard and tights cover the arms and legs.

This bottle was created by Jack Shafton Studios and used in a commercial for Smart and Final Iris Company.

Golf Ball Costume

Polyethylene Foam Sheeting and Flexible White Glue

When she was assigned to create three-and-a-half foot golf ball costumes for dancers to wear in the feature film *Caddyshack II*, Judy Corbett of J & M Costumers Inc. decided to use L-200 polyethylene foam and Phlexglu, building each by the following methods:

1. Using one-inch polyethylene foam sheeting, like Plastazote or L-200, cut twelve circle segments to equal a three-and-a-half-foot diameter sphere.

2. Lop about three inches from the top points in order to end up with a smooth, rounded top. Lop about ten inches from the bottom points to create a twenty-inch diameter leg opening. Butt and glue the edges together with a heavy rubber contact cement ⚠ such as Scotch-Grip 1099. Plug the top opening with a six-inch diameter circle and glue it in place.

3. Make a skullcap of polyurethane one-inch insulation foam, such as Scott Foam, by gluing together two segments and bonding with a contact cement. Cover the cap with cheesecloth brushed with a coat of latex ⚠.

4. Glue the cap to the top of the ball.

5. Get inside the ball to figure out where the arms should protrude and where openings should be placed for the eyes. Make paper patterns for those circles or ovals, place onto form, and cut carefully with scissors.

6. Cut circles of wire screening one inch larger than the eye cutouts. Paint, then bond to inside of ball with cloth and rubber cement.

7. Place a sandpaper disc onto an electric drill to create the golf ball pattern of circles. Sand each circle about a quarter-inch into the foam.

8. Coat the entire ball with Phlexglu for protection and sheen. No need to paint these costumes, for polyethylene foam sheeting is already the correct pale cream color.

Kitchen Utensils, Tableware, and Furnishings

Kydex Acrylic-Polyvinyl Chloride ⚠, Polyurethane Foam Sheeting, Cast Latex Foam ⚠, and Polyurethane-Coated Spandex ⚠

Costume designs for the Broadway production of *Disney's Beauty and the Beast* were an unusual challenge to both designer and craftspersons. Actors portrayed characters who were half-objects and half-people, who transformed into objects and then back again into people. The costumes also needed to reflect the already-popular characters from the animated film. Ann Hould-Ward, who won a Tony for her innovative designs, had six months in which to experiment with prototypes before the usual six or eight weeks needed to build.

Vacuum-forming was done by Nino Novelino at Costume Armour, Inc. in upstate New York. Many of the smaller pieces—like the egg and dart motif on Lumiére and the scrolls on many costumes—were stock pieces found at Costume Armour. The more unusual forms, like sculptural elements of the clock (Kydex with a Mylar lamination), were specially sculpted and formed for this production.

Others who participated in building the original costumes were the Martin Izquierdo Studios (for most painting), Barbara Matera Limited (for beading the Bead-Vac's), La Lame (for custom fabric laminations), John Dodds (prosthetic artist who built parts of headdresses and other special pieces), David Lawrence, (Hair Designer), and Grace Costumes.

Dimensional appliqués from vacuum-formed plastic pieces were selected to link the object parts of a costume to its human parts. As a result, a new technique, "Bead-Vac," was developed. Everybody who is a part of the Beast's household wears costumes decorated by vacuum-formed plastics. These are the steps for creating Bead-Vac:

1. Find or sculpt architectural elements of appropriate size to use as costume decorations. Those for Beauty ranged from about one-by-two inches to three-by-five-inches, with a relief of about one inch. Vacuum-form over them with a thin-gauge lightweight sheet plastic, such as polystyrene.

2. Cut out selected sections from the dimensional vacuum-formed pieces. Design beadwork patterns to blend with the vacuum-formed pieces. Mount the beadwork motifs onto chiffon, and insert them behind the cutouts, bonding them in place with glue. (*Beauty* costume builders alternated between "Green Glue"—3M's Fastbond 30-NF—and Weld-on 10.)

3. The Bead-Vac pieces are then painted with acrylic paint (usually gold) and laden with trimming—braids, rosettes, ribbons, cording, beads, and sequins. Some trimmings are glued onto the painted polystyrene. Others are sewn, and some are both glued and sewn to ensure that the bond survives the heavy dancing.

4. Punch small holes into the edges of the polystyrene forms and sew them either directly onto the costume or onto suede cloth, attaching snaps for easy removability before dry cleaning.

⚠ THIS SUBSTANCE OR PROCEDURE MAY BE HAZARDOUS TO HEALTH AND SHOULD BE USED WITH CARE. PLEASE READ THE APPROPRIATE HEALTH AND SAFETY SECTION.

5. Mingle coordinating motifs made of softer materials with the Bead-Vac to create a unity with the softer parts of the costume. Beading, appliqué, and trapunto were the materials chosen by Hould-Ward.

6. Repeat the same soft embellishments in areas where softness and flexibility are factors. This manner of applying the decorations creates an unbroken flow from the hardness of the object part of the costume to the softness and flexibility of the human actor.

Lumiere

A combination of processes makes up the elegant Lumiere costume. His memorable collar is decorated by vacuum-formed motifs, as well as trapunto, beads, and appliqués. The vacuum-formed egg-and-dart motifs, originally designed as furniture decorations, are cut apart, embellished with gold paint, braids, and Bead-Vac. Golden trapunto, gold beads, and more appliqué radiate around the interior border of his large collar, which is mounted onto a wire-framed leather under-collar. Lumiere's costume parts are carefully designed for laundering and cleaning. The Bead-Vac collar is attached to his vestee; the coat sleeves are part of a jumpsuit that includes the pants. Both sleeves and trousers are decorated with soft decorations that allow for flexibility and mobility. His sleeveless coat is another separate piece. All decorations allow the viewer's eye to move effortlessly from the hard surfaces to the soft areas; the break between hardness and softness is indiscernible.

Vacuum-forming, trapunto, beads, and appliqués decorate a costume worn by Lumiere.

DESIGN: ANN HOULD-WARD FOR
DISNEY'S BEAUTY AND THE BEAST,
ORIGINAL NATIONAL TOURING
COMPANY, 1996.
PHOTO: JOAN MARCUS, ©1996.
PATRICK PAGE AS LUMIERE.

Lumiere's coat sleeve cuffs are sconces—vacuum-formed to hold their shape. A spandex gusset is inserted to offer flexibility. Dripping candle wax, formed from polyurethane foam, completes his hands and blends with the wax-colored hair of his headpiece. The candle-wax headpiece was formed from two-part semi-flexible polyurethane foam by John Dodds in the following manner:

1. Fit the actor in a bald cap. Make a copy, or life cast, of his complete head with alginate. (For information on making life casts, refer to special-effects makeup books listed in the Bibliography and to pages 184-188 of this book.)

2. From the alginate cast, make a positive mold from plaster of Paris.

3. Using the plaster base, sculpt a model of the desired head shape from oil-based clay. To get the effect of the finished image, paint the clay.

4. Make a negative mold over the model from plaster—this may need to be a two-part mold—or sculpt it from silicone ⚠ if it is a complex design with undercuts.

5. Cast the finished piece by first brushing on a thin layer of pigmented casting latex ⚠. When it is thoroughly dry, mix and add pigmented two-part polyurethane foam ⚠.

Dodds worked very closely with David Lawrence, the hair designer. The headpieces were subtly designed blendings of molded polyurethane and actual hairpieces—repeating the constant "blending of the inanimate with the animate." (This phrase was often reiterated by the designer.)

Lumiere's boots are also vacuum-formed, thus retaining visual unity with the rest of his costume.

1. Form a model and make a mold.

2. Using Kydex, vacuum-form a whole boot, one half at a time—front and back. The boots are soleless, like spats. Bond the front and back pieces together. (See the Acrylic-Polyvinyl Chloride section on pages 272-274 for information on adhesives that bond Kydex.)

3. Next, cut the boots horizontally into two pieces at ankle-level. Insert spandex pieces in between the two parts, as hinges, affording the actor movement.

4. Drill two holes to match up with shoe-lace ties, and tie a shoe inside of each "boot."

5. Drill four pairs of holes just above calf level. Sew elastic straps from these holes to a ring of elastic that fits the actor's calf.

Armoire

The costume for Armoire was shaped over a welded metal frame, creating the armature for its actual furniture shape. The remainder of the process is as follows:

1. Build models and then molds for the front doors that actually open and close. Vacuum-form them in Kydex.

2. Build a model and a mold for the panel of drawer units. Mold them from quarter-inch, low-temperature-setting thermo-

Kydex acrylic-polyvinyl chloride, supported by a welded metal frame, is used to create the realistic furniture-shape of Armoire's costume.

DESIGN: ANN HOULD-WARD FOR DISNEY'S BEAUTY AND THE BEAST, ORIGINAL NATIONAL TOURING COMPANY, 1996. PHOTO: JOAN MARCUS, ©1996. MARY STOUT AS ARMOIRE.

⚠ THIS SUBSTANCE OR PROCEDURE MAY BE HAZARDOUS TO HEALTH AND SHOULD BE USED WITH CARE. PLEASE READ THE APPROPRIATE HEALTH AND SAFETY SECTION.

plastic sheeting. This thermoplastic material is easily formed with a hot-air gun or hot water.

3. Build the one drawer that actually opens with the same plastic sheeting supported by a metal frame.

4. Use fabric to create the sides, back, and bottoms of the costume. This allows the actress mobility and comfort. Hang a small Austrian drape cape from the back of her shoulders.

5. Vacuum-form wardrobe legs.

6. Embellish her costume with Bead-Vac and soft appliqués as well as with golden Mylar-coated molding.

7. Paint and airbrush to enhance decorations and dimensionality.

8. For her wig, use a combination of real hair, cast polyurethane-foam prosthetic pieces, and Bead-Vac.

Cogsworth

Cogsworth the clock is bedecked as a grandfather clock of half molded plastic, and half fabric. The front timepiece is of thick molded vinyl and the winder key of rigid Kydex, while the remainder of his period costume is in rich harmonizing fabrics. Transparent vinyl forms the door, while the opaque plastic sheeting shapes the body of the clock box. A long, plastic pendulum hangs inside. A vacuum-formed molding strip edges the timepiece. On his back sits a winder key, attached to a backpack. Use a low-temperature-setting thermoplastic material, like quarter-inch Protoplast, so the shop personnel can mold the actual backpack material directly onto the actor. After molding, the backpack piece is completed by the following method:

Half molded plastics—vinyls and Kydex acrylic-polyvinyl chloride—and half fabrics make up Cogsworth's grandfather-clock costume. A low-temperature-setting thermoplastic forms his hidden backpack.

DESIGN: ANN HOULD-WARD FOR *DISNEY'S BEAUTY AND THE BEAST*, ORIGINAL NATIONAL TOURING COMPANY, 1996. PHOTO: JOAN MARCUS, ©1996. JEFF BROOKS AS COGSWORTH.

1. Trim the edges of the backpack.

2. Make straps with one-inch heavy webbing.

3. Cover backpack and straps with flesh-colored fabric. Attach a seat-belt buckle to the ends of the straps.

4. Make a five-sided aluminum box, and bolt it in place to the back piece.

5. Bolt the Kydex winder to the back of the aluminum box.

Cogsworth's headpieces are a combination of wig and cast polyurethane, painted with acrylic paint and decorated with Bead-Vac and soft embellishments.

Fork

Fork wears a molded backpack underneath his tailcoat. Several of the dancers in this scene, like Spoon and Cake-Server wear such backpacks. After the backpack is completed, an aluminum box, about four-inches square is attached, midback, to hold an oversize silvery fork, vacuum-formed and covered with Mylar film. On his lower body, Fork's coordinating unitard is decorated with embellishments of trapunto and appliqué, which coordinate with his coat and vest, while remaining soft for easier laundering and comfort. Coattails are wired to hold their crisp shape. The costume is built for quick changes, for the dancers in this scene play several roles.

Egg Beater

Shaping for Egg Beater is created with polyurethane and polyethylene foam. Formed over wire frames, the foam forms the mass, the handle, and the large gear. The actual beater shapes resemble paning from Elizabethan trunk hose. Dense polyethylene foam (like Voltek's Minicel L-200) forms the shaping inside for the fabric-covered beaters. Trapunto and Bead-Vac decorate the various parts of his costume as well.

Measuring Spoons

Measuring Spoons are vacuum-formed. They are put onto wire handles that are covered with fabric with trapuntoed hearts. These costumes are further examples of hard shapes that blend into softer structures. The bowl of the largest of the spoons becomes the dancer's headpiece and the spoon surrounds his head and leaves an opening for his face.

Mrs. Potts, Chip, and The Sugar Bowl

The major forms of the costumes of Mrs. Potts and the Sugar Bowl are shaped by metal hooping. The outer porcelainlike surface of their costume as well as Chip's cup-hat is of custom-made fabric from La Lame, a New York City fabric converter. La Lame in New York City is a jobber that custom-coats fabrics and trimmings in addition to being the world's major supplier of ecclesiastic fabrics and trimmings. The fabric is white nylon spandex covered with a thin coating of clear polyurethane foam. The silvery white porcelainlike surface is enhanced at the

Polyurethane-coated nylon spandex, shaped by metal hooping, forms Mrs. Potts' teapot costume. Airbrushed French enamel varnish heightens the porcelain finish.

DESIGN: ANN HOULD-WARD FOR *DISNEY'S BEAUTY AND THE BEAST*, ORIGINAL NATIONAL TOURING COMPANY, 1996. PHOTO: JOAN MARCUS, ©1996. BETSY JOSLYN AS MRS. POTTS.

Martin Izquierdo Studios by judiciously airbrushed French enamel varnish (leather dye and shellac ⚠, on page 152).

Plates

The set of Busby Berkeley Dinner Plates was based on a welded wire structure, covered by dense polyurethane foam, then covered in clear, *polyurethane-coated*, white *spandex*. Embellishments by painter Hochi Asiatico, of Martin Izquierdo Studios, included a metallic holographic heat-transfer foil from Manoukian. To apply the foil, silk-screen the design onto the fabric, with the Manoukian brand adhesive. Use a heat-press machine to apply the foil to the screened areas.

Egg Timer

Egg Timer's costume was basically a vacuum-formed structure. Costume Armour, Inc. sculpted, then cast, the timer shape from clear vinyl. Added dimensional trimming was created from strips of vacuum-formed, gilt-covered sheeting that was bent by a heat gun and glued to the costume.

Napkin Rings

The Napkin Rings' helmets are from molded low-temperature-setting thermoplastic sheeting covered by La Lame fabric. Both are airbrushed with French enamel varnish. Their can-can skirts are of multicolored fabrics.

Piece Of Pizza

Aluminum, Polyethylene Foam, and Latex

When an animated pizza slice was needed for a TV commercial, Judy Corbett, of J & M Costumers, Inc., employed the following process:

A piece-of-pizza costume fabricated from polyethylene foam is supported by an aluminum harness. Upholstery foam, cotton batting, liquid latex, and acrylic compose the toppings.

1. To create the harness, build a fitted, curved aluminum frame to fit over the wearer's shoulders. Attach to it an automobile seat belt that will fit around the chest.

2. To pad the harness frame, glue, with rubber cement ⚠, to a layer of one-inch polyethylene foam. (Corbett uses Voltek's Minicel L-200 and 3M's 826 adhesive.)

3. Cut out two pizza-shaped wedges from the foam.

4. On one piece of foam, cut out holes for the wearer's face and arms. Locate the wearer's head position, and cut an oval that will fit tightly around his face. Now find the elbow level, and cut out two circles large enough to allow some movement for his arms.

5. For the piece of foam which is to be the top of the pizza, cut out some forms from scraps of foam resembling various pizza toppings, like green pepper, olive, and onion slices.

6. Take some cotton batting and soak it in a bowl of liquid latex ⚠, to make the melted cheese.

7. Make an arrangement of the cheese and the other toppings, and then paint with the appropriate colors of acrylic paint.

8. Paint the other piece of foam a light brown "crusty" color, using an acrylic paint. This will be the bottom crust.

9. Glue the edges of the pizza slice together.

10. Determine where the actor's shoulders will be located, and glue the inside of the costume to the foam strap that was placed on top of the aluminum frame. It may be necessary to get inside of the costume for part of this process.

Train Engine

Kydex, Mylar, Spandex, and Iron-On Sequins

For the Broadway production of *Starlight Express*, costumes were made in New York at both Parsons-Meares, Ltd. costume shop and Costume Armour Incorporated. The unitards, appliquéd with iron-on sequins, were partially covered with mechanical-looking train pieces of Kydex acrylic-polyvinyl chloride, Mylar polyester sheet, *spandex*, and tricot.

Leotard

For the character of Joule, John Napier designed a black unitard, especially constructed and fitted to the actress with an under-bust seam. Iron-on sequins were applied to impart a metallic glow to the area above the seam as well as to the uncovered sleeve portions.

Accessories

1. The breast pieces, looking like train wheels, were both spokes and circles of one-inch-high density polyurethane insulation foam. The foam was covered by nylon tricot bonded into place with liquid latex ⚠. To metallize the surface, the tricot was first primed with rubber contact ⚠ cement and then painted with silver acrylic paint.

2. Shaped shoulder pieces were cut out of polyurethane insulation foam. Each was cut in half vertically for mobility, then covered with tricot, adhered with liquid latex, and metallized in the same manner as the wheels.

3. Leather knee pads were covered with clear Kydex and vacuum-formed ⚠ into clear plastic knee-pad shapes. These covers protected the leather but were replaced by new ones every four weeks when they became worn out from the acrobatic stage action.

4. Cast-latex elbow guards were covered in the painted tricot.

5. Leg pieces were shaped from polyethylene foam sheeting (like L-200 sheeting) and covered with shiny vinyl sheeting.

⚠ THIS SUBSTANCE OR PROCEDURE MAY BE HAZARDOUS TO HEALTH AND SHOULD BE USED WITH CARE. PLEASE READ THE APPROPRIATE HEALTH AND SAFETY SECTION.

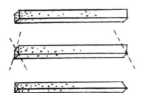

To create "gears," cut four-sided foam strips into three-sided strips.

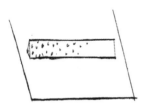

Place the strips, one by one, on the long rectangle of black sequin-covered spandex, leaving enough extra spandex at each end for seam allowance.

With a free-arm sewing machine, stitch the spandex around each foam strip.

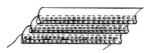

Allow about one-and-a-half inches between each strip.

Sew the strips together into a circle to appear as gears.

PROCESS: COURTESY OF PARSONS-MEARES LTD.

6. Belts were an important part of all of the costumes in this production—with most hidden underneath the leotards. Since skaters linked together, strong belt "handles" on the back of the waist were constructed of leather-covered clothesline rope.

7. Gears, encircling both lower arms and legs, were made of spandex covering polyurethane insulation foam. The foam had been cut into strips of about one inch each to fit loosely around the arms and legs. At this point, the foam naturally had four sides; however, the four-sided foam strips were carefully cut into three-sided strips. With three sides they became more flexible in movement. The cut strips were then placed onto a long rectangle of black spandex previously striped by iron-on sequins. Each foam strip was wrapped by the spandex with a sequin stripe, carefully lined up to its outer surface. The wrapping was stitched with a free-arm sewing machine; a space of about one-and-a-half inches was skipped, and the next strip was wrapped and then stitched into place. The open ends were sewn together to allow each ring to circle the wearer's limbs, appearing to the audience like actual metal machine gears.

All of the materials for costumes in this production were carefully chosen to withstand nightly laundering and to last for years.

Robots

Robot for Honey Nut Cheerios

Polyethylene Foam Sheeting and Plated Jersey

Body

For a Honey Nut Cheerios commercial, Ted Shell, built this metallic-looking robot according to the following method:

1. First construct a box frame from a half-inch aluminum window-screen framing by cutting the framing strips to size and bolting them together. Add two more strips across the top, positioning them to align with the centers of the wearer's shoulders.

2. Attach a harness by suspending it from the aluminum bars across the top of the box frame with bolts. Premade harnessing can be found on sturdy backpacks and on marching-band drums.

3. To create the metal box sides, cut one-inch-thick sheets of L-200 or other polyethylene foam to fit each side of the box. Cut plated jersey pieces of the same dimensions plus an extra six inches: One inch will cover the thickness of the foam, and

two inches will be turned up inside the box. Spray a rubber cement ⚠, like 3M Super 77 Spray Adhesive, thoroughly over the foam. With two people working together, pull the jersey smoothly over each piece of foam. Work should be performed quickly before the adhesive dries.

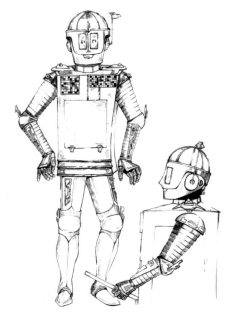

Polystyrene sheet, ventilation tubing, and found items create this robot.

DESIGN AND DRAWING: TED SHELL FOR A HONEY NUT CHEERIOS COMMERCIAL.

Sleeves

1. For the sleeves, first make a pattern shaped to fit the arm. From this pattern, make a new pattern two inches wider and elongate by four inches.

2. Cut the paper pattern into one-and-a-half-inch strips, and, using the strips as patterns, cut strips of the foam sheet. Curve each into a ring, butt the ends together, and glue with a shoemaker's rubber cement ⚠, like Barge.

3. Cover each ring with silver-plated jersey, which is adhered with the sprayed rubber cement.

4. Cover each again with one-inch silver Mylar tape, glued in place. There should be one-eighth inch of jersey left showing at the borders. Use four strips of one-inch elastic to connect the insides of the rings to form a long tubelike sleeve. There should be no spaces remaining between these rings.

Headdress

For the headdress, make an under-helmet from insulation foam laminated with rubber cement. Sculpt a helmet shape from an oil-based plasticine clay, and vacuum-form it from silver Kydex. Premade harnessing can be found on sturdy backpacks and on marching-band drums.

Decorations

To decorate the robot with mechanical parts, find electronic-type panels in toy stores, such as those made for outer space toys. These toys can light up, enhancing the realism of the robot.

Robot for Anheuser-Busch

Polyurethane ⚠, Polyurethane Foam ⚠, and Spandex

This sleek robot costume for Anheuser-Busch's King Cobra Malt Liquor needed to be flexible enough for the actor wearing it to do break dancing, yet strong enough to be worn throughout the filming of a TV commercial and one month of public appearances. To attain the necessary flexibility and strength, Makeup & Effects Laboratories (MEL) worked with reinforced solid flexible-polyurethane foam (Polytech ST 40) and self-skinning polyurethane foam. Following was their manufacturing method:

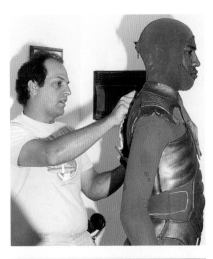

The solid polyurethane armor pieces are fit over a spandex bodysuit.

DESIGN: MAKEUP & EFFECTS LAB INC. PHOTO: COURTESY OF ANHEUSER-BUSCH COMPANIES, INC.

Cast polyurethane and polyurethane foam, built over a full-body cast, are covered by spandex for this Robot costume.

DESIGN: MAKEUP & EFFECTS LAB INC. PHOTO: COURTESY OF ANHEUSER-BUSCH COMPANIES, INC.

1. A body cast of the performer was taken, using plaster bandages. From the interior of the body cast, MEL made an epoxy resin and fiberglass mold.

2. This body cast was then used as the base onto which the sculptor built up the clay model of the costume design.

3. Molds were made—epoxy resin ⚠ reinforced with fiberglass was used for most mold pieces, while silicone was used for the more complex pieces with undercuts.

4. Before casting, the mold makers powdered the mold pieces with bronzing powder and added gray pigment to the polyurethane. They then cut out spandex pieces the size plus at least a half inch of each mold piece. These were added to the molds for reinforcement and later use as attachments to the bodysuit.

5. Thin and more flexible costume pieces were cast in solid flexible polyurethane and the thicker, more solid pieces were of self-skinning polyurethane foam. After casting, the spandex border was trimmed to a one-half-inch overlap.

6. A spandex bodysuit was made to fit the performer. The body-covering pieces were attached to the suit using the spandex overlap for sewing. Other costume parts were attached with liquid polyurethane resin.

After construction was complete, a shiny, metallic look was created by oiling all pieces with silicone. Then, to complete the robot effect, the costume was decorated with electronic gadgets and small pieces of plastic-covered wire.

Robot for Alamo Rent A Car

Polystyrene Sheeting, Ventilation Tubing, and Found Items

This robot was made for an Alamo Rent A Car, Inc. commercial and created at Make-up & Effects Laboratories, Inc. in Hollywood. Because MEL had only a few days' notice, the costume was put together quickly with readily available materials and worn over a partial wet suit. Following is the method used:

1. First, select accordion-type ventilation tubing of eight-inch diameter, or of a diameter large enough to fit the actor closely, and cut it to the length of the actor's arms and legs.

2. Find leftover molds and objects with an interesting mechanical or robotlike appearance to use as molds for forming the robot's body. Vacuum-form polystyrene sheeting ⚠ over these molds.

3. Select wires and electronic objects from an electronic surplus store.

4. Drill holes in the molded polystyrene pieces and wire them together with multiple wires. Allow the wires to remain visible, to add to the mechanical quality. Attach the cut-ventilation tubing to the polystyrene both by sewing it through the drilled holes and bonding with rubber contact cement ⚠. (Barge was used in this case.)

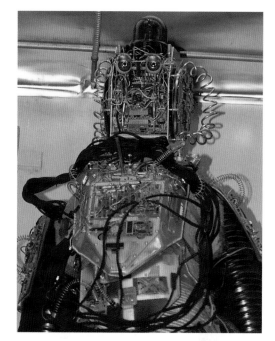

Found objects, such as ventilation tubing, wire, and spare electronic parts are used to create this Robot.

DESIGN AND PHOTO: MAKEUP & EFFECTS LAB INC. FOR ALAMO CAR RENTAL COMMERCIAL.

5. Vacuum-form a polystyrene helmet piece from found objects, as with the body parts. Attach a large piece of accordion tubing to the bottom of the helmet, and stabilize the bottom edge by superglueing ⚠ to it a large metal ring.

6. Decorate all parts with the surplus electronic pieces, and paint as desired.

Space Suits

G.I. Joe

Acrylic, Low-Temperature-Setting Thermoplastic Sheeting, and Vinyl Floor Mat

Astronauts' suits for a G.I. Joe toy commercial incorporated black-spandex unitards for body covering, allowing the headdress and accessories to create the robot appearance. Though each suit was designed differently, the following method was employed to create the suit pictured.

Helmets

The helmet was constructed from a cleverly assembled variety of materials.

1. Use a purchased clear-acrylic hemisphere (available from most retail plastic supply stores) for the front part of the helmet. Cut to desired size, cover the upper two thirds with gray stretch fabric, and cut and shape a piece of vinyl-plastic window screening to form the bottom see-through section. Glue in place with M Scotch-Grip 847 (brown glue ⚠).

⚠ THIS SUBSTANCE OR PROCEDURE MAY BE HAZARDOUS TO HEALTH AND SHOULD BE USED WITH CARE. PLEASE READ THE APPROPRIATE HEALTH AND SAFETY SECTION.

2. Create a positive mold for the back form of helmet out of plasticine clay. Shape a sheet of low-temperature-setting thermoplastic sheeting (in this case, it was Veriform from UnNatural Resources) over the clay mold and paint it.

3. Rivet the two parts together.

4. For the brown piping separating both the front and back sections, slice a one-inch-diameter Ethafoam polyethylene rod in half and cover one half with leather. For the brown strip over the back section, cut and fold another piece of leather, holding it in place with shoemakers' cement ⚠ (like Barge). Glue both strips onto the helmet itself with Scotch-Grip 847.

5. To hold the helmet on the head, use a welding mask. Cut off the face shields from the welding mask, leaving the adjustable headband section.

6. Rivet the adjustable headband section to the interior of the helmet. This will allow it to fit different head sizes.

7. Decorate the helmet with black-rubber electrical cable and parts taken from mechanical toys.

Body Garments

1. The body of the costume is decorated with a variety of plastic and other found objects, which are held in place by either rivets or adhesives.

2. Shoulder guards are roller-blading knee protectors, covered with knit fabric and piped with the leather-covered ethafoam.

3. For the large collar, form low-temperature-setting thermoplastic sheeting over a clay mold, or find an object, like a large salad bowl, for a positive mold.

4. Use black-ribbed, vinyl-sheeting car-floor mats to form the front body covering.

5. Other robotic decorations and accessories used in this group of costumes are aluminum-window-screen framing, vacuum-cleaner hoses and cords, a variety of electrical cords, pieces of toy guns, and other mechanical toy pieces.

These costumes were designed by Mariann Verheyen and constructed at the Martin Izquierdo Costume Shop in New York. Their favorite adhesives are Barge, 3M Scotch-Grip 847 (brown glue), Bridal Adhesive ⚠ from Manny's Millinery, and 3M Jet Melt hot-glue sticks ⚠ numbers 3747 and 3792 (preferred for short-term bonding of metal pieces).

Space Suit for Hasbro Toys

Acrylonitrile-Butadiene Styrene (ABS) and Spandex

Impressive "Transformer" costumes for Hasbro Toys were made at Prop Master Studios, the premier vacuum-forming shop for costumers and prop makers in Los Angeles. Prop Master used the following method:

Body Armor

1. Sculpt the costume shapes from "green" polyurethane rigid foam. The fronts and backs of the pieces should be cut separately. Allow for approximately one-quarter-

inch overlap with which to adhere the segments to one another. Cut them into segments to fit into the vacuum-former.

2. Place the segments into the vacuum-former and cast sheet plastic, like polystyrene ⚠, over them. After casting, scrape and dig out the polyurethane foam until the cast plastic is completely clean.

3. Using these cast-plastic pieces as negative molds, lay up polyester resin ⚠ and fiberglass inside these molds. The polyester resin and fiberglass will form new positive molds over which many duplicates can be vacuum-formed.

4. Vacuum-form ABS sheeting over the fiberglass forms. Prop Master Studios used .090 to .125 mil depending upon the depth of draw of each piece. ABS is available in several colors, though it is also successfully painted with automotive paint, after priming with automotive primer.

Materials for this space suit include acrylic, low-temperature-setting thermoplastic sheeting, and floor matting.

5. Bond parts together with Weld-on #16, or Weld-on's ABS adhesives ⚠, and sand with fine-grit sandpaper for a smooth surface.

6. Use sturdy hooks to attach the arm pieces to the body pieces and corresponding rings to attach the arm pieces to one another. The actor will get into the body costume, and the arms will then be hooked on.

Back Wing Pieces Construct the wings in the same manner as the body armor, then mount them onto an aluminum shoulder harness. Premade harnessing can be found on sturdy backpacks and on marching-band drums. The harness is attached to the actor's body by automobile seat-belt buckles—one part of the buckle on the shoulder harness, and the other part on the back of the plastic armor suit.

Legs and Arms Make sleeves and trousers of silver spandex, and pipe them at every inch. The piping creates an accordion tube that allows enough give to fit actors of different sizes. The piping also enhances the overall mechanical appearance.

Helmet-Mask 1. Form helmets and masks as one-piece units in the same manner as the body. Sculpt them from green foam (rigid polyurethane foam), create a mold from polyester and fiberglass, and then cast the actual piece in ABS.

2. Line the helmets with hard-hat liners. Cut the liners apart and rivet to the helmets. Use a material like low-temperature-setting thermoplastic sheeting to make additional headband and straps to keep the helmet liners in place.

Boots

1. Use the same technique given for the helmet-mask to sculpt and form the boots. Cut out chloroprene rubber (Neoprene) soles and bond them in place with an ABS adhesive or Weld-on #16. They should be roomy enough for the actor to wear sneakers inside.

2. Make one-inch elastic suspenders and attach one end to the boot tops and the other to a waistband.

Accessories

Goggles are like ski goggles, made from transparent smoked acrylic.

Gloves are vinyl ski gloves.

These costumes, weighing one hundred pounds each, are worn by robust six-foot-two actors.

Space Suit for *Running Man*

Butyrate, Vinyl, and Light-Emitting Diodes (LEDs)

For a spaceman costume for the film *Running Man*, Henry Bagdasarian, founder of Prop Master Studios in Los Angeles, devised a cast-plastic costume for the design by Robert Blackman, then decorated it with eight-hundred light-emitting diodes (LEDs), creating a powerful otherworldly look. Below is his technique:

Body Armor

1. With plaster bandages, take a body cast of the actor. (See pages 187-188 for instructions in making a body cast.)

2. Use the interior of this plaster cast to make a polyester resin ⚠ and fiberglass positive mold. Clean out well and then cut away an inch at the shoulder and side edges

3. Place the cast polyester and fiberglass piece into a vacuum-former and form clear butyrate plastic ⚠ sheeting on top of it.

4. Cut four strips of spandex fabric to the size of the shoulder length by one inch plus allowances for turn-unders. Sew heavy-duty zippers to join each pair of spandex strips. Bond these fabric strips to the shoulders with a rubber contact cement ⚠. (Barge was used for *Running Man*.) Repeat this same process for the side edges of the armor.

5. Decorate the armor with LEDs by drilling holes just large enough to insert the LEDs, around the edges of each armor piece. Bond the LED strips to the underside of the armor pieces with rubber contact cement. In *Running Man*, eight-hundred lights, attached to a hidden battery pack, embellished this costume.

Arms and Legs

The arms are covered with vinyl tubes, which are hinged with a series of one-inch spandex strips at the joints. The spandex is piped every inch with upholstery vinyl, forming accordion pleats that enhance the otherwordly look while ensuring flexibility in arm movement.

Helmet

The helmet is also of clear butyrate vacuum-formed over a positive mold of fiberglass and polyester resin.

Superheroes and Antiheroes
Batman

Foamed Latex ⚠ and Spandex-Backed Neoprene

Bob Ringwood, costume designer for the first three *Batman* films made in 1989 and in the 1990s, who also designed for *Dune*, *The Draughtsman's Contract*, *Excalibur*, and many other imaginative films, created the magical costumes for *Batman Forever*. Ringwood, who knows materials well, oversaw the costume construction in a newly built shop near Warner Brothers Studios in Burbank, California. The process for making Batman's costumes was so complex and exacting that it required the hiring of expert specialists and a master mold maker from England. Along with building thirty doubles (identical) costumes for Batman, seven stuntmen each required their own specially fitted costumes. The following is a synopsis of the process that was used.

Body Armor

1. Form life casts of both head and body. Use alginate to cast a mold of the head, and use plaster bandages for the body. Actors were cast from head to toe, with one half a body cast created at a time—the front, and then the back.

2. Cast an oil-based clay body from this model. When the clay sculpture is complete, reduce it about one standard size by carving away the clay, so the costumes will fit tightly over the actor's body.

3. Over the clay model, form an interior mold of silicone rubber ⚠, and over that, a supporting shell of plaster.

4. From the silicone mold, supported by the plaster shell, make the master positive mold from cast epoxy resin ⚠ and fiberglass. Finish it with an auto-body finish, so that molds made from it will be as smooth as metal and the final costume pieces will have a metallic sheen. For *Batman Forever*, this stage of work was performed by a masterful auto-body specialist. His technique was to use several coats of automobile paints, polishing and sanding after each coat of paint with both wet and dry sandpaper.

5. From this master, both a negative mold and a positive core mold are made from resin reinforced with fiberglass. The core mold is of the same shape and size as the actor and made of multiple pieces that are assembled and then bolted together. The inner negative mold of silicone rubber, shaped like the actual costume piece, surrounded by a shell of polyester resin and fiberglass, keeps the outer surface of the costume smooth.

6. Cut a sprue (injection hole) into the top of the mold. The mold is then ready to use.

7. Next make a "core sock," or shaped nylon spandex reinforcement, the shape of the interior mold. Place it very carefully around the inner core before molding. This piece of spandex fabric strengthens the latex costume pieces, which would otherwise tear. Because the core sock is thin and porous, it becomes embedded in the latex foam.

⚠ THIS SUBSTANCE OR PROCEDURE MAY BE HAZARDOUS TO HEALTH AND SHOULD BE USED WITH CARE. PLEASE READ THE APPROPRIATE HEALTH AND SAFETY SECTION.

8. The inner-core pieces are assembled, covered by the core sock. For certain body areas like the head, it is disassembled to fit through the opening of the negative mold. The core mold is then reassembled, and it must be bolted perfectly in order to achieve a wearable costume. Since in some parts of the helmets, the difference between the inside and outside of the mold was only one-sixteenth inch, correct alignment of mold pieces was mandatory. Because of a need for such perfection, the success rate was much less than 100 percent.

9. At this point, the mold is readied for casting. The dense black pigmented latex foam ⚠ is injected through the sprue with a large syringe into the space between the core and the silicone mold.

10. All the pieces are placed inside an oven and baked. Next, they are air-dried, a process lasting about two weeks (depending upon the weather and humidity). Air-drying is preferable to oven-drying, since more time in the oven causes more shrinkage. After drying, the costume parts are rubbed with silicone wax to lend a high-gloss surface. (The cast-latex pieces shrink over time, and after a few months will no longer fit.)

11. The cast-latex armor shapes are now ready to apply over the undersuit, a unitard of spandex-backed Neoprene. To prepare for this step, first glue ⚠ lines of cord onto the fiberglass mannequin of the actor's body. The lines follow the edges of the armor pieces. The undersuit of fitted, spandex-backed black Neoprene is placed on the mannequin of the actor's body, and, by feeling the cord underneath, the costume makers locate the body parts that are soon covered by the costume. Then the armor pieces are glued correctly.

⚠ THIS SUBSTANCE OR PROCEDURE MAY BE HAZARDOUS TO HEALTH AND SHOULD BE USED WITH CARE. PLEASE READ THE APPROPRIATE HEALTH AND SAFETY SECTION.

12. For any pieces that are to be painted, use Skin-Flex or polyurethane paint ⚠. To bond Neoprene to the core sock, use a type A-prosthetic adhesive manufactured for bonding medical prosthetics. In *Batman Forever*, the adhesive held its bond even during scenes filmed under the salt water of the Pacific Ocean. For bonding latex to itself, the adhesive of choice was Pros-Aide prosthetic adhesive.

13. The finished costumes need no openings and no seams, and thus they look quite magical. All pieces stretch enough for actors to slip them on.

14. The breastplates have inserted metal plates for attaching the cape and insignia.

Accessories
1. The insignia, belt, and front lacing are cast of a semiflexible polyurethane ⚠. The coloring is from metallic powder that is brushed into the silicone mold before casting.

2. Gloves are of leather, each one made from about three-dozen separate pieces, and sewn by glove makers.

Cape
Batman's capes are of a latex-coated fabric, matching the texture of his armor. Both the latex and the type of fabrics were chosen to impart the proper weight and movement for specific scenes. For Batman, some capes were made from latex alone ⚠, some of a fine-worsted satin-faced wool embedded into the latex, and others

of a thin black silk and latex. The materials of the cape were designed to suit the demands of the appropriate movement, the wool and latex cape enhancing the most regal moves, while the lighter weight silk lent it floating quality.

The fabrics were laminated on a specially built circular table designed by Ringwood.

1. First, build a table to be approximately seven-eighths of a circle, the same pattern as the finished design of the capes.

2. Cover the table's surface with a heavy hide-grained upholstery vinyl and cut it into segments that are the same pattern as the finished design of the capes. For Batman's capes, the design is composed of triangles. Between each triangle is a shallow crevice of an eighth inch, serving as the molds to form the spine-like ridges on the back of the bat cape.

3. To make a cape, spray black latex through a paint sprayer onto this vinyl- covered table. Allow drying time between spraying, and spray until the latex seems of the correct thickness.

4. After completing the spraying, lay fabric carefully onto the latex.

For Robin's cape, a different method was employed. Nylon spandex fabric was coated with polyurethane by Gem Urethane Co. in New York. The fabric was then cut into gores, and the seams overlapped and sewn together with a close zigzag stitch.

Batman Costume for TV Commercial

Veriform, Latex Sheeting, and Polyurethane Upholstery Foam

This Batman costume outfitted an actor in a commercial for Batman toys made by Hasbro, Inc. The actual suit was constructed from spandex, and the accessories were fashioned at Martin Izquierdo Studios from a variety of materials.

Gauntlets

1. The gauntlets were made of Veriform (UnNatural Resources) low-temperature-setting thermoplastic sheet, molded over the plasticine-thickened arms of a store-window mannequin. Claire Springer, who did this work, first protected the mannequin arms and hands with plastic film. She then covered them with oil-based clay sculpted into gauntlet shapes. Veriform was heated, then formed over these clay gauntlets. (See the Low-Temperature-Setting Thermoplastic Sheetings section on pages 276-279.)

2. Next, winglike projections made from balsa wood were bonded to the Veriform gauntlet shapes with strips of Veriform. The edges were finished off with one-half-inch Ethafoam that was sliced in half.

3. A priming coat of flexible Pros-Aide makeup adhesive was brushed onto all parts, which were then painted with acrylic paint. Polyurethane foam rectangles were Veriform-taped to the gauntlets' interiors for a close fit.

Cape

Batman's cape is of dark-gray thin latex sheeting, which offers both stretch and translucence. The unique collar-hood is made of chloroprene rubber, or Neoprene, which is formed over an aluminum frame.

Hood   The hood was slip cast in a two-part plaster mold from liquid latex ⚠ hardened with an additive (Cementex Latex L-200 with #64 Filler). The hood was then coated with Pros-Aide for a primer and painted with acrylic paint.

Belt   The one-inch-thick belt was formed of semirigid sheet foam and covered by vinyl fabric bonded in place with 3M Scotch-Grip 847. The belt was then hand-sewn for additional stability.

Boots   The boots were based on soft black shoes that were heightened by tightly fitting spandex extensions.

Mighty Morphin Power Rangers

Vinyl-Coated Spandex, Cast Polyurethane ⚠, and Polyurethane Upholstery Foam   The heroes' costumes for the feature film *The Mighty Morphin Power Rangers* were designed by Joseph Porro and constructed at Sticks and Stones in Pacoima, California. These space suits consist of two layers of clothing, both from vinyl-coated spandex—a product of GEM Industries—and are each in a different strong color: yellow, blue, red, black, white, and shocking pink. The first five colors were available, but shocking pink was custom-colored by the fabric manufacturer, and then custom-sprayed ⚠ at Sticks and Stones with a coating of Createx Paint.

The armor pieces are of cast Fast Flex, a polyurethane elastomer from Burman Industries, with accessories mainly of the spandex quilted over polyurethane upholstery foam. Rob Burman, owner of Sticks and Stones, prefers working in polyurethanes and finds Fast Flex brand particularly suited for costume work that must maintain sharp, clean edges. This is the method he followed:

Body Armor   1. Make an under-suit, or unitard, from vinyl-coated spandex.

2. Sculpt armor pieces in plasticine clay on a fiberglass body form (Burman chooses Roma Plastilena clay). Cut the clay-covered form apart into the appropriate individual parts. From these pieces of clay armor, create negative molds from polyester ⚠ and fiberglass by applying the pieces in several layers on top of the armor sculpture. After the new polyester and fiberglass molds are set, use their interiors to cast the polyurethane elastomer. (Be sure to have complete instructions on these techniques from manufacturers of the materials.)

3. When the polyurethane pieces are set, lay on a thin layer of Fast Flex polyurethane. While the polyurethane is still wet, cover them with the vinyl coated spandex. Place them individually into vacuum bags, which suck out the air and hold the pieces together while the polyurethane bonds the spandex to the cast-armor pieces. A vacuum bag is an airtight flexible vinyl bag. It is connected to tubing that is hooked to a vacuum pump (unlike a vacuum cleaner). The pump pulls the air from the bag, causing the interior items—in this case, the vinyl-covered spandex sheeting and the polyurethane armor—to join. This technique is similar to shrink-wrapping. The vacuum pressure causes the fabric to stretch evenly over the poly-

urethane, while displaying every detail of each sculptured curve—the finished look is that of a single piece of plastic armor.

Special Accessories

1. Make knee guards from the same spandex quilted to one-half-inch-thick polyurethane upholstery foam.

2. Gauntlets are custom-made motorcycle gloves, while their long cuffs are made from the same vinyl as the suits. Boots were custom-crafted. For the Mighty Morphin characters, Nike constructed the custom boots. Sticks and Stones painted them afterwards with Createx Paint.

3. Metallize the gold epaulettes on the white suit with bronzing powder. To create these, first sculpt the desired form in Roma Plastilena oil-based clay, to use as models. Over the models, make negative molds of room-temperature-vulcanizing (RTV) silicone ⚠, following the manufacturer's instructions. When the molds are cured, dust in a coating of gold bronzing powder ⚠ and then the polyurethane casting material. When the podlyurethane is poured into the molds, the gold powder will cling to the polyurethane epaulettes, imparting the look of real solid metal.

Each costume required twenty-three armor pieces and accessories, all bonded to the undersuits and each other with Pacer Laboratories' Flex-Zap cyanoacrylate adhesive ⚠.

The Shredder

Polyurethane Foam, Cast Epoxy ⚠, and Spandex

The Shredder's costume was designed by both Vin Burnham and Ray Scott at Jim Henson's Creature Shop in London for the feature film *Teenage Mutant Ninja Turtles II*, but it was built in London and Wilmington, North Carolina, where the film was shot. Although the Shredder actor was a well-built six-feet ten-inch wrestler, for this production, even his well-developed muscles required exaggeration.

Burnham always starts construction of a costume by making a life cast of the performer; she has found from her many years of experience that the life cast is essential to obtain an exactness of fit. All the other elements are made by specialists. In

Built on a full-body life cast, the Shredder's exaggerated muscles are composed of spandex-covered polyurethane foam and vacuum-formed plastic sheetings. Additional costume parts include latex, epoxy, rubber, and metal.

DESIGN: VIN BURNHAM AND RAY SCOTT FOR SHREDDER FROM *TEENAGE MUTANT NINJA TURTLES II*, 1991. PHOTO: JOHN BRAMLEY, ©NORTHSHORE INVESTMENTS LIMITED.

⚠ THIS SUBSTANCE OR PROCEDURE MAY BE HAZARDOUS TO HEALTH AND SHOULD BE USED WITH CARE. PLEASE READ THE APPROPRIATE HEALTH AND SAFETY SECTION.

this case, the life cast was made by Jim Henson's head mold maker, Kenny Wilson, considered by Burnham the ultimate expert in life casting. Burnham and her team, Alli Eynon and Connie Peterson, started by life casting the actor's actual torso, noting that his pectoral muscles were already so distinct that they looked as though they had been sculpted. The torso was cast in fiberglass-reinforced epoxy, which served as a positive mold for the costume's vacuum-formed muscles; these would later be placed on top of a Lycra spandex unitard. Though the actor wore a well fitted unitard, the unitard smoothed out the muscles, since spandex tends to bridge across forms, causing them to lose their definition. Burnham had two costumes built, the second as a backup.

The measurements for the spandex suit were sent from Wilmington, North Carolina, to Phil Reynolds' studio in London, where Reynolds made the suit and returned it to Wilmington. Reynolds makes many ballet costumes and had also made the undersuits for all Batman costumes from the *Batman* films of 1989 and the 1990s, so he knows exactly how spandex behaves.

The actor was clothed in the spandex suit, and the suit covered by the vacuum-formed △ abdominal muscles. The vacuum-formed pieces were covered with spandex glued in place with rubber contact cement △. (Burnham prefers Barge—U.S.—and Evostick or Thixofix—U.K. Thixofix, made by BTR Ltd., is available in British hardware stores.)

For his legs, the muscle size was increased with additional muscle pieces made from reticulated (Scott, or SIF) polyurethane foam. These pieces, independent from the rest of the costume, were covered with spandex and worn underneath the spandex bodysuit.

The shoulder spikes were cast from epoxy (a black, two-part compound by the Devcon Corporation—developed to mend airport luggage carousels). These shoulder pieces were screwed onto shoulder plates of fiberglass reinforced epoxy, which were placed over the unitard.

Boots, based on Japanese *tabis*, were built up about four inches with crepe rubber to make the actor seven feet tall. The massive rubber cloak of latex sheeting was made by Andy Wilkes of Los Angeles (who also made the Catwoman costume). The gauntlets and helmet were of butchers' apron material of flat aluminum discs. (See Metal Mesh in the Chainmail section on page 294.) The apron material was anodized black, and on the middle of each disc a small round highlight was placed to make the material less recognizable and ordinary.

Painting was done by Ed Henze, who emphasized muscle and form with airbrushed textile inks △, adding veins and muscle shadows. A strong and lurid color combination of bright green and purple made the Shredder visible as he was surrounded by gray dust and smoke.

△ THIS SUBSTANCE OR PROCEDURE MAY BE HAZARDOUS TO HEALTH AND SHOULD BE USED WITH CARE. PLEASE READ THE APPROPRIATE HEALTH AND SAFETY SECTION.

Surface Effects

Distressing

Distressing—the term for aging or breaking down fabric—is the fabric modification most often required of costumers. Distressing gives to costumes a sense of age, of character, of having been worn, of belonging to their wearers. Distressing can indicate the most subtle signs of wear on a new and fashionable garment or present the worn-down, worn-out condition of clothing worn by several generations. Distressing can be acomplished with dyes and paints as well as alteration of the costume by physically changing—often by damaging—the structure of its material. This latter step is usually employed after the costume is completed.

A bodice is distressed by airbushed Create. Paint and Rit Dye. Small roses are sewn loosely to simulate aging.

DESIGN: SEAN SULLIVAN FOR *TROJAN WOMEN*, UNIVERSITY OF WASHINGTON SCHOOL OF DRAMA. ARTISTRY AND PHOTO: JOSIE GARDNER.

Breaking down costumes, like most other techniques, should be scaled to the size of the house, the style of production, and the type of media. Theatre effects are usually more exaggerated than those for film and television, and in a large theatre, effects must be even broader and more exaggerated to be visible to an audience. Furthermore, a production in a heightened theatrical style may require stronger costume effects than would a naturalistic drama.

Before starting the aging process, the dyer-painter will analyze how a particular garment would break down naturally and how a particular character would have worn the garment in the situations related to the theatrical piece. Stress and wear will always occur around cuffs, hem, elbows, pockets openings, and on the knees and seat. Garments are usually faded where the sun hits them on the areas of shoulders, shoulder blades, chest, outer arms, hip tops, and the fronts of the thighs. But additional research is important to pinpoint how an individual piece of clothing fits a specific character, and the way the clothing fades, wears, and stretches to accommodate the activities of a particular character—all this information is needed if the designer is to age or distress a costume convincingly within the context of a particular production.

When distressing costumes, maintenance must also be considered. In most cases, coloring agents and aging substances, once applied, need to last though the length of a production run; substances to be subjected to washing and dry cleaning will need to be checked for durability before applying them to the costumes. Refer to the appropriate section of this book for specific recommendations.

Costumes that will not be washed or cleaned during a production can be colored or aged temporarily by a number of media; at the close of the production, the costumes may be cleaned and returned to the stockroom. Certain adhesives and coatings can modify a costume surface temporarily for purposes of aging. Hair-coloring spray, mud, and makeup are almost always removable. Other colorants may be removed by either dry cleaning or washing. Refer to the Colorants section on pages101-183 for specific recommendations.

Natural-fiber fabrics are distressed far more successfully than are synthetics. With natural fibers, even the wrinkling that occurs normally contributes to the realism required in most productions. Polyester fabric and those with a permanent finish are made of tough fibers and so are designed and manufactured to be wrinkle-free; they also resist most dyes and bleaches. Similarly, real leather is weaker and easier to break down than its vinyl imitation, which is commonly known as synthetic leather. Labels must be studied carefully to avoid the difficulties that will arise when working with synthetic textiles.

The aging process begins during the final stages of costume production, after the fittings are completed and the costumes sewn. Distressing is a messy business. Costumes are most efficiently and easily distressed with a mass-production setup. It is also easier to achieve a harmony among the costumes if all are worked on at the same time. If the workplace does not have a special area for this kind of work, drop cloths and newspapers will probably need to be taped in place to protect the floor, walls, and any furniture from paint and dyes. Cover dress forms carefully with plastic dry-cleaning bags. Assemble all necessary brushes, paints, and other tools and supplies into one area. The materials used in this process are often hazardous; read labels carefully and take all safety precautions before commencing the distressing procedure.

Removing Color

Bleach ⚠ kills color as does the sun, fading out the most light-exposed areas of clothing. It is excellent for creating such a color change, but unfortunately it is even stronger than the sun, drying out natural fibers and causing them to disintegrate. (Silk falls apart quickly.) When applying bleach to costumes, first mix the bleach with water in a ratio of no more than 50 percent bleach. Spray it with either a spritzer bottle, an airbrush, or an electric sprayer, or brush or sponge it onto the fabric. Proceed slowly, for just a small amount of bleach at one time will yield strong results. The effects of bleach do not always appear immediately, and the fading process can take time. Take care not to mix bleach with acids, and wear gloves and a respirator mask to avoid irritation.

Color remover ⚠ can also distress sections of costumes. To be effective, it must be hot, and can be applied through judicious dipping, spraying, brushing, or sponging. Color removers and the substances created when complex dye molecules break down into smaller components (seen as loss of color) are very hazardous. A dust mask will provide protection suitable for the substances released during stripping. Wear gloves when dealing with the powders or the water in which stripping has been done, and never mix bleach with color remover.

Coloring

Dyeing is the most commonly used distressing method to produce color change in costumes. It is less destructive than bleach and color remover. Its effects are more subtle than those of paint, since dye, unlike paint, becomes an actual part of the textile fibers. When selecting dyes for distressing, find those that do not require boiling or an immersion period, for distressing is most effectively accomplished by brushing or spraying. Distressing with dyes can simulate stained areas and shadow areas. By creating dyed shadows in those areas that would not receive light (such as under collars, inside folds, beside thick seams, and under armpits) the unshadowed areas appear faded. Shadow colors are usually a darker version of the color of the cloth. When applying any additional coloring agent, work slowly and carefully, for darkly sprayed spots on a costume may look just like sprayed paint or dye and too easily ruin the illusion of age or soil. Overdyeing through immersion can also make costumes look older.

The preferred dyes for aging are those that do not need prolonged heat-setting, that are color fast, and that will withstand laundering or dry cleaning. Dye pastes require steaming. French enamel varnish (see page 152), though quite effective, is not always impervious to most washing and dry cleaning. Textile inks ⚠, such as Versatex, as well as wood stains ⚠ and glass stains ⚠ are thin, like dyes, and serve well in aging textiles. Being transparent, they allow the original fabric texture to remain visible. Stains, inks, and dyes can be brushed, airbrushed, and sponged.

Upholstery dye ⚠, like Fab Spray for Fabric, is transparent and easily sprayed from the aerosol can. Liquid shoe dyes ⚠, like those made by Angelus and Fiebing, are also transparent and can be brushed or sprayed. Shoe dyes are strongly colored and may need thinning with acetone ⚠ before applying. For transparency, use shoe dyes, not shoe makeup or paint, though these opaque substances may also be used for certain distressing procedures, such as adding highlights and soil.

To give white fabrics that yellowed, aged, and lived-in look, dyeing is, of course, an obvious choice, though most commonly used dyes do not adhere to some of the synthetics. Tea and coffee have also enjoyed tinting popularity for many years, but they are only permanent until the next washing or cleaning. At London's National Theatre, another solution for "teching," or ivory-tinting, whites and one successfully used on synthetics is potassium permanganate. This chemical, commonly used in dyes, deodorants, and disinfectants, is pale purple when wet, but turns to ecru when dry. It can be found in some drugstores and chemical suppliers in the United States but is more easily available in England and Europe.

⚠ THIS SUBSTANCE OR PROCEDURE MAY BE HAZARDOUS TO HEALTH AND SHOULD BE USED WITH CARE. PLEASE READ THE APPROPRIATE HEALTH AND SAFETY SECTION.

Paints are easier to apply to selected areas than are dyes, since paints are usually applied with brushes or other applicators; however, some disadvantages of paints are that they sit on top of the fabric, change fabric texture, and usually stiffen fabric. In a large theatre, this will usually not be as apparent as in a small theatre or on film. Nevertheless, change of surface texture can belie the reality of the aging process.

Stove and grill polish is yet another substance that can be rubbed or brushed into fabric to produce a convincing semblance of dirt.

Creating the Appearance of Mud

To produce the effects of mud, or caked-on dirt, mix up a paste that includes an adhesive, a filler, coloring, and some texture. One such mixture is clay, sawdust, pigment powder, with either latex or a PVA glue or coating (fuller's earth can substitute for clay). Another mixture is from vermiculite, acrylic paint, and Phlexglu. (See the *Glitter Mud* section on page 414.) The advantages of using Phlexglu are both its flexibility and its strength through laundering and cleaning.

At London's National Theatre costume shop, mud is made by mixing together PVA, acrylic paint, fuller's earth, dyed sawdust, and water. This mix is pushed into the fabric, more PVA is "sloshed" on top to seal it, and the combination is ironed into the fabric with a warm iron. The National also will lay dyed sawdust on top of the aging costume and then cover it with PVA. Glyndebourne's Festival Opera sometimes uses a combination of white glue with fuller's earth. The Glyndebourne shop also likes to mix Copydex Adhesive (a British brand of latex adhesive) with sawdust and acrylic scenic paint for distressing. They often use it on boots, for they find it can be easily removed when the same boots are needed for a cleaner production, or it can be dissolved from fabric with cleaning fluid or mineral spirits.

The costume shop at Boston's Huntington Theatre often uses Sculptural Arts' Sculpt or Coat for distressing. The coating mixed with sawdust can be placed onto boots or cloth. For their 1991 production of *A Christmas Carol*, designed by Mariann Verheyen, the edges of long, net skirt ruffles were cut into a spiky pattern, with the Sculpt or Coat and sawdust mix applied, then painted with Deka Silk fabric paint.

A less effective method of creating mud is by thickening a muddy color of latex or acrylic paint with a textural material like those mentioned in the above paragraph.

Refer to the charts in the *Adhesives* and *Coatings* sections in this book for qualities of adhesion and durability when creating a long-lasting mud.

Adding Shine That Comes From Age

Substances both plastic and natural can be rubbed onto fabric surfaces to make clothing shiny where needed, such as the seat and knees of worn wool pants and the elbows of old jackets. Among adhesives, white glues are the most successful. Phlexglu is the most durable, lasting through both dry cleaning and washing. A few clear-acrylic coatings, like Createx Clear Ply Adhesive Coating and acrylic gel mediums, also work well. Beeswax and other natural resins have been used for years, though for durability, we recommend brushing a plastic coating onto both sides of the wax. Most waxes can be washed on most surfaces with lukewarm water; do not dry-clean wax until you wish to remove it. For a dirty shine, the National Theatre of London rubs on fireplace-grate polish.

Altering Structure of Material

Breaking down a fabric or a costume surface with tools is another way of producing a distressed look. Some of the most commonly used implements are cheese graters,

Ordinary kitchen and hardware tools can be used for distressing fabrics.

rasps, wire brushes, flames, and sandpaper. A garment can be quickly rubbed with a rasp or grater to create worn spots on hems and other edges, as well as knees and elbows. Sandpaper is less radical in its effects. Wire brushes are effective to wear away already torn, cut, or unfinished edges. If the garment is first soaked in a bath of bleach and water, it will be made more receptive to the wear and tear of the scrapers.

Flames and heat from matches, candles, and propane torches, though difficult to control, are excellent for creating realistic-looking worn edges. Flames and heat are effective on both fabric costumes and hard-surfaced garments like armor made of plastics or metal. Heated plastics can release toxic fumes. Please see appropriate *Health and Safety* section, and take proper precautions.

Doreen Johnson, at the Guthrie Theatre, has effectively used the burning process on the metal armor of the Ghost in *Hamlet*. Have a dish of water close by both for dipping charred edges as well as for avoiding accidents.

The clothes dryer is also effective for aging costumes. As fabric repeatedly bumps against the metal edges of the dryer interior, fibers deteriorate, edges wear out, and clothing soon looks well used.

Water may be used for costume aging. Washing wool garments causes them to wrinkle, shrink, and lose shape. After washing, stretch wool garments to a deformed shape and lay them on a table, or add more wrinkles by tying the garment with cord. Add age by spraying and dipping garments with water or dye.

Metal armor was distressed by burning with an acetylene torch.

DESIGN: ANNE HOULD-WARD FOR THE GHOST IN *HAMLET* AT THE GUTHRIE THEATRE, MINNEAPOLIS. PHOTO: COURTESY OF THE GUTHRIE THEATRE.

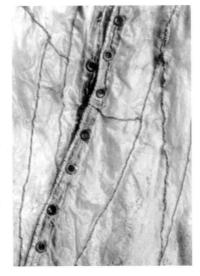

To create this appearance of distressed "salmon skin," rip-stop nylon fabric was painted with textile paints and then sanded.

DESIGN: JOHN BLOOMFIELD FOR THE FILM *WATER WORLD*. PHOTO: RICHARD S. BAILEY.

Inserting rocks or weights in wet pockets and hanging the garments overnight may create the required bagginess. If applied before ironing, vinegar is an excellent solvent for removing creases from pants.

Collaging by appliquéing, or layering materials over each other, is another method of creating an aged look. Cheesecloth is a favored fabric that can be layered onto another and sewn in place by stab-stitching or held with adhesives. Some costume shops find white glue successful for holding cheesecloth to a finished sewn garment. The cheesecloth is then stretched, torn, or worn away by graters in order to simulate decaying fabric. Using this method, someone will need to monitor costumes for durability during the run of a production.

Distressing Accessories

Shoes, bags, and other accessories are distressed in much the same way as are garments. If a character wears a worn-out garment, it is only natural that the matching unshined shoes would have worn soles and even pieced-together shoelaces. Sandpaper, acetone, and paint thinner can wear down the leather, and a power sander may properly age the soles. Spraying or brushing on an adhesive can also further add to a crusty leather finish.

Sanding with a rasp and painting with FEV create this look of wear and tear.

DESIGN: CATHERINE ZUBER FOR *KING LEAR* AT THE AMERICAN REPERTORY THEATRE, CAMBRIDGE, MASSACHUSETTS. PHOTO: RICHARD FELDMAN.

Metal and plastic pieces, such as buckles and armor, can be distressed by sanding, burning, scratching, and painting. Buttons are an important consideration when indicating age on a garment. Broken, missing, discolored, scratched, and unmatched buttons can communicate a strong message, as do all such details.

Distressing Leather

Begin by using a wire brush and/or sandpaper to weaken the leather. Apply shoe cream and petroleum jelly or glycerin to soften it. Select areas of the leather to deform and rub over these with a soldering iron. Coat the leather with waterglass—a silicate of sodium often used for fireproofing and available at chemical suppliers and some pharmacies. Allow the leather to dry; then crumple it. Spray the leather with leather dye, or, for further distressing, spray with a water-based union dye like Rit or Tintex. Another method is to place the leather into a washing machine of cool water and allow it to go through the entire cycle. Agitation of the wet leather will cause it to deform, and the water alone will cause a change in the surface appearance of the leather.

Surface Modification

Leather

When real leather is too expensive or impractical to use for a specific design, shops often create their own leather look by modifying fabrics. Here are just a few techniques, the first from Inge Cahsella, fabric modification artist at the Deutsche Staatsche Oper in Berlin:

This leather was distressed with dye in a washing machine. The dye takes to the leather unevenly, leaving the appearance of a worn surface.

DESIGN: WAYNE FINKLEMAN FOR THE FILM *THE GOLDEN CHILD*.

Canvas, Soap, and Shellac

1. Take canvas fabric and lay it flat on a table. Rub the surface vigorously with a mix of laundry soap and water.

2. The above mix can be merely laundry soap softened by dipping it into water, or it can be soap cut into chips and boiled in water until melted. If the soap mix is boiled, it will need to be strained into a container to remove the lumps, and then cooled before using.

3. To avoid wrinkling, always lay the coated fabric flat on the table to dry.

4. After the fabric is dry, iron directly onto the soaped surface. As it dries, the surface will become browner. Repeat these steps three times.

5. Next, brush the coated fabric with shellac. Allow to dry, then place the iron directly onto the shellacked fabric and iron. Repeat these steps three times also.

Felt, Soap, and Shellac

Felt can be treated just as is canvas in the above process. Inge Cahsella prefers to use felt and repeats the first two stages five to six times.

Suede Cloth, Soap, and White Glue or Acrylic Coating

1. Cotton suede cloth can be coated with any white glue or acrylic coating.

2. When the glue or coating is dry, rub in a layer of saddle soap and then iron the fabric. Then rub in and iron over a second layer of saddle soap.

3. Coat the fabric with yet a third layer of the original glue or coating. After a while, cracks will occur on the surface, simulating the look of worn leather.

Napped Knit Fabric and White Glue

These methods are favored by Gaye Bowen, costume designer and painter, who created "leather" for Shakespeare's *Henry V* while at the University of Texas at Austin:

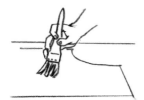

To create the effect of leather on a cloth tunic, first brush fabric with diluted PVA.

Rub soap paste onto the coated fabric.

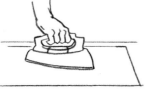

After soap paste is dry, cover the fabric with brown paper and iron.

Color the garment with leather dye solution applied by sponge or brush.

PROCESS: GAYE BOWEN FOR *HENRY V* AT THE UNIVERSITY OF TEXAS AT AUSTIN.

1. Start with a soft, napped fabric, preferably one with a knit backing which eliminates an obvious woven grain line. Brush the right side of the fabric with white glue or polyvinyl-acrylic (PVA) coating. The weight of the fabric and the consistency and amount of coating vary with the desired leather effect. For best results, choose fabric of the desired color range.

2. For soft clothing pieces, use knit suede cloth or knit cotton flannel as the base. Dilute one part PVA with six parts water. Spread the fabric flat onto a horizontal surface; then use a large paintbrush to spread the mixture. In order to avoid creases, do not move the treated fabric until it is absolutely dry.

3. To simulate stiff leather accessories and headgear, start with a heavy, brushed wool. A wool such as this is more compatible with the grain and texture of actual leather than are synthetics or felt. Brush undiluted PVA onto the fabric and allow to dry.

4. To finalize the texture, iron soap paste onto the coated fabric. Make soap paste by cutting the bar into small pieces and boil in a small amount of water until melted. Eliminate lumps by straining the mixture, which will now cool into a smooth paste. Rub the paste onto the fabric, a small amount at a time.

5. When soaping is complete, set the treated fabric by laying it between two sheets of brown paper and ironing it. After the treated fabric has dried, iron a second time without the paper covering. When a smoother surface is desired, the soaping and ironing may need repeating.

6. For coloring the new leather piece, color with leather dye using brush or spray. To achieve maximum depth, dilute leather dye with alcohol, and sponge over the area with a cheesecloth. For additional depth and sheen, add a layer of FEV. (See *French Enamel Varnish* on page 152.)

From the Covent Garden Opera House costume shop come these techniques:

Velvet and Liquid Latex

Velvet fabric also looks like leather if it is brushed with one or two coats of liquid latex.

⚠ THIS SUBSTANCE OR PROCEDURE MAY BE HAZARDOUS TO HEALTH AND SHOULD BE USED WITH CARE. PLEASE READ THE APPROPRIATE HEALTH AND SAFETY SECTION.

- To color, spray the "leather" with liquid leather dye ⚠ diluted with alcohol.
- To create a grainy texture, crumple the piece with a light crushing of the hands, or rub it against itself.

- To texture fake leather more deeply, use a soldering iron rubbed onto the surface to form patterns. This technique is effective on real leather as well.
- For further depth and texture, glue pieces of the same material onto the surface during the first step of coating the fabric with soap.

Patent Leather

To create patent leather, soak pieces of tissue paper in white glue and lay onto canvas fabric. Or paint the canvas fabric with white glue and layer it with pieces of tissue paper. When the glue is dry, paint the layered fabric with enamel paint. Obviously, dry cleaning is out of the question when using this technique.

Futuristic Fabric

Phlexglu and Createx Clear Ply Adhesive Coating on Polyester Fabric

Off on a Tangerine, at the Tiffany Theatre in Los Angeles, was a futuristic story of a world in which natural fibers were so precious that they became the only means of exchange. In the play then, it was important that the costume fabrics appeared obviously synthetic.

1. Starting with a variety of lightweight, soft, and shiny-surfaced knit and woven polyesters, the basic costumes were cut to shape and sewn. The sewn costumes then had to be appliquéd with almost rectangular-shaped fabric pieces that varied from about two-by-three to four-by-six inches. These varied appliquéd pieces, some partially loose, contributed to the illusion of strange clothing, much used and extremely timeworn.

2. In order to work on one side only of the garments, an ironing board was pushed between the thin fabric of the legs of the trousers, one leg at a time. Futuristic authenticity was carried into the costume construction by applying the appliqué with gluing, rather than sewing, using Phlexglu. Each cut rectangle was glued into place, some slightly overlapping the others. When all appliqués were in place, the entire trousers were coated with an additional coating of Phlexglu.

3. A turtleneck shirt was treated similarly: A few appliqués were glued on the shirt, and the appliquéd surface was coated unevenly with Phlexglu and Createx Clear Ply Adhesive Coating acrylic gel. An additional coating of pearles-

Acrylic emulsion, followed by thin layers of textile paints and Phlexglu, lends a futuristic plastic fabric coating for costumes in Off on a Tangerine, *Tiffany Theatre, Los Angeles.*

DESIGN: THE AUTHOR. PHOTO: ROBERT W. ZENTIS.

cent paint and a subtle sprinkling of glitter further disguised the familiar appearance of the ubiquitous turtleneck.

4. The dress that appeared to be made of material obviously synthetic was given an uneven brushing of both glue and paint, and both coatings were sprinkled with glitter.

5. All costumes, once appliquéd and coated, were finally tinted with ombrées of various golden browns. Hems were left uneven, but finished off with a thin border of adhesive to prevent unraveling. Costumes survived several weeks of performance as well as several dry cleanings.

Pleating with Adhesives

White Glue Jack Edwards, designer and costume director at the Guthrie Theatre, used this method to create pleats in his designs for Shakespeare's *A Midsummer's Night Dream*. He dipped cheesecloth into a solution of one-part white glue to two-parts water. He removed the fabric from the solution, and when it was dry, he pinched it into small broomstick pleats. When using this method, it is important to pull the pleats apart before they are completely dry to prevent their sticking together.

At the Bavarian State Opera in Munich, the order of the steps was reversed. A thin fabric was first twisted into broomstick pleats, and then it was coated with the PVA solution. In this instance, too, the pleats had to be separated while still damp so that they would not stick together permanently.

To form broomstick pleating, cut the fabric into desired lengths and sew even basting stitches (usually about an inch apart), carefully opposing one set of basting from the other, so that a top basting thread faces the top basting thread at the other end of the fabric. Pull both sets of threads tightly, and either dip into water and allow to dry, or dip into the above solution before drying. The pleated fabric can be dried in a number of ways:

1. Press with an iron.

2. Loosely coil and placed into a microwave or regular kitchen oven at low setting.

3. Stretch between two hooks or nails.

4. Wrap around a broomstick and allow to dry.

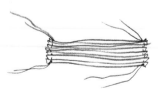

To create broomstick pleating, baste evenly and pull both sets of threads tightly, as the diagram indicates.

Dip into a solution of either water or PVA.

Stretch the pleated fabric while drying. If the fabric has been dipped into a glue solution, separate the pleats before they adhere to each other.

Broomstick pleats, coated in this manner, can usually be only hand-cleaned.

Similarly, for the Berlin Schiller Theater's production of Schiller's *Maria Stuart*, perfect-looking broomstick pleats were made firm and permanent by first forming the pleats and then brushing on a coating of white glue.

Another method, used by the Glyndebourne Festival Opera in England, was followed for creating a heavily sculptured look in Mozart's *Don Giovanni*. A fitted under-tunic was constructed at the same time as an outer layer of heavy, soft fabric. The outer layer was sewn into folds at the shoulder area, then the inner part of the folds were glued into place to the fitted under-tunic.

Pleats are made permanent with an application of white glue.

DESIGN: GÜNTER KRÄMER FOR GISOLA STERN IN THE ROLE OF MARIA STUART, IN *MARIA STUART* AT BERLIN'S SCHILLER THEATER. PHOTO: ANNELIESE HEUER.

Gold Cloth

White Glue, Bronzing Powder, and Nylon Net

Use nylon-net fabric, choosing a color compatible with the desired gold effect. Apply white glue (PVA) by brush, and carefully sprinkle on gold bronzing powder. Stretch the net, shake off the excess bronzing powder, and allow to dry. Layer the net over a solid fabric, and it is ready to use.

Snow and Ice

White Glue, Glass Glue, Styrofoam, and Scenic Paint

Sometimes a situation calls for costumes to be covered permanently with snow and ice. To achieve this effect, the National Theatre in London makes a mix of white glue, glass glue (a product sold in window-glass shops for gluing glass together), crumbled expanded polystyrene foam (such as Styrofoam), and white acrylic scenic paint. (This shop prefers Rosco's.) This mixture can be easily trowled or scooped onto shoulders and hats of winter wear. Obviously, this material cannot be dry-cleaned or laundered.

Zice

This product from Zeller International is a nontoxic granulated powder which is mixed with water to achieve the effect of crushed ice or snowballs. Its companion product, Crystal Zice, simulates water-clear, sparkling pieces of ice which will last only as long as the next dry cleaning or laundering. Both can be trowled onto the garment's surface.

Fake Lace

Acrylic Paint and Transparent Fabric

When lace is unavailable or too expensive, there are methods to achieve its look. At the Teatro San Carlo in Naples, opaque acrylic paint is put onto transparent fabric by stenciling a lace pattern through actual lace, or through a paper cutout of a lace pattern. Organza and tulle are this costume shop's preferred fabric surface for the paint that is applied by airbrush or spray canister.

Heavy Sculptural Look

Canvas, Latex and Tissue Paper

In Germany, larger-than-life figures are often an important part of theatrical productions. Such oversize figures are created with costumes made out of well-padded heavy canvas or duck. The canvas or duck cloth is brush-coated with a layer of liquid latex. On the still-wet latex, tissue paper, torn into bits approximately two-by-three inches is applied. The latex is allowed to dry for several minutes and then painted and latex-coated. More texture can be added with additional layers of paper and latex. For some productions, the peeling tissue paper is a bonus—adding a crackled or degenerating quality, but costumes that must be pristine will need to be watched over carefully by the wardrobe crew.

Glitter Mud

Phlexglu, Acrylic Textile Paint, Vermiculite, and Glitter

When Alan Armstrong designed *Macbeth* for the Alabama Shakespeare Festival, he conceived of the characters as being rooted to the earth and its mud. Costumes were covered with bones, shredded muslin, and collaged with worn found objects and decayed-looking fabric pieces. They were also ombré dyed—dark at the bottom, progressing to lighter at the top.

The Witches were to dance around an actual fire onstage. A brew of Phlexglu, Deka Textile Paint, vermiculite, and glitter was concocted to decorate the hems of their gowns. Phlexglu provided bonding and flexibility, Deka, the color; vermiculite, the texture; and glitter, the light refraction.

Glitter mud at the hem of these skirts is made from a mixture of Phlexglu, acrylic textile paint, vermiculite, and glitter.

DESIGN: ALAN ARMSTRONG FOR THE WITCHES IN *MACBETH* AT THE ALABAMA SHAKESPEARE FESTIVAL. PHOTO: COURTESY OF THE ALABAMA SHAKESPEARE FESTIVAL.

The mix was applied by spatula from the floor-level hem up to the knee-level length of the Witches' gowns. While this paste was still moist, an extra 16th" of glitter was added for additional sparkle and theatricality.

Because the Witches could be endangered by the fire, three coatings of flame retardant were sprayed additionally over the skirt bottoms, which in this case lent further character to the already textured costumes.

When all layers of materials were dry, the entire costumes were ombré-dyed by airbrush.

Slimy Skin

China Silk and Methylcellulose

For the 1988 film *The Blob*, the title character required skin that would ooze and pulsate.

These qualities were achieved by Marilyn Dozer-Chaney for the designer Lyle Conway by using some unusual costume materials. Operated by puppeteers, rather than worn by an actor, the methods used for this prop could easily be applied to a worn costume.

First, china silk was quilted into circles of varying sizes, ranging from two- to nine-inches square. The quilting was done with two layers of fabric without padding or an inner layer. It then was dyed with a pink union dye, like Rit, and spattered with more dye in reds, pinks, and purples. Finally, the entire piece was airbrushed with thinned-out Versatex paint into a pattern of veins and arteries of deeper reds and purples. The back of each circular pocket was slit about a half inch and injected with methylcellulose (a gelatinlike food thickener sold by distributors for special effects in costumes and props).

The methylcellulose would then ooze and slime its way through the front (as well as the back) layer of the china silk.

The puppeteers created a deep rhythmical pulse by manipulating the quilt in a variety of movements.

Synthetic Embroidery

White Glue and Metallic Media

First mix together PVA (white glue) or acrylic emulsion, or rubber cement ⚠ with a metallic medium like glitter, bronzing powder, or metallic acrylic paint. Place this mixture into a squeeze bottle, a cake-decorating instrument, a batik tool, or a sturdy vellum cone made by rolling a six-inch vellum square. The size of the cone point will be determined by the width of the line desired. Any of the utensils suggested above is easier to control than a brush for applying such viscous media. For extra sparkle, sequins and beads can be added while the medium is still moist. To make raised motifs, add Cab-O-Sil ⚠, baking soda, or another filler to the mixture. Precaution: When using Cab-O-Sil and similar lightweight powders, wear a protective mask to avoid inhalation. Cab-O-Sil is amorphous silica and though the degree of its toxicity is arguable, it can stay in the lungs for life!

Inge Cahsella, director of costume crafts at the Komische Oper, Berlin, uses such a vellum cone to create allover designs on fabric. Cahsella finds the cones faster, easier to control, more dispensable, and cheaper than brushes. She also usually applies the synthetic embroidery adhesive to a fabric piece that matches the actual costume or to

⚠ THIS SUBSTANCE OR PROCEDURE MAY BE HAZARDOUS TO HEALTH AND SHOULD BE USED WITH CARE. PLEASE READ THE APPROPRIATE HEALTH AND SAFETY SECTION.

a netting that is eventually hand-sewn to the costume and can be easily removed before dry cleaning.

Hot-Melt Glue ⚠️ and Bronzing Powder Begin by drawing the design onto heavy brown wrapping paper. Next, place a sheet of glass over the brown paper, covering it with two layers of black tulle. Using a hot-glue gun, trace the drawn design onto the tulle. Sprinkle and spread bronzing powder over the hot glue, before it dries. Cut out the tulle, leaving a quarter of an inch around both edges of the design. Baste it onto the costume. Because it cannot survive cleaning fluids, remove it before dry cleaning and then rebaste it before use.

For costumes that do not require dry cleaning, hot glue and bronzing powder can also be applied directly to the costume.

Dimensional embroidery design is made from a mixture of rubber-contact cement mixed with vinyl powder.
COURTESY: KOMISCHE OPER, BERLIN.

Available Paints Puff paint, wet-look paint, and glitter paint are readily available and easy to use in prepackaged squeeze bottles, and most of them are compatible with most fabric surfaces through repeated dry cleanings. The only real disadvantage is the high expense to those on a budget. For more information on these paints, see Flexible Paint in Squeeze Bottles on page 129.

Colored Hot-Glue Sticks ⚠️ Technocraft manufactures several series of colorful metallic hot-glue sticks. Sixteen colors are available in a plain glossy stick, while the eight metallics are from different colors with added glitter. Technocraft is currently developing a line of a more frankly metallic hot glue. In our testing, we found these very easy to use; however, durability in laundering and dry cleaning is not strong on most surfaces. See the Metallic Hot Glue section on page 170.

The border of this dress is painted first with Scribbles metallic paint applied through a squeeze bottle, followed by a coat of Createx Paint applied with a syringe, and finally an application of metallic hot-melt glue over which glitter is sprinkled.
DESIGN AND ARTISTRY: REGAN HAINES FOR *SHE LOVES ME* AT THE UNIVERSITY OF WASHINGTON SCHOOL OF DRAMA. PHOTO: JOSIE GARDNER.

PART FOUR

Appendices

Appendix I: Solvents

Solvents

To those working with plastics and synthetics, a knowledge of the various chemicals they include should be a priority, for most synthetics and plastics contain or are used with solvents.

Solvents are liquid organic chemicals that can dissolve other substances. Solvents hold small solid particles of any given material in a liquid or viscous suspension. For example, acetone, mineral spirits, and alcohol are present in many adhesives, resins, and paints. Solvents hold the solid portions of a material in a fluid state so that the solids can be more easily applied. Upon exposure to air, solvents usually evaporate. Solvents are used for thinning a thick liquid as well as for cleanup. Water may be present in many solutions; these are referred to as "water-based" solutions. Most often the solutions are "solvent-based" and contain hazardous chemicals.

Solvents dissolve materials of similar composition. For example, water and water-soluble solvents usually dissolve water-based substances, and chemically-derived solvents usually dissolve chemical-based substances.

Safety and health precautions must be followed when working with chemically-based solvent materials. The vapors from such materials are injurious to personal and environmental health, and many are flammable as well. In the Health and Safety section on page 00, many of the potential problems, as well as the current regulations regarding the use of such materials, are addressed. Additional information, specific to individual substances, is included in many other sections. This section also includes a safety list. General precautions are included along with a definition in the classifications of solvents.

Some chemical solvents are derived from coal tar and petroleum. From coal tar are extracted benzol, toluol, xylol, and phenol. Examples of petroleum solvents are aliphatic hydrocarbons, chlorinated hydrocarbons, alcohols, ester, ketones, and some of the aromatic hydrocarbons including toluene, xylene, and benzene. Wood distillation is the source of turpentine. The first solvent for practical use was alcohol.

Definition Of Terms

Threshold Limit Value (TLV) TLVs are air-quality standards developed by the American Conference of Governmental Industrial Hygienists and are the American Industrial Hygiene Associaltion's Workplace Environmental Exposure Limits. (See WEEL below.)

TLVs are the amounts of chemicals in the air that most healthy adult workers have been predicted to be able to tolerate without adverse effects. There are three types of TLVs. The most common is TLV-TWA (Time-Weighted Average), averaged over the eight-hour day/forty-hour week.

There are also TLVs for fifteen-minute exposures, TLV-STEL (Short Term Exposure Limits) and TLVs that should not be exceeded for even and instant, TLV-C (Ceiling limits). The eight-hour TLV-TWA is specified unless the initials STEL or C appear after TLV.

In the following charts, the lower the TLV the less is allowed in the workplace air, and the less should be inhaled. Safer substitutes can be chosen by selecting produts with higher TLVs as long as the evaporation rate and other traits are similar. For example, ethyl alcohol (TLV=1000 ppm) would be a better choice than methyl alcohol (TLV=200 ppm).

Flash Point (FP) The lower the FP, the more flammable the material. The FP is the lowest temperature at which a flammable liquid gives off sufficient vapor to form an ignitable mixture with air near its surface or within a vessel. Combustion need not continue.

Evaporation Rate ER ER is the rate at which a material vaporizes or evaporates from a liquid or solid state compared to the evaporation rate of butyl acetate or ethyl ether.

Workplace Environmental Exposure Limit WEEL These standards are based on the same concept as the TLVs but are set by another organization, the American Industrial Hygiene Association. WEELS are used in the following charts when no TLVs are available.

Solvents Charts

Alcohols Alcohols are one of the safer classes of solvents and are hydrocarbons, though they differ greatly from other hydrocarbons.

ALCOHOLS

SOLVENT	COMMON USES	TLV PPM	FP F°	ER	HEALTH AND SAFETY FACTORS
Ethanol, ethyl alcohol, grain alcohol, denatured alcohol	Solvent for shellac.	1000	55	med	The least toxic alcohol.
Isopropyl alcohol, isopropanol, rubbing alcohol	Solvent for some dyes.	400	53	very slow	One of the least toxic alcohols.
Methyl alcohol, methanol, wood alcohol	Alternative fuel for gasoline.	200	52	fast	High dosage or chronic exposure causes blindness. A well-known poison. Absorbed by skin.
n-propyl alcohol, n-propanol	Motor and gasoline additive. Production of chemicals.	200	59	med	Causes cell mutation. Absorbed by skin.
Butanol, n-butanol, n-butyl alcohol	Production of chemicals.	500 (ceiling)	95	slow	Irritation to respiratory system below TLV. Absorbed by skin.

Charts are based on Monona Rossol's charts in *The Artist's Complete Health and Safety Guide*.

Aliphatic Hydrocarbons Aliphatic hydrocarbons are among the least toxic of the solvent classifications. Aliphatic hydrocarbons are also the most economical and the most water-resistant. They dissolve oils, fats, and waxes. Many solvents in this group are chemically derived mixtures from petroleum and are widely used with natural rubber, reclaimed rubber, and SBR adhesives.

ALIPHATIC HYDROCARBONS

SOLVENT	COMMON USES	TLV PPM	FP F°	ER	HEALTH AND SAFETY FACTORS
VM & P naphtha, benzine, paint thinner, odorless paint thinner	Solvent for oil-based paints, oil-based coatings, and some rubber-cement adhesives. Dissolves grease.	300	20-40	med	Comparatively low toxicity; odorless thinner contains no aromatic hydrocarbons; a healthy substitute for turpentine.
n-heptane, normal heptane, heptanes	Solvent for oil-based paints, oil-based coatings, and some rubber-cement adhesives. Dissolves grease.	400	25	fast	Comparatively low toxicity; good substitute for hexanes and other fast-drying solvents.
Kerosene	Solvent for oil-based paints, oil-based coatings, and some rubber-cement adhesives. Dissolves grease.	none	100-150	very slow	Toxicity is low, but it is a known lung irritant and is highly flammable.
Mineral spirits, odorless mineral spirits, Stoddard solvent, and similar petroleum fractions	Usual thinner and cleaner for artists' oil paints.	100	>100	slow	Use with proper ventilation and wear gloves; mineral spirits can contain aromatic hydrocarbons.
Gasoline, (white gasoline)	Grease-spot removal.	300	-45	fast	Do not use. Highly flammable. Contains toxic additions.
n-hexane, normal hexane, commercial hexane	Still used in some rubber-cement and spray can products.	50	-7	fast	Do not use. Nervous system toxin causes disease similar to MS. Highly flammable.

Aromatic Hydrocarbons

Aromatic hydrocarbons are among the most hazardous of solvents and should be avoided when possible. Aromatic hydrocarbons dissolve nonwater-soluble substances such as fats, gasolines, oils, and waxes, including the oils of the skin.

AROMATIC HYDROCARBONS

SOLVENT	COMMON USES	TLV PPM	FP F°	ER	HEALTH AND SAFETY FACTORS
Ethyl benzene, ethyl benzol, phenyl ethane	Styrene production.	100	51	slow	Eye irritation starts at the TLV.
Xylene, xylol, dimethyl benzene	Commercial sprays, lacquer thinner additive.	100	81-90	slow	A narcotic that causes liver and kidney damage, as well as stomach pain.
Toluene, toluol, methyl benzene, phenyl methane	Commercial sprays, lacquer thinner additive.	50	90	med	A narcotic that causes liver and kidney damage.
Styrene, vinyl benzene, phenyl ethylene	Polyester resin-casting material.	20	40	slow	Try to avoid. Possibly cancer producing. Absorbed by skin.
Benzene, benzol	Oil-paint thinner and cleanup. No longer available.	0.5	12	med	Do not use. Causes leukemia and other cancers. Absorbed by skin.

Chlorinated Hydrocarbons

Chlorinated hydrocarbons are highly carcinogenic and should be avoided. Because of their high toxicity and higher price, they are not commonly used. Chlorinated hydrocarbons are nonflammable and deplete the ozone layer.

CHLORINATED HYDROCARBONS

SOLVENT	COMMON USES	TLV PPM	FP F°	ER	HEALTH AND SAFETY FACTORS
1,1,1-trichloroethane, methyl chloroform, chloroform	Dry-cleaning fluid, paint strippers.	350	0	fast	Causes irregular heartbeat and heart arrest.
Methylene chloride, dichloromethane	Solvent for acrylic resin, paint remover.	50	0	fast	Avoid. Metabolizes to carbon monoxide in blood. Possible carcinogen. Stresses heart, causes irregular heartbeat.
Trichloroethylene	Dry-cleaning fluid.	50	0	med	Possible draconian carcinogen. Causes irregular heartbeat.
Perchloroethylene, tetrachloroethylene	Dry-cleaning fluid.	25	0	med	Possible carcinogen. Causes irregular heartbeat and liver damage.
Chloroform	Anesthetic. Used in refrigerants and propellants.	10	0	fast	Avoid. Possible carcinogen.

CHLORINATED HYDROCARBONS

Ethylene dichloride, 1,2-dichloroethane	Anesthetic. Also used to hasten crop ripening.	10	56	med	Intoxicant, causes liver damage, possible carcinogen.
Carbon tetrachloride	Dry-cleaning fluid. Banned in 1960 from consumer products and dry-cleaning.	5	0	fast	Avoid. Carcinogen. Severe liver damage and death result when combined with alcohol. Absorbed by skin.

Esters/Acetates Esters, or acetates, are among the least toxic of the solvents and are irritants rather than toxins. Their formula is similar to ketones, and they are to some degree water-soluble.

ESTERS/ACETATES

SOLVENT	COMMON USES	TLVPPM	FP F°	ER	HEALTH AND SAFETY FACTORS
Ethyl acetate	Solvent for nitrocellulose.	400	24	fast	Least toxic in this class.
Methyl acetate	Paint remover, lacquer solvent, and synthetic flavoring.	200	14	fast	Fairly safe.
Isoamyl acetate, banana oil	Respirator fit testing.	100	64	med	Fairly safe.

Glycols Glycols, also known as dihydric alcohols, vary in toxicity and are commonly found in antifreeze products. They absorb water, evaporate slowly, and are to some degree water-soluble.

GLYCOLS

SOLVENT	COMMON USES	TLV PPM	FP F°	ER	HEALTH AND SAFETY FACTORS
Propylene glycol, 1,2-propanediol	Solvent for lacquer, antifreeze in paints and other products.	50 WEEL*	210	very slow	Least toxic in this class; may cause allergies.
Ethylene glycol, 1,2-ethandiol	Lacquer thinner and antifreeze.	100C Mg/M^3	232	very slow	Lung and eye irritant. At high doses cause neurological damage and blindness.
Diethylene glycol	Antifreeze and food additive.	50 WEEL*	255	very slow	May be more toxic than ethylene glycol, but doesn't cause blindness. Absorbed through skin.
Triethylene glycol, triglycol (technically, a glycol ether)	Antifreeze for dyes.	none	255	very slow	Possible reproductive hazard.

*WEEL is the Workplace Environmental Exposure Limit determined by the American Industrial Hygiene Association when no TLV exists. See page 419.

Glycol Ethers (Cellosolves) Glycol ethers are slow-drying solvents used for some cleanup and in some water-based paint and dye products. They are hazardous, especially to the reproductive system and should be avoided when possible.

GLYCOL ESTERS (CELLOSOLVES)

SOLVENT	COMMON USES	TLV PPM	FP F°	ER	HEALTH AND SAFETY FACTORS
Butyl cellosolve, 2-butoxyethanol, ethylene glycol monobutyl ether	Bonding polycarbonate, solvent in cleaning products (especially spray cleaners).	20	141	slow	Least toxic to reproductive system in this class. Affects blood, liver, kidneys. Absorbed through skin.
Cellosolve, 2-ethoxyethanol, ethyl cellosolve, ethylene glycol monoethyl ether	Magazine transfers in lithography and photo screenprinting; solvent in cleaning products.	5	110	slow	Hazardous to reproductive system for both men and women. Affects blood, liver, and kidneys. Absorbed through skin.
Methyl cellosolve, 2-methoxyethanol, ethylene glycol monomethyl ether	Solvent in cleaning products; dye solvent.	5	102	slow	Hazardous to reproductive system for both men and women. Affects blood, liver, and kidneys. Absorbed through skin.
di- and tri-ethylene and propylene glycol ethers and their acetates	Solvent in cleaning products; dye solvent.				Little known about this group. Possibly harms blood and reproductive systems.

Ketones Ketones vary widely in their toxicity. If their fumes are inhaled over a long time, they are respiratory irritants. Some are soluble in water. They are used with many synthetic rubbers in adhesives and also dissolve other adhesives, coatings, and colorants.

KETONES

SOLVENT	COMMON USES	TLV PPM	FP F°	ER	HEALTH AND SAFETY FACTORS
Acetone, dimethyl ketone, 2-propanone	Dissolving lacquer and many colorants. Nail polish remover.	500	-4	fast	Comparatively low toxicity. Irritating to respiratory tract. Highly flammable.
Methyl ethyl ketone (MEK), 2-butanone	Solvent in adhesives, lacquers, and cleaning fluids.	200	16	fast	Damages nervous system severely when in combination with n-hexane.
Methyl isobutyl ketone (MIBK)	Solvent in marking pens.	50	64	med	May be more toxic when in combination with n-hexane.
Methyl butyl ketone (MBK)	Rarely used today.	5	77	med	Do not use. Causes permanent nerve damage.

MISCELLANEOUS SOLVENTS

SOLVENT	COMMON USES	TLV PPM	FP F°	ER	HEALTH AND SAFETY FACTORS
Turpentine	Oil-paint thinner. General clean-up for oil products.	100	95	slow	Causes allergie symptoms (dermatitis, asthma), kidney and bladder damage. Substitute with odorless paint thinner.
Limonene, d-limonene, citrus oil, citrus turps, menthadiene, dipentene	Oil-paint thinner, pesticide, food additive. Used to produce tumors and birth defects in laboratory testing for cancer in rats. Citrus solvent sold as artists' oil-paint thinner.	30 (WEEL)	unk	very slow	Acutely toxic by ingestion (rats). Inhalation causes liver damage. More toxic than turpentine.
Morpholine	Fungicide and rust preventative.	20	100	slow	Avoid. Absorbed through skin.
Tetrahydrofura, THF	A solvent for vinyl.	200	1.4	very fast	Explosive when old or when exposed to air or water. Highly narcotic.
Dioxane, 1,4-dioxine	Ingredient in photographic emulsions.	25	65	fast	Avoid. Carcinogen. Absorbed through skin.
Cyclohexane, hexamethylene	Wood stain, paint and varnish remover, spot remover.	300	1.4	fast	Not acutely toxic. Chronic effects poorly studied.
Ethyl lactate	Solvent for oil paint and some resins.	see unk above	131	fast	Vapor not acutely hazardous. Absorbed through skin and a skin irritant. Unstudied for long-term hazards.
Lithotine	Turpentine substitute. Contains mineral spirits or benzine and d-limonene, castor oil, and ester gum.				Nonallergenic.

Appendix II: Acids, Alkalis, and Oxidizers

ACIDS

SOLVENT	COMMON USES	HEALTH AND SAFETY FACTORS
Concentrated acetic acid, glacial acetic acid	Solvent in the manufacture of some chemicals.	Highly corrosive. Vapors cause irritation to skin and eyes. Flammable. Must be stored in a cabinet made for flammables.
Dilute acetic acid (5% the strength of glacial acetic acid), vinegar	Dye mordant and food additive.	Mildly irritating to skin and eyes.
Formic acid	Dye mordant.	Highly corrosive to eyes and mucous membranes. May cause mouth, throat, and nasal ulcerations.
Oxalic acid	Bleaching and cleaning agent in the manufacture of dyes and pigments.	Skin and eye contact can cause severe corrosion and ulceration. Inhalation can cause severe respiratory irritation and damage.
Sulfuric acid	Petroleum refining and manufacture of paints, pigments, dyes, and explosives.	Highly corrosive to skin and eyes. Vapors can cause respiratory damage. Heat causes irritating and sensitizing sulfur-dioxide gas.
Tannic acid, tannin	Leather colorant, "tanning."	Slight skin irritant. Carcinogenic in animals.
Uric acid urea	Chemical synthesis and dye assist.	No significant hazards. Evolves hydrogen cyanide gas when heated.

ALKALIS AND OXIDIZERS

SOLVENT	COMMON USES	HEALTH AND SAFETY FACTORS
Ammonia solution, ammonium hydroxide	Present in some latexes; color remover for some dyes. Household cleaner.	Vapors can cause respiratory and eye irritation. Hazardous. Will burn skin. DO NOT MIX WITH BLEACH
Bleach, sodium hypochlorite, (household bleach is 5% sodium hypochlorite)	Household cleaner, fabric whitener for synthetics (destroys silk and other organic fabrics). Some Brands: Clorox, Hylox.	Corrosive to skin, eyes, throat, and mucous membranes. DO NOT MIX WITH AMMONIA for such reaction can release highly toxic gases.
Hydrogen peroxide	Color remover for some fabrics.	Concentrated solutions can cause severe eye and skin damage.
Potassium hydroxide (lye, caustic potash)	Used in manufacture of soap, bleach, dyes, and some paint removers.	Toxic by ingestion and inhalation and corrosive to tissue.
Sodium hydroxide (lye, caustic soda)	Used in manufacture of soap and some textiles.	Poison by ingestion. Corrosive to tissue. Strong irritant to eyes, skin, and mucous membranes.

Appendix III: Stain Removal

Removing stains quickly in an emergency is part of working in most costume shops and wardrobe departments. Stains from makeup, onstage action, and various accidents often require immediate attention, leaving no time to wait for professional dry cleaning.

Soap and water, always the best stain remover, should not be used on fabrics that easily water-spot such as satin, taffeta, or recently dyed fabrics unless first tested with water. To remove stains, place lukewarm water in a jar, add a mild dishwashing detergent (not laundry detergent), and mix well by shaking. Position a soft fabric or towel underneath the stained area to absorb the water and the stain itself. Dip a piece of cheesescloth or a sponge into the solution and feather over the stain; first wet well the actual spot, and then gradually apply the solution more thinly, always working away from the stain's edge.

If the stain is one from a product that soap and water will not remove, refer to the MSDS for the solvent used in the product. Use the same solvent to dissolve and clean the stain. When purchasing spot cleaners, buy those that are biodegradable when possible, which is indicated on the container. Use the same feathering technique with cheesecloth or sponge when removing spots with solvents. On some fabrics, such as many silks and acetates, rings form easily, and the feathering treatment must be applied with special care.

Not all fabrics react similarly to stain-removal products and techniques. Some stains may become permanent, especially if set by heat, or if they have been on the fabric for some length of time. Polyester, for instance, creates a chemical bond with most grease stains. If grease is not removed immediately, it may become permanently affixed.

Costume shops can purchase professional stain-removal solvents, available through costume notions' and dry-cleaners' suppliers. Professional solvents remove more types of stains than the cleaning solvents available in retail stores, for those from retail stores contain a blend of several types of solvents and detergents. Professional solvents are, however, more hazardous and must be used with more caution. Some brands in this category, familiar to many costumers, are Picrin and Ever Blum.

When a garment is stained, first try to absorb any excess fluid with a clean and absorbent cloth or towel. Then use the appropriate cleaning technique, always working with clean materials. When the sponge or cloth becomes stained, use another clean one.

Though chlorine bleach is recommended for some stain removal, do not use on fabrics with either fire-retardant or special-resin finishes, or on silk, wool, or spandex.

Have in the shop a dry spotter, which is handy for many stains. This is a mixture that can be made of one part coconut oil and eight parts dry-cleaning solvent. It must be kept tightly capped. Though coconut oil is preferred, mineral oil also works well.

If detergent is used for removing spots, it should be hand dishwashing liquid mixed with water in proportions of one teaspoon detergent to one cup of lukewarm water. Do not use laundry detergent for spots because it contains optical brighteners that can cause discoloration.

Health and Safety
- Keep dry-cleaning solvents and other solvents away from the skin. They can cause irritation and enter the bloodstream. Use only a small quantity at a time. Do not pour the solvent into a bowl before using because it creates additional toxic fumes.
- Work in a ventilated area.
- Do not mix dry-cleaning solvents.
- After using one solvent, wait until the spot is thoroughly dry before applying another. Mixing solvents this way could cause an explosion.
- Keep away from flames, cigarettes, and electrical equipment like fans and refrigerators.
- Do not drink any kind of beverage or eat food in the proximity of solvents.
- Do not place articles damp with solvents in a clothes dryer.
- Store dry-cleaning solvents and other solvents in well-capped, unbreakable containers in a location where they cannot be ignited.
- If solvents are spilled on the skin, wash off immediately.

Chemical Spots

- These need to be removed immediately.

Acids

All Stains
- Wash or sponge with cold water.
- To restore lost color, hold the cloth over an open bottle of ammonia. If the color changes, apply white vinegar.

Alkalis

All stains
- Sponge with cold water.
- To restore lost color, squeeze on lemon juice and sponge with vinegar. Rinse well with cold water.

Chewing Gum

Washables
- Soak in egg white and then launder in sudsy water.
- Or soak in dry-cleaning solution or turpentine and then in sudsy water.
- Or rub with ice and then rub off chewing gum.

Cleanables
- Swab or sponge with dry-cleaning solution.
- Or rub with ice and then rub off chewing gum.

Citrus Fruit

- Treat immediately with lukewarm suds, or follow directions for fresh and cooked fruits. Citrus fruits can change fabric colors. Use ammonia or baking soda in solution to restore color. Soap and alkalis set some fruit stains.

Coffee, Tea, Soft Drinks, Fresh and Cooked Fruits

Washables
- With white, nonshrinkable fabric, pour boiling water through the fabric. If traces remain, sprinkle with lemon juice and place in sunlight.
- With other fabric, swab or sponge with warm sudsy water and one tablespoon vinegar for up to 15 minutes; or sponge with cool water, then rub in glycerin, let stand one half hour, and then rinse. If traces remain, soak in presoak and water. If some traces still remain, wash in ammonia or hydrogen peroxide in boiling water or in chlorine bleach.

Cleanables
- For fresh stains, swab or sponge with warm water.
- For set stains, rub in glycerin. Allow to stand several hours. Apply a few drops of vinegar. Let remain one minute and then rinse.
- Or apply a spot cleaner with a few drops of vinegar. Cover with a blotter dampened with stain remover and let stand, or push stain remover into fabric until stain is gone. Rinse with water. If traces remain, apply alcohol, and let stand until stain is gone. If traces still remain, moisten with equal parts warm water and presoak. Cover with pad soaked with same solution, and let stand for one half hour. Rinse.

Glue

- Look up specific glues in *Adhesives* section.

Grease Spots

Butter and Butter Substitutes

Washables
- Sponge or soak in soap and warm water.

Cleanables
- Swab or sponge with cleaning fluid.
- Cover both sides of fabric with fuller's earth or a dry spotter. Let stand half an hour and then brush off. Repeat if necessary. If stain remains, sponge again with cleaning fluid.

Candle Wax

- Scrape off wax with a blunt knife before cleaning.

Washables
- Rub with cold lard, dry-cleaning solvent, or turpentine. Wash in sudsy water and rinse.

Cleanables
- Cover both sides with blotters and iron with a warm iron. If traces remain, sponge with cleaning fluid or denatured alcohol, but do not use alcohol on acetate rayon or nonfast dyes.

Chocolate

Washables
- Wash in soap and water. If traces remain, wash in a solution of diluted wood (methyl) alcohol and ammonia.
- Or use processes outlined for gravy and sauces.

Cleanables
- Sponge with dry-cleaning fluid, then sponge with warm water. If traces remain, sponge with mild mixture of bleach and water, and rinse.
- Or use processes outlined for gravy and sauces.

Gravy, Sauces, Salad Dressing, Meat Juice

Washables
- Sponge or wash with mild detergent and cold water.

Cleanables
- Sponge with dry-cleaning solvent. If traces remain, apply dry spotter and cover with absorbent material dampened with dry spotter, or work it into fabric. Keep stain moist and sponge or blot. Then apply dry-cleaning solvent. If traces still remain, repeat process. Sponge with water.
- Or sponge or swab with dry-cleaning solvent. If traces remain, sponge with lukewarm water.

Makeup, Tar, Machine Oil

Washables
- Rub with glycerin or petroleum jelly. Wash in soap and water.

Cleanables
- Sponge on dry-cleaning solvent. If traces remain, apply a dry spotter and cover with a blotter dampened with more dry spotter. Change pads as stains are being picked up. Then clean again with dry-cleaning solvent. When dry, sponge with water. If traces still remain, sponge with denatured alcohol (except on acetate fabric or fabrics dyed with nonfast dye), or sponge with a mixture of bleach and water (if the fabric is compatible with bleach), and rinse well.

Oils and Fats

Washables
- Remove fresh stains with mild detergent and warm water.
- Remove set stains by covering with fuller's earth or other absorbent powder and then swab or sponge with cleaning fluid.

Cleanables
- Sponge on dry-cleaning solvent. If traces remain, apply dry spotter and cover with a blotter dampened with more dry spotter. Change pads as stains are being picked up. Then clean again with dry-cleaning solvent. When dry, sponge with water. If traces still remain, sponge with denatured alcohol (except on acetate fabric or fabrics dyed with nonfast dye), or sponge with a mixture of bleach and water (if the fabric is compatible with bleach), and rinse well.

Inks

- First try a mild detergent and water. If the stains remain, use a presoak or use the solvents listed for each type of ink in the *Colorants* section, or read MSDSs and use the listed solvents.

Mildew

Washables
- Wash with sudsy water. If stains remain, sprinkle with lemon juice and dry in the sun, or soak overnight in a covered container of milk.

- Or rinse with dry-cleaning solvent. Apply dry spotter and amyl acetate, and pat with sponge or cheesecloth. Again apply dry-cleaning solvent, and allow to dry. Apply water, then again apply dry-cleaning solvent and vinegar. If traces remain, pat stain with alcohol, then flush with more alcohol, and allow to dry. If stains still remain, apply chlorine bleach, in a ratio of one part bleach to four parts water, using a dropper. Let it sit on fabric only up to two minutes, then rinse well. Apply one teaspoon vinegar and rinse again.

Mud

For All Fabrics
- Vacuum or brush out any dried particles, then rinse in clear water. If traces remain, rinse or sponge with diluted denatured alcohol.

Perspiration

To restore color
- Dampen with water and hold over ammonia fumes.

To remove odor
- Spray with a special perspirant removal or disinfectant, or wash or sponge with warm sudsy water containing some vinegar.

Washables

- Follow process recommended for urine.

Protein

Blood

- Wear gloves to avoid contact with any blood stains.

Washables
- Soak in cold water, then in a solution of warm soapy water with a small amount of ammonia. If traces remain, wet with hydrogen peroxide, let stand up to 15 minutes, and rinse well.

Cleanables
- Sponge with cold or lukewarm water. If traces remain, sponge with hydrogen peroxide, let stand up to 15 minutes, and rinse well.

- Use only household ammonia. Ammonia can change some colors. If color fades, rinse that area with water, apply a small amount of white vinegar, and rinse again. Avoid inhaling ammonia fumes.

Egg

Washables
- For fresh stains, sponge with cold water. If traces remain, sponge with dry-cleaning solvent. If traces still remain, apply dry spotter, and cover or blot with absorbent material. Continue changing blotters until stain is removed. Soak in a presoak solution and then wash and rinse.

Cleanables • Sponge with cold water. Allow to dry. Sponge with dry-cleaning fluid or mineral spirits. If the stain remains, moisten it with a solution of equal parts of pre-soak and water, let stand up to 30 minutes, and then rinse well.

Milk, Cream, and Ice Cream

Washables • Mild detergent and water. If traces remain, sponge with ammonia and water (one-tablespoon ammonia to one-half-cup water).

Cleanables • For fresh stains, swab or sponge with cold or lukewarm water. If traces remain, sponge with ammonia and water (one-tablespoon ammonia to one-half-cup water).

• For set stains, swab or sponge with stain remover or mineral spirits. Allow to dry. Sponge with cold water.

Scorch

Washables • First wash with soap and water and place in sunlight, if possible. If traces remain on white fabric, dampen a cloth with hydrogen peroxide and lay the cloth on the stain. Cover it with another clean, dry cloth. Press with a medium iron, and rinse well.

• Or swab or sponge with a solution of sudsy water and hydrogen peroxide. Rinse well.

Woolens • Rub with fine emery paper.

Urine and Animal Stains

• Wear gloves to avoid any contact with urine and animal stains.

Washables only • Wash in warm sudsy water with weak ammonia. Rinse. If traces remain, soak in solution of one-quart warm water and one-tablespoon vinegar for up to one hour. Rinse and dry. If traces still remain, apply alcohol and sponge or cover with an alcohol-dampened pad. Let stand until stain is removed. Rinse with water.

• Or wash in warm, sudsy water, then in salt water, and then rinse.

Wine, Liquor, and Soft Drinks

• Immediately, place table salt on the stain to stop its spreading. Then use same methods as for fruit, coffee, and tea stains. do not allow to stand and do not use soap.

Appendix IV: Keeping Actors Safe and Healthy

While fitting actors, observe the following precautions:

- Do not spray any substances other than hair spray. Hair should be sprayed only where ventilation is good.
- Do not put liquid, glue, paint, silicone, or similar materials on an actor's skin.
- Do not stir up dust or release powder into the air, with the exception of small amounts of talcum when necessary.
- Do not apply anything that contains a volatile solvent or other toxic substance.
- The shop or fitting area should be equipped with a first-aid kit. Items that puncture the skin and draw blood should be discarded in a special container.
- When applying paint or dye to fitted costumes like tights and leotards, fit costumes on a dress form or mannequin. Do not apply when the actor is wearing the costume.

When actors are wearing completely encompassing and walk-around costumes, the costumer can take a number of measures to make the actor more comfortable.

- Cut holes—as many as possible—into the costume for air circulation.
- Small fans can be set into a headpiece or into any part of a costume large enough to accommodate them. The fans can be connected to battery packs.
- When noise from a fan or motorized system might disrupt a performance, costumers and dressers can use a battery-operated hair dryer, set on cool, to refresh actors between scenes. Remove the heating element from the hair dryer; then attach the dryer cord to a battery pack.
- Cooling devices are especially designed to work off of battery packs to cool down the performer wearing a heavy costume. Kits and vests are available through Alinco Costumes Inc., and the Actor Climate System is available through Global Effects Lab.
- Allow adequate drying time before permitting actors to wear costumes treated with glue, paint, solvents, etc.

Appendix V: Glossary

ABS Acrylonitrile-butadiene styrene; a polymer of acrylonitrile and styrene liquids and butadiene gas that form a family of resins.

ACCELERATOR A substance that is added to hasten a reaction, for example, that which is added to a resin to speed the curing or hardening process.

ACETONE A colorless, volatile, ketone solvent.

ACRYLICS Clear, brittle organic material formulated from acrylic acid or one of its derivatives. Available as sheeting, liquid or solvent, known as "Lucite," "Plexiglas," and "Perspex."

ADHESIVE An applied substance that holds materials together.

ARMSCYE The armhole of a garment.

ANNEALING Heat-treating acrylic pieces to prevent distortion and crazing occurring over a period of time.

BACKPACK A harnesslike structure worn on the back, usually underneath a covering garment, and often supported by the shoulders, to hold in place large or heavy ornamental pieces, often worn by showgirls and Mardi Gras celebrants.

BLEED Release of color when in contact with water or a solvent; movement of matter within a plastic to its surface.

BOND To adhere, either through chemical or mechanical means.

BURNING RATE The tendency of plastic articles to burn at given temperatures. Some burn quickly at low temperatures, while others melt without actually burning. The latter group is referred to as self-extinguishing.

BUTT A method of joining two items by placing them edge to edge.

CARCINOGEN A substance that causes or has the potential to cause cancer in humans. Findings, which must be listed on MSDSs, are based on a review of all relevant test data by the International Agency for Research on Cancer, the National Toxicology Program, or the Occupational Safety and Health Administration.

CASEIN The first thermosetting plastic, derived from skim milk. Today, soy is also used in casein.

CASTING (NOUN) The process or result of forming an object by pouring a substance into a mold.

CASTING (VERB) To pour a fluid substance into a mold, where it solidifies.

CATALYST A material that facilitates a reaction, but is unchanged once the reaction is completed. Catalysts are commonly known as the chemicals that initiate the curing process or polymerization; also called hardeners or initiators, they are available as liquids or pastes.

CELLULOSE A carbohydrate polymer, derived from plant tissues and fibers, and the main source of celluloid, cellophane, and paper.

CHEMICAL FAMILY A group of elements of a common general type of chemical.

CHEMICAL RESISTANCE The extent to which a material is unaffected by certain chemicals. For example, most plastics are impervious to the effects of moisture.

CLARIFIER An additive used to increase transparency of a material.

CORE An interior mold, used when casting hollow items, such as full bodysuits.

CORE SOCK A shaped nylon-spandex reinforcement that is the shape of an interior mold, used when casting full bodysuits. The fabric, which becomes embedded in the casting material, strengthens the costume pieces.

CRAZING Fine cracks within the surface or layer of plastic.

CURING The process of setting or hardening by chemical reaction, synonymous with *set*.

CYANOACRYLATE An adhesive with an acrylate base used commonly in industry and medicine. Commonly known as *super glue*.

DENSITY The ratio of weight to volume of a substance.

DILUTION VENTILATION A ventilation method that uses vents and air inlets to push fresh air into a room as an exhaust fan is drawing contaminated air out of the same space. Also called *mechanical* or *general ventilation*.

DISPERSION Fine particles of matter suspended in a liquid.

DISTRESSING The process of causing costumes and textiles to appear used or old. Other terms are *aging* and *breaking down*.

DRAPE FORMING Forming thermoplastic sheet by clamping the sheet to a movable frame, heating it, and draping it over the high points of a male, or positive, mold. The vacuum is then pulled to complete the process.

DRAW The process of stretching a thermoplastic sheet of rod, as in vacuum-forming.

DYE A substance that imparts by chemical reaction a transparent color to a material.

ELASTOMER Any polymer with the elastic quality of natural rubber, that can double its length and return to its original size.

ELASTOMERIC Having elastic, rubberlike properties.

EMBEDDING Setting one object into another, such as placing a piece of material into resin while casting.

EMULSION Fine droplet of one liquid within another.

EVAPORATION RATE The rate at which a material vaporizes or evaporates from a liquid or solid state when compared to the evaporation rate of butyl acetate or ethyl ether.

EPOXY A thermosetting plastic, available as a two-component liquid or paste for casting.

EXOTHERM The amount of self-generated heat given off during a chemical reaction.

EXPAND A chemical process that causes plastics to foam.

FABRICATE To work a material into a finished form.

FABRIC HAND The tactile quality of a fabric, including its drapability, firmness, softness, fineness, and resilience.

FABRICATION In special-effects costumes, usually refers to cutting, draping, and gluing foamed plastic sheeting into sculptural costume shapes, in contrast to molding and casting techniques.

FELT-TIP MARKER A metal tube containing an ink-saturated quarter-of-an-inch felt strip which protrudes as a nib.

FIBER A natural or synthetic filament that can be spun into a yarn.

FIBERGLASS A material used for reinforcing thermosetting plastics, made of spun, woven, matted or chopped pieces of glass.

FILLER A substance, often in powder form, added to a liquid resin causing it to be harder.

FILM Sheeting of a thickness of no more than .010 of an inch.

FLAME RETARDANT A chemical used to reduce or eliminate the tendency of a material to burn.

FLAMMABLE Easily ignitable and capable of burning rapidly.

FLASH POINT The lowest possible temperature at which a flammable liquid will combust.

FLEXICIZER An additive that makes a resin or rubber more flexible.

FLOW The movement of material in a semifluid state during setting.

FOAM Rubber or plastics containing many air pockets.

FOAMING AGENTS Chemicals that produce air pockets.

FOUND OBJECTS Cast-off items reused in a manner for which they were not originally intended, such as lipstick cases that serve as decorations on a headdress.

FREE-ARM MACHINE A sewing machine which has, as its table, a base narrow enough to accommodate small clothing parts like sleeves.

GATE Opening in a mold for pouring liquid.

GEL A semisolid state during curing process.

GEL COAT The first layer of unreinforced catalyzed resin applied to the outside of a plastic mold.

GESSO A viscous material, usually a mixture of plaster and adhesive, for coating surfaces preparatory to applying paint or other media.

GLAZING Thin layers of paint that allow underlayers to show through transparently.

GLITTER A type of small metallic flake usually made from colored aluminum, that gives off a visible sparkle or reflection.

GUTTA (Gutta-Percha) A rubberlike material found in the leaves and bark of several tropical trees of the genera Palquium and Pyna, used as a dye resist.

HARDENER A catalyst that speeds up curing time.

HOT-MELT GLUE STICKS Tubes of adhesive, solid at room temperature, that are melted in a special hot-melt resin applicator, commonly known as a *glue gun*.

HOT STAMPING An operation using heat and pressure to apply metal leaf or imitation leaf onto a surface.

HYDROCARBON An organic compound that contains carbon and hydrogen. Hydrocarbons are often solvents and classified as *aliphatic*, *aromatic*, and *chlorinated*.

IMPACT STRENGTH The gauge of resistance to shock by a material.

INFLAMMABLE Catches on fire and continues to burn easily. Synonymous with *flammable*.

INHIBITOR A chemical additive that slows a reaction.

JIG A tool to hold component parts of an assembly during a forming process.

KETONE A class of organic compounds, such as acetone and methyl-ethyl ketone (MEK), commonly used as solvents.

LAMINATE Layers bonded together to form one piece.

LATEX Fine particles of rubber in a water suspension.

LAY-UP In working with reinforced plastics, placing a reinforcing material (like fiberglass) into a mold.

LOCAL-EXHAUST VENTILATION A system, such as a canopy hood over a paint booth, which captures entering air pollutants and exhausts them directly into the outside air.

LUMINESCENT Possessing the quality to glow under ultraviolet light.

MASK To cover and protect a surface.

MAT A randomly distributed group of glass fibers, used in making fiberglass for reinforced castings.

MATERIAL SAFETY DATA SHEET Printed precautions which are required by the Occupational Safety and Health Administration (OSHA) and supplied by manufacturers of hazardous materials.

MELTING POINT The temperature at which a solid liquefies.

MEMORY The tendency of thermoplastic materials to return to their original shape after reheating.

METHYL ETHYL KETONE Methyl ethyl ketone peroxide (MEK) butanone, a ketone solvent and a hardener for resins such as polyester.

METHYL METHACRYLATE A monomer (building block) of a thermoplastic known as an acrylic, also known as *polymethyl methacrylate*.

MITER To bevel, or to cut at similar angles, so that two pieces of material will fit smoothly.

MOCK-UP A garment, usually made of muslin, to try out pattern and test construction, before using actual materials that will go into the finished item.

MOLD (NOUN) A tool for shaping plastic material under heat and pressure.

MOLD (VERB) To shape a piece of malleable material by hand, heat, or pressure.

MOLD, FEMALE A negative mold with a concave working surface.

MOLD, MALE A positive mold with a convex working surface.

MOLD RELEASE AGENT A substance that prevents a material from adhering to a mold; also a *parting agent*.

MONOMER A fairly simple compound that can react with itself or other monomers to form a polymer.

MORDANT A substance that permanently fixes dyes to fabrics and other surfaces.

MOTHER MOLD A rigid support, usually of plaster, which surrounds a flexible or a multiple-part mold. Also referred to as a jacket or main case.

MYLAR The brand name for a polyester resin film sheeting manufactured by E.I. du Pont de Nemours and Company.

NONCONTACT Pertains to one-part rubber-cement adhesives that bond only after the cement has dried. Also referred to as opentime adhesives.

NYLON A generic name for a form of polyamide.

OMBRÉ Shading colors through dyeing or painting so that one color gradually fades into another.

OSHA The Occupational Safety and Health Administration, a federal agency which regulates safety and environmental laws.

OSHACT The Occupational Safety and Health Act that protects those workers using hazardous materials or in dangerous situations.

OXIDATION The addition of oxygen to a compound, often occurring naturally from air and sunlight.

PAPIER-MACHÉ A mixture of adhesive and paper or paper pulp, used for casting and sculpting.

PARTING AGENT Same as mold release agent.

PARTING LINE The line on a mold where the two or more parts meet.

PEARLESCENT PIGMENTS A group of pigments consisting of particles of transparent, high-refraction crystals; the effect is of partial reflection from both sides of each flake.

PIGMENT A coloring agent that is insoluble in the medium in which it is used, unlike a dye.

PLASTIC (NOUN) Any of various man-made compounds, derived chiefly from coal and oil.

PLASTIC (ADJECTIVE) Capable of being shaped or formed.

PLASTIC MEMORY The ability to return to the original form.

PLASTICINE CLAY A synthetic oil- or wax-based clay used in making models for molds.

PLASTICIZER A substance that increases pliability.

PLASTISOL Resin and a plasticizer mixed into a thick mass—typically 100 parts resin to 50 parts plasticizer—used for molding thermoplastic products, chiefly polyvinyl chloride.

POLYMER Any compound consisting of up to millions of repeated linked monomers, or molecular units.

POLYAMIDE Thermoplastic group, e.g., nylon.

POLYESTER A thermosetting or thermoplastic resin, commonly available as a fluid.

POLYETHYLENE A thermoplastic, commonly available as solid or foamed sheeting and rods.

POLYSTYRENE A hard, transparent and brittle thermoplastic, also known as styrene, available as a sheeting or in its expanded, or foam state, commonly known as the brand name "Styrofoam."

POLYURETHANE A thermoplastic resin popular in both its solid and in its expanded, or foamed, states. Also known as *urethane*.

POLYVINYL CHLORIDE (PVC) A widely used thermoplastic, rigid or flexible.

POLYVINYL ACETATE (PVA) A thermoplastic material most familiar to costumers as an ingredient of a class of adhesives, known as *white glues*, and of coatings.

POT-LIFE Length of time a plastic remains in a liquid form before curing.

PPI *Pores per inch*, a measurement used to identify the density of foamed plastic.

PRIMER A first coat of paint or other coating material applied to prepare a surface to ensure a bond with a second material.

PROPERTIES Qualities of materials that enable classification of their differences.

PULL A vacuum-formed piece, as it is pulled from the vacuum-former.

RELEASE AGENT A substance applied to a mold to prevent casting material from adhering to a mold's interior. Also referred to as a *separator* or *parting agent*.

RESIN A complex organic substance (such as acrylic, epoxy, polyester, and polyurethane) that can be mixed with other substances to form plastics.

RESILIENCE The tendency of a material to revert to its original shape.

RTV Room-temperature vulcanizing, referring to rubbers that reach their ultimate inflexibility, strength, and stability at room temperature without being oven-heated.

RESPIRATOR A device that limits inhalation of toxic materials. Respirators range from disposable dust masks to self-contained breathing apparatuses. Respirators should be selected carefully for the specific use.

SEPARATOR Mold-release agent.

SET To convert liquid into a solid state through curing, evaporation, suspension, or gelling.

SETTING TEMPERATURE The temperature at which liquid resin sets into a solid state.

SHELF LIFE The time that liquid plastics remain liquid at average room temperature. Average shelf life is 12 months, though lower temperatures increase and higher temperatures decrease shelf life.

SHELLAC A resin formed as a protective coating by the lac insects in India.

SILICONE A resin derived from silica, having a high resistance to heat and used for making molds, casts, adhesives, and filling gaps.

SILK-SCREEN PRINTING Also called *screen-process printing*; it involves laying a pattern of an insoluble material onto another fabric and blocking off areas with a fluid. As ink is drawn across the screen, it passes through the screen and onto the desired areas.

SIZING A material applied to a surface for filling pores to reduce absorption or to stiffen it.

SLURRY Mixture of a fine material and a liquid.

SLUSH MOLDING A method of casting thermoplastics in which the resin in liquid form is poured into a mold where a viscous skin forms. The excess slush is drained off, the mold is cooled, and the casting removed.

SOLVENT A liquid substance that dissolves other substances.

SPANDEX Textile fibers composed mainly of polyurethane rubber, frequently used in dancewear and swimwear.

SPRUE A funnel-shaped opening at the top of a mold for pouring in liquid casting material.

STABILIZERS Additives that maintain resins in their original, desired properties.

STIPPLE Small, even touches of paint or other colorant applied to produce an even-looking surface.

STYRENE A hard, transparent and brittle thermoplastic, also known as polystyrene, available as a sheeting or in its expanded, or foam state, commonly known as "styrofoam."

STYROFOAM Trade name for expanded polystyrene made by the Dow Chemical Company.

TACK The semidry condition of an adhesive after application.

TACK TIME The time in which an adhesive remains in a semidry condition after application.

TENSILE STRENGTH Resistance against being pulled apart.

THERMOPLASTICS Those plastics that become soft and pliable by heating and hard by cooling.

THERMOSETTING Those plastics that cannot be softened.

THIXOTROPIC The property of a viscous material that is gel-like at rest and fluid when agitated.

THRESHOLD LIMIT VALUE The maximum airborne concentration of a (TLV) material most healthy adults workers have been predicted to tolerate without adverse effects averaged over the eight-hour day, forty-hour work week. Standards are determined by the American Conference of Government Industrial Hygienists.

TOXIC The ability of a material to injure biological tissue.

UNDERCUT Indentations within a form that create reverse curved areas.

UNSTABLE The tendency or a material towards disintegration or other undesirable changes during normal handling.

URETHANE A thermosetting synthetic rubber available as a liquid resin for casting, or in solid and foam sheets. Also known as *polyurethane*.

VACUUM-BAG MOLDING Forming of objects by placing items into an air-tight, flexible bag connected to a vacuum pump. The pump pulls the air from the bag, causing the interior items to bond or mold.

VACUUM-FORMING A method of molding a thermoplastic sheet by clamping it onto a mold, then withdrawing the air beneath it.

VINYL A soft and pliable thermoplastic formed by a combination of plastics.

VISCOSITY Degree of resistance by a liquid to flow.

VISCOUS A high resistance to flow. Low-viscosity fluids are thin, like water. High-viscosity liquids are thick, like syrup.

VOLATILE Vapors that when released can cause an explosion.

WALK-AROUND COSTUME A costume of a character or product used for promotion and usually worn in a commercial environment.

WARPAGE Dimensional distortion in an object after it has been molded.

WATER-SOLUBLE Substances that dissolve in water.

WEB FILM Hot-melt or fusible film, tissue-thin sheets or tapes of adhesive resin, used for bonding fabrics together.

WELDING Joining pieces by a heat-softening process.

WETTING AGENT A chemical that erodes or roughens the surface of a material, allowing it to accept color or other coating.

WORKING LIFE The time length in which an activated resin or adhesive may be handled.

Appendix VI: Resources

Directory to Workshops and Studios

The following costume workshops and studios are mentioned in the text and have been especially helpful in sharing information that has been included within this book.

Alterian Studios
5454 Diaz Street
Irwindale, CA 91706
818-856-3319

Bill Hargate
Costume Shop
1111 N. Formosa Avenue
Los Angeles, CA 90038
213-876-4432

Chip's Character Creations Inc.
7069 Vineland Avenue
N. Hollywood, CA 91605
818-759-1345

Costume Armour Inc.
2 Mill Street
Cornwall on the Hudson, NY 12518
914-534-9120

DNA 69 (Chain Mail)
33 Prince Street
Montreal, Canada
514-866-6969

GM Foam, Inc.
14956 Delano Street
Van Nuys, CA 91411
818-908-1087

J & M Costumers, Inc.
5708 Gentry Avenue
N. Hollywood, CA 91607
818-760-1991

Make-Believe
3229 Pico Boulevard
Los Angeles, CA 90025
310-396-6785

Makeup & Effects Lab Inc. (MEL)
7110 Laurel Canyon Boulevard,
Bldg. E
N. Hollywood, CA 91604
818-982-1483

Martin Izquierdo Studios
118 West 22nd Street
New York, NY 10011
212-807-9757

Michael Curry Design and
Engineering
4511 SE 23rd Avenue
Portland, OR 97202
503-230-0550

Parsons-Meares Ltd.
121 West 19th Street
New York, NY 10011
212-242-3378

Prop Masters Incorporated
912 West Isabel Street
Burbank, CA 91506
818-846-3915

Rodney Gordon
315 W. 35th Street,
10th Floor
New York, NY 10001
212-594-6658

Shafton Inc.
6932 Tujunga Avenue
N. Hollywood, CA 91605
818-985-5025

Stan Winston Studios Inc.
7032 Valjean Avenue
Van Nuys, CA 91406
818-782-0870

Sticks & Stones
10535 Tujunga Canyon Boulevard
Tujunga, CA 91402
818-352-9538

Syren
7225 Beverly Boulevard
Los Angeles, CA 90036
213-936-6693

Total Fabrication
13136 Saticoy Street,
Unit L
N. Hollywood, CA 91605
818-765-0091

Vin Burnham
24 Glyn Mansions
Hammersmith Road
London W 14 8XH
071-792-3102

XFX
8010 Wheatland Avenue
Sun Valley, CA 91352
818-504-2177

Directory to Manufacturers and Distributors

The following list is confined to those manufacturers and distributors who I believe to be the most useful when purchasing and inquiring about the products listed within this book. Many more manufacturers and distributors exist, and some of both may be discovered through the yellow pages, and distributors may be located by contacting manufacturers.

A

A.D.M. Tronics Unlimited, Inc.
224 South Pegasus Ave.
North Vale, NJ 07647
201-767-6040

Activa Products, Inc.
PO Box 1296
512 South Garrett Street
Marshall, TX 75670
903-938-2224

Alcone Company Inc.
5-49 49th Avenue
Long Island City, NY 11101
718-361-8373

**Aleene's,
Division of Artis Inc.**
85 Industrial Way
Buellton, CA 93427
805-688-7339

Alinco Costumes Inc.
5505 S. Riley Lane
Murray, UT 84107
800-845-2272

Allied Plastics, Inc.
9445 North West
East River Road
Minneapolis, MN 55401
612-862-4500/553-7771

**Alucobond
Technologies, Inc.**
PO Box 507, Symsonia Road
Benton, Kentucky 42025
502-527-1376
800-423-0278

American Art Clay Co., Inc.
4717 West 16th Street
Indianapolis, IN 462222
800-374-1600
317-244-6871

American Cyanamid Co.
One Cyanamid Plaza
Wayne, NJ 07470
973-683-2000

Angelus Shoe Polish Co.
8640 National Boulevard
Culver City, CA 90230
310-836-3314

A-R Products, Inc.
11807 7/8 Slauson Avenue
Santa Fe Springs, CA 90670
562-907-7707

Artis, Inc.
85 Industrial Way
Buellton, CA 93427
800-825-3363

Avery Dennison Inc.
1 Clark Highway
Framingham, MA 01702
508-879-0511

B

Ball Consulting, Ltd.
338 14th Street, Suite 201
Ambridge, PA 15003
724-266-1502

Beacon Chemical Company
125 South MacQuesten Parkway
Mount Vernon, NY 10550
914-699-3400

Beacon Chemical Company
Fabri-Tac Division:
301 Wagaraw Street
Hawthorne, NJ 07506
201-427-3700

Bell Chemical Co.
1688 E. 23rd Street
Los Angeles, CA 90011
213-233-1091

Binney & Smith, Inc.
Div. of W. H. Collins
21 Leslie Court
Whippany, NJ 07981
973-887-4900

BJB Enterprises, Inc.
14791 Franklin Avenue
Tustin, CA 14791
714-734-8450

**Blasco, Joe
Makeup Center**
7340 Greenbriar Parkway
Orlando, Florida 32819
407-363-1234

Bond Adhesives Company
301 Frelinghuysen Avenue
Newark, NJ 07114
973-824-8100
800-659-2292

Bostik Inc.
211 Boston Street
Middleton, MA 01949
978-777-0100

British Visqueen Ltd.
(subsidiary of I C I)
ICI Group Headquarters
9 Millbank
London SW1P 3JF
England
441-71-834-4444

Burman Industries Incorporated
14141 Covello Street, Suite 6-A
Van Nuys, CA 91405
818-782-9833

BXL Plastics Ltd.
794 Parklane
Croydon
England CRO IFO
441-81-688-7770

C

Cabot Corporation
700 East U.S. Highway 36
Tuscola IL 61953
800-222-6745

Cadillac Plastic and Chemical Co.
Corporate Offices
2855 Coolidge Highway, #300
Troy, MI 48007
248-205-3100

Canal Rubber Supply Co., Inc.
329 Canal Street
New York, NY 10013
212-226-7339

Cementex Company, Inc.
121 Varick Street
New York, NY 10013
212-741-1770

Chicago Latex Products
345 East Terra Cotta Avenue
Crystal Lake, IL 60014
815-549-9680

Coltene Whaledent Inc.
750 Corporate Drive
Mahwah, NJ 07430
800-221-3046

Ciba-Geigy Corporation
31601 Research Park Drive
Madison Heights, MI 48071
313-585-7200

W. H. Collins Inc.
21 Leslie Court
Whippany, NJ 07981
201-887-4900

ColorCraft, Ltd.
14 Airport Park Road
East Granby, CT 06026
Assistance: 860-653-5505
Ordering: 800-243-2712

Composite Materials Inc.
PO Box 3448
Santa Fe Springs, CA 90670
562-906-2661

Conap, Inc.
1405 Buffalo Street
Olean, NY 14760
716-372-9650

CSL Silicones, Inc.
144 Woodlawn Road West
Guelph, Ontario
Canada N1H 1B5
519-836-9044
or
PO Box 266 Roswell, GA 30077-0266
404-998-2935
or
5800 Fairfield, Suite 260
Ft Wayne, IN 46807
219-456-3438
or
1520 Nutmeg Place, Costa Mesa,
CA 92626
714-957-2935

D

Davis Dental Supply
7347 Ethel Avenue
N. Hollywood, CA 91605
818-765-4994

DeCart, Inc.
(Deka Products)
Lamoille Industrial Park
Morrisville, VT 05661
802-888-4217

Delta Technical
Coatings, Inc.
2550 Pellissier Place
Whittier, CA 90601
626-579-5420

Devcon Corporation
30 Endicott Street
Danvers, MA 01923
978-777-1100

Dexter Adhesives, Inc.
(Hysol Div. for Hysol products)
1 Dexter Drive
Seabrook, NH 03874
800-323-5158
474-5541

Douglas & Sturgess Corp., Inc.
730 Bryant Street
San Francisco, CA 94107
415-896-6283

Dri-Print Foils, Inc.
329 New Brunswick Avenue
Rahway, NJ 07065
732-382-6800

Dow Chemical Co.
2040 Willard H. Dow Center
Midland, MI 48640
800-441-4369

Dow Corning
909 Sylvan Lane
Midland, MI 48640
517-835-5093
800-248-2481

Dritz Corporation
PO Box 5028
Highway Interstate 85
Spartanburg, SC 2930
864-576-5050

Duncan Enterprises
5673 East Shields Avenue
Fresno, CA 93727
559-291-2515

Dupli-Color Products Company
1601 Nicholas Boulevard
Elk Grove Village, IL 60007
708-439-0600

E. I. du Pont de Nemours and Company
1007 North Orange Street
Wilmington, DE 19898
302-774-1000
800-441-7515

Dylon International, Ltd.
Worsley Bridge Road
Lower Sydenham
London, S. E. 26
England
44-416-420-3232

E

Eastman Kodak Company
Eastman Chemical Products, Inc.
Eastman Adhesives Division
c/o Plastics Division
PO Box 431
Kingsport, TN 37662
800-251-0351

Eclectic Products, Inc.
998 South A Street
Springfield, OR 97477
800-767-4667

Elixir Industries
17905 South Broadway
Gardena, CA 90248
310-767-3400

Elmer's Products, Inc.
A Borden Company
1000 Kingsmill Parkway
Columbus, OH 43229
800-848-9400
614-431-6680

Evode Ltd.
Common Road
Stafford ST16 3EH
England
441-01785-57755

EZ International
PO Box 895
Saddle Brook, NJ 07663
201-712-1234

F

Fibermark Inc.
45 North 4th Street
Quakertown, PA 18951
215-536-4600

Fiebing Company, Inc.
421 South Second Street
Milwaukee, WI 53204
414-271-5011

Flecto Company Inc.
1000 Forty-fifth Street
Emeryville, CA 94608
510-655-2470

Foamex Products, Inc.
1800 East Second Street
Eddystone, PA 19022
800-767-4997

Four D Rubber Company Limited
Delves Road, Heanor Gate
Industrial Estate
Heanor, Derbyshire DE75 TSJ
England
01773-763134

Fred Frankel & Sons, Inc.
19 W. 38th Street
New York, NY 10018
212-840-0810

G

Gaylord Bros.
P. O. Box 4901
Syracuse, NY 13221
315-457-5070

Gebr Lutt Ges Gmbh & Co.
Focher Strasse 179
D-42719 Gelingem
Germany
02-12-313828

General Electric Company
GE Silicones:
260 Hudson River Road
Waterford, NY 12188
800-255-8886

Plastics Group:
One Plastics Avenue
Pittsfield, MA 01201
800-451-3147

Gibbon Inks
and Coatings Ltd.
Screen Division
25 Dear Park Road
Wimbledon, London SW193UD
0181-542-8531

Global Effects Lab
7119 Laurel Canyon Blvd., #4
North Hollywood, CA 91605
818-503-9273

GM Foam, Inc.
14956 Delano Street
Van Nuys, CA 91411
818-908-1087

Golden Artist Colors, Inc.
Bell Road
New Berlin, NY 13411
607-847-6154

Goodrich, BF
Adhesive Systems Division
Akron OH, 44318

West Coast Office and Warehouse:
On-Hand Distributors, Inc.
26945 Cabot Road, 106
Laguna Hills, CA 92653
714-582-6939
800-323-5158

H

Hastings Plastics Company
1704 Colorado Avenue
Santa Monica, CA 90404
310-829-3449

Head Lite Corp.
2415 Ventura Drive
St. Paul, MN 55125
612-730-7000
800-777-5630

Henkel Home Improvement & Adhesive Products
Cromwell Road
St. Neotf Cambs, PE 192JW
England
44-1480-408-323

Hexcel Corp.
5794 West Las Positas Avenue
Pleasanton, CA 94588
510-847-9500
Duxford, Cambridge
England CB24QD
44-1223-833-141

I

ICI Americas Inc.
Concord Plaza
3411 Silverside Road
PO Box 15391
Wilmington, DE 19850
302-887-3000
800-822-8215

ICI/ Imperial Chemical Industries Ltd.
ICI Group Headquarters
9 Millbank
London SW1P 3JF
England
441-71-834-4444

IPS/Industrial Polychemical Service Corporation
455 West Victoria Street
Compton, CA 90237
310-366-3300

Iron Horse Safety Specialties
P. O. Box 551548
Dallas, TX 75355
800-323-5889

J

Jeweltrim, Inc.
19 W. 38th Street
New York, NY 10018
212-840-0810

Johnson & Johnson Orthopaedics
Raynham, MA 02767
800-526-2459

K

Kiwi Brands Inc.
447 Old Swede Road
Douglassville, PA 19518
610-385-3041
800-289-5494

Kishigo, M. L., Manufacturing Co.
2901 South Daimler Street
Santa Ana, CA 92705
800-338-9480

Krazy Glue, Inc.
53 W. 23rd Street
New York, NY 10010
212-807-3884

Kleerdex Company
6685 Low Street
Bloomsburg, PA 17185
717-387-6997
800-682-8758

Koh-I-Noor Inc.
100 North St.
Bloomsbury, NJ 08804
908-479-4124

L

Le Franc & Bourgeois
U.S. Distributor:
Koh-I-Noor Inc.
100 North Street
Bloomsbury, NJ 08804
908-479-4124

Liquitex
Binney & Smith, Inc.
Div. of W. H. Collins
21 Leslie Court
Whippany, NJ 07981
201-887-4900

Lockfast Inc.
4430 Mitchell
North Las Vegas, NV 89031
800-626-0034

Loctite Corporation
North American Group
1001 Trout Brook Crossing
Evergreen, CO 80439
888-261-2578

Lumered
292 Smith Street
Woodbridge, NJ 07095
732-634-1313

M

Macklenburg-Duncan
4041 North Santa Fe
Oklahoma City, OK 73118
800-241-0528 (in CA)
800-654-0007 (Outside CA)
800-654-8454 (Customer Service)

Magic American Chemical Corp.
23700 Mercantile Road
Cleveland, OH 44122
800-321-6330

Manny's Millinery Supply Company
63 West 38th Street
New York, NY 10018
212-840-2235

MarChem Corporation
2500 Adie Road
Maryland Heights, MO 63043
314-872-8700

McCloskey Division of The Valspar Corporation
1191 Wheeling Road
Wheeling, IL 60090
800-345-4530

Miles Inc.
Mobay Road
Pittsburgh, PA 15205
800-622-6004

Modern Options, Inc.
2325 Third Street, #339
San Francisco, CA 94107
415-252-5580

Monsanto Company
800 North Lindbergh Blvd.
St. Louis, MO 63141
314-344-9300

Mydrin, Incorporated
5901 Telegraph Road
Los Angeles, CA 90040
213-724-6162

N

National Hair Technologies, Ltd.
300 Canal Street
Lawrence, MA 01840
808-686-2964

Norcostco
Headquarters:
3203 North Highway 100
Minneapolis, MN 55422
612-533-2791
Other stores include:
333-A Route 46 West
Fairfield, NJ 07004
973-575-3503
or
3603 West Magnolia Boulevard
Burbank, CA 91505
818-567-0753

O

On-Hand Distributors, Inc.
1247 Rand Road
Des Plaines, IL 60016
312-296-0140
800-323-5158

P

Pacer Technology
9420 Santa Anita Avenue
Rancho Cucamonga, CA 91730
909-987-0550

Palmer Paint Products, Inc.
1291 Rochester Road
Troy, MI 48083
248-588-4500

Pellon Corporation
1040 Sixth Avenue
New York, NY 10018
212-391-6300

Permaflex Products Co., Inc.
28 Industrial Boulevard
Paoli, PA 19301
215-647-3578

Pierce & Stevens Corp.
710 Ohio Street
PO Box 1092
Buffalo, NY 14240
716-631-8991 or 716-856-4910

Pink House Studios, Inc.
35 Bank Street
St. Albans, VT 05472
802-524-7191

Plaid Enterprises
1649 International Court
PO Box 7600
Norcross, GA 30093
800-241-5202

Polymerics, Inc.
24 Prime Parkway
Natick, MA 01760
800-458-7010

Polytek Development Corp.
55 Hilton Street
Easton, PA 18042
908-236-2990

Polyurethane Specialties Company
624 Schuyler Avenue
Lyndhurst, NJ 07071
201-438-2325

R

Red Spot Paint and Varnish Company, Inc.
Research Center
1111 East Louisiana Street
Evansville, IN 47711
812-428-0965

Reichold Chemicals Incorporated
524 N. Broadway
White Plains, NY 10603
914-682-5700

West Coast Distributor:
H. H. Gerisch Products
20814 South Normandie Avenue
Torrance, CA 90502
310-320-5479

Ridlen (AAI) Adhesives
2952 Blystone Lane
Dallas, TX 75220
800-445-0609

Rilsan Corporation
139 Harristown Road
Glen Rock, NJ 07452
201-447-3300

Rohm and Haas Company
Independence Mall West
Philadelphia, PA 19105
215-592-3000

Rosco Laboratories Inc.
36 Bush Avenue
Port Chester, NY 10573
914-937-1300
or
1135 N. Highland Ave
Hollywood, CA 90038
213-462-2233

**Ross Adhesives Division
of the American Glue
Corporation**
25300 Northline Road
Taylor MI 48180
800-387-5275

S

Safe Reflections, Inc.
1714 Gervais Avenue East
St. Paul, MN 55109
612-773-8199
800-773-8199

Safety Effects
116 Venture Court, #3
Lexington, KY 40511
800-929-3975

**Safety Flag Company
of America**
P. O. Box 1088
390 Pine Street
Pawtucket, RI 02862
401-722-0912
800-556-7584

**Sculptural Arts
Coating, Inc.**
PO Box 13113

Greensboro. NC 27415
800-743-0379

Sennelier S. A.
3 Quai Voltaire 7e
Paris, 75007
France
42-60-29-38

Shell Chemical Company
777 Walker Street
Houston, TX 77002
713-241-6161

Sherman Foam
17 Toms Wood Road
Chigwell
Essex IG 7 5PQ
England
44-0181-559-1942

Sherwin-Williams Co.
101 West Prospect Avenue
Cleveland, OH 44115
216-566-2000

Siphon Art Products
365 Pittsburgh Avenue
Richmond, CA 94801
510-236-0949

Slomons Laboratories, Inc.
1000 Zekendorf Boulevard
Garden City, NY 11530
or
32-45 Point Avenue
L. I. C., NY 11101
212-784-0205
or
9-11 Linden Street
Newark, NY 07102

Smith & Nephew Roylan Inc. EBI
One Quality Drive
P.O. Box 1005
Germantown, WI 53022
800-558-8633

Smooth-On, Inc.
1000 Valley Road
Gillette, NJ 07933

800-762-0744 (Order Desk)
800-766-6841 (Technical Assistance)

Spectra Dynamics Products
415 Marble N. W. Avenue
Albuquerque, NM 87102
505-843-7202

Stabond Corporation
14010 S. Western Avenue
Gardena, CA 90249
310-770-0591

Stanley-Bostich Inc.
Route 2
East Greenwich, RI 02818
401-884-2500

**Swift Adhesives & Coatings
Division of Eschem, Inc.**
3100 Woodcreek Drive
PO Box 1546
Downers Grove, IL 60515
800-659-2292

T

3M Company
Product Information Center:
Building 304-01-01
St. Paul, MN 55144-1000
Main Offices:
800-364-3577

Occupational Health &
Environmental
Safety System Division:
800-328-1667
Industrial Specialty Division
(Adhesives):
800-362-3550

U

**Uncommon
Conglomerates, Inc.**
400 Western Avenue North
St. Paul, MN 55103
612-227-7000

Union Carbide
39 Old Ridgebury Road
Danbury, CT 06817
800-568-4000

Uniplast, Inc.
Department D
616 111th Street
Arlington, TX 76011
817-640-3204

Uniroyal Technology Inc.
312 North Hill Street
Mishawaka, IN 46544
219-256-8000

**UnNatural Resources
for Meta-Lites**
13 Forest Street
Caldwell, NJ 07006
973-364-1006
for all other products:
730 Bryant Street
San Francisco, CA 94107
415-896-6283

V

Vagabond Corporation
36374 Montezuma Valley Rd.
Ranchita, CA 92066
760-782-3136

Velcro USA Inc.
406 Brown Avenue
Manchester, NH 03103
603-669-4880

Voltek
Division of Sekisui
America Corp.
100 Shepard Street
Lawrence, MA 01843
978-685-2557

W

Walco Materials Group
2221 Las Palmas Drive, Suite J
Carlsbad, CA 92009
619-930-2575

Ward Engineering
13444 Wyandotte
N. Hollywood, CA 91605
818-503-7940

Wilhold Glues, Inc.
8707 Millergrove Drive
Santa Fe Springs, CA 90670
or
2943 W. Carroll Avenue
Chicago, IL 60612

Windsor & Newton, Inc.
11 Constitution Avenue
PO Box 1396
Piscataway, NJ 08855
732-562-0770

Witco Corporation
Organics Division
520 Madison Avenue
New York, NY 10022
212-755-4593
or
56200 W. 51st Street
Chicago, IL 60638
800-231-1542
or
3230 Brookfield Street
Houston, TX 77045

Z

Zeller International Ltd.
Main Street Box Z
Downsville, NY 13755
800-722-USFX
607-363-7792

Zeta Trikotagenfabrik
Linkenheimerweg 51
D 7520 Bruchsal
Germany 07251-2446
49-725-12446

Zynolyte Products Co.
2320 East Dominiguez Street
Carson, CA 90749
310-513-0700

Product List

The following products, some trademarked and registered, are mentioned in the book. I have done my best to include and represent all of them correctly.

#74 Flexible Latex Molding Compound; A-R Products, Inc.

10-76; Ball Consulting, Ltd.

280 Latex; A-R Products, Inc.

3-Dimensional Fabric Paint, Glittering; Aleene's® Product of Duncan Enterprises

3M™ 8010 Reflective Ink

3M™ High Strength Adhesive 90; 3M™ Company

3M™ High Tack 76; 3M™ Company

3M™ Scotchlite™ Reflective Material; 3M™ Company

3M™ Super 77 Spray Adhesive; 3M™ Company

481 Tacky; Bond™ Adhesives Company

5-Minute Epoxy Gel; Devcon®

5-Minute Epoxy; Devcon®

732 Multi-Purpose Sealant; Dow Corning®

A-1 Urethane Varnish; A-1 Paint & Varnish Company

Acrifix® 90; Rohm & Haas G.m.b.H.

Acrylic Scenic Paint; Oleson Paints

Ad Marker®; Chartpak

Adapt-It®; UnNatural Resources®

Aleene's® Mosaic Crackle; Aleene's® Product of Duncan Enterprises

Aleenes'® Flexible Stretchable Fabric Glue; Aleene's® Division of Artis, Inc.

Altra-Form®; UnNatural Resources®

Amway™ L.O.C.; Amway™ Corporation

Angelus® Brand Leather Dye; Angelus® Shoe Polish Company

Aqualyte™; Zynolyte® Products Company

Aquapellets®; Smith & Nephew Rolyan® Inc. EBI

Aquaplast®; Smith & Nephew Rolyan® Inc. EBI

Araldite®; Ciba-Geigy Corporation

Artist's Choice™ Paints; Sculptural Arts Coating, Inc.

Artist Color Gel Medium; Rotring®

Artist Color Opaque Acrylic; Rotring®

Artistic Acrylic Colors; Cal Western Paint, Inc.

Artists' Acrylic Color, Grumbacher®, Inc.

Artists' Acrylic Colours; Windsor & Newton®, Inc.

Barge® All-Purpose; Cement; Pierce & Stevens Chemical Corporation

Batman™; Warner Communications, Inc.

Beauty and the Beast™; Walt Disney Productions

Bic® Accountant; Bic® USA

Bond™ 527; Bond™ Adhesives Company

Bond™ 634; Bond™ Adhesives Company

Bond™ Rhinestone Adhesive #916; Bond™ Adhesives Company

Bostik® 3851; Bostik® Inc.

Bostik® 6330; Bostik® Inc.

Bridal Adhesive; Manny's Millinery Supply (MANCO)

Bridal Glue; Washington Millinery

Bullwinkle©; Universal City Studios, Inc.

Cab-O-Sil®; Cabot Corporation

Cadco® ABS; Cadillac® Plastic and Chemical Company

Cadco® Acrylic Adhesive SC-125; Cadillac® Plastic and Chemical Company

Cadco® PS-30; Cadillac® Plastic and Chemical Company

Catalin Styrene; Catalin Corporation of America

Catwoman™; Warner Brothers Communications

Celastic®; The Celastic® Corporation

Celluclay® Instant Papier Mâché; Activa Products

Cement II; Rohm and Haas G.m.b.H.

Claycrete®; American Art Clay Company, Inc. (AMACO®)

Clear Caulking; Hercules® Chemical Company, Inc.

Cloth Tape; Dritz® Corporation

Cloud Cover®; Cerulean Blue, Ltd.

Color-Lac K-C-I; John Lincoln Company

ColorCraft Textile Pigment; ColorCraft Ltd.

Colourseal®; Evo-Stick®, Evode Ltd.

Copper Topper®; Modern Options®, Inc.

Copydex Adhesive; Henkel® Home Improvement & Adhesive Products

Cova® Color; Tandycrafts®, Inc.

CPG® International Design Art Marker; A. W. Faber-Castell GmbH & Co.

Crackle and Age It; Bond™ Adhesives Company

Crackle Finish Kit; Accent

Crackle Surface Mosaic; Aleene's™ Product of Duncan Enterprises

Craft and Hobby Glue; Macklenburg-Duncan

Crayola™ Craft Fabric Crayons; Binney & Smith®

Crayola™ Transfer Crayons; Binney & Smith®

Createx Air Brush Paint; Colorcraft, Ltd.

Createx Clear Ply Adhesive Coating; ColorCraft, Ltd.

Createx Colors Fabric Paint; ColorCraft, Ltd.

Createx Colors Glitter Paint; ColorCraft, Ltd.

Createx Fluorescent Textile Colors; ColorCraft, Ltd.

Createx Metallic Colors; ColorCraft, Ltd.

Createx Pearlescent; ColorCraft, Ltd.

Createx Transparent Airbrush Colors; ColorCraft, Ltd.

Cryla Artists' Acrylic Colors; George Rowney® & Company Limited

Crystal Zice; Zeller International Ltd.

CSL™ Miracle Colour Up; CSL™ Inc.

Darn Fabric Mender; Woodhill Permatex

Decart® Badger® Air Tex Fabric Paint; Deka®-Textilfarben GMBH

DecoColor® Opaque Paint Marker; Marvy, Uchida® of America, Corporation

Deft™ Safe & Easy Biodegradable Wood Stain; Deft™, Inc.

Deka® Permanent Fabric Fluorescent Paint; Decart, Inc.

Deka® Permanent Fabric Paint; Decart Inc.

Deka®-Flair; Decart®, Inc.

Deka®-Fun; Decart®, Inc.

Deka®-Perm Air Fabric Paint; Decart®,Inc.

Delta™ Swell™ Stuff; Delta™ Technical Coatings, Inc.

Dental Dam; The Hygienic Corporation

Design® Art Marker; Eberhard Faber Incorporated

Designer Foam; Stro-Fab, Inc.

Desira Plast; Gebr Lutt Ges Gmbh. & Co.

Devcon® 2-Ton Epoxy; Devcon® Corporation

Devcon® Rubber Adhesive; Devcon® Corporation

Devcon® Super Glue for Wood & Leather; Devcon® Corporation

Devcon® Super Glue Gel; Devcon® Corporation

Devcon® Super Glue; Devcon® Corporation

Dimensional Bedazzlers; Lumured

Dimensional Fabric Paint; Binney & Smith®, Inc.

Dr. Ph. Martin's®; Salis International

Duco® Cement; E.I. du Pont de Nemours and Company, Inc.

Duracell® Batteries; Duracell® Company

Duro® Household Cement; Loctite® Corporation

Duro® Master Mend; Loctite® Corporation

Duro® Quick Mix Syringe E-Pox E5; Loctite® Corporation

Duro® Super Glue Gel; Loctite® Corporation

Duro® Vinyl Adhesive; Loctite® Corporation

Dylon™ Color Fun Fabric Paint; Dylon™ International Ltd.

E-Z Foil; Dri-Print Foils, Inc.

Eastman®; Eastman® Corporation

Easy Leaf®; Madana Manufacturing Company

Elbetex; LeFranc & Bourgeois

Elmer's® Glue-All; Elmer's® Products, Inc.

Elmer's® Washable Glue Stick; Elmer's® Products, Inc.

Epolite™; Hexcel® Corporation

Epoxy Adhesive, Ross® Chemical Company

Ethafoam®; Dow® Chemical Company

Everblum®; Albatross® USA

Evo-Stick® for Fabric; Evode Limited

EZ Foil; DriPrint®Foils, Inc.

Ezeform®; Smith & Nephew Rolyan Inc. EBI

Fab Spray for Fabric; Zynolite® Products Company

Fabri Tac™; Beacon™ Chemical Company

Fabric Cement; Magic Mender

Fabric Glue #430; Bond™ Adhesives

Fabric Stiffener; Aleene's®, Division of Artis, Inc.

Fabric-Form™; UnNatural Resources®

Fashion Foil; Jones Tones™ Inc.

Fast Flex; BJB Enterprises, Inc.

Fastbond™ 30-NF; 3M Company

Fastbond™ 48-NF; 3M Company

FGR-95; Ball Consulting, Ltd.

Fiebing's® Leather Dye; Fiebing® Company, Inc.

Finity; Windsor & Newton®

Fleck Stone™; Plasti-cote Company, Inc.

Flex-Zap®; Pacer® Technologies

FloralPro™; Adhesive Technologies Inc.

Fluorescent Neon Acrylic Paint; Palmer Paint Products, Inc.

Foamall; Woodall Industries, Inc.

Folk Art™ Crackle Medium; Plaid™ Enterprises

Forton® Modified Glass Reinforced Gypsum System (MG); Ball Consulting, Ltd.

Frame Fast® Activator; Uncommon Conglomerates, Inc.

Frame Fast® Screen Adhesive, Uncommon Conglomerates, Inc.

Fray Check™; Dritz® Corporation

Friendly Plastic®; American Art Clay Company, Inc. (AMACO®)

FW® Nonclogging Drawing Ink (Waterproof);Steig® Products

G-S Hypo-tube Cement; Germanow-Simon

G. I. Joe™; Hasbro®, Inc.

Galeria; Windsor & Newton®

Gel Medium; Golden® Artist Colors, Inc.

Gel Medium; Windsor & Newton®

Gem Tac™; Beacon™ Chemical Company

George Screen and Fabric Printing Color; George Rowney® & Company Limited

Gesso; Golden® Artist Colors, Inc.

Gesso; Lascaux®

Gesso; Modern Masters® Custom Paint and Chemical Company

Gesso; The Art Store®

Get Set®; Bond™ Adhesives Company

Gibbons Ink; Gibbons Inks and Coatings

Glass Stain; Stain Glass Products

Glue Stick Purple; 3M™ Company

Glue Stick White; 3M™ Company

Glue-Stic; Avery Dennison® Incorporated

Golden® Artist Colors; Golden® Artist Colors, Inc.

Gothic Casein Fresco Colors; Gothic Ltd.

Great Glass Stain; Plaid® Enterprises

Gripflex Paints; Wyandotte Paint Products Company

Heat N Bond™; Thermo O Web

Heirloom® Satin Varnish; McCloskey Division of the Valspar Corporation

Heirloom® Wood Stain; McCloskey Division of the Valspar Corporation

Hem N Trim®; Dritz® Corporation

Hexcelite®; AOA, Division of Biomet® Corporation

Higgens® Waterproof Drawing Ink; Eberhard Faber®, Inc.

Hot Stitch® Fusible Web; Aleene's®, Division of Artis, Inc.

Hot Stitch® Glue; Aleene's®, Division of Artis, Inc.

Hot-Melt Glue Sticks; Stanley Fastening Systems

Household Glue and Seal II; General Electric®, Silicone Products Division

Household Goop™; Eclectic Products Inc.

Hydrocal®; United States Gypsum Company

Iddings Deep Colors; Rosco Laboratories, Inc.

Instant Vinyl®; W.H. Collins

Jacquard® Textile Color; Ruppert, Gibbon & Spider Inc.

Jet-Melt™ Adhesive 3762; 3M™ Company

Jet-Melt™ Adhesive 3764; 3M™ Company

Jewel & Fabric Glue; Jurgen

Jewel Glue; Delta™ Technical Coatings, Inc.

Jewel-glue; Ridlen Adhesives, Inc.

Jewel-It; Aleene's, Division of Artis, Inc.

Jewelry and More; Creatively Yours®, Division of Loctite® Corporation

Jiffy Mixer; Jiffy Mixer Company Inc.

Jurek Professional Airbrush Colours; Medea Airbrush Products

King Cobra Malt Beer; Anheuser-Busch Companies

Kitchen Aid™; Whirlpool™ Corporation

Koh-I-Noor® Pens; Koh-I-Noor®

Kralastic®; United States Rubber Company

Krazy Glue®; Krazy Glue®, Inc.

Krylon®; Krylon® Products Group

Kwik Seal®; DAP®, Inc.

Kydex®; Kleerdex Company

L-200 Casting Latex; Cementex Corporation

Latex Rubber Sheet; Four D Rubber Company Limited

Let's Grip®; General Electric® Company

Lexan®; General Electric Company

Lincoln Shoe Dressing; John Lincoln Company

Lindy®; Lindy® Manufacturing Company

Liquid Acrylic Colours; Windsor & Newton®

Liquid Beads™ Press & Peel Foil; Plaid® Enterprises, Inc.

Liquid Latex; Alcone Company Inc.

Liquid Stitch®; Dritz® Corporation

Liquitex™ Acrylic Gel Medium; Binney & Smith®, Inc.

Liquitex™ Artists' Acrylic Colors; Binney & Smith®, Inc.

Liquitex™ Concentrated Artist Color; Binney & Smith®, Inc.

Liquitex™ Gesso; Binney & Smith®, Inc.

Loctite® 404; Loctite® Corporation

Loctite® 480; Loctite® Corporation

Lucite®; E.I. du Pont De Nemours & Company Inc.

Luma Inks; Steig Products

Luma; Daler-George Rowney & Company Limited

Lumiere™; The Walt Disney Company

Lumiere® Fabric Paints; Cerulean Blue, Ltd.

Lustran®; Monsanto® Company

Magic Marker®; Berel Corporation

Magic Mender; EZ International

Magique; Tandycrafts, Inc.

Magix® Shoe Color Spray; Kiwi® Brands Inc.

Magna-tac Bridal Glue; Beacon Chemical Company, Inc.

Marvy® Fabric Marker; Uchida Corporation

Meltonian® Water and Stain Protector; Magid Corporation

Merlon®; Mobay® Chemical Corporation

Meta-Lites™; UnNatural Resources®

Metal Master; Modern Options®, Inc.

Metallic Fabric Paint; Liquitex®, Division of Binney & Smith®, Inc.

Metallic Leaf; Old World Art

Metlyn® Stanfix®; Ross® Chemical Company

MF-415; Ball Consulting, Ltd.

Mini-Luster Rub-On; Crafts Products, Inc.

Minicel® L-200; Voltek, Division of Sekisui America Corporation

Minicel® L-300; Voltek, Division of Sekisui America Corporation

Minicel® L-400; Voltek, Division of Sekisui America Corporation

Minwax® Wood Finish; The Thompson Minwax Company

Miracle Coulour-Up; CSL™, Inc.

Mix Master®; Sunbeam® Oster Household Products

Modeling Clay; Aken Products, Inc.

Modern Options™, Inc. Patina Antiquing Kit; Modern Options, Inc. Paint and Chemical Company

Mrs. Potts™; The Walt Disney Company

Mylar®; E.I. du Pont de Nemours and Company, Inc.

Naugahyde®; Uniroyal Engineered Products

Neoprene; E.I. du Pont de Nemours and Company, Inc.

No-Fray Spray; Sprayway®, Inc.

No-Sew Fabric Glue; Aleene's, Product of Duncan Enterprises

No. 1 Pottery Plaster; United States Gypsum Corporation

Nu-Life™ Color Spray; Magid® Corporation

Off-Broadway Paint; Rosco Laboratories, Inc.

OK to Wash-It; Aleene's®, Division of Artis, Inc.

Ole-Bond™; Uncommon Conglomerates, Inc.

Orc®; Daivd & Asociates

Orhoplast® II; Johnson & Johnson® Orthopaedics

Orhoplast®; Johnson & Johnson® Orthopaedics

Pactra® Latex Plus; Pactra® Industries

Pantone®; Pantone®, Inc.

Papermate®; Write® Brothers

Para Casein Paint; Alcone Company Inc.

Patina-It; A-West

Peintex; Sennelier® A. S.

Pelikan® A; Pelikan® A.G.

Pellon®; Pellon® Corporation

Pentel® Fabric Fun; Pentel® Company, Ltd.

Permanent Fabric Paint; Decart, Inc.

Permatex® Form-A-Gasket® Blue Silicone Sealant; Permatex® Division of Loctite® Corporation

Perspex®; Imperial Chemical Industries Ltd. (ICI)

Phlexglu™; Spectra Dynamics Products

Phlexglu™ Plasticizer; Spectra Dynamics Products

Picrin®; R. R. Street & Co., Inc.

Pilot® Metallic Markers; Pilot® Corporation of America

Plastazote®; BXL Plastics Ltd.

Plasti Dip®; PDI Inc.

Platamid Hot Melt; Rilsan® Corporation

Plexi 400 Stretch Adhesive; Tom Jones

Plexiglas®; Rohm and Haas Company

Polane®; The Sherwin-Williams® Company

Polyamide Powder; Bostik® Inc.

Polyflex®; Smith & Nephew Rolyan® Inc. EBI

Polyform®; Smith & Nephew Rolyan® Inc. EBI

Polymark® Dimensional Fabric Paint; Polymark® Product of Duncan Enterprises

Polymer Medium; Golden® Artist Colors, Inc.

Polyshield®; Aervoe Pacific Company, Inc.

Pow'r Stix®; H.B. Fuller Company

Press-In-Place Caulk™; 3M™ Company

Prima® Acrylic Colors; Martin/F. Weber Company

Primo Primer and Sealer; Modern Options, Inc.

Prismacolor Spray, CSL™ Inc.

Prismacolor®; Berol Corporation

PROfab™ Textile Inks; PROfab

Pronto™ Instant Adhesives; 3M™ Company

Pros-Aide® Prosthetic Adhesive; A.D.M. Tronics Unlimited, Inc.

Protoplast; UnNatural Resources®

Quick N' Tacky; Delta™ Technical Coatings, Inc.

Quicktite®; Loctite® Corporation

Rain Guard Water Repellent; Dorfman Pacific

Removable Glue Stick; Avery Dennison® Incorporated

Res Q-Tape™; Seams Great Corporation

Riddler™; Warner Communications

Rit® Liquid Dye; CPC International Inc.

Rocco™ Airbrush Ink; Atelier de Paris

Roll Leaf; Admiral Coated Products, Inc.

Roma® Plastilena; Sculpture House

Rotring Art Pen Ink; Rotring GmbH

Royalite® Acrylic PVC; Uniroyal Chemical Company Inc.

Royalite®; Uniroyal Chemical Company Inc.

Rub 'n Buff®; American Art Clay Company, Inc. (AMACO®)

Saran Wrap®; Dow Brands® L.P.

SC-40; Polytek™ Development Corporation

Scotch™ Brand Adhesive Transfer Tape 924; 3M™ Company

Scotch-Grip™ 4475 Industrial Adhesive; 3M™ Company

Scotch-Grip™ Plastic Adhesive 1099; 3M™ Company

Scotch-Grip™ Plastic Adhesive 2262; 3M™ Company

Scotch-Grip™ Rubber and Gasket Adhesive 847; 3M™ Company

Scotch-Weld™ Epoxy Adhesive 2216; 3M™ Company

Scotch-Weld™ Urethane Adhesive 3549; 3M™ Company

Scotchgard™; 3M™ Company

Scotchpak™ Heat Sealable Polyester Film; 3M™ Company

Scott® Foam; Scott® Paper Company

Scribbles®; Scribbles® Product of Duncan Enterprises

Sculpey® Metallic Daubing Paint; Polyform Products Company

Sculpt or Coat; Sculptural Arts Coating, Inc.

Se-Lin® Tape; Gaylord Bros.

Seal and Gasket Silicone II; General Electric®, Silicone Products

Sequin and MicroTransfers; Jeweltrim, Inc.

Seta Scrib Fabric Marker; Pébéo® Industries

Sharpie® Fine Point Permanent Marker; Sanford® Corporation

Shout; S.J Johnson & Sons, Inc.

SIF®; Foamex® Products, Inc.

Sintra®; Allucabond Technologies, Inc.

Skin-Flex Paint; BJB Enterprises, Inc.

Sobo; Delta® Technical Coatings, Inc.

Solvoset; Alcone Company

SP 500; Spartech Corporation

SP 900; Spartech Corporation

Speedball Fabric Painters; Hunt Manufacturing Company

Stabond 836; Stabond Corporation

Stabond C-148; Stabond Corporation

Stabond U-148; Stabond Corporation

Starlight Paints Shoe Color; Starlight Paints

Stitch Witchery; Bostick® Inc.

Stitchless™ Fabric Glue; Delta Technical Coatings, Inc.

Stop Fraying; Aleene's®, Division of Artis, Inc.

Styrofoam®; Dow® Chemical Company

Sun Burst™ Colors; American Art Clay Company, Inc. (AMACO®)

Super Glue; Devcon Corporation

Super-Saturated Roscopaint; Rosco Laboratories, Inc.

Superman™; Warner Communications

Tandy's® Pro Dye; Tandycrafts™, Inc.

Tectron Fabric Protector; Glue Magic Products, Inc.

Teflon®; E.I. du Pont de Nemours and Company

Tempo Display Loop Fabric; Lockfast Inc.

Tensol No. 7; Imperial Chemical Industries Ltd. (ICI)

Texticolor; Sennellier® S.A.

The Thing™; Marvel Characters, Inc.

The Transformer; Hasbro, Inc.

Thixofix; BTR Ltd.

Tin-Fix; Sennelier® S.A.
  Tintex Dye; Kiwi Brands, Inc.

Treasure Gold®; Plaid® Enterprises

Trymer® Designer Foam; Dow® Chemicals

Tuffak®; Rohm and Haas Company

Tulip® Crystal Fabric Paint; Tulip® Product of Duncan Enterprises

Tulip® Glitter Fabric Paint; Tulip® Product of Duncan Enterprises

Tulip® Iridescent Fabric Paint; Tulip® Product of Duncan Enterprises

Tulip® Pearl Fabric Paint; Tulip® Product of Duncan Enterprises

Tulip® Puffy Fabric Paint; Tulip® Product of Duncan Enterprises

Tulip® Slick Fabric Paint; Tulip® Product of Duncan Enterprises

Turpenoid™ Natural; Martin F. Weber Corporation

Turpenoid™; Martin F. Weber Corporation

Tyvek; E.I. du Pont de Nemours and Company

UHU Glu Stic; Eberhard Faber®

Ultracal; United States Gypsum Company

Unique Stitch™; W. H. Collins, Inc.

Urethane Bond; Conap® Inc.

Valu Kid™; K.V. Mart Company

Vara-Form™; UnNatural Resources®

Varabond; Mann Bros.

Varathane® Diamond Wood Stain; The Flecto Company, Inc.

Varathane®; The Flecto™ Company, Inc.

Vaseline®; Cheesebrough-Ponds USA Company

Velcro® Adhesives; Velcro® USA Inc.

Velcro®; Velcro® USA Inc.

Velverette; Delta Technical Coatings, Inc.

Versatex™ Airbrush Ink for Fabrics; Siphon Art Products

Versatex™ Textile Paint; Siphon Art Products

VF-812; Ball Consulting, Ltd.

Vibrathane; United States Rubber Company

Victory 1991; Bond™ Adhesive Company

Victory Vinyl Repair Kit; Bond™ Adhesives

Volara®; Voltek, Division of Sekisui America Corporation

Vulcabond 36; Stabond Corporation

Vulcabond V-36; Stabond Corporation

W/290 H Witcobond; Witco Corporation

Water and Stain Protector; Cadillac Shoe Products, Inc.

Water Repellent Shield; Cadillac Shoe Products, Inc.

Water-Based Urethane Adhesive; Uncommon Conglomerates

Waterproof Victory; Bond™ Adhesives Company

WC-575; BJB Enterprises, Inc.

Weather Guard; CSL™, Inc.

Weld-On® 10; Industrial Polychemical Service Corporation, Inc. (IPS®)

Weld-On® 1001; Industrial Polychemical Service Corporation, Inc. (IPS®)

Weld-On® 16; Industrial Polychemical Service Corporation, Inc. (IPS®)

Weld-On® 3; Industrial Polychemical Service Corporation, Inc. (IPS®)

Weld-On® 4; Industrial Polychemical Service Corporation, Inc. (IPS®)

White Glue; Aleene's® Product of Duncan Enterprises

White Glue; Ross® Chemical Company

White Stuff®; Uncommon Conglomerates

Wonder Tape; W. H. Collins, Inc.

Wonder Under™; Pellon® Corporation

Wonder Web™; Pellon® Corporation

X-Lite®; Smith & Nephew Roylan Inc. EBI

Zap-A-Gap®; Pacer® Technology

Zeta™; Zeta™ Trikotagenfabrik

Zice; Zeller International

Zout; J.C. Caret Division of Sun Luster Inc.

Source Materials and Consultants

The following bibliography is divided by subject. Within each subject, books, periodicals, government publications, videos, and/or consultants are listed. Periodicals are suggested for ongoing useful information, rather than for specific articles.

Adhesives

Books B.S. Jackson, Editor. *Industrial Adhesives and Sealants*. London: Hutchinson Benham, 1976.

Theatre Crafts. *How-To*. New York: Theatre Crafts Books, 1984.

Giles, Carl and Barbara. *Glue It!* Blue Ridge Summit, PA: Tab Books Inc., 1984.

Consultants Bill Mason. UnCommon Conglomerates, St. Paul, MN. 612-227-7000.

Artists' Materials

Books Meyer, Ralph. *The Artist's Handbook of Materials and Techniques*. Rev. Ed. New York: Viking Penguin, 1991.

Casting From Life

Books Baygan, Lee. *Techniques of Three-Dimensional Makeup*. New York: Watson-Guptill, 1982.

Kehoe, Vincent J.-R. *The Technique of the Professional Makeup Artist*. Newton, MA: Focal Press, 1955.

Savini, Tom. *Grande Illusions, The Art and Technique of Special Makeup Effects*. Pittsburgh: Imagine, Inc., 1983.

Periodicals *Make-up Artist Magazine*. Sun Valley, CA: Make-up Artist Magazine.

Videos *Better One-Piece Head Molds from Life*. St. Albans, VT: Distributed by Pink House Studios, Inc. and *Make-up Artist Magazine*.
Success with Full Body Molds and Forton Castings. St. Albans, VT: Distributed by Pink House Studios, Inc. and *Make-up Artist Magazine*.

Costume Crafts

Books Emery, Joy Spaniel. *Stage Costume Techniques*. Englewood Cliffs, NJ: Prentice-Hall, Inc., 1988.

Ingham, Rosemary. *The Costume Technicians' Handbook*. Rev. Ed. Portsmouth, NH: Heineman, 1992.

Ingham, Rosemary and Covey, Elizabeth. *The Costumer's Handbook*. Rev. Ed. Englewood Cliffs, NJ: Prentice-Hall, Inc., 1993.

Smith, C. Ray. *The Theatre Crafts Book of Costumes*. Emmaus, PA: Theatre Crafts Books, 1973.

Periodicals *American Craft*. New York: American Craft Council.

Costume Business. Jacksonville, FL: Festivities Publications Inc.

Fiberarts. Asheville, NC: Altamont Press.

Theatre Crafts International (TCI). New York: Intertec/Primedia Company.

Theatre Crafts Magazine. Now known as *Theatre Crafts International (TCI)*.

Dyeing and Painting

Books

Belfer, Nancy. *Designing in Batik and Tie Dye*. Englewood Cliffs, NJ: Prentice-Hall, Inc., 1977.

Broughton, Kate. *Textile Dyeing: The Step-by-Step Guide and Showcase*. Cincinnati, OH: Rockport Publishers, 1997.

Dryden, Deborah. *Fabric Painting and Dyeing for the Theatre*. Rev. Ed. Portsmouth, NH: Heinemann, 1993.

Kennedy, Jill and Varrall, Jane. *Everything You Ever Wanted to Know About Fabric Painting*. Cincinnati: North Light Books, 1994.

Tuckman, Diane and Janas, Jan. *The Complete Book of Silk Painting*. Cincinnati, OH: North Light Books, 1992.

Ward, Nancy. *Fabric Painting Made Easy*. Radnor, PA: Chilton Press, 1993.

Periodicals

Surface Design Journal. Oakland, CA: Surface Design Association.

Health and Safety

Books

McCann, Michael. *Artist Beware: The Hazards and Precautions in Working with Art and Craft Materials*. New York: Watson-Guptill, 1979.

Rossol, Monona. *The Artist's Complete Health and Safety Guide*. New York: Allworth Press, 1990.

——. *Stage Fright, Health and Safety in the Theatre*. New York: Allworth Press, 1991.

Periodicals

ACTS FACTS. New York: Arts, Crafts, and Theatre Safety.

Art Hazard News. New York: Center for Safety in the Arts.

Government Documents

U.S. Department of Labor, OSHA. *Hazard Communication. A Compliance Kit*. Washington, DC: Superintendent of Documents, U.S. Government Printing Office.

Worker's Compensation Board of British Columbia. *WHMIS Core Material: A Resource Manual for the Application and Implementation of WHMIS*. Richmond, BC, Canada: Community Relations Department, Workman's Compensation Board.

Videos

First Steps. Artsafe Australia. Distributed in U.S. by Arts, Crafts and Theater Safety (ACTS). New York.

Play It Safe - Introduction to Theatre Safety. Distributed by Theatre Arts Video Library. Leucadia, CA.

Consultants Monona Rossol. President, Art, Crafts and Theater Safety (ACTS). NY. 212-777-0062. Services also available through United Scenic Arts Union (USA). 212-581-0300.

Dr. Randall W.A. Davidson. Risk International & Associates. Pomona, CA. 909-625-5961.

Jewelry

Books Hollander, Harry. *Plastics for Jewelry*. New York: Watson-Guptill Publications, 1974.

von Neumann, Robert. *Design and Creation of Jewelry*. Rev. Ed. Radnor, PA: Chilton Book Co., 1972.

Plastics

Books Bryson, Nicholas L. *Thermoplastic Scenery for the Theatre Vol. I*. New York: Drama Book Specialists, 1972.

Cherry, Raymond. *General Plastics, Projects and Procedures*. Bloomington, IL: McKnight & McKnight Publishing Co., 1967.

James, Thurston. *The Prop Builder's Molding & Casting Handbook*. White Hall, VA: Betterway Publications, Inc., 1989.

Newman, Thelma R. *Plastics As An Art Form*. Philadelphia: Chilton Books, 1964.

Newman, Thelma R. *Crafting With Plastics*. Philadelphia: Chilton Books, 1975.

Roukes, Nicholas. *Crafts in Plastics*. New York: Watson-Guptill Publications, 1970.

Time-Life Books. *Working With Plastics*. Chicago: Time-Life Books, 1981.

Videos *Mold Making and Casting*. Ambridge, PA: Distributed by Ball Consulting Ltd.

The Special Makeup Effects Artist's Guide to Using GM Foam. Van Nuys, CA: Distributed by GM Foam Inc.

The User's Guide to Reducit®, Rubber Molds and Innovative Plastic Support Structures. St. Albans, VT: Distributed by Pink House Studios, Inc. and *Make-up Artist Magazine*.

The Videoguide to Special Makeup Effects. 4 Volume Set. Van Nuys, CA: Videfx. Distributed by Burman Industries Inc.

Printing

Books Croner, Marjorie. *Fabric Photos*. Loveland, CO: Interweave Press, 1989.

Prop Making

Books Govier, Jacquie. *Create Your Own Stage Props*. Englewood Cliffs, NJ: Prentice-Hall, Inc., 1984.

James, Thurston. *The Theater Props Handbook*. White Hall, VA: Betterway Publications, Inc., 1987.

———. *The Prop Builder's Mask Making Handbook*. White Hall, VA: Betterway Publications, Inc., 1990.

Motley. *Theatre Props*. New York: Drama Book Specialists, 1975.

Special Effects

Periodicals *Cinefex . . .the Journal of Cinematic Illusion*. Riverside, CA: Cinefex 62.

INDEX

W